INDUSTRIAL PRODUCTIVITY

Work Methods, Times, and Their Application
in Planning and Continuous Improvement

José Agustín Cruelles Ruiz

Industrial productivity

Copyright © 2014 **José Agustín Cruelles Ruiz**

First edition: 2014

Published by © **MCB Press**, 2014 owned by Marcombo

Distributed in USA and Canada by ATLAS BOOKS, 30 Amberwood Parkway, Ashland, Ohio 44805. To contact a representative, please e-mail us at order@bookmasters.com.

Distributed in Europe by MCB Press. To contact a representative, please contact us at info@mcb-press.com, Facebook or Twitter.

www.mcb-press.com

Layout: Paul Creuheras
Cover Designer: Ndenu

All rights reserved. No part of this book may be reproduced, stored in a retrieval System, or transmitted in any form or by any means, without the prior written permission of the Publisher, except in the case of brief quotations embedded in critical articles or reviews.

ISBN: 978-84-267-2105-1

Printed in EU

INDUSTRIAL PRODUCTIVITY

Work Methods, Times, and Their Application in Planning and Continuous Improvement

José Agustín Cruelles Ruiz

Dedication

I gave this book the best I had; however much or little, it has been my best. During its development I devoted most of my free time; I reworked chapters after finishing them, revising each between five and seven times. And yet it will have defects—errors and imperfections.

The book is not intended to be a technical and engineering exhibition. Its greater focus is on being didactic, useful, easy, and educational, which I believe should be the mission of those who aim to train. I cannot judge its success; I will leave that task to others.

So far this book has been my work of my life, and I therefore dedicate it to my mother who made me feel big when circumstances made me small.

It is also dedicated to Ana Rosa, who gives me stability and serenity. I do not know, in other circumstances, what I would have done or where would I be or even if could have written this book.

And to my children who approached it with great enthusiasm, constantly asking me how it was going. Now that I have finished, I will devote more time to you.

January 16, 2014

Acknowledgments

To the colleagues who helped in the preparation of the content: Gregorio Ordóñez Recio, Agustín Lizasoain, Raúl Álvarez Silva, and José Fuentes Redondo.

To Alvaro Javier González Endemaño, who put enormous effort into the technical translation of the text and images.

To customers who trust in us, especially to those who had a special role during the start-up of this project.

To Jeroni Boixareu who gave me this opportunity.

To Carlos Torres Barroso, for writing the prologue and for trusting enough in this material to make a special edition.

To the International Labor Organization for providing us with chapters of Introduction to Work Study, about issues that needed to be included in this book, but to which I could not contribute anything new.

To Ramon Forn Valls for being my MTM instructor.

Contents

Prologue .... **XIII**

1. Introduction to Industrial Productivity **1**
    1.1. Introduction 1
    1.2. History of Scientific Work Study 3
    1.3. Why Does Productivity Matter? Productivity Is Not Optional 8
    1.4. The Future of Scientific Work 10
    1.5. Definitions 10
    1.6. Structure of This Book 14

2. The Theory of Waste Measurement **29**
    2.1. Introduction and Definition 29
    2.2. Waste in Work Design 36
    2.3. Waste in Manufacture 45
    2.4. All Waste Coefficients: Combination and Criteria for Their Use 58
    2.5. The Identification of Waste and Its Reduction 61
    2.6. The Theory of Waste Measurement and Subsequent Communication 62

3. Diagnosis of Productivity **67**
    3.1. Introduction: Diagnosis of Unproductiveness 67
    3.2. Report and Points of the Unproductiveness Diagnosis 68
    3.3. Waste Maps and Improvement Deposits 79
    3.4. Influence of Productivity in Production Costs 94
    3.5. Productivity, a Human Problem 98
    3.6. Process of Problem Solving 99

4. Continuous Improvement Evolution and Systems Approach **115**
    4.1. Introduction 115
    4.2. Stages and Evolution of Continuous Improvement 118
    4.3. System Concepts and System Approaches 119
    4.4. Decision Making: Events That Trigger It 144

5. The Study of Methods **157**
    5.1. Definition 157
    5.2. Systematic Procedure for Methods Study 158

5.3. Method Record 171
5.4. Processes 192
5.5. Record of Actual and Proposed Processes and Procedures 210

6. Methods Analysis 217
6.1. The Concept of Analysis 218
6.2. Interrogatory Technique.. 218
6.3. Checklists: Background Questions... 220
6.4. Operation Analysis 230
6.5 Study of Movements 235
6.6. Analysis of Micro-Motions... 243

7. Design of the Improved Method 261
7.1. Introduction 261
7.2. Creativity and Generation of Ideas 264
7.3. Catalog of Solutions 277
7.4. Evaluate and Present Correctly the Improvement Proposals, Including Their Economical, Technical, Social, Ecological, Legal, and Ethical Justifications 298
7.5. The Study–Analysis–Improvement Proposal Simplified Cycle 305

8. Improvement in Setup Times of Machines - SMED: Agile Manufacturing.. 309
8.1. Introduction. What Is SMED?.. 310
8.2. Convenience of SMED 311
8.3. The SMED System: Description of Stages 312
8.4. Techniques for Applying the SMED System 317
8.5. The Correct Machine Election: The Best Exchange Is the One Not Made 325
8.6. Practical Cases 326

9. Balancing Improvements in Tasks with Several Participants............. 341
9.1. Introduction: Reduction of Delay Time 342
9.2. Improvement of Assembly Line Works... 342
9.3. Improvement of Simultaneous Person-Person Tasks 357
9.4. Improvement of Simultaneous Person-Machine Tasks........................... 360

10. Process Improvement Criteria... 373
10.1. Introduction: The Concept of Process Improvement........................... 374
10.2. Balancing of Tasks from the Process 380

10.3. Reduction of Stocks in Process 386
10.4. Reduction of Available Space and Transfers 388
10.5. Implementation of Means to Automate or Facilitate Transport 403

11. The Most Important Improvement: Ergonomics 415
11.1. Introduction 416
11.2. Objectives of Ergonomics 417
11.3. Benefits of Ergonomics 418
11.4. Person-Machine-Work Environment Systems 418
11.5. Analysis and Improvement of the Ergonomic System 420
11.6. Ergonomics and Safety 432
11.7. Ergonomics and Fatigue 435
11.8. Images and References 437

12. Innovation and Implementation 443
12.1. Introduction and Definition 444
12.2. Implementation and Resistance to Change 448

13. Study and Analysis of Administrative Processes 457
13.1. Introduction 457
13.2. Elaboration and Representation of an Administrative Process 459
13.3. Improvement of Administrative Processes 468

14. Foundations of Work Measurement 479
14.1. Definition and Evolution of Time Measurement 479
14.2. Concept of Standard Time 480
14.3. Importance of the Standard Time (ST) 484
14.4. General Methods to Measure the Standard Time (ST) 485
14.5. Systematic Procedure for Timekeeping 492

15. Prerequisites for Determining the Standard Time 499
15.1. Trained Analyst, Required Competencies 499
15.2. Qualified Operator, Learning Curve 501
15.3. Normal Work Pace, Scales, and Valuation Methods 502
15.4. Execution Standard, Work Specification, and Standard Operation Procedure 514
15.5. Physical Work Environment, Applicable Requirements and Standards, and Organizational Aspects 516
15.6. Materials for the Time Study 517

16. Time Study with Timekeeping 521
16.1. Introduction: Timekeeping Techniques 521
16.2. Stages of the Timekeeping Study 523
16.3. Time Studies with Machines 568

17. Work Sampling and Structured Estimating 583
17.1. The Need for Work Sampling 583
17.2. A Few Words About Sampling 584
17.3. Establishing Confidence Levels 584
17.4. Determination of Sample Size 587
17.5. Making Random Observations 589
17.6. Conducting the Study 592
17.7. Rated Work Sampling 596
17.8. Group Sampling Techniques 596
17.9. Using Work Sampling 597
17.10. Structured Estimating 598

18. Predetermined Time Standards 601
18.1. Definition 601
18.2. Origins 602
18.3. Advantages of PTS Systems 603
18.4. Criticisms of PTS Systems 604
18.5. Different Forms of PTS Systems 605
18.6. Use of PTS Systems 608
18.7. Application of PTS Systems 616

19. Development of Standard Data and Time Formulas: Methods Study and Parameterized Times 629
19.1. Introduction and Concepts 629
19.2. Principles for Elaborating Standard Data and Time Formulas 630
19.3. Handling of Variable Elements: The Study of Methods and Parameterized Times 640
19.4. Archive and Use of Standard Data and Time Formulas 642
19.5. Presentation of Results 643
19.6. Examples of Parameterized Studies 647

20. Operations: Production Management 659
20.1. Introduction and Concepts 659

20.2. Aggregate Production Planning 661
20.3. Master Production Schedule (MPS) 674
20.4. MRP *(Material Requeriments Planning)* 679
20.5. Manufacturing Resource Planning (MRPII) 683
20.6. Bottleneck management 696

21. Productivity Control and Incentive Systems 707
21.1. Introduction and Concepts 707
21.2. Convenience of Productivity Control 714
21.3. Convenience of the Incentive Systems 715
21.4. Productivity Control 716
21.5. Productivity Control Implementation 743
21.6. Incentive Systems 757
21.7. Characteristics, Implementation, and Maintenance of an Incentive System 768

Synthesis 787

Solutions 797

Appendix 811

Prologue

The manufacturing industry is rapidly moving, like other sectors, into a globalized world where the lack of differentiation with regard to competence can only be accommodated by being highly efficient in cost management.

Even those with a vision of offering something new and different in the market will only be able to continue if their vision goes hand in hand with efficiency.

In current times, the need to be cost efficient is indisputable; however, the lack of competitiveness has been a criticism commonly used to attack the industrial sector both internally and externally.

Over and above other social-labor considerations, the industry has made an effort to optimize productive processes. It can be said that in many cases, the assembly lines and productive processes are optimized, but improving auxiliary or indirect activities around the proper productive process still has a long way to go.

The imperative need to optimize the process as a whole, both direct operations as well as auxiliary or indirect aspects, combined with the known reality of the process and the adequacy of the associated resources, directly affects cost efficiency.

Gaps in the previously mentioned factors or deficiencies in real knowledge, apart from potentially erroneous tactical or strategic decisions, require that supporting technological tools, especially enterprise resource planning (ERP) systems, be properly engaged to avoid negatively influencing the production quality and service levels and inventories or creating inefficiencies and thus inducing other costs.

In the following pages you will find concepts related to industrial productivity and the way toward excellence in industrial processes. Indra, one of the world's leading technology companies, is aware that technology is not an end in itself, but a means to obtain results at a business level. A key element for technology is that it be accompanied by excellence in the process and by proper resource training.

Carlos Torres Barroso - Director of Industry of Indra
April 16, 2014

Chapter 1

Introduction to Industrial Productivity

1.1. Introduction

Competitiveness, or being competitive, is a term with many variations. A company can be competitive in a number of ways:

1. Low manufacturing costs
2. Low costs of raw materials
3. Proximity to clients and, therefore, low costs of distribution
4. Short delivery deadlines
5. Quality of product
6. Innovation
7. Technology
8. Design
9. After-sales service

According to Michael Porter, to be competitive is to be differentiated. Each of the ways in the previous list constitutes for itself an almost infinite discipline.

Companies may choose any of the different existing strategies to be competitive and then specialize and become strong in that line.

Low manufacturing costs are also called operative effectiveness. According to Michael Porter, operative effectiveness is not competitiveness. In other words, a company that is highly productive in making something nobody wants, the company is not going to compete. Under the assumption that the good or service produced is something society needs, cost reduction is a step toward competitiveness.

This book's goal is to focus on the reduction of manufacturing costs to gain operative effectiveness.

Consider here that we are speaking about competitiveness. For example, nowadays more competition comes from emerging countries—China, India, Brazil, and others—in the manufacturing of products. On many occasions it may seem that the battle is lost because their manufacturing costs, due to low labor costs, are much lower than the Europeans. However, products manufactured in distant countries have certain competitive disadvantages:

- *Delivery deadlines, which are solved with large warehouses that, of course, also have a cost*
- *Cost of transportation that keeps rising along with fuel prices*
- *Few possibilities for personalization*
- *A cheaper but less productive workforce*

The price, for the moment however, continues to be a determining factor, and consumers and manufacturers keep choosing products from, for example, China.

Years of observation of the industrial sector lead to the conclusion that manufacturing wastes exist, which implies a great potential for improvement. This news is good in part. This waste can be attributed to both the labor force and managers, and its most evident cause is a **lack of cultural productivity**. Neither in engineering universities nor in business colleges do they raise awareness about operative effectiveness and its importance. Lack of awareness of the problem precludes efforts to solve it.

A company can fix its competitive strategy in one and only one of these attributes. However, this reality does not imply that the rest can be abandoned; they must be addressed as well. For example, some companies use the strategy of innovation, bringing to the market highly differentiated products with, at least in origin, enough margins. But those companies who disregard operative effectiveness are not able to control manufacturing costs, leading the company out of business or making it vulnerable to takeover by others who do control their productivity. For companies whose only strategy has been to reduce costs, if their products have not been differentiated from the competition and the entire sector has followed the same path, the result is sales without margin. In this scenario only clients and equipment suppliers benefit from buying increasingly cheaper.

So, it is clear that balance is necessary.

This book has three ambitious objectives:

1. That readers learn how to recognize and reduce costs and manage the deadlines of manufacturing.
2. To differentiate through its pedagogy, which helps readers understand everything that is explained, not only in each chapter, but in the book as a whole.
3. That the book becomes a working and consultation tool, a support that the reader can use indefinitely.

To achieve these objectives, the book must be correctly structured and guided, allowing the student to always know where he or she is.

Section 1.3, *Productivity is not optional,* explains why an industrial company must adopt this strategy as a pillar of its viability and competitiveness.

1.2. History of Scientific Work Study

The following characters, events, and methodologies in the evolution of industrial organization are addressed in this section.

Adam Smith (1723–1790)

Frederick Winslow Taylor (1856–1915)

Frank Bunker Gilbreth (1868–1924)

Charles Bedaux (1887–1944)

Henry Gantt (1861–1919)

MTM (1940s)

PERT-CPM (program evaluation and revision technique) (1957)

MRP (1940s)

MRP II (mid-1970s)

ERP (enterprise resource planning) (1990s)

Ergonomics (twentieth century)

International Labor Organization (1919)

JIT (just-in-time) (1970s)

Lean manufacturing (1990s)

SMED (1990s, after JIT).

A brief overview of each follows.

- Adam Smith (1723–1790)

    Adam Smith was born July 7, 1723, in Kirkcaldy, Scotland. He studied in the universities of Glasgow and Oxford. He is considered the father of political economy. He was one of the promoters of specialized work, which is discussed widely in his book *The Wealth of Nations*. In this book he writes about the importance of the contribution of machines (created by artisans to streamline work). Mechanization simplifies the task, and its use is centered on fast and easy execution methods. In one of the examples from the book—*the pin factory*—he says that one worker manufacturing pins can make fewer than 100 per day, while dividing the work by specific task allows for the manufacture of 10,000 pins daily.

- Frederick Winslow Taylor (1856–1915)

    Taylor was born in Germantown, Pennsylvania and is considered the father of scientific work organization.

    After abandoning his law studies because of a sight problem, he found employment in the metalworking industry in Philadelphia. After a period of time in metalwork, he began a machinery workshop where he observed workers performing their roles when cutting metal. From these observations, Taylor analyzed the work, decomposed it in simpler tasks, timed the execution of each task, and set the fulfillment times required of the workers for these tasks.

    This analysis of work organization also allowed for modifying tasks when it was necessary in order to reduce and optimize timing, thereby eliminating unnecessary displacements and reducing time spent in activity or tool changes. In addition, salary could be established per manufactured part based on estimated time, which would serve as an incentive for workers to improve work pace.

    Taylor fought actively to impose this method in his workshop. He studied engineering during the night shift, in parallel with his work, and went on to work as engineering chief at Bethlehem Steel Company from 1898 to 1901. There he successfully developed his methods and published several scientific work organization books, including his masterpiece *The Principles of Scientific Management* (1911).

    After these works, his methods became famous, because entrepreneurs saw in them the possibility to control production processes, improve productivity by reducing costs, and allow for hiring a less-qualified workforce, due to tasks being increasingly simpler and more repetitive.

- Frank Bunker Gilbreth (1868–1924)

  Gilbreth, an American engineer, established the modern technique of human body movement used to execute a determined labor operation in order to improve it by eliminating unnecessary movements, simplifying necessary ones, and establishing an optimum movement sequence. In collaboration with his wife, he developed techniques—such as cinematographic study of movements, or cyclographic and cronocyclographic analysis techniques—used in the study of movement trajectories made by operators.

  He collaborated with Taylor in work organization studies and established simplification principles that help to reduce execution times and fatigue. His wife, Lillian Evelyn Moller, continued his work and conducted the divulgation of labor organization concepts specially oriented to valuing the human factor.

- Charles Bedaux (1887–1944)

  This French engineer was influenced by Taylor and Gilbreth. He introduced the concept of evaluation and classification of working time, which gave place to large improvements in the productivity of employees.

  In 1916, Bedaux established a management consulting company in Cleveland, and his great success led to the creation of branch offices around the world. The Bedaux method links timing with activity appreciation or operator performance. In the 60–80 scale of Bedaux activity, 60 corresponds to normal activity and 80 to optimum activity. With this method, productivity of operators can be measured by comparing accomplished work with normal time.

- Henry Gantt (1861–1919)

  Henry Gantt was an American mechanical engineer who collaborated with Taylor in the study of industrial work organization. He created the Gantt chart, a graphic diagram for planning task sequences in almost any project. He published his main work, *Work, Wages, and Profits,* in 1913.

- MTM

  MTM had its origin in the United States during the 1940s. It was developed by Maynard, Schwab, and Stegermerten of the Council of Engineering Methods while they were consulting for Westinghouse Brake and Signal Corporation. Published in 1948, *Methods-Time Measurement* clearly defined MTM and its rules of application as applied in the United States and other industrialized countries. In 1951, the *USA/Canada MTM Association for Standards and Research* was formed by MTM users. Afterwards derived systems were developed: the MTM-2, MTM-3, MTM-V, MTM-C, MTM-M, and others.

- PERT-CPM

    Program evaluation and revision techniques (PERT) method, also named critical path method, has two origins.

    The U.S. Army began development of PERT in 1957 to control execution times of its space exploration projects. It was first used with Polaris and currently is used in the whole space program.

    The critical path method (CPM) is the second origin of the current method. Its development also started in the United States in 1957 at an operations investigation center for the DuPont and Remington Rand firm, with the goal of controlling and optimizing the operation costs through adequate planning of the project's component activities.

    From the combination of the two previous methods the critical path method was formed, which is nowadays used for management and control of projects.

- MRP

    MRP started during World War II, when the U.S. government used recently created computers in the 1940s for the logistics of unit operations in wartime. These solutions were the origin of the *material requirements planning systems*.

    After the war, MRP was integrated into the productive sectors as companies realized that these systems would better manage and control their logistics, inventory, and diverse activities.

    The continuous development of computers influenced the growth of these systems, and more and more companies began to use them.

    In the 1960s and 1970s, MRP helped many companies to decrease their level of inventory through material planning based on manufacture demands, allowing them to stock up only the necessary materials for manufacture.

- MRP II

    Manufacturing resource planning (MRP II) was born from MRP in the mid-1970s. This new system was based on demand. It allowed, on top of planning material demands, the management of any necessary resources for the manufacturing process. It was born from MRP's deficiency of calculating material quantities but not resources for a manufacturing process. MRP II uses standard times for its elaboration.

- ERP

    Enterprise resource planning (ERP) systems were born in the 1990s and are information management systems that integrate and automate many of the business practices associated with operative or productive aspects of a company. ERP integrates production, sales, purchases, logistics, accounting, project management, geographic information systems (GIS), inventories and warehouse control, orders, payrolls, and so on.

These systems arose out of the need for support of business clients, quick response times to their problems, as well as an efficient handling of information that allows making timely decisions and a decrease in total operation costs.

- Ergonomics

  The term *ergonomics* can be defined as "human adaptation to environment." Work ergonomics has always been applied. From ancient times, humans' working limits were already known. In 1949 the Ergonomics Research Society was founded in England; the Japanese Ergonomics Society followed in 1964.

  An example of ergonomic development would be the combat planes in World War I and World War II. In the beginning, planes were designed with no ergonomic base—the only concern was that they could fly—but the necessity of advantage over enemy planes quickly became evident. The control panel had to be such that with a glance all flight variables (height, pressure, fuel level, etc.) could be observed. Control levers and triggers to fire weapons were designed with adapted forms for the pilots, and seat designs began taking into account comfort. We could say that it was the first step toward modern ergonomics.

  Nowadays ergonomics is applied in any type of design, from houses to offices to products, such as ergonomic chairs and hand-adapted work tools, all with the goal of total improvement of comfort.

- ILO

  The International Labor Organization was created in 1919 at the end of World War I. Its foundation initially was a response to humanitarian concerns. Workers' situations, which were exploited without regard for their health, family life, and professional and social progress, were becoming less acceptable. This concern is clearly reflected in the Preamble of the Constitution from the ILO, which states that "conditions of labor involving injustice, hardship and privation to large numbers of human beings exist."

  It was also based on political motivations. Without improvement in the situation of workers, whose number grew constantly due to the industrialization process, they would end up creating social conflicts, which could lead even as far as revolution. The Preamble states that the discontent caused by injustice "constitutes a threat to international peace and universal harmony."

  The third motivation was economic. Any industry or country adopting social reforms would be at a disadvantage compared to its competitors, due to the inevitable consequences of such measures on production costs. The Preamble states, "If any nation would not adopt humane conditions of labor, this is an obstacle for other nations who wish to improve the fate of workers in their own countries."

- JIT

  Just-in-time is a Japanese manufacturing management method developed in the 1970s. Its goal is to produce only when product is demanded. It was first adopted in Toyota's industrial plants by Taiichi Ohno. Because of its success, Taiichi Ohno was named the father of JIT.

  After World War II, Japan was totally destroyed, so they had to maximize the few resources they had left. For this reason they began designing industrial practices like JIT that could help them restore old companies and establish new ones by working in the most efficient way possible and thereby rebuilding their economy.

  With the introduction of JIT many of their problems were solved. For example, the handling of large inventories required management and storage, with their consequent costs and potential delays in deliveries. In this new production process, activities pulled from materials required in previous processes.

- Lean Manufacturing

  Lean manufacturing can be understood as "skinny" manufacturing that takes all the "fat" or extra steps/materials out of a given process. It is a set of production techniques that arose from the Toyota system in the 1990s, which improve and optimize operative processes of any industrial company regardless of its size in order to obtain much shorter reaction times, better quality, better customer service, and lower costs.

- SMED

  Single-minute exchange of die (SMED) was born by the need to achieve JIT production. It is a set of techniques developed to drastically reduce preparation times for machines, which significantly increases the flexibility of manufacturing processes, trying to do more varied and smaller batches. Its development was primarily the work of Shigeo Shingo.

1.3. Why Does Productivity Matter? Productivity Is Not Optional

An extract from the chapter addressing the competitive advantages of various nations, Michael Porter's *Competitive Advantage: Creating and Sustaining Superior Performance* provides the following analysis. From studies of the 10 most competitive countries that have higher quality of life over a span of four years, Porter concluded:

> *National prosperity is created, not inherited. It does not grow out of a country's natural endowments, its labor pool, its interest rates, or its currency's value, as classical economics insist on.*
>
> *A nation's competitiveness depends on the capacity of its industry to innovate and upgrade. Companies gain advantage against the world's best competitors because of pressure and challenge. They benefit from having strong domestic rivals, aggressive home-based suppliers, and demanding local customers. . . .*
>
> *The only meaningful concept of competitiveness at the national level is productivity. The principal goal of a nation is to produce a high and rising standard of living for its citizens. The ability to do so depends on the productivity with which a nation's labor and capital are employed. Productivity is the value of the output produced by a unit of labor or capital. Productivity depends on both the quality and features of products (which determine the prices that they can command) and the efficiency with which they are produced. Productivity is the prime determinant of a nation's long-run standard of living; it is the root cause of national per capita income. The productivity of human resources determines employee wages; the productivity with which capital is employed determines the return it earns for its holders.*
>
> *A nation's standard of living depends on the capacity of its companies to achieve high levels of productivity and to increase productivity over time. Sustained productivity growth requires that an economy continually upgrade itself. A nation's companies must relentlessly improve productivity in existing industries by raising product quality, adding desirable features, improving product technology, or boosting production efficiency. They must develop the necessary capabilities to compete in more sophisticated industry segments, where productivity is generally high. They must finally develop the capability to compete in entirely new, sophisticated industries.*

And if productivity is so important: Why do companies and administrations pay insufficient attention to it? In my opinion, the reason is a lack of awareness of its importance. Why, then, is the education in this field so deficient?

1.4. The Future of Scientific Work

In some countries more than others technicians have been in the background, above them are executives and traders, and a whole generation has been the victim of the financial "engineering." Such an approach fails to work because it is a game about winning money without giving anything in return. When problems occur, and they do occur, it is necessary to put the "mechanics" to work and begin to solve the failures. It is time for technicians and scientists to act and bureaucrats to step aside and let them work.

Technicians and scientists will solve problems, new products will be invented, productivity will be increased, and raw materials and energy will be better utilized. All these efforts combine to solve the imbalance and to reducing the enormous amount of debt. It is important that technicians acquire leadership and work at the forefront of the improvements required by society and the planet.

It is a unique moment for technicians and scientists; they are more necessary than ever. This notion is an important one that must stand at the center of productivity issues.

Money merchants and mutual funds sales forces have lost their position; there is no money in circulation with which to speculate. It is time for real economy, real wealth, represented by goods and technology. And given the scarcity of everything, scientists and technicians are the ones who are able to provide solutions.

1.5. Definitions

The reader must be clear about certain concepts before continuing with the introduction. These concepts coincide with the development of this book. While assimilation of the following definitions may be difficult at first, these concepts will become clearer through examples provided.

Process

A manufacturing process is the set of tasks to which a material or materials is submitted from the moment the manufacturing order is given until it is delivered to the client (internal or external).

1. Introduction to Industrial Productivity

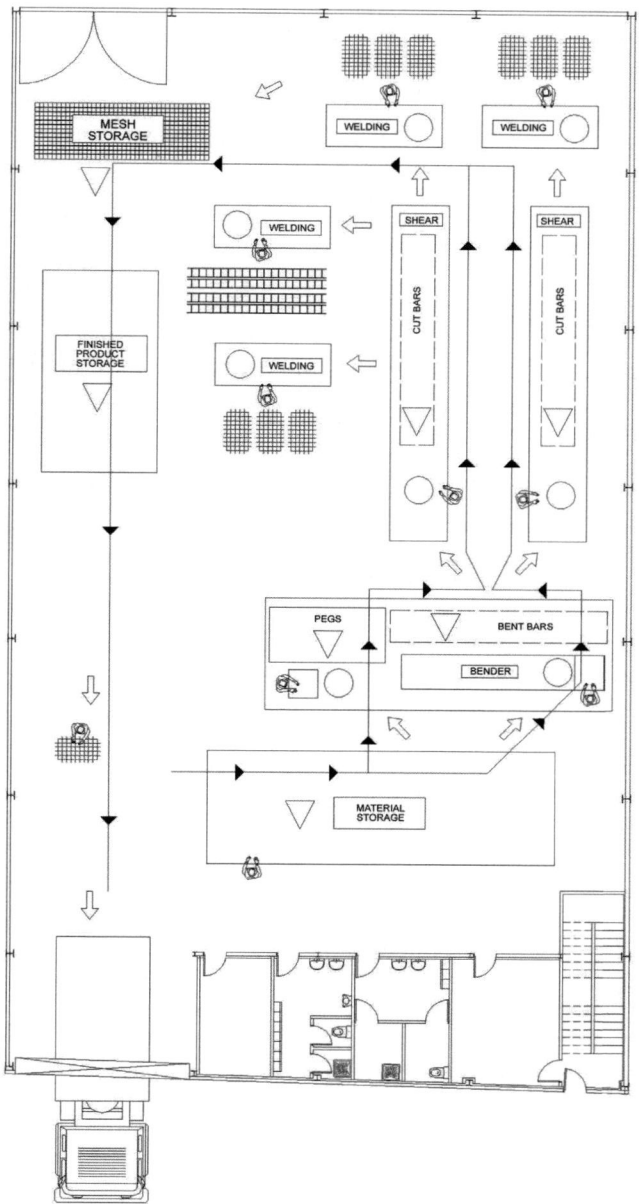

Figure 1.1. Rebar production process layout

Task

A task is a work unit of operations, consisting of an operator or team of operators and/or machines that work on a material or materials. A task is composed by operations. If they are material transformation tasks, they are value-adding (VA) activities.

Figure 1.2. Welding task

Non-value-adding tasks (NVAT)

Within the process, it is that task that does not change the state of the material (e.g., transport, stockpile, or search for) or tasks that change the state of the material in a manner that is pointless. Moving material with the pallet truck from one section to another is an NVAT, as is palletizing or placing material on shelves..

Operation

Every task consists of a number of different movements to carry it out. Classified and disaggregated, these movements constitute the operations of the task. Detail and grouping of movements and micro-motions can assume a variety of levels based on the analysis methodology used. In fact, an operation can be divided into micro-operations. If the operation adds transformation to the material, it is a value-adding operation (VAO).

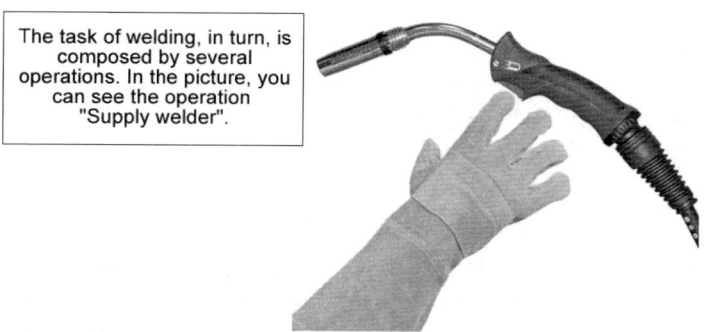

Figure 1.3. Welder supply operation

Non-value-adding operations (NVAO)

This operation does not transform the material or, if it does, it does so uselessly. For example, an NVA task would be displacement of an operator to fetch a component 10 feet from the task location or the repair of a recurrent error by a supplier or previous task.

Process diagram

This graphic form of representing a manufacturing process can be presented schematically or in a layout.

Method

A specific sequence of operations fulfills a certain task.

Standard time (ST)

A standard is the required time for an average operator, fully qualified and trained, and working at a normal pace, to fulfill a task according to the established method. It is determined by adding the assigned time for each of the elements that compose the task. It is measured in person-time (person-hours or person-minutes) and in machine-time.

Best standard time

This measure is calculated by subtracting the sum of times of all non-value-adding operations of the specific method from its standard time. It is the sum of time of the VA operations and may be referred to a task or a process.

Waste

According to Toyota waste is "everything that is not the minimum quantity of equipment, materials, parts, space and time of the operator that is totally essential to add value to the product." Hence, waste time is reduced by eliminating non-value-adding operations.

Minimum amount of necessary time (MANT)

The manufacture of a product or service is a process composed of several tasks necessary for its fulfillment. Each of the tasks will have an associated standard time as determined by a time and methods study. MANT is the sum of the best standard times of the tasks involved in the process:

$$MANT = \sum \text{Best Standard Time i}$$

Formula 1.1

> All the time it takes to perform above the MANT is waste. The aim should be ZERO WASTE and this book will address the methodologies and tools to achieve this goal.

1.6. Structure of This Book

As discussed, the aim of this book is to recognize and reduce manufacturing costs and deadlines. Because this book is about work times and standards and, supposing the materials used are constant, cost reduction will be achieved by the reduction of execution time.

The goal then is shown graphically in Figure 1.4.

1. Introduction to Industrial Productivity

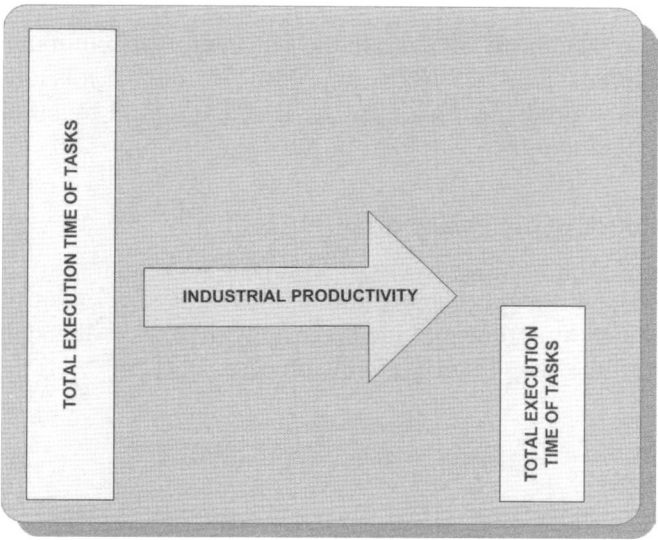

Figure 1.4. *Book aim: Reducing execution time of tasks*

This overall aim, or result, is divided into four main stages, which are addressed in the book's four parts.

Part I: Productivity Diagnosis

The first part of this book is a methodology to identify, from the total amount of time that is spent in manufacturing, what is necessary time, what is waste or time lost, and what are the causes of this waste.

To be able to improve manufacturing times, it is necessary to disaggregate where time is lost and the causes. From that point, solutions can be determined and improvement attempted. In this first part the concept of *waste measurement theory* is introduced, which breaks down the time components involved in manufacturing. Figure 1.5 shows this step graphically. The first time division made is as follows:

1. Standard time, the necessary time to carry out a task or set of tasks, with current methods and means

2. Waste time, spent in addition to the standard time

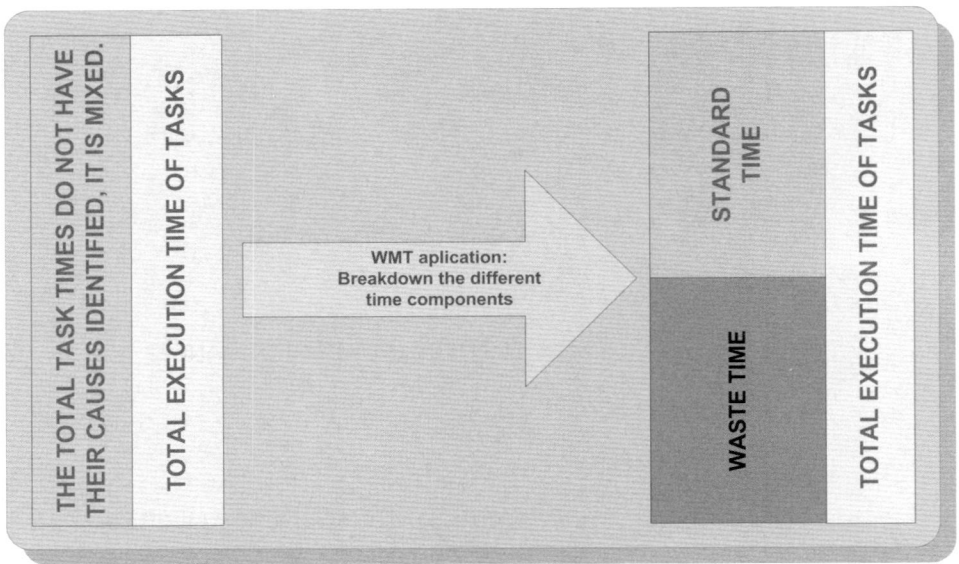

Figure 1.5. Waste measurement theory applications for diagnosis

Waste exists that is implicit within standard time. Given a working method, the standard time does not have to be the lowest, so a **working method design waste** exists. Figure 1.6 includes this *Waste in work design*. Standard time actually includes two components:

1. Minimum amount of necessary time (MANT) = $\sum$ Best standard time.
2. Waste in work design: in the method and the process.

Another time division is made to separate waste into two primary causes, which are shown in Figure 1.6:

1. Waste from low performance
2. Waste from management failures

1. Introduction to Industrial Productivity

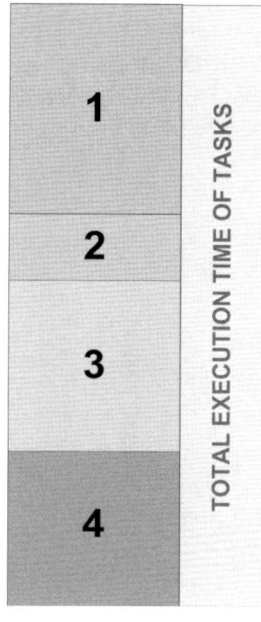

1. MANT
2. WASTE IN WORK DESIGN
3. WASTE BY LOW PERFORMANCE
4. WASTE BY MANAGEMENT FAILURES

Figure 1.6. Time breakdown into causes

Once the breakdown of what is happening is obtained, it is important to determine how to reduce each component of manufacturing time. The remaining parts of the book explain how to act on each of the components. This figure will serve as guide for the reader to identify which is the aim of the chapter he is studying.

Part II: Study, Analysis, and Improvement of Methods

In any task, the first thing to do is to study its work method, define it, and then take that analysis and criticism and use it to improve the current method. In this part, action is taken upon the standard time in order to improve it. **The aim of the study and analysis of methods is to reduce the standard time**. Figure 1.7 illustrates that an action is being taken on waste. Action on the standard time comes from improvement in methods—in other words, by acting on waste reduction in the working method.

In this second part ergonomic improvements will also be studied. They provide the most effective and useful way for the employee to improve a method.

Industrial Productivity

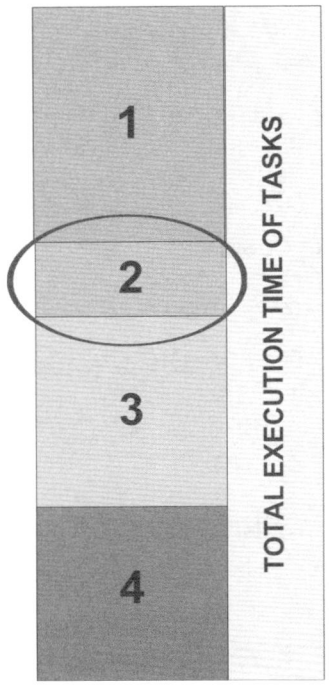

1. MANT
2. **WASTE IN WORK DESIGN**
3. WASTE BY LOW PERFORMANCE
4. WASTE BY MANGEMENT FAILURES

Figure 1.7. Action on the task's standard time

Part III: Time Study

In order to define and improve the working method of a task, it is necessary to measure the time required for its execution, either per unit or per batch, which can be accomplished through a time study. In this part, work and action will be assessed to determine standard time and techniques for its measurement will be learned. Initially, to measure is not to improve. However, simply quantifying the operations of a task will inevitably bring a reduction of time; by having the information broken down, decisions may be made.

The image corresponding to this part is also shown in Figure 1.8. Actions are performed on the standard time, not explicitly to improve it, but to quantify it.

That which is measured and observed is improved.

Part IV: Application of Methods and Standards

The standard time on its own does not provide any value. Times must be used to manage production, and the goal of applying calculated time is to reduce manufacturing wastes: management failures waste and low-performance waste. The solutions for these two wastes are, respectively, operation planning and productivity control. Times and methods, then, allow these two functions to be put into practice, in addition to reducing standard time.

Operation planning tries to assign resource quantities, eliminate bottlenecks, and make decisions to take action on poor management waste. Its part in attacking total execution time is represented in Figure 1.8, graphically and qualitatively.

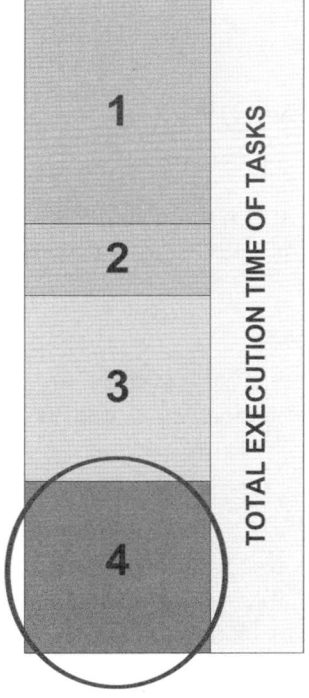

1. MANT
2. WASTE IN WORK DESIGN
3. WASTE BY MANAGEMENT FAILURES
4. **WASTE BY LOW PERFORMANCE**

Figure 1.8. Action on waste for management failures

Productivity control enforces standard times by the comparison between required times and accomplished work (measured in time) and acts on low-performance waste, as graphically shown in Figure 1.9.

Industrial Productivity

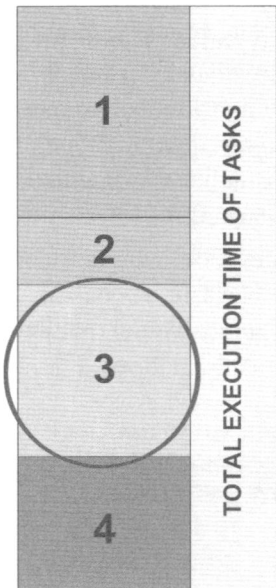

1. MANT
2. WASTE IN WORK DESIGN
3. **WASTE BY MANAGEMENT FAILURES**
4. WASTE BY LOW PERFORMANCE

Figure 1.9. Action on low performance waste

Link between the actions

Methods and times, operation planning, and productivity control are three indispensable functions in radical reduction of the execution times of tasks. They are the three pillars of productivity. In the following scenarios, one of the pillars is missing.

Scenario 1: Standard times and operation planning tools are available but not productivity control. With the standard time of each task and the manufacturing shipments necessary, resources are calculated to be able to undertake the work. Workload and necessary capacity are calculated, but a lack of productivity control fails to ensure that standard times will be met, which is the equivalent of not having them. Therefore more time will be spent, resources will be insufficient, and bottlenecks will be generated, which will leave the next stations without work, generating downtime and jeopardizing deadlines. The final execution time will be much higher than planned.

Scenario 2: Standard times and productivity control are available but planning of operations is lacking. Operators will comply with the standard times when they can fulfill them. However, for periods of time a lack of balance between workload and capacity or because of missing material means workers are idle. When previous sections are not properly sized, and other factors will arise. In such circumstances operators often refuse to be under a control system whose standards are impossible to meet. Without proper planning, balance and saturation will be lacking and will result in waiting times and down times in such a way that the total execution time exceeds standard time.

Scenario 3: Productivity control and planning tools are available, but not standard times. This scenario is essentially impossible. Without standard times, any planning or productivity control systems are meaningless, although many plant managers try to make this shortcut work. They inevitably fail in the attempt, often without realizing it.

We can conclude, therefore, that industry cannot be productive if one of these pillars fails. By default, standard time is the raw material for all the processes. Figure 1.10 illustrates this conclusion.

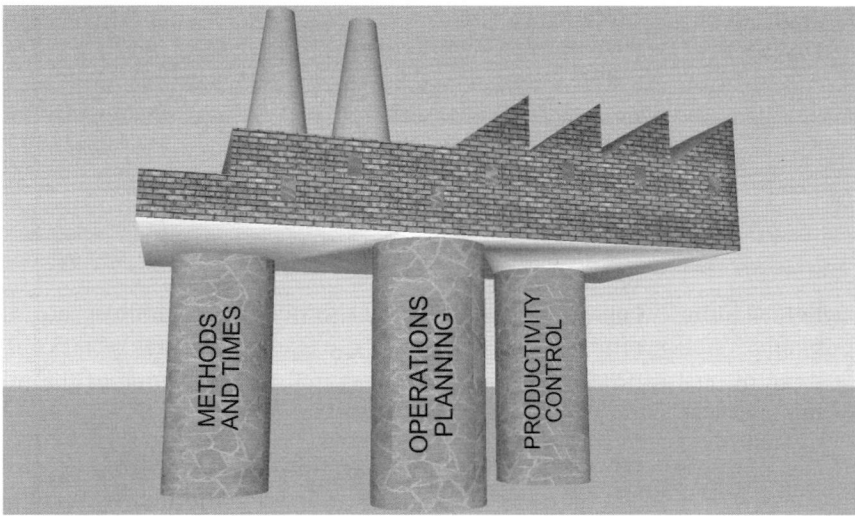

Figure 1.10. The three pillars of productivity

Finally, applying the three functions (the scientific work study) achieves reduction in the total execution time.

Because this book is extensive, it is important to have a graphic guide to tell us each moment where we are. The following list is our guide. It will appear at the beginning of each part of the book to signal which we are in. (See also Figure 1.11.)

Industrial Productivity

1. MANT
2. Waste in Work Design
3. Waste from Low Performance
4. Waste from Management Failures

Part	Aim	Initial Situation	Final Situation
Part 1: Productivity Diagnosis	We start with manufacturing execution times and want to know what caused them.	TIEMPO TOTAL DE EJECUCIÓN DE LA TAREA/S	1, 2, 3, 4
Part 2: Study, Analysis, and Improvement of Methods	We study and improve the work method of a task to reduce its necessary execution time. The same occurs with processes.	1, 2, 3, 4	1, 2, 3, 4
Part 3: Time Study	With a defined and improved method, we time the task through various techniques to be able to establish a standard, which implies time improvements.	1, 2, 3, 4	1, 2, 3, 4

1. Introduction to Industrial Productivity

Part 4: Application of Methods and Standards [Operations Planning]	With standard times, we can manage production, measurement, make decisions, etc. Waste from management failures is reduced.		
[Productivity Control]	With standard times, productivity can be better controlled, reducing the waste from low performance.		

***Figure 1.11.** Guide for navigating through the book*

If we compare the initial situation in Part 1 with the final situation in Part 4, the graphic result is as shown in Figure 1.12.

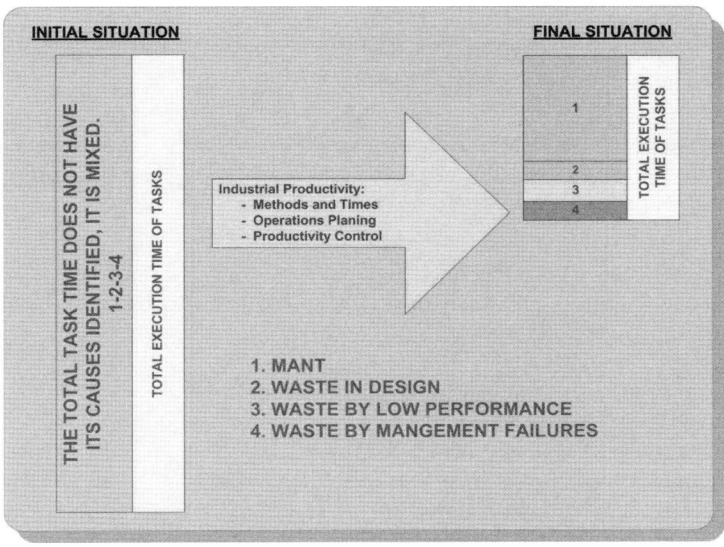

***Figure 1.12.** Result in execution time when applying scientific study of work*

Throughout the book, example cases, modified or invented with pedagogic purposes, will be presented and are applicable to many real-world cases. Although their efforts to take in risk in order to produce products the world needs or wants are admirable, industrialists and manufacturers sometimes make mistakes. The examples presented are an attempt to help readers avoid making these common mistakes.

Bibliography

Drucker, Peter, *The Effective Executive* (New York: Harper & Row, 1967).

Porter, Michael, *Competitive Advantage* (New York: Free Press, 1985).

Smith, Adam, *The Wealth of Nations* (London: 1776).

Womak, James P. and Daniel T. Jones, *Lean Thinking* (New York: Simon & Schuster, 1996).

PART I
PRODUCTIVITY DIAGNOSIS

1. MANT
2. WASTE IN WORK DESIGN
3. WASTE BY LOW PERFORMANCE
4. WASTE BY MANAGEMENT FAILURES

Part	Aim	Initial Situation	Final situation
➡ Part 1: Diagnosis	We start from a manufacturing execution times and we want to know what caused them.	TIEMPO TOTAL DE EJECUCIÓN DE LA TAREAS	1 / 2 / 3 / 4
Part 2: Methods	We study and improve the work method of a task to reduce its necessary execution time. The same with processes.	1 / 2 / 3 / 4	1 / 2 / 3 / 4
Part 3: Time measurement	With a defined and improved method we time the task through various techniques to be able to establish a standard, this implies time improvements.	1 / 2 / 3 / 4	1 / 2 / 3 / 4
Part 4: Operations planning	With standard times we can manage production, dimensionate, make decisions, etc. Waste by management failures is reduced.	1 / 2 / 3 / 4	1 / 2 / 3 / 4
Part 4: Productivity control	With standard times productivity can be controled reducing the waste by low performance.	1 / 2 / 3 / 4	1 / 2 / 3 / 4

Chapter 2

The Theory of Waste Measurement

2.1. Introduction and Definition

In this first part of the book, a methodology for diagnosing productivity is outlined. The diagnosis is especially important to be able to adopt measures; it is the first step for improvement. However, what is really going to be constructed is **a methodology to measure unproductiveness.** For that reason, we will consider absolute productivity to be the execution of manufacturing work according to the "best feasible standard time." All time spent over this amount is considered waste.

Because the best standard time and the time spent are known quantities, the calculation of unproductiveness will not be more difficult than a simple subtraction. The diagnosis must be much more: it must identify the causes and be quantifiable by indicators. In this way, the causes of that unproductiveness can be attacked.

To measure unproductiveness, the following *theory of waste measurement* is developed. Valuable information is found in the study of details. Therefore, the proposed diagnosis methodology needs to start in observation and information collection in the workplace, with each machine. **As is shown in Figure 2.1, the product that is manufactured has an associated intrinsic time, which is the MANT, or how the International Labor Organization (ILO) denominates "work content." Time greater than the MANT is attributed to waste and its causes.**

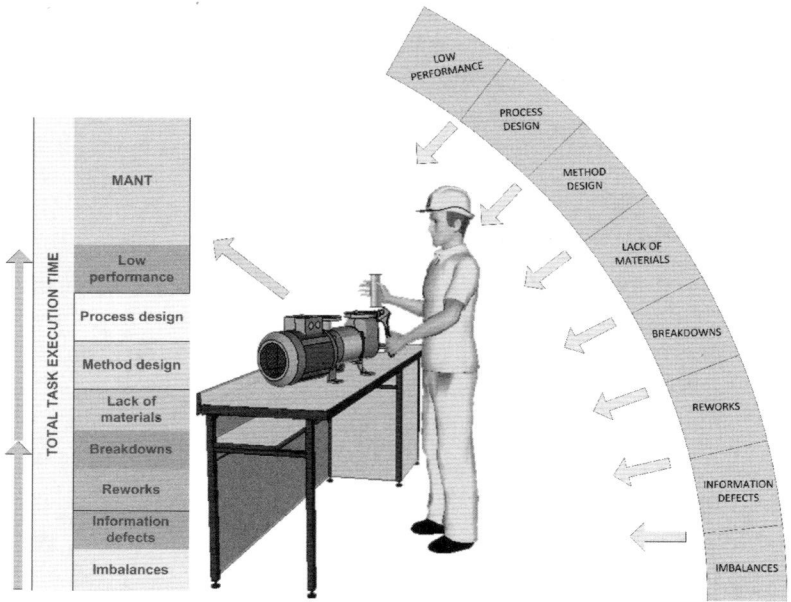

Figure 2.1. Observation of the workplace and waste causes.

The *theory of waste measurement* was developed by Zadecon (Industrial Organization Engineering) in 2008 to measure the unproductiveness in manufacturing and then be able to measure the available improvement capacity of the system using indicators and common criteria.

The only way for management to diagnose the state of an industrial company is through detailed observation of its productive tasks. As shown in Figure 2.1, incidences of unproductiveness can be detected through observation. These incidences can include lack of materials, information errors, maintenance failures, lack of work, bottlenecks, defects in quality, absence of method, a wrong method or process, and low performance. All these factors are what cause, along with their subcauses, a high component of waste within the work performed .

This chapter will describe a method for waste calculation in industries or other types of workforce activities; *the goal of the rest of the chapters of this book is its elimination.* The concept of waste in industrial activities is not new; the goal of waste management and elimination has been used by several authors and numerous companies as a management tool.

The theory of waste measurement (WMT) includes the following aspects:

1. **Waste measurement methodology.** Even though great progress has been made from Taylor to Taiichi Ohno, a common methodology for quantifying waste does not exist. These data are important for evaluating the state of a factory and its improvement potential.

2. **A breakdown of this measurement in terms of its causes and variation from established indicators.** Waste has certain causes that can be separated and quantified. Well identified, these causes can be scientifically targeted for radical reduction. Once causes are identified, work must be done where more problems are being generated and where changes in global waste can be effected.

3. **Creation of visual systems: Waste maps.**

4. **A standard methodology of productivity and waste diagnosis.** Really, when the department of operations or consultants and operation engineers act to improve their factories or processes, what they focus on is reducing wastes. With this theory, the methodology to diagnose is based on waste measurement, from which potential improvements will emerge. It is critical for effective use of these indicators that they be understandable by all.

5. **Identification of the different methodologies that exist for waste reduction.** Tools of operations management serve to reduce production waste in terms of its causes. Within the first part of the book, these tools will be identified by referring to them and the chapters in which they are covered.

This chapter and the next introduce the rest of the book. References will therefore be made to concepts that belong to the following chapters; definitions considered necessary will also be inserted. This first part is the most important of the book, the one that indicates why and how we must act, that generates motivation. After studying the book, rereading this first part will help in acquiring a proper vision.

The point here is not about process improvement or continuous improvement or process reengineering and cost reduction or anything that may be or seem positive. It is about something negative: THE WASTE THAT EXISTS. Logically, once known, it will give information to act and perform improvements to eliminate or reduce it. Manufacturing time reduction can be treated two ways:

1. Improve current situation. It may seem the current situation is good and what is needed is to improve it.

2. Eliminate/reduce the wastes that cause the current situation. It is supposed that the current situation is bad and must be made productive.

The theory of waste reduction is based on the second approach. Even though the result of both is qualitatively the same, quantitatively it is not, and quantity matters. When speaking about losses human beings react differently from the way they act when speaking about possibilities of improvement. Why? Because we assume not winning, but losing is not assumed. Therefore, speaking about a possibility of improvement is speaking about something that really is not necessary to be done. If we speak about losses we are having, we may speak about necessary actions.

Remember that we are diagnosing unproductiveness, the diagnosis of what is being lost.

When it comes to risk, a man prefers not winning the double of what he is willing to lose. It seems that it has an anthropologic explanation: prehistoric men who preferred to conserve what they already had survived in higher proportion, even if it meant forgoing hunting and experiencing the pain and suffering that hunger caused. Therefore, we will speak about losses and not about improvements because only pain leads to change. To diagnose losses is much more convincing for inspiring action than diagnosing improvement possibilities.

It is about measuring what *is* against what *needs to be*. The losses lie in that chasm between one point and the other. Neither analytic nor accounting management quantify those losses, but they really are there and are important because the day any of the competitors, who also have them, eliminate them, then the accounts will reflect the hard reality that will oblige all others to cut prices or shut down.

> **Waste = Losses**
> **(which will be reflected in accounts sooner or later)**

The aim of scientific work study and operations management must be to reduce waste and execution times.

A product's total manufacturing time is composed of three components:

- Standard time: Breakdowns into the "best standard time" (MANT) and the defects in method.

- Low-performance time: The time spent due to below-normal performance that adds to total time of the operation.

- Management failures time: The errors in operations planning cause an increase in execution time.

- Execution time = Standard time + Low-performance time + Management failures time.

Sun Tzu: "Therefore I say: **Know your enemy** and know yourself; in a hundred battles you shall never be defeated."

> The first goal is to know the waste:
> With the *theory of waste measurement* (WMT), waste will be identified and quantified

In Figure 2.2, is presented the first breakdown that must be reached:

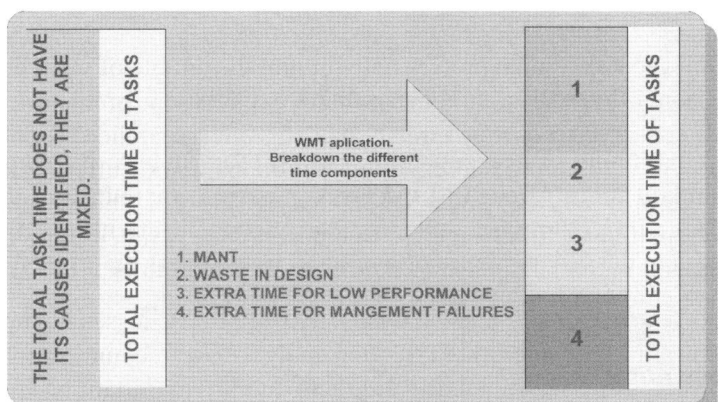

Figure 2.2. Breakdown of total execution time into the four large components

The waste is great, but once discovered and localized it can be "removed" from the factory.

Once identified, waste becomes available improvement.

Definitions

The two concepts already defined in the introduction are worth repetition here. Following this reminder, new definitions and concepts will be provided.

Waste

According to Toyota, waste is: "everything that is not the minimum quantity of equipment, materials, parts, space, and time of the operator, which are totally essential to add value to the product." The object of the WMT is the measurement of workforce waste, which, by definition, is the cause of unproductiveness.

Minimum amount of necessary time (MANT)

According to the previous definition, the first place to look for waste is its relationship to the minimum amount of necessary time (MANT) for the fulfillment of each task that composes the manufacture of a product or the development of a service. From there, the function of the time spent allows us to deduce the waste.

A product or service comes out of a process composed of several tasks for its fulfillment. Each of the tasks will have a standard time associated that will be the result of a study of times and methods and the elimination of non-value-adding operations. Then, the minimum amount of necessary time (MANT) of a process is:

Industrial Productivity

$$\text{MANT} = \sum \text{Best Standard Time i}$$

Formula 2.1

The minimum amount of necessary time (MANT) is equal to the summation of the best standard times of each of the tasks needed to manufacture the product or provide the service through a determined process. To clarify this formula we proceed to graph the task structure of a product in a process diagram. An example diagram for a generic product can be found in Figure 2.3.

Explanatory note

Hereafter the expression $\sum$ Standard Time will appear repeatedly and refers to:

3. For processes and for design at work, the sum of the standard times of the tasks that compose a process, which normally refers to a product unit.
4. For a certain manufacturing, the sum of standard times of some tasks multiplied by the number of times that the task is repeated for certain products, which is referred to as a particular manufacturing shipment, with its batch dimensions and different references.

Analogously it applies to the concept MANT.

With the examples provided in this chapter this concept will be clarified.

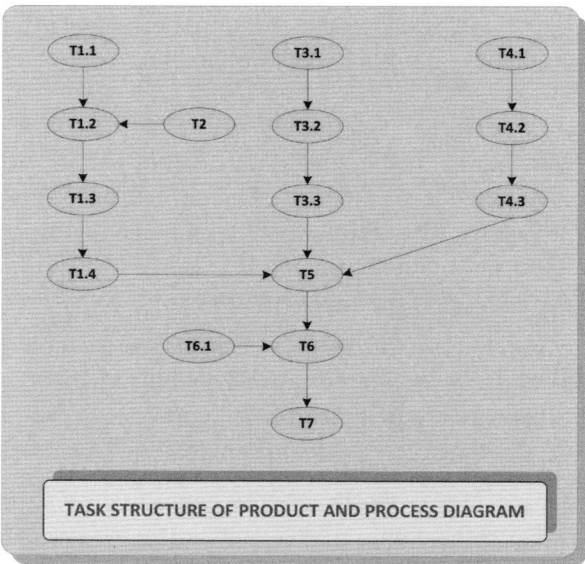

Figure 2.3. Task structure for a generic process

2. The Theory of Waste Management

For the tasks in Figure 2.3, a hypothetic standard time can be calculated for the minimum amount of standard time (MANT) that Toyota defines. Any additional time spent becomes waste.

Task	Best Standard Time (minutes)
T1.1	7
T1.2	5
T1.3	9
T1.4	5
T2	5
T3.1	8
T3.2	5
T3.3	9
T4.1	3
T4.2	1
T4.3	3
T5	2
T6	10
T6.1	7
T7	21
CMTN	100

Figure 2.4. Best standard times and MANT of the product structure

Therefore, for a hypothetic product and from the best standard time of the tasks needed for its manufacture, it has been determined that the MANT is 100 person-minutes.

The waste in the manufacturing time is the time spent in a process above the MANT; this waste has origins or causes that are divided into two large groups.

1. Waste in work design, which in turn is divided into:
   - Waste in the work method of the task
   - Waste in the process

2. Waste in manufacture, which in turn is divided into:
   - Waste from management failures
   - Waste from low performance

The *waste in work design* quantifies the amount of time spent without adding value to the product due to poor design of the method and/or process. The operators can work diligently and the factory be well managed, but a loss of time is inherent in the poor execution of tasks and the process they follow.

The *waste in manufacture* measures the time used over and above the standard time for the designed methods and processes, which is based on the development of everyday production. These losses in time may be the result of low performance of operators, that is, lack of materials, down time, lack of work, bottlenecks, malfunctions, and so on.

> The theory of waste measurement says:
> 3. Waste exists in the use of time.
> 4. Waste can be measured by concrete causes and determined from coefficients.
> 5. Such coefficients can constitute a tool for measuring the state of the factory from which to act for its management and improvement.

2.2. Waste in Work Design

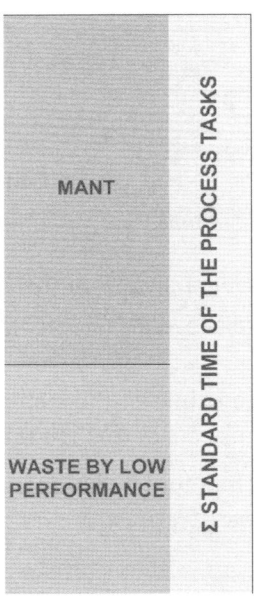

Figure 2.5. Waste in standard time by work design

This figure can be converted to a mathematical model that answers the following equation:

$$\sum \text{Standard Times} = \text{CwD} \times \text{MANT}$$

Formula 2.2

2. The Theory of Waste Management

Where:

CwD is the coefficient of waste for work design, which is always greater than 1. It is a dimensionless number that indicates waste, or the amount of time from a poor design of work that deviates from the minimum amount of time that could be used to develop a process.

The waste in work design arises from two sources:

1. Tasks inside the operations fail to add value to the product, which is referred to as waste in the work method.
2. Tasks within a process fail to add value; for example, an operator dedicated to transporting parts from one workstation to another or tasks that are exclusively of warehouse management.

Every task can be represented by the following methodology:

Icon	Type of task
 ◯	Value adding task.
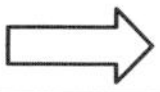 ⇨	Displacement.
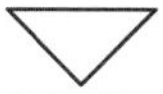 ▽	Storage.
 D	Delay or wait.
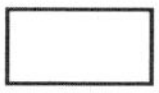 ▭	Inspection.
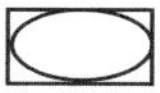 ◌	Inspection-Operation.
 B	Search.
 ⍉	Eliminable task.
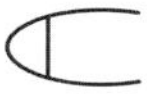 C	Communication.

Figure 2.6. *Operation symbols*

Every operation or task that does not correspond to the circle of value-added operations implies waste in the work design.

The process studies the set of tasks, and inside the process are non-value-adding tasks. Even within value-adding tasks are operations, some of which add value and others that do not. The following figure contains an explanatory graphic.

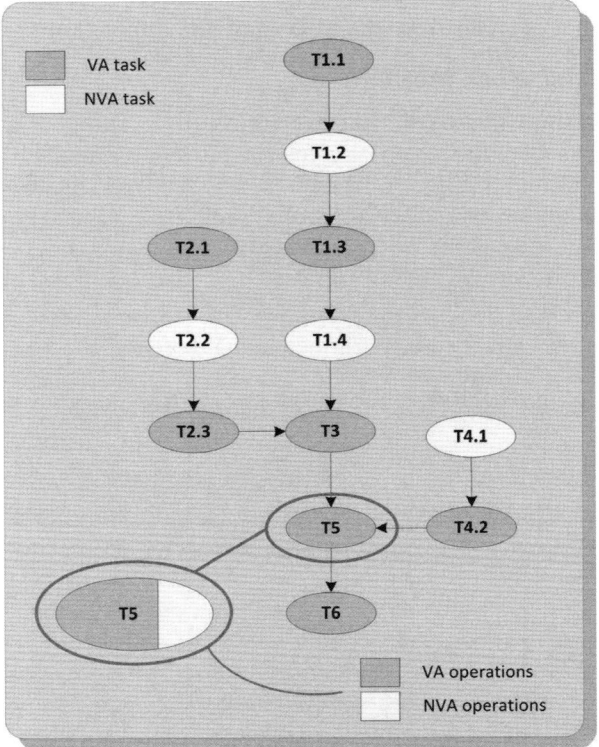

Figure 2.7. Hypothetical process with value-adding and non-value-adding tasks

Many different processes can be used to make a certain product. A task within a process can have one standard time or another or even be different tasks. When choosing between one process or another, we opt for the one whose summation of standard times is lower. For example, it is thought that manufacturing in large batches saves time. It is true that value-adding tasks are made more quickly by the effect of specialization; however, if many intermediate stocks are generated, new displacements, and searches and storage tasks appear, the process can come to have more wastes overall. **When comparing standard times, what is important is the sum of the group of processes.**

To establish criteria and fix variables, the following order of priorities is recommended:

    1. Optimize the process.

    2. Optimize the methods.

2. The Theory of Waste Management

Research has shown that the most efficient way to eliminate wastes is to focus on the total. Once the process is improved, action has to be taken on each task and its method. The loss of the vision of the process as a whole has on occasion made for efficient tasks at the expense of the whole.

2.2.1 Waste in the Work Method

A work method is the sequence of operations to fulfill a certain task. The operations can be classified according to typology and operations symbols previously shown.

Everything within the task that does not correspond to a value-adding operation represents waste of method design. To correctly understand this concept, we show a work method and its time breakdown.

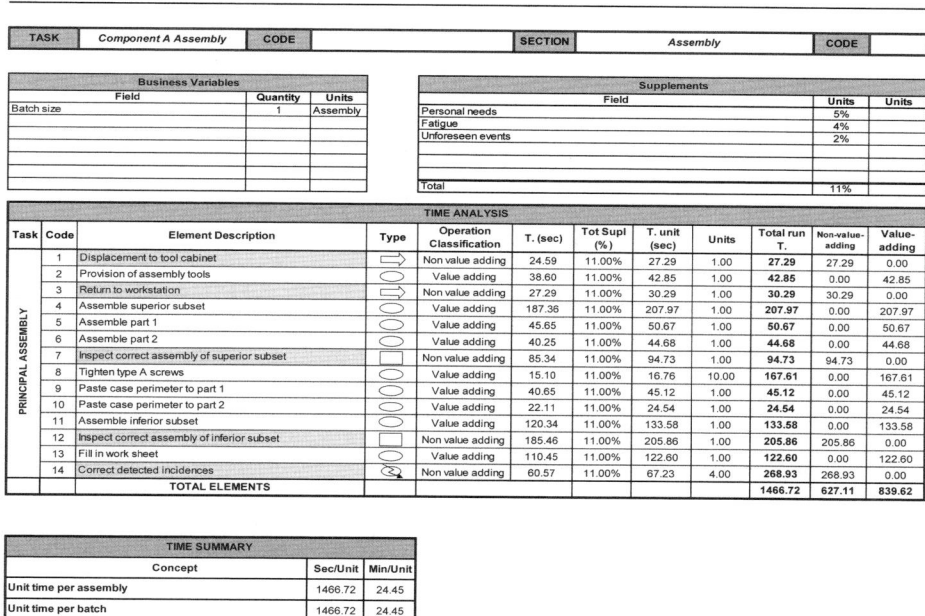

Figure 2.8. Example of work methods and task times

Within this method, non-value-adding operations such as displacements, inspections, and operations that should not be done are revealed. The corresponding time of these operations is waste. As a result, breakdown and quantification must be done. If a column for "operation classification" is added and completed with the data "value-added" and "non-value-added," the standard time of the task can be quantified in a final report by the current method, which will include the best standard time and the time waste for method. From here, a first indicator can be determined, *coefficient of waste for method (CwM)*, which will quantify the waste in relation to the best standard time.

For a certain task:

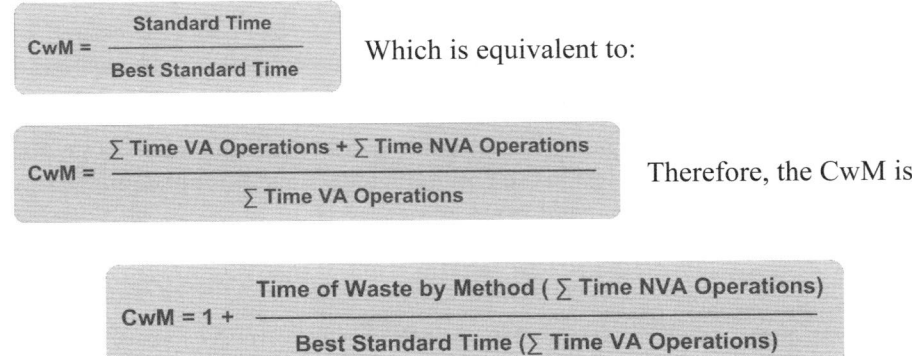

$$CwM = \frac{\text{Standard Time}}{\text{Best Standard Time}}$$

Which is equivalent to:

$$CwM = \frac{\sum \text{Time VA Operations} + \sum \text{Time NVA Operations}}{\sum \text{Time VA Operations}}$$

Therefore, the CwM is:

$$CwM = 1 + \frac{\text{Time of Waste by Method } (\sum \text{Time NVA Operations})}{\text{Best Standard Time } (\sum \text{Time VA Operations})}$$

Formula 2.3. *Calculation of the coefficient of waste for method (CwM)*

Visually, we have the next column:

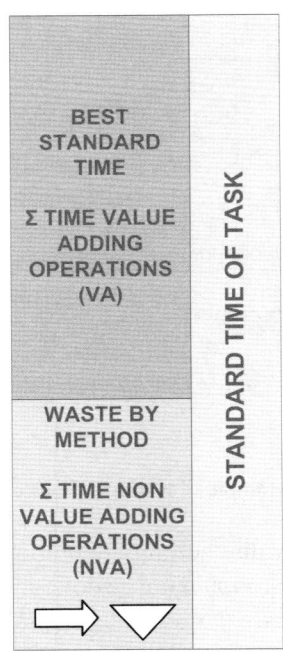

Figure 2.9. *The waste from method of a task*

The previous is applied to the method under study.

2. The Theory of Waste Management

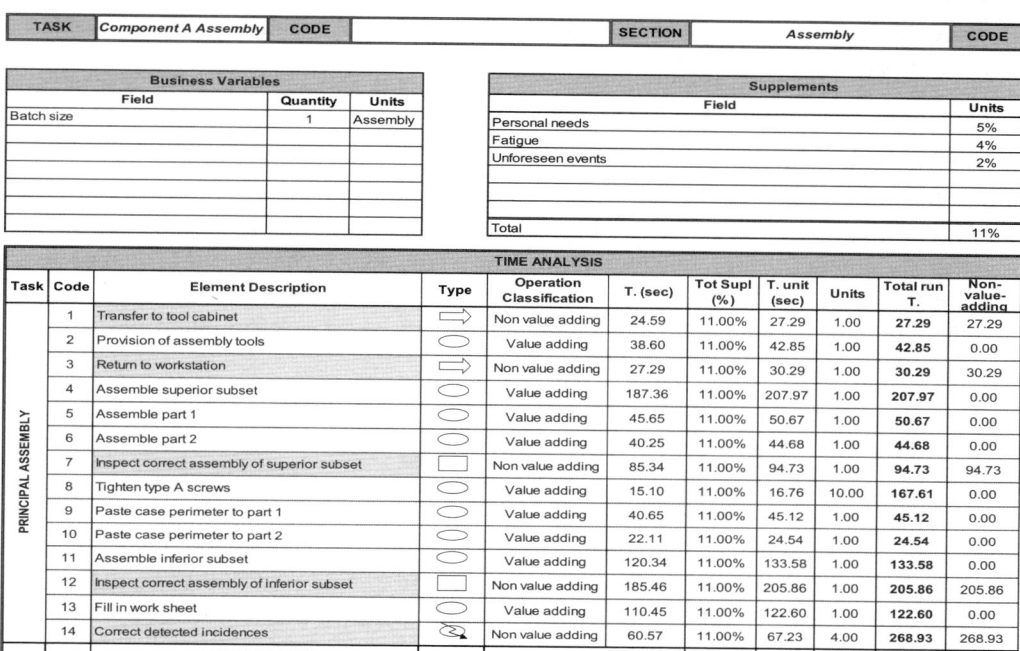

Figure 2.10. Classification of VA operations and NVA operations

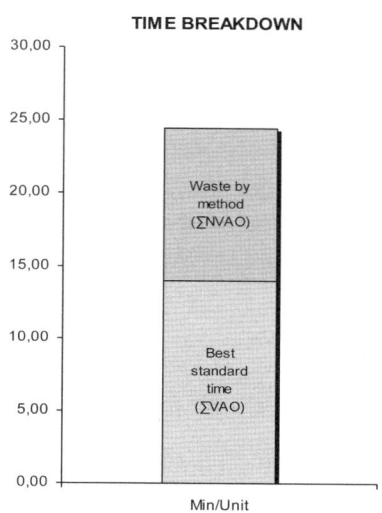

Figure 2.11. Time breakdown: Waste – Best Standard Time

The best standard time only sums the times for operations that, if not done, would leave the product incomplete. All others must be eliminated.

CwM must tend to 1, meaning that everything above it manifests waste in the method and, therefore, potential for improvement.

The definition of the best standard time does not contemplate other possible improvements such as the ones that could emerge from materials that are more appropriate, from a better technology that, for example, allowed a higher rate of progress, a better design in engineering, and so on. Those elements that cannot be quantified will not be considered in the waste quantification. At some point we must stop and fix variables, that is, the best standard time is the one given for a task with specific materials and technology.

2.2.2. Waste in the Process

The design of the manufacturing plant, the stock policy, the distance between tasks, and other variables can cause added waste for the type of process from which it derives. The tasks can be classified the same way as the table of operations. Given the process definition, **waste for process will be considered the time that all those tasks occupy inside the process that do not add any value**. These tasks can include transportation between sections, storages, and delays.

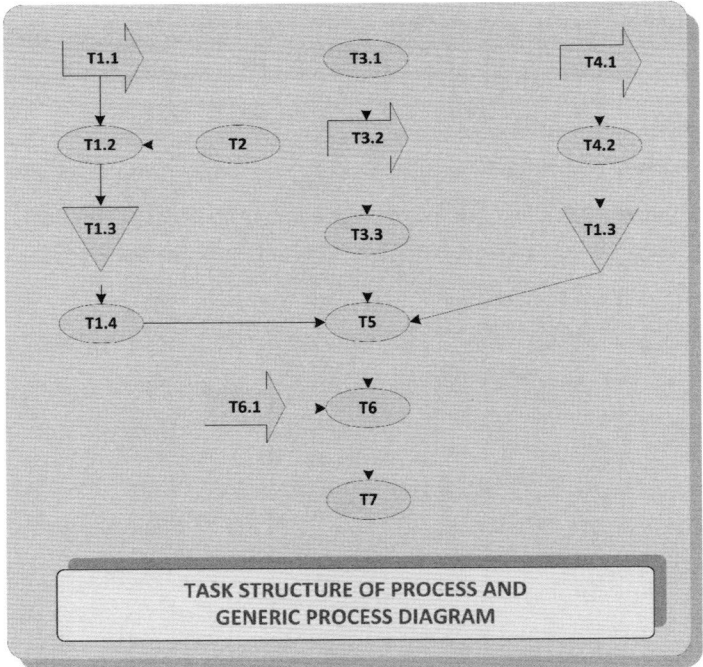

Figure 2.12. Structure of process with symbols

2. The Theory of Waste Management

As can be observed in the previous process, non-adding-value tasks exist, such as displacements and storages. The corresponding time to those tasks is waste. In the process map, eliminating the tasks that should not exist will be done. From here an indicator for evaluating the process design can be obtained: *Coefficient of waste for process (CwP)* will quantify how much time is waste with respect to the time of the perfect process—that is, the process that includes only value-adding tasks.

For a certain process:

$$\sum \text{Standard Time} = \text{CwP} \times \sum \text{Standard Times of VA Operations}$$

Which equals:

$$\text{CwP} = 1 + \frac{\sum \text{Time NVA Tasks}}{\sum \text{Time VA Tasks}}$$

Formula 2.4. *Calculation of the coefficient of waste for process (CwP)*

If the standard times of each task are known, as shown in the following table, the coefficient can be deduced.

Task	Best Standard Time (minutes)	Symbol
T1.1	7	
T1.2	5	
T1.3	9	
T1.4	5	
T2	5	
T3.1	8	
T3.2	5	
T3.3	9	
T4.1	3	
T4.2	1	
T4.3	3	
T5	2	
T6	10	
T6.1	7	
T7	21	
TOTAL PROCESS	100	

Figure 2.13. *Standard time and typology of tasks*

For the type of task, we have the next apportionment:

- Time dedicated to added value = 66 minutes
- Time without added value = 34 minutes

$$CwP = 1 + \frac{34}{66} = 1.51$$

Equally, a representative bar can be contributed.

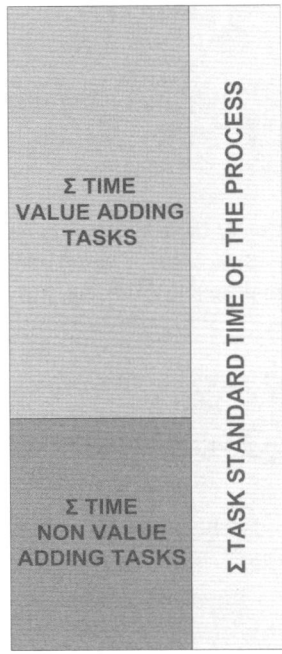

Figure 2.14. Waste in the process

The process is represented visually with non-value-adding tasks crossed out, with its coefficient of waste for process quantified.

2. The Theory of Waste Management

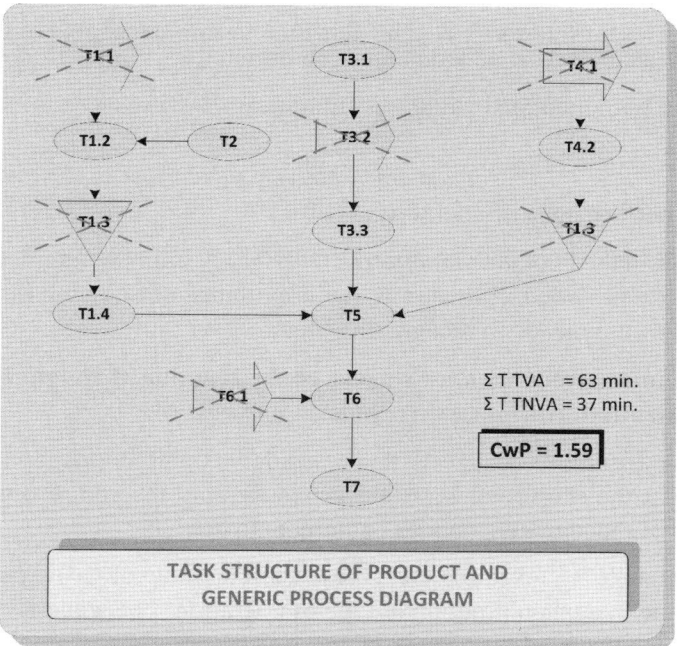

Figure 2.15. Process diagram with CwP

CwP must tend to 1; that is, everything above it manifests the current waste for process and, therefore, the potential for improvement.

The CwP measures how poorly the process is designed, meaning the amount of displacements and storages that are within the process. The more intermediate stocks a process has and the farther from one another are the workplaces, the higher will this coefficient be, unrelated to how well designed the tasks are individually. The CwP measures how poorly tasks are related among themselves.

2.3. Waste in Manufacture

The wastes treated so far are those due to the design of the task and the process in itself; they are constant wastes for certain conditions and a way of working. Insofar as no change occurs in these ways of working or in the conditions or means of the factory, the coefficients of waste, CwM and CwP, will not vary.

In this section a different waste from the previous ones will be studied, a dynamic waste that changes every day. To be able to define this concept, variables need to be fixed and what has been studied in section 2.2 must be blocked out. Starting from a process and methods, which are constant, a new waste surfaces. It is the waste in manufacturing and consists of the time spent above the standard times of a process's tasks, whatever the methods and process. It is a waste added to the one already present due to its design. For this reason, concepts are not going to be mixed.

This waste can be divided in two major causes:

1. Management failures
2. Low performance of operators

An excerpt from the book *Introduction to Work Study* from the International Labor Organization is provided. It illustrates the importance of knowing the causes and how scientific study leads to recognizing them:

> **Work measurement may start a chain reaction throughout the organization.** How does this come about?
>
> The first thing to realize is that breakdowns and stoppages taking effect at the shop-floor level are generally only the end results of a series of management actions or failures to act.
>
> Let us take an example of excessive idle time of an expensive machine in a batch production type of operation. This excessive idle time was revealed by a study taken over several days. The piece of plant is very productive when operating but takes a long time to set up. It is found that a great deal of the idle time is due to the fact that the batches of work being put on this machine are very small, so that almost as much time is spent in resetting it to do new operations as is spent in actual production. The chain of reactions resulting from this discovery may be something like this:
>
> **The work study department**
>
> reports that work measurement reveals that the machine is idle for excessively long periods because of small orders coming from the planning department. This is substantially increasing the cost of manufacture. It suggests that the planning department should do some proper planning and either combine several orders for the same product into one large order or make more for stock.
>
> **The planning department**
>
> complains that it has to work on the instructions of the marketing department, which never seems to sell enough of any one product to make up a decent-sized batch and cannot give any forecast of future orders so that more can be made for stock.

The marketing department

says that it cannot possibly make forecasts or provide large orders of any one product as long as it remains the policy of top management to accept every variation that customers like to ask for. Already the catalogue is becoming too large: almost every job is now a "special."

The managing director

is surprised when the effect of marketing policy (or lack of it) on the production costs is highlighted and says that the aim was to prevent orders going to competitors by being as obliging to customers as possible.

One of the principal purposes of work study will have been served if the original investigation leads the managing director to think again about marketing policy. Enthusiastic work study persons may, however, find it well to pause a moment and think about the fact that such chains of reaction tend to make someone ask: "Who started this, anyway?" People do not like being "shown up". This is one of the situations in which a good deal of tact may have to be used. It is not the task of a work study specialist to dictate marketing policy, but merely to bring to the attention of management the effect of that policy on the company's costs and hence on its competitive position.

Thus it can be seen that the purposes of work measurement are to reveal the nature and extent of ineffective time, from whatever cause, so that action can be taken to eliminate it; and then to set standards of performance of such a kind that they will be attainable only if all avoidable ineffective time is eliminated and the work is performed by the best available method and by appropriately trained and capable personnel. (ILO, 1992, p. 245).

As can be seen the cause of time loss in production can be far away from the workplace. At the workplace the effect is seen, from a simplistic point of view the blame will fall on the operator or the production manager, nevertheless, blaming does not solve anything. The WMT exists to find and quantify the real causes of waste. Only in that way it may be solved. The following excerpt is provided from the same book.

Work measurement, as the name suggests, provides management with a means of measuring the time taken in the performance of an operation or series of operations in such a way that ineffective time is shown up and can be separated from effective time. In this way its existence, nature and extent become known where previously they were concealed within the total. One of the surprising things about plants where work measurement has never been employed is the amount of ineffective time whose very existence is unsuspected—or which is accepted as "the usual thing" and something inevitable that no one can do much about—that is built into the process. Once the existence of ineffective time has been revealed and the reasons for it tracked down, steps can usually be taken to reduce it.

Here work measurement has another role to play. Not only can it reveal the existence of ineffective time; it can also be used to set standard times for carrying out the work, so that, if any ineffective time does creep in later, it will immediately be shown up as an excess over the standard time and will thus be brought to the attention of management.

Earlier it was mentioned that method study can reveal shortcomings of design, material and method of manufacture, and, as such, affects mainly technical people. Work measurement is more likely to show up management itself and the behaviour of the workers. Because of this it is apt to meet with far greater resistance than method study. Nevertheless, if the efficient operation of the enterprise as a whole is being sought, the application of work measurement, properly carried out, is one of the best means of achieving it.

It is unfortunate that work measurement—and in particular time study, its principal technique—acquired a bad reputation in the past, especially in trade union circles. This was because in many early applications it was directed almost exclusively to reducing the ineffective time within the control of the operatives by setting standards of performance for them, while the ineffective time within the control of management was virtually ignored. The causes of ineffective time over which management has some control are much more numerous than those which lie within the direct control of the workers. Furthermore, experience has shown that, if causes of ineffective time such as hold-ups due to lack of raw materials or to plant breakdowns are allowed to go on without real efforts being made to eliminate them, operatives tend to get discouraged and slack, and "workers' ineffective time" increases. This is only to be expected: the attitude taken by the workers is, quite simply: "Well, if we are going to be stopped from doing our jobs by something which we can do nothing about and which it is management's job to put right, why should we work harder? Let management put its own house in order first." It is an argument that can hardly be countered. (ILO, 1992, p. 244).

2. The Theory of Waste Management

What does the excerpt mean?

1. The majority of waste that occurred during manufacture is caused by management failures.
2. These management failures cause waste from low performance in the operators (and largely justified).
3. Therefore, waste from management failures has a multiplying effect. For example, an hour lost from lack of materials will cause an added loss of time in discouragement and excuses.

A dimensionless parameter is now going to be defined, which will be called *coefficient of waste in manufacturing/production* (CwF). It articulates the relationship between the real required time during manufacturing and the sum of standard times.

Therefore,

$$\text{Real Manufacturing Time} = \text{CwF} \times \sum \text{Standard Times}$$

Formula 2.5. Coefficient of waste in manufacture

CwF is always larger than 1 and is broken down into the following factors:

$$\text{CwF} = 1 + \text{Cact} + \text{Cm}$$

Formula 2.6. CwF breakdown

Where:

4. Cact: the coefficient that measures the waste for unproductiveness caused by low performance of workforce.
5. Cm: the coefficient that measures the waste caused by management negligence.

It can be represented graphically, as shown in Figure 2.16.

Industrial Productivity

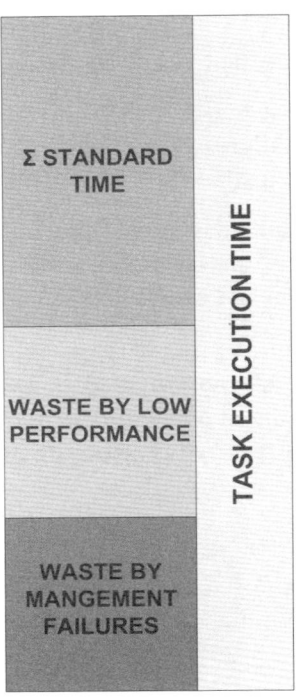

Figure 2.16. Breakdown of the execution time into standard time and waste in manufacturing

The waste starts in this case from the summation of standard times, which in turn, as seen in the previous paragraph, contains waste for work design. Based on Figure 2.16 and from Formulas 2.5 and 2.6, the value of coefficients Cm and Cact will be calculated:

According to Formula 2.5: Real Manufacturing Time = CwF x ∑ Standard Time

Then:

$$CwF = \frac{Real\ Time}{\sum Standard\ Time}$$

Formula 2.7.

According to Figure 2.16:

Real Time = ∑ Standard Time + Low Performance Time + Management Failures Time

Formula 2.8.

Dividing the equation between $\sum$ Standard Time results in:

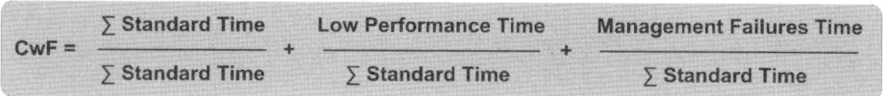

Formula 2.9.

Taking into account Formula 2.6:

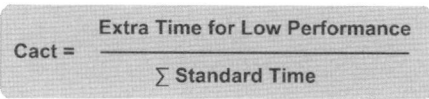

Formula 2.10.

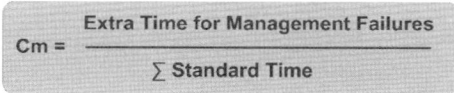

Formula 2.11.

Therefore, all the manufacturing waste is divided in two groups and is measured from these two coefficients. To be able to measure how much waste was due to one cause or the other, we define the following:

- Controlled time (CT) is measured in person-time, in which operators have been able to produce with total normality and without incidences and, therefore, a production proportional to that time and the standard time of the products manufactured.

- Incidence time (IT) is measured in person-time, in which, by management failures (lack of work, of materials, etc.), the operators have not been able to produce with normality.

- Presence time (PT) is measured in person-time, during which the operators were in the factory.

$$\text{Presence Time} = \text{Controlled Time} + \text{Incidence Time}$$

Formula 2.12.

Presence time is the time that the company will have to pay at the end of the month, with or without production. Presence time is the equivalent to the

Industrial Productivity

time spent to execute tasks, well or poorly spent. It is the number of hours to be allocated among total production.

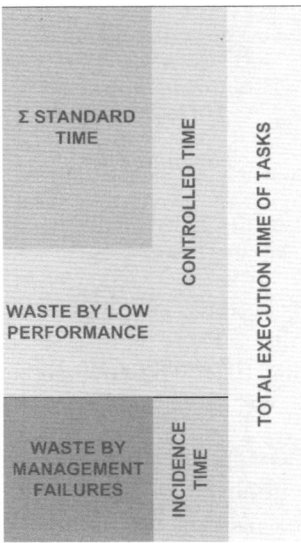

Figure 2.17. Identification of causes for time spent in manufacturing

To be able to calculate the waste in manufacturing it is necessary to control all the components of time that are shown in Figure 2.17. This control is named *productivity control*. In the fourth part, a complete chapter is dedicated to control methodologies and their implementation. However, due to its importance in diagnosis, the concept is introduced in advance. Productivity control could be defined as:

"A comparison system between the work performed in time without incidences (controlled time) and the one that should have been done and which also measures the incidence time and identifies its causes."

2.3.1 Manufacturing Waste from Low Performance

This type of waste is due to, simply, the fulfillment of tasks in a time greater the standard with no other cause than poor performance. Workforce can only cause waste within the controlled time, this is, within the time during which they were able to be productive, or during the presence time and with no incidences.

Activity is the measure of the performance of operators; this concept is developed in the fourth part. Among the different measurement scales of activity, the 60-80 and the 100-133 are the most commonly used. For intuitive ease in this explanation, the 100-133 will be used, because 100 is the normal activity. Activity is the ratio

2. The Theory of Waste Management

between the performed work (measured in standard time) and the time spent to perform the work. In the 100-133 scale it would be expressed as:

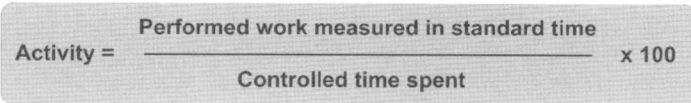

$$\text{Activity} = \frac{\text{Performed work measured in standard time}}{\text{Controlled time spent}} \times 100$$

Formula 2.13.

Therefore, whenever Activity falls below 100, it is an indication of waste from low performance.

The previous activity is the activity calculated with hindsight in function of performed work and spent time. There is also an observed activity, which the analyst observes while timing. It will be covered in the third part of the book. However, the *definition of activity* is anticipated for its relevance.

A single operation, even if it is performed by the same operator, can be subject to variations in the real execution times. Hence, the need for quantification and classification of different work paces is the concept of activity.

Activity is work pace in its broadest sense, which depends on the following factors:

- Fidelity to the method
- Movement precision
- Movement speed
- Perseverance

Insofar as the highest levels of those factors are reached, activity will increase and the execution time will diminish. The more accurate the method, the more precise and quick will be the movements, resulting in lower execution time and higher activity levels.

To be able to calculate the Cact, it is necessary to start from the classification and register of hours, obtained from the productivity control system. A hypothesis is fixed, which is that the activity will always be under 100, indicating low-performance waste. Sometimes the activity is higher than normal. In this case, operators are supposed to perceive an incentive or bonus but it is a scenario not taken into account in this part of methodology development. In the fourth part of the book, in the chapter *Productivity Control and Incentive Systems*, these concepts will be developed with greater detail.

What has to be calculated is the time spent above the standard for the activity.

Waste from Low-Performance Time = Controlled Time – $\sum$ Standard Time

Industrial Productivity

If the equation is divided between $\sum$ Standard Time:

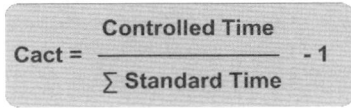

Formula 2.14.

It is possible that Controlled Time is lower than $\sum$ Standard Time, then Cact will be negative, but, as has been indicated previously, this scenario is not going to be considered in this part.

2.3.2 Waste from Management Failures: Incidences

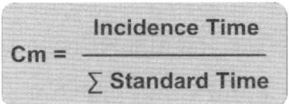

Formula 2.15.

Incidence time (IT) is caused by failures in the management of the company. The possible management failures that can cause noncontrolled time include the following:

- **Lack of materials (Clm):** Materials do not arrive on time to the workplace and cause operator stoppage. It can be the result of a failure in purchasing management or an upstream mismanagement that prevents materials from reaching the workplace.

- **Imbalance between workload and available capacity (Cim):** In all productive processes, a limiting task determines the amount of production that can be made in the rest of the tasks, no matter their capacities. The greater the difference in capacity between the different phases, the greater the imbalances will be. In these cases, rather than explicit stops, what happens is a lowering of the pace to "stretch the available work." The imbalance can also be caused by lack of workload, failing to match existing capacity, caused by lack of orders, an oversizing of productive capacity, a bottleneck, and so on.

- **Stops for breakdowns (Cmt):** Breakdowns cause stops that are not imputable to low performance.

- **Defects of information (Cdi):** They can cause stops or unnecessary work.

- **Reprocesses (Crp):** It is the time spent to redo work due to a failure in quality.

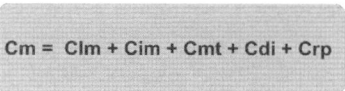

Formula 2.16.

The coefficient of each management failure will be calculated from the time wasted by such failure divided by the $\sum$ Standard Time.

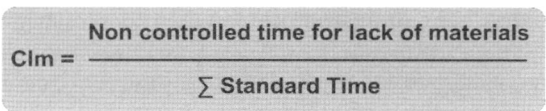

Formula 2.17.

Analogously it will be done to the rest of coefficients.

CwF must tend to 1 from Cm and Cact, which tend to 0.

As in the previous cases, we proceed with an example of calculation of these coefficients.

2.3.3 Example of CwF Calculation

The control of productivity is a tool for comparing the work performed measured in standard time with the controlled time spent. If the time from the work performed is higher than the time spent, then this scenario is of high performance, otherwise, we will be facing waste from low performance. The productivity calculation in this case will be made for tasks or phases and not for operators because what is being calculated is the waste of the system and not the caused by each operator. Although they are calculations that can be made in parallel, what matters from the CwF is the calculation of productivity of the system.

For this calculation, the next data collection is needed:

1. Assistance reports in which the total dedication time is indicated
2. The annotation in the reports of incidence hours and their causes
3. Actual production

From these three inputs, the different coefficients that compose the CwF can be obtained.

With the equations from the previous section we should be able to calculate the coefficient of manufacturing waste in any situation; however, the following example is given to help comprehend how to make these calculations.

Example

Suppose that during a given week of the year we want to calculate the waste that has been produced in manufacturing the product whose structure is shown in Figure 2.12 and whose sum of standard time is 100 person-minutes. The data are as follows:

- *Four operators work in the manufacturing of this product, and during the specified week they all worked 8 hours per day.*
- *The registered incidence hours in the reports are the following: Monday, 3 hours due to lack of materials; Tuesday, 4 hours due to information errors; Wednesday, 7 hours due to a machine breakdown; Thursday, 0 hours; and Friday, 6 hours due to imbalance between tasks.*
- *The production data were the following: Monday, 12 units; Tuesday, 16 units; Wednesday, 15 units; Thursday, 14 units; and Friday, 14 units.*

With these data and the available standard time, CwF and its components can be calculated.

Coefficient of Waste in Manufacture CwF

In total, 71 units were manufactured during the week. If standard time is 100 minutes per unit, the $\sum$ Standard Time for 71 units is 7,100 minutes. The time spent is 4 operators × 8 hours/day × 60 minutes/hour = 9,600 minutes.

$$CwF = \frac{\text{Real time}}{\sum \text{Standard times}} = \frac{9,600}{7,100} = 1.35$$

This initial data indicate that the manufacturing remittance has cost, in terms of direct labor, 1.35 times what is contemplated as standard. It is necessary to apportion more CwF for this information to be useful.

Coefficients of Waste Cact and Cm

CwF = 1 + Cact + Cm; so Cact + Cm = 0.35, which is the quantity by which unit cost and the standard time of manufacturing are determined.

$$Cact = \frac{\text{Controlled Time}}{\sum \text{Standard Time}} - 1$$

Controlled time = Presence time – Incidence time

Presence time = 9,600 minutes

2. The Theory of Waste Management

Incidence time = 20 hours x 60 = 1,200 minutes

Controlled time = 9.600 − 1.200 = 8,400 minutes

$$Cact = \frac{8,400}{7,100} - 1 = 1.18 - 1 = 0.18$$

$$Cm = \frac{\text{Incidence Time}}{\sum \text{Standard Time}} = \frac{1,200}{7,100} = 0.17$$

To better explain these coefficients, consider the following:

- *A coefficient of waste in manufacturing of 1.35 indicates that, for every 100 minutes manufactured in standard time, the costs are actually equivalent to 135 minutes.*
- *A Cact of 0.18 indicates that, due to low performance of the operators, for every 100 minutes manufactured in standard time, 118 have been spent, that is, 18 more minutes than the standard.*
- *A Cm of 0.17 indicates that, due to management errors, for every 100 minutes manufactured in standard time, 117 have been spent, that is, 17 more than the standard.*

Cm Apportionment

Cm has several possible causes, which appear in the reports as the amount of incidence hours. For example, to calculate Clm, the incidence minutes from lack of materials (180) have to be divided between the $\sum$ Standard Time (7,100). The same calculations are made for other causes as well.

Concept	Incidence Hours	Incidence Minutes	Coefficient	Coefficient Value
Lack of Materials	3	180	Clm	0,025
Information Errors	4	240	Cdi	0,033
Breakdowns	7	420	Cmt	0,060
Imbalances	6	360	Cim	0,051

***Figure 2.18.** Cm breakdown*

The sum of coefficients results in 0.17, which is equal to, logically, Cm.

In percentages, it can be said that 2.5% of the excess costs are the result of material shortages, 3.3% are caused by errors in information, 6% by breakdowns, and 5% by workload imbalances.

2.4. All Waste Coefficients: Combination and Criteria for Their Use

To summarize information provided in the previous chapter, two grand typologies of waste exist:

- Waste in work design (measured by CwD), which is caused by the waste in process (measured by CwP) and by the waste in method (measured by CwM)

- Waste in manufacturing (measured by CwF), composed by management failures and low performance

These waste typologies, although they are cumulative to the unproductiveness of the industry, are totally independent from one another. Having a task method and a defined process, the way in which the daily manufacturing is managed does not depend on those designs. Therefore, this book tries to contribute easy and applicable solutions, no combination between them is proposed because it would complicate the calculation and make its use more difficult. What is proposed is establishing some simple criteria for their use.

For Waste for Work Design

The wastes by method and by process can be linked, and therefore, the following criteria are adopted as steps to follow:

4. Reduce to the minimum waste for process: CwP tends to 1.
5. Reduce to the minimum waste for method: CwM tends to 1.

Among the alternatives that this analysis gives us, we will choose the one that results in the lowest sum of standard times, keeping in mind all the tasks of the process.

For the Waste in Manufacture

Regardless of the previous criteria, the aim is to reduce to the minimum the waste in this area; therefore, CwF tends to 1.

In General

The criterion is simple and, because of its simplicity, will be effective: **Eliminate all causes of waste, whatever their origin.** However, conceptually, the existing relationship among the coefficients can be modeled. Take into account the following equations:

$$\sum \text{Standard Times} = \text{CwD} \times \text{MANT}$$

Formula 2.18.

$$\text{Real Manufacturing Time} = \text{CwF} \times \sum \text{Standard times}$$

Formula 2.19.

So then:

$$\text{Real Manufacturing Time} = \text{CwF} \times \text{CwD} \times \text{MANT}$$

Formula 2.20.

These two coefficients, multiplied and greater than 1, represent the relationship between the time required to manufacture in a process and the minimum amount that is really necessary. CwF x CwD provide the indicators of total waste. This effect is graphically presented in Figure 2.19:

Industrial Productivity

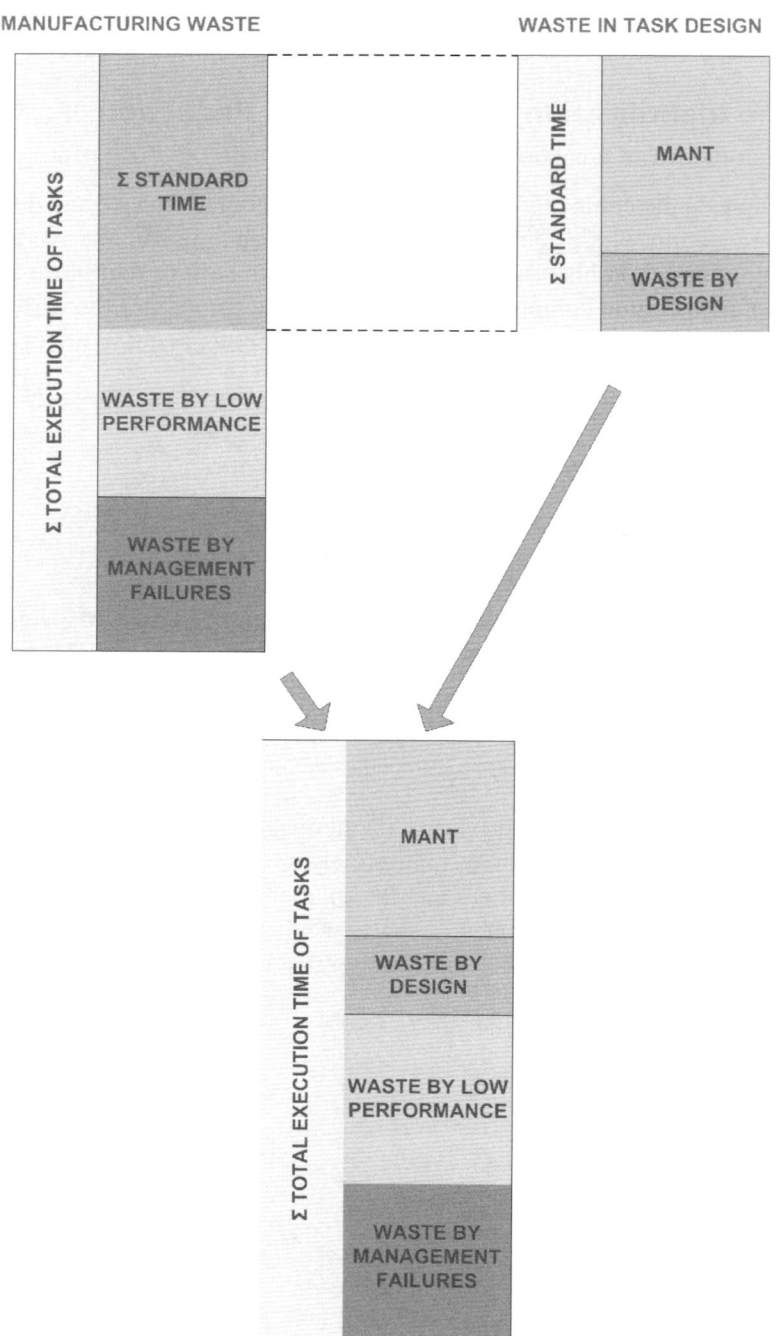

Figure 2.19. Accumulation of the effects of waste on MANT

In Chapters 3 and 4, these concepts are widely developed with examples of application.

2.5. The Identification of Waste and Its Reduction

The higher the waste breakdown in a factory, the smaller the size of it.

For example, some companies believe that they do not have waste and do not care about its reduction. These companies confuse standard time with the average times of execution based on historical figures. They do not believe that those historical times contain a certain component of waste. In these companies the waste has the shape (symbolically) of Figure 2.20. It is an amorphous being, without apparent limits, and is largely out of control.

Figure 2.20. Shape of waste in companies that do not identify or quantify it

Figure 2.21 shows the size and shape (symbolical) of waste in companies that searched for it and break it down. Figuretively speaking it shows how, the more apportioned the waste or its causes are, the smaller it is. It becomes a waste under control, bounded. This difference in the two types of companies seems logical because the breakdown provides information that makes it possible to attack and eliminate the waste.

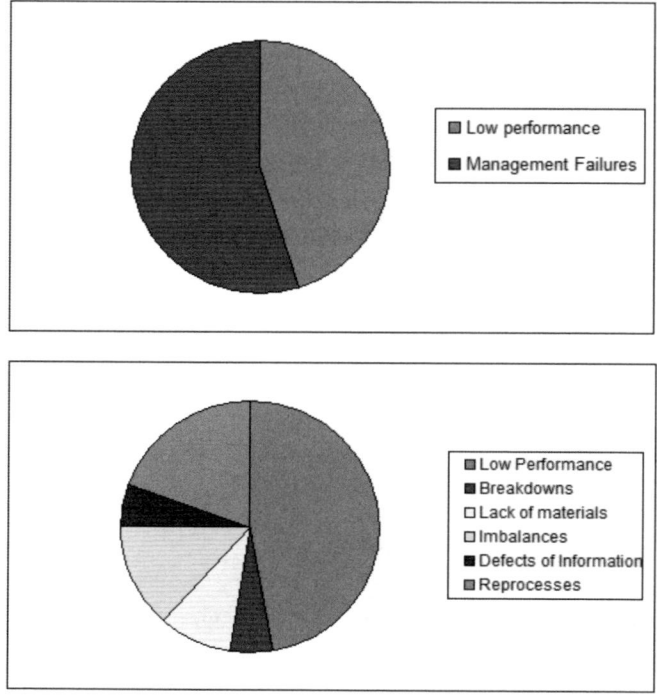

Figure 2.21. Shape of waste in companies that measure and pursue it

2.6. The Theory of Waste Measurement and Subsequent Communication

Before editing this book, I passed around a copy of the draft of the WMT method to collaborators from industrial organization engineering. These individuals in turn passed on some copies to industrial clients and managers.

One of these technicians found a great utility in the method and shared it with the rest. It was the communication element. By distributing the WMT document to different company agents and knowing these individuals had read it, he could easily speak about what was being done incorrectly.

Thanks to WMT he did not need to personalize about who was doing what wrong. Simply, by having worked on diagnosing the state of the factory, he was able to focus on the different wastes and in what sections they were produced. All the conversational partners took notice. It may seem obvious, but it is not. Let us consider that all of us in our workplaces suffer insecurities and make mistakes, this tendency makes it more difficult to solve the problems and communicate.

Political problems within companies, the pacts of silence, the internal myths (which perpetuate the assumption that people in charge do everything right while others always do it wrong), the unpleasant things a technician must tell his or her boss or client, will be addressed when we speak about waste with the language this theory has created. The WMT is not about opinions; it is a scientific measurement of waste, of its causes and where it is produced.

Maybe the best contribution that WMT can make is that it serves as a communication tool for the difficult topic of wastes and losses. The language and key words will make it possible to speak more easily about what is happening, and thanks to that language, the problems that have existed in silence for years can begin to be solved.

Questions

1. What aspects of task execution time are vulnerable to waste?
2. What two main types of waste exist?
3. How are those wastes classified in turn?
4. Indicate three causes of waste from management failures.
5. Indicate three types of operations that would be waste in the work method.
6. What is low-performance waste?
7. How has time without waste been defined?
8. Within a process, non-value-adding tasks, by definition, imply waste; however, can waste exist in value-adding tasks? Explain.
9. What time factor within manufacturing makes C_m higher?
10. How and where can information be acquired about waste and its causes?

Problems

1. Given the following method diagram and the time of each operation, indicate which operations are value-adding and which are not, marking the corresponding box. Calculate the CwM.

Industrial Productivity

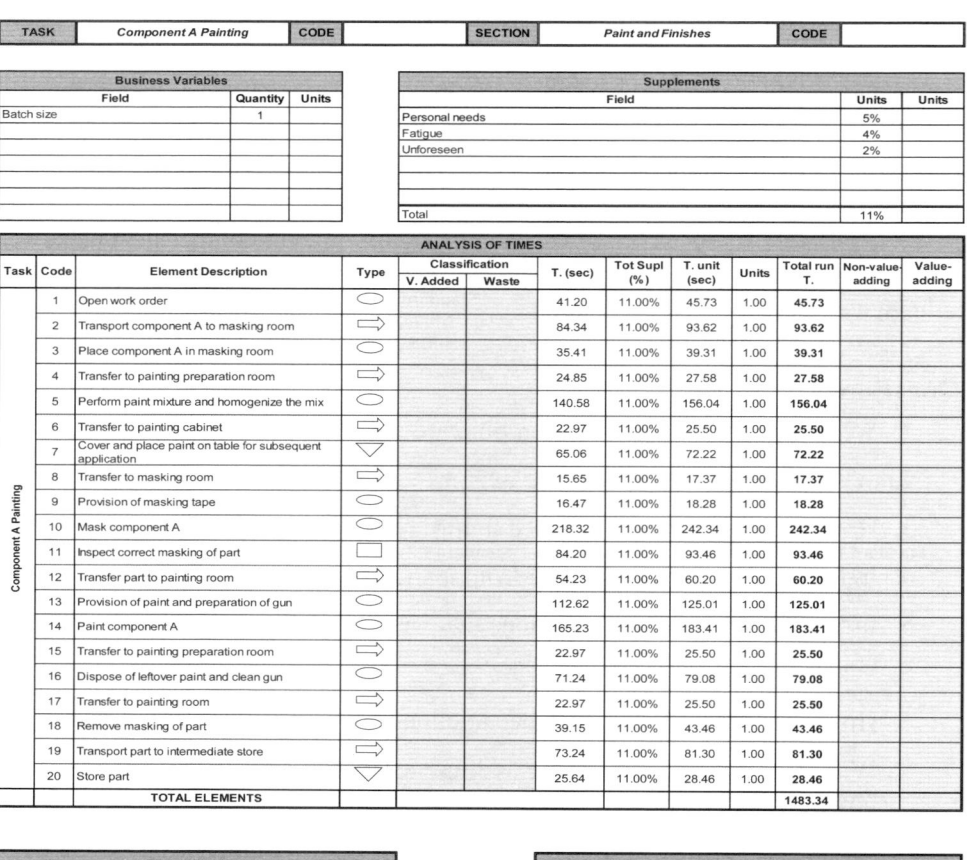

Figure 2.22. Problem 1: Method diagram

2. Given the process diagram (Figure 2.23), indicate which tasks are value-adding and which are not by marking the corresponding box. Calculate the CwP.

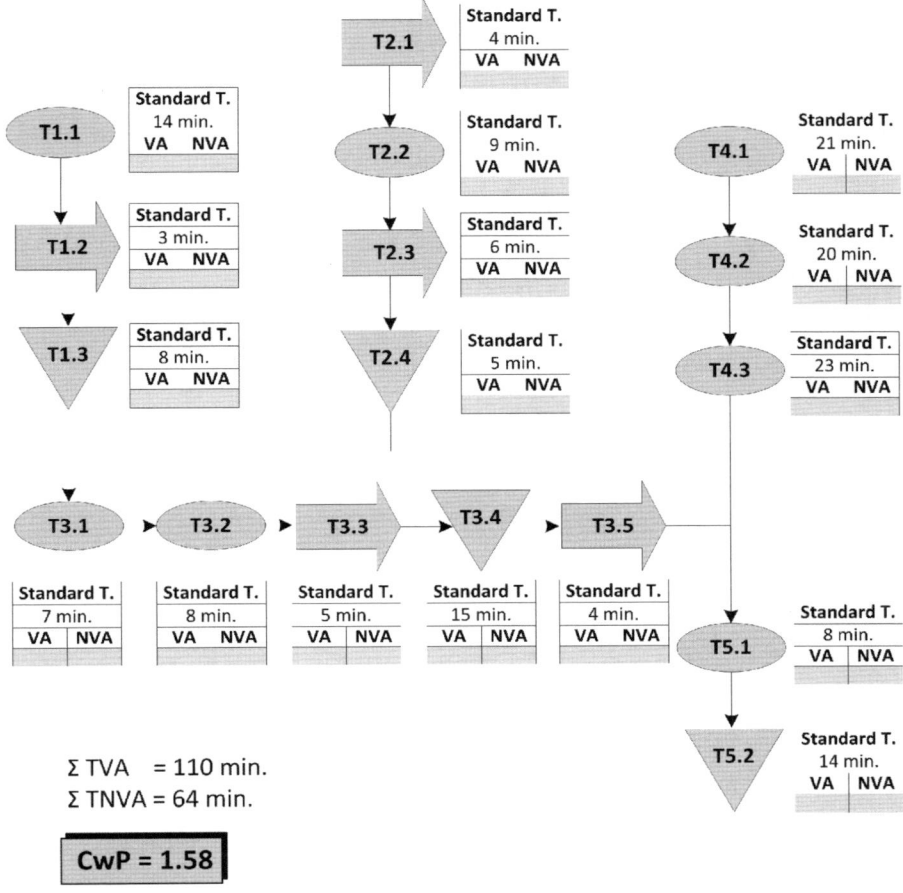

Figure 2.23. Problem 2. Process diagram

3. During month of February 2010, five factory operators manufactured 3,000 B1c type parts, whose standard time was 12 person-minutes. From work reports, the following data are noted:

- The five operators worked the whole month (20 workdays), and each worked 8 hours per day. There was no absenteeism.

- The incidence person-hours from the reports, divided by causes, are the following:

- 10 hours lost for task imbalance.
- 5 hours lost for lack of materials.
- 11 hours lost for breakdowns.

With these data, calculate the CwF, Cact, and Cm and all the components of Cm.

Bibliography

Kanawaty, George, *Introduction to Work Study* (Geneva, International Labor Organization, 1992).

Chapter 3

Diagnosis of Productivity

3.1. Introduction: Diagnosis of Unproductiveness

What does it mean to make a diagnosis of the state of manufacturing?

To identify the state of the factory and analyze the possibilities for improvement are the main focus for diagnosis. This activity is generic and no common methodologies exist; professionals use their own approaches, which are generally quite qualitative. In this book, our approach to describing the state of productivity involves identifying and quantifying the waste. The possibilities and proposals for improvement will be oriented to the elimination of such waste.

In this chapter, the methodology used to diagnose unproductiveness is the *theory of waste measurement* seen in the previous chapter. **It is about having a method and common indicators that can give a qualitative and quantitative vision of the state of a factory's unproductiveness.**

This approach is developed in the following manner:

- An index for a report for diagnosing unproductiveness
- A visual system named "Waste maps"

Part of the discussion includes how unproductiveness influences the costs and how it affects human elements. Finally, a section is dedicated to the solution to problems detected during diagnosis.

3.2. Report and Points of the Unproductiveness Diagnosis

To further apply the concepts explained in Chapter 2—the *waste measurement theory*—it is necessary to create a list of points to develop for discovering the waste. By giving expression to the data in a simple and legible way, the recipient is better able to understand what is unproductiveness (i.e., the waste) and, therefore, how much it can be improved and what steps to follow. It is convenient to create a standard report for identifying waste.

The following index of a diagnosis report for unproductiveness will serve as a guide for the analyst. Afterwards, each of the points in the diagnosis will be explained.

Diagnosis report on unproductiveness (WTM):

1- Introduction, background and definitions.
2- Samplings and observations performed.
3- Diagnosis of unproductiveness: Current situation.
   3.1- Diagnosis of unproductiveness by work design.
      3.1.1- Diagnosis of task method unproductiveness (CwM).
      3.1.2- Diagnosis of process unproductiveness (CwP).
      3.1.3- Quantification of total waste in work design (CwD).
   3.2- Diagnosis of manufacturing unproductiveness.
      3.2.1- Diagnosis of management failures (Cm).
         a- Information defects
         b- Workload imbalances
         c- Lack of materials
         d- Breakdowns
         e- Reworks
         f- Estimation of total incidence time
      3.2.2- Diagnosis of low performance (Cact).
      3.2.3- Quantification of total manufacturing waste (CwF).
   3.3- Unproductiveness report from the various waste coefficients obtained.
   3.4- Waste map and improvement deposits.
4- Problem solutioning: Actuation proposal on each waste.
5- Paln of action to undertake diverse actions.
6- Estimation of achievable improvement.

Figure 3.1. Index of an unproductiveness diagnosis report according to the WMT

Introduction and Background

At this point of the report, the issues that motivate the diagnosis study of a certain factory need to be described. The details of the company and the section(s) of the factory that are the focus of the diagnosis need to be articulated as well. The essential points contained in this section include:

3. Diagnosis of Productivity

- Issues that motivate this diagnosis
- Details of the company
- Data from the person in charge of the company
- Author of the diagnosis
- Brief presentation of the author

For the comprehension of the report, some concepts must be clear for the recipient, which will be defined at this point:

- Process
- Task
- Non-value-adding task
- Operation
- Non-value-adding operation
- Waste (according to Toyota)
- Standard time
- Minimum amount of necessary time (MANT)
- Introduction to WMT and description of the different wastes

Sampling and Observations Made

This section of the report covers the processes and tasks that have been observed and the diagnosis as measured. Information needed to clarify the issues should be included, but the minimum for data collected should cover:

- Observed processes
- Observed tasks
- Shifts
- Information and lists provided by the company
- Interviews made for obtaining information
- Other information of interest

Diagnosis of Unproductiveness: Current Situation

What follows is an explanation of how to proceed to calculate each coefficient of waste that has been defined in the WMT in order to measure unproductiveness.

Industrial productivity

Diagnosis of Unproductiveness by Work Design

Diagnosis of Unproductiveness of the Task Method

For the tasks that will be observed, time spent in value-adding operations and in non-value-adding operations will be calculated. The sources of information used here are the study of methods and times of the company or, if it does not have one, an estimation of times. For the second case, at diagnosis level it will not be necessary to make a precise measurement, but an estimate. For each task observed, the CwM will be calculated. This summarized information can be presented in the following format:

Task	Standard Time	$\sum$ VAO Times	$\sum$ NVAO Times	Task Symbol	CwM
Task 1					
Task 2					
Task 3					
Task 4					
Task 5					
Total					

Figure 3.2. *Data from the sampling of waste from method and calculation of the weighted average value of CwM*

The CwM data of the "Total" row represent the weighted average value of waste from method based on the total of sampled tasks. **An explanation will be included of what each of the following concepts mean, according to material covered in Chapter 2:**

- $\sum$ VAO times
- $\sum$ NVAO times
- Waste from method and CwM

From the studied tasks, a task diagram and times that justify the results will be provided. For a task that is non-value-adding, its CwM is infinite. The reason is that it spends time and does not contribute with any value.

3. Diagnosis of Productivity

Diagnosis of Process Unproductiveness (CwP)

For processes that will be observed, the time spent in both value-adding and non-value-adding operations will be calculated. The source of information used here is the map of processes of the company with times for each task. If a process map is not available, then visualize the process and apportion the different tasks to create a map that includes the estimated time for each task. For each process observed, the CwP is calculated. This summarized information can be shown in the following format (see Figure 3.3):

Process	Standard Time	$\sum$ VAO Times	$\sum$ NVAO Times	CwP
Process 1				
Process 2				
Total				

Figure 3.3. *Data from the sampling of waste from process and calculation of the weighted average value of CwP*

The CwP data of the "Total" row represents the weighted average value of waste from process based on the total of sampled processes. **An explanation will be included of what each of the following concepts mean, according to material covered in Chapter 2:**

- $\sum$ VA time
- $\sum$ NVA time
- Waste from process and CwP

From the studied processes, their process diagram and times that justify the results will be provided.

Quantification of Total Waste from Work Design (CwD)

For the processes in which tasks have been studied, the total waste from work design can be calculated from the formula we already know:

$$\sum \text{Standard times} = \text{CwD} \times \text{MANT}$$

Formula 3.1

Diagnosis of Unproductiveness in Manufacturing

Diagnosis of Management Failures (Cm)

As discussed, a series of causes contribute to poor management. When being diagnosed, each of the causes will have to be listed and treated. Management failures can cause waste in the following ways:

- Defects of information
- Workload imbalances
- Lack of materials
- Machine breakdowns
- Reprocesses

In such cases, it is difficult to assign to each cause its exact value, because it is an action of diagnosis. For example, a defect of information can cause a wrong change of tool that requires the operation to be repeated.

For this reason when diagnosing, it is recommended to try to deduce Cm and roughly try to describe how it affects each of the causes. To have an idea of the Cm and its causes, interviewing the operators is recommended. They will have information about everything but may try to blame the management for all the existing waste. Even if their comments need to be taken in context, they are in a position to provide insight into a company's management problems. As is represented in Figure 2.1, information will be obtained from workplace observation.

Following the list of possible management errors, a position-by-position sampling will gather downtime information about the causes. This way, a first approximation will be obtained of the different coefficients of waste from management.

As previously noted, it is difficult to distinguish the causes of downtimes, therefore, another exercise will quantify downtime without breakdown in order to deduce the total incidence time.

The purpose of this exercise is to obtain the Cm in a global way and then contrast it with the different coefficients that compose it. From the attempt to deduce all the coefficients, the reasons for such waste from management can be discerned. The sampling is shown in Figure 3.4.

3. Diagnosis of Productivity

Task	Standard Time	Incidence Time Observed	Possible Causes	Cm
Task 1				
Task 2				
Task 3				
Task 4				
Task 5				
Total				

Figure 3.4. Data from the sampling of waste from management failures and calculation of the weighted average value of Cm

The Cm data of the "Total' row represent the weighted average value of waste from management failures from the total of the tasks sampled. Commentaries will be provided about the incidences observed in each of the tasks, referring to the possible causes of waste from management failures and a percentage approximation of its weight: information defects, workload imbalances, lack of materials, machine breakdowns, and reprocesses. Based on the various management coefficients, corrective measures will be proposed to reduce the global Cm. Logically, more improvement with less effort will obtained if we attack the highest coefficients, which is where more potential improvement will be.

At this point, greater clarification of the Cm and its meaning needs to be provided.

Diagnosis of Waste from Low Performance

As previously mentioned, low performance appears in many activities and industries and constitutes an important component of waste. Whoever conducts the factory diagnosis must make a sampling of various workplaces, focusing on activities that have more weight within the productive process. It is not about making the time study; remember that it is a diagnosis and not a detailed study.

When appreciating the activity of several workstations, we can deduce an average appreciated activity (AAA) and from it obtain the first coefficient, Cact.

We assume the activity has been measured in the 100-133 scale.

Industrial productivity

Remembering the Cact formula:

$$Cact = \frac{\text{Controlled Time}}{\sum \text{Standard Time}}$$

Formula 3.2

If we take into account that Standard Time = Activity / 100 x Spent Time, where Spent Time coincides with Controlled Time, then:

$$\text{Controlled Time} = \frac{\sum \text{Standard Time}}{\text{Activity}} \times 100$$

Formula 3.3

Based on this formula, $C_{act} = \frac{100}{C_{act}} - 1$, as we are dealing with the diagnosis and we consider activities in average and approximately (AAA), or $C_{act} = \frac{100}{AAA} - 1$.

The 100 appears in the formulas because the activity is being quantified by the 100-133 scale. If we worked in the 60-80 scale, 60 would have to be substituted for 100.

Figure 3.5 provides a table in which the sampling of each of the tasks is noted.

Task	Standard Time	Appreciated Activity	Comments	Cact
Task 1				
Task 2				
Task 3				
Task 4				
Task 5				
Total				

Figure 3.5. *Data from the sampling of waste from performance and calculation of the weighted average value of Cact*

3. Diagnosis of Productivity

The Cact data of the "Total" row represents the weighted average value of waste from low performance in the sampled tasks.

At this point, an explanation of the Cact and its meaning needs to be provided.

Quantification of Total Waste in Manufacture

By obtaining a coefficient of waste in manufacture $CwF = 1 + Cact + Cm$, how much the standard times will be maximized once manufacturing is finished can be known.

Report of Unproductiveness from the Different Coefficients Obtained

At this point, the coefficients of waste obtained from the samplings are listed: CwM, CwP, CwD, Cm, Cact, and CwF.

The meaning of each of the coefficients will be explained along with the implications of the results. Additional information required includes the unproductiveness percentage and, therefore, the improvement potential:

- Unproductiveness percentage for task design: Knowing the CwM, the unproductiveness percentage is $(CwM - 1) \times 100$, which provides an idea of the method improvement that can be obtained.
- Unproductiveness percentage for process design: Knowing the CwP, the unproductiveness percentage is $(CwP - 1) \times 100$. This unproductiveness can be addressed through process improvement.
- Unproductiveness percentage for management failures: $Cm \times 100$.
- Unproductiveness percentage for low performance: $Cact \times 100$.

$$\text{Percentage of Total Unproductiveness} = ((CwD \times CwM) - 1) \times 100$$

Identified Unproductiveness = Improvement Potential

Note: The effects of CwM and CwP can be added only when calculating the weighted average of the diagnosis. Precise calculation requires caution in determining whether this sum gives erroneous results. The CwP calculates the waste of all the process while the CwM calculates the waste of each task. This concept will be clearer when detailing the waste maps tool.

Waste Maps and Improvement Deposits

Waste maps are a visual tool designed to expose in a clear way the existing wastes. Waste maps reflect the processes studied and appear in the diagnosis report.

Due to their extension, they will be studied in section 3.3, where the recommended formats will be found.

Problem Solutions: Proposed Actions for Each Waste

At this point of the report, possible solutions will be proposed for each waste so that recipients make the most convenient and critical decisions. In Section 3.6 *Troubleshooting Process* you will find an index of solutions to waste problems. This index provides a guide to the remaining parts of this book. The way to transfer the solution of problems will be to list, for each task, the solution proposals to waste from method, low performance, and management (see Figure 3.6):

Task 1

Diagnosis	Improvement Proposal
Method Design	
Management Failures	

3. Diagnosis of Productivity

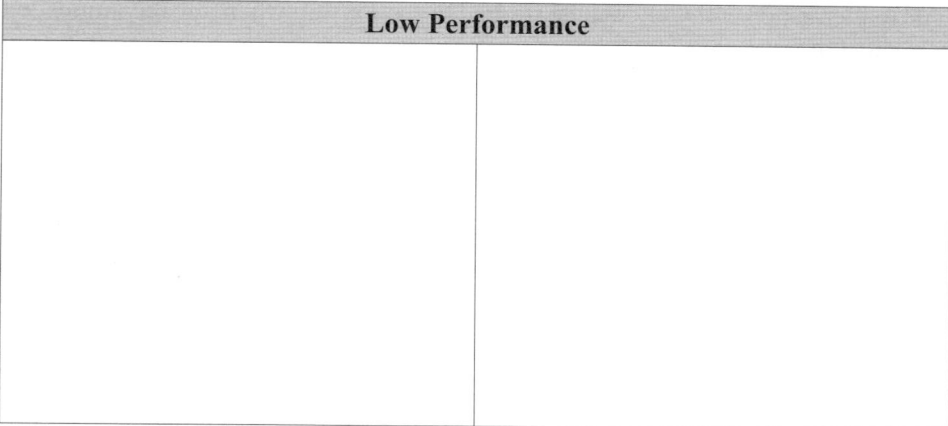

Low Performance	

Figure 3.6. *Table of proposed solutions to detected problems in the diagnosis of each task*

A table can be completed for each sampled task. Once all tasks are assessed, the same will be done with the studied processes. Generally, the incidences and other detected wastes in the tasks are closely related with the process; however, the proposals will be made independently for the processes (Figure 3.7).

Process 1

Diagnosis	Improvement Proposal
Method Design	

Industrial productivity

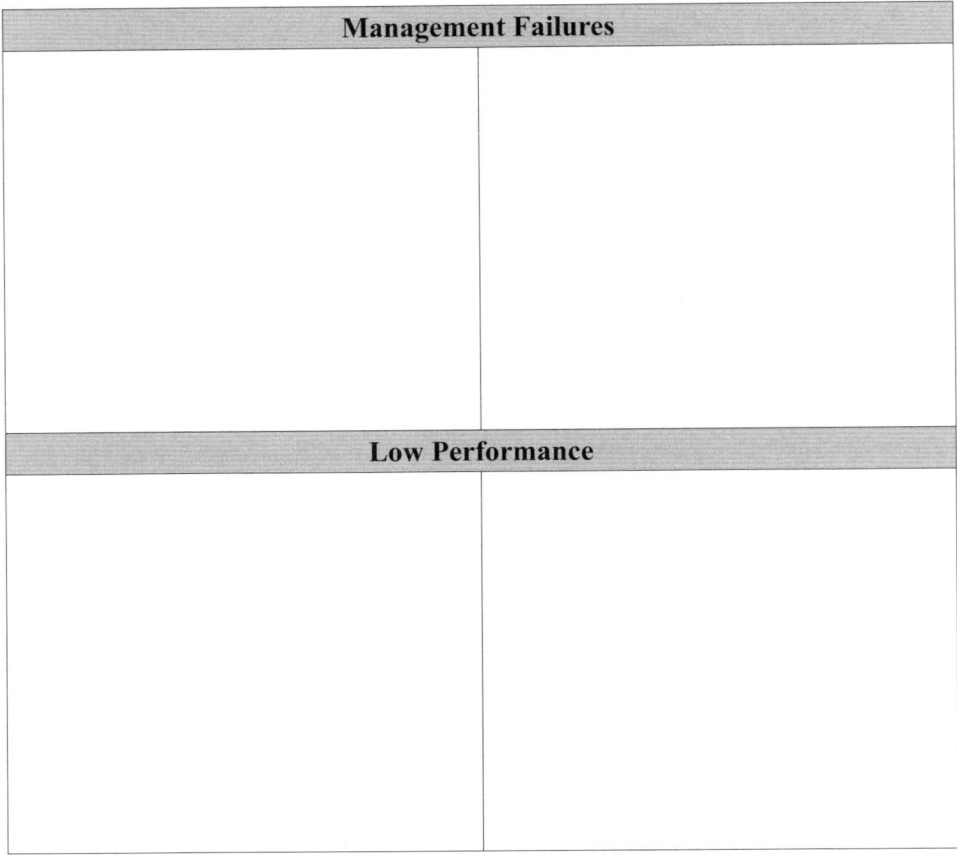

Figure 3.7. Table of proposed solutions to detected problems in the diagnosis for each process

Plan to Carry Out the Different Actions

From all the improvement proposals that emerge from the report, priorities need to be set. For this exercise, two criteria will be followed:

1. Pareto principle: 20% of solutions will solve 80% of the problems.

2. Cost-benefit criteria: The improvements whose cost-benefit is lower will be prioritized.

Once improvement prioritization is done, each proposal is assigned:

- Start and end dates
- Person in charge
- Dedicated hours of the person in charge

- Budget
- Other resources

Finally, a Gantt diagram of the improvement implementations can be provided.

Estimation of Improvements

From the unproductiveness report from the different coefficients of waste, a total estimation will be obtained of the improvements that can be achieved from the diagnosis.

3.3. Waste Maps and Improvement Deposits

It is necessary to create a visual of everything treated so far, to be able to have a more global control of waste that takes place in every task and has diverse classifications. An overload of lists and numeric data can cause a loss of analysis capacity.

As discussed, two groups of waste are waste from work design and the waste that occurs in manufacturing. The first is static and given a certain design, it does not change. The second changes every day in accordance to how manufacturing is managed. For this reason, three waste maps will be made:

1. Waste map for work design
2. Waste map for manufacturing management
3. Total waste map

Maps 1 and 2 are the important ones because they show information destined to different managers. For example, the waste from work design is the responsibility of the methods and processes engineering department. In maps 1 and 2 all the possible breakdown must be given. Map 3 adds the quantity of all the wastes but will not be as useful for analysis and decision making because the results affect various managements differently.

The waste maps will also show the quantification of improvement potential from the diagnosed unproductiveness and through another visual tool called "improvement deposits." The improvement deposits must be scaled with the quantity of person-time.

3.3.1. Waste Maps for Work Design

The waste from work design is the responsibility of the methods and processes engineering department, and its maps will be the reference of the mentioned department. As discussed, the maps will be drawn on the processes in two possible versions: process on plan or process on diagram.

1. Company
2. Author of the diagnosis
3. Type of map
4. Name of the process at analysis
5. Date
6. Revision
7. Reason for revision

Information about waste from process:

8. Total standard time of the studied process
9. Tasks that should not exist crossed out on the map
10. Sum of standard time of non-value-adding tasks (that should not exist)
11. Sum of standard time of value-adding tasks
12. Coefficient for process, CwP
13. Improvement deposit of process (it corresponds with the sum of standard times of non-value-adding tasks)

Information about waste from method in each task:

14. Name of the task
16. Current standard time
16. Sum of time for non-value-adding operations
17. Best standard time
18. Coefficient by method, CwM
19. Improvement deposit of method (it corresponds with the sum of standard times of non value-adding operations).

Information about total waste from work design:

20. Total sum of the standard times of all tasks
21. Total sum of the best standard times MANT
22. Coefficient for work design, CwD
23. Deposit of total improvement

The example provides the waste map of a process in its two possible versions.

Figure in the next page

Industrial productivity

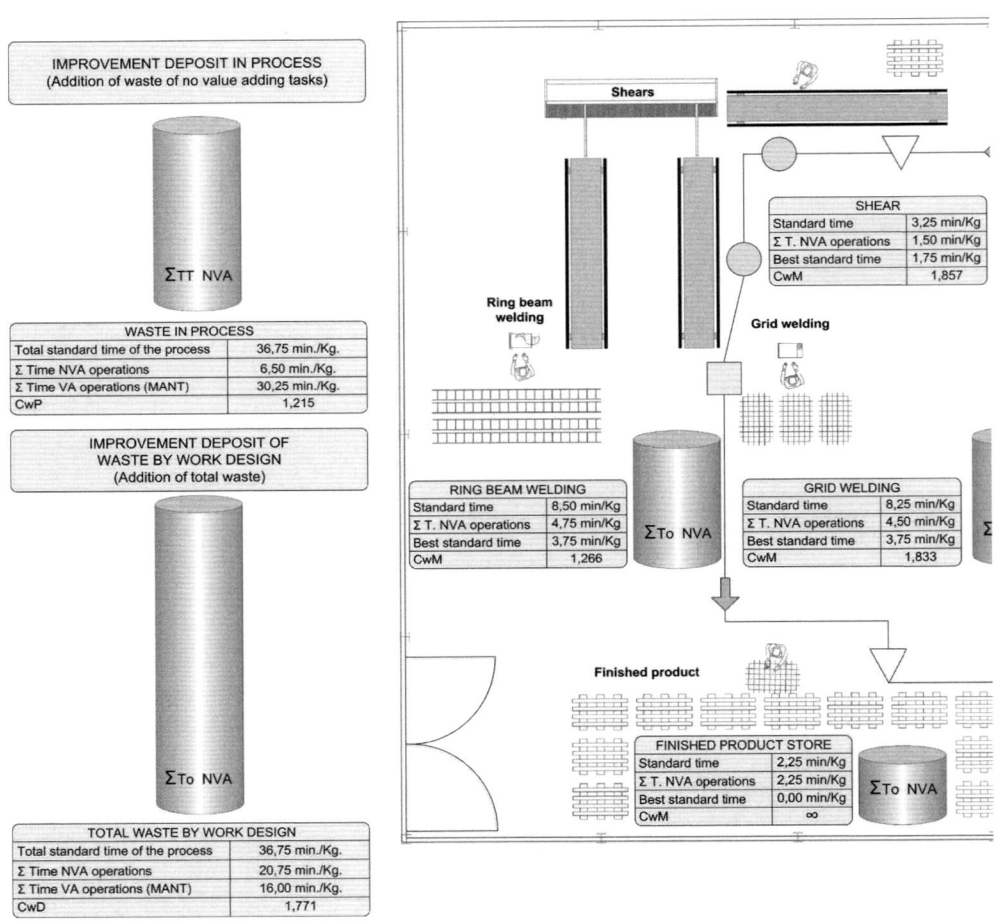

Figure 3.8. *Waste map in plan view by work design*

3. Diagnosis of Productivity

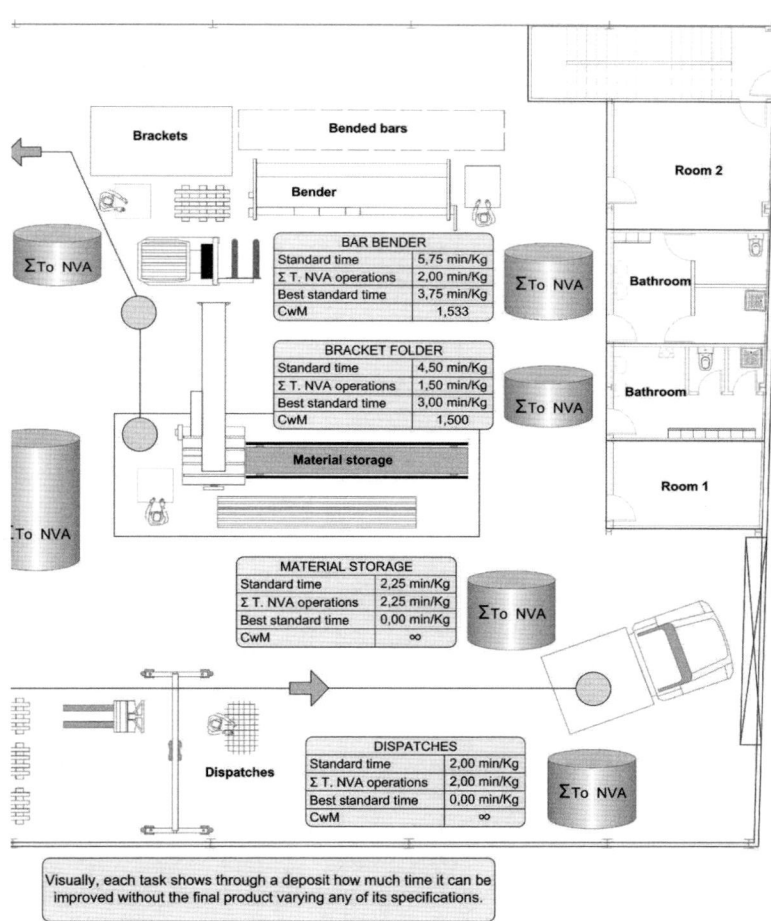

Visually, each task shows through a deposit how much time it can be improved without the final product varying any of its specifications.

Industrial productivity

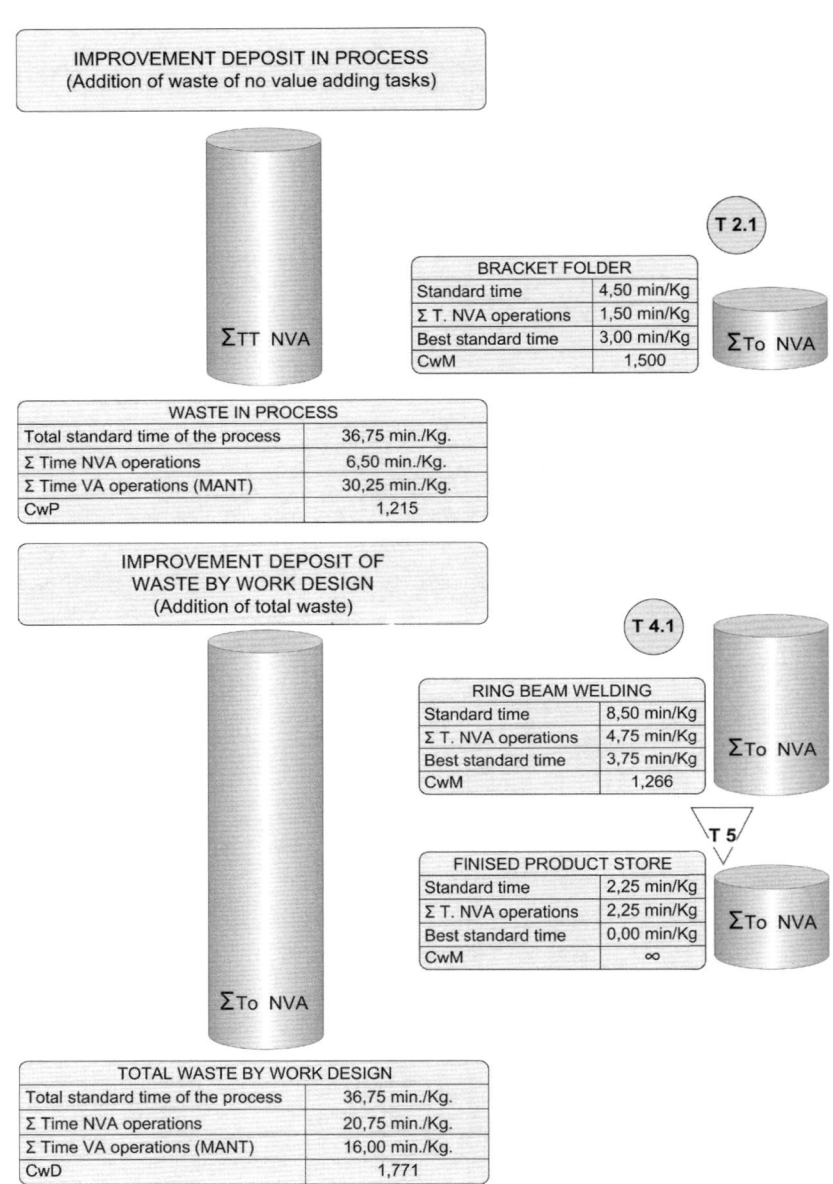

Figure 3.9. Waste map diagram by work design

3. Diagnosis of Productivity

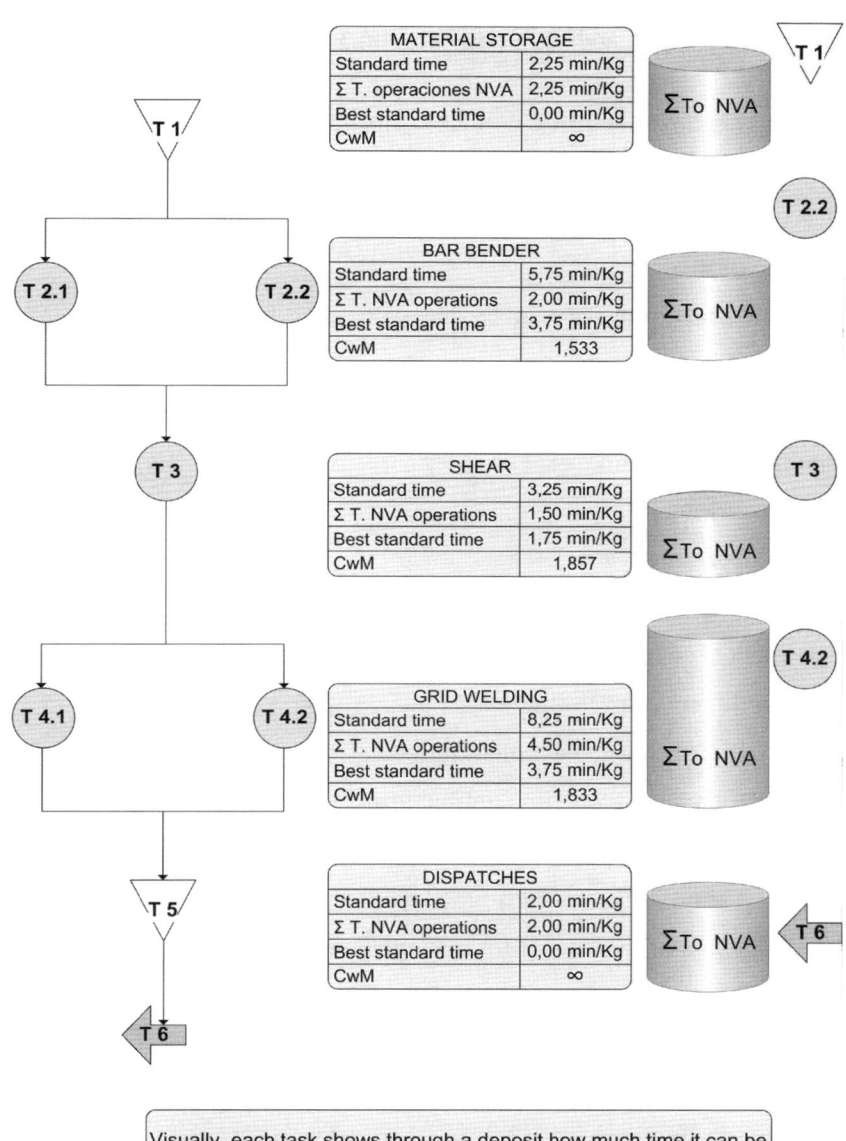

Visually, each task shows through a deposit how much time it can be improved without the final product varying any of its specifications.

3.3.2. Waste Maps in Manufacturing

The waste in manufacturing is the responsibility of the methods and processes engineering department and its maps will be the reference of the mentioned department.

The waste map in manufacturing will have this preliminary information:

1. Company
2. Author of the diagnosis
3. Type of map
4. Name of the process in analysis
5. Date
6. Period under study

Information about waste in task:

7. Name of the task
8. Standard time
9. Spent time for management failures (incidence time)
10. Spent time for low performance
11. Coefficient of performance, Cact
12. Coefficient for management failures, Cm, and its breakdown
13. Coefficient of waste in manufacturing, CwF

Information of total waste from work design:

14. Total sum of the standard times of all tasks
15. Total sum of time spent for management failures (incidence time)
16. Total sum of time spent for low performance
17. Coefficients of waste in manufacturing of all tasks
18. Deposit of total improvement in manufacturing

3. Diagnosis of Productivity

Figure in the next page

Industrial productivity

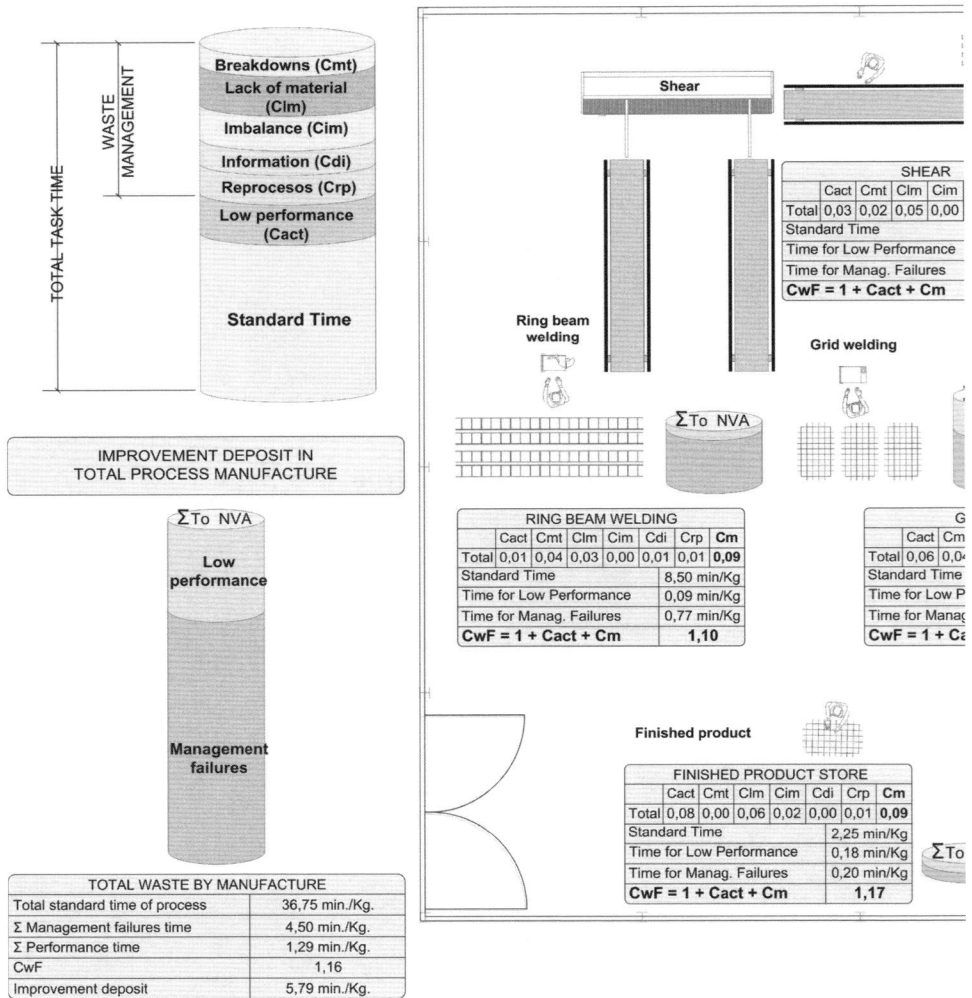

Figure 3.10. Waste map in plan view in manufacturing

3. Diagnosis of Productivity

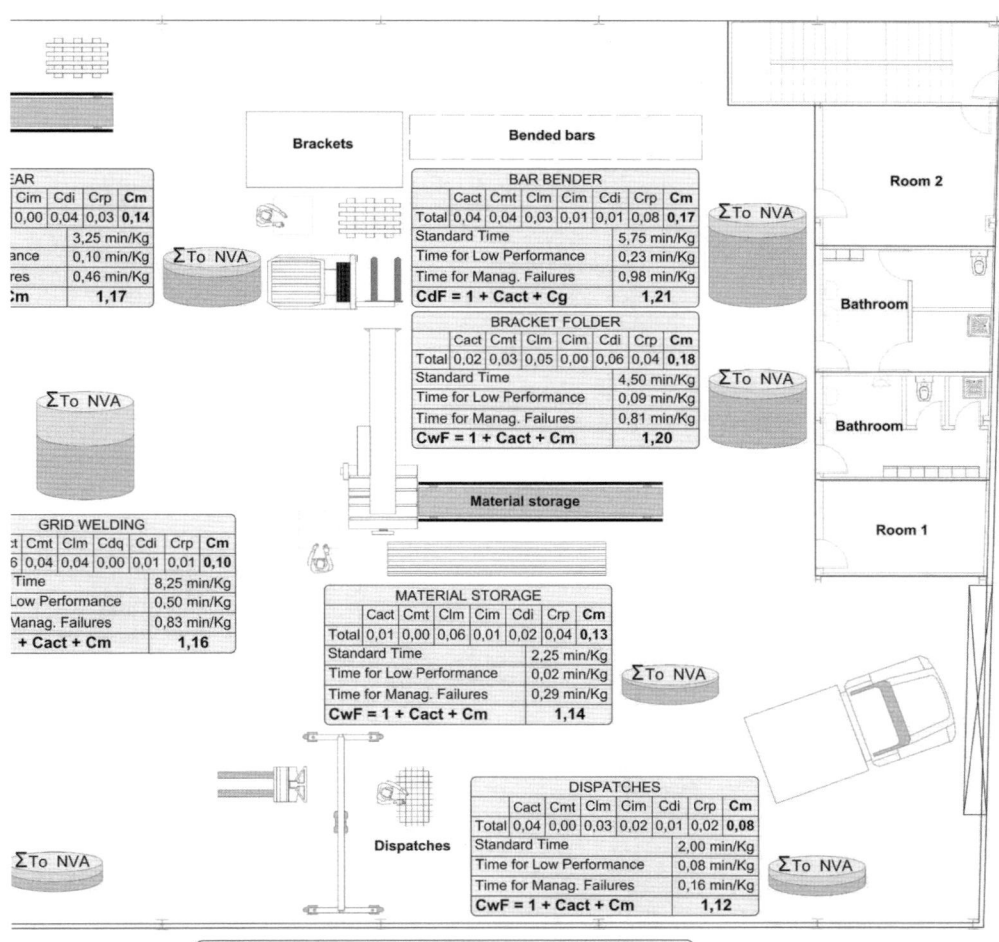

Visually, each task shows through a deposit how much time it can be improved without the final product varying any of its specifications.

89

Industrial productivity

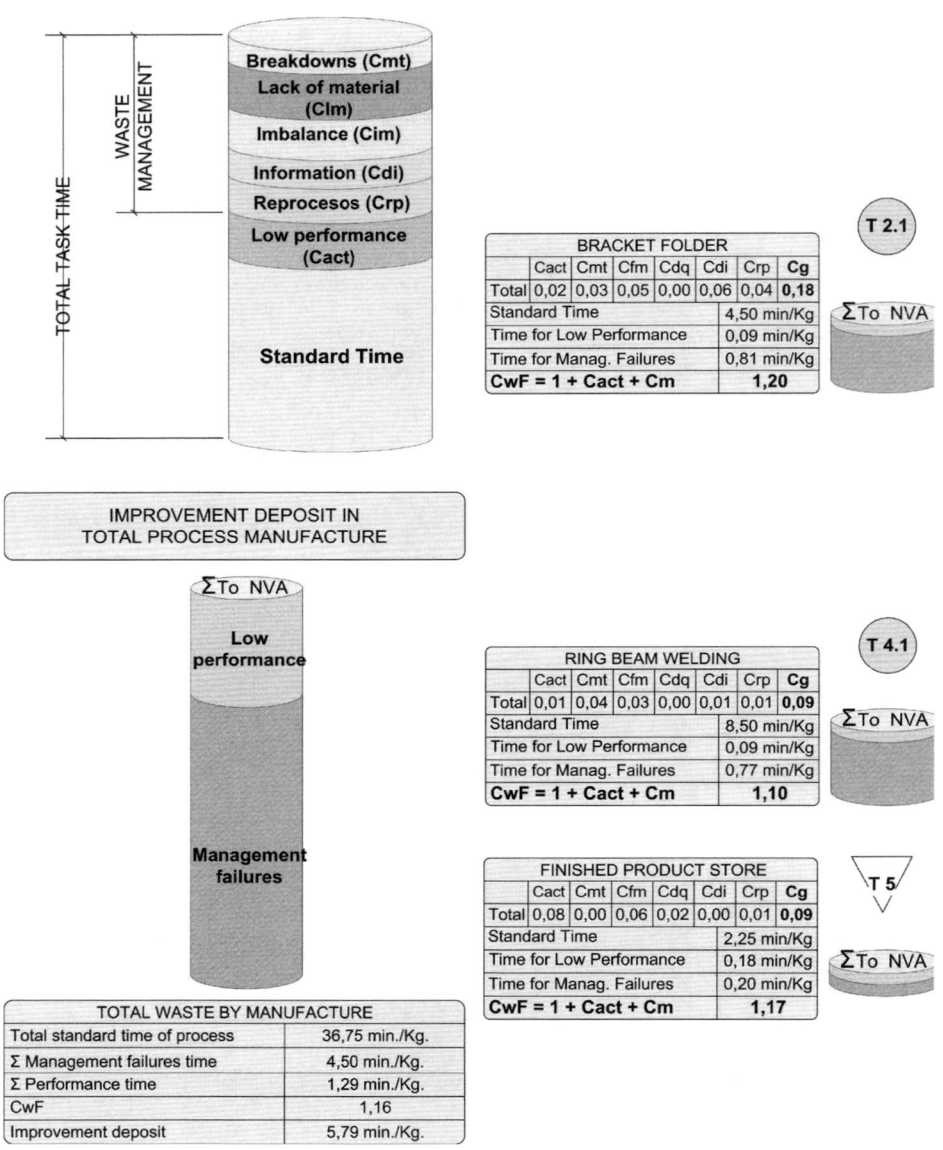

Figure 3.11. Waste map diagram in manufacturing

3. Diagnosis of Productivity

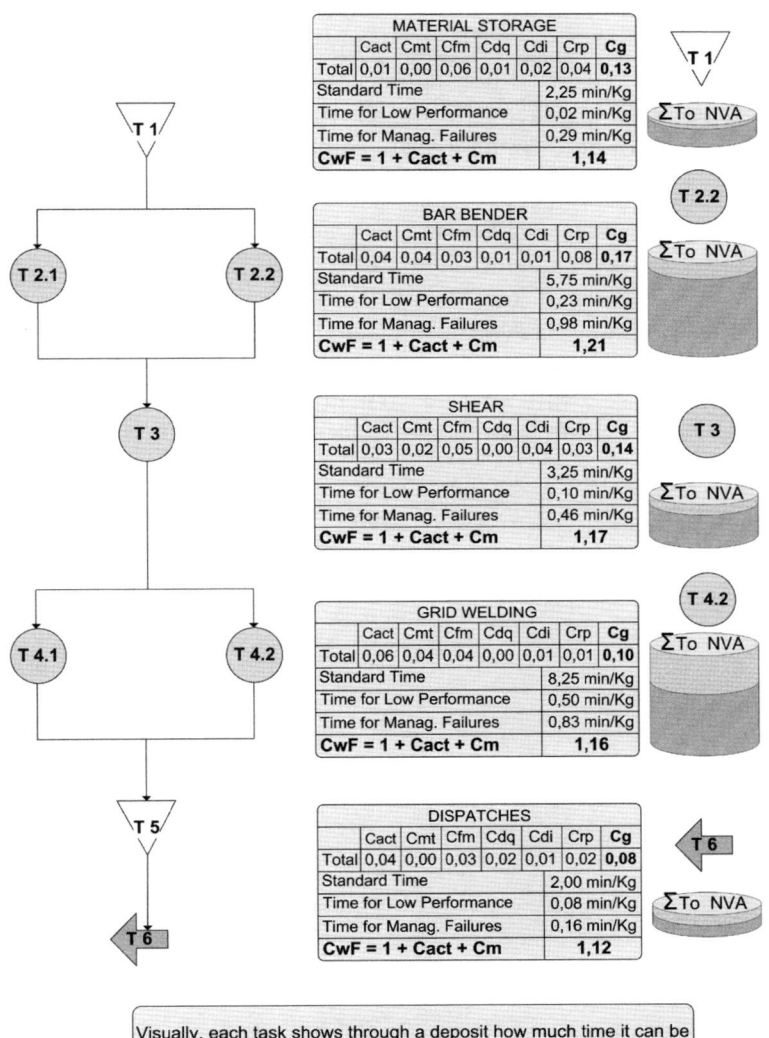

Visually, each task shows through a deposit how much time it can be improved without the final product varying any of its specifications.

3.3.3. Total Waste Map

Although we must act on wastes separately, as seen in previous chapters, it will be great to have a view of the total existing waste to which are added, for each task and for the entire process, their improvement deposits. Although this map cannot be an action tool because it mixes different responsibilities, it is convenient to have the reference of how much it can be improved; these data are motivating and, because they are calculated and justified, provide credibility. The global waste data will change the reality and context of the people in charge and the way they view the possibilities of improvement. Fifty percent improvements will seem credible.

On many occasions, improvement objectives are imposed with no justification, therefore nobody believes them and they are not achieved. When carrying out the theory of waste measurement, all unproductiveness is quantified and the potential improvement calculated, the resulting data are surprising and may even seem exaggerated, but they have been calculated scientifically and are true. Obtaining this information removes excuses that prevent the pursuit of improvement. To avoid repetition, data will not be listed in this type of map. The map in Figure 3.13 shows the sum of waste from the previous maps, the total waste is data that force action.

3. Diagnosis of Productivity

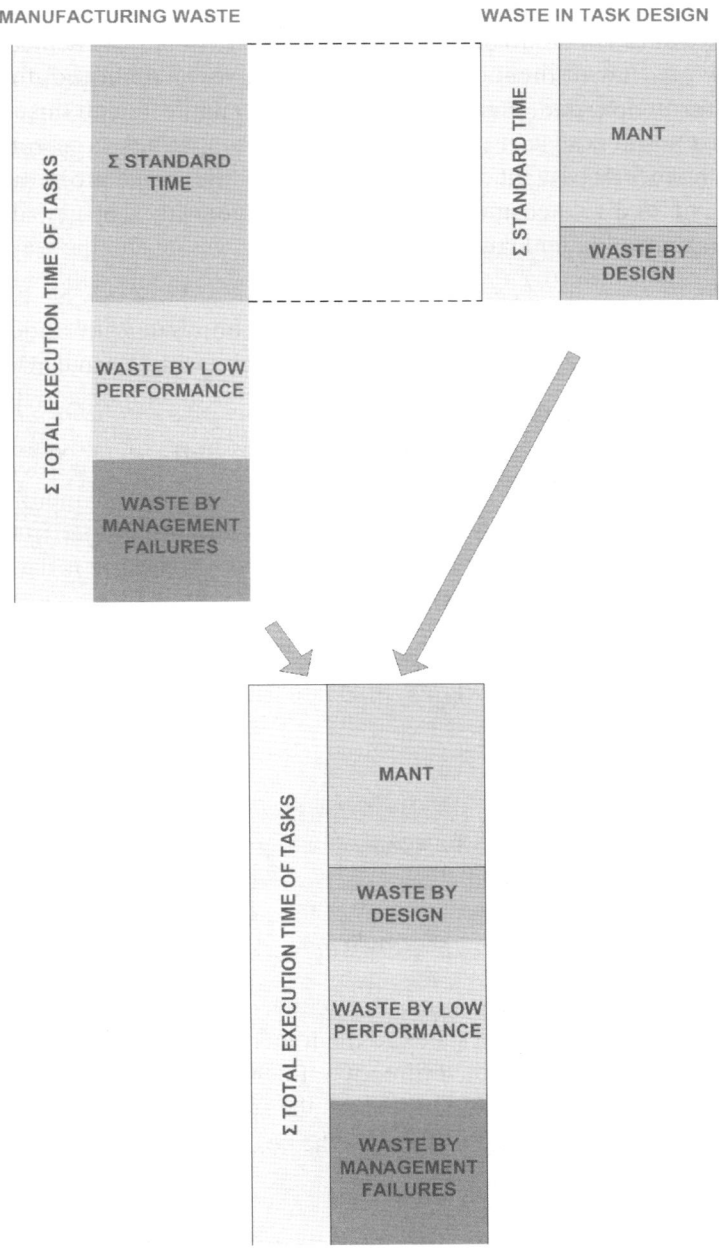

Figure 3.12. Wastes overlap

Waste maps provide a visual scorecard of the state of the factory that greatly facilitates the decision making.

3.4. Influence of Productivity in Production Costs

Production costs are the sum of three major components: materials, manufacturing (machinery and workforce), and general expenses. Supposing the constant materials for a determined product design, the manufacturing cost is directly proportional to the time spent executing manufacture. Besides, general expenses also decline with the execution times, as in the same installations more can be produced and so dilute energetic expenses, management, property amortization and/or rentals, machinery amortisation, and so on.

As unproductiveness has been calculated from the WMT, it can be affirmed that manufacturing costs are directly proportional to the waste coefficient. Besides, general expenses per manufactured unit also increase with unproductiveness.

Therefore, although may seem obvious: *Costs increase with unproductiveness.* **The purpose of this book, then, is to teach how to reduce costs and manufacturing deadlines.**

If standard time is fixed as reference for the calculation of the standard cost and this formula is taken into account:

Standard cost of manufacture = $\sum$ Standard person-time x Operator-hour cost + $\sum$ Standard time-machine i x Machine-hour cost i

Real Manufacturing Time = CwF x $\sum$ Standard Times

It can be said that:

> Real Cost of Manufacturing = CwM x Standard Cost of Manufacturing

Formula 3.4.

On the other hand, if standard times are reduced by an improvement of work method and process design, the standard manufacturing cost will be reduced. The two major types of waste handled directly influence the standard manufacturing cost. The waste from work design influences the standard manufacturing cost and the waste from manufacturing influences the real manufacturing cost, factored from the standard.

3.4.1. The Theory of Waste Measurement as a Tool for Cost Calculation

One of the most difficult measures to calculate is the manufacturing cost per reference and per task. Even though the standard cost can be calculated once the standard time is obtained, the real cost is more difficult to calculate.

The attempts to find out the costs of direct labor in manufacturing have been many in the industries, and the majority of them have failed because technicians and economists have surrendered at the difficulty of implementation.

Efforts have generally been concentrated on working with excessive detail, trying to know from each batch, task, and reference the start and end times to determine its cost. Complex information systems have been developed and time control readers placed everywhere around the factory. Sometimes, different report systems have been developed that make the operator write down the starting and ending hour of the work package, increasing the administrative workload and recollecting false data. The errors in these cases may exceed 50 percent.

Logically, with the increase of references and the reduction of batch sizes, this data collecting has gotten more complicated, but being complex does not make it more effective.

From the exposition of this methodology, this system of data collecting is not recommended for the following reasons:

1. For starters, the philosophy is reactive; it works after the event based on what has happened and not on what should happen.

2. It needs a high level of investment and imposes a high administrative workload for data management.

3. The handled and returned data are excessive. Too much information is disinformation.

4. The returned data are incorrect:

    a. A batch made at 10:00 a.m. tends to be faster than one made after lunch. Should we assign more cost for this reason to the last reference? It seems unfair.

    b. If during a batch, the operator has had a momentary decrease in productivity, this batch will have low productivity and therefore an elevated cost. It is also unfair; fatigue must be daily prorated and detailed and *online* data collecting does not do it.

    c. On most occasions, the most important influence is not clear: the batch's beginning and ending criteria.

    d. During a certain batch, a management failure could have occurred that increases that batch's cost. It is unfair to impose on the part or task the additional cost, because it is a general negligence that could have occurred at any moment and that, therefore, could have affected any batch; it is just a matter of chance.

> e. Cost assignment for different time per unit readings for the same reference are impractical.

5. If any historical list of real manufacturing times is observed for the same reference, one concludes that it is impossible to obtain coherent data.

These reasons show why measuring in detail the time spent in each batch is a waste of time and money and why it never works. It returns incongruent, excessive, false, and useless data that lead to wrong conclusions and worse solutions. Through WMT this difficult problem can be solved by doing things, simply, right.

> Manufacturing costs cannot be determined if first we do not have the standard times per reference and a productivity control system. Manufacturing cost is impossible to know a priori, at best we can work with it as an objective.

Then, how to know the real cost?

- A priori: From the standard cost and from a waste coefficient objective in manufacturing (CwFo).
- A posteriori: From productivity control, by which we will obtain the Cact, the total of incidence hours, therefore Cm and in total CwF, that multiplied by the standard manufacturing cost will return the real cost.

This methodology of cost calculation responds to the following principle:

Supposing the standard times are well measured, neither the wastes from management nor the wastes from performance are applicable to a punctual aspect, but to a general behavior. The fact that a management error or a lack of performance has been produced at a certain time does not mean it has to be charged to the batch that was being done at that precise moment. Pointing to that level of detail is, apart from being difficult and costly, a source of information errors.

In the value of standard time, certain factors need to be considered, such as fatigue, personal necessities, and so on. Therefore, productivity needs to be measured by comparing fulfilled production with time spent within a day, week or month, not by batch; **to control productivity by batch is an error** that gets bigger when the batch is smaller.

Based on all these points, it follows that we can determine with hindsight, and without major complications, the production cost, and we can have a priori a cost objective. Therefore, if productivity control is done and the factory CwF is calculated, a CwFo can be applied (objective waste coefficient in production) to the standard time and cost to know the objective costs.

In some companies, standard costs are fed with the historical costs that the ERP returns. This practice does not inform but misinforms, as previously mentioned.

3.4.2. The CwFo for Cost Attribution

If we assume a CwF, that is, a waste in production, it can be converted into the CwFo from which to attribute costs:

$$\text{Objective Cost} = \text{CwMo} \times \text{Standard Cost}$$

Formula 3.5.

CwFo stands as an objective of CwF for the factory or all process. As we concluded in the previous section, waste is not produced per reference or section, it is produced by processes; it is produced by the entire factory, its managers, and its operators, which implies for every reference:

$$\text{Objective Cost } i = \text{CwMo} \times \text{Standard Cost } i$$

Formula 3.6.

To calculate the cost, the CwF of each task must not be distinguished. From here on, the following points must be taken into account:

- The standard cost depends on the standard time that, while it is not improved or changed, is a constant.
- The production cost depends on how it is managed each day, from the amount of waste in manufacturing generated or avoided, and it is not a constant. Each day it must be addressed.
- It must be assumed that the responsibility of the cost lies with factory managers. The cost is not such by its own, it is done by those who manage the production.

So then to calculate the real costs, waste must be taken into account. To calculate costs a priori, cost objectives must be assumed because real cost will not be known until a certain manufacturing remittance is made. **The cost is one of the least safe results. To control costs is a competitive advantage by itself.**

A CwFo must be assumed and enforced. To do so, a management methodology must be adopted based on a scorecard in which the different coefficients are controlled after the data reading. Work must be done every day to maintain the CwF under the CwFo. In Chapter 4, the systems approach develops this methodology in depth. If CwF is less than CwFo, the manufacturing costs are less than assumed. If CwF is greater than CwFo, we have a deviation problem that can result in income loss per product, failure to meet deadlines, and so on.

The advantage of this methodology is that CwF can be calculated daily. The monitoring can be done and the deviations obtained *with a unique indicator.* **To calculate the costs per batch and/or per reference requires such a magnitude of data that may be so contradictory that, finally, it is not done.**

3.5. Productivity, a Human Problem

Unproductiveness is a human problem.

Productivity, as happiness, does not exist; it is a path to follow.

The greatest problem that productivity encounters in an industry is the lack of *cultural productivity* in its organization, from management to production workforce. When the existing problem remains unknown, it acquires enormous dimensions. In these cases, the simple acquisition of concepts by management and middle managers turns around the way the problem is treated. With no conscious recognition of the problem, it is not given any treatment; and a problem that is not faced grows indefinitely.

As seen in WMT, several groups cause unproductiveness. After defining standard time, unproductiveness can be caused by either poor management or by the workforce. Both causes are linked, and the growth of waste due to one of the causes results in a growth in the other. Operators can never have a good performance if management does not do its job well. How can performance be demanded of an operator who always lacks materials to do assigned work or whose tools or machines are always damaged or who sees how managers are highly unproductive?

Productivity must be stressed at all levels of the company to be able to implement it. The culture of productivity must defend the principle that the workday's objective is not to remain a certain amount of hours inside a building but to contribute with a value that, when speaking about manufacturing, is measurable.

Within the concept of WMT, the path toward productivity means making the coefficients CwM, CwP, and CwF reach 1 as an ultimate objective. Staying on that path permanently then is one of the strategic foundations of the industrial company.

3.6. Process of Problem Solving

Given the diagnosis, what are the problems? In quantitative terms, and for what is being discussed, high waste coefficients are problems. Because a certain level of waste is unavoidable, as zero is perfection, a maximum objective of waste will have to be articulated. In this section, a catalog of solutions is provided for each type of waste. Although many responses to the problems are provided in this book, which it is its principal aim, some others are not the object of this content. Having advanced in quite a number of concepts, this section will serve to reference the different chapters of the book indicating what waste issue it solves in a more precise way. It is important for a better assimilation of the structure of the book and the aim of each of the chapters and sections.

3.6.1. Problem-Solving of Waste in Method CwM

The second part of the book focuses on the study, analysis, and improvement of methods.

- In Chapter 5, study methods are discussed. It is necessary to know how the task is performed and from there to be able to diagnose and improve it.

- Chapter 6 discusses method analysis to detect incidences in the method in order to know what to solve.

- In Chapter 7, the design of the improved method is demonstrated. To improve a method has no other objective than to reduce its waste, to reduce the CwM. Methodologies are used to stimulate ideas and a catalog of solutions for common problems. Due to the extension of some improvement methodologies, they have been explained in separate chapters. Chapters 7, 8, 9, and 11 are dedicated to method improvement.

- Chapter 12 shows how the implementation of designed improvements is established.

The third part provides a time study of the established methods.

Problem-Solving Process of Waste from Method

If the CwM of a task is greater than a certain goal, it is appropriate to set in motion the problem-solving process.

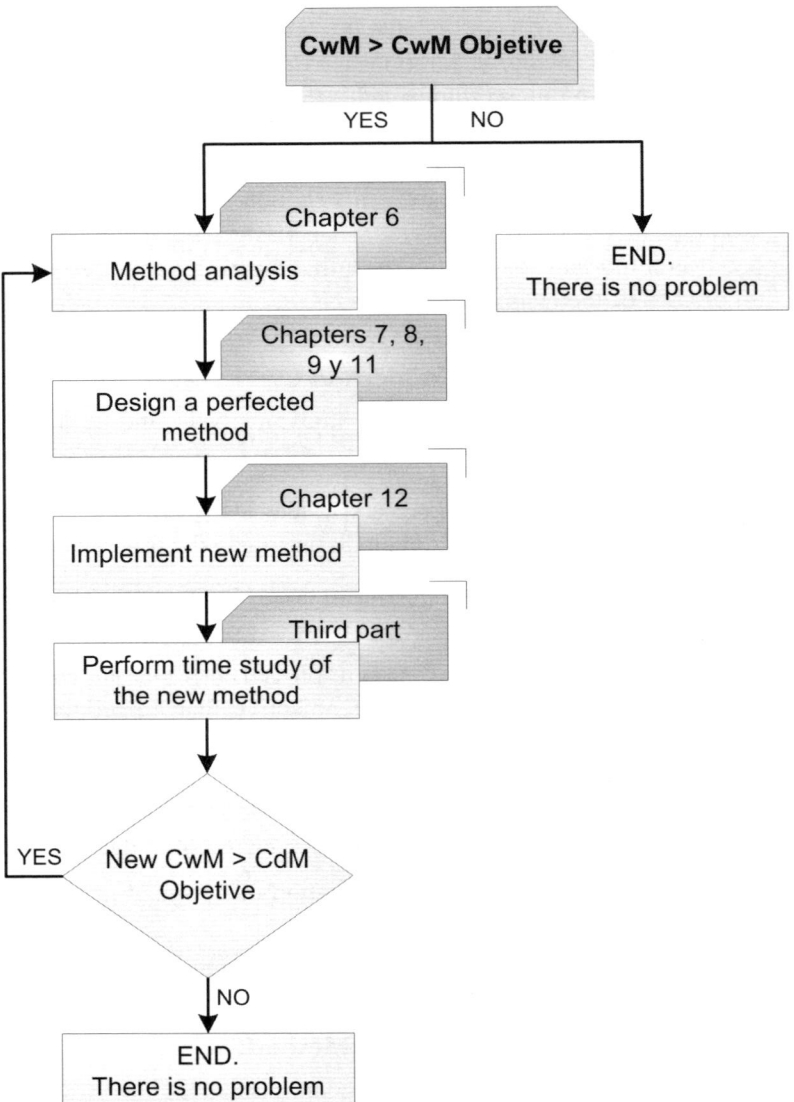

Figure 3.13. Problem-solving process of waste from method

3.6.2. Problem-Solving of Waste in the Process CwP

In the second part is where processes are also studied because somehow the process is a method on a larger scale:

- In section 5.4, the study and mapping of processes is described in order to have a map of how materials move and of which tasks are necessary to finish a certain product.
- In Chapter 10, a catalog of solutions is available for process improvement. The application of what is described in this chapter improves the problems of waste in the process.

Problem-Solving Process of Waste from Process

If the CwP of a task is greater than a certain goal, it sets in motion the problem-solving process.

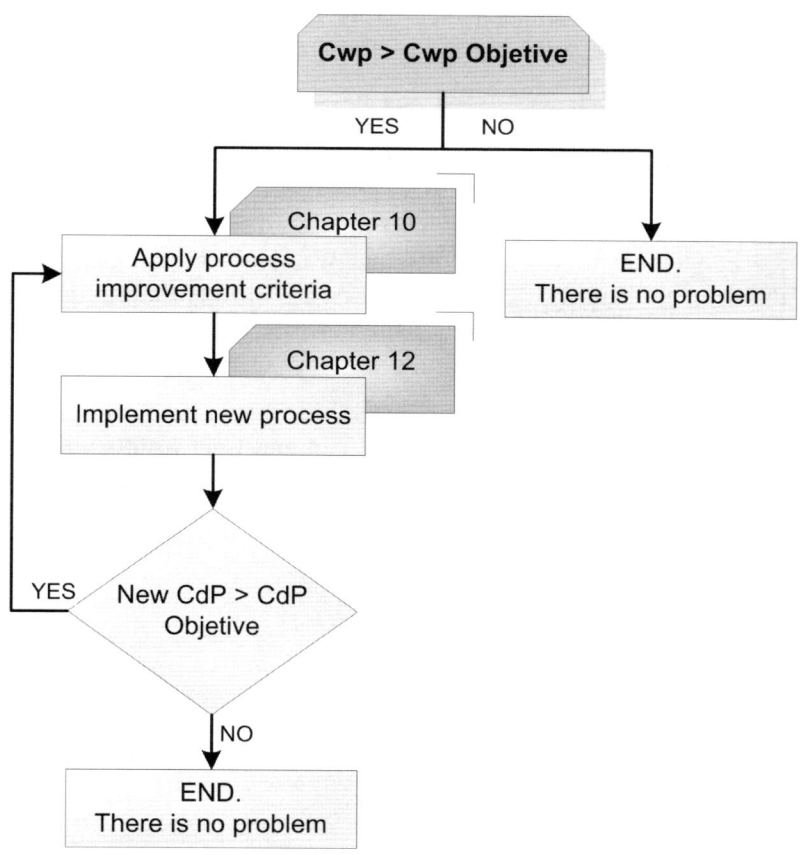

Figure 3.14. Problem-solving process of waste from process

3.6.3. Problem-Solving of Waste in Manufacture, CwF

The fourth part of the book describes the application and use of the calculated standard times. The CwF may have two origins: management failures and low performance:

- The problems of management failures arise out of deficient management of operations. Based on gained experience, the imbalance between the workload and capacity and the lack of materials are the major causes of waste from management failures. In Chapter 20, the planning of operations from the use of standard times for the optimization of capacity and decision making is shown. The improvement in operation planning reduces the Cm, coefficient of waste from management failures.

- The problems of low performance normally are caused by lack of productivity control. Chapter 21 is dedicated to productivity control and incentive systems for the performance improvement of operators, to reduce the Cact.

Problem-Solving Process of Waste from Manufacture

If the CwF of a process is greater than a certain objective, it triggers the problem-solving process. As seen on repeated occasions, CwF = 1 + Cact + Cm. Therefore, it will be convenient to work on different waste objectives, one for the Cact and another for the Cm, because their causes are different and require different treatment. For this reason, a problem-solving process will be implemented for each of the causes: management failures and low performance.

The CwF is not a static coefficient; it depends on how manufacturing developed over a certain period. For each period. the Cm and Cact results will have to be observed and assessed as over or under the objective. If they are over, the problem-solving process will be launched.

3. Diagnosis of Productivity

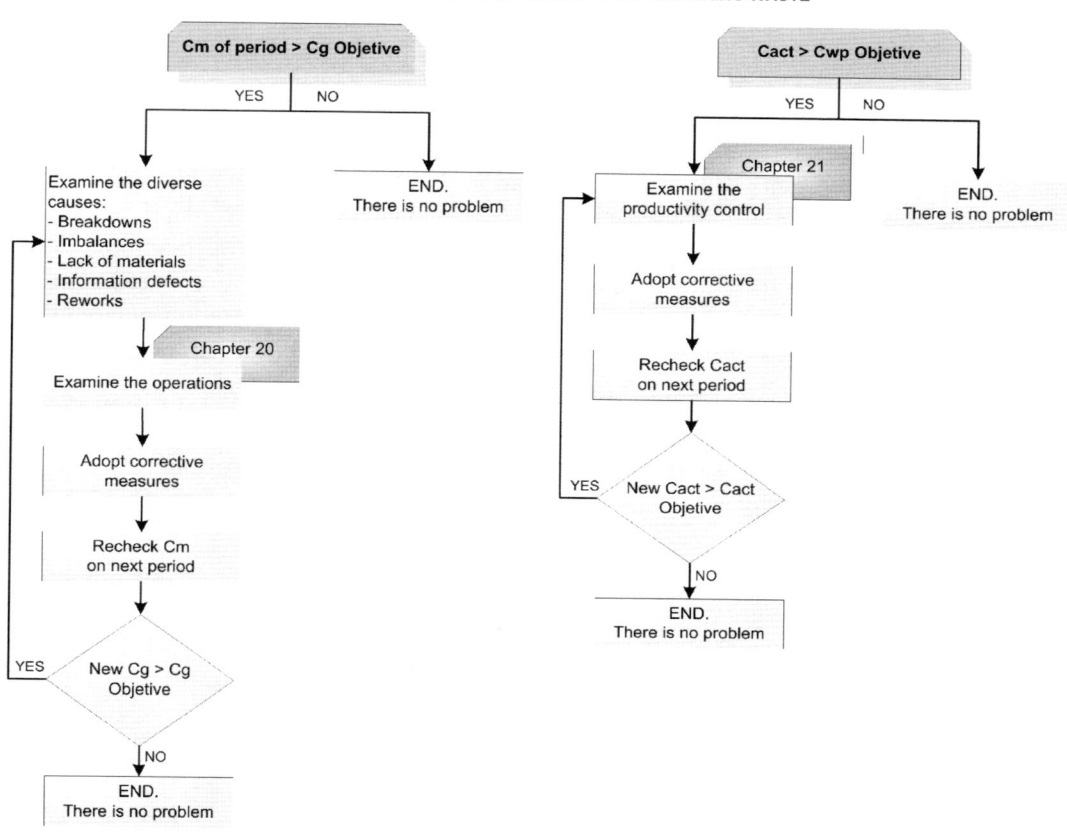

Figure 3.15. Problem-solving process of waste from manufacturing

3.6.4. Suggestions and Ideas

Besides what has been discussed previously, solution ideas for problems may be totally original and not registered in the standard processes. People who live daily with these problems and suffer the consequences of such problems are a valuable source of solutions and creativity; for them, solving the problems is an authentic need. Those affected generate many ideas and suggestions. *The problem is that these ideas often get lost because no defined process by which to register or apply those solution ideas exists.*

To avoid the loss of these ideas, we propose a simple procedure to register suggestions for continuous improvement. First, a form for recording improvements will be created. Workers identify the need to improve a process or situation based on:

Industrial productivity

- Repeated incidences
- Dissatisfaction of internal/external customer
- Detection by made error
- Creativity

All factory personnel will have these forms available to record their ideas. Once identified, the opportunity for improvement or problem solving must be noted for its subsequent presentation. A basic format for improvement annotation is shown in Figure 3.16.

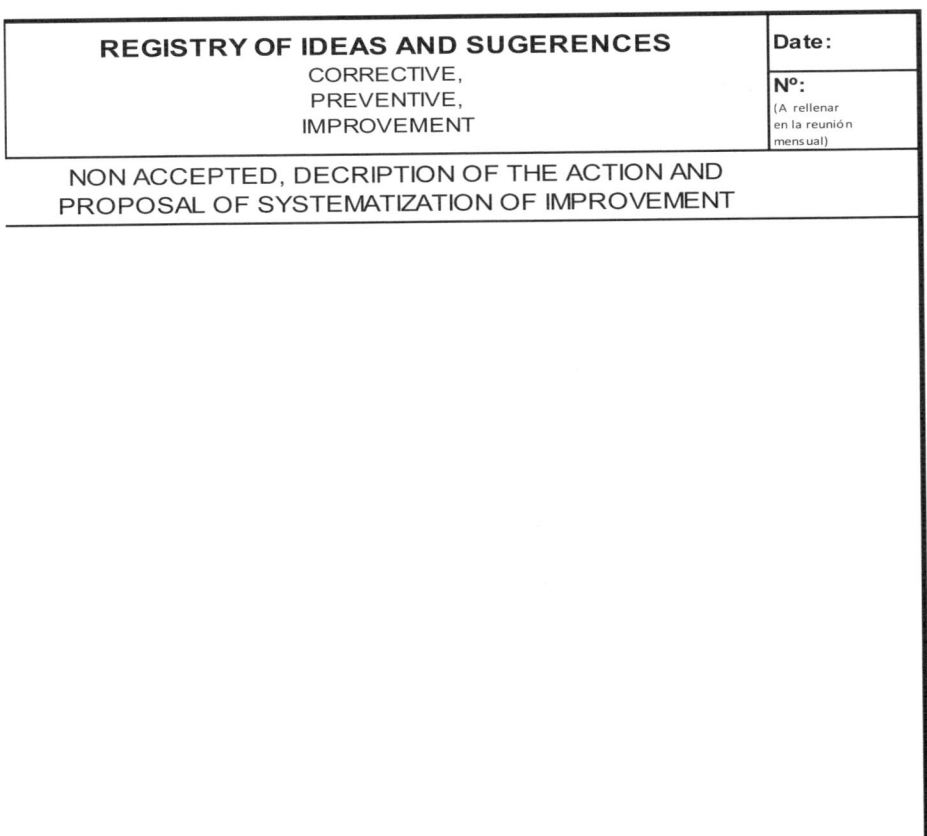

Figure 3.16. Register of ideas and suggestions

As can be observed, this form is driven by articulation of "Nonconformance, Description of Action, and Proposed Improvement."

The idea, if it may, must be accompanied by a standardization proposal, which is the point the improvements. The standardization contributes to consistency in the process in such a way that once proposals are implemented, they require no further thought but become automatic as part of the process. Otherwise, such suggestions remain difficult or impossible to implement.

3.6.5. Selection of Improvements

The ideas and proposals of problem solutions will be presented at improvement meetings; the ones approved will be filed as **pending proposals of improvement approved**. Once the improvement has been made, they will be passed on to **implemented proposals of improvement.** Figure 3. 17 provides a format for registering decisions made and improvements to be performed.

CONTINUOUS IMPROVEMENT MEETING		
Meeting date:		Date of next meeting:
Meeting participants		
Position:	**Name:**	**Signature:**

Summary of improvements to perform
Summary of improvements to perform
Description, date, and supervisor

Figure 3.17. Continuous improvement meeting file

Finally, the resolutions adopted in the improvement meetings and the revision of pending issues will be registered and archived in a folder created for this purpose.

3.6.6. Start-Up of Improvements

In case the improvement proposals have notable substance, they can be archived as **continuous improvement projects**, and one or several managers will be assigned to their implementation. In Chapter 12, where implementation of work method improvements is discussed, an implementation file is developed, which can be applicable here.

Register of Improvement Start-Up   **Date:**

Task or process affected	
Person in charge of the improvement	
Brief description of the improvement (see improvement record)	
Other participants	
Time assigned (hours)	
Budget assigned	
Deadline	

Gantt Diagram of Start-Up

Figure 3.18. Register of improvement start-up

Industrial productivity

> It is important to have a process through which improvements are shepherded and implemented.

The process flowchart of the start-up of an improvement is shown in Figure 3.19. With this chart, each member of the organization will know what steps to follow when he or she comes up with an idea.

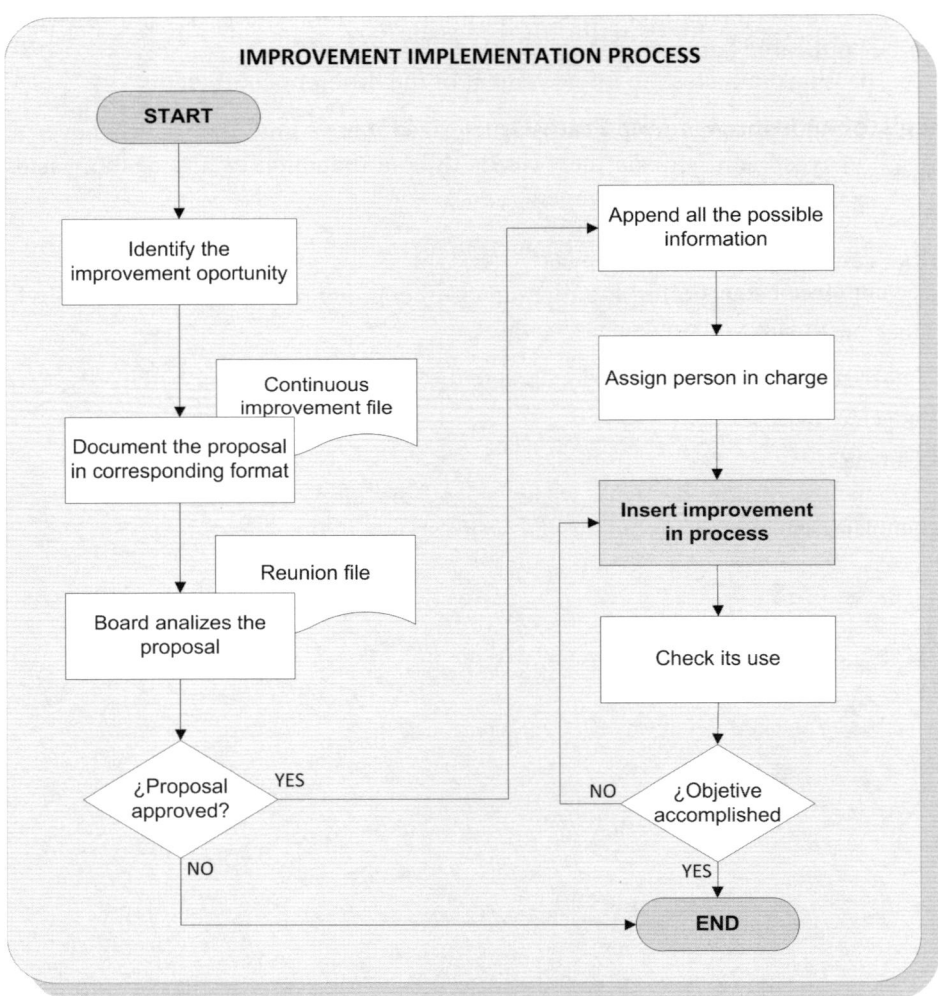

Figure 3.19. Improvement implementation process

Questions

1. What indicators are used to diagnose unproductiveness?

2. What is the diagnosis report of productivity?

3. What are waste maps?

4. What types of waste maps are used?

5. What is the relationship between the coefficient of waste, Cact, and the observed activity in the 100-133 scale?

6. What activates the improvement of the different coefficients?

7. Since through WMT is parameterized where time is lost, whenever an investment is made there needs to be a reduction of any of the wastes. Comment on this statement.

8. Who is responsible for each group of waste?

9. How often should the director of operations revise the results of CwF? Explain your answer.

10. Why is it incorrect to calculate the production cost per batch?

Problems

1. Given the following two waste maps, develop the diagnosis report of unproductiveness according to the script shown in this book.

Industrial productivity

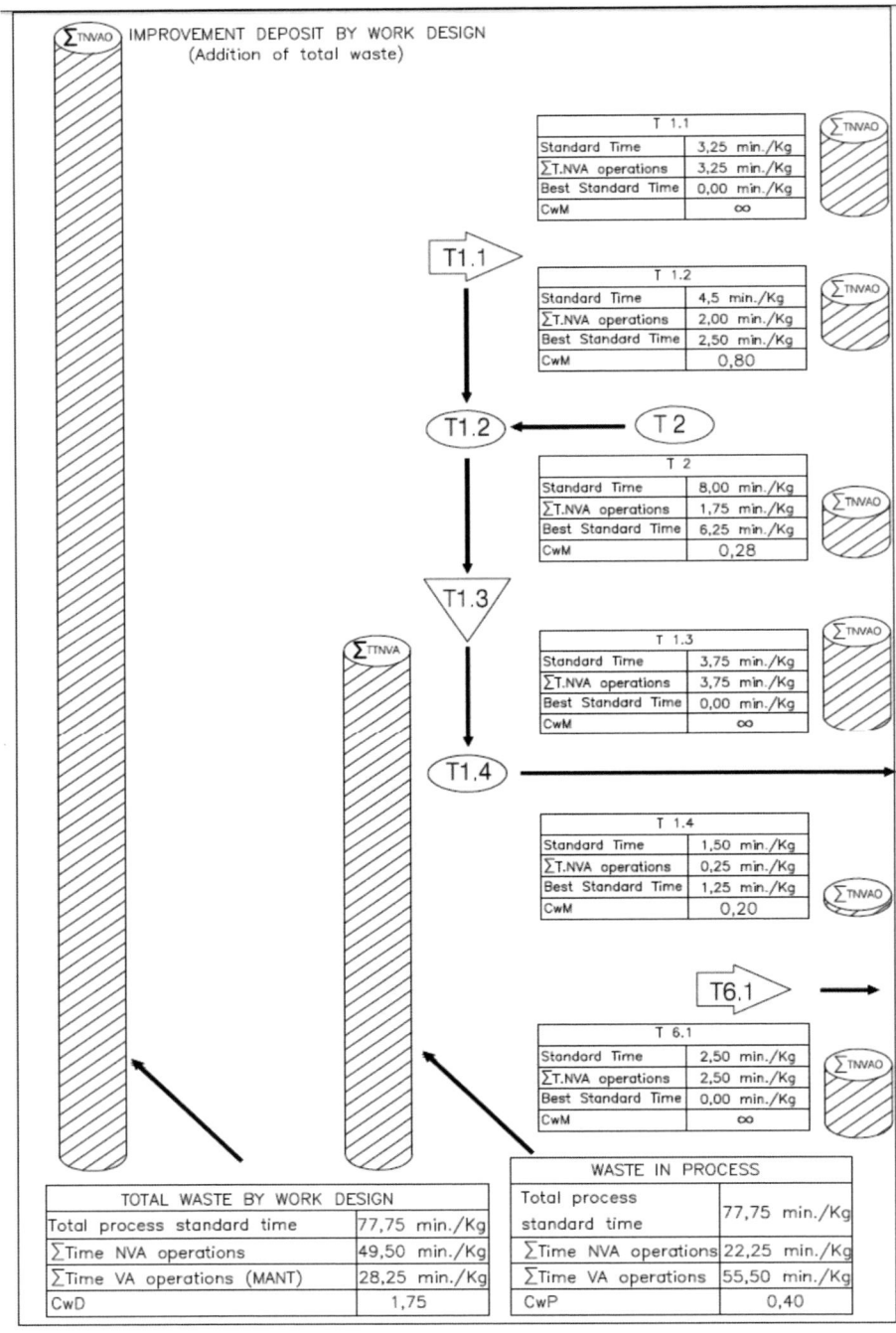

Figure 3.20. Problem. Waste diagram for work design.

3. Diagnosis of Productivity

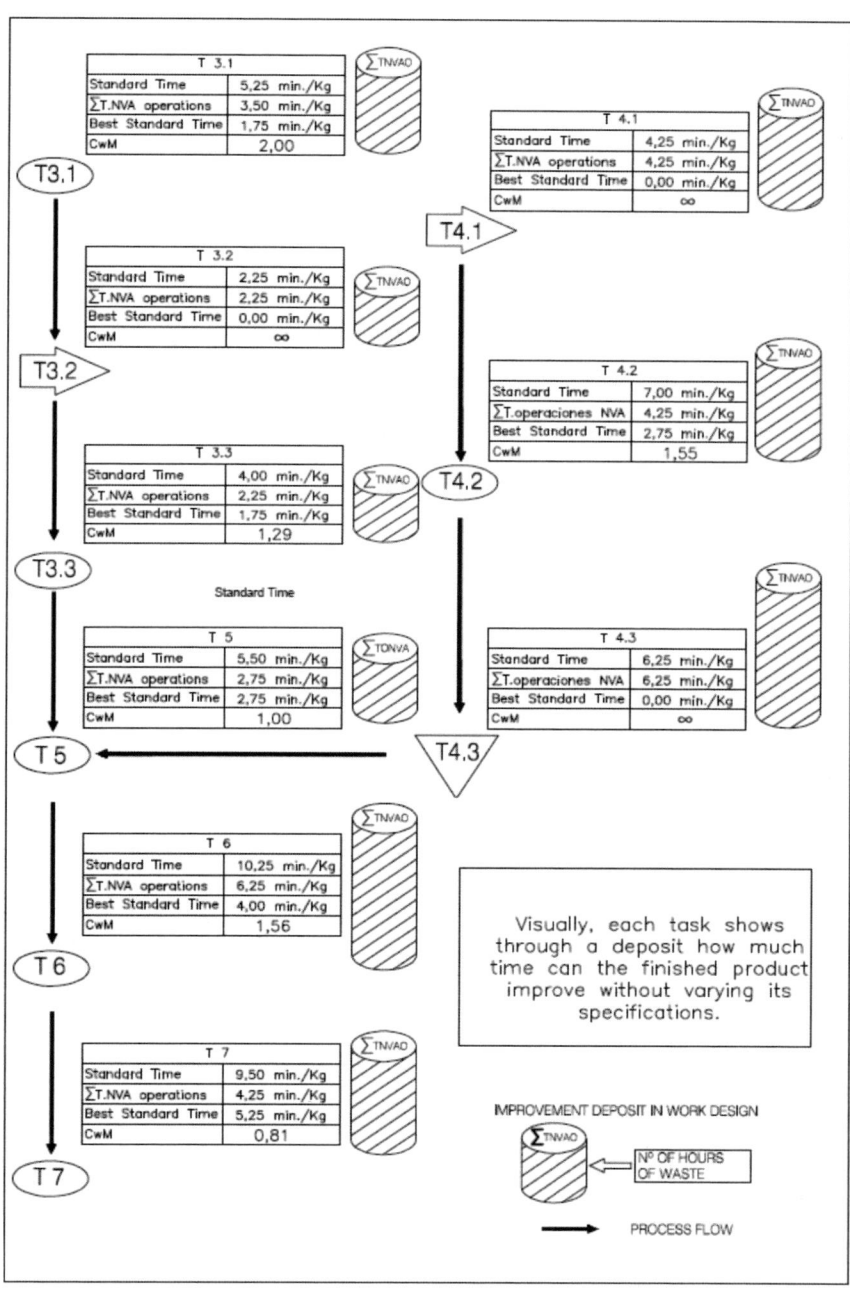

Industrial productivity

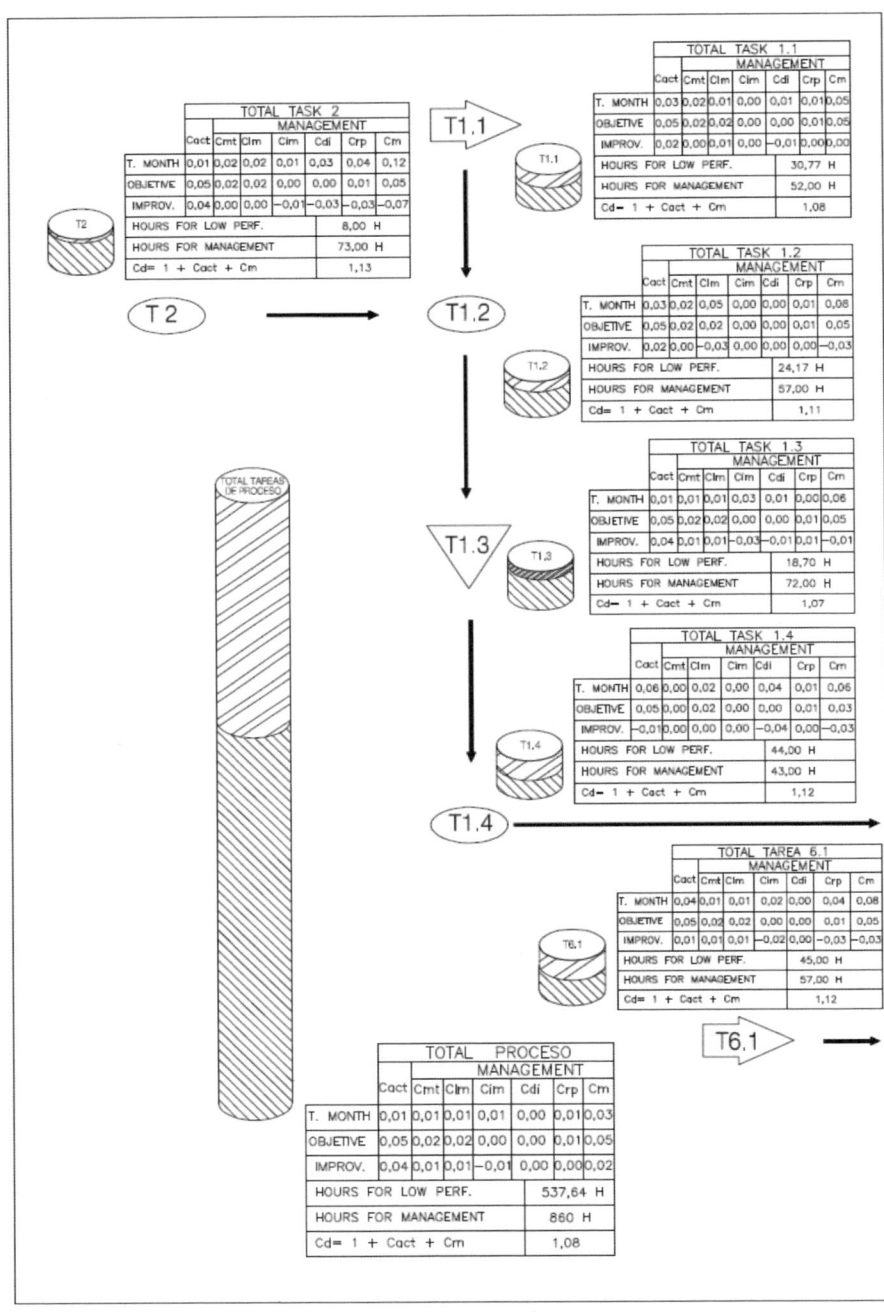

Figure 3.21. Problem: Waste diagram in manufacturing

3. Diagnosis of Productivity

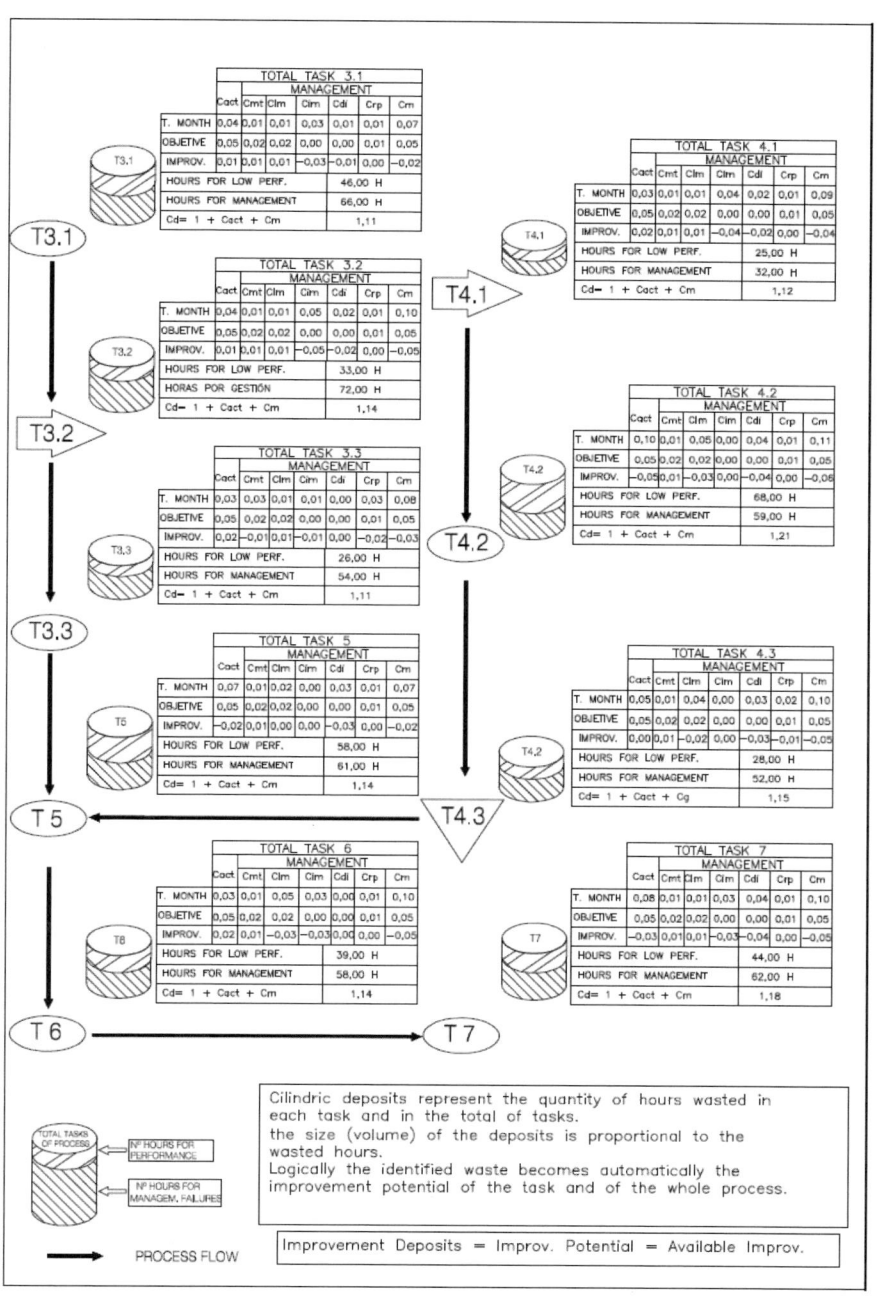

Chapter 4

Continuous Improvement Evolution and Systems Approach

4.1. Introduction

Once we have the unproductiveness diagnosis, its quantification, and the origin of its causes, it is necessary to systematize the productivity improvement. If we do not, the diagnosis information and improvement proposals will come to nothing. It is highly recommended that continuous improvement is seen as a sustainable activity over time and not as a quick fix or patch against a problem. In this chapter, we will learn:

- To register the evolution of waste in production.
- To fix criteria for acting on different wastes.
- To assign people in charge of the improvement of different wastes.
- To prepare procedures and systematize them so that continuous improvement becomes part of the company's management style rather than a one-time project or extra work.

Because this chapter about continuous improvement, it is necessary to speak about *Kaizen*.

Kaizen emerged in Japan out of its need to reach the levels of western industrial powers and earn a living for its large population, which lives in a country of small size and limited resources. Today the entire world needs to improve day by day. The environmental pollution, the continuous growth of population worldwide, and the depletion of traditional resources more easily exploited make the search for solutions necessary, which can only be reached by the continuous improvement in resource use in a world accustomed to extravagance and waste.

These changes and necessities will be lethal for all those who do not comprehend them appropriately. Many individuals fight each day to subsist in the world; they try to sell better and more economical products and services. They use all means at hand. If a warrior is trained daily to survive, trying to improve, because there lays his survival possibilities, in the same way companies and individuals must train and improve each day in order to survive. Food, clothes, health, and a home are not things simply "given."

Kaizen must not only be understood by entrepreneurs and workers, but also by leaders, educators, students, and opinion makers. The country must not only improve itself, but also encourage and empower its citizens to achieve continuous improvement as the only possible alternative in a world with many issues.

The world is being flooded by products from countries such as China, India, Thailand, Malaysia, Indonesia, and Pakistan, among others. Much of the world's population does not even know where to locate these countries on a map, which is a serious issue. In a time of great commercial struggles and rapid growth of world trade, to ignore global competitors is no longer valid. Trying to close the doors to the rest of the world is dangerous and can lead to problems for a country or region in the medium to long term. The two types of countries are those who improve continuously, trading and competing globally, achieving greater standards of living and comfort, and those others that stubbornly refuse change and integration into the global world, watching their standards of living decline along with their capacity to compete.

In a world of rapid change and transformations—technological, cultural, political, and social—not making every possible effort to quickly adapt to those changes is an attitude that could be classified either as arrogance or as plain stupidity.

The great economic commotion that took place in 1973 when, after a large period of economic growth, the price of fuel rose precipitously, jeopardizing Western economies, was based on a wide use of petroleum as input for the production of energy. Within this framework, the companies that were more flexible with more capacity and able to adapt rapidly emerged triumphant. Large U.S. factories of both cars and appliances subject to the introspective paradigms mentioned earlier, suffered the brunt of strong growth of Japanese companies that sold U.S. and European consumers on their sophisticated and much more affordable products.

That great ability of Japanese companies was due to the use of the kaizen system, based on a new philosophy that used many tools, methods and administrative instruments. It not only took corporate America but storm, but also upended their concepts of management.

So one by one, Western industries in automobiles, motorcycles, watches, cameras and video cameras, photocopiers, and many others were falling under Japanese competition. Companies such as Toyota, Honda, Yamaha, Minolta, Sharp, Seiko, Daihatsu, and Nippon Steel, among many others, invaded and displaced Western brands in public opinion and on shelves. Products that before were considered cheap and of low quality grew in market value, due to the favourable relationship between their quality and price.

The country that until recently received the great gurus of the West in terms of quality, such as Deming and Juran, now exported its advisors and knowledge to Western nations. Figures such as Ohno, Ishikawa, Taguchi, and Karatsu became renowned.

Same example and discipline for quality and productivity improvements emerged in countries such as South Korea, Singapore, and Hong Kong.

Kaizen in Action

To make continuous improvement possible and to achieve it at the highest levels, a number of factors are required, apart from diligence and discipline, and include the start-up of the following major systems:

1. Total quality control/Total quality management
2. A just-in-time production system
3. Total productive maintenance
4. Policy deployment
5. A suggestion system
6. Small-group activities

Kaizen refers to the improvement of all aspects that influence the entrepreneurial process. This topic is extensive and beyond the scope of this book. This chapter will focus on the continuous improvement of work execution time and eliminating waste within it.

4.2. Stages and Evolution of Continuous Improvement

Continuous improvement referred to here is the continuous improvement in productivity. Given the approach discussed so far, it is the constant reduction of waste. Figure 4.1 shows the stages through which waste reduction passes.

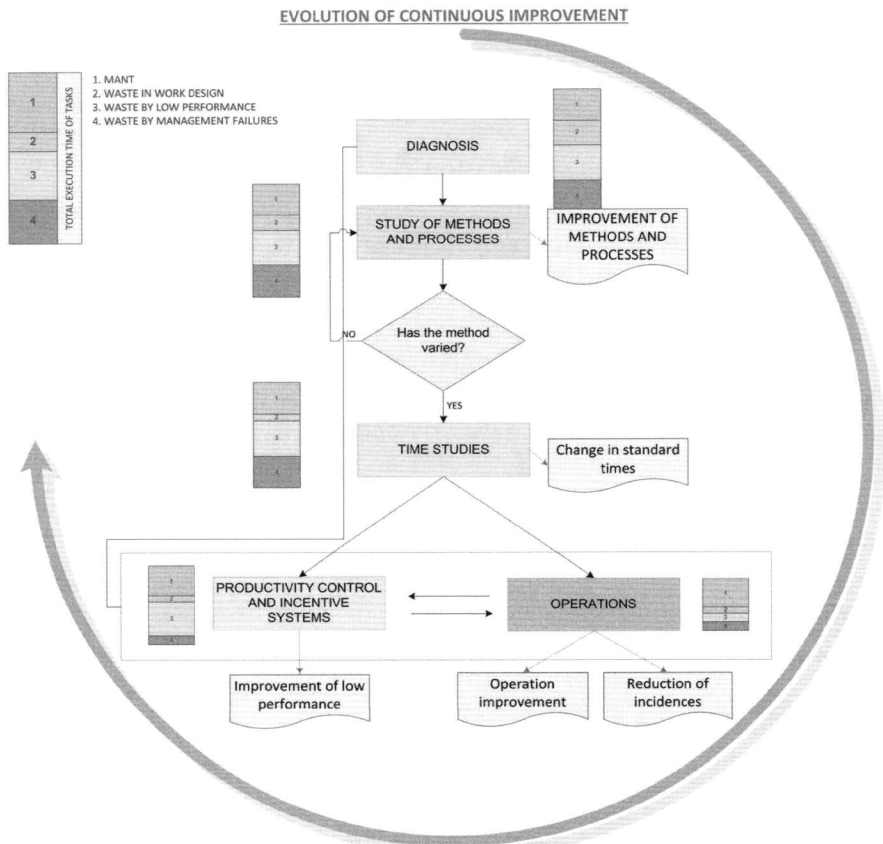

Figure 4.1. Stages of continuous improvement

As you examine Figure 4.1, you can see the stages through which waste reduction passes and how they match with the parts that compose this book. The purpose of each is explained next:

Diagnosis Phase

The diagnosis phase brings to light the level of waste of the factory and its different typologies. *Management is responsible for this phase* and based on the results will makes decisions about what to do and what part of the waste to attack. It corresponds to the first part of the book.

4. Continuous Improvement Evolution and Systems Approach

Phase of Methods and Process Engineering

During this phase, waste from method, CwM, and waste from process, CwP, are reduced. *The actions are the responsibility of the department of engineering processes, methods, and times.* The improvement of methods and/or processes will result in a new standard time for the tasks and the overall process. This phase corresponds to the second and third parts of the book. With the improvements, standard times will be passed to the new operations department for modification in data, feeding the productivity control system and operations planning.

Phase of Standard Times Application

The application of the standard times affects productivity control and operations planning. Improvement in the standard times should reduce the costs resulting from the application of the new times. *This application is responsibility of the director of operations.*

On the other hand, regardless of improvements in the standard times, CwFo (defined in the previous chapter), must be improved by increasing the productivity of manufactured resources and production planning. It corresponds to the fourth part of the book.

Repetition of the Cycle

Management should propose reductions of all the waste coefficients every period. These waste reduction proposals should be assigned with managers, time, resources, and dates in order to carry out the changes that bring these improvements.

The Path Toward Productivity

The path toward productivity never ends. Being productive is not an absolute term, but depends on how productive the competition is, which is why you cannot stop efforts at continuous improvement. Repeating the cycle is necessarily a permanent habit.

It is not about implementing this methodology of continuous improvement, but living in it. This culture of productivity *affects all departments and members of the company.*

4.3. System Concepts and System Approaches

The culture of productivity depends largely on the people who exercise it and it is of great value for the competitiveness of a company and its continuous improvement. However, it is highly desirable to support this culture with systems. A system is defined as:

«A group of parts or elements organized and related that interact together to achieve a goal. Systems receive (input) data, energy, or environmental matter and provide (output) information, energy, or matter».

The system that achieves continuous improvement is not only a question of will but also of methodology. For any event to be performed and maintained over time and that does not depend on the will of people, it is necessary to build a system. **This section describes a type of system for implementing continuous improvement of productivity.**

The two major groups of waste—waste in work design and waste in manufacturing—both have the same impact on manufacturing costs; however, their treatment will be different because by nature they are different. Although they have been described previously, we reiterate those descriptions here:

- Waste in work design is static, no matter what happens, it is a matter of design. By the method or process specified, latent waste already exists, and while no change is made in the design, waste will always be the same.

- Waste in manufacturing is dynamic and changes with each period of measurement and control. This waste is the time it takes above and beyond the designed standard time for manufacturing, regardless of the waste that the standard time already has.

- To clarify, one waste is known *a priori*, the other *after manufacturing*.

4.3.1. Systems for Continuous Improvement in the Design of Work

The engineering department of methods and processes will perform time studies of the different tasks. The results of the times are represented in the data-picking tables. Derived from the data table for each relevant process of the company is a waste map. Finally, a summary table of the waste of each process is provided. This implementation of a system of continuous improvement requires the establishment of parameters that mark the evolution of improvement. Logically, the trend will be seen over time. It is important that each table and waste map mark the factor *Date* in order to record the state of work design at each moment and its evolution. Then, the tables of the state of work design at each moment must be supplemented with tables that display the evolution of improvement.

The work design does not change alone; therefore, criteria or events that trigger their revision must be established.

The system should establish the criteria and/or revision orders of methods and processes of work for its improvement. These criteria can include:

- Periodic or annual analysis of the methods of all weighing tasks and processes.

4. Continuous Improvement Evolution and Systems Approach

- Based on the waste coefficient, a periodic analysis of the methods and processes, noting those tasks and processes whose waste coefficient ratio is greater than an objective coefficient. According to this criterion, effort would be invested in those places where it would be easier to achieve waste reduction. This would require defining some objectives:

    - Objective coefficient in method: CwMo

    - Objective coefficient in process: CwPo

    - Objective coefficient in work design: CwDo

- After change has occurred, instead of analyzing the method in order to change it, if it changed through the introduction of a new technology or change of materials, the method will be restudied and times will be measured again.

- For incidences in costs: If the company cannot be competitive in their product offerings, it must analyze what is happening and ask whether it is because of manufacturing costs. If so, methods and processes should improve.

To manage all these variables and their analyses, a scoreboard is needed. Figure 4.2 displays the productivity state in work design.

Scorecard indicators of waste in work design:

a. The column Standard Time shows the standard time of each task in the process and of the total process per manufactured unit.

b. Σ VAO Times is the time for the value-adding operations of each task and the total process.

c. The Σ NVAO Times is the time for the non-value-adding operations of each task and the total process.

d. Task symbol shows the type of task icon in question (storage, inspection, movement, operation, etc.).

e. Finally, the CwM is calculated, which is the last column. It is applied to the tasks, not the process. In case the task is non-value-adding, CwM will be infinite.

f. For the total of the process, the coefficients CwP and CwD will be obtained.

g. The analysis of waste in work design can be complemented with its waste map to a specified date. On the map, the tasks with coefficients higher than the objectives can be highlighted.

STATE OF WASTE IN WORK DESIGN

Process:

Date:

Revision:

Reason for revision:

Task	Standard Time	Σ VAO Times	Σ NVAO Times	Task Symbol	CwM
Task 1					
Task 2					
Task 3					
Task 4					
Task 5					
Total Process	**CwP**				
	CwD				

Notes:

- The value-adding time equals the best standard time.
- In case of non-value-adding tasks, all the standard time adds no value and the CwM tends to an infinite value.

Figure 4.2. State of waste in work design of a process

For each process, a table tracks the status of waste and its waste map for design in the task, as shown in Figure 3.9: *Waste map diagram by work design* from the previous chapter.

Regardless of what triggers a revision, each time one occurs, a change will be generated in the status of waste in work design. This change must be recorded and data provided in a table that has the most relevant indicators for the study of the evolution of continuous improvement in work design. For this reason, it is important to include the factor Date in the previous table and compare the data.

The data from which historical analysis will be done are the CwM, CwP, and CwD, the absolute value of the task times and their sum. To each task, a comment

4. Continuous Improvement Evolution and Systems Approach

is added to note the reason for the revision. This activity may return paradoxical data, as if the standard time of a task is reduced and its CwM increased, which can occur because new value-adding operations are identified that return a bigger waste, while the relevant datum in this record is the absolute standard time. The tables for recording the evolution of a continuous improvement process in work design would have a structure as Figure 4.3.

This table is done for each process. The following table of continuous improvement shows graphic evolution of standard time for a certain process.

Task	DATE 1 Standard Time	CwM	Revision Motive	DATE 2 Standard Time	CwM	Revision Motive
Task 1	20	1.25		18	1.13	Machine acquisition
Task 2	18	∞		18	∞	
Task 3	21	1.24		21	1.24	
Task 4	19	1.27		19	1.27	
Task 5	20	1.43		20	1.43	
Total Process	98	1.58		96	1.55	
	CwP	1.23		CwP	1.23	
	CwD	1.58		CwD	1.55	

Task	DATE 3 Standard Time	CwM	Revision Motive	DATE 4 Standard Time	CwM	Revision Motive
Task 1	18	1.13		18	1.13	
Task 2	0	0.00	Workstation redistribution	0	0.00	
Task 3	21	1.24		21	1.24	
Task 4	19	1.27		19	1.27	
Task 5	20	1.43		15	1.07	Method improvement.
Total Process	78	1.26		73	1.18	
	CwP	1.00		CwP	1.00	
	CwD	1.26		CwD	1.18	

Task	DATE 5		
	Standard Time	CwM	Revision Motive
Task 1	18	1.13	
Task 2	0	0.00	
Task 3	19	1.12	Method improvement
Task 4	18	1.20	Method improvement
Task 5	15	1.07	
Total Process	70	1.13	
	CwP	1.00	
	CwD	1.13	

Figure 4.3. Example: Evolution table of continuous improvement in work design

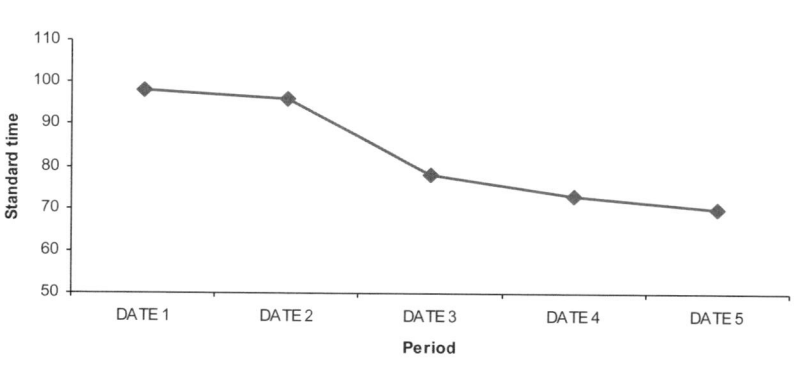

Figure 4.4. Example: Evolution graphic of continuous improvement of a process

> This productivity culture occurs when you cannot stop improving and changing. Many companies measured and improved their working times long ago and thought the work was done. Today their competitors have evolved and have complicated things. It is therefore absolutely necessary to systematize the work of improvement. Having launched an improvement, the only work that remains is **improve more.**

4.3.2. Systems for Continuous Improvement in Manufacturing

Manufacturing waste changes every day, every period of productivity control (waste measurement) depends on how the production has been managed and on the problems that arose. After establishing the periods of productivity control, which may well be daily, the system will calculate the waste each period. This section addresses this task of how to establish the calculation system for the CwF. It requires a daily data collection in order to know what happened and to analyze it. As in the case from the previous section, the evolution of continuous improvement shall be recorded over time. Because manufacturing waste changes every day, data collecting must be constant.

The system must establish criteria that trigger corrective actions based on each existing waste. These may include the following:

- When waste coefficients are greater than the established target ratios and assumed in the costs, as seen in section 3.4.2; it would require the definition of some objectives:
    - Objective coefficient in management (which in turn will have to be broken down into all possible causes): Cmo
    - Objective coefficient for low performance: Cacto
    - Objective coefficient in total manufacture: CdFo
- Periodically, based on reduction of objective waste coefficients imposed by management.
- Due to changes that cause a shift in the objective coefficients; for example, if a new machine has been purchased, a reduction in the waste coefficient for maintenance (Cmt) can be forced in order to recoup the investment.

Due to the difficulty and data loading, we will first explain how to calculate the waste of a certain period and later how to represent and visualize the evolution of continuous improvement in manufacturing.

4.3.2.1. Calculation of Waste Coefficients in Manufacturing for a Given Period

The measurement and control of waste shall be by task and for the whole process. Three charts and graphs are associated with each task and process:

1. Attendance reports:

   a. From each operator, the amount of hours present in the factory.

   b. Workdays from the month under study; 20 have been reflected.

   c. The column of Tot Att notes the sum of attendance of all the operators each day.

   d. The column of Tot Abs shows the hours of absenteeism in each day.

   e. The row Total sums the daily quantities of each column, returning the quantities by month.

2. Incidents record and production fulfilled:

   a. In the Incident Hours columns, the hours stopped because of incidences are inserted according to their causes (Breakdowns, Material shortages, Imbalance, Defects in information, and Reprocesses) and adds them in the column Total.

   b. The column Control H indicates the controlled hours that arise from subtracting the incidence hours from the attendance hours. Controlled hours are the hours during which the operator can produce normally.

   c. Production Units are the number of units that have been manufactured each day within the phase or task under study.

3. Scorecard indicators:

   a. The column ST x Units represents the production measured in standard time, in person-hours. It is calculated by multiplying the standard time (in minutes) by the units produced and divided by 60, to turn into hours.

   b. Activity arises from the division of production measured in time (ST x units) between the controlled hours. It measures the performance of operators.

   c. Cact is the waste coefficient for activity, as explained in Chapter 2.

   d. The Management Coefficients are those that arise from the incidents of poor management and calculation is based on the Incidence Hours in the previous table and in the function of the cause.

   e. Finally we get the column CwF from the formula CwF = 1 + Cact + Cm.

   f. Total month i data are the result of indicators in the month is obtained.

   g. In the row Objective, the objective waste of each indicator is recorded.

   h. Improvement on objective shows what margin was obtained between the real results and the objective. Whenever these data are negative, it means a worse result compared to the objective.

   i. Previous period (i - 1) notes the data from the previous period.

   j. Improvement on previous period indicates the most immediate evolution of the indicators and whether they have been better managed than in the previous control period. Whenever this datum is negative, it means no.

   k. Accum. previous periods calculates the indicators from all previous periods; it must take data from all previous periods. **This datum is a valid reflection of management and costs, because data from a relatively short period may be contaminated by a single incident or other aspects.**

l. Improv accum periods - object calculates the improvement of the accumulation against an objective. This comparison indicates status against the objectives throughout the year under study.

4. Waste coefficient graphs:

For the calculation indicators and comparatives described, pie charts and bar charts are shown for a better visualization of results.

5. Waste maps and improvement deposits:

From each period and for each process under study a waste map in manufacturing will be presented according to the data obtained. The difference with the previously seen maps is that coefficients greater than the objective coefficient are identified.

Chapter 21 discusses the control of productivity, taking into consideretion data collection, legal issues, and other relevant factors. The tables that will then be developed, and that have been previously described, are for the calculation of manufacturing waste and keeping a full methodology for productivity control. The information must be obtained from each task in order to make the calculation of manufacturing waste. Not all tasks are displayed, some examples will be shown. Finally, the calculation of the total process tasks is done; this calculation is the most important of all.

An example will be developed of waste analysis of a process task-by-task and by process in a given period of time. Figure 4.7 captures the process under study.

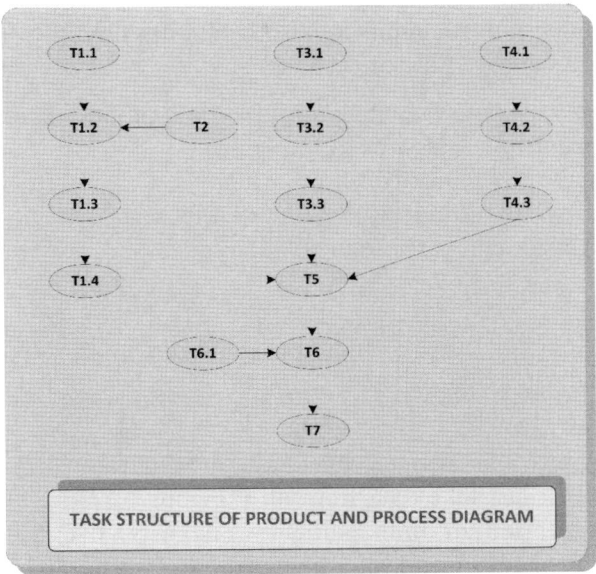

Figure 4.7. Structure of product tasks and process diagram

Industrial Productivity

Task	Standard Time (minutes)	N° Operators
T1.1	7	7
T1.2	5	5
T1.3	9	9
T1.4	5	5
T2	5	5
T3.1	8	8
T3.2	5	5
T3.3	9	9
T4.1	3	3
T4.2	1	1
T4.3	3	3
T5	2	2
T6	10	10
T6.1	7	7
T7	21	21
$\sum$ MANT	100	100

Figure 4.8. Standard times of tasks and of the total process

In order to facilitate the calculations, has been considered the same number of operators than the standard time of each task.

On the following pages are the tables for tasks in a month under study with the data collection occurring as previously explained.

4. Continuous Improvement Evolution and Systems Approach

LOGO	COMPANY NAME		Process				Task	1.1
	Responsible:						Month	Month i
Attendance Sheet									
Operator/Day	Opr 1.1.1	Opr 1.1.2	Opr 1.1.3	Opr 1.1.4	Opr 1.1.5	Opr 1.1.6	Opr 1.1.7	Tot Att	Tot Abs
1	8	8	8	8	8	8	8	56	0
2	8	0	8	8	8	8	8	48	8
3	8	8	8	8	8	8	8	56	0
4	8	8	8	8	8	8	8	56	0
5	8	8	8	8	8	8	8	56	0
6	8	8	8	8	8	8	8	56	0
7	8	8	4	8	8	0	8	44	12
8	8	8	8	8	8	8	8	56	0
9	8	8	8	8	8	8	8	56	0
10	8	8	8	8	8	8	8	56	0
11	8	8	8	8	8	8	8	56	0
12	8	8	8	8	8	8	8	56	0
13	8	8	8	8	8	8	8	56	0
14	8	8	8	8	8	8	8	56	0
15	8	8	8	8	8	8	8	56	0
16	8	8	8	8	8	8	8	56	0
17	8	8	8	8	8	0	8	48	8
18	8	8	8	8	8	8	8	56	0
19	8	0	8	8	8	8	8	48	8
20	8	8	8	8	8	8	8	56	0

Figure 4.9. Attendance report

- The column Tot Abs calculates the daily absenteeism from the amount of hours that should have been minus the real assistance.
- The number of columns corresponds to the number of operators at work in the task; in this case 7.

Industrial Productivity

LOGO	COMPANY NAME		Process			Task	1.1
	Responsible:					Month	Month i

Incidence Sheet (Hours at No Control) and Performed Production

| Day | Incidence Hours |||||| H Control | Production |
	Breakd.	Lack mat.	Imbal.	Informat.	Reworks	Total		Units
1	3	1	0	0	0	4	52	430
2	0	0	0	0	0	0	48	405
3	0	0	0	8	0	8	48	387
4	4	0	0	7	0	11	45	360
5	0	0	0	0	0	0	56	465
6	0	3	0	0	3	6	50	405
7	0	0	0	0	0	0	44	399
8	4	0	0	0	0	4	52	421
9	0	0	0	0	0	0	56	461
10	0	3	0	0	0	3	53	475
11	0	0	0	0	0	0	56	460
12	5	0	0	0	0	5	51	422
13	0	0	0	0	3	3	53	425
14	0	3	0	0	0	3	53	425
15	3	0	0	0	0	3	53	463
16	0	0	0	0	0	0	56	451
17	0	0	0	0	0	0	48	420
18	2	0	0	0	0	2	54	435
19	0	0	0	0	0	0	48	410
20	0	0	0	0	0	0	56	463
TOTAL	21	10	0	15	6	52	1032	8582

Figure 4.10. Incidents record

The column Control H comes from subtracting attendance hours.

In terms of production, it is noted, for simplicity, the production of a single reference, in the case of any ordinary factory that manufactures more than one reference in each phase or task. The production of every article or reference should be recorded afterwards in order to calculate the production measured in standard time (Quantity x Standard Time ST x Units).

4. Continuous Improvement Evolution and Systems Approach

Manufacturing Waste Scorecard

Day	ST x Units	Activity	Cact	Cmt	Clm	Cim	Cdi	Crp	Cm	CwF
1	50.17	96.47%	0.04	0.06	0.02	0.00	0.00	0.00	0.08	1.12
2	47.25	98.44%	0.02	0.00	0.00	0.00	0.00	0.00	0.00	1.02
3	45.15	94.06%	0.06	0.00	0.00	0.00	0.18	0.00	0.18	1.24
4	42.00	93.33%	0.07	0.10	0.00	0.00	0.17	0.00	0.26	1.33
5	54.25	96.88%	0.03	0.00	0.00	0.00	0.00	0.00	0.00	1.03
6	47.25	94.50%	0.06	0.00	0.06	0.00	0.00	0.06	0.13	1.19
7	46.55	105.80%	-0.05	0.00	0.00	0.00	0.00	0.00	0.00	0.95
8	49.12	94.46%	0.06	0.08	0.00	0.00	0.00	0.00	0.08	1.14
9	53.78	96.04%	0.04	0.00	0.00	0.00	0.00	0.00	0.00	1.04
10	55.42	104.56%	-0.04	0.00	0.05	0.00	0.00	0.00	0.05	1.01
11	53.67	95.83%	0.04	0.00	0.00	0.00	0.00	0.00	0.00	1.04
12	49.23	96.54%	0.04	0.10	0.00	0.00	0.00	0.00	0.10	1.14
13	49.58	93.55%	0.07	0.00	0.00	0.00	0.00	0.06	0.06	1.13
14	49.58	93.55%	0.07	0.00	0.06	0.00	0.00	0.00	0.06	1.13
15	54.02	101.92%	-0.02	0.06	0.00	0.00	0.00	0.00	0.06	1.04
16	52.62	93.96%	0.06	0.00	0.00	0.00	0.00	0.00	0.00	1.06
17	49.00	102.08%	-0.02	0.00	0.00	0.00	0.00	0.00	0.00	0.98
18	50.75	93.98%	0.06	0.04	0.00	0.00	0.00	0.00	0.04	1.10
19	47.83	99.65%	0.00	0.00	0.00	0.00	0.00	0.00	0.00	1.00
20	54.02	96.46%	0.04	0.00	0.00	0.00	0.00	0.00	0.00	1.04
TOTAL MONTH i	1001.23	97.02%	0.03	0.02	0.01	0.00	0.01	0.01	0.05	**1.08**
OBJECTIVE			0.05	0.02	0.02	0.00	0.00	0.01	0.05	*1.1*
IMPROVEMENT OVER OBJECTIVE			0.02	0.00	0.01	0.00	-0.01	0.00	0.00	*0.02*
PREVIOUS PERIOD (MONTH i - 1)			0.06	0.03	0.01	0.00	0.02	0.00	0.06	*1.12*
IMPROVEMENT OVER PREV. PERIOD			0.03	0.01	0.00	0.00	0.01	-0.01	0.01	*0.04*
ACCUM. PREVIOUS PERIODS			0.05	0.03	0.01	0.00	0.02	0.00	0.06	*1.10*
IMPROV. ACCUM. PERIODS - OBJECT.			0.00	-0.01	0.01	0.00	-0.02	0.01	-0.01	*0.00*

Figure 4.11. Scorecard indicators of waste in manufacture

Industrial Productivity

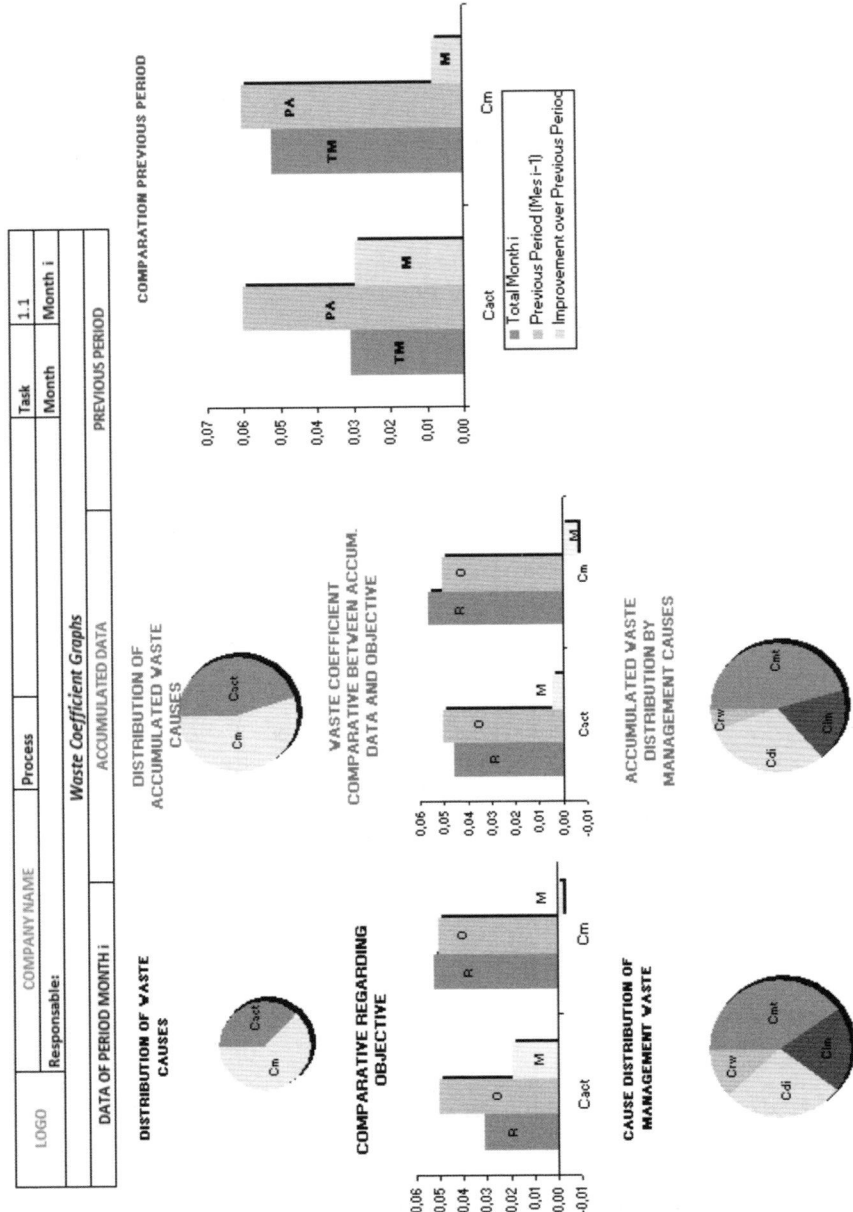

Figure 4.12. Graphics of waste coefficients

The previous tables and figures address the waste analysis in one of the tasks (the rest would be done similarly). The following tables and figures will show the

4. Continuous Improvement Evolution and Systems Approach

analysis of the overall process, which is what really matters for evaluating the waste in manufacturing.

It is important to see that data collecting for the total process is not done directly. The calculations in this case are done by adding the data from all the tasks of the process and thereafter all indicators are calculated.

LOGO	COMPANY NAME	
	Month	Month i
Addition of Attendance in all Sections		
Day	Total Attendance	Total Absenteeism
1	800	0
2	754	46
3	800	0
4	764	36
5	741	59
6	725	75
7	800	0
8	780	20
9	780	20
10	800	0
11	800	0
12	722	78
13	744	56
14	800	0
15	744	56
16	732	68
17	800	0
18	800	0
19	800	0
20	748	52
TOTAL	**15434**	**566**

Figure 4.13. Attendance report in all sections

Industrial Productivity

LOGO	COMPANY NAME		Process	TOTAL OF PROCESS	
	Supervisor			Month	Month i

Incidence Summary (Noncontrolled hours)

Day	Incidence Hours						H Control
	Breakd.	Lack mat.	Imbal.	Informat.	Reworks	Total	
1	10	12	6	0	0	28	772
2	0	0	0	0	0	0	754
3	0	0	0	8	0	8	792
4	40	0	7	0	0	47	717
5	0	0	0	0	0	0	741
6	0	51	0	0	3	54	671
7	0	0	0	0	0	0	800
8	0	0	8	32	0	40	740
9	0	0	0	0	0	0	780
10	0	3	0	0	43	46	754
11	0	0	0	0	0	0	800
12	5	0	51	0	0	56	666
13	32	0	0	0	3	35	709
14	0	0	7	0	0	7	793
15	3	0	41	0	0	44	700
16	0	0	0	0	0	0	732
17	0	0	0	0	0	0	800
18	2	62	0	0	0	64	736
19	0	0	0	33	0	33	767
20	0	0	0	0	33	33	715
TOTAL	92	128	120	73	82	495	14939

Figure 4.14. Incidents record of all sections

For the total process, there is no Units column; the production is calculated by adding the ST x Units from all the tasks of the process. The following table shows this column as $\sum$ ST x Units.

4. Continuous Improvement Evolution and Systems Approach

LOGO	COMPANY NAME	Process		Task	
	Responsible:			Month	

Manufacturing Waste Scorecard

Day	ST x Units	Activity	Cact	Management Coefficients				
				Cmt	Clm	Cim	Cdi	Crp	Cm
1	876.40	113.52%	-0.12	0.01	0.01	0.01	0.00	0.00	0.03
2	752.08	99.75%	0.00	0.00	0.00	0.00	0.00	0.00	0.00
3	720.87	91.02%	0.10	0.00	0.00	0.00	0.01	0.00	0.01
4	692.42	96.57%	0.04	0.06	0.00	0.01	0.00	0.00	0.07
5	709.20	95.71%	0.04	0.00	0.00	0.00	0.00	0.00	0.00
6	699.97	104.32%	-0.04	0.00	0.07	0.00	0.00	0.00	0.08
7	702.52	87.81%	0.14	0.00	0.00	0.00	0.00	0.00	0.00
8	764.63	103.33%	-0.03	0.00	0.00	0.01	0.04	0.00	0.05
9	753.53	96.61%	0.04	0.00	0.00	0.00	0.00	0.00	0.00
10	691.92	91.77%	0.09	0.00	0.00	0.00	0.00	0.06	0.07
11	764.52	95.56%	0.05	0.00	0.00	0.00	0.00	0.00	0.00
12	687.50	103.23%	-0.03	0.01	0.00	0.07	0.00	0.00	0.08
13	692.62	97.69%	0.02	0.05	0.00	0.00	0.00	0.00	0.05
14	763.02	96.22%	0.04	0.00	0.00	0.01	0.00	0.00	0.01
15	766.68	109.53%	-0.09	0.00	0.00	0.05	0.00	0.00	0.06
16	775.42	105.93%	-0.06	0.00	0.00	0.00	0.00	0.00	0.00
17	757.57	94.70%	0.06	0.00	0.00	0.00	0.00	0.00	0.00
18	709.08	96.34%	0.04	0.00	0.09	0.00	0.00	0.00	0.09
19	756.83	98.67%	0.01	0.00	0.00	0.00	0.04	0.00	0.04
20	742.57	103.86%	-0.04	0.00	0.00	0.00	0.00	0.04	0.04
TOTAL MO	14,779	98.93%	0.01	0.01	0.01	0.01	0.00	0.01	0.03
OBJECTIVE			0.05	0.02	0.02	0.00	0.00	0.01	0.05
IMPROV. OVER OBJECTIVE			0.04	0.01	0.01	-0.01	0.00	0.00	0.02
PREVIOUS PERIOD (MONTH i - 1)			0.02	0.01	0.01	0.05	0.02	0.00	0.09
IMPROV. OVER PREV. PERIOD			0.01	0.00	0.00	0.04	0.02	-0.01	0.06
ACCUM. PREVIOUS PERIODS			0.02	0.01	0.01	0.03	0.01	0.00	0.06

Figure 4.15. Manufacturing waste scoreboard, all sections

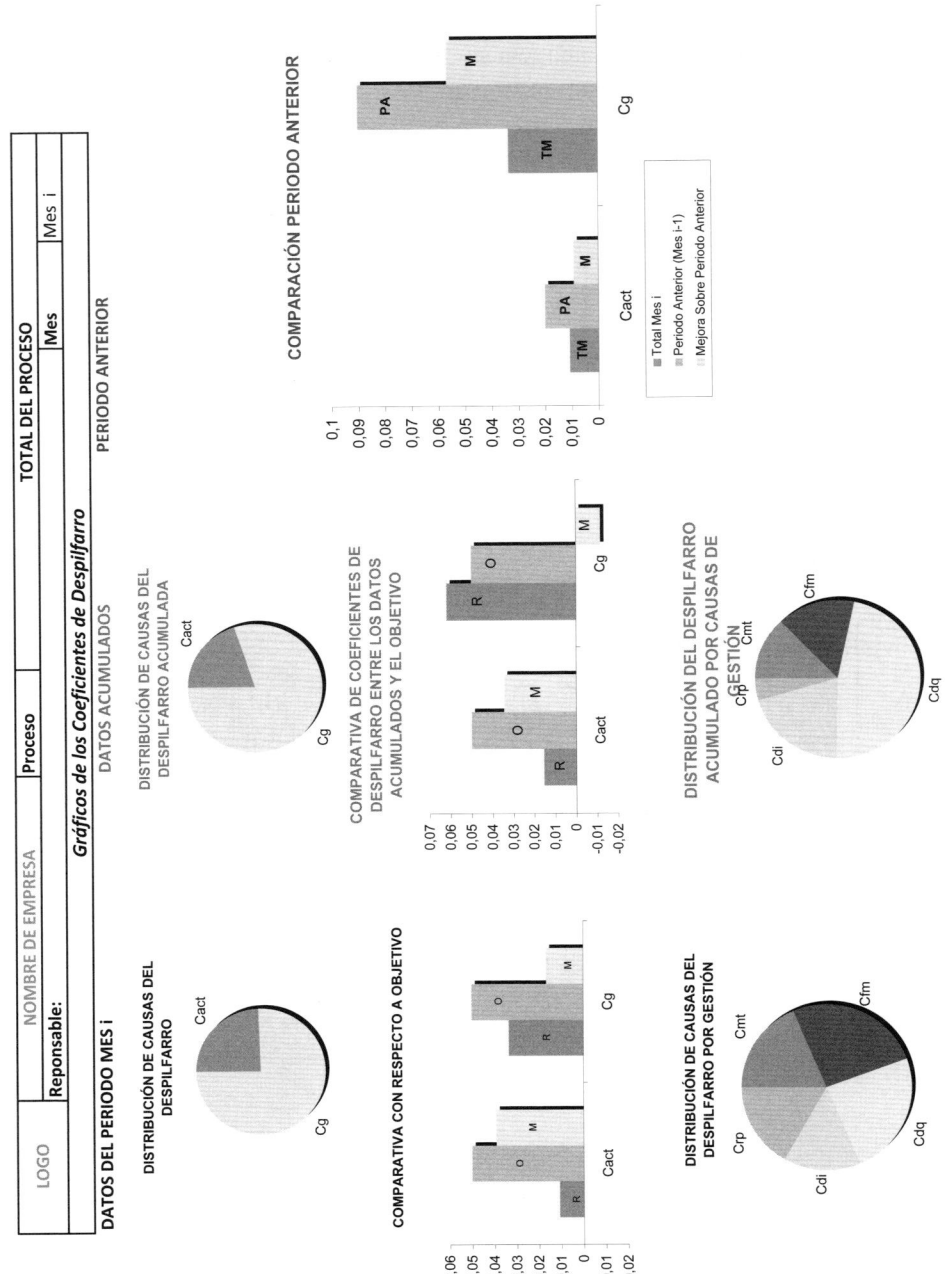

Figure 4.16. *Waste coefficient graphs of the whole process*

As can be observed, the quantity of data is large. This process should be totally automatic and simplified; it is not difficult. Reducing the problem to each day of work, the operations manager can analyze concrete data and, based on these analyses, acquire information and make decisions. Of course, hindsight explanations are always better, but here issues are anticipated. The head of operations must supervise and correct daily, and the manager should see the results at least once a month. It is not a burdensome amount of work, and it provides helpful information. The consequences of not looking at it generate much more work than looking at it.

Total month i	14.779	98,93%	0,01	0,01	0,01	0,01	0,00	0,01	0,03	*1,04*
Objetive			0,05	0,02	0,02	0,00	0,00	0,01	0,05	*1,1*
Improvement over objective			0,04	0,01	0,01	-0,01	0,00	0,00	0,02	*0,06*

Figure 4.17. *Extract from total process results: Results concentration tool*

In this case, the waste map is essential to be able to synthesize the results from the calculation process. The next figure shows the visual result. In the table of waste coefficients from each task, the shaded cells, indicating the waste coefficient that is above the objective, stand out.

To be able to reduce the waste in the process, it is necessary to know what happens in each task. The map provides the most visual assessment, which in this case is essential.

- Low performance
- Management failures
    - Lack of materials
    - Imbalance in workload
    - Defects of information
    - Reprocesses and quality errors
    - Maintenance

Each department will measure responsibility for the waste in manufacturing, as well as in comparison to some objectives.

The breakdown of the causes constitutes a production management scorecard.

Industrial Productivity

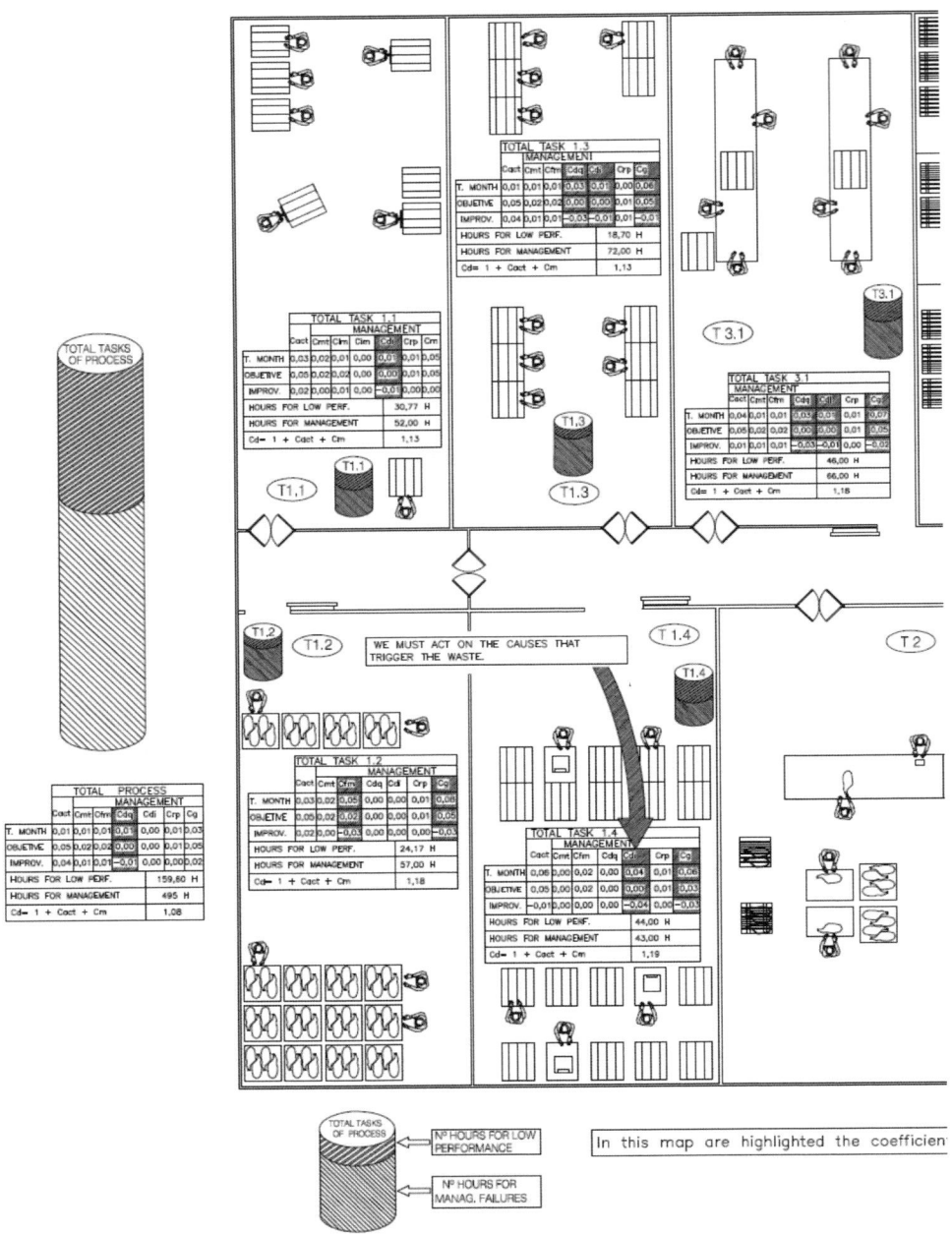

Figure 4.18. Manufacturing waste map

4. Continuous Improvement Evolution and Systems Approach

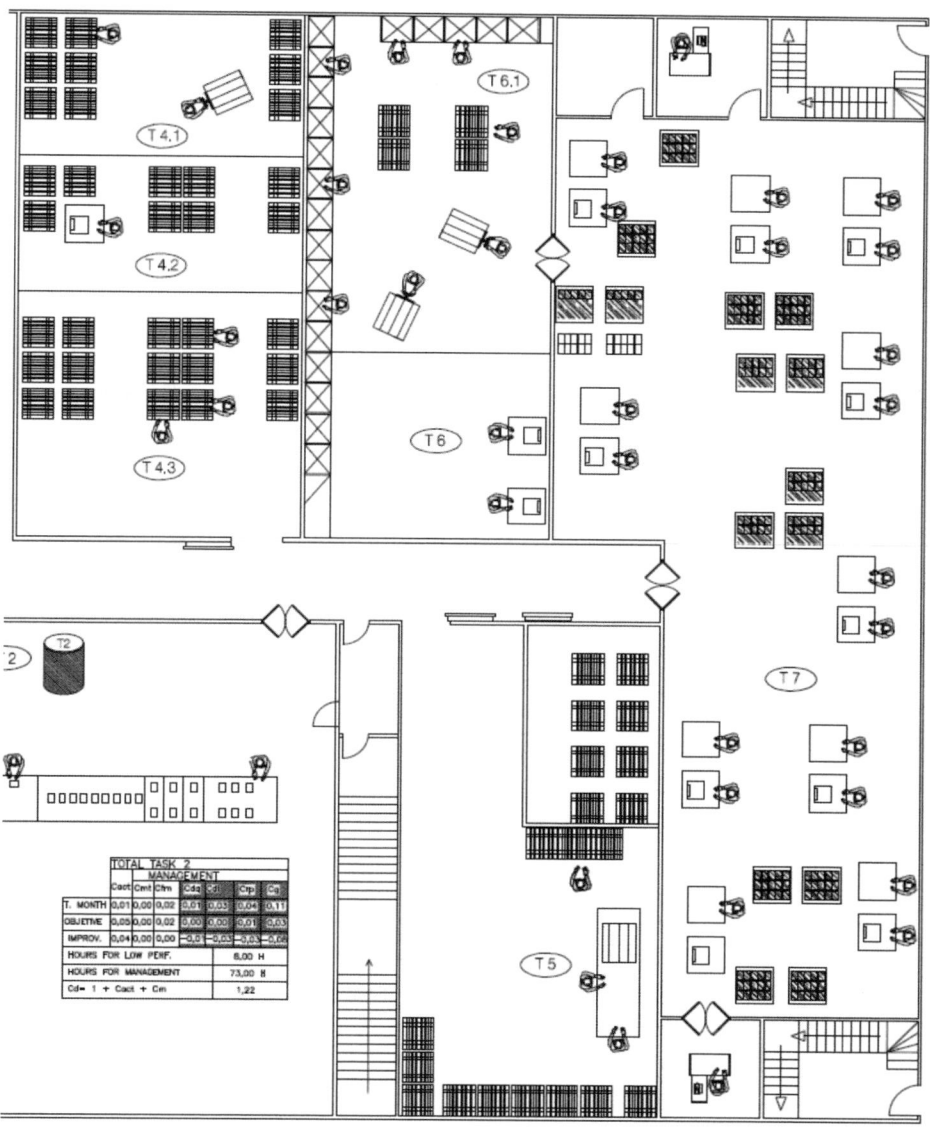

icients above the objective.

4.3.2.2. Evolution of Continuous Improvement in Manufacturing

The previous tables and maps reflect the analysis of a certain period, but as continuous improvement is being discussed, the evolution of waste in manufacturing through time has to be captured in different periods. Analysis of two types of data is made:

1. Data from the period
2. Accumulated data

The accumulated data are the result of analyzing waste from the beginning of the analysis to the present; it includes what happened in all the periods. The purpose of both types of data and their evolution are different. The accumulated CwF is the valid datum for the calculation of current real costs. The accumulated data by period help to show the results of one-time wastes and what effects a certain corrective measure can have. Imagine that last month money was invested in a tool that generates fewer machine stops for a certain task; it would be convenient to know what effects it has had in the Cm in the next period and whether the investment is amortizing. Or, if measures have been taken on low performance in a specific section, knowing whether their evolution have had effect on the Cact.

Evolution must be shown by task or process. Figures 4.19 through 4.26 show examples of formats used for expressing the evolution of waste coefficients in manufacturing.

4. Continuous Improvement Evolution and Systems Approach

LOGO	COMPANY NAME		Process		Task	
	Responsible:				Month	
Waste Coefficients by Month						
Coefficients	Month 1	Month 2	Month 3	Month 4	Month 5	Month 6	Month 7
Cact	0.04	0.04	0.02	0.03	0.03	0.04	0.02
Cmt	0.02	0.01	0.01	0.02	0.02	0.02	0.01
Clm	0.02	0.03	0.03	0.02	0.01	0.02	0.01
Cim	0.03	0.04	0.04	0.03	0.02	0.05	0.04
Cdi	0.01	0.01	0	0	0.02	0	0
Crw	0.01	0.01	0.01	0.01	0	0	0.01
Cm	0.09	0.1	0.09	0.08	0.07	0.09	0.07
CwF	1.13	1.14	1.11	1.11	1.1	1.13	1.09

Figure 4.19. Waste coefficients by month

LOGO	COMPANY NAME		Process		Task	Task i
	Responsible:				Month	Several
Accumulated Waste Coefficients by Month							
Coefficients	Month 1	Month 2	Month 3	Month 4	Month 5	Month 6	Month 7	Month 8
Cact	0.04	0.04	0.03	0.03	0.03	0.03	0.03	0.03
Cmt	0.02	0.02	0.01	0.02	0.02	0.02	0.02	0.02
Clm	0.02	0.03	0.03	0.03	0.02	0.02	0.02	0.02
Cim	0.03	0.04	0.04	0.04	0.03	0.04	0.04	0.04
Cdi	0.01	0.01	0.01	0.01	0.01	0.01	0.01	0.01
Crw	0.01	0.01	0.01	0.01	0.01	0.01	0.01	0.01
Cm	0.09	0.10	0.09	0.09	0.09	0.09	0.08	0.09
CwF	1.13	1.14	1.13	1.12	1.12	1.12	1.12	1.12

Figure 4.20. Accumulated waste coefficients by month

Industrial Productivity

LOGO	COMPANY NAME		Process			Task	Task i
	Responsible:					Month	Several
Monthly Waste Coefficients vs. Objectives							
Coefficients	Month 1	Month 2	Month 3	Month 4	Month 5	Month 6	Month 7	Month 8
Cact	0.01	0.01	0.03	0.02	0.02	0.01	0.03	0.02
Cmt	0	0.01	0.01	0	0	0	0.01	0
Clm	0	-0.01	-0.01	0	0.01	0	0.01	0
Cim	0	-0.01	-0.01	0	0.01	-0.02	-0.01	-0.01
Cdi	0	0	0.01	0.01	-0.01	0.01	0.01	0.01
Crw	0	0	0	0	0.01	0.01	0	0
Cm	0	-0.01	0	0.01	0.02	0	0.02	0
CwF	0.04	0.03	0.06	0.06	0.07	0.04	0.08	0.05

Figure 4.21. Waste coefficients by month versus the objectives

LOGO	COMPANY NAME		Process			Task	Task i
	Responsible:					Month	Several
Monthly Accumulated Waste Coefficients vs. Objectives							
Coefficients	Month 1	Month 2	Month 3	Month 4	Month 5	Month 6	Month 7	Month 8
Cact	0.01	0.01	0.02	0.02	0.02	0.02	0.02	0.02
Cmt	0.00	0.01	0.01	0.01	0.00	0.00	0.00	0.00
Clm	0.00	-0.01	-0.01	-0.01	0.00	0.00	0.00	0.00
Cim	0.00	-0.01	-0.01	-0.01	0.00	-0.01	-0.01	-0.01
Cdi	0.00	0.00	0.00	0.01	0.00	0.00	0.00	0.01
Crw	0.00	0.00	0.00	0.00	0.00	0.00	0.00	0.00
Cm	0.00	-0.01	0.00	0.00	0.00	0.00	0.01	0.01
CwF	0.04	0.04	0.04	0.05	0.05	0.05	0.05	0.05

Figure 4.22. Accumulated waste coefficients by month versus the objectives

4. Continuous Improvement Evolution and Systems Approach

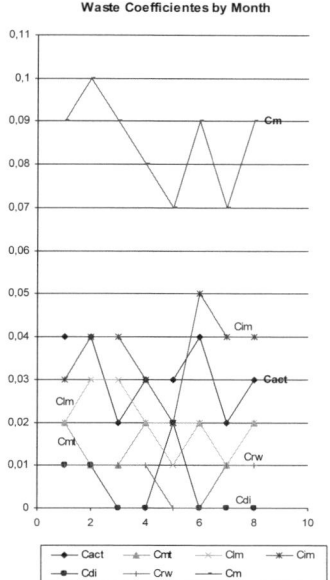

Figure 4.23. *Graph of waste for month*

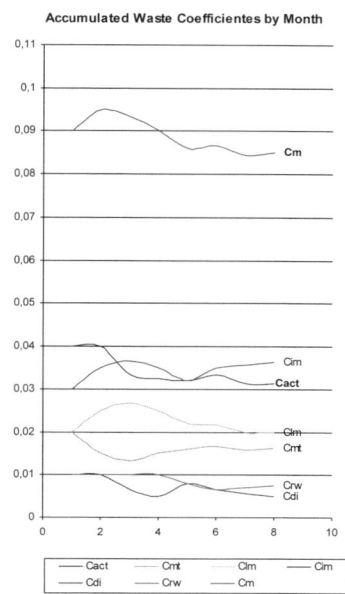

Figure 4.24. *Graph of accumulated coefficients by month*

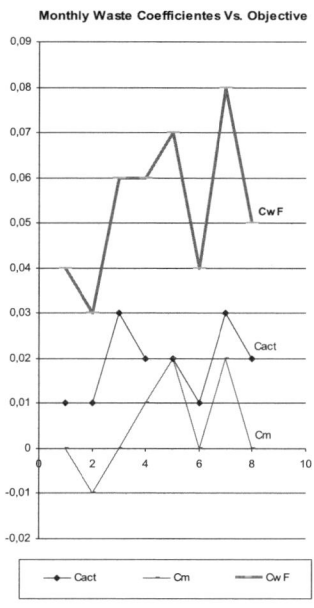

Figure 4.25. *Graph of monthly coefficients versus objectives*

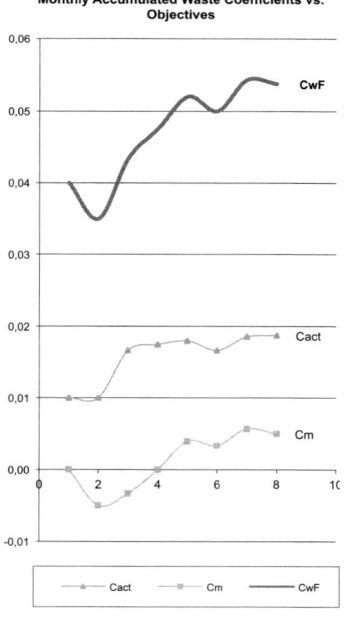

Figure 4.26. *Graph of monthly-accumulated coefficients versus objectives*

4.4. Decision Making: Events That Trigger It

Decision making and subsequent actions must be tailored to a procedure. *Figure 4.27: Procedure of continuous improvement* details the responsibilities, participants, milestones, and other factors necessary for continuous improvement of a procedure. An explanation about the procedure includes the interpretation of the tables shown in section 4.2 and a recommendation of its use by every position within the industrial company.

4. Continuous Improvement Evolution and Systems Approach

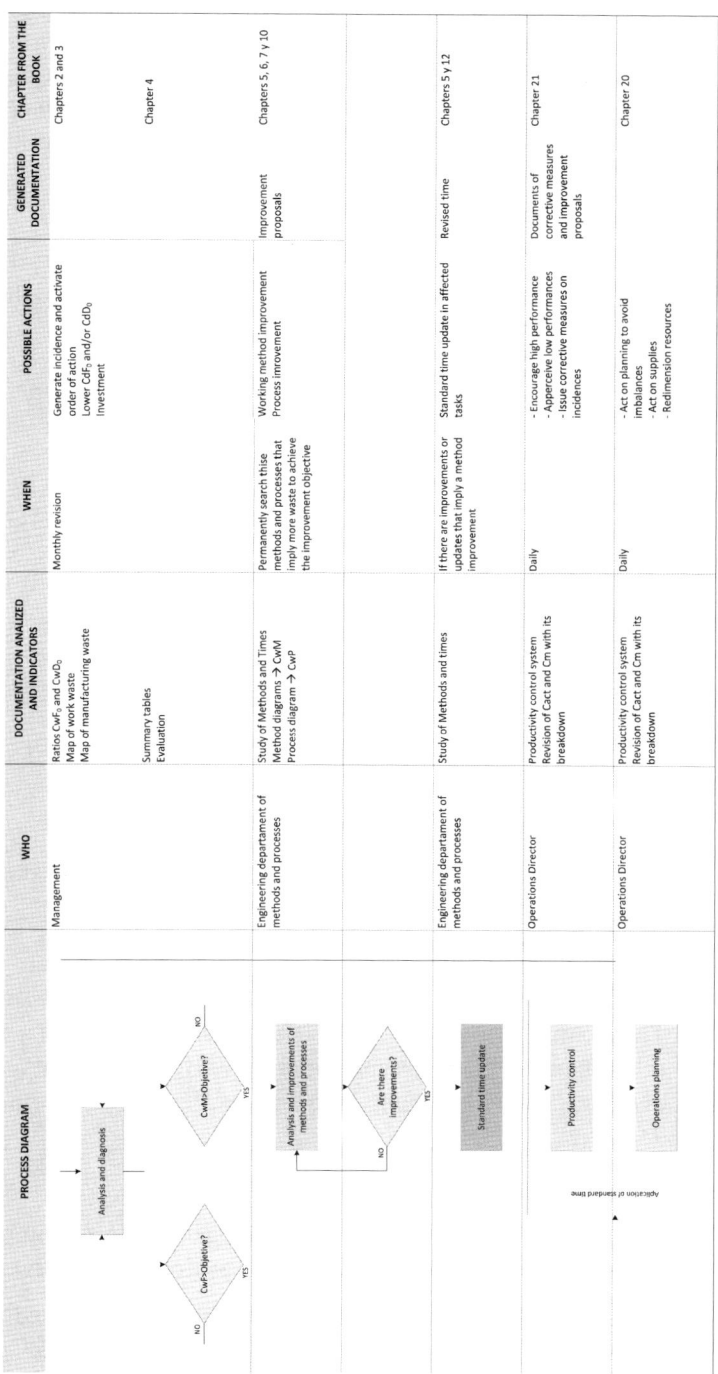

Figure 4.27. Continuous improvement procedure

Clarifications and Recommendations about the Procedure and Waste Calculations

Logically the data the WMT returns need to be analyzed, and then, based on the results, actions carried out for their reduction. The analysis should have a greater or lesser detail based on the responsibility of the analyst in question.

CEO (Chief Executive Officer)

The CEO of an industrial company cannot be unaware of what occurs in his or her factory. Thereby, CEOs must revise periodically the existing waste data.

- Information analyzed:
    - Waste maps of work design and manufacturing and their corresponding tables
    - Waste evolution tables
    - Comparison of the result of all processes in all periods with the objective waste coefficients
    - Compare CwF with CwFo and CwD with CwDo
- When analyzed:
    - Maximum, monthly
    - When incidences in costs make waste analysis a priority
- Possible actions:
    - Communications, requests of reports to operations department, establishment of corrective measures to deal with the principal waste cause, etc.
    - In order to reduce objective costs, management can force continuous improvement by reducing objective waste coefficients. These improvements have to be substantiated in a cause-effect relation or the people responsible for performing them will become discouraged. This means investments, learning and improvement deadlines, new tools, etc.
- Generated documentation:
    - Each management revision must generate a compliance or noncompliance report, based on the results of the analysis.
    - Might generate a communication of objective waste reduction.

4. Continuous Improvement Evolution and Systems Approach

Responsible for Methods and Process Engineering

The engineering department of methods and processes will be in charge of measuring the work and, from the methods and process improvements, reducing the standard time. The purpose of these activities is to reduce waste in work design. Once work is designed, waste is constant and does not change from month to month unless changes occur in the operative method or in the process. Therefore, another constant must be imposed, an objective improvement, ergo, to improve the standard times a certain percentage each year.

- Information analyzed:
    - Method diagrams (CwM) and process diagrams (CwP)
    - Waste maps in work design and comparison with objectives
    - Evolution tables of wastes in work design

- When:
    - Permanently, the work of reducing standard times is constant.
    - The engineering manager must search the processes and tasks with more weight and more waste and dedicate study to these processes and tasks. The more waste found in a task or process, the easier it will be to improve; therefore, the work of selection is important.

- Possible actions:
    - Order the study of methods of certain tasks or processes
    - Request investments for the reduction of standard times
    - Order time studies

- Generated documentation:
    - Proposals for methods improvement
    - Implementation orders
    - Diagrams of revised methods
    - Diagrams of revised processes
    - Actualized standard times

COO (Chief Operating Officer)

The COO must revise the CwF and its components daily and make corrective measures daily. The manufacturing waste is constantly changing and, if not monitored, has uncontrollable growth. Multiple factors can affect the increase in CwF, and they can emerge in unanticipated ways. To avoid this, must be done

147

almost immediately an anticipative work, analysis and correction. The tasks and causes of deviations from the objective must be identified, which means identifying the waste coefficients that compose the CwF from each task that are above the target. Efforts must focus on the causes of waste in these tasks.

In turn, operations management is affected by the possible variations in standard time after the improvements in methods and processes. Each time revisions are made in the standard time they must be updated in the productivity calculation, waste in manufacturing, and productivity planning systems. In the same way, a reduction in the standard times that is inserted in the system and does not increase the CwF should be reflected by manufacturing execution times that are lowered in the same proportion.

- Information analyzed:
    - Waste maps in manufacturing
    - Tables of waste in manufacturing
    - For the totality of the process and for each task
    - Compare it with the objective
- When:
    - Daily
- Possible actions:
    - Reorganize shifts to balance load and capacity
    - Modify plans
    - Increase the capacity of bottlenecks
    - Warn teams with low performance
    - Or provide incentives to those whose activity is above normal
    - Repair a machine that returns a low performance
    - Warn a supplier for defects in the supply that cause waste in our manufacturing
    - Request investments for breakdown reduction
    - Update the standard times in the production and productivity control management system
- Generated documentation:
    - Launches of work orders and revisions
    - Warnings
    - Incentives

4. Continuous Improvement Evolution and Systems Approach

- Improvement proposals from the organization
- Possible penalization of a supplier

> Without a daily control of waste, it will not be possible to reach the waste objective. The inputs for its calculation must be automated and simplified as possible.

The Cause-Effect Measurement

Undertaking actions generally supposes a cost. Management can know, with the use of the defined indicators, the state of the production and whether the necessary objectives are being met.

On the other hand, objectives do not have to be static. They can be broken down to determine where the problems are being produced in order to set goals for lowering the CwFo and the CwDo. The reduction of these coefficients will measure the continuous improvement that is happening.

We know the Cm breaks down into other waste coefficients. For example, we detect that within a Cm, whose objective is 0.15, 0.08 is provided by Cmt because of a machine that causes constant breakdowns (or because the maintenance team does not enough resources to repair all the breakdowns and make the necessary preventive maintenance). We can simulate the benefits that will come from a CwFo = 1.30 – 0.06 = 1.24 (supposing that it is to reduce the Cmt from 0.08 to 0.02, that is, a 0.06). Then, with the production we have, we will know whether the necessary investment to address this improvement will be recouped. **A clear cause-effect relationship is necessary. If for example we invest in a new machine to reduce breakdown stops, CwFo has to be reduced in such a way that the investment can be recouped.**

For example, if an imbalance arises from a lack of workload for the workforce capacity and the company decides to sell more and invests in marketing or hiring a new sales agent or lowering the prices, this shift should be compensated with a decrease in the coefficient of imbalance (Cim).

This approach would solve many problems some managers have after investing in a piece of equipment based on pressure from their middle managers. From the coefficients of waste, management will know what it needs to ask in exchange for making an investment. Or if they hire another person for maintenance, that person's salary must be paid by the reduction in waste. **Anything not compensated this way will be an investment not recouped or an expense that will punish the income statement.**

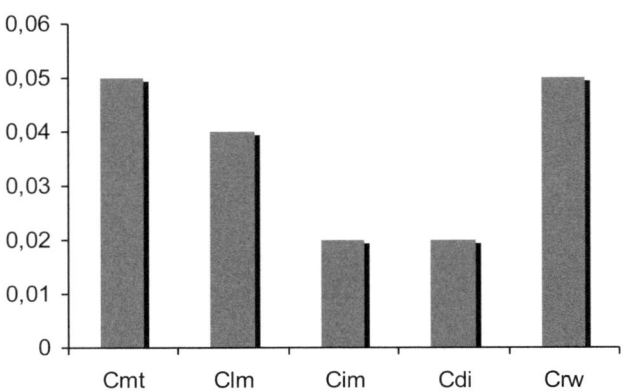

Figure 4.28. Initial state of waste

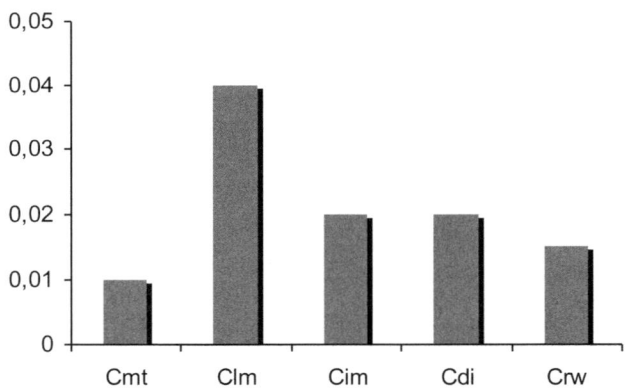

Figure 4.29. State of waste after the investment

When making an investment in a new machine, for example, maintenance waste (perhaps reprocesses) must be reduced. The graph shows how these waste coefficients are reduced. No reduction of the coefficients implies that the investment is not being recouped.

Questions

1. What Japanese technique corresponds to continuous improvement as a permanent management method?

2. What stages does continuous improvement have for the improvement of manufacturing times?

3. What is recorded in the state of waste in process work design?

4. What does the evolution of continuous improvement record in the work design of a process?

5. What does the state of waste in manufacturing record?

6. What does the CEO have to revise about the continuous improvement of manufacturing times? How often must a CEO do this?

7. What should any investment or improvement action reflect?

8. Most of the content in this chapter was explained in the previous chapter: waste measurement and the process of solving the waste. What does this chapter provide?

Bibliography

Acina, José Domingo. *Calidad y mejora continua. Actividades I. (San Sebastian,* S.A. Editorial Donostiarra, 2007).

Imai, Masaaki. *Kaizen: The Key to Japan's Competitive Success* (New York, Random House, 1986).

Suzaki, Kiyoshi. *New Manufacturing Challenge: Techniques for Continuous Improvement* (New York, The Free Press, 1987).

PARTE II

STUDY, ANALYSIS, AND IMPROVEMENT OF METHODS

1. MANT
2. WASTE IN WORK DESIGN
3. WASTE BY LOW PERFORMANCE
4. WASTE BY MANAGEMENT FAILURES

Part	Aim	Initial Situation	Final situation
Part 1: Diagnosis	We start from a manufacturing execution times and we want to know what caused them.	TIEMPO TOTAL DE EJECUCIÓN DE LA TAREAS	1, 2, 3, 4
Part 2: Methods	We study and improve the work method of a task to reduce its necessary execution time. The same with processes.	1, 2, 3, 4	1, 2, 3, 4
Part 3: Time measurement	With a defined and improved method we time the task through various techniques to be able to establish a standard, this implies time improvements.	1, 2, 3, 4	1, 2, 3, 4
Part 4: Operations planning	With standard times we can manage production, dimensionate, make decisions, etc. Waste by management failures is reduced.	1, 2, 3, 4	1, 2, 3, 4
Part 4: Productivity control	With standard times productivity can be controled reducing the waste by low performance.	1, 2, 3, 4	1, 2, 3, 4

Chapter 5

The Study of Methods

5.1. Definition

The study of methods of a task is the systematic investigation of the operations that compose it, their typology, materials, and tools used.

The study of methods breaks the task into reasonable steps of operations. This way it is better understood how the task is executed and thereby serves to unify an operations method for all those involved in its execution. It is also the starting point for its improvement. In addition, it is important to note that to describe the modus operandi is in itself an improvement, probably the most important.

The nine chapters of the second part discuss the work methods:

- Methods study
- Methods analysis
- Improvement proposals
- Improvement implementation

Industrial productivity

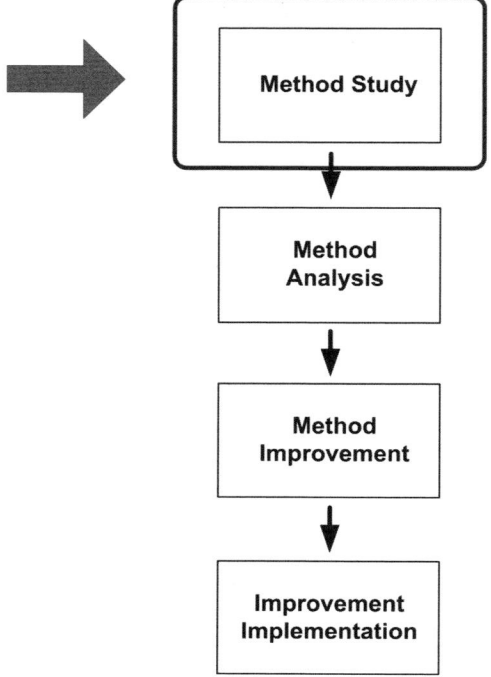

Figure 5.1. Current phase: Method study of a task

In each of nine chapters, we will identify where we are in order to guide readers' way through an extensive amount of material.

In this chapter you will learn to:

- Perform method studies of tasks, their record, and representation.
- Perform process studies, their record, and representation.

5.2. Systematic Procedure for Methods Study

The following outline provides a structure to use when performing a methods study for a certain task. We recall here the definition of a task.

> A task is a work unit of operations, consisting of an operator or team of operators and/or machines work on material or materials. A task is composed of operations.

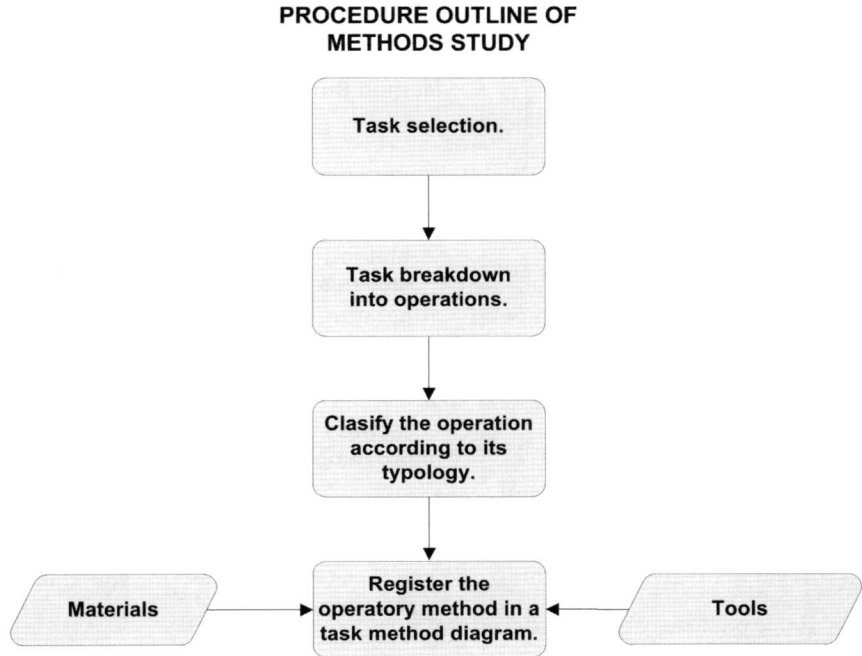

Figure 5.2. Outline of the procedure for studying methods.

5.2.1. Selection of the Task

Any task performed in a working environment can be the object of study with the purpose of improving the way it is done; in other words, to study its working method in order to be more efficient. With this premise, the analyst would face a great mission, even unlimited, which may not be an especially productive approach. However, focusing in some tasks, the analyst can achieve significant results in the work study in a short period of time. Several factors are taken into account when choosing what task to study:

- Ergonomics
- The CwM (coefficient of waste from method), which is the potential for improvement
- The weight of the task in the productive process

The first factor is ergonomics. Extensive studies in prevention show that much absenteeism is motivated by discomfort and injuries due to an inadequate way of performing the work or unfavorable conditions for the worker. It is essential that management realize the relevance of the adapting the workplace to the worker, improving worker welfare, work quality, and, therefore, worker performance.

Good working conditions positively affect professional performance and reduce absenteeism in a noticeable way, avoiding risks of illness and work accidents. The improvements in ergonomics include:

- Reduction of accident risks
- Illumination conditions
- Postures in the workplace
- Reflections in computer screens
- Humidity and environmental temperature adequate to the type of task performed
- Circulation of air in closed spaces
- Noise conditions in the installation
- Regulations for visualizing screens
- esign of the workplace and study of the different ways to position objects in such a way as to facilitate the productive task and work adequately
- Back postures adapted to each task
- Optimum ways to transport loads, handle weights, push objects

All these aspects have influence when adapting a workplace to the operator and not the other way round, translating into lower absenteeism rates and greater productivity and motivation of the operator.

The improvements in ergonomics favorably influence the social environment: it is the "best of improvements." The analyst must start with the tasks that generate more absenteeism: injuries and/or low motivation.

The second factor is the CwM. As described in previous chapters, a work method is the sequence of operations defined to fulfill a certain task. All the operations that form a task and that do not provide a value-adding activity pose waste for method design. This concept is explained widely in Chapter 2, section 2.2.1.

The *coefficient of waste from method* quantifies the amount of waste based on the best standard time.

What has been shown here is the methods study of a task, which is what is explained in this chapter. When selecting the task, the method may be observed in order to study it, if it is already recorded. If not recorded, the selection criteria from waste in the method must be derived through the assessment of estimations and samplings.

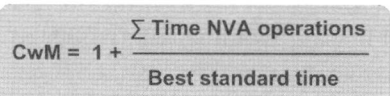

$$CwM = 1 + \frac{\sum \text{Time NVA operations}}{\text{Best standard time}}$$

Formula 5.1

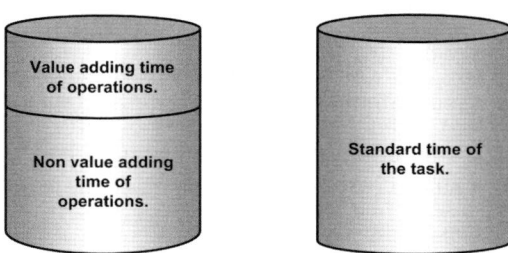

Figure 5.3. *Identification of non-value-adding time*

The coefficient CwM must tend to 1, anything above the unit manifests the amount of current waste from method and, therefore, the potential improvement. The higher the CwM coefficient of a task, the easier it will be to improve it.

The third factor is the weight of the task in the productive process. Because it constitutes a loss of time to start or carry out a large investigation, the economic importance of the task must be notable. It is necessary to ask:

- Will it be profitable to start a method study for this task?
- Will it be profitable to continue with this study?

Among other evident aspects of the study, the following can be mentioned:

- Essential operations as a source of benefits or cost, or operations with the maximum rates of waste
- Bottlenecks that are hindering production activities or long-term operations
- Activities that involve repetitive work with high employment of workforce or activities that probably will not last long
- Material transports that travel long distances between workplaces or that involve large amounts of person-hours or require repeated manipulation of material. This point would be the equivalent of a high CwM, or many non-value-adding operations.

This criterion is normally subject to the Pareto principle or the ABC analysis of tasks. In summary it can be said that a small number of tasks involve the major part of the workload. It could be quantified as the 20 percent of tasks involve the 80 percent of the workforce time spent and that the remaining 80 percent only uses the 20 percent of the workforce. Therefore, before starting any methods studies, this classification must be done.

On the other side, the criterion of cost/benefit can also be applied. It is possible that a task has little weight in the production of the factory but, nevertheless, costs little to study. In this case, the task could be selected for study.

In conclusion, the first criterion for the study of a task from a social, ethical, and economic point of view is ergonomics. Priority must be granted to tasks with greater ergonomic and health consequences. An ergonomic and safe workplace is a productive workplace.

On the other hand, the amount of waste due to poor design is the first motive from an economic point of view; a high CwM is cause for task study. At last, the task must have a relevant weight within the production process or, if not, that it is easy to study, so that the time dedicated to the study is profitable.

5.2.2. Data Collection and Breakdown of the Task into Operations

Once the task to study is selected based on the three factors described in the previous section, the limits of the study will be fixed and will highlight exactly what will be covered. Questions to ask include the following:

- Is the whole sequence of the task examined or just a part of it?
- What part of the task?
- Will the movements of materials or people be the object of study?

These questions have an impact on a better knowledge of the situation and promote, as consequence, a greater specification of the field under study. Then, a set of guidelines will be described that the analyst must take into account when breaking down a task into a variety of operations:

1. Before proceeding to the division of a task into small operations, the analyst must observe the operator during several work cycles. If possible, it is better to determine the operations that the task is composed of before starting the study.

2. The manual operations must be differentiated from those done with a machine. In manual activities, operators can reduce the execution time according to their interest, ability, or dexterity. However, machine-times can be beyond the control of the operator when they depend on the technical characteristics of the machine and, therefore, the operator cannot exercise any influence over them, although it is important to note that paying attention to a machine makes it work better.

3. Manual operations with the machine stopped and with the machine running must be differentiated from one another. The manual operations performed with the machine stopped can affect the duration of the activity deployed by the operator. The manual operations executed while the machine is working do not modify the duration of the cycle, but influence the capacity of the operator.

4. The operations that require different efforts will be separated from others, with the purpose of facilitating the work of the analyst in the fulfillment of the future time study, which will determine the standard time of execution of the task and allow for the application of different coefficients for fatigue. This point will be discussed in the third part of the book dedicated to the studies of times.

5. The operations that compose a working process must be easily identified, based on the operation limits through the initial and final targets.

6. The operations must be within a range of 8 to 100 seconds. These limits are so because timings of less than 8 seconds are difficult to measure, because the targets of the operation are diffuse and complicated to establish and, as a consequence, measurement mistakes can be made. For operations whose execution time is higher than 100 seconds, the performance of operators can vary during that time interval.

The task breakdown into operations is necessary to:

- Describe the operations sequence.
- Know exactly the action involved in the work.
- Classify the operation according to its typology, to give it its corresponding treatment.
- And to be able to perform the time measurement.

Here we break down the task of assembling a hot tub into one of its operations.

Task: Shower Assembly
Operation Description
Take a frame and place on work table.
Search instructions to check model of screw.
Take pneumatic screwdriver. Fix the regulator to cover with two screws, leaving screwdriver in tool.
Assemble cover to frame, passing radio cable through the inside opening window.
Take screwdriver and fix cover with two screws to frame.
Wait until trolley is free.
Transfer to frame trolley.
Turn frame trolley.

Figure 5.4. Apportionment of a task into operations

5.2.3. Classification of Operations

The operations or elements of work can be classified by function of the following criteria:

- In relation to the work cycle:
    - *Regular:* Those elements that always appear in each work cycle and, therefore, their frequencies are constant and regular.
    - *Irregular:* Necessary operations that do not happen every cycle, nor do they happen regularly or periodically. To calculate their effects it is necessary to have pertinent statistical probabilities.
    - *Frequency:* Operations that do not happen every cycle but do occur in a regular and predictable way. Their effects can be calculated precisely.
    - *Strange:* Elements that are not needed to complete the work cycle but that happen. Therefore, as much as possible, they must be eliminated.

- In relation to the operator:
    - Manual elements are performed with the intervention of the operator and can be without machine, also called *free*, whose duration depends on the activity of the operator; and with **machine**, in which

the worker who feeds or controls the machine intervenes. These last are also classified in elements with the machine stopped or with the machine running. These elements or operations must be clear when performing the study of times, in order to avoid committing any error.

- The machine elements are work elements performed by the machine. They can be done with an *automatic machine* that does not require the intervention of the operator, or with *manual advance machine*, in which the machine works with the help of an operator at certain moments.

- In relation to the operation typology the operator performs.

Both for tasks and for operator-performed operations, common symbols of classification are used. In the case of studying methods, the types of operations *the operator can make* are classified:

- Value-adding operations: All necessary actions to satisfy the specifications of a product and transform it, such as drilling, screwing, sanding, painting, etc.

- Displacement of operator: When an operator moves in his or her workplace to perform an operation.

- Storage: When an operator makes a storage operation.

- Delay or wait: Time dedicated by the operator to waiting because of a machine cycle.

- Inspection: Does not contribute to the transformation of material into finished product. It only serves to ensure that an operation has been correctly executed concerning quality and quantity.

- Inspection-operation: Confirming that the specification of the product is met, sometimes performed while the product is transforming.

- Search: Operator action of looking for materials, tools, information, etc.

- Removable operations: Operations that need not be performed and, therefore, could be eliminated.

- Communication.

Depending on the typology of the operation, this should be identified with a symbol. Such symbols are showed in the following table:

Industrial productivity

Icon	Type of Task
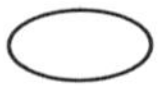 ◯	Value-adding operation
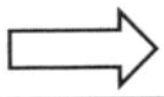 ⇒	Transfer
 ▽	Storage
 D	Delay or wait
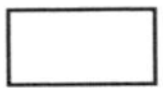 ▢	Inspection
 ▢◯	Inspection/Operation
 ᗒ	Search
 ⪖	Removable operation
 ⊂	Communication

Figure 5.5. Symbols for the type of operations

The normalized operations and typology are the first five operations. The four remaining are provided in this book because they happen frequently. Classifying them specifically allows for more precision within the work study.

5. The Study of Methods

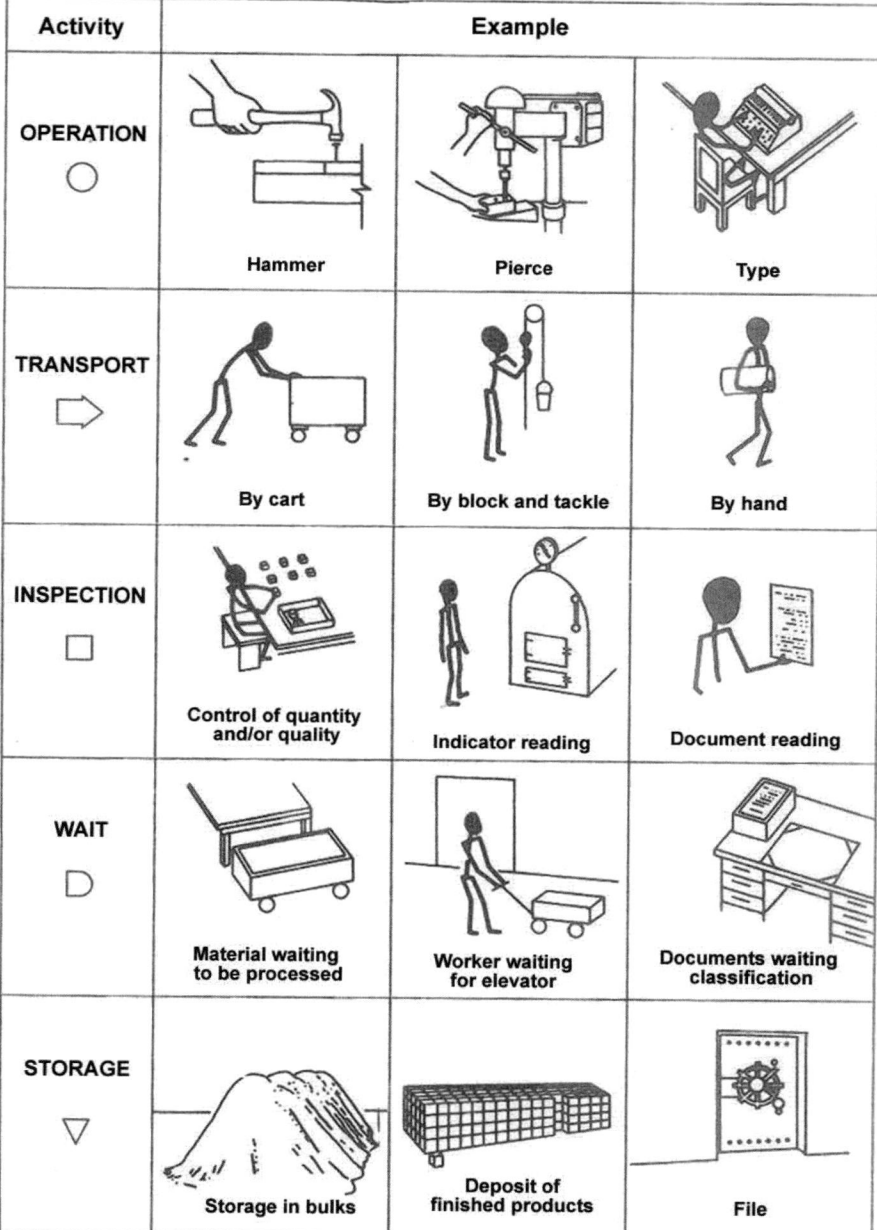

Source: Ralph M. Barnes, Motion and Time Study, 7th ed. (New York: John Wiley, 1980).

Figure 5.6. Types of operations

Industrial productivity

In Figure 5.7, each operation of the task from Figure 5.4 is identified with its corresponding symbol.

Task: Shower Assembly	
Operation Description	**Type**
Take a frame and place on work table.	 ◯
Search instructions to check model of screw.	 ▭
Take pneumatic screwdriver. Fix the regulator to cover with two screws, leaving screwdriver in tool.	 ◯
Assemble cover to frame, passing radio cable through the inside opening window.	 ◯
Take screwdriver and fix cover with two screws to frame.	 ◯
Wait until trolley is free.	 D
Transfer to frame trolley.	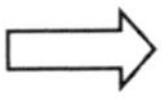 ⇨
Turn frame trolley.	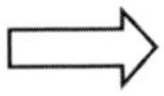 ⇨

Figure 5.7. Breakdown into operations with symbols

5.2.4. Formats for Data Collecting: Examples

With the breakdown criterion and the symbols of operations we are able to perform the data collecting for the study of methods. This section contains with practical examples.

5. The Study of Methods

Example

Diagram:	Initial
Product:	Bicycle
Work:	Handlebar and brake assembly
Method: Current/Proposed (X)	
The current method is performed	
Place:	
Assembly line	
Operator:	
Juan Salinas	
Composed by:	
Frances Long	
Approved by:	
Al Mason	

SUMMARY

Activity		Current	Proposed
Operation	○	147.66	-
Transport	⇨	32.00	-
Wait	D	0.00	-
Inspection	□	20.87	-
Storage	▽	5.11	-
Distance (meters)		40.00	-
Time (Min-Person)		3.43	-
Cost	$	18.50	-
Workforce	$	1.06	-
Material	$	26.32	-
Total	$	27.38	-

Description of the Operation	Type of Operation	Distance (meters)	Unitary Time (sec.)	Units	Operation Time (sec.)	Observations
Grab cart.	○		1.98	1.00	1.98	
Take fork truck and assemble.	○		27.00	1.00	27.00	
Tighten break nuts.	○		2.46	3.00	7.38	
Fit faceplate in brake nuts.	○		2.85	3.00	8.55	
Assemble fork in the chassis.	○		3.02	1.00	3.02	
Place front wheel.	○		3.13	1.00	3.13	
Screw in two nuts in wheel axis.	○		12.60	2.00	25.20	
Tighten nuts. Spin wheel.	○		17.81	2.00	35.62	
Deposit in cart.	▽		1.45	1.00	1.45	
Grab cart.	○		1.45	1.00	1.45	
Check, adjust, and spin bycicle.	□		12.58	1.00	12.58	
Place model sticker on bycicle.	○		1.84	1.00	1.84	
Place EEC sticker.	○		5.66	1.00	5.66	
Regulate break pads.	□		8.29	1.00	8.29	
Loosen circlip.	○		4.70	1.00	4.70	
Take the handlebars. Insert cable in brake lever.	○		6.23	1.00	6.23	
Insert cable in circlip. Tighten circlip and put cap on.	○		15.90	1.00	15.90	
Transfer toward cart.	⇨	20.00	16.00	2.00	32.00	
Deposit set in cart.	▽		3.66	1.00	3.66	

Figure 5.8. Format example of data collecting for open work

Industrial productivity

Figure 5.8 shows the format type for the data collection of the method of the task once completed. We will now see the format type for the data collection of tasks with several participants (either machines or operators).

Format

Format of data collecting for tasks with several particpants					
Diagram:		SUMMARY			
Product:		Activity		Current	Proposed
Work:		Operation	○	0.00	-
Method: Current/Proposed		Transport	⇨	0.00	-
		Wait	D	0.00	-
Place:		Inspection	□	0.00	-
		Storage	▽	0.00	-
Operator:		Distance (meters)		0.00	-
		Time (Min-Person)		0.00	-
Composed by:		Cost		$ -	-
		Workforce		$ -	-
Approved by:		Material		$ -	-
		Total		$ -	-
Operation Observations	Distance (meters)	Time (minutes)	Operator 1	Operator 2	Operator 3
	Value-adding time (minutes)				
	Wait time (minutes)				

Figure 5.9. Basic format for the data collection of tasks with several participants

Figure 5.10 shows the same format once the data collecting is performed, where waiting times for each participant are recorded.

Example

Format of data collecting for tasks with several participants

Diagrama:	Initial revision.		SUMMARY			
Producto:	Steel tank	Activity		Current	Proposed	Economy
Trabajo:	Pumping inspection	Operation	◯	605.00	-	-
Method: Current/Proposed ✗		Transport	⇨	0.00	-	-
The current method is performed		Wait	D	942.00	-	-
Place:		Inspection	□	35.00	-	-
Pumping Area		Storage	▽	0.00	-	-
Operators:		Distance (meters)		0.00	-	-
Maintenance team		Time (min-person)		1,582.00	-	-
Composed by:		Cost		$ 20.00	-	-
Marie Samson		Workforce		$ 527.33	-	-
Approved by:		Material		$ 125.30	-	-
Jacinto Vedarte		Total		$ 652.63	-	-

Operation Observations	Distance (meters)	Time (minutes)	Operator 1	Operator 2	Operator 3	Operator 4
Operators 2, 3, and 4 must wait until operator 1 disassembles the tank protectors.		60.00	Disassemble protectors	Wait	Wait	Wait
				Wait	Wait	Wait
After disassembling the protectors, the operator can perform maintenance tasks. Operator 3 remains waiting until operator 2 loosens a stopper from the tank.		40.00		Loosen caps with spanner	Wait	Wait
		40.00	Maintenance tasks		Install pipes	Wait
		40.00			Disassemble stopper	Wait
		20.00		Wait	Wait	Wait
While operator 4 performs the quality inspection, the rest remain waiting.		35.00	Wait	Wait	Wait	Quality inspection
		18.50	Wait	Adjust stoppers		Wait
Once the first stopper is closed, the operator can install the protector of that stopper, eliminating the wait and reducing the cycle.		26.00	Wait		Remove pipes	Wait
		52.00	Wait	Close stoppers	Wait	Wait
			Wait		Wait	Wait
		64.00	Intall protectors	Wait	Wait	Wait
				Wait	Wait	Wait
	Value-adding time (minutes)		264.00	216.50	124.50	35.00
	Waiting time (minutes)		131.50	179.00	271.00	360.50

Figure 5.10. Completed format

5.3. Method Record

Once the data collecting is completed, it is time to record the work methods. The record format could be similar to the one shown in the previous section or according to the level of detail desired. At this point, we will list and develop the information and formats for a study of methods. It contains complete information

Industrial productivity

about the method. Based on the cost/benefit criteria, an analyst could use all the formats or only the most basic, which are the study of methods and the summary. At this step of the study of methods, with the elaboration of the working method of the task, suggestions for improvement will emerge. The main objective here is to capture the operations method in order to standardize the way of working.

Capturing the method on paper and identifying each operation with its corresponding symbol shows which tasks are subject to influence for a future improvement in method, which includes all those operations whose symbol is not a circle, or a value-adding operation.

Due to the characteristics of every studied task, the analyst will encounter situations where the operator intervenes alone and must operate with a machine in an assembly line or with several operators in parallel. Therefore, it will be necessary to make distinctions in work typologies.

A complete study of methods will have the following sections:

1. *Document 1 – Task data and summary of the study of methods:* This sheet contains summarized data of the task and the study and shows the summary of the result and the method graph. (Later this concept will be clarified.)

2. *Document 2 – Method study of the task:* On this sheet is recorded what the operator does, broken down into operations and quantified, with comments and particular proposals for improvement. It is the most important information.

3. *Document 3 – Sketch of the part and sketches of the workplace:* The graphic representation will help in better comprehension of the method.

4. *Document 4 – Other data of the operations:* Auxiliary information can be relevant for the study of methods, but that cannot be put in the preceding documents it due to lack of space. This document includes information about number of operators, tools used, machines, materials, and other necessary information for each operation.

5. *Document 5 – Ergonomic considerations of the task*: This general questionnaire about the operator, task, and environment provides information about ergonomic aspects to be analyzed.

6. *Document 6 – Task rationale:* This sheet records how the task is executed, what conditions it has, restrictions, frequency motives, incidentals, etc. It is important for the latter time study.

7. *Document 7 – General improvement proposals:* The document of the methods study can present proposals for improvement in each operation; however, these must be completed with general proposals. Once all

sheets are filled in, we possess a greater vision of the task; thereby ideas can emerge that affect the task globally and not by operation.

The completion of all these sections concludes the study of methods. However, sometimes the assigned time for the study or the weight of the task does not permit this level of information and detail. In that case, at least Documents 1 and 2 will be completed.

In Document 1 we introduce a concept that is "the graph of the method." The graph of the method is a visual tool for tasks that involve more than one participant. To provide a better vision of participant interaction, the graph indicates simultaneous tasks, person-machine tasks, and assembly line works. It is not necessary in open work.

Figures 5.11 through 5.17 show sample sheet formats for the complete study of methods.

Industrial productivity

Example

Document 1 - Task data and summary of the methods study: Insert placement

Task data

Company	Smith Tools
Address	49 Ringtone Street
Location	Liverpool
Zipcode	49002
Telephone	92522883
Task name:	Insert placement
Area-Section:	Decorative assembly
Task code:	90/39A00

Workstation description:
Workstations lack tools and supplies, causing the operator to make continued searches and transfers.

Study data

Information file name:	
Analyst/Author:	Peter Smith
Date of data collection:	2012/03/05
Process date:	2012/03/08
Nº Revision:	009
Date of revision:	2012/03/13
Motive for revision:	

Parameters of order / product

Description of ordered parameter	Quantity	Units
Quantity of panels to process.	2.00	panel
Quantity of inserts per panel.	4.00	inserts

Technical parameters

Description of technical parameter	Quantity
Speed on foot.	0.80
Distance from Assembly Area 1 to 2.	120.00
Distance from Injected Area to supervisor.	10.00
Distance from drilling workstation to packaging	20.00

Supplements

Rest supplements	Quantity
Personal needs.	5%
Fatigue.	4%
Being on foot.	2%
Total rest supplements.	**11%**

Statistical parameters

Description of statistical parameter	Quantity
Quantity of inserts injected per kit.	264.00
Average quantity of inserts per panel.	24.00

Summary table of methods

Description	Min/Unit
Standard time.	*16.68*
Workforce cost ($/hour)	*35.00*
Workforce cost per unit ($/unit)	*9.73*
Total displacements (meters)	*149.25*

Classification of operations		Min/Unit
Total value-adding operations.	○	*7.17*
Total non-value-adding operations.	☁	*8.25*
Total displacements.	⇨	*1.99*
Total storages.	▽	*0.79*
Total waits.	D	*0.00*
Total inspections.	□	*0.00*
Total inspection-operation.	⌀	*1.26*
Total searches.	B	*0.55*
Total removable operations.	⌇	*4.92*
Total communications.	C	*0.00*
Waste by method coefficient (CwM)		*1.98*

Figure 5.11. Document I – Task data and summary of the study of methods

5. The Study of Methods

Document 2 - Study of task methods: Place insert

Description of Operation	Type of Operation	Distance (meters)	Unit Time (sec.)	Units	Operation Time (sec.)	% Operation in Task
Provision panel. Remove protector paper.	○		10.73	2.00	21.46	1.07%
Provision set of bits for drill.	○		6.79	1.00	6.79	0.34%
Transfer toward following workstation.	⇨	20.00	18.40	1.00	18.40	0.92%
Deposit panel on worktable.	○		2.19	1.00	2.19	0.11%
Search and provision of plans.	⊟		66.60	1.00	66.60	3.33%
Perform drill markings with pencil and ruler.	⌇		237.13	2.00	474.26	23.69%
Store plans in closet.	▽		62.58	1.00	62.58	3.13%
Take panel.	○		2.30	2.00	4.60	0.23%
Transfer toward manual mechanizing area.	⇨	100.00	92.00	1.00	92.00	4.60%
Deposit bits and panel on auxiliary table. Clear working area.	▽		6.65	1.00	6.65	0.33%
Assemble bit on column drill.	○		35.09	1.00	35.09	1.75%
Place wooden piece in column drill base.	○		8.63	1.00	8.63	0.43%
Perform a predrill in panel to place floating inserts.	○		17.69	8.00	141.51	7.07%
Exachange bit for bidiametral bit in column drill.	○		30.91	1.00	30.91	1.54%
Perform a predrill in panel to place floating inserts.	○		14.78	8.00	118.24	5.91%
Disassemble bidiametral bit. Remove panel.	○		5.98	1.00	5.98	0.30%
Store bits. Turn off column drill.	▽		15.92	1.00	15.92	0.80%
Transfer toward working area from manual mechanization area.	⇨	120.00	110.40	1.00	110.40	5.51%
Deposit panel on worktable. Store bits on workbench.	▽		9.17	1.00	9.17	0.46%
Take seat. Turn panel over on worktable. Provision tweezers.	○		5.51	2.00	11.03	0.55%
Remove material leftovers from performed holes with help of tweezers.	⌇		14.48	8.00	115.80	5.78%
Provision floating inserts. Extract set of inserts.	○		18.05	2.00	36.09	1.80%
Fit floating inserts in performed holes.	○		15.37	8.00	122.97	6.14%
Provision glue kit. Prepare it for use mixing in machine. Remove plunger.	○		97.00	1.00	97.00	4.85%
Put on work gloves.	○		27.42	1.00	27.42	1.37%
Assemble aplicator in kit. Assemble kit in aplication gun. Connect to compressed air intake.	○		30.44	1.00	30.44	1.52%
Apply glue in hole. Check glue emerges from other hole.	○		6.51	8.00	52.12	2.60%
Clean excess glue in inserts with paper.	○		10.36	8.00	82.89	4.14%
Free panel to dry glue.	○		7.26	2.00	14.51	0.72%
Provision panel and take seat. Provision pliers.	○		5.51	2.00	11.03	0.55%
Remove insert protection plates. Check correct positioning of insert.	◌		18.85	8.00	150.77	7.53%
Transfer panel to following workstation.	⇨	10.00	9.20	1.00	9.20	0.46%
Return to workplace.	⇨	10.00	9.20	1.00	9.20	0.46%
			Total task execution time:		2,001.81	100.00%
			Standard time:		1,000.91	

Figure 5.12. Document 2 – Methods study of the task

175

Industrial productivity

As you can see, the total execution time of the task does not match the standard time of the summary table. The reason is that the time calculation is made for two parts; therefore, the result must be divided by that amount. Another way to do it is by unit. For this approach, cyclic operations will have unit frequencies and those who do not will have a fraction. The result in either case is the same. In this book we choose to calculate the total frequencies for the batch and then divide by the number of units. This approach makes it easier to take into account the size of the batch.

Example

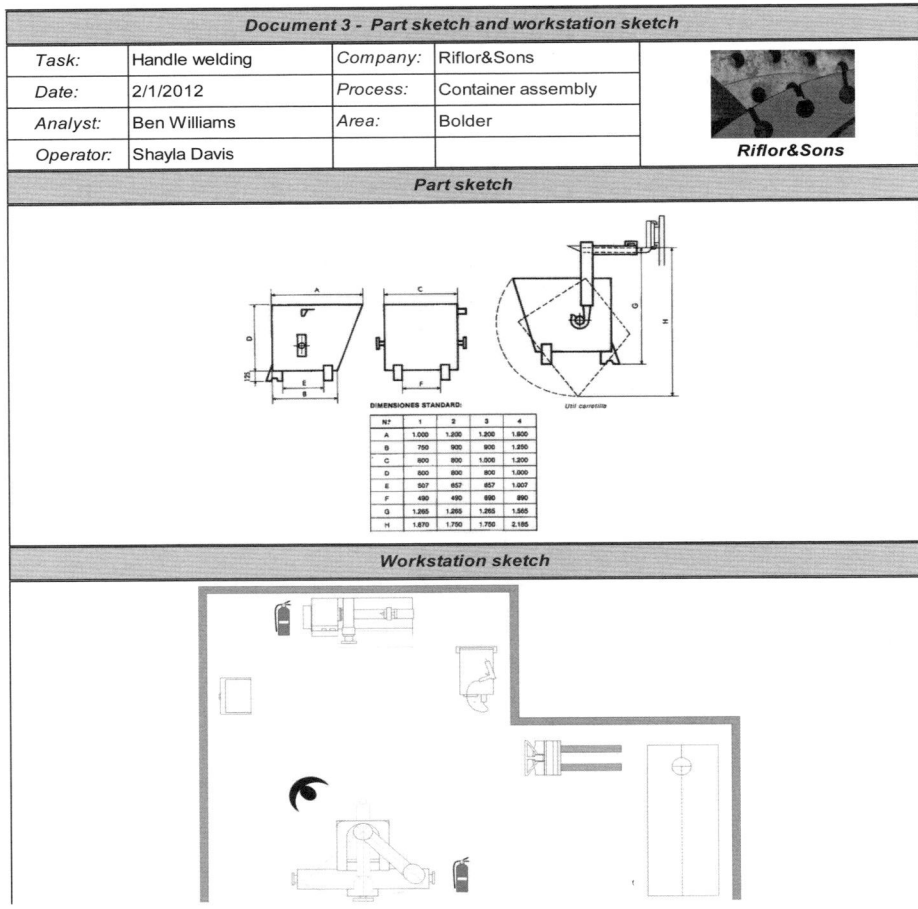

Figure 5.13. Document 3 – Sketches of the part and workstation

Example

	Document 4 - Other data of the operations				
Task:	Assembly of chain	Company:	Moore Bicycles		
Date:	2011/04/22	Process:	Mountain Line		
Analyst:	Tanya Elliot	Area:	Final assembly		
Operator:	Doug Anderson				**Moore Bicycles**
Nº	Description of the Operation	Nº Operators	Tools	Machines	Materials
	Take Altus change and place in circlip.	1			Altus chain
	Provision a screw.	1			4.8 mm screw
	Tighten change in circlip with help of screwdriver.	1	Screwdriver		
	Mesh bycicle chain.	1			
	Actuate pedal with hand and check correct assembly.	1			
	Read tracing label with scanner.	1	Code reader		

Figure 5.14. Document 4 – Other data of the operations

Industrial productivity

Example

Document 5 - Ergonomic considerations									
Task:	Chain assembly		Company:	Moore Bicycles					
Date:	2011/04/22		Process:	Mountain line					
Analyst:	Tanya Elliot		Area:	Final assembly					
Operator:	Doug Anderson							*Moore Bicyles*	
Operator data									
Name:		Frank Walker		Age:	36	Sex:	Man	Height: 1.75	Weight: 85
Education:			Bachelor degree					Physical	High **Medium** Low
EPI		Gloves	Ear plugs	Glasses	Helmet	Shoes	Others		
Ergonomic considerations									
Illumination:									
Poor illumintaion in the workplace.									
Temperature:									
Climatized.									
Noises:									
Ear plugs available to protect the operator.									
Positions:									
No awkward positions are performed.									
Weights:									
The operator must stand weights less than 1 kilogram.									
Other aspects:									

Figure 5.15. Document 4 – Other data of the operations

Example

Document 6 - Task rationale				
Task:		Company:		
Date:		Process:		
Analyst:		Area:		
Operator:				
Task rationale				

This document describes task singularities and method information that co needs to be clarified, for example:

- *Frequencies*
- *Whether any time of the operation can change*
- *What changes can the method have as a function of the product variables*
- *Etc.*

Figure 5.16. *Document 6 – Task rationale*

Industrial productivity

Example

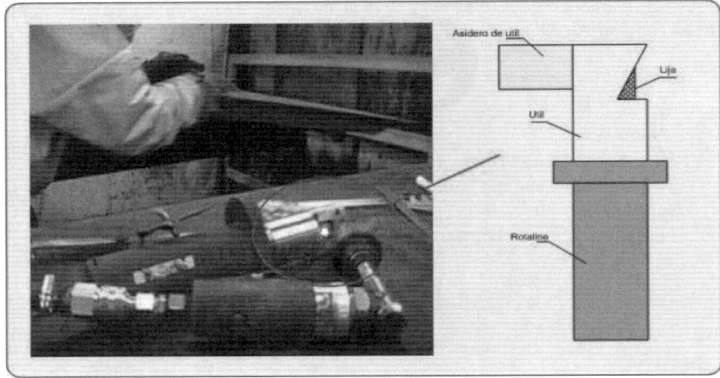

Document 7 - General improvement proposals			
Task:	Make chamfer to fairing	Company:	Motoban United
Date:	10/20/2011	Process:	Mechanized
Analyst:	Clarice Young	Area:	Finish
Operator:	Dwayne King		
General improvement proposals			

Initial Situation: To make a chamfer in the internal fairing of a motorbike, the operator marks the boundary of the chamfer with the aid of a gauge. After marking the chamfer, the o

Proposed Situation: The proposal is to manufacture an auxiliary tooling that is installed in the grinder. Such auxiliary tooling must have an indent with the shape of the chamfer to mechanise, so that the operator must only make several passes over the fairing.

Figure 5.17. Document 7 – General improvement proposals.

The following sections discuss singularities of the methods study and of the methods record for different task typologies:

- Open work
- Assembly-line work
- Simultaneous person-person work
- Simultaneous person-machine work

From all the studied documents, certain ones have a difference based on their typology. The rest of the formats are common in all the studies. It is important to into account that, although a minimum amount of information must be met, flexibility can be used when representing it. The task rationale is broad because

5. The Study of Methods

combinations of the four principal typologies are found in the same task or because other type of additional information can be relevant. This flexibility can only be obtained when the analyst has a high level of experience.

5.3.1. Method Record in Open Work

A work is designated as free when it has no cause that limits the operator in the amount of work that operator can potentially do. In an open work system, the amount of work performed by the operator depends exclusively on that person. Open work is, in general, purely manual and usually involves only one operator.

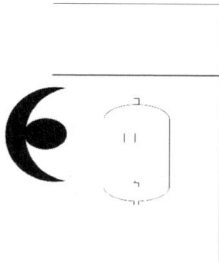

Figure 5.18. Open work

About open work, it needs to be said that the typology is exposed in the development of the different documents of the study of methods. Therefore developing it again would be repetitive.

5.3.2. Work-Method Record in Assembly Line

Assembly line work is performed by several operators in succession, making each of them a part of the task in a specialized way.

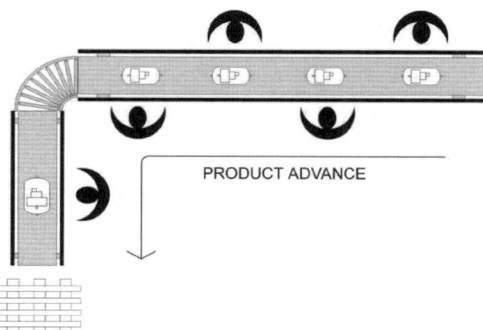

Figure 5.19. Assembly line

Industrial productivity

The product advances from workplace to workplace through the line until the totality of the task is completed. In these cases, operators do not have the same amount of control over the work saturation and the whole line operates at the pace of the slowest workplace. Figure 5.19 shows the progress in the manufacturing process of a product. Such a product circulates through the assembly line, and in each of the workplaces, the operator executes an individual part of the task. The time the operator spends performing the task is what determinates the saturation regarding the remaining workplaces of the production line. The method graph in this case is similar to the one shown in Figure 5.20.

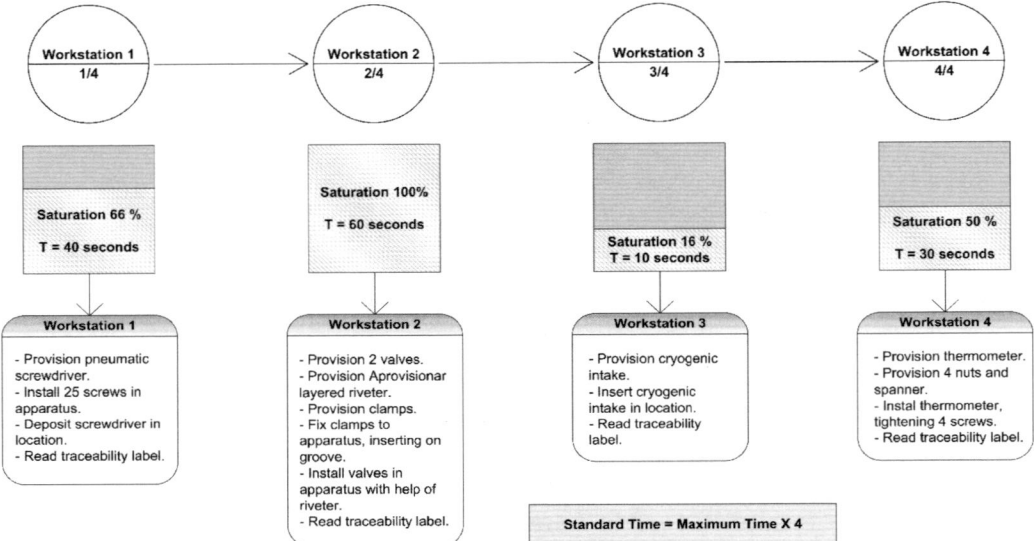

Figure 5.20. Method graph of the task

In this type of work, standard time is derived from the following equation:

$$\text{Standard Time} = \text{Maximum cycle time} \times N^\circ \text{ operators}$$

The format of document 1 for assembly lines is shown in Figure 5.21.

Example

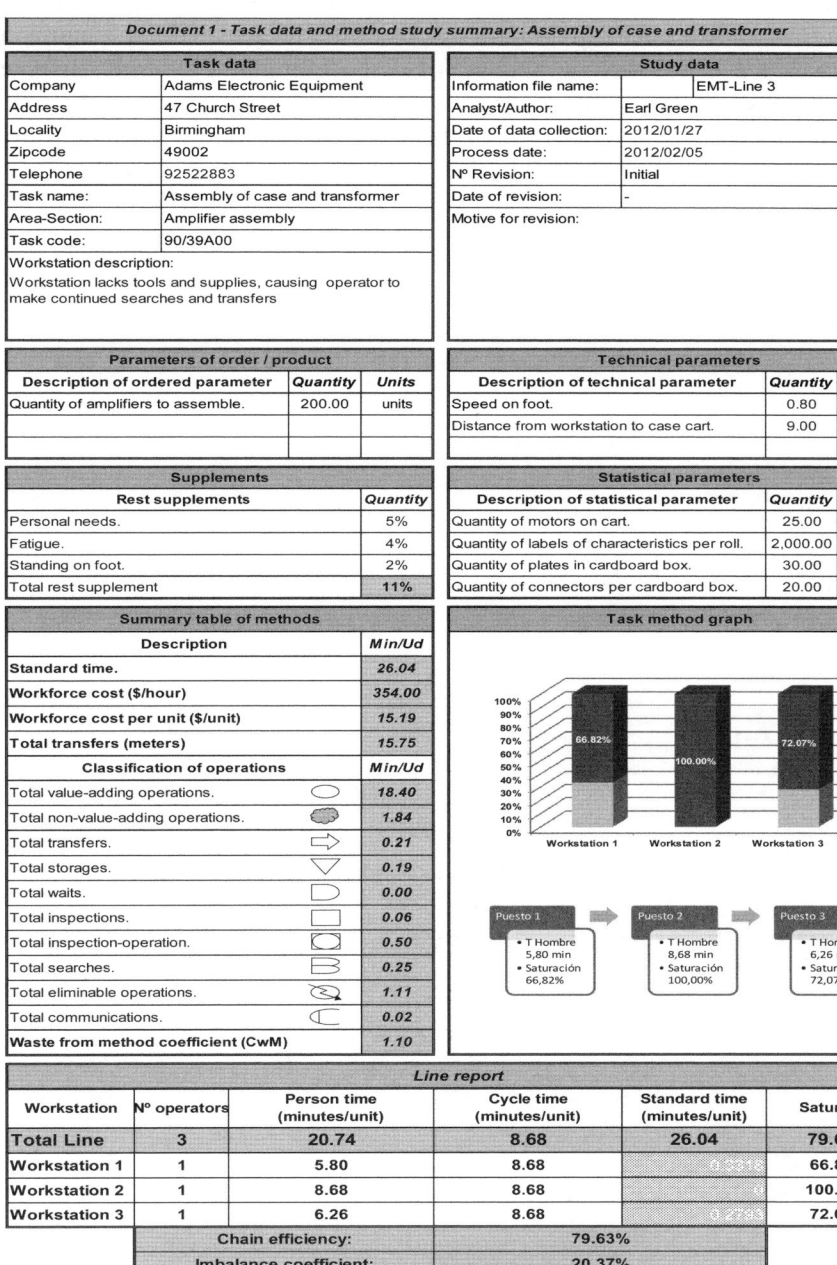

Figure 5.21. *Document 1: Data entry of task, summary table of the methods study, and method graph of the task and assembly line report*

Industrial productivity

Being several actors it is made necessary to show a report of the line for a better clarity. The report mentioned details and shows the information from each workstation of the line, indicating data such as saturation, efficiency, and imbalance coefficient of the assembly line. There data are clear improvement indicators for closer review and will be developed in following chapters. In addition to this information, the person-time of each workstation is also detailed. Next, the methods study justifying each workplace will be shown.

Document 2 - Method study of the task: Case and transformer assembly - Workstation 1						
Description of the Operation	Type of Operation	Distance (meters)	Unit Time (sec)	Units	Operation Time (sec)	% Operation in Task
Take case from cart, perform visual inspection. Place on work table.			17.64	200.0	3,528.11	5.07%
Take motor from cart and unroll cable.			14.37	200.0	2,874.22	4.13%
Introduce motor in case interior, insert cable.			35.21	200.0	7,042.67	10.12%
Screw the motor to the case with two screws through one side of the amplifier.			19.40	200.0	3,879.67	5.57%
Take metal plate and present in case.			16.79	200.0	3,358.36	4.82%
Screw protection plate to case (install 10 screws).			73.82	200.0	14,764.58	21.21%
Search and paste specifications label.			14.78	200.0	2,956.08	4.25%
Introduce cables of transformer inside case.			5.56	200.0	1,111.17	1.60%
Turn amplifier.			5.65	200.0	1,130.00	1.62%
Fix motor to case through the front side, installing four screws.			20.40	200.0	4,080.56	5.86%
Fix motor to case with two screws through opposite side.			19.40	200.0	3,879.67	5.57%
Take metal plate and present in case.			16.79	200.0	3,358.36	4.82%
Screw protection plate to case (place 10 screws).			28.62	200.0	5,724.58	8.22%
Turn amplifier. Leave inferior part of the amplifier upside.			12.32	200.0	2,463.67	3.54%
Introduce net cable in case.			8.19	200.0	1,638.50	2.35%
Transfer amplifier to following workstation.			19.02	200.0	3,803.58	5.46%
Move new case to process.		9.00	8.14	200.0	1,627.20	2.34%
Write down performed work.			52.79	1.00	52.79	0.08%
Remove separation cardboard from cart motors.			34.27	1.00	34.27	0.05%
Change motor cart.			239.25	8.00	1,913.96	2.75%

Figure 5.22a. Document 2: Methods study of the task - Workstation 1

5. The Study of Methods

Change roll of characteristics labels.	○		44.64	0.10	4.46	0.01%
Provide protector plates.	○		46.12	6.67	307.44	0.44%
Turn case cart.	⇨		70.40	1.00	70.40	0.10%
			Total task execution time:		69,604.29	100.00%
				Person time:	348.02	sec/unit

N° Operators	Person time (seconds/unit)	Person time (minutes/unit)	Saturation
1	348.02	5.80	66.82%

Figure 5.22b. *Document 2: Methods study of the task - Workstation 1*

Time has been calculated for 200 units, so time per unit is divided by this number.

Document 2 - Method study of the task: Case and transformer assembly - Workstation 1

Description of the Operation	Type of Operation	Distance (meters)	Unit Time (sec)	Units	Operation Time (sec)	% Operation in Task
Take case from cart, perform visual inspection. Place on work table.	○		17.64	200.0	3,528.11	5.07%
Take motor from cart and unroll cable.	○		14.37	200.0	2,874.22	4.13%
Introduce motor in case interior, insert cable.	○		35.21	200.0	7,042.67	10.12%
Screw the motor to the case with two screws through one side of the amplifier.	○		19.40	200.0	3,879.67	5.57%
Take metal plate and present in case.	○		16.79	200.0	3,358.36	4.82%
Screw protection plate to case (install 10 screws).	○		73.82	200.0	14,764.58	21.21%
Search and paste specifications label.	⊐		14.78	200.0	2,956.08	4.25%
Introduce cables of transformer inside case.	○		5.56	200.0	1,111.17	1.60%
Turn amplifier.	○		5.65	200.0	1,130.00	1.62%
Fix motor to case through the front side, installing four screws.	○		20.40	200.0	4,080.56	5.86%
Fix motor to case with two screws through opposite side.	○		19.40	200.0	3,879.67	5.57%
Take metal plate and present in case.	○		16.79	200.0	3,358.36	4.82%
Screw protection plate to case (place 10 screws).	○		28.62	200.0	5,724.58	8.22%
Turn amplifier. Leave inferior part of the amplifier upside.	↷		12.32	200.0	2,463.67	3.54%
Introduce net cable in case.	○		8.19	200.0	1,638.50	2.35%
Transfer amplifier to following workstation.	⇨		19.02	200.0	3,803.58	5.46%
Move new case to process.	⇨	9.00	8.14	200.0	1,627.20	2.34%
Write down performed work.	⊏		52.79	1.00	52.79	0.08%
Remove separation cardboard from cart motors.	○		34.27	1.00	34.27	0.05%
Change motor cart.	○		239.25	8.00	1,913.96	2.75%
Change roll of characteristics labels.	○		44.64	0.10	4.46	0.01%
Provide protector plates.	○		46.12	6.67	307.44	0.44%
Turn case cart.	⇨		70.40	1.00	70.40	0.10%
			Total task execution time:		69,604.29	100.00%
				Person time:	348.02	sec/unit

N° Operators	Person time (seconds/unit)	Person time (minutes/unit)	Saturation
1	348.02	5.80	66.82%

Figure 5.23. *Document 2: Methods study of the task – Workstation 2.*

185

Industrial productivity

Document 2 - Method study of the task: Case and transformer assembly - Workstation 3					
Description of the Operation	Type of Operation	Distance (meters)	Unit Time (sec)	Units	Operation Time (sec)	% Operation in Task
Take pneumatic riveter from intermediate workstation.	◯		5.90	200.0	1,180.22	1.57%
Rivet frame to the case, practice three rivets.	◯		24.67	200.0	4,934.33	6.57%
Take a rivet to pneumatic riveter and leave on tooling on intermediate table.	◯		10.67	200.0	2,134.44	2.84%
Take amplifier and place in position 3	◯		16.54	200.0	3,308.39	4.41%
Screw grid to the case, by screwing 4 screws.	◯		65.73	200.0	13,145.67	17.51%
Place line label.	◯		10.98	200.0	2,196.72	2.93%
Place amplifier vertically.	◯		18.68	200.0	3,735.28	4.98%
Proviside two buttons from box. Detach plastic	◯		21.22	200.0	4,243.78	5.65%
.Place a button on the tool assembly table. Perform visual inspection.	◯		12.18	200.0	2,435.78	3.24%
Assemble button on the tooling.	◯		14.22	200.0	2,843.83	3.79%
Center central support screw	◯		7.09	200.0	1,418.78	1.89%
Take tray and present in tooling.	◯		13.12	200.0	2,624.11	3.50%
Take elbow screwdriver and three screws.	◯		7.28	200.0	1,456.44	1.94%
Merge button and tray tightening three screws.	◯		16.42	200.0	3,284.23	4.38%
Place screwdriver in location.	▽		3.86	200.0	772.17	1.03%
Take processed tray. Assemble it in amplifier.	◯		19.78	200.0	3,955.00	5.27%
Take hook and remove pods.	◯		12.12	200.0	2,423.22	3.23%
Screw the pods to the trays.	◯		48.52	200.0	9,704.72	12.93%
Take inner filter and put in amplifier.	◯		15.08	200.0	3,015.56	4.02%
Remove the tray. Verify proper installation.	☐		3.89	200.0	778.44	1.04%
Take external filter and put in amplifier.	◯		12.12	200.0	2,423.22	3.23%
Place wire and stack in belt.	◯		13.03	200.0	2,606.67	3.47%
Open button box.	◯		46.93	2.9	134.08	0.18%
Change line label roll.	◯		56.50	0.1	5.65	0.01%
Adhere label of No quality in amplifier.	◯		8.95	1.0	8.95	0.01%
Empty rivets inside the riveter. Store in box.	▽		25.64	1.00	25.64	0.03%
Fix tray rubbing regulating sliding screws.	◯		27.62	1.00	27.62	0.04%
Fill job sheets.	⊏		190.97	1.00	190.97	0.25%
Replace racks in top of workstation.	◯		53.52	1.00	53.52	0.07%
			Total task execution time:		75,067.44	100.00%
			Person time:		375.34	sec/unit

Nº Operators	Person time (seconds/unit)	Person time (minutes/unit)	Saturation
1	375.34	6.26	66.82%

Figure 5.24. Document 2: Methods study of the task – Workstation 3

5.3.3. Record of simultaneous person-person work methods

In some cases a group of operators interacts in parallel on a product. This situation is involves simultaneous work.

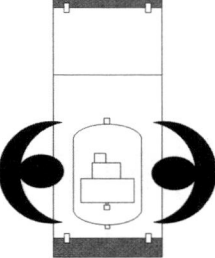

Figure 5.25. Simultaneous person-person work

The method graphs of simultaneous tasks represent this type of task. They can be defined as those graphs that record the respective operations of various objects according to a common time scale, to show the correlation among them. Thus, with the mentioned graphs, the waiting times from any of the operators become evident, in order to try to reduce them and improve their performance through a higher saturation. In this case, the simultaneous person-person task is shown.

This type of tool is extremely useful when organizing operator teams or for maintenance works when expensive machinery can only be stopped in emergencies. For simultaneous tasks, standard time follows this formula:

Standard time = Cycle time x N° Operators

In the following figure it is clarified. The study of methods in a simultaneous task can constitute its method graph.

Industrial productivity

Example

Subtasks of Operator 1	Minutes / Unit	State	State	Minutes / Unit	Subtasks of Operator 2
Waiting time.	0.00			1.11	Search for Quality Operator.
Waiting time.	0.00			1.11	Notify quality operator.
Transfer from Quality Area to template location.	1.18			1.18	Transfer to subframe assembly area.
Provide mudguard positioning template.	0.36			0.36	Clear work area. Remove tools from part.
Transfer toward subframe assembly area.	0.43			0.43	Clear work area. Remove tools from part.
Assemble positioning template. Bridle bolts in direction bearings.	1.13			1.13	Assemble positioning template. Bridle bolts in direction bearings.
Check alignment of mudguard and template.	1.35			1.35	Check alignment of mudguard and template.
Waiting time.	0.00			0.67	Provide compressed air intake and pneumatic drill.
Waiting time.	0.00			1.73	Perform two holes through mudguard and subframe. Pinch.
Waiting time.	0.00			0.89	Change tool toward front side.
Waiting time.	0.00			3.16	Perform two holes through mudguard and subframe. Pinch.
Use gauge and record measures on control sheet. Attach label and validate.	2.49			0.00	Waiting time.
Remove bolts. De-bridle mudguard positioning template.	0.79			0.79	Remove bolts. De-bridle mudguard positioning template.
Transfer to template location.	0.43			0.00	Waiting time.
Deposit positioning template on location.	0.67			0.00	Waiting time.
Move to PC to clock in.	0.74			0.00	Waiting time.
Clock in.	0.57			0.00	Waiting time.
Move to quality area.	0.74			0.00	Waiting time.

Workstation	N° Op.	Person Time Operator 1 (min/unit)	Saturation	Workstation	N° Op.	Person Time Operator 2 (min/unit)	Saturation
1	2	10.88	55.65%	1	2	13.92	71.20%

Cycle time (minutes/unit)	19.55
Standard time (minutes/unit)	39.11

Figure 5.26. Method graph of simultaneous person-person tasks

The work cycle will always be studied in order to break the process into operations. The times of each operation will be measured, and operations and waiting times of the operator or machine classified separately to try to reduce them.

In Figure 5.26, each of the subtasks the operators perform is detailed. Depending of the duration of these subtasks, each of them could have their pertinent study of methods associated. In the case shown they are not included, being low duration operations, but would be analogous to what was done in the example of assembly line tasks.

5. The Study of Methods

Report of simultaneous task				
	Nº Operators	Person Time (min/unit)	Cycle Time (min/unit)	Standard Time (min/unit)	Saturation
Total Task	2	24.81	19.55	39.11	63.43%
Operator 1	1	10.88	19.55		55.65%
Operator 2	1	13.92	19.55		71.20%

Figure 5.27. Report of simultaneous task

The previous illustration also shows the studied task report, indicating the number of operators of the task and the standard time. In a summary of participants, the person-time of each operator is quantified, as well as saturation.

Before the previous example, we have to differentiate two types of operations within simultaneous tasks. They are dependent operations and independent operations:

- *Dependent operations* are those that must be executed simultaneously by the intervening operators due to the characteristics of the operation. They cannot be done by a unique operator or would take much longer if they could be done that way. Operators must help each other to execute them. An example may be flipping a part with large dimensions or positioning a large part on the processed item.

- *Independent operations* are those that can be executed individually, without the help of a second operator. An example can be the sanding of a wooden panel of large dimensions, which can be sanded by two operators or by a single operator.

It is most convenient when tasks within a simultaneous process are independent insofar as possible.

5.3.4. Record of Simultaneous Person-Machine Work Methods

Generally, in the tasks where worker and machine participate, normally it is the last one that sets the pace of work for the operator, limiting the skills and dexterity of the operator.

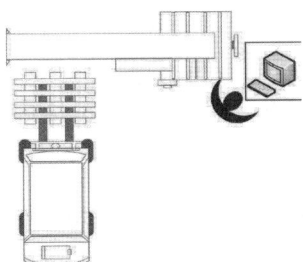

Figure 5.28. Simultaneous person-machine work

Industrial productivity

As explained in the previous point, the analyst must take into account all the indications explained when performing the breakdown of the task into operations: observe the operator for various cycles, differentiate manual operations from the ones done with the machine, distinguish manual operations with the machine stopped and running, define initial milestone and final milestone, and so on. In this case, the method graph is also the graph of simultaneous person-machine tasks.

Once the breakdown is done, the analyst has on one side a group of operations performed by the operator and on the other side, the operations made by the machine, as shown in the following chart of the task method.

Example

Task method graph: Table packaging

Operator				Packer		
Subtasks of Operator	Sec/Unit	State	State	Sec/Unit	Subtasks of Machine
Take table from packaging area and transport to packer.	33.30			-	Pause time.
Place quality labels on table.	66.60			-	Pause time.
Insert table in packer and push start.	22.20			-	Pause time.
Waiting time.	-			100.00	Packaging time per unit.
Remove table from packer.	33.30			-	Pause time.

Report on simultaneous task

Workstation	N° Interveners	Working Time (sec/unit)	Cycle Time (sec/unit)	Standard Time (sec/unit)	Saturation
Total task	2	255.40	255.40	255.40	50.00%
Operators	1	155.40	255.40		60.85%

Figure 5.29. Method graph of simultaneous person-machine task and task report

Within the work cycle, it is observed that the machine can work in two ways:

- Machine running: MR
- Machine stopped: MS

For the method summary and cost calculation, the cost per hour of the machine needs to be taken into account in such a way that it is multiplied by the cycle time and results in the machine cost per unit, which, added to the workforce cost, will result in the direct manufacturing cost.

5. The Study of Methods

Method summary table	
Description	*Min/Unit*
Standard time.	*4.26*
Workforce cost ($/hour).	*21.00*
Workforce cost per unit ($/unit).	*1.49*
Machine cost ($/hour).	*12.00*
Machine cost per unit ($/hour).	*0.85*
Total Cost ($/unit).	*2.34*

Figure 5.30. Summary table of methods for simultaneous person-machine tasks

For cases in which the costs of running machine and stopped machine are significantly different (by wear of tools, energy consumption, etc.), it could be interesting to breakdown the machine-running cost and machine-stopped cost, respectively).

In the previous example, the tasks performed by the operator are machine-stopped operations. Figure 5.31 shows a task with worker and machine operating simultaneously.

Example

Task method graph: Pattern cutting							
Operator				Tanned cutting machine			
Subtasks of Operator	Sec/Unit	State	State	Sec/Unit	Subtasks of Machine		
Put fabric roll.	39.67			-	Waiting time.		
Remove fabric roll.	36.67			-	Waiting time.		
Load orders.	30.77			-	Waiting time.		
Calibrate laser after putting roll.	7.09			-	Waiting time.		
Order change.	56.82			-	Waiting time.		
Change of labels in cutting head.	9.44			-	Waiting time.		
Fix fiberglass sheet.	7.06			-	Waiting time.		
Open documentation.	20.10			-	Waiting time.		
Provide very small patterns.	430.67			217.17	Cutting time.		
Provide small patterns.	151.86			-	Cutting time.		
Provide medium patterns.	96.51			53.04	Labelling time.		
Roll small kits.	590.63			-	Labelling time.		
Roll small kits.	65.63			104.84	Labelling time.		
Record spent material and print stickers.	77.77			-	Waiting time.		
Fill and seal guidelines.	234.19			-	Waiting time.		
Seal guidelines.	20.10			-	Waiting time.		
Bag kits.	421.51			-	Waiting time.		
Bag kits and add label.	53.68			-	Waiting time.		

Figure 5.31. Method graph of simultaneous person-machine task

Analogously, the report of simultaneous person-machine task highlights the level of saturation of each participant, indicating also the standard time of the task.

Report on simultaneous task					
Workstation	Nº Interveners	Working Time (min/unit)	Cycle Time (min/unit)	Standard Time (min/unit)	Saturation
Total task	2	45.42	39.17	39.17	57.98%
Operators	1	39.17	39.17		100.00%
Machines	1	6.25	39.17		15.96%

Figure 5.32. Report of simultaneous person-machine task

5.4. Processes

5.4.1. Introduction to Processes

This section tries to set the general guidelines to take into account when studying a new process, without going into technical details of manufacturing and particular products.

A manufacturing process is the group of tasks to which a material or materials are subjected from the time the manufacturing order is given and until it is served to the client (internal or external).

To be able to define correctly the production processes, normal symbols are used, which is the same as those used for the operations with the difference being that they do not define operations but tasks. On the other hand, symbols can also indicate what the material is doing.

In the following table, the mentioned symbols can be seen:

Icon	Type of Task
◯	Value-adding operation
⇨	Transfer
▽	Storage
D	Delay or wait
▢	Inspection
◌	Inspection/Operation
⟳	Removable operation

Figure 5.33. Task symbols

The steps that the material follows are tasks upon which workers and/or automatic machines perform. The following table shows examples of what the symbols represent:

	Industrial Production (Factory)	Material Services (Restaurant)	Processes with Documents (Administration)
Operation	Chassis welding.	Fill a cup with icecream scoops.	Introduce the data of a receipt.
Transfer	Cart full with chassis transported to paint area.	Tray with icecream cups transported to customer table.	Transport a pack of receipts to filing cainet.
Storage	Welded chassis stored in a cart waiting to be full.	Icecream cups in tray waiting for the rest to be ready.	Receipts in a folder waiting to be uploaded to computer.
Delay or wait	Chassis waiting for the welding machine to be ready to start working.	Icecream cups waiting for liquid caramel.	Receipts waiting in a folder for the sales manager to sign them.
Inspection	Quality control of welding.	Control of size and number of icecreams scoops.	Check of calculations and data of receipts.

Figure 5.34. Examples of symbols

In the manufacturing of any type of production, we can find transfers, storages, inspections, and delays. These symbols are intended to quickly identify what types of tasks compose a process The process is represented at a section or factory level.

5.4.2. Study and Construction of a Certain Process

To transform raw materials into a finished product it is necessary to perform a series of transformations in a certain order. When defining a productive process, the order in which these transformations will be performed is determined and also the quantity and quality of all the elements that participate.

The first step in building a process is to determine the structure of materials of the product to manufacture. Throughout this section, we will work with the design of the manufacturing process of a simple bicycle. Let us see in the following graphs how the production process design evolves.

Industrial productivity

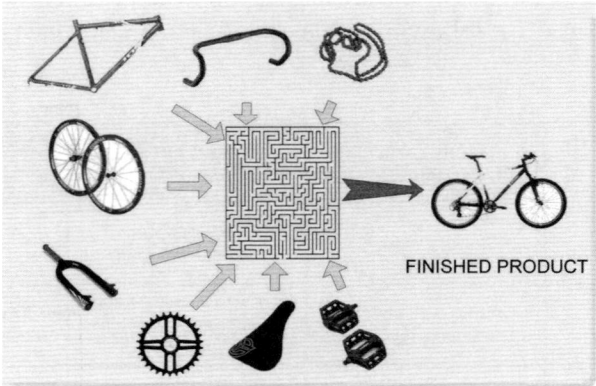

Figure 5.35. Determination of product structure I

The first step will be to bring order to this chaos and design the structure of the item to be manufactured by determining what the product is composed of and in what order will the parts be assembled.

The **product structure** is a file that shows the sequence in which raw materials are manufactured and assembled, parts bought, and necessary subassemblies formed in order to arrive at the final product. Each element from the product structure has an associated number that corresponds to the amount of necessary units for the next phase. A figure with a possible product structure is shown in Figure 5.36:

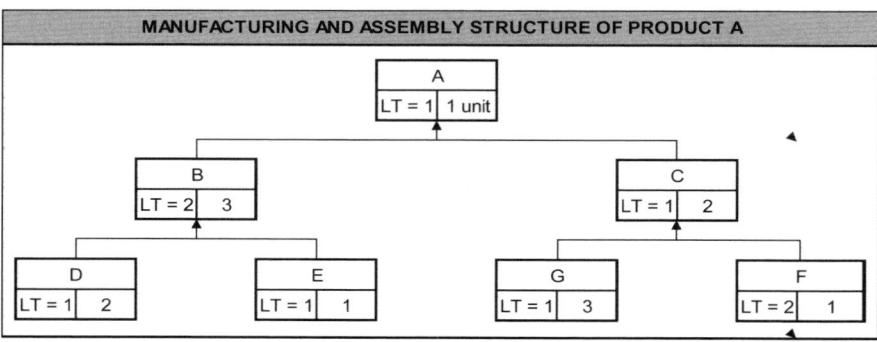

Figure 5.36. Manufacturing structure and assembly of product A

At this point a production process is the group of steps that a material or materials follow for the creation of a product or service, beginning from the work-order generation and finishing with its complete assembly.

Having in mind both definitions, the product structure for the assembly of the bicycle is the following:

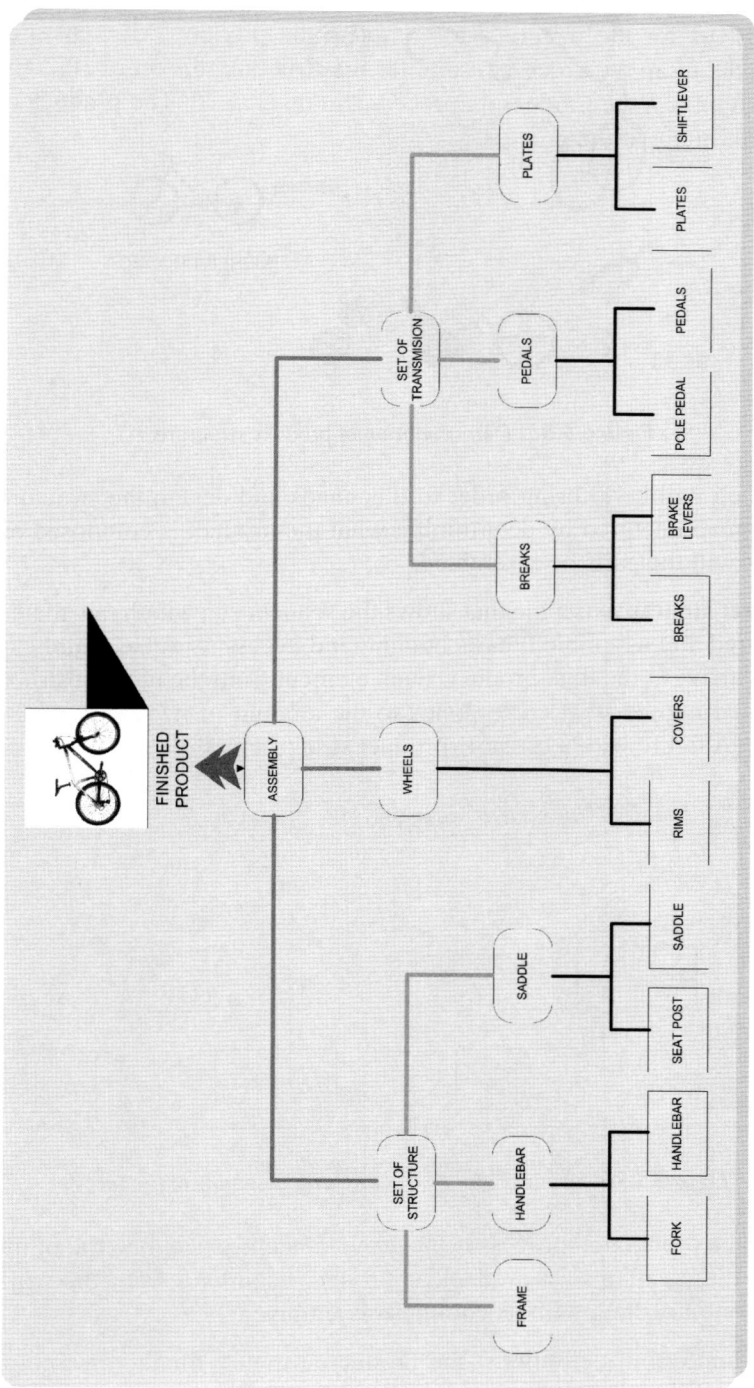

Figure 5.37. Structure of bicycle manufacturing and assembly

When designing a manufacturing process, the product structure represents the minimum steps for the materials to complete the product. All steps are value-adding, so the more the process resembles the structure, the more efficient it will be. Using symbols, the production process can be charted. The product structure "evolves" throughout the process.

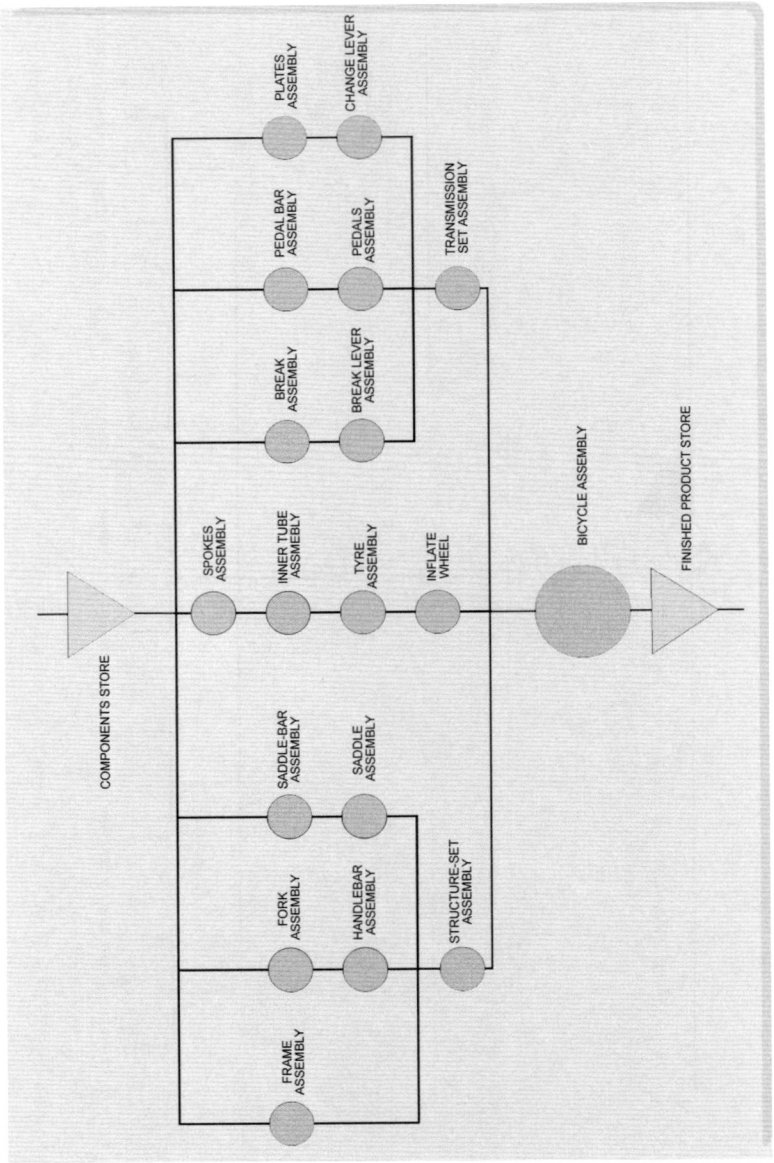

Figure 5.38. *Evolution of product structure I*

5. The Study of Methods

In the next step, because different work paces exist, storehouses are introduced with the intention of "improving the process."

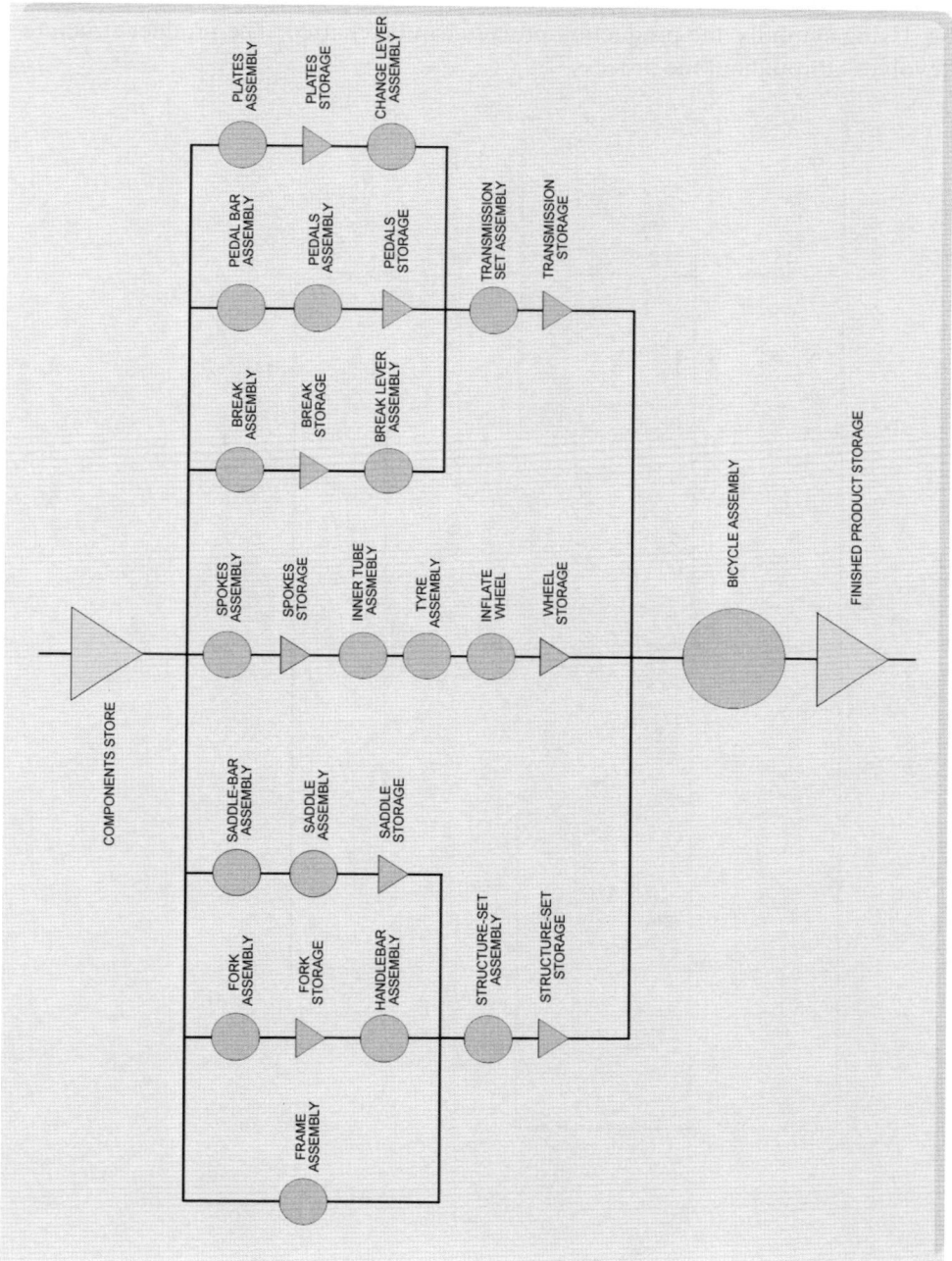

Figure 5.39. Evolution of product structure 2

Industrial productivity

Last, storehouses create all kinds of wastes, especially those involving transfers.

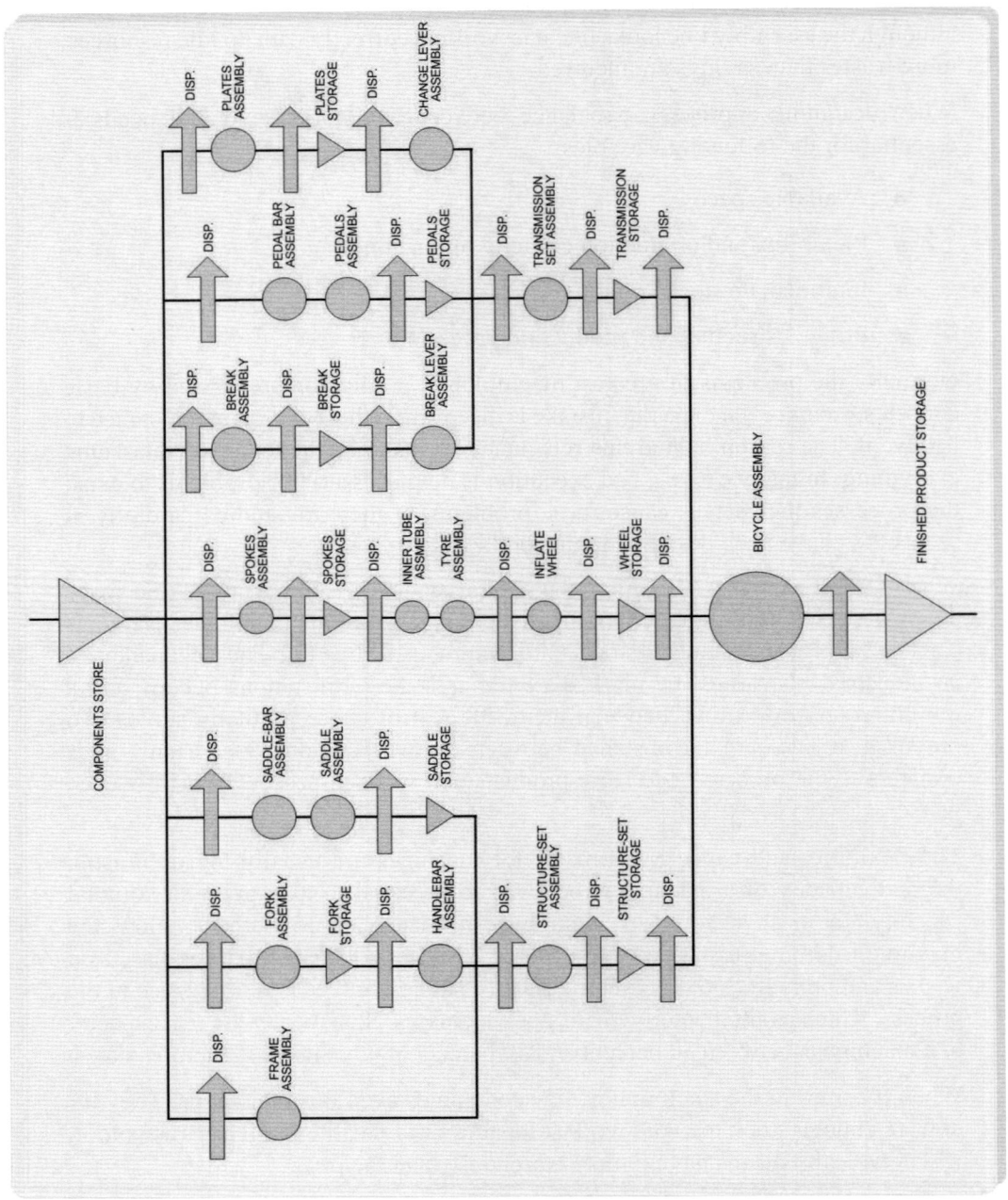

Figure 5.40. Evolution of product structure 3

As observed in this example, the process is generated from the product structure, but for a variety of reasons, non-value-adding operations are introduced until, although the assembly line looks like it is working correctly with no idle resources, more wastes than savings are incurred.

When designing a process, a balance between availability and real needs is essential for the following variables:

- Available space
- Flexibility and production capacity of machines
- Intermediate stocks policy
- Product structure and production programming

Normally the problems of greatest magnitude in production are caused by basic concepts, so that even once the mistake is discovered, there is certain reluctance to believe it. The reason behind this reluctance seems to be the tendency to assume everything. In many cases, a bad execution is not necessary for problems to exist, the processes themselves cause these problems. If they are studied carefully, it seems they have been designed to that end.

When setting a process in motion, the natural tendency is to occupy all the space available, to not have into account for changes in tools in calculating the machine's capacity, and to accumulate stock until warehouses are full. The occupancy of an industrial plant must be marked by the area the workstations occupy and a minimum space to move between them, the rest of space normally serves two purposes: to increase the distance between the workstations, which only adds transfers to the process or to store products and work-in-process, which is even worse.

The flexibility and capacity estimates for machines are usually too optimistic; the real capacity of a machine is believed to be equal to its maximum nominal capacity. In most sectors, an average performance of 15 percent below the maximum nominal capacity is considered a success. This estimate is based on wishes and opinions, not in objective data or studies, and causes imbalance in the process, which result in intermediate stock increases. Statistically the real capacity of a machine is between 30 percent and 50 percent of what its manufacturer states.

When it comes to the stock policy, few companies even raise this issue. They try to have enough stock to avoid work stoppages or to be able to fill any rush order, which typically means having more warehouse than factory.

Another problem detected when designing productive processes is the lack of global vision of production; in other words, the same importance is given to every phase when in some cases it is necessary to "sacrifice" the productivity of some to benefit the process as a whole. To design a process correctly, it must be done keeping in mind economy in all aspects, which is the basis of LEAN philosophy, meaning we must not provide the process with unnecessary resources because an excess always has negative repercussions. Oversized installations pose an important drag, not only when recouping expenses, but they also often harm the plant's operations.

In the majority of cases, facilities, infrastructures, and machinery are acquired and studied in order to adjust the product and the process to the acquired goods. It should be just the opposite; some of the previously mentioned variables should be fixed in order to determine what type of facilities and assets are needed.

Normally the steps taken to design a process include those noted in Figure 5.41

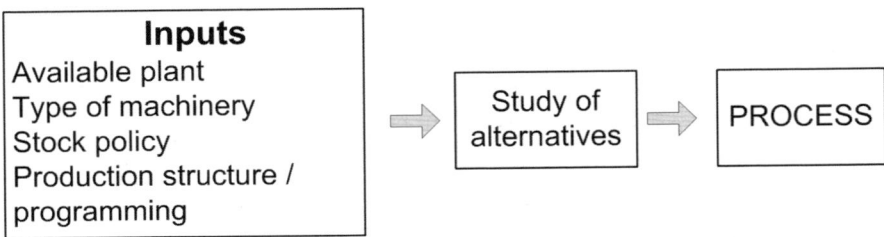

Figure 5.41. Steps for process fulfillment 1

The process is consequence of various factors. Its definition and determination are almost an accident.

The necessary steps include those chosen in Figure 5.42:

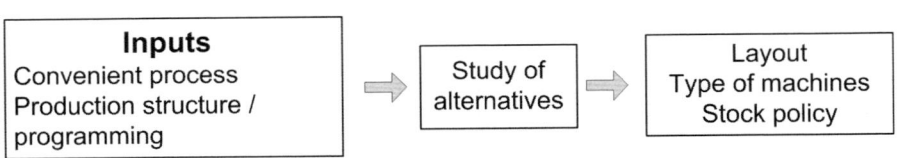

Figure 5.42. Steps for process fulfillment 2

In this case the process is a cause and not a consequence, and therefore it determines the remaining factors. Designing a new process demands consideration of the relationship represented in Figure 5.43:

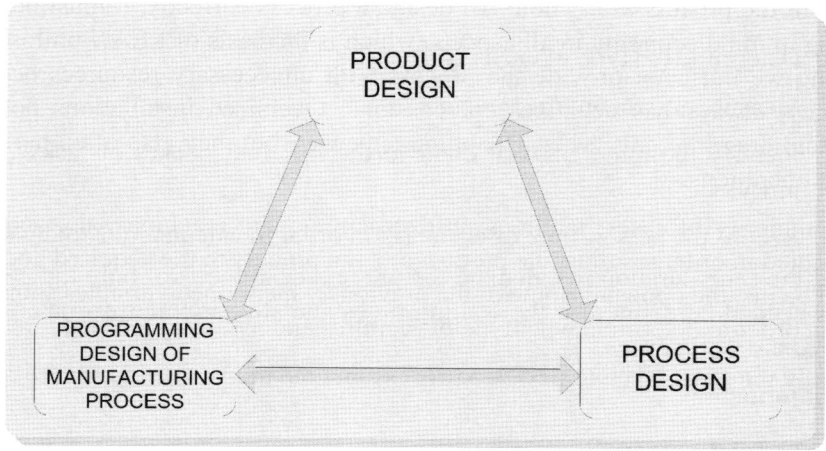

Figure 5.43. Process fulfillment diagram

In summary, a process cannot be correctly designed without taking into account the rest of variables that influence it. But neither can all be studied at the same time. Some of these variables need to be fixed, always maintaining an austere nature that does not condemn the system to failure from the start for a bad design. In Chapter 10, the criteria for process improvement will be discussed.

5.4.3. Mapping and Process Record

Having already explained the concept of process creation from the product structure, this section will explain several representation standards of process diagrams. **The process diagram is the graphic representation of such process.**

The steps to follow for process mapping are:

- Name the process.
- Define the initial milestone of the process.
- Describe the process briefly.
- Define the final milestone of the process.
- Identify the inputs of the process.
- Identify the outputs of the process.

- Identify all tasks.
- Determine the type of each task.
- Measure and record the transfers.
- Identify the materials that enter in the different phases or tasks of the process.
- Record the person-time of each task in order to calculate the total cost.

Record the time duration to calculate the process deadline. Not only the person-time is needed here, but also the waiting times and storage times of materials in intermediate warehouses.

Other information:

- Used machinery
- Process suppliers: Subcontracted phases
- Clients of the process

Based on these factors, representing the result in a process diagram is shown in Figure 5.44. This case includes two documents:

1. Document 1: Data entry sheet and process summary
2. Document 2: Process diagram

The process diagram can be represented as a diagram, flowchart, or layout, using the map of the factory.

Example

Document 1 - Process data: Window assembly			
General data of process		**Study data**	
Company	Ventanalia	Informatic file name:	
Address	132 Queens Road	Analyst/Author:	David Scott
Location	Leeds	Date of data collection:	2013/08/01
Zipcode	49002	Process date:	2013/08/09
Telephone	9.3E+07	N° Revision:	009
Task name:	Window assembly	Date of revision:	2013/09/23
Area-Section:	Line 1	Motive for revision:	
Task code:	90/39A00		
Summary table of process		**Particular data of process**	
Description	Min/Unit	Initial milestone:	Launching production order.
Standard time (person time)	102.2	Final milestone:	Stored window.
Process time (minutes)	5,862.2	Inputs:	Bars Ref 35 y bars Ref 36.
Workforce cost ($/hour)	35.0	Outputs:	Model A window.
Workforce cost per unit ($/unit)	59.6	Machinery:	Table saw and welder.
Total displacements (meters)	21.0	Outsourcing:	Nelson Portlocks
Classifcation of operations	Min/Unit	Process client:	Dispatch
Total value-adding operations. ○	66.7	Process providers:	Ferrygor and Smith Crystal
Total non-value-adding operations.	35.5	Process description:	
Total displacements. ⇨	16.8	For PVC window manufacturing, the material to be processed in three lines is received. Each line cuts the bars for welding and then inspect them. Afterwards, mechanisms are assembled before assembling the window completely.	
Total storage. ▽	3.3		
Total waits. D	0.0		
Total inspections. □	15.4		
Total inspection-operation.	0.0		
Process Waste Coefficient (CwP)	**1.53%**		

Figure 5.44. Document I: Data entry sheet and process summary

Note:

- The standard time refers to the cost of the whole process in person-time.
- The process time is the time that elapses from the work order until the product is delivered. It is the delivery time of the process.

Industrial productivity

Example

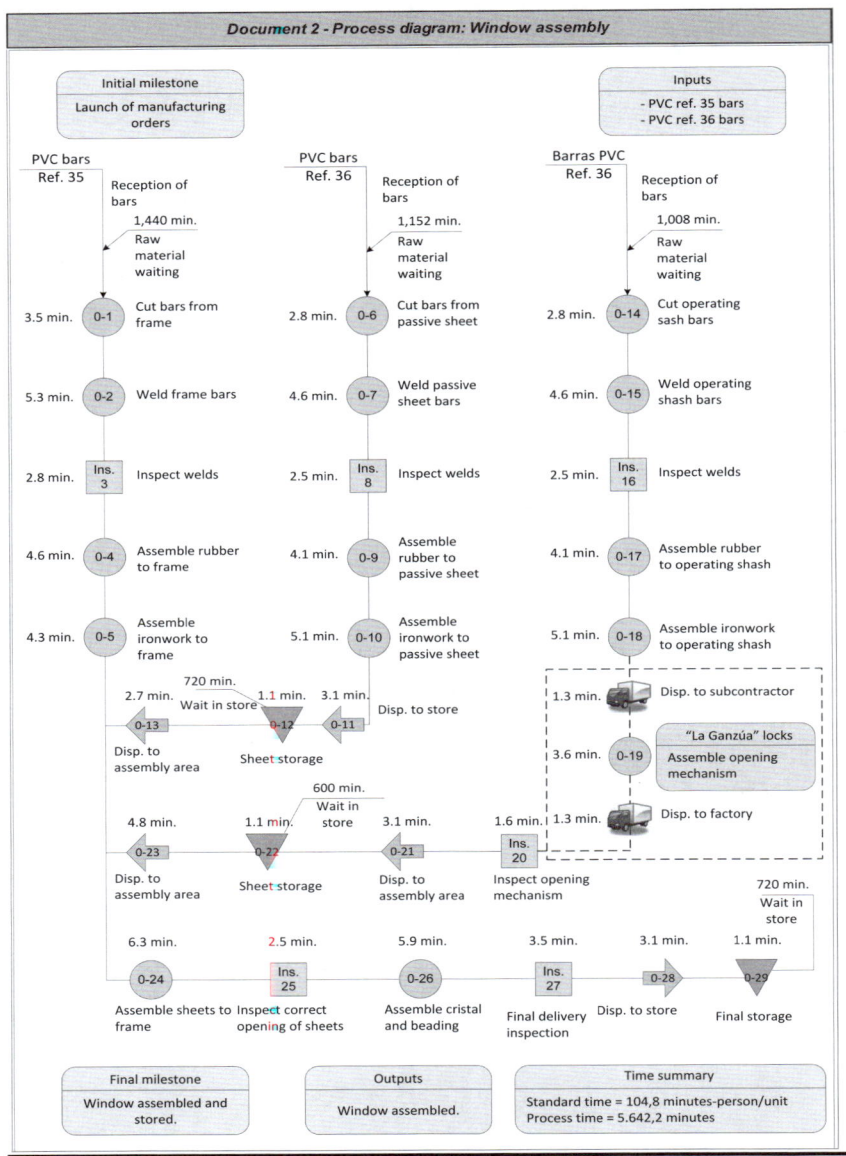

Figure 5.45. Document 2: Process diagram

The following diagram shows the manufacturing process for grills and rebar hoops for the construction of buildings. In this case, the different tasks to execute are directly represented on the factory layout.

Example

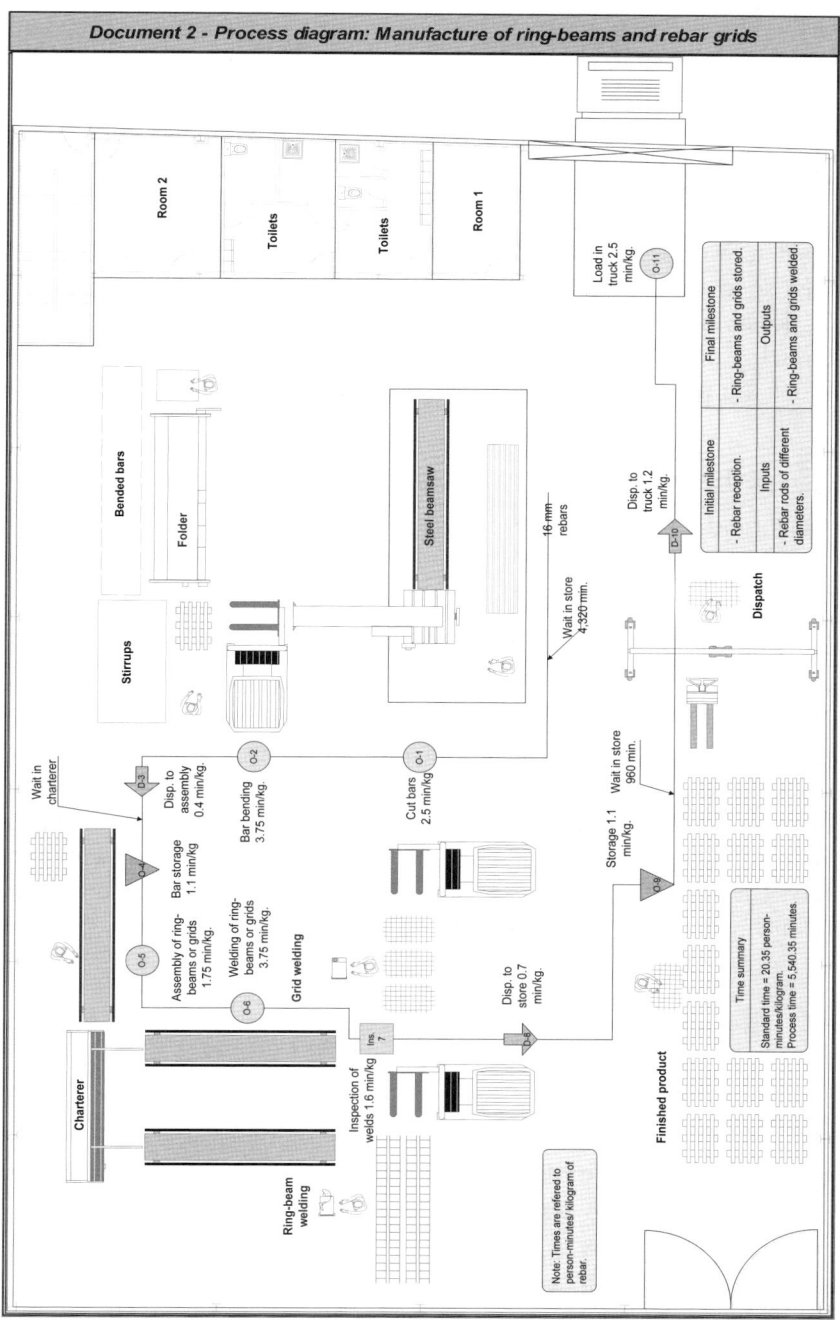

Figure 5.46. Process rebar manufacturing layout

Industrial productivity

These types of diagrams serve to watch and understand more quickly the flow of work and materials. Besides, they are useful for detecting the displacements and storages performed due to the layout.

5.4.4. Process Layout

After seeing the concepts, must be exposed the methodologies and criteria for layout design come next. The layout of a factory is the plant view and distribution of machines and workplaces in the factory.

Layout is determined in process design; it is not a map where system components are placed spontaneously, or at least it should not be. The arrangement should make it possible for production to consume the minimum amount of space while reducing the movement of materials. Given these parameters, the existing dispositions are practically infinite, but can be grouped into the following three groups:

- Assembly line disposition *(flow shop)*
- Distribution in sections *(job shop)*
- Fixed position

5.4.4.1. Assembly Line Disposition (Flow Shop)

This typology is oriented to the product. The companies that use this typology normally manufacture to stockpile, using always the same installations to obtain the same product, with an assembly line disposition of machines. They are products whose process requires a similar sequence of operations, which determines the order of the workstations. The product moves from one workstation to another, being able to bypass some if it does not have to undergo that workstation's operation. The crucial aspect is to coordinate the operations performed in the workstations, what is known as line balancing (Machuca, 1995).

Figure 5.47. Flow shop production

The workflow in this type of distributions can adopt diverse forms, depending on which adapts better to each concrete situation:

Figure 5.48. Line production

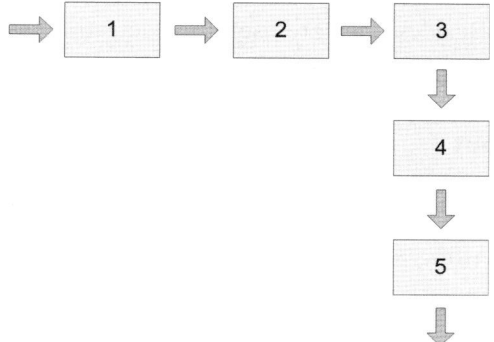

Figure 5.49. L-shape production

The most flexible disposition for regulating the productive capacity is the U-shaped typology, because the number of operators that attend it can vary without posing a productivity loss. An example is shown in the following image:

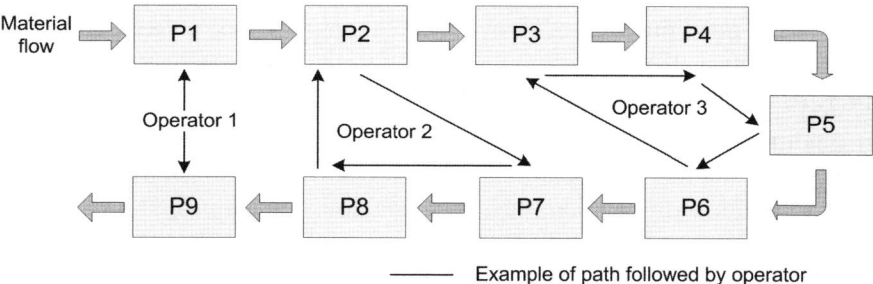

Figure 5.50. Example of balancing with three operators

The distribution through the flow shop typology presents the following advantages and disadvantages:

Advantages

- Reduced material handling
- Low existence of on-going works
- Minimum manufacturing times
- Simplification of programming systems and productivity control
- Simplification of tasks: highly specialized work allows rapid learning by low-skilled workers

Industrial productivity

Disadvantages

- Lack of flexibility in the process (a simple change in the product may require major changes in the facilities)
- Poor flexibility in manufacturing times (production flow cannot be faster than the slowest activity)
- High investment (specific equipment)
- Dependence of the whole on each of the parts: stopping a machine or a lack of staff or parts in any workstation can stop the entire chain
- Monotonous work (which can affect staff morale)

5.4.4.2. Distribution in Sections (Job Shop)

This typology is oriented to the process. The companies that use this typology often manufacture on request, working with small batches of dissimilar items that have different step sequences through the machines or workstations. The operations and equipment corresponding to the same type of activity are grouped in areas (e.g., lathes, forging, heat treatment, painting, etc.) through which the different elaborated products pass, organized in batches, as required or not by each activity (Machuca, 1995).

The products have to move from one area to another in accordance with the sequence of operations that are reflected in a variety of material flows between workshops.

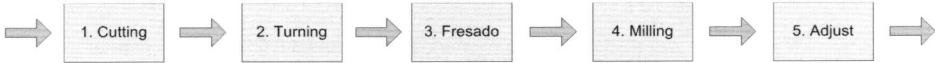

Figure 5.51. Manufacturing process

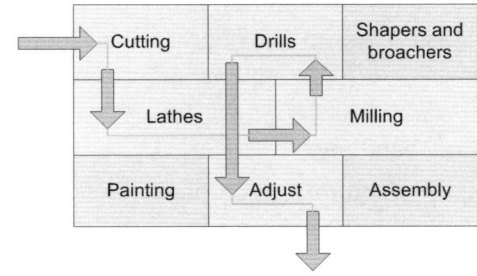

Figure 5.52. Manufacturing process for distribution in sections

Distribution in a job shop typology presents the following advantages and disadvantages:

Advantages

- Flexibility in the process through versatile equipment and qualified staff
- Reduced investments in equipment (universal and usually less expensive)
- Improved reliability (failure of a machine or supply does not involve a process stop)
- Increased workforce motivation from diversity of the tasks assigned to workers

Disadvantages

- Low efficiency in material handling (long displacements and cross-flows)
- High execution times (job often left waiting on the various work areas)
- Difficult to program and control production
- Higher cost per unit of product (more qualified workforce and inefficient material handling)
- Low productivity (uniqueness of job requiring different organization and training from operators)

5.4.4.3. Fixed Position

This type of disposition is used in situations of the impossibility or high cost of product transfer, so the machines and workers are who move to the product's location. The two basic types of distribution depend on the elaborated product:

- Construction projects (buildings, roads, bridges, etc.)
- Manufacturing projects through fixed position (shipyards, aeronautical, locomotives, etc.)

Because manufacturing times of products that are executed in fixed positions (buildings, industrial constructions, boats, etc.) are high, this process diagram is oriented to representing the different actions on a timeline, which will serve to plan all the works. The diagram used to perform this planning is called a Gantt diagram.

Figure 5.53 shows a Gantt diagram, which plans the necessary activities for the construction process of an industrial plant.

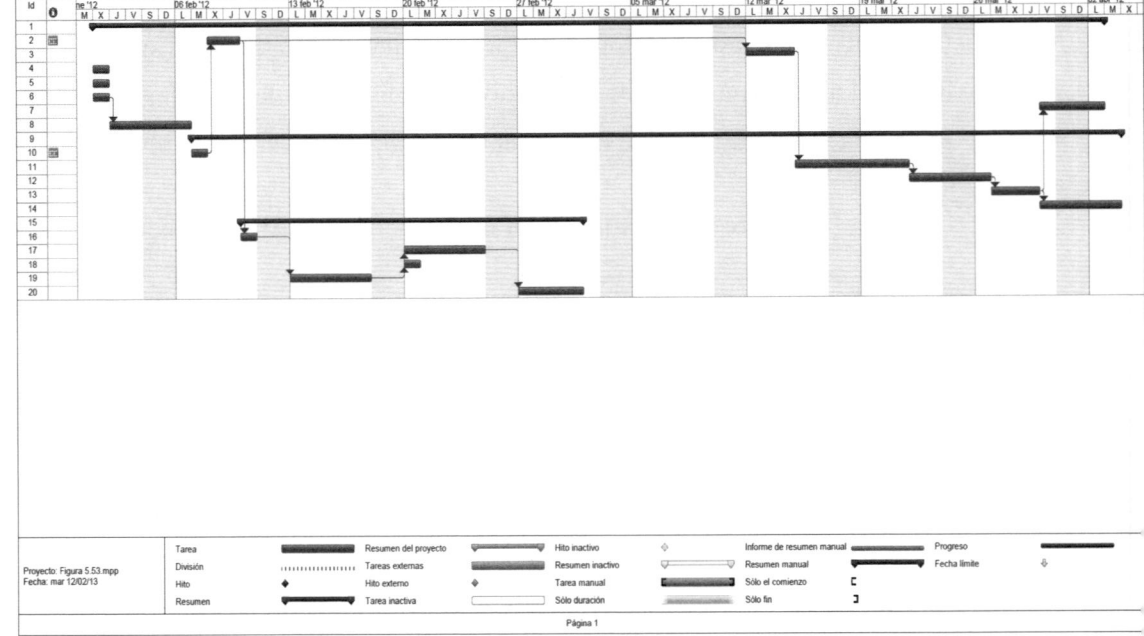

Figure 5.53. Diagrama de Gantt.

5.5. Record of Actual and Proposed Processes and Procedures

The record of methods and processes has been demonstrated throughout the whole chapter. In this section will be seen how the current and improved process is recorded. It will also show Document 1, which is the entry sheet and summary of the study of methods or process.

A comparison is made in the summary table. Later, the current and improved study of methods or process will be shown. Here, however, we will limit the discussion to the data entry sheet and summary.

Once the improved method or process is implemented, it would become the current method, changing the number of the revision and noting the motive for the revision, the date, and everything that affects the new method.

Example

Document 1 - Process data: Window assembly			
General data of process		**Study data**	
Company	Ventanalia	Informatic file name:	
Address	132 Queens Road	Analyst/Author:	David Scott
Location	Leeds	Date of data collection:	2013/08/01
Zipcode	49002	Process date:	2013/08/09
Telephone	92522883	Nº Revision:	009
Task name:	Window assembly	Date of revision:	2013/09/23
Area-Section:	Line 1	Motive for revision:	
Task code:	90/39A00		

Summary table of process	Current	Improv.	Economy	Particular data of process	
Description	Min/Unit	Min/Unit	Min/Unit	Initial milestone:	Manufacturing order.
Standard time (person time)	113.4	95.3	18.1	Final milestone:	Stored window.
Process time (minutes)	4,433.4	1,547.9	2,885.5	Inputs:	Ref 35 and Ref 36 bars.
Workforce cost ($/hour)	35.0	35.0	35.0	Outputs:	Ventana model A.
Workforce cost per unit ($/unit)	66.2	55.6	10.6	Machinery:	Table-saw and welder.
Total transfers (meters)	18.5	11.6	6.9	Outsourcing:	Packaging and customer shippi
Classification of operations	Min/Unit	Min/Unit	Min/Unit	Process client:	Dispatch
Total value-adding operations.	66.7	66.7	0.0	Process providers:	Ferrygor and Smith Crystal
Total non-value-adding operations.	4,366.7	1,481.2	2,885.5	Process description:	
Total transfers.	14.8	9.3	5.5		
Total storage.	4,336.5	1,456.5	2,880.0		
Total waits.	0.0	0.0	0.0		
Total inspections.	15.4	15.4	0.0		
Total inspection-operation.	0.0	0.0	0.0		
Process Waste Coefficient (CwP)	39.1%	16.2%	22.9%		

Figure 5.54. Document 1: Process data and summary table after improvement

Questions

1. What are the stages of the study of methods?
2. What information is found in a complete study of methods?
3. What is the method's graph?
4. How many different operations have been classified?
5. Is the summary of working methods always the same for any type of task?
6. What types of task have been defined?
7. What difference is found between the representation of a process and the representation of a method?
8. What basic information is needed for designing a process?
9. What are the four types of processes?
10. Why is it recommended to record the methods and processes as they change?

Industrial productivity

Problem 1: Production process of steel boxes

Steel plates are received and unloaded in the Reception Department. Each 25 plates come in light packaging of the same dimensions as the plates, 90 x 220 centimeters. Packages corresponding to the order are moved from the delivery truck and stacked on the loading dock; when the forklift operator is free, that worker stores them in the warehouse.

The package unloading operation takes, on average, 4.812 minutes, and the round-trip (120 meters) to the warehouse takes 5.1 minutes.

From the storage, plates are distributed in batches of 10, taking 1.15 minutes. In the shears, this batch waits for 95.1 minutes. The operation of cutting each plate into four pieces takes 2.472 minutes. When the batch is ready, the forklift operator moves the pieces of plate to the press to cut them in shape, taking 2.028 minutes.

At the press, the material waits for 115.14 minutes. The press operator uses the whole batch and places it on the table of the press, which takes 0.36 minutes. Subsequently cuts the piece, using a time of 0.66 minutes. After cutting all the pieces, the entire batch is transported to the stuffing section (2.50 minutes).

In this section, the batch waits an average of 2 hours; moreover, the operator must move to put the whole batch on top of the table, taking 0.36 minutes. The stuffing of each piece is precisely 1.11 minutes. Once the whole batch is prepared, the forklift operator moves it to the welding department (2 minutes). In this department, the material awaits for 151 minutes.

The welding operator spends 3 minutes per box; once the batch is completed, it is transferred to the finishing bench, a distance of 23.2 metres that takes 2.14 minutes. In the finishing operation 1.2 minutes are spent per box for deburring, securing the handle, and so on. At this same bench, a quality inspector occasionally performs a piece-by-piece inspection that takes 0.48 minutes.

Once the complete batch is inspected, the forklift operator transfers it to the degreasing workstation, a distance of 10.4 meters that takes 1.272 minutes. This batch waits for 2.01 hours.

In the degreasing area, each part takes 2.64 minutes to process and each one is moved by hand 0.60 meters to a conveyor belt drying oven, taking 0.21 minutes.

The drying takes 4.764 minutes and at the exit, when a complete batch is assembled, it is transferred by forklift 7.3 meters toward the painting area, taking 1.05 minutes.

In the painting area, it waits for 2 hours. The gun-painting takes 0.558 minutes, the operator transfers each part 0.60 meters to leave it on the drying oven, taking a total of 5.01 minutes for the batch.

The drying takes 5.16 minutes and from there, the batch is transferred 20.6 meters to the expedition storage (1.98 minutes).

Required: Portray the task process using the data-collecting format shown in the chapter.

Format for data collecting in free labor					
Diagram:		SUMMARY			
Product:		Activity	Current	Proposed	Saving
Work:		Operation ◯		-	-
Method: Current/Proposed		Transport ⇨		-	-
		Wait D		-	-
Place:		Inspection ☐		-	-
		Storage ▽		-	-
Operator:		Distance (meters)		-	-
		Time (min-person)		-	-
Composed by:		Cost		-	-
		Workforce		-	-
Approved by:		Material		-	-
		Total		-	-

Description of the Operation	Type of Operation	Distance (meters)	Unit time (sec)	Units	Operation Time (sec)	Observations
					0.00	
					0.00	
					0.00	
					0.00	
					0.00	
					0.00	
					0.00	
					0.00	
					0.00	
					0.00	
					0.00	
					0.00	
					0.00	
					0.00	
					0.00	
					0.00	
					0.00	

Figure 5.55. Example of format

Problem 2: Construction of concrete wall

In the construction of a concrete wall (without mechanical elements) 2 meters high, four operators work the following way with a single bucket.

Industrial productivity

- First worker: removes the concrete on one plate and fills a bucket; fills the bucket in 5 seconds and after filling it, kneads the concrete for 15 seconds; and is inactive the remaining time.

- Second worker: transports the bucket; spends 10 seconds to bring the bucket when it is filled by the first and 2 seconds to deliver it to the third worker, who is halfway up the shuttering; waits until third worker empties it and then takes 7 seconds to pick it up and return it to the first worker.

- Third worker: uses 2 seconds to take the bucket delivered by the second worker, elevates it and pours it into the shuttering, and returns the bucket afterwards; a cycle that takes, in total, 9 seconds.

- Fourth worker: tamps down the concrete when the previous worker finishes pours it, taking 10 seconds.

Required: Portray the task process using the data-collecting format shown in the chapter.

Format for data collecting in tasks with several participants					
Diagram:		**SUMMARY**			
Product:	**Activity**		**Current**	**Proposed**	**Saving**
Work:	Operation	◯	0.00	-	-
Method: Current/Proposed	Transport	⇨	0.00	-	-
	Wait	D	0.00	-	-
Place:	Inspection	▫	0.00	-	-
	Storage	▽	0.00	-	-
Operator:	Distance (meters)		0.00	-	-
	Time (min-person)		0.00	-	-
Composed by:	Cost		$/hour	-	-
	Workforce		$/hour	-	-
Approved by:	Material		$/hour	-	-
	Total		$/hour	-	-

Observations of Operation	Distance (meters)	Time (Minutes)	Operator 1	Operator 2	Operator 3	Operator 4
	Value-adding time (minutes)					
	Waiting time (minutes)					

Figure 5.56. Example of format

Bibliography

Aguirre de Mena, Juan M., María Mercedes Rodríguez Fernández, and Dolores Tous Zamora, *Organización y métodos de trabajo* (Ediciones Pirámide, 2002).

Dominguez Machuca, José, *Dirección de operaciones. Aspectos tácticos y operativos en la producción y los servicios* (New York: McGraw-Hill, 1995).

Harris, Rick, Chris Harris, and Earl Wailson, *Making Materials Flow* (Cambridge, MA: Lean Enterprise Institute, 2003).

Jones, Dan and Jim Womack, *Seeing the Whole* (Cambridge, MA: Lean Enterprise Institute, 2003).

Kanawaty, George, *Introduction to Work Study*. (Geneva: International Labor Organization, 1992).

Martín López, Milagro, María Elena Robles Rábago, Francisco José González Domínguez, and Juan Manuel Crespo Pérez, *Métodos de Trabajo: Casos Prácticos*. (Ediciones Pirámide, 2001).

Rother, Mike and Rick Harris, *Creating Continuous Flow* (Cambridge, MA: Lean Enterprise Institute, 2001)

Rother, Mike and John Shook, *Learning to See Value* (Cambridge, MA: Lean Enterprise Institute, 1999).

Chapter 6

Methods Analysis

Once the study method of a certain task has been made, the next step will be to analyze the method according to an improvement objective. The methods analysis will be our next step within the second stage.

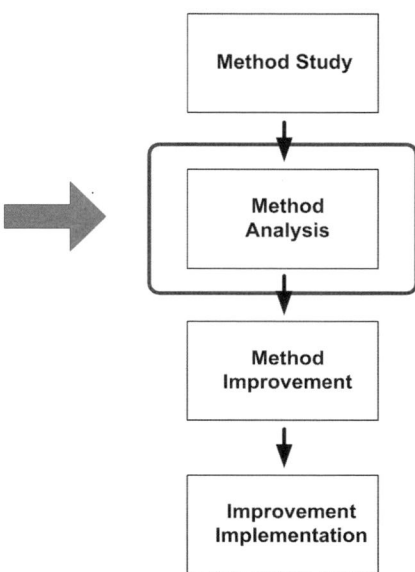

Figure 6.1. Second stage diagram: Methods analysis

6.1. The Concept of Analysis

During the study of task method, the next objective is to detect the operations that do not add value to the product and to improve the ones that do add value. The methods analysis does not treat the improvement of these operations; it is a diagnosis system that detects what can be improved. Once this analysis is made, the next step is to focus on improvement, which will be seen in Chapter 7.

The working method analysis must identify where to improve the methods and procedures, as well as equipment design, installations, and materials, to reduce unnecessary worker fatigue and economize in the use of material, machines, and workforce. Increasing the security of the process and creating the best working conditions can make the process easier, quicker, simpler, and safer.

The analysis does not make improvement proposals, but it identifies the potential points for improvement.

6.2. Interrogatory Technique

The critical analysis of the defined working method is a stage of the working method analysis technique that applies once all the necessary information for the study of the task method has been collected. According to the International Labor Organization (ILO), this stage of method analysis consists of a critical and systematic analysis of the current method, which allows for the discovery of improvements to apply to the method. The interrogatory technique is the means to carry out a critical exam, successively submitting each operation to a series of systematic and progressive questions.

The interrogatory technique has two types of questions to formulate: preliminary questions and background questions. The preliminary questions correspond to the first stage of the interrogatory, where systematically and for each recorded operation, the purpose, place, succession, person, and means of implementation used in the task are examined with the intention of eliminating, combining, arranging, or simplifying that operation.

The preliminary questions will therefore be:

    1. Purpose:
- What is really done?
- What is really obtained?
- Why is it made?

2. Place:
    - Where is it done?
    - Why is it done there?
3. Succession:
    - When is it done?
    - Why is it done at that moment?
4. Person:
    - Who does it?
    - Why does that operator do it?
5. Method:
    - How is it done?
    - Why is it done that way?
6. In relation to materials and transportation:
    - Are they appropriate?
    - Could less expensive ones be used?
    - Could others that generate fewer wastes be used?
    - Are adequate means of transportation used?
    - Is the warehouse situated in an adequate, logical location?
7. In relation to operations:
    - Could it be done in a quicker and less expensive way?
    - Is the best procedure used?
8. In relation to the employee:
    - Is the worker specialized in the work?
    - Could a less-qualified worker perform at this workstation, thereby reducing costs for the company?
9. In relation to the tools and equipment:
    - Are they in good shape to use?
    - Are the tools used the most advanced, the most appropriate?
    - Is adequate maintenance done?

10. In relation to the working conditions:

   - Are physical working conditions good: ventilation, illumination, temperature, noises, etc.?
   - Is the working environment safe and motivating?

11. In relation to product design:

   - Is the best design the one that is used?
   - Can the product be changed in ways (other than weight and volume) that result in lower costs for the company without changing price for the customer/client?

The background questions compose the second phase of the interrogatory.

The objective is to dig deeper and detail the preliminary questions to determine whether improving the actual method would make it feasible and preferable to replace the place, succession, person, and/or means used.

In this second stage of the interrogatory that asks what is done and why is it done, the analyst moves on to determine what quantity of improvement exists and, therefore, what should be done. Thus, drilling down deeper in the obtained answers provides even more information about the place, succession, person, means, and so on. In the following section a complete catalog of test lists is provided and includes background questions regarding the task and operation.

6.3. Checklists: Background Questions

The tables or lists of issues that follow will help the analyst in an analysis of methods, with the purpose of improving and eliminating operations that do not add value. Such questions will be centered in analyzing the group of operations to manufacture the final product and also the environment in which the mentioned product or service is elaborated.

Fomato

Checklist regarding operations			
Task:		Company:	
Date:		Process:	
Analyst:		Area:	
Operator:			
Operations			
What is the purpose of the operation?			
Is the result obtained by the operation necessary? If so, what makes it necessary?			
Is the operation necessary because the previous operation was not performed correctly?			
Is the operation instituted to correct a condition that has now been corrected otherwise?			
If the operation is being carried out to improve appearance, does the additional cost provide extra marketability			
Can the purpose of the operation be carried out in another way?			
Is the operation being performed to satisfy the requirements of all users of the product, or is it made necessary by the requirements of one or two customers only?			
Does a subsequent operation eliminate the necessity for this operation?			
Was the operation established to reduce the cost of a previous or subsequent operation?			
Would adding an additional operation make other operations easier to perform?			
Can the operation be performed in another way to obtain the same or even better results?			
Have conditions changed since the operation was added to the process?			
Could the operation be combined with a previous or subsequent operation?			
Can the operation analyzed be combined with another operation? Can it be eliminated?			
Can it be broken up and the various parts of the operation added to other operations?			
Can a part of the operation being performed be completed more effectively as a separate operation?			
Is the sequence of operations the best possible or would changing the sequence improve the operation?			
Could the operation be done in another department to save the cost of handling?			
If the operation is changed, what effect will it have on the other operations? On the finished product?			
If a different method of production is used, will it justify all the work and activity involved?			
Can the operation and inspection be combined?			
Comments			

Fourth Edition Copyright © 1992, International Labor Organization

Figure 6.2. Checklist referring each operation made by the operator

Industrial Productivity

Format

Checklist regarding products and parts design				
Task:		Company:		
Date:		Process:		
Analyst:		Area:		
Operator:				
Operations				
Can the design be changed to simplify or eliminate the operation?				
Can the number of component parts be reduced?				
Can certain component parts be standardized?				
Can a standard part be substituted by another cheaper or better material?				
Has Pareto analysis been used to detect the products or parts that are most valuable?				
Comments				

Fourth Edition Copyright © 1992, International Labor Organization

Figure 6.2. *Checklist for component design, product, or article*

Format

Checklist regarding quality requirements				
Task:		Company:		
Date:		Process:		
Analyst:		Area:		
Operator:				
Operations				
Has an agreement been reached by all concerned as to what constitutes acceptable quality?				
What are the inspection requirements for this operation?				
Can the operator inspect his or her own work?				
Are tolerance and other standards appropriate?				
Can standards be raised to improve quality without unnecessary cost?				
Will lowering standards reduce cost considerably?				
Can the finished quality of the product be improved in any way above the present standard?				
Can the quality be improved by using new processes?				
Are the same standards necessary for all customers?				
Will change in standards and inspection requirements increase or decrease the defective work and expense in the operation, shop, or field?				
What are the main causes of rejections for the part?				
Would a change in the composition of a product render it less susceptible to quality variances?				
Comments				

Fourth Edition Copyright © 1992, International Labor Organization

Figure 6.3. *Checklist of quality requirements*

Format

Checklist regarding materials utilization				
Task:		Company:		
Date:		Process:		
Analyst:		Area:		
Operator:				
Operations				
Is the material being used suitable for the job?				
Could a less expensive material be substituted and still do the job?				
Could a lighter-gauge material be used?				
Is the material purchased in a condition suitable for use?				
Could the supplier perform additional work on the material that would improve usage and decrease waste?				
Is the material sufficiently clean?				
Is the material bought in amounts and sizes that give the greatest utilization, limiting scrap, offcuts, and short ends?				
Is the material used to the best possible advantage during cutting and processing?				
Are indirect materials used in connection with the process—oils, water, acids, paint, gas, compressed air, electricity—suitable, and is their use controlled and economized?				
How does the cost of material compare with the cost of labor?				
Can the design be changed to eliminate excessive loss and scrap material?				
Can the number of materials used be reduced by standardization?				
Can the part be made from scrap material or offcuts?				
Can the scrap be salvaged for further processing?				
Can the scrap be sorted out for sales at a higher price?				
Is the supplier of the material performing operations on it that are unnecessary for the process?				
Is the material supplied of consistent quality?				
Could a more careful inspection of incoming materials decrease difficulties now being encountered in processing?				
Is the material free from sharp edges and burrs?				
What effect does storage have on material?				
Could sampling inspection combined with supplier rating reduce inspection costs and delays?				
Could the part be made more economically from offcuts in some other gauge of material?				
Comments				
Fourth Edition Copyright © 1992, International Labor Organization				

Figure 6.4. Checklist of raw materials

Format

Checklist regarding workplace layout			
Task:		Company:	
Date:		Process:	
Analyst:		Area:	
Operator:			
Operations			
Does the plant layout aid in efficient material handling?			
Does the plant layout allow for efficient maintenance?			
Does the plant layout provide adequate safety?			
Is the plant layout suitable for appropriate sequencing of operation? Can parts of an intermittent operation be changed to a line operation layout for major products or parts?			
Does the plant layout help social interaction between the operators?			
Are materials conveniently placed at the workplace?			
Are tools prepositioned to save mental delay?			
Are suitable jigs and fixtures available at the workplace to facilitate work, particularly in assembly operations?			
Are adequate working surfaces provided for subsidiary operations (e.g. inspection and deburring)?			
Are facilities provided for the removal and storage of scrap and waste?			
Is adequate provision made for the comfort of the operator (e.g. fan, duckboard, or chairs)?			
Is the lighting adequate for the job?			
Has provision been made for the storage of tools and gauges?			
Has provision been made for storage of operators' personal belongings?			
Comments			

Fourth Edition Copyright © 1992, International Labor Organization

Figure 6.5. *Checklist for layout of work space*

Format

Checklist regarding materials handling				
Task:			Company:	
Date:			Process:	
Analyst:			Area:	
Operator:				
Operations				
Is the time spent in bringing material to the workstation and in removing it large in proportion to the time used to handle it at the workstation?				
If not, could material handling be done by the operators to provide a rest through change of occupation?				
Should hand, electric, or forklift trucks, or conveyors or chutes be used?				
Should special racks, containers, or pallets be designed to permit the handling of material with ease and without damage?				
Where should incoming and outgoing materials be located in the work area?				
Can material be transferred from a central point by means of a conveyor?				
Is the size of the container suitable for the amount of material transported?				
Can a container be designed to make material more accessible?				
Could a container be placed at the workstation without removing the material?				
If an overhead travelling crane is used, is the service prompt and accurate?				
Can gravity be utilized by starting the first operation at a higher level, and using suitable chutes or conveyors?				
Are truck loading and unloading stations located appropriately?				
Would a turntable eliminate walking?				
Can incoming raw material be delivered at the first workstation to save double handling?				
Could operations be combined at one workstation to save double handling?				
Would a container of standard size eliminate weighing?				
Are containers uniform to permit stacking and eliminate excessive use of floor space?				
Could material be bought in a more convenient size for handling?				
Would signals (i.e., lights, bells, etc.) notifying workers that more material is required, reducing delays?				
Can the location of stores and stockpiles be altered to reduce handling and transport?				
Comments				
Fourth Edition Copyright © 1992, International Labor Organization				

Figure 6.6. Checklist for environment and working conditions

Format

Checklist regarding work organization				
Task:		Company:		
Date:		Process:		
Analyst:		Area:		
Operator:				
Operations				
How is the job assigned to the operator?				
Are things so well controlled that the operator is never without a job to do?				
How is the operator given instructions?				
How is material obtained?				
How are drawings and tools issued?				
Are time controls used? If so, how are the starting and finishing times of the job checked?				
What delays at the drawing room, tool room, and storeroom are possible?				
Is the material properly positioned?				
If the operation is being performed continually, how much time is wasted at the start and end of the shift by preliminary operations and cleaning up?				
What clerical work is required from operators for filling in time cards, material requisitions, and the like? Can some of these operations be computerized?				
How is defective work handled?				
How is the issue and servicing of tools organized?				
Are adequate records kept on operator performance?				
Are new employees properly introduced to their surroundings, and do they receive sufficient training?				
When workers do not reach a standard of performance, are the details investigated?				
Are suggestions from workers encouraged?				
Do the workers really understand the incentive plan under which they work?				
Comments				

Fourth Edition Copyright © 1992, International Labor Organization

Figure 6.7. Checklist relative to the manipulation of raw materials

Format

Checklist regarding working conditions				
Task:			Company:	
Date:			Process:	
Analyst:			Area:	
Operator:				

Operations
Is the lighting even and sufficient at all times?
Has glare been eliminated from the workplace?
Is the proper temperature for comfort provided at all times? If not, can fans or heaters be used?
Would installation of air-conditioning equipment be justified?
Can noise levels be reduced?
Can fumes, smoke, and dirt be removed by exhaust systems?
If concrete floors are used, are duckboards or matting provided to make standing more comfortable?
Can a chair be provided?
Are drinking fountains with cool water provided and are they located nearby?
Has due consideration been given to safety factors?
Is the floor safe, smooth but not slippery?
Have operators been trained to work safely?
Is operator clothing suitable from a safety standpoint?
Does the plant present a neat and orderly appearance at all times?
How thoroughly is the workplace cleaned?
Is the plant unduly cold in winter or stuffy in summer, especially on the first morning of the week?
Are dangerous processes adequately guarded?

Comments

Fourth Edition Copyright © 1992, International Labor Organization

Figure 6.8. *Checklist relative to operator productivity*

Format

Checklist regarding job enrichment				
Task:		Company:		
Date:		Process:		
Analyst:		Area:		
Operator:				
Operations				
Is the job boring or monotonous?				
Can the operation be made more interesting?				
Can the operation be combined with previous or subsequent operations to enlarge it?				
What is the cycle time?				
Can the operator do his or her own setting?				
Can the operator do his or her own inspection?				
Can the operator deburr his or her own work?				
Can the operator service his or her own tools?				
Can the operator be given a batch of tasks and do his or her own scheduling?				
Can the operator make the complete part?				
Is job rotation possible and desirable?				
Can group work be encouraged?				
Are flexible working hours possible and desirable?				
Can buffer stock be provided to allow variations in work pace?				
Does the operator receive regular information about his or her performance?				
Comments				

Fourth Edition Copyright © 1992, International Labor Organization

Figure 6.9. *Checklist for task enrichment*

Through these lists of questions the analyst is better able to detect the possibilities for improvement in the actual operations method. The correct formulation of the question will bring with it the idea for the incidence improvement. A good analysis translates into proposals of improvement more easily.

6.4. Operation Analysis

Following all indications described earlier and making use of the available tools, the analysis of the operations method can be made. Next we will observe a methods study of a task submitted for examination. All the operations that are non-value-adding or involve inspection-operation suppose waste and constitute the potential for improvement available within the task.

Description of Operation	Type of Operation	Total Corrected Time (sec)
Provide panel. Remove protector paper.	○	21,46
Provide set of bits for drill.	○	6,79
Transfer to following workstation.	⇨	18,40
Deposit panel on worktable.	○	2,19
Search and supply of plans.	▤	66,60
Perform drill markings with pencil and ruler.	⟲	474,26
Store plans in closet.	▽	62,58
Take panel.	○	4,60
Transfer to manual mechanizing area.	⇨	92,00
Deposit bits and panel on auxiliary table. Clear working area.	▽	6,65
Instal bits on column drill.	○	35,09
Place wooden piece in column drill base.	○	8,63
Perform a predrill in panel to place floating inserts.	○	141,51
Exchange bidiametral bit for normal bit in column drill.	○	30,91
Perform a predrill in panel to place floating inserts.	○	118,24
Disassemble bidiametral bit. Remove panel.	○	5,98
Store bits. Turn off column drill.	▽	15,92
Transfer to working area from manual mechanization area.	⇨	110,40
Deposit panel on worktable. Store bits in workbench.	▽	9,17
Take seat. Turn panel over on worktable. Provide tweezers.	○	11,03
Remove material leftovers from preformed holes with help of tweezers.	⟲	115,80
Provide floating inserts. Extract set of inserts.	○	36,09

Fit floating inserts in preformed holes.	◯	122,97
Provide glue kit .Prepare it for use mixing in machine. Remove plunger.	◯	97,00
Put on work gloves.	◯	27,42
Assemble aplicator in kit. Assemble kit in aplication gun. Conect to compressed air intake.	◯	30,44
Apply glue on hole, check glue emerges from other hole.	◯	52,12
Clean excess of glue in inserts with paper.	◯	82,89
Free panel, to dry glue.	◯	14,51
provide panel and take seat. provide pliers.	◯	11,03
Remove insert protection plates. Check correct positioning of insert.	◯	150,77
Transfer panel to following workstation.	⇨	9,20
Displacement towards workplace.	⇨	9,20

Figure 6.11. *Methods study of a task with identification of non-value-adding operations*

All the operations within a task will be analyzed in order to eliminate the ones with no added value (those that appear shaded in the previous figure) and improve the ones that do add value:

- Provide panel. Remove protection paper:
    - Could the supplier provide the panel without protection paper?
- Provide set of bits for drill:
    - Could the location of the bits be annexed to the workstation?
- Transfer to following workstation:
    - Could the workstation be closer, so the distance between is less?
- Deposit panel on worktable:
    - Could the workstation be closer to avoid the supply of the panel?
    - Could the two workstations be grouped into one to eliminate all transfers and supplies?
- Search and supply of plans:
    - Could the plans be printed automatically with the production order to eliminate searching and time to supply them?

- Perform drill markings with pencil and ruler:
    - Could we produce a standard template to avoid the measurement and marking of the component?
    - Could the supplier mark the component in its manufacturing?
- Store plans in closet:
    - If the plans are supplied with the production order, is it necessary to save the component plans?
- Take panel:
    - Could we place the column drill in the workstation and avoid having to supply the panel?
- Transfer to manual mechanizing area:
    - Can we place the column drill in the workstation and avoid traveling that distance?
- Deposit bits and panel on auxiliary table. Clear working area:
    - Could we place the column drill in the workstation and avoid the exchange of bits?
- Install bits in column drill:
    - Could the bits be installed permanently in the column drill?
- Place wooden piece in the column drill base:
    - Can the wooden plug be left permanently in the column drill?
- Perform a predrill in the panel to place floating inserts:
    - Could this operation be eliminated by making a unique hole in the component?
- Exchange bidiametrical bit for normal bit in column drill:
    - Could this operation be eliminated by making a unique hole in the component?
- Perform a predrill in panel to place floating inserts:
    - Could the supplier supply it already drilled?
    - Could this operation be eliminated by making a unique hole in the component?

- Disassemble bidiametrical bit. Remove panel:
  - Could the supplier provide it already drilled?
- Store bits. Turn off column drill:
  - Could a column drill be located in the workstation for that operation, avoiding the bit exchange?
  - Could the bit be installed permanently in the column drill?
- Transfer to working area from manual mechanization area:
  - Can we place the column drill in the workstation and avoid travelling that distance?
- Deposit panel on worktable. Store bits in workbench:
  - Can we place the column drill in the workstation and avoid travelling that distance?
- Take seat. Turn panel over on worktable. Provide tweezers:
  - Could we use bits of more quality to avoid the creation of burrs in the panel?
- Remove material leftovers from preformed holes with the help of tweezers:
  - Could bits of more quality be used to avoid the creation of burrs in the panel?
  - Could paper tape be used to avoid material pieces from coming off while drilling?
- Provide floating inserts. Extract set of inserts:
  - Could the supplier provide the panel already processed?
- Fit floating inserts in preformed holes:
  - Could the quality of the hole be improved to reduce the time for this operation?
- Provide glue kit. Prepare it for use mixing in machine. Remove plunger:
  - Could the kit be supplied already mixed?
  - Could the length of the operation be reduced by a faster tool?

- Put on work gloves:
- Assemble applicator in kit. Assemble kit in application gun. Connect to compressed air intake:
    - Could the application gun be connected permanently?
    - Is it possible to supply the kit with a disposable applicator?
- Apply glue to hole, check for glue to emerge from the other end:
    - Can the application process be improved to reduce the length of the operation?
- Clean excess glue from inserts with paper:
    - Could the application process be improved to eliminate this operation?
- Release panel for drying:
    - Is it possible to let the panel in its place until the adhesive is dry?
- Provide panel and take seat. Supply pliers:
    - Is it possible to use other types of inserts to avoid this operation?
- Remove insert protection sheet from plates. Check correct position of insert:
    - Is it possible to use other types of inserts to avoid this operation?
- Transfer panel to following workstation:
    - Can the next workstation be nearer?
    - Could we install an automatic transportation system (by gravity or conveyor belt)?

Questions have been formulated for each and every operation that appears in the methods study, in order to reduce waste or eliminate the operation. It is always easier to improve the non-value-adding ones, but everything has to be questioned.

Using this exercise of questioning every operation, wouldn't any method previously analyzed be improved? Maybe a desired answer is not found in every question; if so, it means the entire task is not needed (which sometimes happens). However, the questions are important in the pursuit of ambitious goals.

6.5 Study of Movements

Frank. B. Gilbreth was the founding father of this modern technique that studies movement, which can be defined as the study of human body movements involved in performing a task, with the goal of improving it, eliminating unnecessary movements and simplifying the necessary ones, and establishing the most favorable sequence or succession to achieve maximum efficiency.

More than anyone else, the Gilbreths, Frank and his wife Lillian, helped the industry recognize the importance of a thorough study of the human movements in relation to their capacity to increase the production, decrease the fatigue and instruct operators about the best method to carry out a task.

The movements study can affect three fields:

- Utilization of human body
- Distribution of the workplace
- Machines and tools models

The three serve, indistinguishable from one another, in workshops and offices. And although not always, they can be applied as the basis for efficiency improvement and for decreasing labor fatigue. The study of movements differentiates within each operation (as described in Chapter 5), in the study methods of the task, a new classification of micro-operations and micro-motions.

Based on the Gilbreths' work, micro-motions can be analyzed to economize the movements. In the next section the analysis of micro-motions is studied. Even though Chapter 6 refers to the analysis and not the improvement proposals, for reasons of coherence this part of the economy of movements is treated here. In Chapter 7 further reference will be made to this point in the catalog of improvement solutions.

Motion economy:

1. Utilization of the human body

Whenever it is possible:

- Both hands must start and complete their movements simultaneously.
- Never must both hands be inactive at the same time, except during rest periods.
- The movement of the arms must be made simultaneously and in opposite and symmetrical ways.

- The movement of hands and body must fall into the lowest possible category to execute the work satisfactorily. It must be considered that, to achieve an effective use of the workplace, it is important that the movements effectuated by the operator are the ones that cause the least fatigue. It is convenient, therefore, to relate the normal and maximum working zones with the next categories (from lower to higher, when movements made to fulfill an operation belong to the three first categories, better advantages will be obtained) of movements:

    - Movements in which only fingers are used.
    - Movements in which only fingers and wrist are used.
    - Movements in which only fingers, wrist, and forearm are used.
    - Movements in which only fingers, wrist, forearm, and arm are used.
    - Movements in which fingers, wrist, forearm, arm, and body are used.

- Impulses must be taken advantage of when they benefit the worker, but must be reduced to a minimum if they have to be counteracted by muscular effort.
- Continuous and curved movements are preferable to straight ones in which sudden and abrupt changes of direction have to be made.
- Free oscillation movements are quicker, easier, and more exact than restrained or controlled ones.
- Pace is essential for a smooth and automatic implementation of repetitive tasks, when possible they must be done at an easy and natural pace.
- Labor must be arranged in such a way that eyes move between comfort limits and it is not necessary to constantly change focus.

2. Workplace distribution

- A defined and permanent place for all tools and materials is imperative, with the purpose of acquiring habits.
- Tools and materials must be placed in advance where they will be needed, in order to avoid having to look for them.
- Deposits and means of "gravity supply" must be used, so materials get as close as possible to the place of usage.
- Tools, materials, and controls must be located in the most used working area and as close to the workers as possible.

6. Methods Analysis

Figure 6.12. *Normal work area in the horizontal plane*

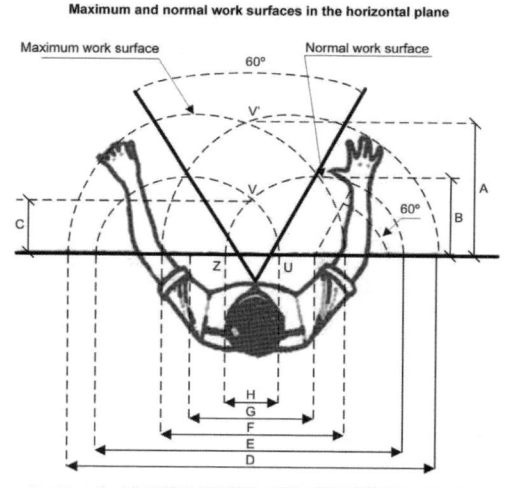

	WOMAN Height: 1.59 m. Weight: 54 kg.	MAN Height: 1.68 m. Weight: 68 kg.
A	0,480	0,550
B	0,300	0,335
C	0,200	0,240
D	1,370	1,550
E	1,100	1,350
F	0,640	0,720
G	0,550	0,600
H	0,200	0,240

Figure 6.13. *Maximum and normal work area in the horizontal plane*

237

Normal and maximum working area in the vertical plane

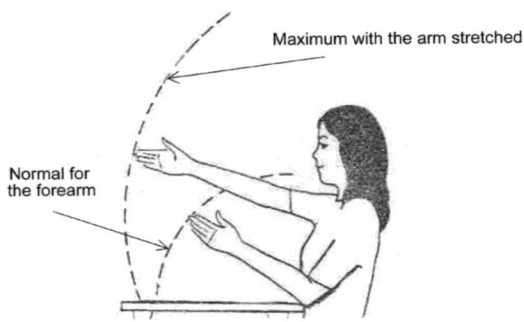

Figure 6.14. *Normal work area in the vertical plane*

Maximum and normal work surfaces in the vertical plane

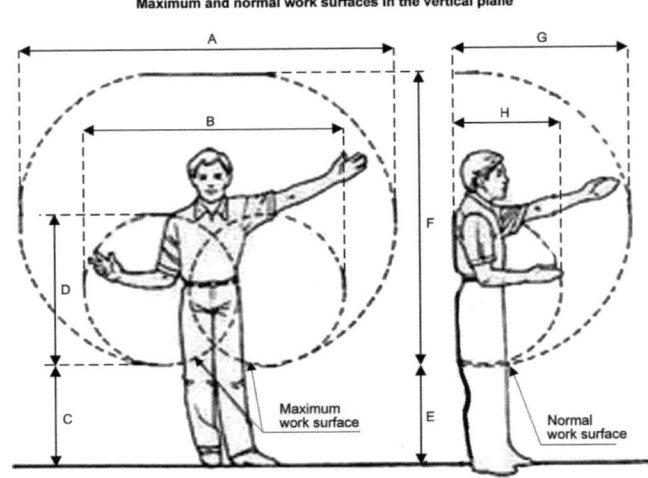

	WOMAN Height: 1.59 m. Weight: 54 kg.	MAN Height: 1.68 m. Weight: 68 kg.
A	1,400	1,550
B	1,100	1,350
C	0,880	0,770
D	0,720	0,800
E	0,630	0,700
F	1,260	1,400
G	0,730	0,800
H	0,430	0,500

Figure 6.15. *Maximum and normal work area in the vertical plane*

- Materials and tools must be placed in such a way that the sequence of movements for their use is as comfortable as possible.

- When possible, use of ejectors and devices that allow the operator to "drop" the finished work without needing to use the hands to dispatch it is beneficial.

- Luminaires must be provided for enough light, as well as a suitable chair with the adequate height so that the employee can sit comfortably. The height of the workplace and chair must be combined in such a way that the operator can work alternatively sitting and standing.

- Adequate ventilation and temperature are essential.

- The workplace color surface must be clearly distinguished from the color of the task being made as a way to reduce eyesight fatigue.

- A good working pace is essential to carry out a task smoothly and automatically. Work must be organized so that it allows obtaining an easy and natural pace when possible.

3. Design of machines and tools

- It is advisable to avoid holding components and thereby occupying the hands when those components could be held with a template, item, or foot-activated device.

- Whenever possible, two or more tools must be combined into one.

- Whenever each finger makes a specific movement, like when typing, workload must be distributed according to the inherent capacity of each finger.

- Handles, like the ones used in cranks and large screwdrivers, must be designed so that the greatest possible surface is in contact with the hand. It is of special importance when a lot of strength must be applied on the handle.

- Levers, crossbars, and steering wheels must be placed in positions that allow the operator to manipulate them with a minimum change of the body position and a maximum of mechanical advantages.

When designing work tools and templates that will be used to perform an operation in a repetitive way, such as cutting materials into a certain shape, it is convenient that the analyst has the support of the area supervisor when designing the device. The supervisor is closer to the operations and can give useful opinions that the analyst perhaps did not take into account. It is also highly recommended to take into account the suggestions of the operator who executes the task. On the other hand, generally the analyst is not an expert designer, so the help of a tool designer will contribute to obtaining a more cost-effective device.

Industrial Productivity

Other recommendations about the workplace layout and the simplification of movements:

- If both hands perform analogous work, a reserve of materials and components for each hand must be provided.
- When sight is needed to select material, it should be located, to some extent, where the operator can see it without necessity of moving his or her head.
- Instead of a transfer in only a circle arc, it is preferable to use two circle arcs.
- In the conception of the workplace, ergonomic rules must be applied.
- The nature and shape of the material influences its location in the workplace. To distribute the material, it is advisable to use drawers like the ones showed in Figure 6.16.

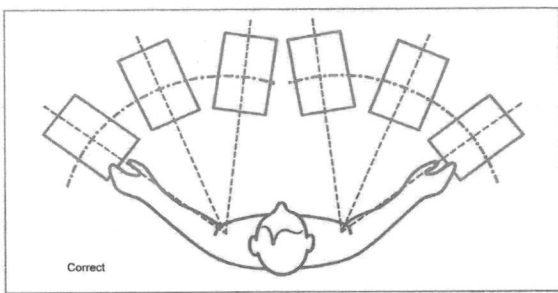

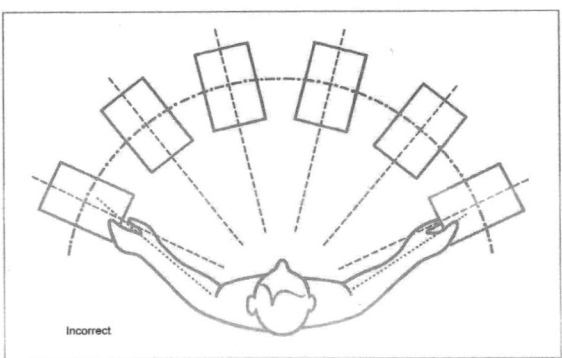

Copyright (C) International Labour Organisation 1992

Figure 6.16. Recommended disposition in two circle arcs

6. Methods Analysis

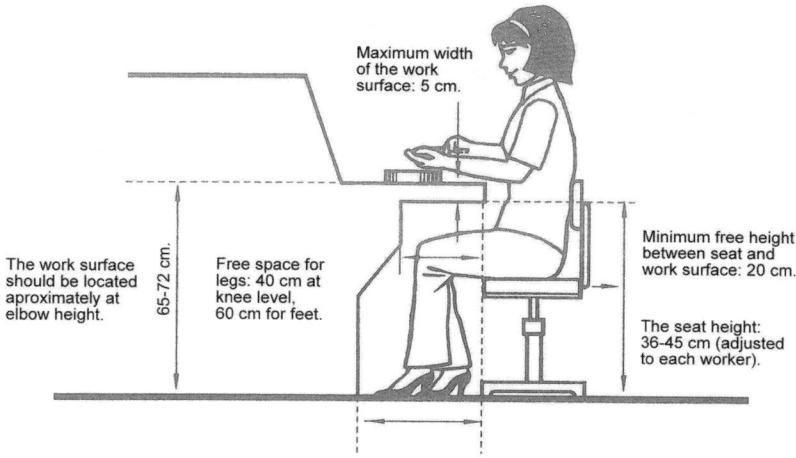

Source: International Labor Organization, copyright © 1992.

Figure 6.17. *Recommended dimensions for effectuating tasks in sitting position*

- Manual tools must be held in a way that does not alter the minimum pace or symmetry of movements. The operator must take or deposit the tool as the hand passes from a stage of work to the next, without making a special path. Natural movements are curved and not straight: tools must be located in the arc movement, but not in the way of any material that needs to slide through the workbench.

- Tools must be located in such a way that it is easy to grab them and then put them back in their place; when it is possible they will go back to their place with an automatic device or making the most of the hand movement when it is going to take the next part.

- Finished work must:
    - Drop freely into dumps or slides.
    - Drop into a slide when the hand initiates the first movement of the next cycle.
    - Be located in a container prepared in such a way that minimizes hand movements.
    - Be located in a container where the next operator can grab it easily, if it happens to be an intermediate operation.

The potential use of knee pedals or levers must always be studied and consideration given to using mechanisms of closure or graduation or other devices to withdraw the completed work.

Industrial Productivity

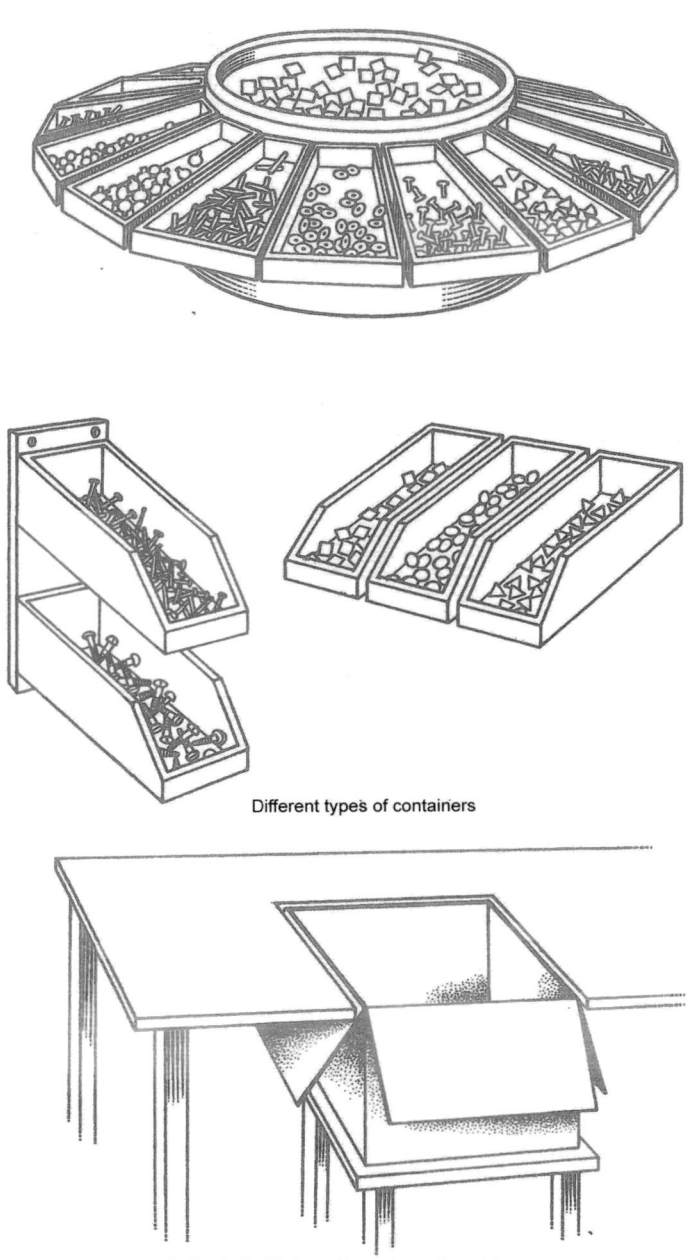

Different types of containers

Device to facilitate package in cardborad boxes

Copyright (C) International Labour Organisation 1992

Source: International Labor Organization, copyright © 1992.

Figure 6.18. *Containers and devices for economizing movements*

Copyright (C) International Labour Organisation 1992

Source: International Labor Organization, copyright © 1992.

Figure 6.19. *Example of workplace arrangement*

6.6. Analysis of Micro-Motions

So far tasks have been broken down into operations, but these operations can be further broken down into micro-motions. This level of detail gives as a new vision about how to optimize work. An value-adding operation, according to previously discussed criteria, contains micro-motions with no added value. With analysis we will be able to improve those operations. This concept is shown in Figure 6.19. When the analyst has to analyze tasks where brief operations are repeated many times, the operation must be examined with great detail to determine where is it possible to save movements and effort, arranging the succession of gestures so that the operator can execute the operation with the least effort and fatigue.

Example

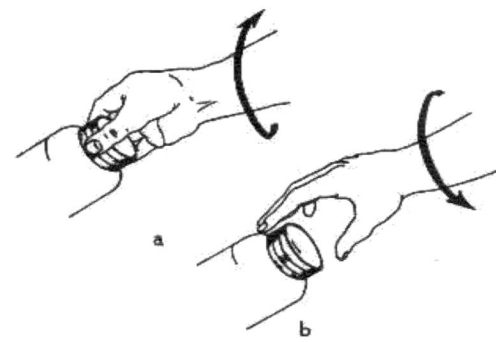

Breakdown of the operation "open bottle" into micro-operations				
Micro-operations	○	⇨	▢	▽
Hold cap.	•			
Turn hand counterclockwise.	•			
Release cap.	•			
Turn hand clockwise.	•			
Hold cap.	•			
Turn hand counterclockwise.	•			
Release cap.	•			
Turn hand clockwise.	•			
Hold cap.	•			
Turn hand counterclockwise.	•			
Move hand toward table.		•		
Place cap on table.				•

Summary table of methods		
Classification of micro-operations		Units
Total value-adding operations.	○	10.00
Total transfers.	⇨	1.00
Total storages.	▽	1.00
Total waits.	▢	0.00
Total		12.00

Figure 6.20. Breakdown of an operation into micro-operations

The Gilbreths developed an analysis technique to study the trajectory of movements made by an operator, which consists of fixing a small electrical lamp to the finger or body part being studied and later recording photographically the movements while the operators carry out the work or operation. These photographs provide a permanent record of motion trajectory and can be analyzed for potential improvement.

Gilbreth labelled each fundamental movement as a **therblig**, and concluded that every operation is composed of a series of 17 basic divisions. At the same time they can be divided in efficient therbligs and inefficient therbligs (it is analogous to the distinction between added value and no added value). Efficient therbligs contribute directly to the advance or development of the work. These therbligs frequently can be reduced, but it is difficult to eliminate them completely. Inefficient therbligs do not contribute to the advance of the process and must be eliminated.

The 17 fundamental movements are described here:

1. Search.

This basic element of an operation is the part of the cycle in which eyes or hands try to find an object. It starts the instant in which the eyes move in an attempt to locate an object, and ends the instant that they fix on the object found.

Search is a therblig that the analysis seeks to eliminate. Well-structured workplaces allow work to be accomplished continuously, so it is not necessary that the operator engage in this element. Positioning each tool and component in a precise location is a practical way to eliminate the search element in a workplace.

A new employee or one unfamiliar with the process has to perform search operations periodically, until developing enough skill.

> The expert motion analyst will pose the next questions, trying to reduce or eliminate the duration of the search:
> - Are all articles perfectly identified? Could labels and colors be used?
> - Is it possible to use transparent containers?
> - Could a better workplace distribution eliminate searches?
> - Is illumination used correctly?
> - Could the set up of tools and parts be completed earlier?

As can be observed, these analysis checklists are similar in nature and purpose as those previously discussed, but here they are oriented to micro-motions.

2. Select.

This therblig is performed when the operator has to choose between two or more similar parts. This therblig generally follows the search, and it is difficult to determine even through the procedures of a micro-motion study when the search finishes and the selection starts. Frequently, the selection can exist without the search element, especially when it is a selective assembly. Select is also classified as an ineffective therblig and must be eliminated when possible from the work cycle through a better distribution of the workplace and a better control of the parts.

> To eliminate this therblig the analyst must ask:
>
> - Are the most common parts interchangeable?
> - Could the tools and parts be standardized?
> - Are parts and materials kept in the same box?
> - Would it be possible to use a rack or tray to facilitate the collocation of parts?

Among the factors that can hinder the execution of the selection, the analyst will find an inadequate distribution of the workplace, materials and parts without classification, or disorganization. However, the fulfilment of this micro-motion would improve with the placement of the material deposits in semicircles within the normal and maximum work areas.

3. Grasp.

This elementary movement that the hand makes when it closes its fingers around a component or part is an efficient therblig and generally cannot be eliminated; in many cases, however, it can be improved. It starts when fingers of one or both hands start to close around an object to get control of it, and ends the instant in which this control is achieved.

The grasp element almost always is preceded by "transport empty" and followed by "hold." Detailed studies have demonstrated that several forms of grasping exist, some of which require three times the amount of time that others do. The number of grasping operations should be minimized in the work cycle, and the parts to grasp must be prepared in such a way that the least amount of time can be spent in this operation. This goal is achieved when the object assumes a fixed location and remains in place, not interfering with the worktable, the box, or the surroundings.

The next questions are used to check out and try to help improve the grasp therblig executed during a cycle:

- Would it be advisable for the operator to take more than one object or part at a time?
- Could a contact grasp be used instead of a rise grasp? In other words, could the objects be brought closer by sliding them instead of grabbing and carrying them?
- Would it be feasible to simplify the operation of grabbing small parts by putting a flange to their box?
- Could tools or parts be brought closer to make their separation easier?
- Could vacuum or magnetic devices, or rubber thimbles be used?
- Would it be possible to use a conveyor?
- Has the template been designed so that the part can be grabbed easily when removed?
- Would it be feasible for an operator to place a tool or part in a way that it facilitates the grabbing operation for the next operator?
- Could the tools be provided in an oscillating stand?
- Could the surface of the workbench be covered with a material that helps fingers grab small parts more easily?

4. Reach/transport empty.

The reach therblig corresponds to the movement of an empty hand, without resistance, toward an object or withdrawing from it. The basic division "reach" was named "transport empty" in Gilbreth's original list. Today, most method specialists accept the shorter term. Reach starts the instant the hand moves toward an object or place, and ends when it stops its movement on arrival at the object or place. This element normally is preceded by "release load" and followed by "grasp." It is natural that the time required to reach depends on the distance covered by the hand. Such time depends also, to a certain degree, on the type of reach. Like grab, reach can be classified as an efficient therblig and generally cannot be eliminated from the work cycle. However, it can be reduced by shortening the distance required and giving fixed locations to the objects. This fundamental principle is the goal for making workplaces in which minimum "reach" times are obtained.

5. Move/transport loaded.

The basic division that corresponds to a loaded hand movement can be in the form of pressure. "Move" was initially named "transport loaded." This therblig starts when a loaded hand moves toward a place or general location, and ends the instant in which the movement stops as it reaches its destination. "Move" is normally preceded by "grasp" and followed by "release load" or "position."

The required time to move depends on the distance, the weight that is moved, and the type of movement. Move is an effective therblig and difficult to eliminate from the work cycle. Still, its execution time can be reduced by shortening the distances, lightening the load, or improving the type of movement through gravity conduits or conveyor belts at the final point of the movement so that it is not necessary to materially carry the object that needs to be moved to a specific location. Experience has proven that move operations to a general location are performed quicker than those that move to a specific location.

> Both move and reach therbligs can be improved by asking and answering the following questions:
>
> - Could these therbligs be eliminated?
> - Could the distances be conveniently shortened?
> - Are the best means of transportation being used (such as pliers, holders, etc.)?
> - Are the appropriate parts of the body used, like fingers, wrist, forearm, or shoulder?
> - Would it be possible to use gravity conduits?
> - Could the transportation be made by mechanized equipment and pedal apparatus?
> - Could the transportation time be reduced by transporting bigger quantities of elements?
> - Is the time increased due to the nature of the transported materials, or by having to place it in a determined position?
> - Can abrupt changes in direction be avoided?

6. Hold.

Hold is the basic division that takes place when one hand supports or exercises control over an object, while the other hand executes useful work. Hold is an inefficient therblig and generally can be eliminated from the work cycle by designing a template or holding device that holds the part on which an operator

6. Methods Analysis

is working, instead of having to use the hand. Also, a hand is hardly an efficient holding device, so the methods analyst must always be alert to avoid a hold as part of the work assignment.

Hold starts the instant in which one hand exerts control over the object, and ends the moment in which the other hand completes the work on it. A typical example occurs when the left hand holds a bolt or gland stud while the other one screws it in. During the assembly of nut and bolt, the left hand will be using the hold therblig.

> This element can nearly always be eliminated by answering these questions:
> - Can a mechanical template, a press or clamp, a pin, a hook, a zipper, a clip, or nothing at all be used?
> - Could friction be used?
> - Would it be feasible to use a magnetic device?
> - Could dual attachment devices be used?

7. Release load.

This element is the basic division that occurs when the operator stops controlling the object. Release load is the therblig that is executed in the shortest time and little can be done to alter the time of this effective therblig.

Release load starts the moment in which fingers start to separate from the load, and ends the instant that fingers are free from it. This therblig nearly always is preceded by "move" or "position" and followed by "reach."

> To improve or eliminate the release load duration, the analyst asks the following questions:
> - Can release load be performed while walking?
> - Could a mechanical ejector be used?
> - Are the boxes that are the destination for the part after releasing the load adequate and have an adequate size?
> - After finishing the release, are hands left in an advantageous position for the next therblig?
> - Could several objects be released at once?

Industrial Productivity

8. Position

This working element consists of placing an object in such a way that it is left properly oriented in a specific location.

The therblig "position" occurs when the hand or hands try to place the part in a way that the next operation can be executed more easily. In fact, position can be the combination of several quick movements. "Position" is generally preceded by "move" and followed by "release load," and starts as soon as the hand or hands that control the object begin to agitate, turn, or slide the part to orientate it to the adequate position and ends as soon as the hand starts to withdraw from the object.

> "Position" can generally be eliminated or improved answering these and other verification questions:
>
> - Could we use means such as a guide, funnel, nozzle, swing bracket, locating pin, recess, cotter, wedge, pilot or marking signals, or bevels?
> - Could it be possible to change the tolerances?
> - Could the hole be countersunk?
> - Could a template be used?
> - Do burrs from the orifice increase the problem to position?
> - Could the item be used as a pilot?

9. Preposition.

This work element consists of placing an object in a predetermined place in a way that it can be grasped and moved to the position where it has to be held, when necessary.

The prepositioning occurs frequently with another therblig, normally "move." It is the basic division that prepares a part so that it ends up in a convenient position on its arrival. It is difficult to measure the necessary time for this element, because it is a therblig that can hardly be separated. Prepositioning can take place when aligning a screwdriver, while it moves toward a screw that must be loosened.

> The next questions will help the analyst study the prepositioning therblig:
>
> - Can a tool-holder device be used in the workstation to hold tools with their handles upwards?
> - Could the tools be hung?

- Is it possible to use a guide?
- Is it possible to use cartridge supplies?
- Could an automatic device be used to pile up parts?
- Would it be feasible to use a revolving device?

10. Inspect

This therblig is included in the operation to secure an acceptable quality through a regular verification made by the worker who performs the operation.

An inspection is carried out when the main purpose is to compare a given object with a pattern or standard. Usually it is not difficult to distinguish when this work element happens, because eyes get fixed on the object and a noticeable delay happens between movements while the mind decides whether to accept or reject the particular part. Time spent in inspection depends on the severity of the standard and how the part differs from it. If an operator had to draw blue marbles from inside a box, he would lose little time deciding what to do with a red marble. However, if he chose a purple marble, he would hesitate longer in deciding to accept or reject it.

The analyst can reduce the duration of this "inspect" therblig as a result of considering the following questions:

- Could the inspection be eliminated or combined with another operation or therblig?
- Could gauges be used or multiple-type checks?
- Would inspection time be reduced with better illumination?
- Are objects inspected at the correct distance from the operator's eyes?
- Would an outline help the inspection?
- Could a photocell or "electronic eye" be used?
- Would the production volume justify an automatic electronic inspection?
- Would a magnifying glass facilitate the inspection of small parts?
- Is the best inspection method available being used?
- Has the use of polarized light, acoustic tests, performance or behavior tests, template gauges, etc., been considered?

11. Assemble.

The assemble element occurs when two corresponding parts are united. It is another effective therblig and can be easier to improve than to eliminate. The assembly can be preceded by "position" or "move," and generally is followed by "release load." It starts the instant in which both parts are brought in contact, and ends when they complete the union.

12. Disassemble.

This element is precisely the contrary of "assemble." It occurs when assembled parts are separated. This basic division generally is preceded by "grasp" and followed by "move" or "release load." The disassembly has an effective nature and improvement possibilities are more probable than the elimination of this therblig. The disassembly starts the moment in which one or both hands get control of the object, after grabbing it, and ends once the disassembly finishes, which is generally evidenced by the beginning of "move" or "release load."

13. Use.

This therblig is completely effective and takes place when one or both hands control an object during the part of the cycle in which productive work is executed. When both hands hold a melted part against a grinding wheel, "use" will be the therblig that indicates the action of both hands. After a screwdriver has been positioned in the groove of a screw head, the element "use" will start the instant the screw starts to move. The duration of this therblig depends on the type of operation, as well as the dexterity of the operator. "Use" can be detected easily, because this therblig makes the operation progress toward its final objective.

> When studying these last three effective therbligs—assemble, disassemble, and use—the following questions must be considered:
> - Could a template or holding device be used?
> - Would the activity or the kind of work justify the use of automated equipment?
> - Would it be practical to perform the assembly of several units at the same time?
> - Would it be possible to use a more efficient tool?
> - Would it be feasible to use blocks?
> - Does the tool operate with the supplies and speeds of highest efficiency?
> - Should a mechanized or electric tool be used?

14. Unavoidable delay.

An unavoidable delay is an interruption that the operator cannot avoid in the continuity of work. It corresponds to downtime in the work cycle experienced by one or both hands, depending on the nature of the process. For example, when an operator drills with his or her right hand a part placed in a template, an unavoidable delay appears in the left hand. Because the operator cannot control the unavoidable delay, its elimination from the cycle requires the process to change somehow.

15. Avoidable delay.

All downtime that occurs during the work cycle and for which only the operator is responsible, intentionally or not, is classified as avoidable delay. In this way, if an operator suffers from a coughing fit during work, this delay is classified as avoidable because normally it would not appear in the cycle. The majority of possible avoidable delays can be eliminated by the operator without changing the process or method by which the work is done.

16. Plan.

The plan therblig is the mental process that occurs when the operator stops to determine the next action to follow. Planning can appear at any stage of the cycle and normally is easily discovered in the form of hesitation, after having located all the components. This therblig is characteristic of inexperienced operators and generally is eliminated from the cycle by an adequate training of the workforce.

17. Rest.

This kind of delay rarely appears in the work cycle, but it does appear periodically when recovering from fatigue is necessary. The duration of rest to cope with fatigue will vary, naturally, according to the type of work and the characteristics of the operator who undertakes it.

> To reduce the number of times the "rest" therblig appears, the analyst must consider:
>
> - Is the best classification used for the order of muscle use?
> - Are conditions of temperature, humidity, ventilation, noise, illumination, and others satisfactory?
> - Are workbenches set at a convenient height?
> - Is it possible that the operator can alternatively sit and stand while working?
> - Does the operator have a comfortable chair, with an adequate height?
> - Are mechanical means used to handle heavy loads?

Figure 6.21 shows a table with the previously described 17 therbligs, identifying each one with its corresponding symbol according to the UNE 52002 standard.

Format

Name of Therblig	Symbol	Graphic symbol
Search	Sh	
Select	St	
Find	F	
Grasp	G	
Transport empty	TE	
Transport loaded	TL	
Hold	H	
Release load	RL	
Position	P	
Preposition	PP	
Inspect	I	
Assemble	A	#
Disassemble	DA	#
Use	U	U
Unavoidable delay	UD	
Avoidable delay	AD	
Plan	Pn	
Rest	R	

Figure 6.21. *Therbligs and their UNE 52002 standard symbols*

Nowadays using video for recording motion is increasingly widespread. Video is also used to record the transfers of workers and materials in certain workplaces. The analyst can quickly realize a variety of useful data that will help in analyzing operations and devising new work methods.

Video presents a series of advantages in comparison to direct observation of tasks:

- Records more details than human eyes.
- Leaves a more exact record than timing methods.
- Provides a real document.
- Contributes to improvements for work specialists.

In conclusion, it is important to note that micro-motion analysis will always be able to find margin for improvement within the micro-operation. The possibilities of improvement are high.

The recording and analysis of micro-motions is shown in the following example of "opening a door with its key." Once a record of micro-operations is made, the analysis seen in this chapter will be applied to each as a way to improve the task.

Example

Breakdown of the operation "open lock with its key" into micro-operations

N°	Micro-operations	Symbol	Graphic symbol
1	Move hand toward pocket.	AL	⌣
2	Look inside pocket (select between coins, car keys).	S	→
3	Grasp key-ring inside pocket.	T	∩
4	Move key-ring toward viewing area.	AL	⌣
5	Place key-ring in searching position.	P	9
6	Select key from inside key-ring.	S	→
7	Grasp selected key.	T	∩
8	Place key in previous position.	PP	8
9	Move toward lock.	M	⌒
10	Place in previous position, in front of lock.	PP	8
11	Position key inside lock.	P	9
12	Turn key to open.	U	U
13	Open door (with the other hand).	M	⌒
14	Turn key to extract it from lock.	PP	8
15	Extract key from lock.	M	⌒
16	Move toward pocket.	M	⌒
17	Position in pocket.	P	9
18	Release keys in pocket.	SL	⌒
19	Take hand from pocket.	M	⌒

Figure 6.22. Breakdown of operation into micro-motion

All micro-operations with the potential for improvement will be analyzed in order to reduce or eliminate the duration of that therblig:

- Search inside the pocket.
    - Is it possible to have an exclusive pocket for keys and avoid looking for them?
- Select the key.
    - Could we avoid having so many keys on the key ring that are not used and only have the ones normally used, so that the "select" operation is not necessary?
    - If the previous question was affirmative, perhaps the movement of the hand from the pocket to a vision zone and the prepositioning of the key ring to a search position can be avoided.
- Position the key inside the lock.
    - It is an effective therblig and cannot be eliminated; nonetheless, is the lock cylinder correctly greased for the positioning?
- Turn the key to open.
    - This therblig is also effective and cannot be eliminated: however, is the lock cylinder correctly greased for the turn to be made in the shortest time possible?
- The opening operation requires little concentration, if we open with the opposite hand to the one that is operating, could operations 14 to 19 be made in parallel with 13? This way we would have a bimanual diagram.

Example

Sheet for hand movement analysis

Operation:	Open door with its key	Company:	
Date:	2011/04/27	Task:	
Analyst:	Jeremy Rogers	Process:	
Operator:	Luke Stewart	Area:	

N°	Movement Analysis of Left Hand	Graphic Symbol	Time (sec)	N°	Time (sec)	Graphic Symbol	Movement Analysis of Right Hand
1	Move hand toward pocket.		1.2				
3	Grasp key-ring inside pocket.		0.9				
7	Grasp selected key.		0.5				
8	Place key in previous position.		0.2				
9	Move toward lock.		0.6				
10	Place in previous position, in front of lock.		1				
11	Position key inside lock.		0.6				
12	Turn key to open.		0.3				
14	Turn key to extract it from lock.		0.8	13	0.8		Open door (with the other hand).
15	Extract key from lock.		0.6	13	0.6		Open door (with the other hand).
16	Move toward pocket.		0.4	13	0.4		Open door (with the other hand).
17	Position in pocket.		0.8	13	0.8		Open door (with the other hand).
18	Release keys in pocket.		0.4	13	0.4		Open door (with the other hand).
19	Take hand from pocket.		0.9	13	0.9		Open door (with the other hand).

Figure 6.23. Bimanual diagram of the operation

Frequently the analyst must perform method studies of diverse difficulty; in general an analyst will be able to verify how the most obvious detail goes unnoticed by the operator performing the task.

In assembly works, the repetition and duration of micro-motions make the construction of a bimanual diagram especially helpful in analyzing the micro-motions of the left and right hand in parallel. This diagram is especially important when both hands are engaged in different micro-operations. Therblig symbols from Figure 6.22 would be used, as they were in Figure 6.23.

Industrial Productivity

Format

	Sheet for hand movement analysis							
Operation:			Company:					
Date:			Task:					
Analyst:			Process:					
Operator:			Area:					
N°	Movement Analysis of Left Hand	Graphic Symbol	Time (sec)	N°	Time (sec)	Graphic Symbol	Movement Analysis of Right Hand

Figure 6.24. Basic format for bimanual diagram operations

Questions

1. What is methods analysis? What is obtained with it?
2. What methodology is used for detecting possible improvements in a method or operation?
3. What type of operations must the analysis of methods detect?
4. Indicate five preliminary questions for the analysis of methods.
5. Indicate four types of checklists for background questions.
6. Is an operation divisible into other elements? What are they called?
7. How many types of micro-motions did the Gilbreths define?
8. From this classification, how many types contribute to added value?

9. Is the following statement true? "If an operation can be carried out with only hand movements, it is better than if we have to use the forearm."

10. List the five types or levels of movements that are defined in motion economy.

Problems

1. Analyze the method from problem 1 of Chapter 5, making use of the tools shown in this chapter.

2. Analyze the method from problem 2 of Chapter 5, making use of the tools shown in this chapter.

3. Make a study of methods and list the therbligs for both hands for the operation of making a phone call from a public phone. The phone number is memorized so consulting the directory is not necessary.

4. Give an example of each type of therblig corresponding to operations with which you are familiar.

Bibliography

Aguirre de Mena, Juan M. María Mercedes Rodríguez Fernández, and Dolores Tous Zamora, *Organización y métodos de trabajo* (Ediciones Pirámide, 2002).

Gilbreth, Frank B. and Lillian Moller Gilbreth, *Cheaper by the Dozen* (New York: Thomas Y. Crowell Co., 1948).

Kanawaty, George, *Introduction to Work Study* (Geneva, International Labor Organization, 1992).

Martín López, Milagro; María Elena Robles Rábago, Francisco José González Domínguez, and Juan Manuel Crespo Pérez, *Métodos de trabajo: Casos Prácticos* (Ediciones Pirámide, 2001).

Chapter 7

Design of the Improved Method

7.1. Introduction

The two previous chapters discussed the study of methods and its analysis. The study of methods allows the operations to be known. Later, the described and current method will undergo critique through the different interrogatory lists. This task is what we have named analysis. This analysis shows the deficiencies or the improvable areas within the method under study. In this chapter, we will work on correcting any identified deficiencies.

> A detected deficiency becomes an available improvement and we have to materialize it.

If, for example, the diagnosis of an operatory method shows too many transfers, what the analyst has to do is find out the solution and devise an improvement that can be put into practice.

Devising improvements requires creative work because the engineer is faced with a challenge of nonexisting solutions that first have to be conceived. However, as in the case of method analysis in which, thanks to checklists, all deficiencies can be identified, the creativity can follow a systematic strategy. Like everything that follows a method, the chances of success are greater.

Industrial Productivity

In this chapter different methodologies of idea generation will be shown, which will help to improve the methods, along with practical examples of success. A catalog of common solutions will be given for the existing methods.

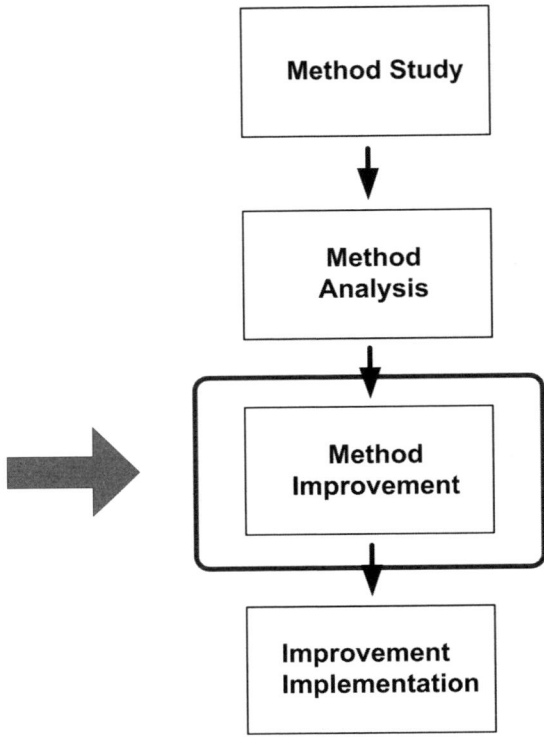

Figure 7.1. Phase 3 of the methods creation process

As a fundamental principle, improving an existing method will consist of eliminating all the non-value-adding operations and, once all the possible non-value-adding operations are eliminated, improving the value-adding ones. Figure 7.2 shows the operations method that underwent the interrogatory method in Chapter 6.

7. Design of the Improved Method

Example

Document 2 - Study of task methods: Place insert

Description of Operation	Type of Operation	Distance (meters)	Unit Time (sec)	Units	Operation Time (sec)	% Operation in Task
Provision panel. Remove protector paper.	○		10.73	2.00	21.46	2.13%
Provision set of bits for drill.	○		6.79	1.00	6.79	0.67%
Deposit panel on worktable.	○		2.19	1.00	2.19	0.22%
Take panel.	○		35.09	1.00	35.09	3.48%
Assemble bit on column drill.	○		8.63	1.00	8.63	0.86%
Place wooden piece in column drill base.	○		17.69	8.00	141.51	14.05%
Perform a predrill in panel to place floating inserts.	○		30.91	1.00	30.91	3.07%
Exachange bit for bidiametral bit in column drill.	○		14.78	8.00	118.24	11.74%
Perform a predrill in panel to place floating inserts.	○		5.98	1.00	5.98	0.59%
Disassemble bidiametral bit. Remove panel.	○		5.51	2.00	11.03	1.10%
Take seat. Turn panel over on worktable. Provision tweezers.	○		18.05	2.00	36.09	3.58%
Provision floating inserts. Extract set of inserts.	○		15.37	8.00	122.97	12.21%
Fit floating inserts in performed holes.	○		97.00	1.00	97.00	9.63%
Provision glue kit. Prepare it for use mixing in machine. Remove plunger.	○		27.42	1.00	27.42	2.72%
Put on work gloves.	○		30.44	1.00	30.44	3.02%
Assemble applicator in kit. Assemble kit in application gun. Conect to compressed air intake.	○		6.51	8.00	52.12	5.18%
Apply glue on hole. Check glue emerges from other end	○		10.36	8.00	82.89	8.23%
Clean excess glue in inserts with paper.	○		7.26	2.00	14.51	1.44%
Free panel to dry glue.	○		5.51	2.00	11.03	1.10%
Provision panel and take seat. Provision pliers.	○		18.85	8.00	150.77	14.97%
			Total task execution time:		1,007.04	100.00%
			Standard time:		503.52	

Figure 7.2. Basic example of method improvement— eliminate any non-value-adding operation

As confirmed by the data, once the improvement of the operatory method of the task under study has been implemented, a reduction of almost 50 percent in the execution time was achieved through the elimination of non-value-adding operations.

Industrial Productivity

Eliminating and/or reducing these operations is sometimes easy and immediate but other times will require creativity and innovation. The definitions of these two terms are the following:

- *Creativity* is the process or mental game, free from censorship and restriction, that allows unlimited idea creation.
- *Innovation* is the applicability of creative ideas with the purpose of achieving the objectives of a person or organization effectively.

7.2. Creativity and Generation of Ideas

In order to be creative it is necessary to have a process for the generation of ideas. The proposed process has four steps:

1. Finding the problem
2. A clear enunciation of the problem and of the desired situation
3. The generation of ideas
4. The selection of ideas

In this section the four steps will be applied to the improvement of methods through practical examples.

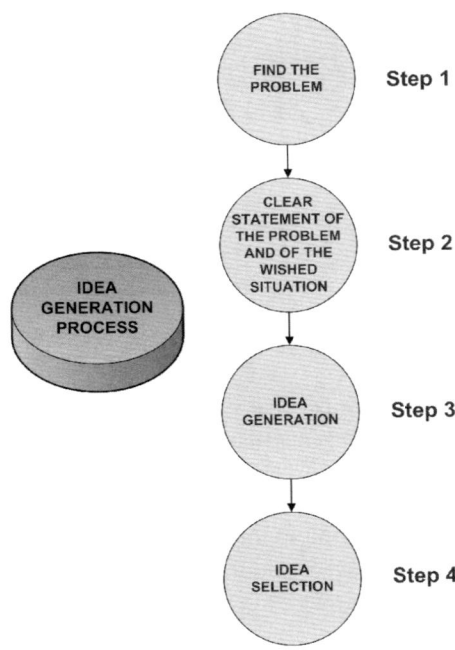

Figure 7.3. Steps for generating ideas

7.2.1. Finding the Problem

Evidently, before looking for the solution, the problem needs to be discovered. The problem is the first source of creativity and, later, of innovation.

It can be said that finding the problem has already been studied in the previous chapter, meaning that the analysis of methods, the interrogatories, help to find where the problem is. In general, the problems in working methods are:

- Operations that should not be done
- Tasks of no added value
- Inadequate materials
- Value-adding tasks that can be improved

Next, Figure 7.4 details the result of the criticism of the operative method from Figure 7.2, or the problems the analyst detected as a result of using the tools explained in the previous chapters.

Example

Document 2 - Method study of the task: Place Insert				Problem definition
Description of Operation	Type of Operation	Operation Time (sec)	% Operation in Task	Particular Problems
Provision panel. Remove protector paper.	○	21.46	1.07%	
Provision set of bits for drill.	○	6.79	0.34%	
Transfer toward following workstation.	⇒	18.40	0.92%	The operator must travel 20 meters.
Deposit panel on worktable.	○	2.19	0.11%	
Search and provision of plans.	▷	66.60	3.33%	Search for plans that are not found in their location.
Perform drill markings with pencil and ruler.	⊘	474.26	23.69%	The operator needs to make marks to be able to perform the drills.
Store plans in closet.	▽	62.58	3.13%	This operation can be eliminated as consequence of the improvement of the previous ones.
Take panel.	○	4.60	0.23%	This operation can be eliminated as consequence of the improvement of the previous ones.
Transfer toward manual mechanizing area.	⇒	92.00	4.60%	The operator must travel 100 meters.
Deposit bits and panel in auxiliary table. Clear working area.	▽	6.65	0.33%	The operator must travel 100 meters.
Assemble bit on column drill.	○	35.09	1.75%	
Place wooden piece in column drill base.	○	8.63	0.43%	
Perform a predrill in panel to place floating inserts.	○	141.51	7.07%	
Exachange bit for bidiametral bit in column drill.	○	30.91	1.54%	
Perform a predrill in panel to place floating inserts.	○	118.24	5.91%	
Disassemble bidiametral bit. Remove panel.	○	5.98	0.30%	
Store bits. Turn off column drill.	▽	15.92	0.80%	The operator must travel 120 meters.
Transfer toward working area from manual mechanization area.	⇒	110.40	5.51%	The operator must travel 120 meters.
Deposit panel on worktable. Store bits on workbench.	▽	9.17	0.46%	The operator must travel 120 meters.
Take seat. Turn panel over on worktable. Provision tweezers.	○	11.03	0.55%	
Remove material leftovers from performed holes with help of tweezers.	⊘	115.80	5.78%	The operator must reprocess the item because of the state of the screws.
Provision floating inserts. Extract set of inserts.	○	36.09	1.80%	
Fit floating inserts in performed holes.	○	122.97	6.14%	
Provision glue kit. Prepare it for use mixing in machine. Remove plunger.	○	97.00	4.85%	
Put on work gloves.	○	27.42	1.37%	
Assemble applicator in kit. Assemble kit in application gun. Connect to compressed air intake.	○	30.44	1.52%	

***Figure 7.4a.** Outcome of criticism to the existing operatory method*

7. Design of the Improved Method

Apply glue in hole. Check glue emerges from other end.	○	52.12	2.60%	
Clean excess glue in inserts with paper.	○	82.89	4.14%	
Free panel to dry glue.	○	14.51	0.72%	
Provision panel and take seat. Provision pliers.	○	11.03	0.55%	
Remove insert protection plates. Check correct positioning of insert.	○	150.77	7.53%	
Transfer panel to following workstation.	⇒	9.20	0.46%	The operator must travel 10 meters.
Return to workplace.	⇒	9.20	0.46%	The operator must travel 10 meters.

Figure 7.4b. *Outcome of criticism to the existing operatory method*

Next to each operation is a description of the problem that was detected. In addition, general problems of the task can also be described, not only of the operation.

> Without problem detection, no possibility for improvement will be discerned.
>
> DETECTED PROBLEM = AVAILABLE IMPROVEMENT

7.2.2. The Clear Statement of the Problem and of the Desired Situation

There are no erroneous solutions, only poorly stated problems. A correctly stated problem is a solved problem. After finding out the problem, time should be invested in stating it properly.

Poorly stated problem:

"The transfers between the assembly area and the components shelf are excessive; the assemblers have to walk too much."

Correctly stated problem:

"The distance between the assembly workstation and the location of the covers is 20 meters, in the final stage of the assembly task, when placing the covers they have to move two times, representing a transfer distance of 80 meters."

Other examples of problem statement:

1. Having analyzed the work diagram of two operators in parallel it is observed that Operator 2 presents a saturation of 31 percent, meaning that 69 percent of the time the operator is idle, a great part of the process is the delay.

2. The task of riveting from the inside requires that the operator holds a lantern, enabling the operator to only operate with one hand and wasting the capacity of working with both hands in parallel.

Industrial Productivity

In the articulation of the problem, which defines the current situation, the desired situation must be stated so the analyst can focus effort in the desired situation. For the enumeration of the two previous problems, the objectives for the desired situation can be:

1. That the saturation of operators is at least 90 percent in this first phase of improvement.
2. That the operator can completely use both hands.

Example

Document 2 - Method study of the task: Place insert				Problem definition
Description of Operation	**Type of Operation**	**Operation Time (sec)**	**% Operation in Task**	**Problem - Possible solution**
Transfer to following workstation.	⇨	18.40	0.92%	The operator must travel 20 meters. Solution: Group the two workstations.
Search and provision of plans.	◻	66.60	3.33%	Search for plans that are not found in their location. *Solution: Design a template to mark the drills.*
Perform drill markings with pencil and ruler.	◯	474.26	23.69%	The operator needs to make marks to be able to perform the drills. *Solution: Design a template to mark the drills.*
Store plans in closet.	▽	62.58	3.13%	This operation can be eliminated as consequence of the improvement of the previous ones. *Solution: Design a template to mark the drills.*
Take panel.	◯	4.60	0.23%	This operation can be eliminated as consequence of the improvement of the previous ones. *Solution: Design a template to mark the drills.*
Transfer toward manual mechanizing area.	⇨	92.00	4.60%	The operator must travel 100 meters. Solution: Transfer the drill to the workstation.
Deposit bits and panel in auxiliary table. Clear working area.	▽	6.65	0.33%	The operator must travel 100 meters. Solution: Transfer the drill to the workstation.
Store bits. Turn off column drill.	▽	15.92	0.80%	The operator must travel 120 meters. Solution: Transfer the drill to the workstation.
Transfer toward working area from manual mechanization area.	⇨	110.40	5.51%	The operator must travel 120 meters. Solution: Transfer the drill to the workstation.
Deposit panel on worktable. Store bits on workbench.	▽	9.17	0.46%	The operator must travel 120 meters. Solution: Transfer the drill to the workstation.
Remove material leftovers from performed holes with help of tweezers.	◯	115.80	5.78%	The operator must reprocess the item because of the state of the screws. *Solution: Buy screws of better quality.*
Transfer panel to following workstation.	⇨	9.20	0.46%	The operator must travel 10 meters. Solution: Group the two workstations.
Return to workplace.	⇨	9.20	0.46%	The operator must travel 10 meters. Solution: Group the two workstations.

Figure 7.5. Solution to encountered problems in the operatory method

7.2.3. Generation of Ideas

Once the problem is stated precisely, the next step is to look for the cause or causes that, in turn, will have other causes. One of the keys for comprehending the problem consists of dividing the problem into smaller parts. One of the best approaches follows a cause-effect analysis of the problem. For problem solving it is essential to know the underlying causes. There are two tools:

- Ishikawa diagram
- The exercise of why

Ishikawa/Fishbone diagram

The objective of this technique is to help enumerate all the causes of the problem. With the use of this technique, additional advantages are obtained:

- Prompts new ideas about the possible causes.
- Helps to establish a logical sequence for manipulating the different parts of the problem.
- Prevents analysts from getting stuck in the problems that revolve around the same cause without finding a solution.
- Allows exploration of the problem from a holistic perspective.
- Helps to create solutions without having to go to the next parts of the cycle.

The fishbone diagram is a creation of Kaoru Ishikawa, professor at the University of Tokyo. It is named in this way because of its resemblance to the head and spine of a fish. On paper a straight line is drawn representing the backbone. Subsequently, lines are traced at 45° angle, with each line representing a possible cause of the problem. Each cause, in turn, can have more causes, so more ramifications will be traced from each possible cause to enumerate them. It does not matter whether a particular cause appears more than once. On the contrary, it must be emphasized because it may imply that it is the cause of the problem. Decomposing the problem in this way and fragmenting it into its main elements may facilitate the discovery of the cause.

Industrial Productivity

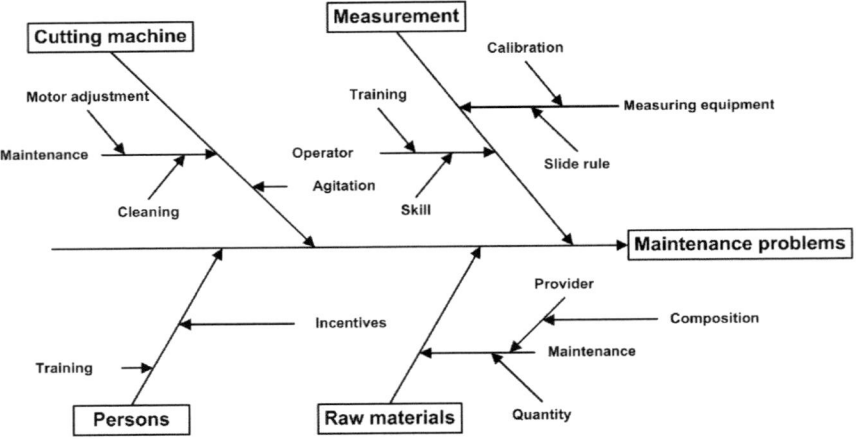

Figure 7.6. Ishikawa diagram or fish diagram

In the particular case of this chapter, the objective is bounded: it is the improvement of methods and processes, approached in such a way that a list of generic causes for the problems can be prepared and then illustrated in a fishbone diagram with their principal "predetermined" causes in order to work toward solutions:

- Poor design in the workplace
- Disorder
- Defective materials
- Imbalance between tasks
- Distant previous and subsequent tasks
- Distant location of materials
- Nonergonomic postures
- Delays
- Excessive storage
- Unnecessary inspections
- Searches
- Communications
- Undefined operatory method

7. Design of the Improved Method

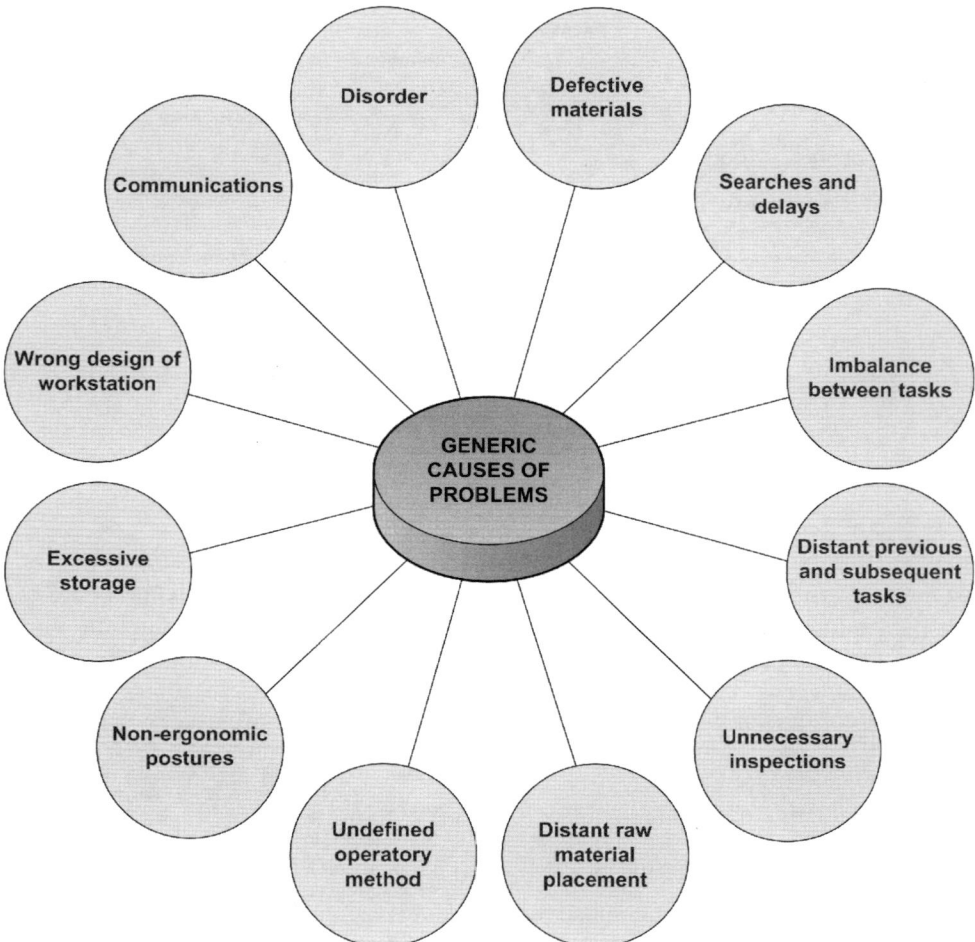

Figure 7.7. Generic causes for the problems.

And for one of these problems there exists one or several solutions. This chapter provides a table cataloging problems, causes, and solutions.

The Exercise of "Why"

The exercise of "why" can be used to fragment completely the causes. It consists of asking why five consecutive times, similar to the way children ask for explanations or clarifications and do not stop asking "Why? Why?" until they believe they have reached the core of the matter.

The exercise of "why" is combined with the fishbone diagram and often provides satisfactory, simple, and even unexpected results. The cycle follows this pattern:

Industrial Productivity

- Problem.
- Cause 1.
- Why does cause 1 happen?
- Cause 1.1 and cause 1.2.
- Why do cause 1.1 and cause 1.2 happen?
- Cause 1.1.1, cause 1.1.2, and cause 1.2.1.

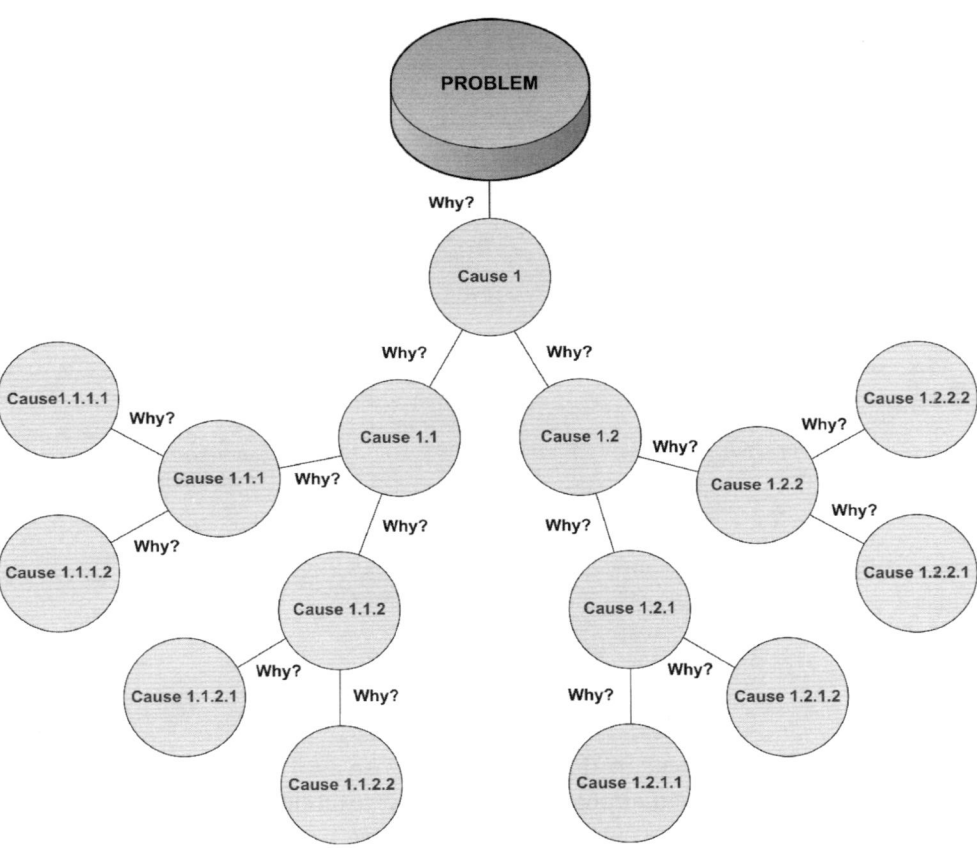

Figure 7.8. Outline of the "why" exercise

Each cause will have a cause, and it in turn may have several causes. A clear example is illustrated in Figure 7.9 and shows how to reach the origin of the problem using the exercise of "why."

7. Design of the Improved Method

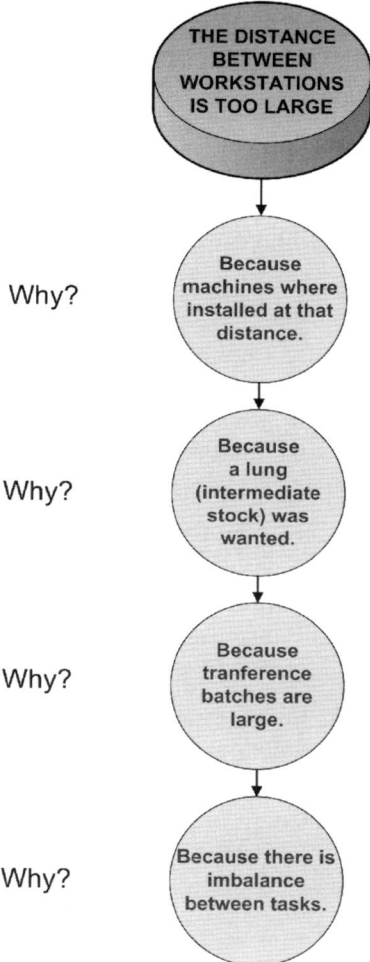

Figure 7.9. The exercise of "why"

In Figure 7.9 we see how making use of the "why" exercise reaches the origin of the problem, which allows us to act upon it. This exercise is fundamental, because if we do not reach the principal cause and the analysis stays at a previous step, cause may be mistaken with effect, resulting in action being taken on an effect and undoubtedly causing a failure in the improvement attempt, because the real cause is still not solved.

Once the cause is found, one can proceed to find the solution and the method improvement. This improvement will emerge from one idea. The generation of ideas must also follow a systematic procedure.

> Once the real underlying cause is found, the solution to the problem will be almost immediate.

The Generation of Ideas

Once the cause of a nonconformity or improvable situation is detected, it is time to eliminate it. How? At this point, several methods can be used to help in the generation of good ideas.

The "How" Diagram

The "how" diagram represents a similar approach to the "why" diagram. The only difference is that it tries to identify the diverse steps that must be taken when implementing a solution. It is a technique used in creative circles; it provides an opportunity to select ideas in a practical way and to sort out the results.

The procedure starts with an agreement between the participants about the cause to address. At this point, it is systematically questioned on how to solve it. Several routes are identified and each route presents several possible subroutes in response to "how." During the exhaustive discussion of each ramification, a convergent process can be used to narrow down the list of possibilities.

The "how" can then be restarted in that more narrow field of analysis in order to access some additional and more detailed steps of implementation. This method, well used, can constitute a valuable help for the selection of solutions and the initial preparation of an implementation plan. Figure 7.10 represents the "how" diagram.

7. Design of the Improved Method

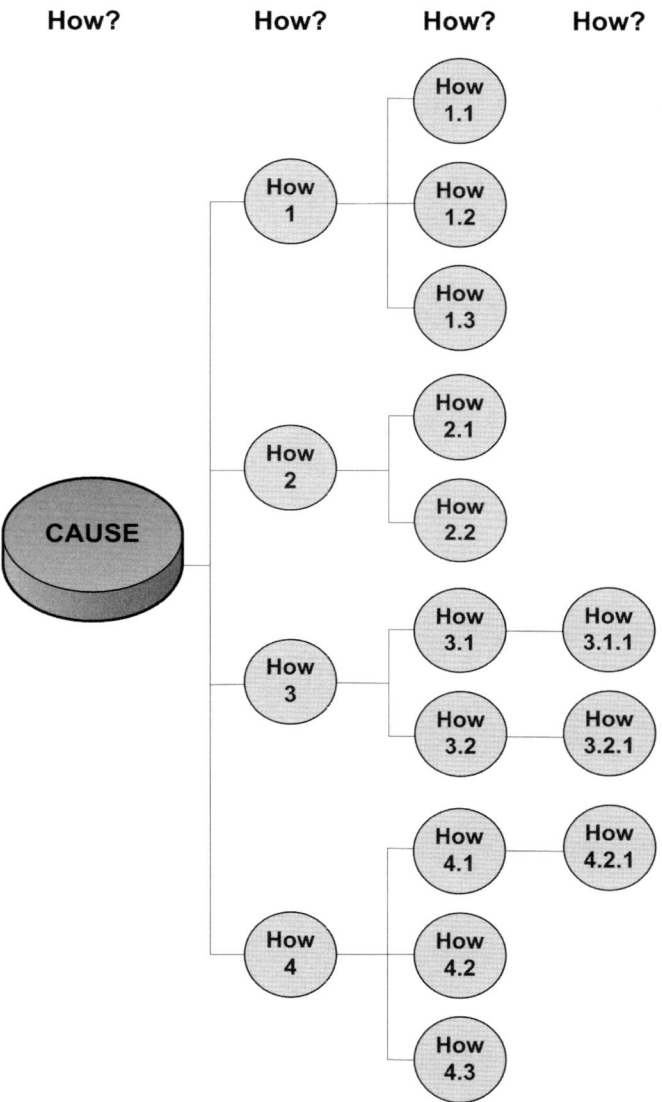

Source: "APRENDER A GENERAR IDEAS. Innovar mediante la creatividad" from Fabio Gallego Reinoso. Ed Paidós.

Figure 7.10. *"How" diagram in relation to a decision to solve a problem*

Industrial Productivity

The cause needing a solution is placed in the beginning of the diagram and from there on ideas for its solution are generated. Once a level of ideas considered executable has been reached, we will go on to select and implement the chosen idea.

Example

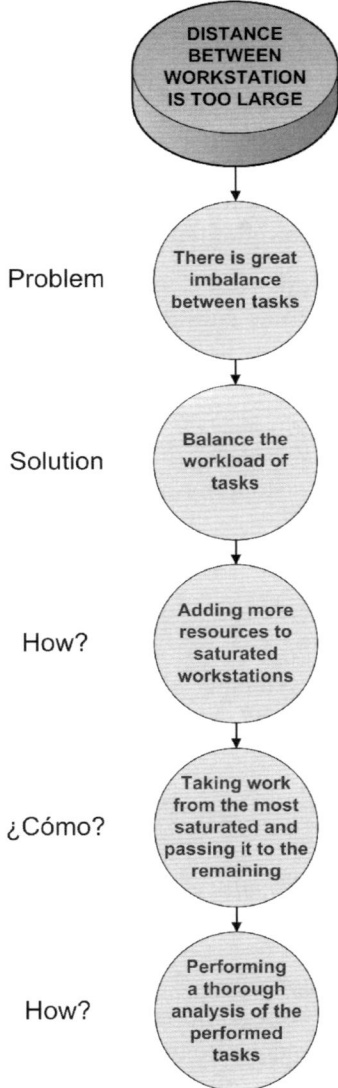

Figure 7.11. Exercise of "how" diagram

Indicating "how" we solve each of the whys found, we will manage to discover the solution to the origin of the problem. Frequently, when indicating how we solve one cause, implicitly we will solve another cause.

In the generation of ideas, quantity is equal to quality. The more ideas are contributed, however absurd and simple they may seem, the more likely a good idea will be found. Besides, the combination of two or more ideas can return additional applicable ideas.

7.3. Catalog of Solutions

Creativity can provide radical solutions and unexpected method improvements; however, several techniques have developed solutions for each type of problem in the designing of working methods, and these solutions have already been accepted. **It is important to keep in mind that creativity and cataloged solutions are nonexclusive; they are totally complementary.**

In designing the improved method, some solutions are generally applicable to all working methods. For all, the outline **common problems–causes–solutions** will be followed. This catalog of solutions provides a starting point for the generation of proposals for method improvement:

- The 5 S methodology
- The principles of motion economy
- Improvements in the designing of materials and material handling
- Benchmarking
- Work tools—tool catalogs
- Fast machine and tools exchange: SMED
- Work balancing with more than one participant
- Process improvement
- And the most important: IMPROVEMENT IN ERGONOMICS

Next is shown a table where common problems, the causes that normally cause them, and the catalog solutions are reflected. The analyst will search in that table for the solution to some problems. Normally, the application of one of the solutions will lead to the resolution of more than one problem. It is also probable that applying independently only one solution is not possible; additional solutions are sometimes necessary to complement one another.

Format

Problem - Analysis	Cause	Solution from Catalog
Excess transfers, delays, and communications due to prolonged searches	Disorder	*5 S*
Operator fatigued, excess of micro-operations moving parts of the body Inefficient therbligs	Poor design of the workstation	*Economy of movements*
Variety of raw materials and components, excess of residues and leftovers Excess time dedicated to handling	Materials that compose the product, nor their handling, have not been studied	*Design of the materials and handling*
Different operatory methods for the same task or objective	Lack of methods study, difficult procedures, or handicraft tasks	*Benchmarking*
Dangerous, heavy, and uncomfortable tools	Possession and use of such tools	*Study of tool catalogs*
High setup times for machines and tool changeovers	Lack of task method for changeover	*SMED*
In tasks with more than one participant: high waiting times in some of them	Simultaneous tasks or imbalanced assembly lines	*Balancing of tasks with more than one participant*
Excessive intermediate stock, transfer and transport tasks with high impact on time, production prevision out of control, large working areas	Process poorly designed or not designed	*Process improvement*
Occupational accidents, injuries, fatigued operators at the end of the day, standard times not met	Poor design of the workstations, insecure jobs, heavy and uncomfortable tools	*Ergonomics improvement*

Figure 7.12. Catalog of solutions

7.3.1. The 5S Methodology

5S is a methodology to ensure that work areas are systematically kept clean and tidy. It is an important tool if methods and processes are to be maintained and ensured. The main principle of 5S is "there should be a *place* for everything and everything should be in *its place.*"

> The objective of the 5S system is to reduce the execution time of the tasks due to searches, communications, waits, transfers, and errors caused by disorder.

The five stages of the process are:

- **1S – Seiri:** Separate the necessary from the unnecessary.
  And when in doubt, throw it out.
- **2S – Seinton:** Order, define the best place for everything.
  A place for everything and everything in its place.
- **3S – Seiso:** Cleaning of areas and elements.
  To be effective you must be clean.
- **4S – Seiketsu:** Create and establish the cleaning standards.
  Standardize the methods.
- **5S – Shitsuke:** Educate and communicate to sustain the four first in the long term.
  Maintain the standards.

The 5S methodology can be immediately implemented in the whole department, allowing for everyone to get involved in this activity. It is easy to understand and to carry out. To raise awareness and inform all personnel of the progress of the 5S implementation, a graph that reflects the five stages is designed. For effectiveness, it is located in the working area in plain sight. When one stage is implemented, it is identified on the graph, keeping all participants completely informed. Figure 7.13 provides a graph that will serve as a reference with further explanations of each of the stages.

Graph of 5S Follow-Up				
1º Sorting	2º Set in order	3º Systematic cleaning	4º Standardizing	5º Sustaining

Figure 7.13. Initial 5S graph

Separate the necessary from the unnecessary

And when in doubt, throw it out.

This stage distinguishes the necessary elements from the unnecessary ones in the workplace, separating them and getting rid of the latter, trying to avoid a future appearance of it. In this stage, all the unnecessary elements for the execution of work will be removed from the workplace. The team and/or worker will perform the following:

1. Define the place where the unnecessary elements are located.
2. Create the norms for objects and material that are not essential for the area.
3. Identify the unnecessary elements and label them in red.
4. Remove the identified elements.
5. Take responsibility [managers and team leaders] for the marked elements, which may include returning them to their area, creating a common area, or disposal.
6. Publish the 5S circle in common areas and stamp the first S.

Graph of 5S Follow-Up					
1º Sorting OK	2º Set in order	3º Systematic cleaning	4º Standardizing	5º Sustaining

Figure 7.14. Graph with first S completed

Order, define the best place for everything

A place for everything and everything in its place.

This S establishes the place assigned for each element, through either labels or visual marks. At this stage, the workspace is organized to avoid wasting time and energy. The team and/or worker will:

1. Mark common areas, labeling drawers and identifying everything that belongs to that area.
2. Create a standard for the selected area, a reference in case something is not in its place or has not been returned. It must be obvious when something is not in its place and each item must be labeled so that the place where it belongs is obvious.

7. Design of the Improved Method

3. Constantly protect the fulfillment of this S in the selected area.
4. After one or two weeks to confirm the fulfillment of this S, the stamp can be placed in the circle of the 5S graph.

Graph of 5S Follow-Up				
1º Sorting **OK**	2º Set in order **OK**	3º Systematic cleaning	4º Standardizing	5º Sustaining

Figure 7.15. Graph with second S completed

Cleaning of areas and elements

To be effective you must be clean.

This S sets the basic cleaning of the work area, establishing the frequency for such cleaning on a regular basis. Activities range from the cleaning of tools and worktable to the scrubbing of floors. The team must perform the initial cleaning and later create the cleaning plan, which may be achieved the following way:

1. Establish a special time for the initial cleaning.
2. Create the cleaning plan (it can be daily, weekly, monthly, etc.).
3. Place the stamp on the third part of the 5S graph.

The 5S is a team process, but also involves the individual compromise of workers in their own areas. The important point is to identify what needs to be cleaned, how it needs to be kept clean, and by whom. All the former, together with a visual table help to ensure that the process is followed.

Graph of 5S Follow-Up				
1º Sorting **OK**	2º Set in order **OK**	3º Systematic cleaning **OK**	4º Standardizing	5º Sustaining

Figure 7.16. Graph with third S completed

281

Industrial Productivity

Create and establish the cleaning standards

Standardize the methods.

To standardize implies creating norms for keeping an area organized, neat, and clean, and includes determining visual and obvious standards. In order to standardize the methods, it is necessary to carry out the procedures in which the standards will be given by corresponding technical instructions.

Example

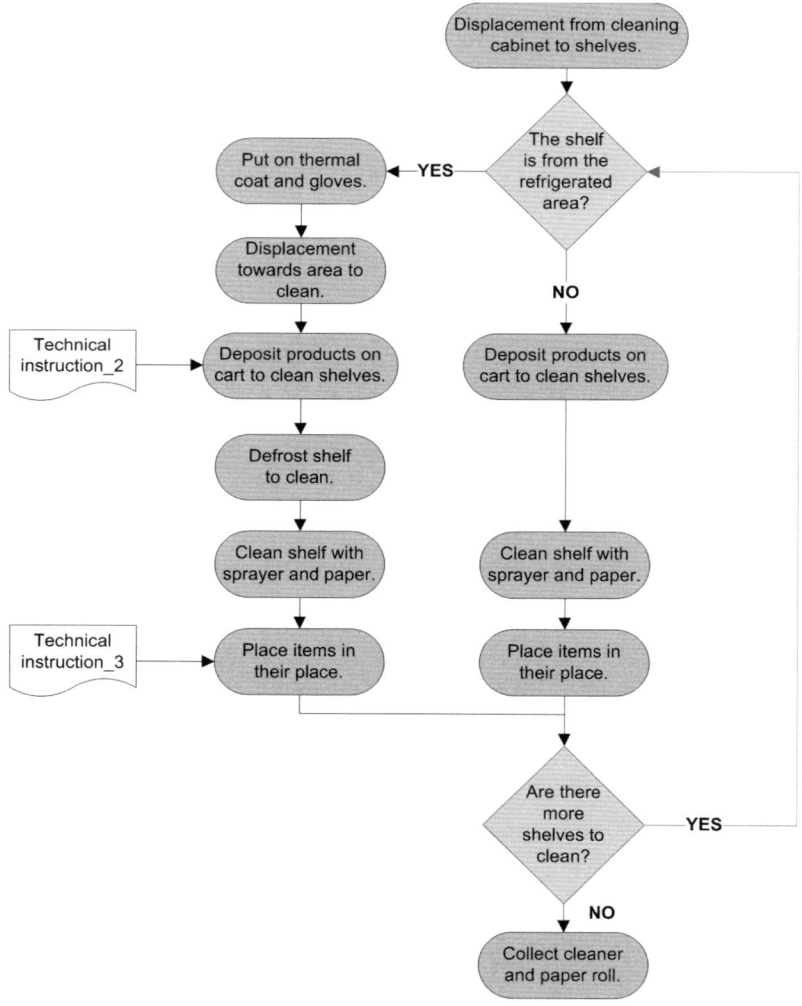

Figure 7.17. Process of cleaning shelves

In Figure 7.17, the logical sequence of each of the operations that compose the task of cleaning shelves is evident.

> Once the ordering procedure is determined, we have to define who will perform it, when (frequencies), and how much time is assigned. Without these assignments, the procedure will not take place, because more "urgent" things will interfere and the 5S will not be maintained.

Therefore, the following points need to be fulfilled:

1. Identify the selected area.
2. Specify (prepare a list on paper) the tasks and when they would have to be done.
3. Decide who will perform the tasks; indicate it in a column.
4. Decide the frequency and the necessary resources; indicate it in a column.
5. Indicate how much time will be dedicated.
6. Publish the standard time of the selected area.
7. Place the stamp on the fourth part of the 5S graph.

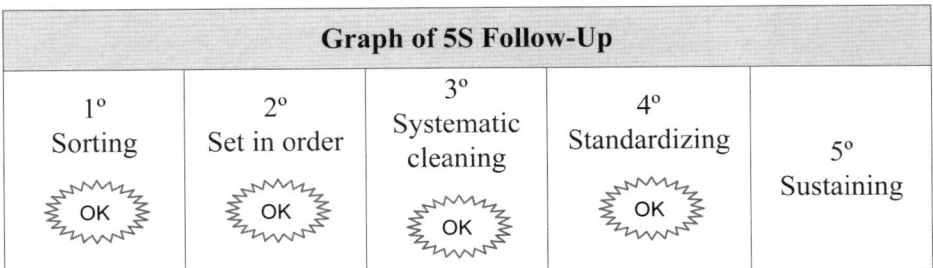

Figure 7.18. Graph with fourth S completed

Educate and communicate to sustain the four first in the long term

Maintain the standards.

This stage focuses on turning the proper maintenance of the procedures into habit, that is, to work permanently in accordance with the established standards, monitoring the 5S methodology and elaborating actions for continuous improvement. Once implemented, the new method must be maintained, which necessitates periodic audits. This S presupposes that all employees are trained in the 5S methodology.

Industrial Productivity

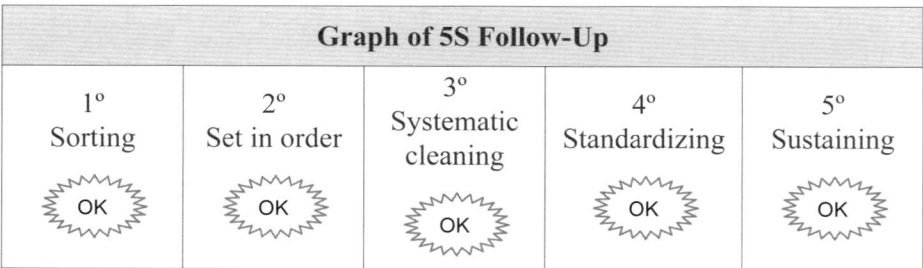

Figure 7.19. Graph with fifth S completed

The benefits of the 5S methodology include the following:

- Involves all employees in a simple and useful tool.
- Helps eliminate wastes.
- Softens the workflow.
- Reduces the stress of employees who no longer have to perform frustrating tasks.
- Increases the time dedicated to value-adding tasks.
- Reduces the risks of accidents.
- Improves the quality of production.

In summary, the 5S improvement program instills order and thereby reduces the number of tasks corresponding to search, archive, move, and communicate. Operation tasks are also more efficient due to cleanliness.

Application of the 5S system is shown in the following images.

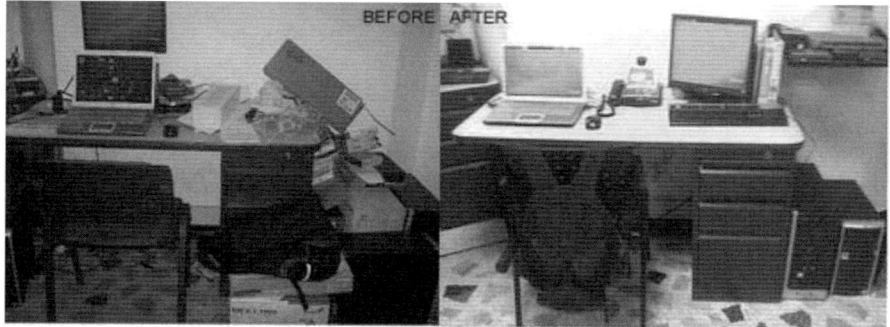

Figure 7.20. Image of workplace before and after applying the 5S methodology

7. Design of the Improved Method

Figure 7.21. Second S application: A place for everything and everything in its place

In Figure 7.21, on the left, apparently the elements deposited on the shelves are ordered; however, nothing has a specific place assigned on the shelf. Then, in the image on the right, on top of being ordered, each book has a place assigned. In this case within the shelf named "Engineering–Civil works," each of the shelves is labeled with several subcategories, and in turn each book is codified within that subcategory.

Figure 7.22. Example of 5S implementation

285

Industrial Productivity

Figure 7.23. Examples of 5S implementation

Figure 7.24. Example of 5S implementation

7. Design of the Improved Method

Industrial furniture products can be of great help for the improvement of order, material identification, and tools used.

Example

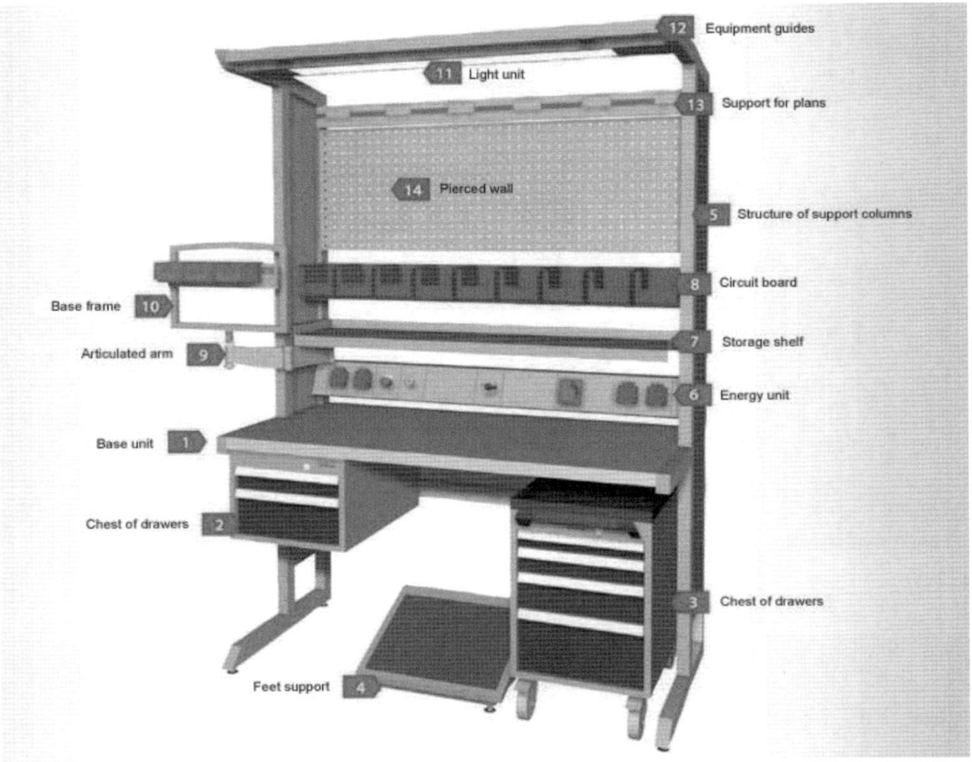

Source: © **Hoffmann** Group
Figure 7.25. Example of combinable workplace

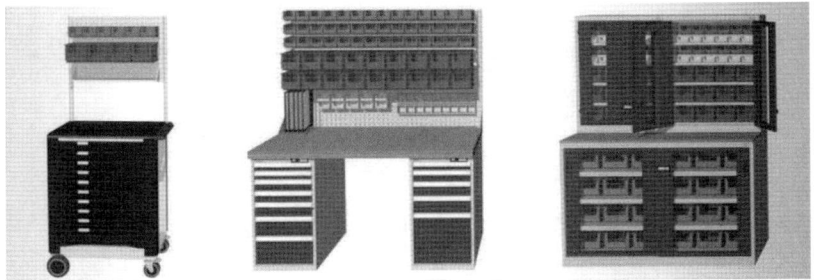

Source: © **Hoffmann** Group
Figure 7.26. Devices with storage boxes in sight

Industrial Productivity

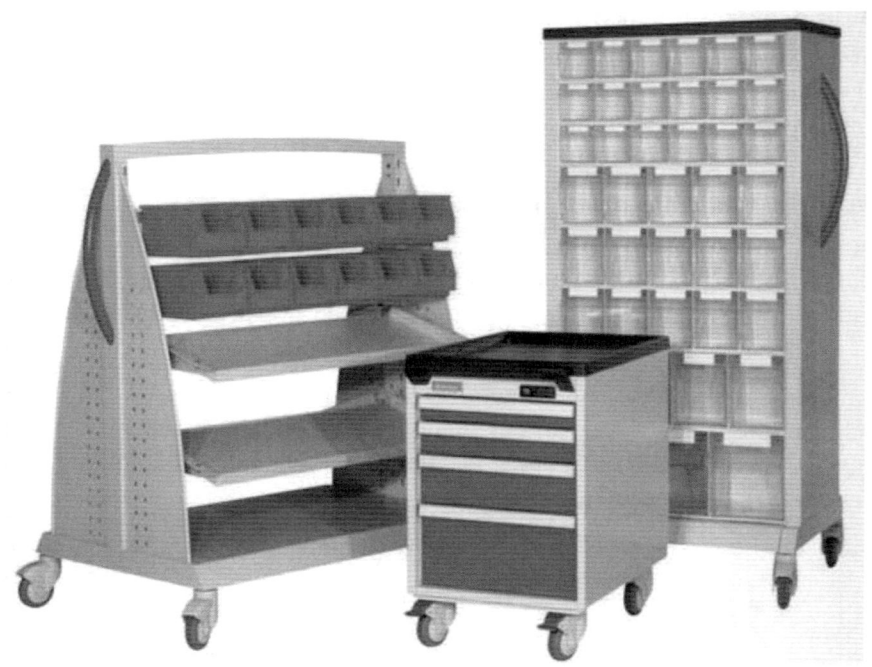

Source: © Hoffmann Group
Figure 7.27. Combinable and storage trolleys

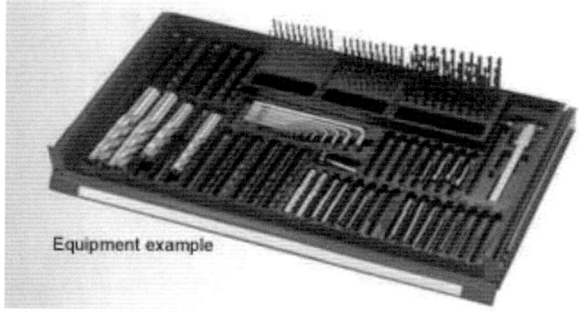

Source: © Hoffmann Group
Figure 7.28. Separators

7.3.2. Application of the Rules of Motion Economy

The rules of motion economy, which were discussed in detail in section 6.5, are a great tool for the design of workplaces. To eliminate and reduce movements implies more time to operate, to add value to the product. These rules are simple and their results are significant.

7.3.3. Improvements in the Use and Design of Materials

A way to reduce operation times and total manufacturing costs is to improve the purchase, design, handling, and types of materials. To do so, a series of rules and recommendations are recommended:

1. Avoid the transformation of material

If cutting, milling, grinding, and similar operations can be avoided by purchasing the material with specific measures or a specific treatment, then that change should be made.

The supplier may charge more for these materials;, if it reduces the processing cost and internal manipulation, then it may be cost beneficial to purchase the higher-priced materials. Maybe the supplier would not increase the charges. Perhaps making the change to those specifications for our convenience would not actually cause an increase in costs for the supplier.

Viewing suppliers as part of the process includes analyzing how they can provide raw materials efficiently to the process being improved.

Even packaging should be analyzed. In some circumstances, a supplier spends lots of money in packaging that is unnecessary for us. Because the cost of this packaging is included in the product price, cost could be reduced by eliminating it. Another aspect that would be eliminated is the work of unpacking.

2. Design of components

To reduce the number of assembly operations and therefore, their time, a series of aspects are studied relative to the components that can be more influential in the method improvement. These include the following:

- Use of lighter and more flexible materials when possible.

- Reduced tolerance requirements. On many occasions the product engineering departments, when in doubt, apply tolerances that do not correspond to a real need. This problem entails a totally unnecessary increase in time. This time can be multiplied by two, three, or more depending on the required tolerances.

- Reduced number of parts to assemble. For this, manufacture components that include all the parts or order them that way from the supplier.

- Product engineering. It must be designed not only thinking about the final product, but also taking into account how the components are assembled or manufactured.

- Reduced variety of components, always trying to unify when it is viable. Larger batches of components can be achieved, resulting in a reduction in the unit time. Subsequent management, searching times for components, obsolescence risk, and size of the stores are also reduced.

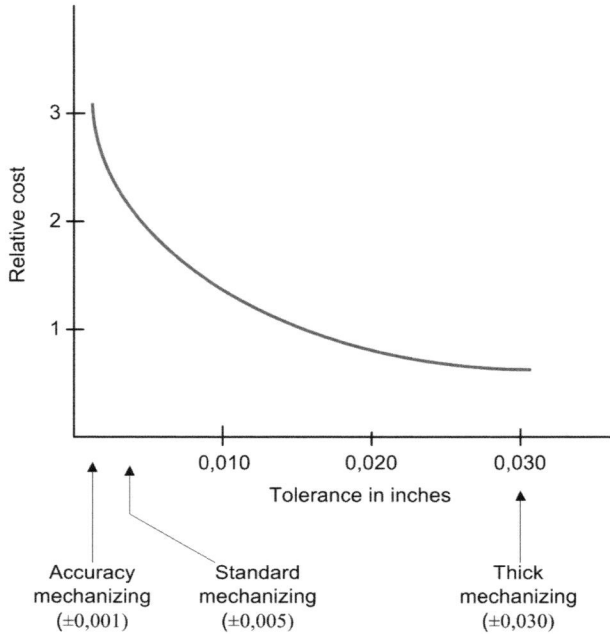

Figure 7.29. *Relation between cost and required tolerance*

3. Reduce the cost of materials

The standards for cost reduction of materials are simple; however, it is important to remember them.

- Purchase if possible in multiples, trying at the same time to avoid residuals.
- Use optimization programs for an efficient use of bars and surfaces to minimize waste.
- Purpose the residuals of smaller components.
- Reduce the variety of materials and components used. This approach results in less stock, and larger batches can be purchased from suppliers, reducing the purchase price. On the other hand, the raw material storage unit will be much easier to manage.
- Search for suppliers that integrate more into the process, thereby reducing supply costs.

- Search for cheaper materials.
- Search for materials that are easier to process.

4. Reduce the transport of materials

The time dedicated to the transport of materials from the warehouse to the factory, from one workstation to another, from the factory to the warehouse of finished products, and so on is often ignored and is high. It can become, in extreme cases, as much as 60 percent of the total manufacturing time; only a 40 percent of the time is it adding value to the product. The rules to reduce this time include the following:

- Do not ignore the time spent in transport, workstation positioning, warehouse positioning, and taking materials from the stores. To calculate these times will raise awareness of the cost involved.
- Avoid as far as possible leaving materials in the ground.
- Reduce the buffer stock. The less intermediate stock there is, the less will be required for material transport and material handling to and from the warehouses (see Chapter 10, *Process Improvement Criteria*).
- Force the reductions of factory space; more available space means more space to be occupied by materials (see Chapter 10, *Process Improvement Criteria*).
- Use automatic or mechanized means for material transport; the most interesting for the reduction of time are those that involve no intervention from the operator (see Chapter 10, *Process Improvement Criteria*):

    - Conveyor belts

    - Roller tracks

    - Worms

    - Air chains

    - Gravity falls

- Move materials once, which could be achieved with no intermediate stocks—the material would move from workstation n to $n + 1$ and nothing more, not as often occurs where it moves from workstation n to a buffer and from the buffer to workstation $n + 1$.
- Apply the concepts of motion economy.
- Whenever possible, make the transport of material form part of the manufacturing process, performing operations, and transformations.

- The 5S methodology facilitates the handling of materials.
- Industries with a vast variety of item references and/or components computerize material management in order to control search and inventory.
- Design the layout keeping in mind the criterion of minimum transfer of materials.
- Do not damage materials when handling: the transport operations, storage, turnover, and so on of materials sometimes cause damages and pose expensive repair operations. We must have:
    - Tools that exert less pressure and have a greater product-gripping surface
    - Tweezers and padded edges
    - Shelves to avoid stacking too much weight

7.3.4. Benchmarking

Benchmarking can be defined in business administration as a systematic and continuous process to evaluate comparatively the products, services, and processes of work in organizations. It consists of taking "comparators" or benchmarks to those products, services, and processes of specific companies that demonstrate best practices in the area of interest in order to transfer the knowledge of the best practices and their application.

In the area of work methods, it would consist of comparing some methods with others while performing the same task. The key then is to match the best-performing methods. We have to be careful with the use of this tool for improving methods. Initially the analyst must have clear criteria of motion economy and elimination of non-value-adding operations that are universal to any method. However, for some tasks the application of this criterion is not easy, especially when the task is "artisanal" or we are using a material not commonly used. In this case, each operator does the work as able or in the way he or she was taught.

For these labors, benchmarking can be a useful tool. From the analysis of several operators we deduce the best way of doing things within the method and establish that best way as standard. The concept is difficult to understand, perhaps for its simplicity; therefore a case of benchmarking application is shown applied to method improvement.

7.3.5. Work Tools—Tool Catalogs

The analyst of working methods must have access to all the information about manual tools, because they are a possible source of method improvement for ergonomic reasons, weight, speed, material termination, and so on. We must have

7. Design of the Improved Method

technical catalogs from leading manufacturers. What follows are some pictures and features of working tools and industrial furniture. There are also some references for manufacturers and/or distributors.

Distributor/Manufacturer	Web address
Hoffmann Group	www.hoffmann-group.com
JG Herramientas SAC	www.jgherramientas.com
Grupo Urrea	www.urrea.com
Hilti	www.hilti.es
Kaiser + Kraft	www.kaiserkraft.com

Figure 7.30. Tabla de fabricantes/distribuidores de herramientas.

Gauge	Fast-measuring device	Laser-measuring device	Torque screwdriver
Digital display with high contrast, with readings of 0.01 mm.	Quick interior measurement apparatus of 3 points.	Versatile device for outdoors and indoors.	Upon reaching the set torque, the screwdriver is triggered audibly.
Pneumatic drill	**Universal laser**	**Infrared thermometer**	**Portable briefcase**
High-performance with high-running smoothness.	Auto-leveling cross-lines laser.	Infrared thermometer with switchable optics for remote measurements.	Polypropylene bucket with aluminium handle for transport.

293

Industrial Productivity

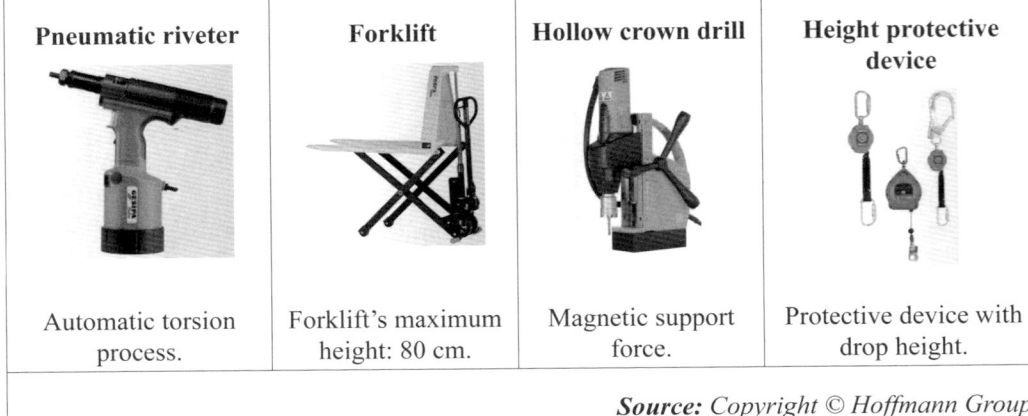

Figure 7.31. Catalogs of industrial tools

7.3.6. Quick Change of Machines and Tools: SMED

A typical task given in manufacturing, even more when the process contains many tasks done by the same machine, is the exchange of format or tools to manufacture a new batch.

These tasks are scarcely given the right attention, which causes the machine to remain stopped for a long time while the exchange is done. A stopped machine means no units produced: unbilled units.

The SMED methodology tries to reduce the time of change in format for a machine, especially the time the machine is not working. It is based on some stages and is the proposal for improvement suggested when one of the problems the factory has is few effective hours of machine operation and long times for preparation.

Due to its length, the explanation of this methodology requires its own chapter—Chapter 8.

7.3.7. Balancing of Tasks with More Than One Participant

In Chapter 5, in the study of methods, tasks are classified into four types:

1. Open work
2. Simultaneous tasks: person-machine
3. Simultaneous tasks: person-person
4. Assembly line works

Of the four types of tasks, the last three have more than one participant. This situation always generates imbalances in the workload; that is, for the same cycle

7. Design of the Improved Method

time, the activity times of the participants are different from one another. This situation causes a non-value-adding operation: **the delay.** Delay can be reduced through workload balancing:

- Changing the order of the operations
- Studying the saturation
- Removing operations from the most saturated workstation
- Passing them to the least saturated
- Doubling stations
- Unifying workstations

Thus, balancing will ensure that for the same amount of operators, cycle time is reduced, specifically due to the elimination of delays.

This improvement will be explained in Chapter 9.

7.3.8. Process Improvement

The improvement in methods affects how the task is being performed. The improvement in processes affects the whole task carried out for a determined product or service. It studies the optimization of movements and transformations that the material suffers as a whole. These movements and transformations are determined by the size of the factory, the balance of tasks, the methods of internal transportation, and the intermediate stock policy. **The improvement in processes consists in eliminating all the tasks done on the material that do not pose any transformation of it, or non-value-adding activities.** The methods of improvement are the following:

- Balance of workstations
- Reduction of space and transports
- Reduction of intermediate stocks
- Implementation of automatic transport means

This improvement will be explained in Chapter 10.

7.3.9. Improvement in Ergonomics (the Most Important Improvement)

The word *ergonomics* comes from the Greek words *ergon,* meaning "work," and *nomos,* meaning "natural laws." Frederick Taylor took the first steps in the study of the labor activity with his work *Scientific Management,* where he applied the design of elemental work devices, such as shovels of different shapes and sizes.

Industrial Productivity

Ergonomics is a scientific-technical discipline—a design that studies the shortlist or system formed by persons in their operational framework—related to the handling of equipment and machines within a specific work environment.

According to the Spanish Ergonomics Association, ergonomics is the multidisciplinary knowledge applied to the suitability of products, systems, and artificial environments to the needs, constraints, and characteristics of their users, optimizing the efficiency, safety, and welfare.

We believe that ergonomics is the most important improvement that can be made from the scientific study of work, because it manages to make physical labor more comfortable and safe for the operator. Both of these conditions will result in increased productivity. Nobody can work fast if they feel uneasy and fear an accident or if they feel fatigue in their muscles and joints. ERGONOMICS IS A MORAL OBLIGATION FOR THE ANALYST.

Chapter 11 discusses improvement in ergonomics.

What follows is an example of improved method design.

Narrative

Redistribution of tanned cutting area in footwear factory

This story will study how the work method was improved in a footwear factory. This improvement references the cutting and marking section where operators cut the different parts of a shoe (instep, heel, etc.) with the help of dies. Another operator, with the help of a cardboard pattern and a pen, marks the sewing line for the next operator.

Figure 7.32 shows the distribution of the cutting area.

7. Design of the Improved Method

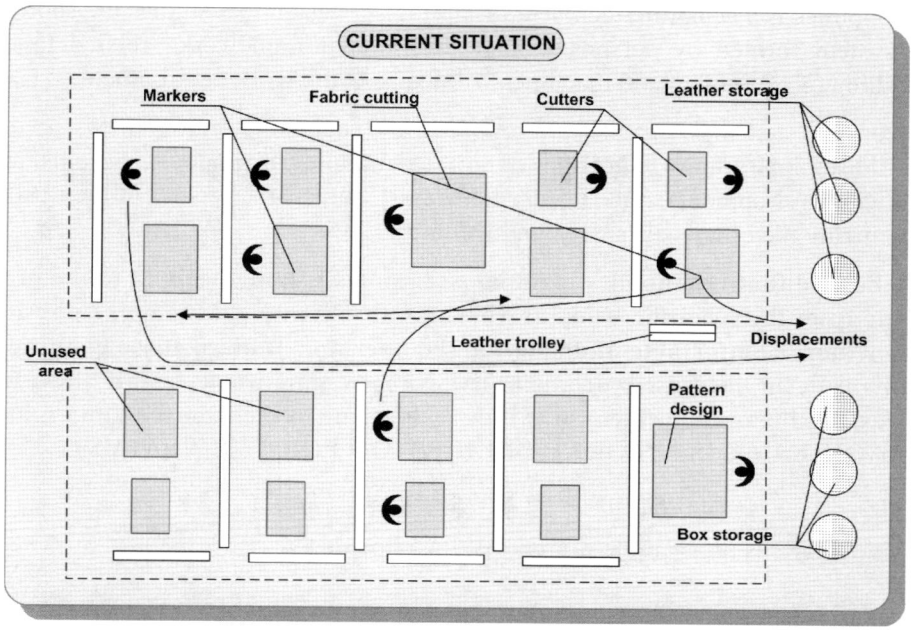

Figure 7.32. *Initial situation of tanned cutting area*

As can be observed from Figure 7.32, the distribution and order of the section was nonexistent. Each cutting operator must keep the material in a box and travel toward the storage place, to stock up the next tanned parts. This operation required that the marking operator had to move away from a workplace in order that the other operator could exit his or her area.

On the other hand, the marking operator did not have enough space to perform the task. This operator had to improvise and deposit the marked material on the table of a colleague, so in turn the other operator had to search for another site for his or her material.

The result was that operators continuously carried material back and forth in the section, wasting time and money on transports not needed.

After studying the methods and times within the factory, the subject of this report, the proposal to factory management was the following.

Industrial Productivity

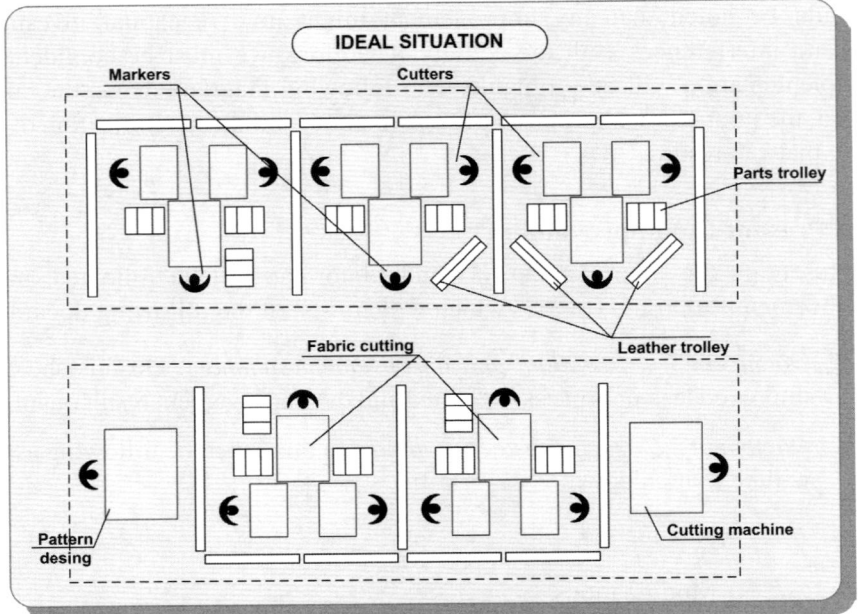

Figure 7.33. Proposed situation of tanning cut area

Apparently, everything is much more ordered and better distributed in the same space. Now, marking operators have enough space to deposit processed materials without having to bother their colleagues.

The same situation occurs with cutting operators. They did not need to move in search of leather, because it was supplied by an operator with a trolley, so that as soon as they ended one part, they deposited it on a trolley and were supplied the next tanned, thereby eliminating many transfers.

7.4. Evaluate and Present Correctly the Improvement Proposals, Including Their Economical, Technical, Social, Ecological, Legal, and Ethical Justifications

The acceptance of an idea must pass across a whole filter and interrogatory. The result should be able to be simulated after applying the idea under study. In the case of the study of methods and their improvement, it can be done with certain precision. The method study has a sequence of broken down operations; the improvements consist of eliminating some of them or improving them, which will provide an idea of what time reduction can be obtained in quantitative terms.

It should be noted that any improvement might involve capital investment, time, and interferences with the activity. Therefore, we must be confident that its implementation will be profitable. The following diagram shows the current method, the improvement proposal of such method, and the quantification of time saving that can result.

7.4.1. Present the Improvement

For presenting the improvement, a standard format will be followed, named "Improvement Proposal Format," which will consist of the following documents:

- *Document 1 – Task data and improvement summary.* On this sheet, the improved task or process is defined and the improvement result quantified.
- *Document 2 – Aspects to keep in mind.* On this sheet the following aspects will be written down:

    - Advantages

    - Modifications

    - Objections

    - Social aspects and ergonomics

    - Ecological aspects

    - Investment and amortization

- *Document 3 – Improvement description.* This document will describe and develop the improvement that will be carried out. The current method and the improved method will be developed.
- Document 4 – Improvement sketch.

Figure 7.34 contains an improvement proposal example.

Example

IMPROVEMENT PROPOSAL

Document 1 - Task data and improvement summary: Decorative assembly

General data of task

Company	Carter&Sons
Address	29 North Street
Location	Durham
Zipcode	49002
Telephone	92522883
Task name:	Decorative assembly
Area-Section:	Line 1
Task code:	90/39A00

Description of improvement

Problem definition:
The column drill is located 120 meters from the workstation, which poses great waste in time. In addition, the operator must make measurements to perform the drill.

Summary table of improvement

Description	Current Min/Unit	Proposed Min/Unit	Improvement Min/Unit	%
Standard time (person time)	15.42	5.91	9.51	62%
Workforce cost ($/hour)	35.00			
Workforce cost per unit ($/unit)	9.00	3.45	5.55	62%
Total transfers (meters)	2.49	0.00	2.49	100%

Classification of Operations	Min/Unit	Min/Unit	Min/Unit	%
Total value-adding operations	7.17	5.91	1.26	18%
Total non-value-adding operations	8.25	0.00	8.25	100%
Total transfers.	1.99	0.00	1.99	100%
Total storages.	0.79	0.00	0.79	100%
Total waits.	0.00	0.00	0.00	0%
Total inspections.	0.00	0.00	0.00	0%
Total inspection operation.	1.26	0.00	1.26	100%
Total searches.	0.55	0.00	0.55	100%
Total removable operations.	4.92	0.00	4.92	100%
Total communications.	0.00	0.00	0.00	0%
CwM	1.54 %	1.00 %	0.54	

Brief development of improvement:
It is proposed to move the drill next to the workstation, because that drill is only used for this operation. It is proposed to make a template in order to avoid making measurements.

Acceptance of improvement

Accepted:	☒ YES		☐ NO
Acceptance date:	2/13/2012		
Accepted by:	Lewis Cox		
Implementation responsibiliy:	Marc Peterson		
Implementation deadline:	1 week		
Implementation date:	2012/08/16		
Assigned person-hours:	18 person-hours		
Assigned budget:	$1,200		

Quantification of the expected improvement

N° units performed / year:	3,960.00
Savings expected per unit ($/unit):	5.55
Annual expected saving ($/year):	21,978.00

Improvement implementation registry

Date 1:	Implemented: ☐ YES ☐ NO	Implementation level (%):
Date 2:	Implemented: ☐ YES ☐ NO	Implementation level (%):
Date 3:	Implemented: ☐ YES ☐ NO	Implementation level (%):

Implementation level is the percentage between obtained and expected improvement.

Budget spent: .... $
Hours spent: .... person-hours
Final improv. obtained: .... $/unit
Annual savings obtained .... $/year

Brief description of obtained results:

Figure 7.34. Document 1 – Task data and improvement summary

7. Design of the Improved Method

IMPROVEMENT PROPOSAL
Document 2 - Aspects of the improvement to take into account: Decorative assembly
Advantages (Economy, surface saved, work hours, surplus equipment, material saved, security, etc.)
With the improvement proposal ongoing, the standard time of the task is to be reduced to 9.51 minutes, which poses a workforce savings equivalent to $5.55/unit.
Modifications (Changes regarding teams, transfers, standards, forms, etc..)
Tthe column drill should be transferred to the decorative-assembly area, thereby eliminating transfer distances of 240 meters per part.
Disadvantages (annual implementation costs, new material, new staff, etc.)
Investment spending corresponds to the cost of the steel plate for the drill tooling. This template will be made by the engineering department by CNC machining. These expenses include the hours spent by the engineering staff and production worker. For transportation and operation of the drill column, maintenance personnel will be needed. It is necessary to install a power point and an extension for compressed air intake. The cost of this action is estimated to be $80 annually.
Social and ergonomic aspects (eliminated risks and ergonomic improvements will be indicated)
This action prevents the risk to the operator posed by moving through an area traveled by forklifts.
Ecological aspects (contribution to the environment will be indicated)
Does not include.
Investment and amortization (cost of the investment and amortization will be quantified)
A priori the cost of the investment is assumed at $1,200. With the implementation of the improvement, the expected monetary savings is $5.55, with a production of 3,960 units per year. With these data, the repayment period is 20 days.

Figure 7.35. Document 2 – Aspects to keep in mind

Industrial Productivity

IMPROVEMENT PROPOSAL
Document 3 - Description of task improvement: Decorative assembly
Description and initial situation (explained through text, study of current method, etc.)
The study of current methods reveals that many operations do not add value to the product but nevertheless extend the duration of the operation.
Description and proposed situation (explained through text, study of proposed method, etc.)
It is proposed to move the drill next to the operator's working area, thus eliminating the risk on the journey and reducing the duration of the task. Besides, it is intended to make a template for drilling the part, eliminating measurement operations. Attached is a sketch of the part, in document 4.

Figure 7.36. Document 3 – Improvement description

7. Design of the Improved Method

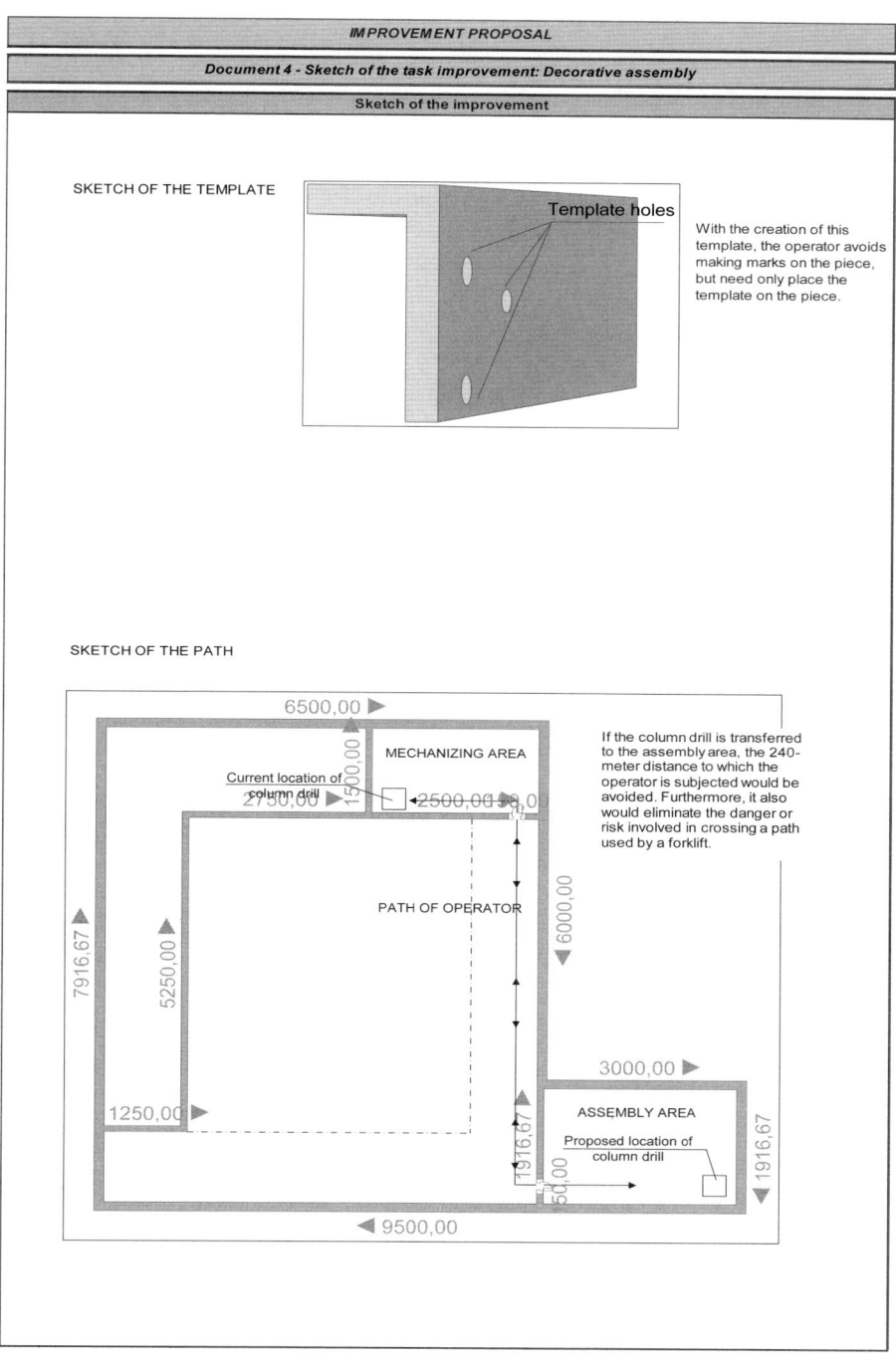

Figure 7.37. Document 4 – Improvement sketch

7.4.2. Improvement Evaluation

Once the improvement proposal has been detailed according to the previous formats, the improvement is subject to acceptance or rejection. Consequently, management will need to have some criteria. Figure 7.38 shows a method for filtering, evaluating, and approving an idea. When making a decision among several ideas, **choose the simplest and the one involving less investment; the best investment is the one not done.**

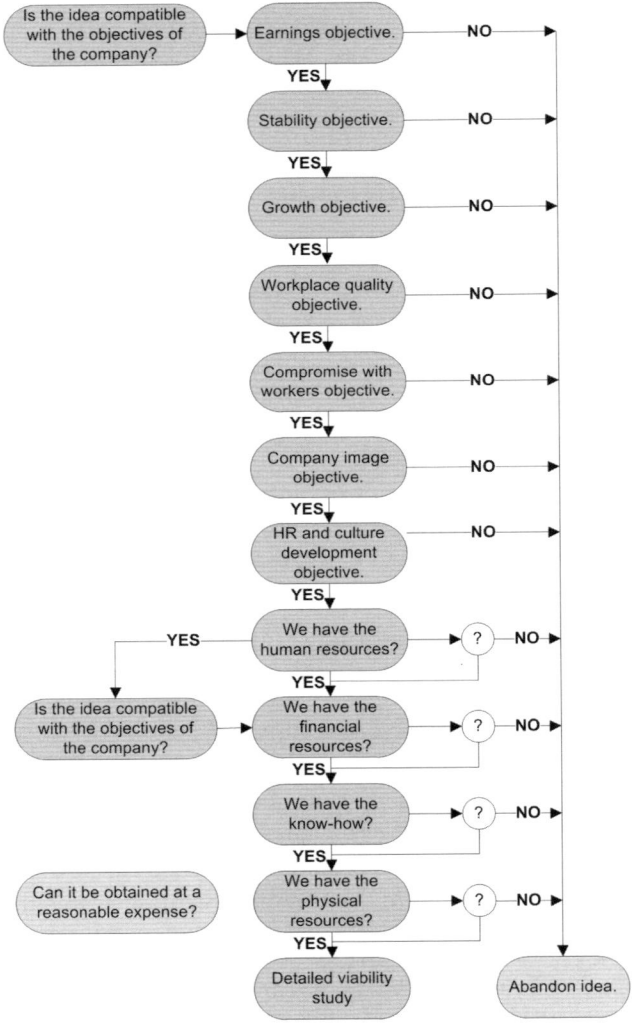

Source: "LEARNING TO GENERATE IDEAS. Innovate through creativity" of Fabio Gallego Reinoso. Ed Paidós.

Figure 7.38. Outline: Study of idea feasibility

7. Design of the Improved Method

Once an idea is accepted or denied, the field "Improvement acceptance" is completed in the improvement proposal format in Document 1.

Acceptance of improvement	
Accepted:	☒ YES ☐ NO
Acceptance date:	2012/07/19
Accepted by:	Lewis Cox
Implementation responsibility:	Marc Peterson
Implementation deadline:	1 week
Implementation date:	2012/08/16
Assigned person-hours:	18 person-hours
Assigned budget:	$1,200

Figure 7.39. Improvement acceptance

7.5. The Study–Analysis–Improvement Proposal Simplified Cycle

The cycle studied to this point presents the following main steps:

1. Study of methods
2. Analysis of methods
3. Design of improved method—improvement proposals

Because the analyst is subjected to cost/benefit limitations, sometimes not enough time is available to perform the entire cycle meticulously, step by step and operation by operation. In large companies where many operators work, a small percentage of improvement will, in absolute terms, be a great economic improvement; however, in smaller companies, where the improvement is not as scalable, analytical work may not be profitable. In these cases, the analyst should be more productive and focus on the most noticeable improvements.

The experienced analyst should be agile in the development of the cycle and perform the three steps simultaneously: study the method, analyze it, and make improvement proposals.

Industrial Productivity

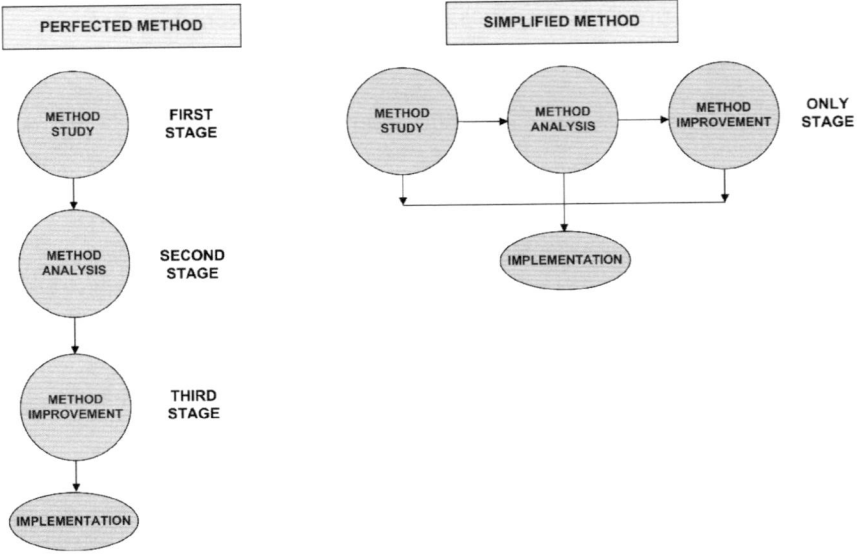

Figure 7.40. Simplified method

Questions

1. Is any method or process improvable?
2. What is the first step for improving a situation?
3. What tools are used to define the problem?
4. Once a problem is defined, how can ideas be generated for its resolution?
5. Describe four types of solutions oriented to the improvements of methods and processes that can be preestablished in the improvement catalog.
6. What is the basic principle of the 5S?
7. What does benchmarking involve?
8. Of all the improvements that can be applied, which is the most important?
9. Describe the simplified method for the study, analysis, and improvement of methods, and its importance.
10. Conceptually, on what does improvement of a method or process depend?

Problems

1. Given the working method shown and the applied analysis, make improvement proposals for the operations that need them.

7. Design of the Improved Method

Document 2 - Method study of the task			
Code Op	Description of Operation	Total Corrected Time (sec)	% Operation in Task
0010	Take case from cart, perform visual inspection. Place on worktable.	3,528.11	5.07%
0020	Take motor from cart and unroll cable.	2,874.22	4.13%
0030	Introduce motor in case interior, insert cable.	7,042.67	10.12%
0040	Screw the motor to the case with two screws through one side of the amplifier.	3,879.67	5.57%
0050	Take metal plate and present in case.	3,358.36	4.82%
0060	Screw protection plate to case (install 10 screws).	14,764.58	21.21%
0070	Search and paste specifications label.	2,956.08	4.25%
0080	Introduce cables of transformer inside case.	1,111.17	1.60%
0090	Turn amplifier.	1,130.00	1.62%
0100	Fix motor to case through the front side, installing four screws.	4,080.56	5.86%
0110	Fix motor to case with two screws through opposite side.	3,879.67	5.57%
0120	Take metal plate and present in case.	3,358.36	4.82%
0130	Screw protection plate to case (place 10 screws).	5,724.58	8.22%
0140	Turn amplifier. Leave inferior part of the amplifier upside down.	2,463.67	3.54%
0150	Introduce net cable in case.	1,638.50	2.35%
0160	Transfer amplifier to following workstation.	3,803.58	5.46%
0170	Provide for new case in process.	1,627.20	2.34%
0180	Write down performed work.	52.79	0.08%
0190	Remove separation cardboard from cart motors.	34.27	0.05%
0200	Change motor cart.	1,913.96	2.75%
0210	Change roll of characteristics labels.	4.46	0.01%
0220	Provide protector plates.	307.44	0.44%
0230	Turn case cart.	70.40	0.10%
	Total task execution time:	69,604.29	100.00%

Figure 7.41. Working method under study

2. The following layout shows a working method with its displacements. Propose, through a sketch, a new layout that reduces or eliminates operations time. Explain and justify.

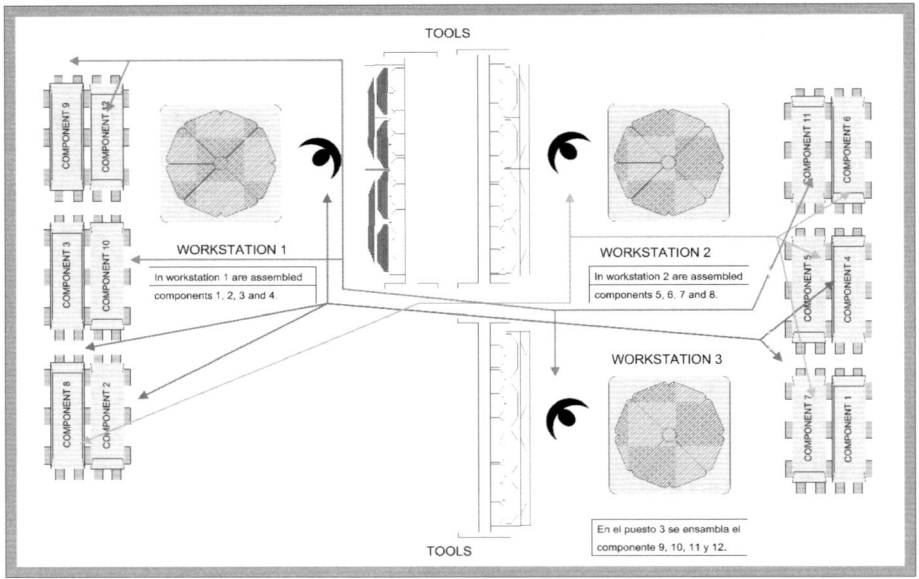

Figure 7.42. Simplified method

Bibliography

Aguirre de Mena, Juan M., María Mercedes Rodríguez Fernández, and Dolores Tous Zamora, *Organización y métodos de trabajo*. (Ediciones Pirámide, 2002).

Gallego, Fabio, *Aprender a generar ideas: Innovar mediante la creatividad*. (Ediciones Paidós Ibérica S.A., 2001).

Hirano, Hiroyuki, *5 Pillars of the Visual Workplace* (Tokyo: Nikkan Kogyo Shimbun Ltd., 1990).

Martín López, Milagro, María Elena Robles Rábago, Francisco José González Domínguez, and Juan Manuel Crespo Pérez,. *Métodos de trabajo: Casos Prácticos*. (Ediciones Pirámide, 2001).

Chapter 8

Improvement in Setup Times of Machines - SMED: Agile Manufacturing

In this chapter, we will discover one of the most important tools that the analyst can use to improve the working method, the SMED. The SMED will help reduce the time used for performing the format changes of the machine, achieving enormous improvements and investing in it few resources.

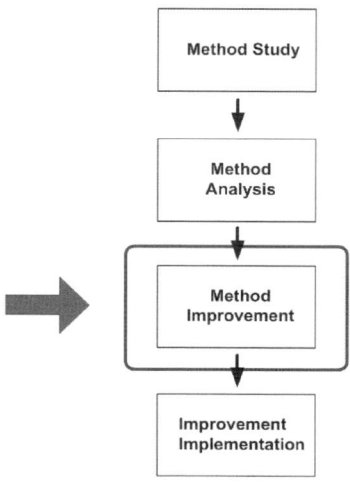

Figure 8.1. Outline of the second part. Method improvement

8.1. Introduction. What Is SMED?

Within the possible method improvements, a particularly relevant one is the SMED system. It is a methodology designed to improve the duration of setup tasks for machines and tools in order to maximize machine use, reduce batch sizes, reduce costs, and increase flexibility in customer service. SMED is an acronym for single-minute exchange of die. This concept introduces the idea that generally any exchange of machine or initialization of a process should take no longer than 10 minutes, "single-minute" meaning duration of only one digit. The origin of this concept is attributed to Shigeo Shingo, one of the major contributors, along with Taiichi Ohno, of just-in-time (JIT), Toyota's production system.

The goal of SMED techniques is to reduce drastically tool setup times in the preparation of machines and production lines, enabling smaller, yet economical, batches.

The principal function and objective of this chapter is to describe the fundamentals and theories of the SMED system, along with concrete examples of improvements. However, awareness of these specific techniques is not enough to secure an adequate start-up. An effective implementation is only possible when the full scope of these techniques is understood. For this, the following fundamental conditions must be given:

- Become aware of the importance the reduction of preparation times has for the company and its activities.

- Raise awareness of the problem for employees and provide training in order to increase productivity and reduce costs by reducing preparation times, eliminating the belief in the impossibility of achieving this goal.

- Stress the reduction of time for both preparations and global processes of productive operation, based on the tremendous effects on productivity, cost, deadline fulfillment, and satisfaction levels. For this reason, treatment is established as a matter of strategic nature.

It should be noted that you cannot reach the range of "less than 10 minutes" in all types of machine preparations, but the application of SMED techniques will significantly reduce changeover times and preparation in all cases.

> Without SMED, a company cannot achieve agile manufacturing. If machine preparation times are not low enough, the company will only be able to make profitable manufacturing batches if they are large. When batches are large, the manufacturing cannot be agile.

8.2. Convenience of SMED

Nowadays, customers desire a wide variety of products, in limited quantities and within a short period. They expect high quality, good prices, and quick deliveries (quality, cost, and time). For companies that want to increase their flexibility and at the same time reduce their stock levels, it is critical to reduce times to the minimum, for both tool exchanges and preparations. To eliminate the concept of batch manufacturing, minimizing the preparation times for machines and materials is essentially the SMED philosophy.

SMED helps companies to satisfy these needs with less waste, making cost-effective the production of goods in small quantities or batches. Numerous companies produce goods in large batches simply because the tool exchange and machine preparation costly.

To demonstrate the relative importance of batch size increases, Figure 8.2 provides a comparative table. It demonstrates how low preparation times leads to smaller savings from increasing the batch size.

Preparation Time	Batch size	Cycle of part	Total time of part
4 hours	100	1 min	1 min + (4 x 60/100 units) = 3.4 min
4 hours	1,000	1 min	1 min + (4 x 60/1,000 units) = 1.24 min
4 hours	10,000	1 min	1 min + (4 x 60/10,000 units) = 3.4 min
3 minutes	100	1 min	1 min + (3/100 units) = 1.03 min
3 minutes	1,000	1 min	1 min + (3/1000 units) = 1.003 min

Figure 8.2. Influence of machine exchange in batch time

Production in large batches has several disadvantages:

- *Stock wastes:* The storage of what is not sold costs money and immobilizes resources of the company without adding any value to the product.
- *Delay:* The customers must wait for the company to produce full batches instead of manufacturing the necessary quantities for each moment.
- *Quality reduction:* The storage of unsold products increases the possibilities of deterioration or breakage, increasing costs.

The application of SMED techniques radically changes the production system of any company. When the tool exchanges can be made quickly, they will be done whenever necessary, which means companies can produce in small batches and realize the following advantages:

- *Flexibility:* Companies can meet the changing demands from customers without having large stocks.
- *Fast deliveries:* Production in small batches means shorter manufacturing deadlines and less waiting time for all the customers.
- *Elevated productivity:* Shorter preparation times and tool exchanges reduce the downtimes of equipment, increasing the productivity rate.

It is noteworthy that currently the SMED philosophy not only applies to tool exchanges and machinery and equipment preparations in companies of any field, but also to the preparation and implementation of operating rooms, air shipment operations, race cars, and other activities related to services.

The most notable benefits that this tool brings include the following:

- Reduced preparation time, making it productive time
- Reduced size of inventory
- Reduced size of production batches
- Reduced costs
- Shorter delivery times
- More balanced workloads in production on a time interval
- Greater competitiveness

8.3. The SMED System: Description of Stages

8.3.1. Initial Situation

Traditionally, preparation procedures were believed to be varied and complex as a function of the type of industry, machinery, equipment, and tools. However, if we analyze these procedures in depth, we can observe how a sequence of operations is repeated. Such sequence is shown in Figure 8.3.

Operation	% Time
Preparations, postprocess adjustments, and verifications	30
Assemble and disassemble tools	5
Center, size, and fix other conditions	15
Production of trial parts and adjustments	50

Figure 8.3. Approximated distribution of exchange time of machine

1. *Preparation, postprocess adjustment, and verification:* In this first step we ensure that all necessary components are available and in working order. This process also includes the removal and cleaning process once the exchange is done.

2. *Assembling and disassembling tool:* It includes the removal of parts and tools once the batch being manufactured is finished and placing the parts and tools needed for the next batch.

3. *Center, size, and place other conditions:* Includes all measurements and calibrations needed to perform a production operation.

4. *Production of test parts and adjustments*: After a test part, appropriate adjustments are made. Such adjustments are easier with greater accuracy of the preceding measurements and calibrations.

This last point, production of test parts and adjustments, has the most variable frequencies and duration, because it depends on the ability of the operator. The greater difficulty of a preparation operation lies in the correct adjustment of the equipment.

At this preliminary stage, we will discover the absence of any operatory method or instruction defined around the tool exchange. Exchange operations that could be done during the running time of the machine are done in the downtime.

In these preparatory operations, traditionally, different classes of wastes are produced:

- Finished products are transported to the warehouse or the following batch of raw material is brought from the stock after finishing the previous batch and with the machine stopped, so precious time is wasted during this machine stoppage.

- The blades, molds, or other tools are delivered after the internal preparation has begun or a defective part is discovered after assembly and testing.

The result is the necessity of starting the process over. Moreover, in these cases the waste may be greater if you have already taken the parts you do not need to store.

- With regard to tools, we could try to use a template that does not have the accuracy needed or needs to be repaired, has screws missing, or a nut that does not tighten enough.

- Many circumstances similar to those described can be found in which errors, lack of availability, or inadequate verification of equipment produce substantial delays in preparatory operations.

- Businesses managers or production engineers do not traditionally spend their time and expertise on analyzing preparation operations. Often, these tasks are assigned to workers, assuming they are aware and willing to carry out preparations as quickly as possible.

8.3.2. Stages of SMED

Stage 1: Separation of internal and external operations

A machine exchange is a task that, as any of the others that have been studied, follows a sequence of operations. These operations of the machine exchange task can be divided in internal or external:

- Internal operations: those that need to be done with the machine stopped (e.g., an exchange of a blade in a lathe).

- External operations: those that can be done with the machine working—the most common is the transfer to tool storage for the next batch.

It is the most important step when performing the SMED system. A special effort in meticulously differentiating all operations that really are external can result in a 30 percent to 50 percent reduction in the internal preparation time.

Stage 2: Conversion of internal and external times

The following step is to detect what internal operations can be performed while the machine is working and can pass to external. This conversion is achieved through method improvement or a simple modification of equipment or tools.

Stage 3: Perfect internal and external operations

The objective of this stage is to perfect the aspects of preparation operations, including all the elemental operations (both internal and external), using generic actions that will be described in the following section. Additionally, preparation will improve through analysis criteria and method improvements.

The graph in Figure 8.4 summarizes the three stages of SMED.

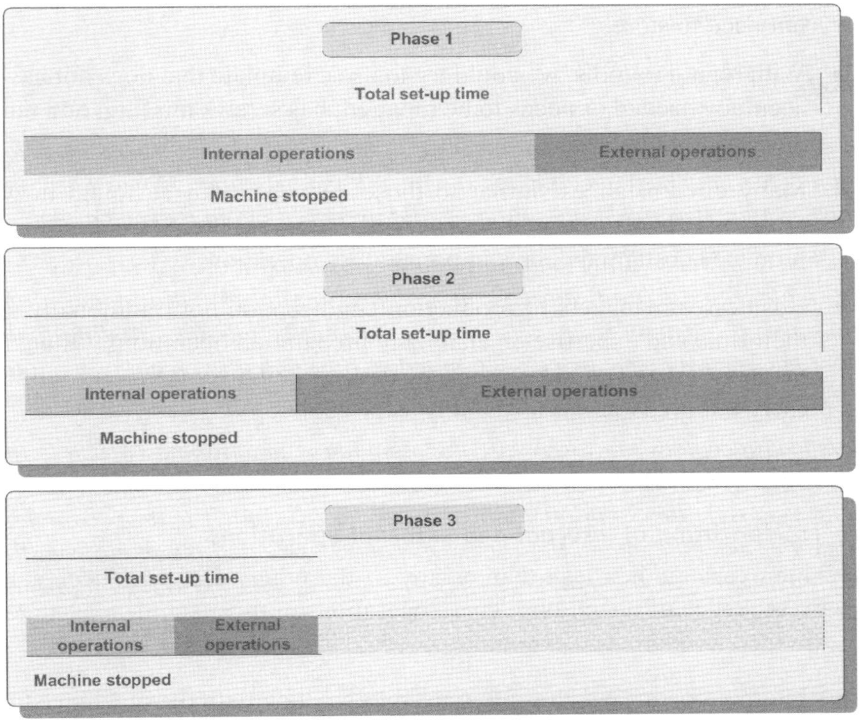

Phase 1
Total set-up time
Internal operations | External operations
Machine stopped

Phase 2
Total set-up time
Internal operations | External operations
Machine stopped

Phase 3
Total set-up time
Internal operations | External operations
Machine stopped

Figure 8.4. Time reduction in the different stages of SMED

The following two examples illustrate the concepts discussed.

Example

In the metal industry, machinery known as injection presses inject the liquid metal into molds. After cooling, the mold is opened and the solidified part is removed.

When the type of part to manufacture changes, it is necessary to change the mold or tool. After the change, due to the low temperature of the new mold, the first castings manufactured do not meet the necessary quality standards. Currently, the only source of heat for the mold is the injected metal, which means wasting several cycles (time) and discarding several castings (raw material).

The solution to the low temperature of the mold was to install a grid suspended above the casting oven, which effectively preheated the mold with heat dissipating from the oven. The new mold enters the machine at sufficient temperature to achieve required quality for the first casting. This

Industrial Productivity

alteration—building a grid with sufficient strength to support the weight of the mold—will eliminate internal preparations and results in greater efficiency of the machine.

Example

In a factory of prefabricated concrete tubes, a unique mold was used for each type of part, so once the mold was full and the concrete was hard, the finished tube was taken out and the mold prepared again for a new cycle.

The cycle of tube filling and hardening consumes about 25 minutes, but the mold release and subsequent preparation, because all operations are carried out with a crane, consumes about 21 minutes. Adding these amounts, the cycle per piece is 46 minutes, of which 45 percent of the total cycle time the machine is stopped by the exchange.

Because operators are idle while the machine is functioning (which is the necessary set time of concrete in order to be minimally hardened for its mold release), the solution proposed was to give each team two molds. Once the machine ended the cycle, operators extracted the mold from the pit, leaving it near the machine. They then inserted the second mold, which was already prepared, and started the machine again.

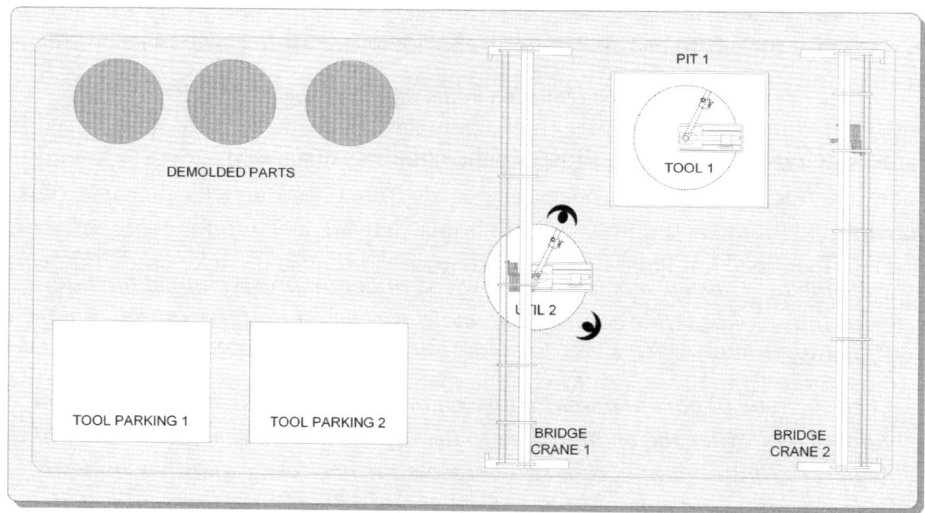

Figure 8.5. *Layout of prefabricated concrete factory*

The change drastically reduced preparation time from 21 minutes to no more than 3 minutes, or 14 percent of its initial cycle. Daily production increased from 9 units to 15 units per shift. Increasing the number of workers in the workstation was unnecessary because their labor in performing the operations of mold release took place during machine time.

8.4. Techniques for Applying the SMED System

This section provides improvement activities for each of the SMED stages.

8.4.1. Stage 1: Separation of Internal and External Operations

The techniques described next are useful to ensure that the operations that can be performed externally are really performed when the machine is running:

Use of checklists: Checklists are effective when ensuring out that all necessary parts and steps to start work are available. A checklist must include:

- Participant names
- Specifications
- Necessary tools
- Pressure, temperature, and other variables
- Numeric values of all measurements

Checklists prevent mistakes and related losses by not taking anything for granted. It is important to establish a checklist for each machine and avoid the use of a single list for the entire factory. Generic checklists are more likely to be confusing, wasting time, and consequently it would never be used.

Perform functional checks: Checklists are an effective way to make sure everything is where it should be, but does not ensure that the means are in perfect working order. Therefore, it will be necessary to do functional checks during external preparation. Frequent failures involve tools that are not working properly or a template that does not have the required accuracy. These mistakes inevitably will result in lost time.

Transportation improvement of tools and other parts: The auxiliary tools need to be transported from the warehouse to the machine and, once used, returned to their initial position.

Standardization of the preceding techniques.

8.4.2. Stage 2: Conversion of Internal and External Times

To perform this methodology we cannot limit ourselves to seeing the problems and their solutions from the point of view of the SMED system. We must use improvement tools and other instruments. However, it must be clear that creativity, at this point, is a fundamental component, because the situations faced are innumerable, and no book can cover them all. Furthermore, technological advances change the possible solutions.

As will be seen in the following examples, the task of preparation follows an operatory method similar to the one described in Chapter 5. Through the analysis seen in Chapter 6 and the methodologies used generate ideas for improvement, discussed in Chapter 7, we can work to achieve this stage. Initial areas for improvement in this stage include the following:

- **Reevaluation to check that no erroneous step has been taken in the preliminary phase**
- **Presetting of tools**
- **Elimination of adjustments:** The operations of adjustment represent 50–70 percent of the internal preparation time. It is important to reduce this time to shorten the total duration of the preparation.

Adjustments are normally associated with the relative position of parts and auxiliary tools, but once the exchange is done, it is delayed for some time in order to manufacture the first valid unit. Although called *adjustment*, it actually refers to nonconformities that, through trial and error, are eliminated until the product meets the required specifications. (It also uses an extra amount of material.)

We start from the premise that the best settings are the ones not needed, so we fix the positions. The key is to recreate the same conditions as the last time the product was manufactured. Because many adjustments can be made with the machine running, all holes should be standard and space required to accommodate different tools specified.

8.4.3 Stage 3: Perfect Internal and External Operations

After concluding the first stage (separation of internal and external operations) and the second (conversion of internal and external operations), we can proceed to perform improvements in the elementary operations of preparation. Although they may be subject to the analysis of methods and the improvement proposals, the basic solutions for the SMED follow.

1. Improvement proposals for the operations of external preparation

Improved operations can be achieved by improving the storage and transport of parts and tools. For small tools, templates, and gauges, it is vital to consider the management all these elements. It is necessary to ask questions like the following:

- What is the best way to organize all these elements?
- How can we have all elements in perfect condition and ready for the next operation?
- How many of these elements do we need to have in stock?

With the following example we will explain a method for improving storage and internal transport:

The operations of storage and internal transportation of tools can consume a great deal of time, especially if the company has a large number of tools. Storage and transportation can be improved by marking tools with color codes and location numbers from the shelves where they are to be stored, as shown in Figure 8.6:

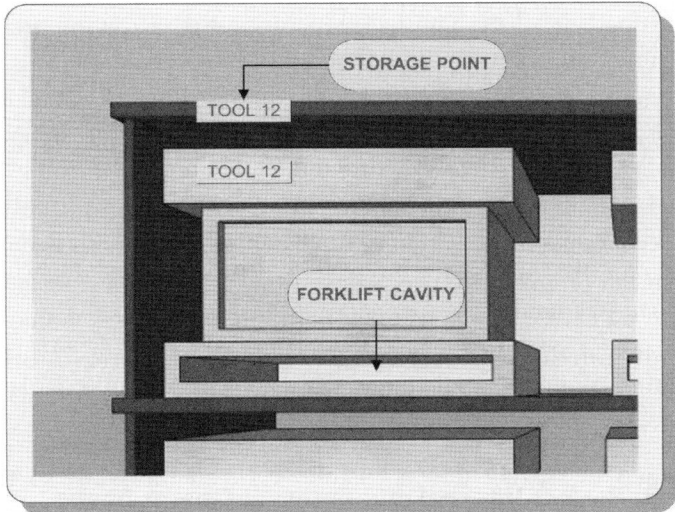

Figure 8.6. Positioning of tools for machine exchange

The method can be improved even more if a logical order is followed in the positioning of tools on the shelf, placing frequently used tools in the most accessible way. The solutions for improving external preparations include:

- Implementing 5S for tools
- Applying rules from motion economy and reducing transfers
- In general, applying the analysis and improvement of methods to reduce times

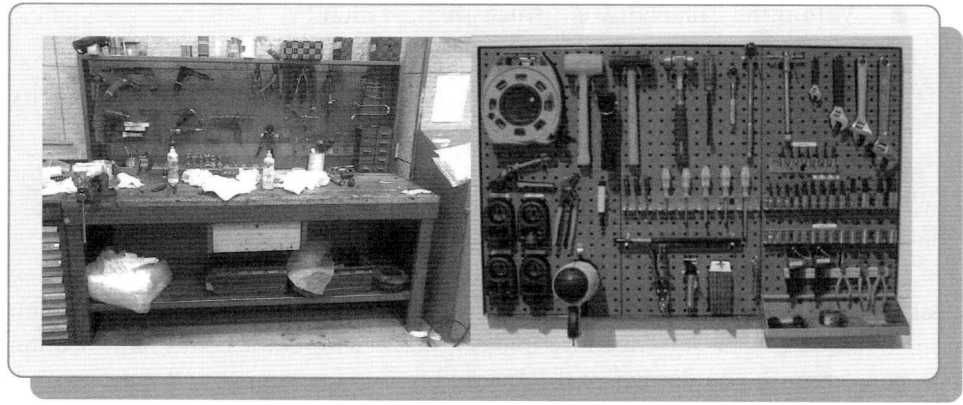

Figure 8.7. Disorder vs. order in tool location

2. Improvement proposals for operations of internal preparation

Actions designed to improve the most frequently used internal operations by the SMED system include the following:

- **Execution of operations in parallel:** The operations that need more than one operator help to accelerate some works. With two operators, an operation that consumes 12 minutes will not be fully completed in 6, but maybe in 8, thanks to movement savings.

- **Use of functional moorings:** Fastening devices serve to keep objects fixed somewhere with a minimum amount of effort (clamps).

- **Task standardization:** Preparation procedures are standardized and reflected in writing that is visible (e.g., on the wall) so they may be consulted by operators.

- **Standardization of functional dimensions:** Matching the functional measures of several auxiliary tools to reduce preparation time. Spacers will be used at shorter dimensions or parts will be shortened when they are longer than those chosen as standard. Use of patterns and precision templates minimize preparation time.

- **Rapid fasteners:** Substituting nut-and-bolt fasteners with faster ones and reducing the potential for time lost for any incident (breakage or missing parts).

- **Complementary tool:** For example, for attaching a drill to the spindle of a lathe or for attaching the die to a press, intermediate tools can be designed to enable the tasks of adjustment and calibration outside the machine.

8. Improvement in Setup Times of Machines - SMED: Agile Manufacturing

- **Automate, mechanize processes:** Hydraulic systems, pneumatic, position sensors, artificial vision systems, etc.
- **Place a low-capacity, flexible machine in parallel with large-capacity ones:** This concept is explained in the next section.

In traditional preparations, screws are often used to fasten tools directly to the machine. However, in the preparations applied in the SMED system, screws are considered "enemies," based on the following reasoning:

- Screws and nuts become loose; they may fall and roll under the machines, into holes, or under floorboards.
- Screws do not harmonize. Bolts and screws are not always standardized. Finding and adjusting the bolts and screws correctly poses an investment in search time, which translates into waste.
- Most importantly, tightening a screw is time consuming.

The following proposals show ways to improve or directly substitute for traditional screws.

The first would be to reduce their number required by the part. A meticulous consideration of magnitude and direction of acting forces must be performed. Figure 8.8 converts 10 screws to 4.

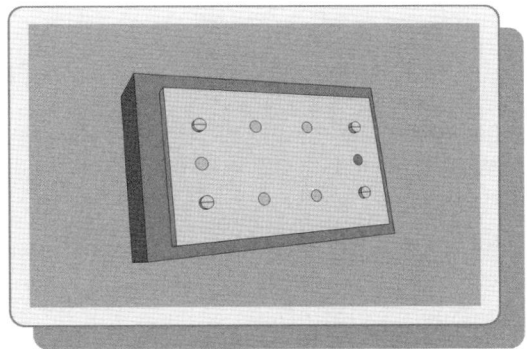

Figure 8.8. Reduction in the number of screws

When the pressure or force exerted on the part is significant and the number of screws cannot be reduced, the use of pear-shaped holes allows screws from any part to be loosened in a single turn.

321

Industrial Productivity

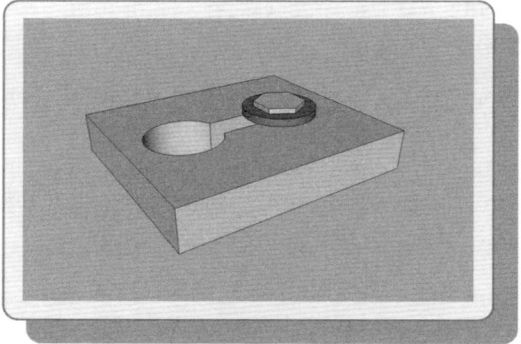

Figure 8.9. Single-turn screws

Another improvement is the use of U-shaped washers. They require making the hole large enough for the screw and nut set to fit loosely. In this way, the screw is inserted with the nut mounted, the washer is placed, and with less than one turn, the part remains fastened. This measure reduces the fastening time and avoids the problems that emerge from separating the screw from the nut (centering problems or loss of parts).

Different types of type U washers are shown in Figure 8.10.

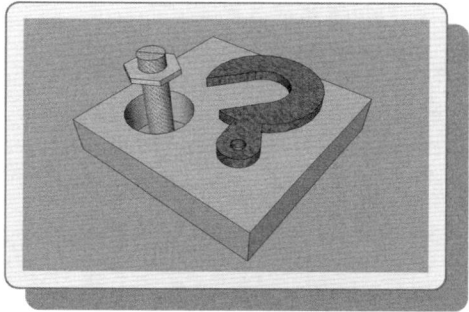

Figure 8.10. U-type washer

8. Improvement in Setup Times of Machines - SMED: Agile Manufacturing

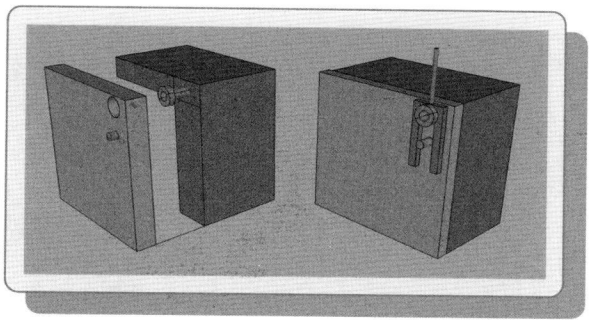

Figure 8.11. U-type washer

Another way to reduce the number of tightening turns to fasten a screw would be to use grooved threads. This method achieves tightening a bolt with less than a lap (Figure 8.12).

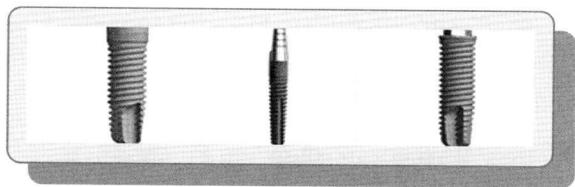

Figure 8.12. Grooved threads

In order to achieve this type of screw, grooves must be mechanized along the bolt to divide it into sections, making equivalent grooves in the female thread of the nut. This way the screw would be inserted, matching the area of the screw thread with nut slots, and once in the final position, the nut would be tightened with less than one turn.

Fast-tightening systems can be substitute for the traditional bolt.

- Spring mooring (Figure 8.13)

Industrial Productivity

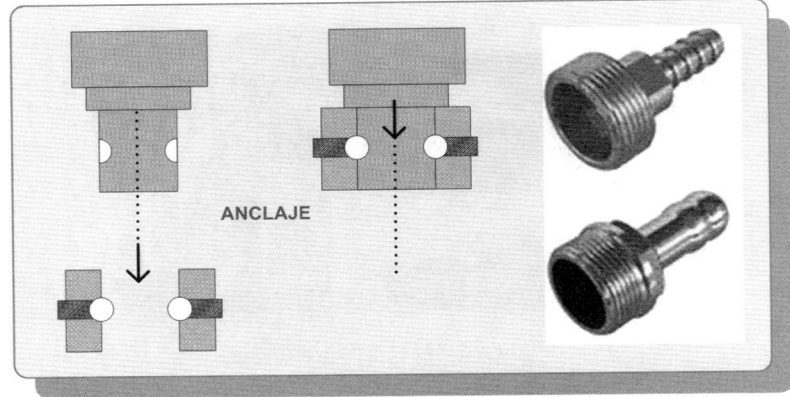

Figure 8.13. Spring mooring

- Triggers, which can apply pressures of more than 500 kg (Figure 8.14)

Figure 8.14. Triggers

- Cams (Figure 8.15)

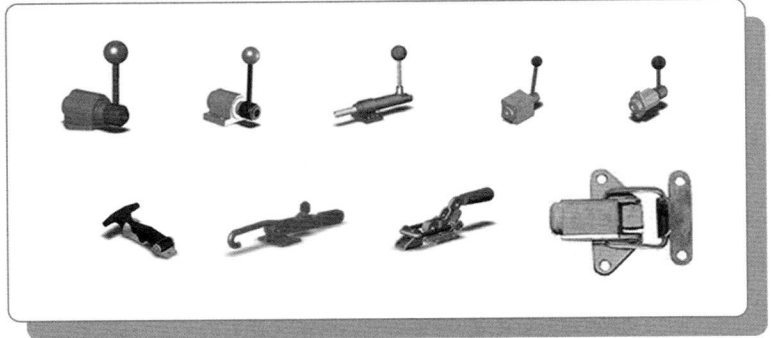

Figure 8.15. Cams

- Wing nut closure (Figure 8.16)

8. Improvement in Setup Times of Machines - SMED: Agile Manufacturing

Figure 8.16. Wing nut closure

While the SMED system is specifically for time reduction in machine exchanges, the way it reflects the operatory method is like any other task. From the method description, application of improvements can begin.

8.5. The Correct Machine Election: The Best Exchange Is the One Not Made

Any discussion of how to improve a machine exchange needs to address whether those changes are necessary. Manufacturers have obsessed about the acquisition of machines with great productive capacity. These machines are often sold at trade fairs where the salesperson has everything perfectly prepared for the machine to work at full speed and without stops. The problem emerges when this equipment is installed in the factory and encounters an increasingly varied mix of production and with increasingly smaller batches. In this circumstance, a commonly heard phrase is "We spend more time exchanging the formats than producing."

Generally, the more capacity a machine has, the more time it needs for exchanging the tool. When opting for one machine over another, it is important to keep in mind not only its productive capacity but also its flexibility in the exchanges.

A low-cost solution to machine exchanges for occasional small batches could be parallel placement to high-capacity machines of more economical but lower capacity and lower exchange time. That approach, paradoxically, as a function of the batch sizes, will produce more.

Factories normally keep the old machines with lower capacity in an auxiliary warehouse for that purpose. Occasionally, to repurpose these machines and place them in parallel with high-capacity ones can be useful for deriving the production as a function of the batch size, especially custom and urgent deliveries.

8.6. Practical Cases

Example

Method improvement in the exchange of tools in a metal laminates conforming machine.

In Figure 8.17, the study of methods performed in one of the tasks can be checked. The operation consists of installing a series of tools or profiles in the machine, depending on the type of metal coil to manipulate. Once the profiles are installed and the coil is loaded, the cycle of manipulation of the coil starts. At the end of the process, the used profiles were disassembled, the coil was unloaded, and the depleted material was unsubscribed.

8. Improvement in Setup Times of Machines - SMED: Agile Manufacturing

Document 1 - Task data and summary of the methods study

Technical parameters	
Coil width:	1250 mm
Longitudinal speed crane:	1 m/s
Transversal speed crane:	0.5 m/s
Time up/down crane:	29 sec
Speed passing plate:	3.29 s/ml
Steel density:	7850 Kg/m3
Coil weight:	8000 Kg
Profiling machine power:	15 Kw
Power of crane:	15 Kw
Energy cost:	0.085 $

Statistical parameters	
Distance to coil store	30 m
Distance of coil transport	10 m
N° coils that are moved in store:	4
D. store	15 m
Coil changeovers per order	1.5
Profile changes per order	0.25

Profile and order parameters:	
Plate thickness:	0.75 mm
Profile type:	
N° Plates/Package:	24.00
Total meters of order:	2000.00 m
Plate average length:	7.00 m
Different measures:	2.00 Units
Order weight:	14,718.8 Kg / 14.7 Tn

Document 2 - Methods study of the task

Task	Operation Description	Type of Operation	Distance (meters)	Unit Time (sec)	Units	Operation Time (sec)	N° of Operators	Person Time (sec)	Operation Code
PROFILING	Inspect note.			25.00	1.00	25.00	1.00	25.00	
	Place crane.		45.00	74.00	1.00	74.00	1.00	74.00	CRANE
	Change profile.			3605.96	0.25	901.49	2.00	1802.98	CRANE
	Remove current coil.			258.00	1.00	258.00	2.00	516.00	CRANE
	Weigh and discharge.			15.00	1.00	15.00	2.00	30.00	CRANE
	Transport to store.			108.00	1.00	108.00	2.00	216.00	CRANE
	Unleash.			62.64	1.00	62.64	2.00	125.28	CRANE
	Take new coil.			427.92	1.50	641.88	2.00	1283.76	CRANE
	Transport to table.			108.00	1.50	162.00	2.00	324.00	CRANE
	Place on table.			37.50	1.50	56.25	2.00	112.50	CRANE
	Place on mandrill.			105.90	1.50	158.85	2.00	317.70	
	Place plate on profiling machine.			182.50	1.50	273.75	2.00	547.50	
	Program machine.			148.00	1.00	148.00	2.00	296.00	
	Collect data of new coil.			112.00	1.50	168.00	2.00	336.00	
	Take to sampling area.			15.00	1.50	22.50	2.00	45.00	
	Make free check.			122.60	1.50	183.90	2.00	367.80	
	Profile.			3.29	2000.00	6580.00	2.05	13489.00	CRANE
	Measure change.			100.00	1.00	100.00	2.05	205.00	
	Wait to pack.			0.00	1.00	0.00	2.05	0.00	CRANE
	End of note.			25.00	1.00	25.00	2.00	50.00	
	TOTAL					9,964.26		20,163.52	

Figure 8.17. Study of methods and times of the profile operation

Observing the previous study of methods and times, we can check how, in the operation of "profile exchange," approximately 3,600 seconds were spent, regardless of the thickness of the metal sheet. We will perform a particular methods study of this operation to analyze and reduce the time. In Figure 8.18, this detail is indicated.

Industrial Productivity

Document 1 - Task data and summary of the methods study

Techincal parameters		Statistical parameters	
Axes per cassette	5	Nº cassettes to change	4
Bridge crane long. speed	1 m/s	Packages per hook:	2
Bridge crane transv. speed	0.5 m/s	Transversal placement:	12.5 m
Raise/lower crane	29 sec		

Document 2 - Methods study of the task

Task	Operation Description	Type of Operation	Distance (meters)	Unit Time (sec)	Units	Operation Time (sec)	Nº of Operators	Person Time (sec)	Operation Code
PROFILE CHANGEOVER	Inspect note.			25.00	1.00	25.00	1.00	25.00	
	Place bridge crane.	⇨	45.00	128.00	1.00	128.00	1.00	128.00	
	Hook tool.	○		114.00	1.00	114.00	1.00	114.00	
	Transfer to remove arms.	⇨		15.00	1.00	15.00	1.00	15.00	
	Remove arms.	○		20.00	5.00	100.00	1.00	100.00	
	Hook cassette.	○		47.28	8.00	378.24	1.00	378.24	
	Transport.	⇨		96.25	8.00	770.00	1.00	770.00	
	Unleash in store.	○		32.67	4.00	130.68	1.00	130.68	
	Transport.	⇨		30.33	8.00	242.64	1.00	242.64	
	Drop to train.	○		48.75	4.00	195.00	1.00	195.00	
	Put arms.	○		90.00	4.00	360.00	1.00	360.00	
	Put principal arm.	○		178.00	1.00	178.00	1.00	178.00	
	Use gauge.	○		42.07	20.00	841.40	1.00	841.40	
	Put stoppers.	○		31.00	1.00	31.00	1.00	31.00	
	Remove tool.	○		97.00	1.00	97.00	1.00	97.00	
	TOTAL					3,605.96		3,605.96	

Figure 8.18. Detailed study of the profile exchange

Once the breakdown of operations is made, the following step identifies what operations can be performed while the machine is running (and that are currently made with the machine paused) and can be eliminated because they are non-value-adding. For this purpose, we will use the diverse tools described in this book.

Observing the operation, we see how all the previous tool preparations can be performed while the machine is operating. They include note inspection, bridge crane position, tool engage, transfer to remove arms, and remove arms; these operations of internal preparation will automatically become operations of external preparation.

After the conversion of internal operations into external, the method of profile exchange would be as follows:

8. Improvement in Setup Times of Machines - SMED: Agile Manufacturing

Document 1 - Task data and summary of the methods study

Techincal parameters	
Axes per cassette	5
Bridge crane long. speed	1 m/s
Bridge crane transv. speed	0.5 m/s
Raise/lower crane	29 sec

Statistical parameters	
N° cassettes to change	4
Packages per hook	2
Transversal placement	12.5 m

Document 2 - Methods study of the task

Task	Operation Description	Type of Operation	Distance (meters)	Unit Time (sec)	Units	Operation Time (sec)	N° of Operators	Person Time (sec)	Operation Code
	Hook cassette.	○		47.28	8.00	378.24	1.00	378.24	
	Transport.	⇒		96.25	8.00	770.00	1.00	770.00	
	Unleash in store.	○		32.67	4.00	130.68	1.00	130.68	
	Transport.	⇒		30.33	8.00	242.64	1.00	242.64	
	Drop to train.	○		48.75	4.00	195.00	1.00	195.00	
	Put arms.	○		90.00	4.00	360.00	1.00	360.00	
	Put principal arm.	○		178.00	1.00	178.00	1.00	178.00	
	Use gauge.	○		42.07	20.00	841.40	1.00	841.40	
	Put stoppers.	○		31.00	1.00	31.00	1.00	31.00	
	Remove tool.	○		97.00	1.00	97.00	1.00	97.00	
	TOTAL					3,223.96		3,223.96	

Figure 8.19. Improvement in the profile exchange

After the implemented improvement, time is reduced by 12 percent.

The following step in the reduction of machine exchange duration will be to improve and reduce the time of internal tasks. For the example shown, if two bridge cranes were available for the cassettes exchange, several tasks could be performed while the machine was operating. For this, the operations that the first bridge crane should perform would be to remove the cassettes from the previous batch, while the second bridge crane supplies the cassettes of the following batch.

With this improvement applied, the study of the operation would return the following results:

Industrial Productivity

Document 1 - Task data and summary of the methods study

Techincal parameters	
Axes per cassette	5
Bridge crane long. speed	1 m/s
Bridge crane transv. speed	0.5 m/s
Raise/lower crane	29 sec

Statistical parameters	
N° cassettes to change	4
Packages per hook	2
Transversal placement	12.5 m

Document 2 - Methods study of the task

Task	Operation Description	Type of Operation	Distance (meters)	Unit Time (sec)	Units	Operation Time (sec)	N° of Operators	Person Time (sec)	Operation Code
	Unleash in store.	○		32.67	4.00	130.68	1.00	130.68	
	Transport.	⇨		30.33	8.00	242.64	1.00	242.64	
	Drop on train.	○		48.75	4.00	195.00	1.00	195.00	
	Use gauge.	○		42.07	20.00	841.40	1.00	841.40	
	Put stoppers.	○		31.00	1.00	31.00	1.00	31.00	
	Remove tool.	○		97.00	1.00	97.00	1.00	97.00	
	TOTAL					1,537.72		1,537.72	

Figure 8.20. Second improvement in the profile exchange method

As can be seen, the operation time has been reduced by approximately 58 percent. On the other hand, the time study of the complete task would be as follows:

8. Improvement in Setup Times of Machines - SMED: Agile Manufacturing

Document 1 - Task data and summary of the methods study

Technical parameters

Coil width:	1250 mm
Longitudinal speed crane:	1 m/s
Transversal speed crane:	0.5 m/s
Time up/down crane:	29 sec
Speed passing plate:	3.29 s/ml
Steel density:	7850 Kg/m3
Coil weight:	8000 Kg
Profiling machine power:	15 Kw
Power of crane:	15 Kw
Energy cost:	0.085 $

Statistical parameters

Distance to coil store	30
Distance of coil transport	10
N° coils that are moved in store	4
D. store	15
Coil changeovers per order	1.5
Profile changes per order	0.25

Profile and order parameters:

Plate thickness:	0.75 mm
Profile type:	
N° Plates/Package:	24.00
Total meters of order:	2000.00 m
Plate average length:	7.00 m
Different measures:	2.00 Units
Order weight:	14,718.8 Kg / 14.7 Tn

Document 2 - Methods study of the task

Task	Operation Description	Type of Operation	Distance (meters)	Unit Time (sec)	Units	Operation Time (sec)	N° of Operators	Person Time (sec)
PROFILE	Inspect note.	□		25.00	1.00	25.00	1.00	25.00
	Place crane.	⇒	45.00	74.00	1.00	74.00	1.00	74.00
	Change profile.	○		1537.72	0.25	384.43	2.00	768.86
	Remove current coil.	○		258.00	1.00	258.00	2.00	516.00
	Weigh and discharge.	○		15.00	1.00	15.00	2.00	30.00
	Transport to store.	⇒		108.00	1.00	108.00	2.00	216.00
	Unleash.	▽		62.64	1.00	62.64	2.00	125.28
	Take new coil.	○		427.92	1.50	641.88	2.00	1283.76
	Transport to table.	⇒		108.00	1.50	162.00	2.00	324.00
	Place on table.	○		37.50	1.50	56.25	2.00	112.50
	Place on mandrill.	○		105.90	1.50	158.85	2.00	317.70
	Place plate on profiling machine.	○		182.50	1.50	273.75	2.00	547.50
	Program machine.	○		148.00	1.00	148.00	2.00	296.00
	Collect data of new coil.	□		112.00	1.50	168.00	2.00	336.00
	Take to sampling area.	⇒		15.00	1.50	22.50	2.00	45.00
	Make free check.	○		122.60	1.50	183.90	2.00	367.80
	Profile.	○		3.29	2000.00	6580.00	2.05	13489.00
	Measure change.	○		100.00	1.00	100.00	2.05	205.00
	Wait to pack.	D		0.00	1.00	0.00	2.05	0.00
	End of note.	□		25.00	1.00	25.00	2.00	50.00
	TOTAL					9,447.20		19,129.40

Figure 8.21. Result of profiling time after the improvement in profile exchange

331

Example

Method improvement in press exchange

In this example, we will see the obtained improvement in a manufacturing company of embossed sheet components. Before performing the improvement study in the workstation, the operator performed the sequence of operations as can be seen in Figure 8.22.

Document 2 - Methods study of the task							
Description of Operation	Type of Operation	Distance (meters)	Unit Time (sec)	Units	Operation Time (sec)	Type
Complete documentation.	○		106.69	1.00	106.69	TB
Clock in task.	○		60.24	1.00	60.24	TB
Remove processed material and leave it next to bending machines.	○		49.39	1.00	49.39	TB
Check tool to use.	○		156.62	1.00	156.62	TD
Disassemble dies.	○		50.83	1.00	50.83	TD
Install dies.	○		66.81	1.00	66.81	TM
Search and place gauges.	○		182.96	1.00	182.96	TB
Remove material coil to the rear of machine.	○		98.80	1.00	98.80	TB
Introduce coil/band.	○		121.89	1.00	121.89	TB
Adjust feeder.	○		358.55	1.00	358.55	TB
Program task.	○		143.54	1.00	143.54	TB
Process part.	○		34.24	1.00	34.24	TB
Control part.	○		306.99	1.00	306.99	TB
Clock in task.	○		67.24	1.00	67.24	TB
TOTAL OPERATIONS					1,804.78	

Total Basis Time	1,530.52
Total Disassembly Time	207.45
Total Asssembly Time	66.81
Initial Time	1,804.78

Figure 8.22. Methods study of press exchange

As observed, when performing the study, the type of each operation was defined with the purpose of facilitating the conversion of internal operations into external.

Before starting the operation, the operator revised what kind of tool to install in the machine in order to start the task. This operation was done while the machine was paused, so it was initiated when the machine was running. In the same way, the removal of processed material was initiated while the machine was operating, with no impediment in doing it that way.

The next operation eliminated was "search and place gauges." Once the dies were installed, the operator had to adjust them to the machine. For

8. Improvement in Setup Times of Machines - SMED: Agile Manufacturing

this, the operator used a group of gauges and inserted them according to their necessity. To eliminate these adjustments, what was done was to perform a series of marks in the machine and tool, so now the operator just had to match both marks, eliminating the placement of gauges.

To reduce the time of "adjust feeder," we opted for the same solution as in the previous case. A series of marks were done in the machine, reducing the time of adjustment.

To shorten the execution time of the remaining operations, it was decided that they would be performed by two operators, reducing the time to half in most cases.

After this first step, the time study showed the data provided in Figure 8.23.

Document 2 - Methods study of the task						
Description of Operation	Type of Operation	Distance (meters)	Unit Time (sec)	Units	Operation Time (sec)	Type
Complete documentation.	○		106.69	1.00	106.69	TB
Clock in task.	○		60.24	1.00	60.24	TB
Disassemble dies.	○		50.83	1.00	50.83	TD
Install dies.	○		66.81	1.00	66.81	TM
Remove material coil to the rear of machine.	○		49.40	1.00	49.40	TB
Introduce coil/band.	○		60.95	1.00	60.95	TB
Adjust feeder.	○		71.71	1.00	71.71	TB
Program task.	○		143.54	1.00	143.54	TB
Process part.	○		17.24	1.00	17.24	TB
Control part.	○		153.50	1.00	153.50	TB
Clock in task.	○		67.24	1.00	67.24	TB
TOTAL OPERATIONS					848.14	

Total Basis Time	730.50
Total Disassembly Time	50.83
Total Assembly Time	66.81
Initial Time	848.14

Figure 8.23. Reduction of time in press exchange after applying first phase of SMED

The following step will be to polish all aspects of the operations; the immense majority of external and internal operations will be improved. Consequently the operations "dismount the dies," "install the dies," and "adjust feeder" are now performed with two operators, reducing the time to half.

333

To improve the work cycle of the machine, a new computer program was installed that eliminated diverse pauses in the process of sheet metal transformation.

With all these improvements, the study reflected the following data:

Document 2 - Methods study of the task						
Description of Operation	Type of Operation	Distance (meters)	Unit Time (sec)	Units	Operation Time (sec)	Type
Complete documentation.	○		106.69	1.00	106.69	TB
Clock in task.	○		60.24	1.00	60.24	TB
Disassemble dies.	○		25.42	1.00	25.42	TB
Install dies.	○		33.41	1.00	33.41	TD
Remove material coil to the rear of machine.	○		49.40	1.00	49.40	TD
Introduce coil/band.	○		60.95	1.00	60.95	TM
Adjust feeder.	○		35.86	1.00	35.86	TB
Program task.	○		100.48	1.00	100.48	TB
Process part.	○		8.62	1.00	8.62	TB
Control part.	○		46.05	1.00	46.05	TB
Clock in task.	○		67.24	1.00	67.24	TB
TOTAL OPERATIONS					594.34	

Total Basis Time	450.59
Total Disassembly Time	82.81
Total Assembly Time	60.95
Initial Time	594.34

Figure 8.24. *Reduction of press exchange times after applying second phase of SMED*

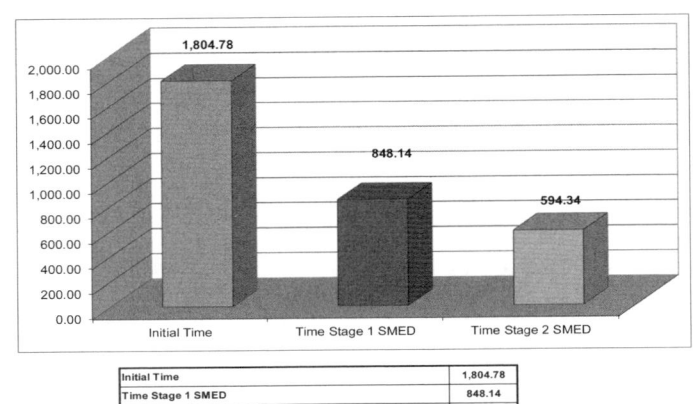

Initial Time	1,804.78
Time Stage 1 SMED	848.14
Time Stage 2 SMED	594.34

Figure 8.25. *Graph of time reduction in press exchange*

As can be seen in the summary table (Figure 8.25), the execution time of the task was reduced by 20 minutes with the use of SMED techniques.

Example

Implementation of working method in beverage bottling plant.

The following examples are about the implementation of a working procedure in a juice bottling plant. The container in which the juice is bottled can have different shapes and sizes. For this reason, constant exchanges must be made in the format of the bottling machine, including exchanges in the head or cap.

When performing the format change to the machine, the operators lacked a working procedure or technical instruction that clearly indicated what they had to do. Therefore, procedure duration was variable and depended on the dexterity of the operators. A study of methods and times was done and from this study, such procedure was elaborated for operators.

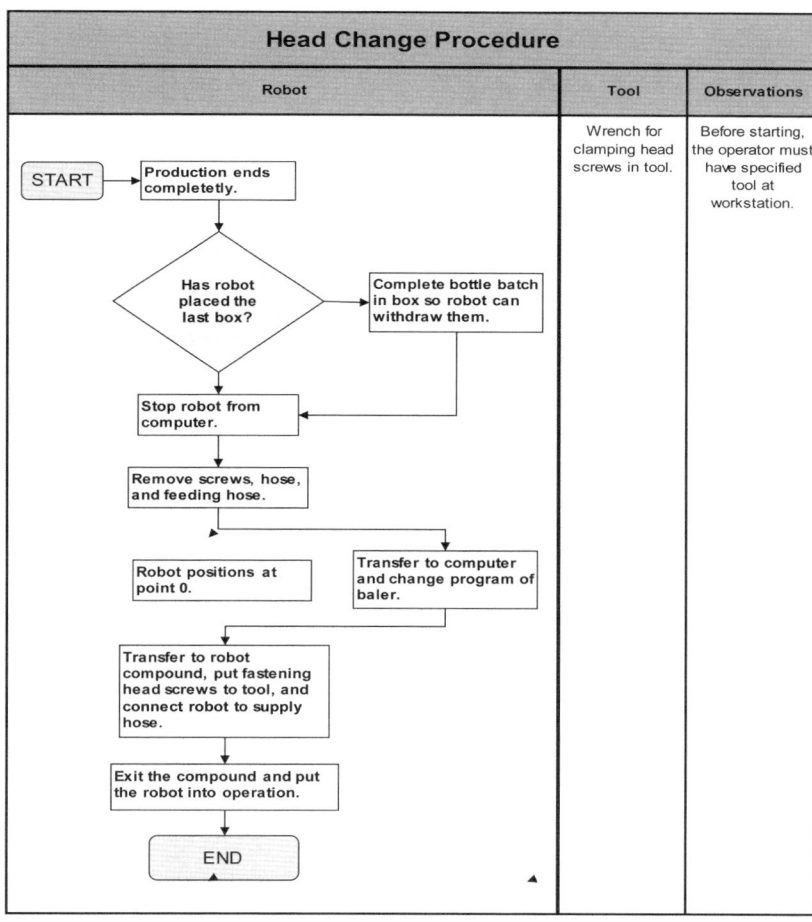

Figure 8.26. *Head exchange procedure*

Industrial Productivity

Documento 2 - Estudio de métodos de la tarea					
Descripción Operación	Tipo	Dist (m)	T. unit(seg)	Unidades	T.Corr. Total
Completar lote de botellas en caja para que el robot las retire.	○		64,19	1,00	**64,19**
Parar el robot desde el ordenador.	○		41,13	1,00	**41,13**
Entrar en recinto de robot.	○		3,91	1,00	**3,91**
Quitar tornillos de sujeción del cabezal al útil.	○		85,66	1,00	**85,66**
Desconectar latiguillo de robot.	○		9,20	1,00	**9,20**
Desconectar manguera de alimentación de robot.	○		15,09	1,00	**15,09**
Salir de recinto de robot.	⇨		8,06	1,00	**8,06**
Activar robot para que vaya a punto 0.	○		3,23	1,00	**3,23**
Cambiar programa de enfardadora 1.	○		18,03	1,00	**18,03**
Desplazamiento a ordenador.	⇨	20,00	16,00	1,00	**16,00**
Cambiar programa de enfardadora 2.	○		3,72	1,00	**3,72**
Desplazamiento a recinto de robot.	⇨	20,00	16,00	1,00	**16,00**
Poner tornillos de sujeción de cabezal a útil.	○		113,13	1,00	**113,13**
Conectar latiguillo de robot.	○		2,91	1,00	**2,91**
Conectar manguera de alimentación de robot.	○		18,20	1,00	**18,20**
Salir del recinto del robot.	⇨		9,48	1,00	**9,48**
Poner en funcionamiento el robot.	○		21,97	1,00	**21,97**
TOTAL OPERACIONES					**449,91**

Figure 8.27. Method study of the head exchange task

With this measure, all operators worked in the same way. The workstation was given a checklist for the operators to follow before the format exchange in the machine in order to avoid time wastes or unnecessary delays from lack of materials or tools.

Checklist That Precedes Head Exchange	
Check	Checked
Prepare key to tighten head fastening screws to tool.	
Prepare instructions for batch.	

NOTE:

1. This checklist will be done when 2,500 bottles are left for batch exchange.
2. Machine will not be stopped without having verified the checklist.

Figure 8.28. Checklist of external operations

For the top exchange, the same methodology was followed.

8. Improvement in Setup Times of Machines - SMED: Agile Manufacturing

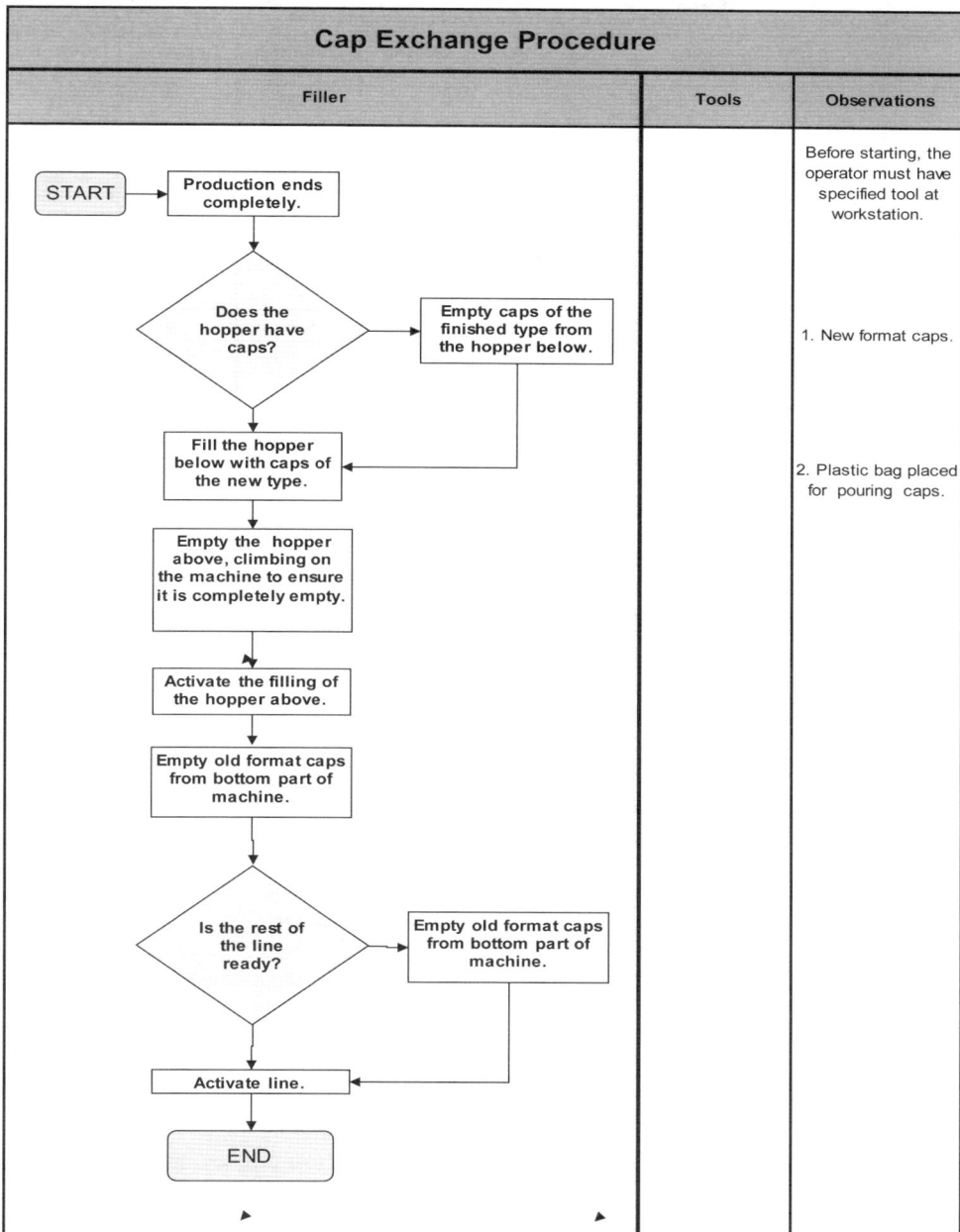

Figure 8.29. Top exchange procedure

The working procedure was defined.

337

Industrial Productivity

Document 2 - Methods study of the task

Description of Operation	Type of Operation	Distance (meters)	Unit Time (sec)	Units	Operation Time (sec)
Empty finished format caps from the bottom hopper.	○		23.20	1.00	23.20
Fill bottom hopper with new format stoppers.	○		36.20	1.00	36.20
Empty the above hopper, climbing on the machine to ensure it is completely empty.	○		45.32	1.00	45.32
Activate the above hopper filling.	○		3.00	1.00	3.00
Empty previous format caps from machine.	○		43.31	1.00	43.31
Place a bottle right before the packaging section.	○		3.21	1.00	3.21
Activate line.	○		1.31	1.00	1.31
Move to computer.	⇨	19.00	15.20	1.00	15.20
Change batch number in computer.	○		78.94	1.00	78.94
TOTAL OPERATIONS					**249.69**

Figure 8.30. Methods study of the top exchange task

Checklist That Precedes Cap Changeover

Checking	Checked
Prepare plastic bags for cap pouring.	
Prepare instructions for batch.	

NOTE:
1. This checklist will be done when 2,500 bottles are left for batch exchange.
2. Machine will not be stopped without having verified the checklist.

Figure 8.31. Checklist for external operations of top exchange

Questions

1. What is the SMED?
2. What is the difference between internal operation and external operation setup?
3. Define the three stages of SMED.
4. Why does the SMED reduce the stock of the company?

8. Improvement in Setup Times of Machines - SMED: Agile Manufacturing

5. Are the principles of analysis and improvement of methods applicable to machine exchange tasks?
6. Describe three solutions for the improvement of external and internal operations.

Problem

Given the following method diagram of machine exchange, describe what actions you would carry out to apply the different stages of SMED. Quantify what improvement can be realized. The method in question indicates each of the operations an operator has to perform in exchanging the tool in a forming machine. Before the exchange, the operator must wait until the tools are cold in order to be able to exchange them.

Document 2 - Methods study of the task

Description of Operation	Type of Operation	Distance (meters)	Unit Time (sec)	Units
Turn off machine after use.	○		15.32	1.00
Wait until tool is cold.	D		300.25	1.00
Move to location of toolbox.	⇒	25.00	20.00	1.00
Provide gloves.	○		14.32	1.00
Provide toolbox.	○		12.35	1.00
Move to workstation.	⇒	25.00	20.00	1.00
Grab wrench and disassemble type 1 tools loosening nuts.	○		63.23	1.00
Move in search of type 3 tools.	⇒	46.50	37.20	1.00
Provide type 3 tools.	○		43.31	1.00
Move to workstation.	⇒	46.50	37.20	1.00
Assemble type 3 tools tightening nuts with wrench.	○		52.00	1.00
Move to toolbox.	⇒	25.00	20.00	1.00
Store toolbox.	○		3.65	1.00
Move to workstation.	⇒	25.00	20.00	1.00
Provide type 1 tools.	○		6.25	1.00
Move to location of type 1 tools.	⇒	54.50	43.60	1.00
Store type 1 tools.	○		43.31	1.00
Move to workstation.	⇒	54.50	43.60	1.00
Activate start button.	○		6.00	1.00
TOTAL OPERATIONS				

Figure 8.32. Tool exchange method.

Bibliography

Hirano, Hiroyuki, *5 Pillars of the Visual Workplace* (Tokyo: Nikkan Kogyo Shimbun Ltd., 1990).

Liker, Jeffrey K., *The Toyota Way* (New York: McGraw-Hill, 2006).

Shingo, Shigeo, *A Revolution in Manufacturing: The SMED System* (New York: Productivity Press, 1985).

Shingo, Shigeo, *Quick Changeover for Operators: The SMED System* (New York: Productivity Press, 1996).

Womak, James P. and Daniel T. Jones, *Lean Thinking* (New York: Simon & Schuster, 1996).

Chapter 9

Balancing Improvements in Tasks with Several Participants

In this chapter, we will look at improving the tasks involving several participants operating in parallel or operating in line. We will try to balance such tasks and eliminate the possible waiting times the participants might encounter. All the tools available for this purpose will be described in this chapter.

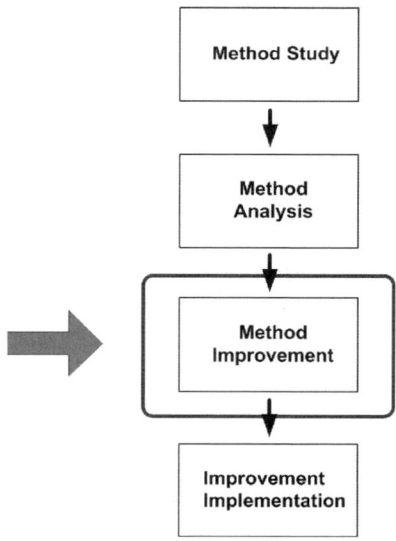

Figure 9.1. *Second part outline. Methods improvement*

341

9.1. Introduction: Reduction of Delay Time

As we have seen in the previous chapters of the book, in tasks where several participants operate simultaneously, imbalance often occurs in the various workloads. This situation occurs for both assembly line work and work in which the participants carry out their tasks in parallel. In both cases, that situation is not ideal when different workloads produce imbalances and, consequently, waits and delays in the workplace; less workload means less saturation.

> **The main objective of method improvement in tasks where several participants operate is to reduce the delay times to which the participants may be subjected due to the action of others, either in simultaneous tasks or in line tasks.**

In this chapter, methods and rules necessary to reduce the times of delay caused by imbalances will be discussed. We introduce the concept of coefficient of imbalance, which is the proportion between delay time of one participant and the total duration of the cycle. It can also be extrapolated to the total of participants. The sum of saturation and the imbalance equals 100 percent; saturation is the equivalent of chain efficiency.

9.2. Improvement of Assembly Line Works

The balancing of workloads or of productive capacities of the different stages of a line manufacturing process is one of the essential aspects that must be addressed in order to make adequate use of resources.

> **Line balancing means "equal productive capacity of each of the tasks in the sequence of a line."**

If equal production times characterize all the stages, it is said that the line balancing is perfect (impossible to achieve), but if not, the rhythm of production is constrained by the stage with more workload (limiting operation), causing a waste in resources (workforce and machines) and, consequently, increasing the costs. In this chapter we explain the existing tools that address these delays in order to reduce them.

Although the problem of balancing the production lines can be subject to different approaches according to the circumstances of each case, we can determine two general approaches:

- Start from a given demand of production in order to determine the factors to combine, and then assign resources to achieve that demand.
- Based on combinations of the resources available, calculate the production that is obtained.

To balance a line, the following options are available:

1. **Divide the task:** Could a task be divided in such a way that the units can be processed in two workstations? In this case, the work would be divided into several workstations.

2. **Redistribute the operations:** Removing several operations of an oversaturated workstation and incorporating them in an upstream or downstream workstation whose saturation is low, balancing the production line.

3. **Use parallel workstations:** Given the level of saturation of the workstation, work may need to be assigned to two or more workstations so they operate in parallel. This technique consists in duplicating the workplaces. It would be equivalent to assigning more operators.

4. **Workplace grouping:** In some situations, the workplaces could be grouped into one, achieving greater saturation of the newly created workplaces and redistributing the remaining resources in other workstations of the line.

5. **Redesign:** Sometimes an analyst can be forced to redesign the working method to try to reduce the imbalance times.

To implement an assembly line, it is essential to know the product and its components as well as the machines and tools necessary for the assembly of such product.

Example

We have an assembly line of three operators. On this occasion, to improve the performance of the production line after performing the exhaustive analysis, we opted to eliminate one of the stations, redistributing the operations performed in that station between the remaining workplaces. Next, the study of methods of the line and data of each workstation before designing the improvement are shown.

Document 2 - Method study of the task: Shower assembly - Workstation 1					
N°	Description of Operation	Unit Time (sec)	Frequency		Operation Time (sec)
1	Take case from cart, perform visual inspection. Place on worktable.	18.86	1	1	18.86
2	Fold front fold with both hands.	9.22	1	1	9.22
3	Take window glass, verify visually, and mount jonquil on each side.	26.69	1	1	26.69
4	Tighten jonquils in tool until it butts with the glass, and remove from tool.	9.92	1	1	9.92
5	Assemble both stoppers in window set.	16.17	1	1	16.17
6	Assemble window set in case, matching the drills.	9.50	1	1	9.50
7	Take pneumatic screwdriver and place 2 screws to attach the window to the case.	33.14	1	1	33.14
8	Turn case placing vertically.	5.83	1	1	5.83
9	Place 2 screws in back to attach window to case.	29.80	1	1	29.80
10	Move hood toward intermediate position.	6.83	1	1	6.83
11	Take a frontal and place on worktable.	14.61	1	1	14.61
12	Take a commuter and assemble on frontal.	16.17	1	1	16.17
13	Take pneumatic screwdriver and attach the commuter to frontal with 2 screws, leaving screwdriver in tool.	39.92	1	1	39.92
14	Assemble frontal in case, inserting cable and opening window.	23.75	1	1	23.75
15	Take screwdriver and attach the frontal with 2 screws to the case.	36.56	1	1	36.56
18	Take hood with both hands and transfer to intermediate table of workstation 2.	11.80	1	1	11.80
19	Move to case cart.	7.44	1	1	7.44
42	Turn case cart (1).	55.00	1	40	1.38
43	Remove attaching clips from case cart (1).	7.05	1	40	0.18
44	Provide 20 commuters in carboard box.	51.09	1	20	2.55
45	Provide 20 glasses aproximately.	73.86	1	20	3.69
46	Provide box with 24 frontals.	117.09	1	24	4.88
47	Provide jounquils.	95.75	2	60	3.19
48	Provide brakes.	122.86	2	80	3.07
101	Introduce biometric work code.	25.56	1	217	0.12
102	Perform reading of fingerprint in biometric.	7.06	1	217	0.03
				Person Time:	335.30

Figure 9.2. Study of methods of workstation I

9. Balancing Improvements in Tasks with Several Participants

Document 2 - Method study of the task: Shower assembly - Workstation 2

N°	Description of Operation	Unit Time (sec)	Frequency		Operation Time (sec)
20	Take cart wrap, visually inspect and place in tool, unwinding cable.	24.30	1	1	24.30
21	Assemble two lamps.	20.98	1	1	20.98
106	Place red LED light.	21.38	1	1	21.38
22	Take case from intermediate workstation and place in wrap, matching the holes.	22.25	1	1	22.25
23	Screw case and wrap with 12 screws.	83.39	1	1	83.39
24	Take feedthrough bracket and mount at the rear of the case.	37.69	1	1	37.69
25	Take wrap assembly + case, remove from tool and transfer to the auxiliary table of workstation 3 and turn.	21.14	1	1	21.14
	Perform 180 degree turn to take the label (2).	6.56	1	1	6.56
104	Take double label printer, separate. Paste traceability label on back or side and the characteristics label inside the apparatus. Take warranty booklet, paste label and insert. (The operator can wear protective gloves.)	50.51	1	1	50.51
27	Take sleeve and place inside the hood.	5.80	1	1	5.80
28	Push/pull the hood toward workstation.	5.42	1	1	5.42
29	Turn and move toward the wrap cart.	5.53	1	1	5.53
49	Provide with hook 36 wraps from cart with 108 units.	176.25	1	108	1.63
99	Provide feedthrough bracket.	60.97	1	100	0.61
51	Open box of bulbs.	89.15	1	150	0.59
98	Provide sleeves.	60.58	1	150	0.40
52	Place box of bulbs in workstation, removing cardboard protection.	38.21	1	25	1.53
53	Remove bars from wrap cart.	17.79	3	54	0.99
105	Fill in job sheet.	214.53	1	217	0.99
101	Introduce biometric work code.	25.56	1	217	0.12
102	Perform reading of fingerprint in biometric.	7.06	1	217	0.03
				Person Time:	311.85

Figure 9.3. Study of methods of workstation 2

Document 2 - Method study of the task: Shower assembly - Workstation 3

N°	Description of Operation	Unit Time (sec)	Frequency		Operation Time (sec)
31	Move hood to workstation 3 using both hands.	10.58	1	1	10.58
34	Take instructions manual and introduce in apparatus.	8.88	1	1	8.88
26	Open box of connections without removing any screws, connect, close box, and place net cable.	45.53	1	1	45.53
32	Place 2 screws in connection box to close it.	28.44	1	1	28.44
33	Take net cable and hose with tweezers inside the case.	31.58	1	1	31.58
35	Take plate holder and assemble with 5 rivets on hood.	86.22	1	1	86.22
37	Take and assemble light plate.	17.89	1	1	17.89
38	Take three filters and assemble in hood.	36.97	1	1	36.97
39	Place net cable correctly and close window.	11.86	1	1	11.86
40	Take and place hood to line.	6.30	1	1	6.30
41	Perform 180 degree turn and initiate the work cycle.	5.69	1	1	5.69
55	Empty 75 rivets from riveter interior.	22.69	5	75	1.51
54	Return instructions manual to workstation.	99.30	1	22	4.51
56	Provide workstation with several light plates.	107.08	1	60	1.78
57	Provide plate holders from tray to table.	76.62	1	25	3.06
58	Replenish filters on top of workstation.	47.36	3	15	9.47
97	Replenish filter box.	13.03	3	55	0.71
101	Introduce biometric work code.	25.56	1	217	0.12
102	Perform reading of fingerprint in biometric.	7.06	1	217	0.03
				Person Time:	311.15

Figure 9.4. Study of methods of workstation 3

Line report

N°	Workstation	Person Time (min/unit)	Cycle Time (min/unit)	Saturation
Total	Total Line	15.97	5.59	95.27%
1	Workstation 1	5.59	5.59	100.00%
2	Workstation 2	5.20	5.59	93.00%
3	Workstation 3	5.19	5.59	92.80%
	Standard Time (min/unit)		16.77	
	Efficiency of the line		95.27%	
	Imbalance coefficient		4.73%	

Figure 9.5. Line report

9. Balancing Improvements in Tasks with Several Participants

Justification of calculations for the team of three operators:

- *Standard time = Maximum standard times of the workstations (5.59) x (1 + 1 + 1) = 16.7 minutes/units*
- *Coefficient of imbalance = 100 x [(3 x 5.59) – (5.59 + 5.20 + 5.19)] / (3 x 5.59) = 4.73%*
- *Efficiency of the line = [100 x (5.9 + 5.20 + 5.19)] / (3 x 5.59) = 95.27%*

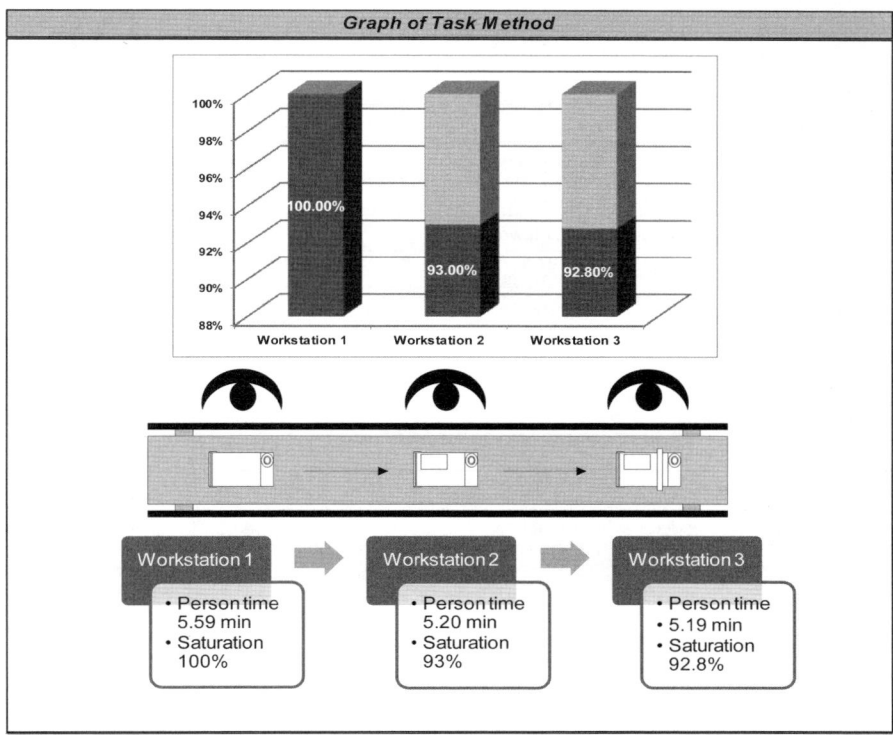

Figure 9.6. *Graph of the method of the task*

Proposed improvement: Unify the workstations; pass from three workstations to two. Operations are distributed in the new definition of workstations (see Figure 9.7).

347

Document 2 - Method study of the task: Shower assembly - Workstation 1

Nº	Description of the Operation	Unit Time (sec)	Frequency		Operation Time (sec)
1	Take case from cart, perform visual inspection. Place on working table.	18.86	1	1	18.86
2	Fold the front fold with both hands.	9.22	1	1	9.22
3	Take window glass, verify visually, and mount jonquil on each side.	26.69	1	1	26.69
4	Tighten jonquils in tool until it butts with the glass and remove from tool.	9.92	1	1	9.92
5	Assemble both stoppers in window set.	16.17	1	1	16.17
6	Assemble window set in case, matching the drills.	9.50	1	1	9.50
7	Take pneumatic screwdriver and place 2 screws to attach the window to the case.	33.14	1	1	33.14
8	Turn case placing vertically.	5.83	1	1	5.83
9	Place 2 screws in back to attach window to case.	29.80	1	1	29.80
10	Move hood toward intermediate position.	6.83	1	1	6.83
11	Take a frontal and place on working table.	14.61	1	1	14.61
12	Take a commuter and assemble on frontal.	16.17	1	1	16.17
13	Take pneumatic screwdriver and attach the commuter to frontal with 2 screws, leaving screwdriver in tool.	39.92	1	1	39.92
14	Assemble frontal in case, inserting cable and opening window.	23.75	1	1	23.75
15	Take screwdriver and attach the frontal with 2 screws to the case.	36.56	1	1	36.56
17	Take hood with both hands and transfer to intermediate table of workstation 2.	21.38	1	1	21.38
18	Move to case cart.	11.80	1	1	11.80
	Change from workstation 1 to workstation 2.	10.97	1	1	10.97
20	Take cart wrap, visually inspect and place in tool, unwinding cable.	24.30	1	1	24.30
21	Assemble two lamps.	20.98	1	1	20.98
22	Take case from intermediate workstation and place in wrap, matching the holes.	22.25	1	1	22.25
150	Take screwdriver and screws.	7.38	1	1	7.38
151	Place screw in case.	5.96	7	1	41.72
152	Deposit screwdriver and screws.	3.60	1	1	3.60
	Change from workstation 2 to workstation 1.	10.97	1	1	10.97
42	Turn case cart (1).	55.00	1	40	1.38
43	Remove attaching clips from case cart (1).	7.05	1	40	0.18

44	Provide 20 commuters in carboard box.	51.09	1	20	2.55
45	Provide 20 glasses aproximately.	73.86	1	20	3.69
46	Provide box with 24 frontals.	117.09	1	24	4.88
47	Provide jounquils.	95.75	2	60	3.19
48	Provide brakes.	122.86	2	80	3.07
49	Provide wit hook 36 wraps from cart with 108 units.	176.25	1	108	1.63
51	Open box of bulbs.	89.15	1	150	0.59
52	Place box of bulbs in workstation, removing cardboard protection.	38.21	1	25	1.53
53	Remove bars from wrap cart.	17.79	3	54	0.99
101	Introduce biometric work code.	25.56	1	217	0.12
102	Perform reading of fingerprint in biometric.	7.06	1	217	0.03
				Person Time:	496.15

Figure 9.7. Study of methods of workstation 1 (unified)

Document 2 - Method study of the task: Shower assembly - Workstation 2

N°	Description of the Operation	Unit Time (sec)	Frequency		Operation Time (sec)
150	Take screwdriver and screws.	7.38	1	1	7.38
151	Place screw in case.	5.96	5	1	29.80
152	Deposit screwdriver and screws.	3.60	1	1	3.60
24	Take feedthrough bracket and mount at the rear of the case.	37.69	1	1	37.69
25	Take wrap assembly + case, remove from tool, and transfer to the auxiliary table of workstation 3 and turn.	21.14	1	1	21.14
	Perform 180 degree turn to take the label (2).	6.56	1	1	6.56
104	Take double label printer, separate. Paste traceability label on back or side and the characteristics label inside the apparatus. Take warranty booklet, paste label. and insert. (The operator can wear protective gloves.)	50.51	1	1	50.51
26	Open box of connections without removing any screw, connect, close box, and place net cable.	45.53	1	1	45.53
27	Take sleeve and place inside the hood.	5.80	1	1	5.80
34	Take instructions manual and introduce in apparatus.	8.88	1	1	8.88
	Change from workstation 2 to 3.	10.89	1	1	10.89
31	Move hood to workstation 3 using both hands.	10.58	1	1	10.58

32	Place 2 screws in connection box to close it.	28.44	1	1	28.44
33	Take net cable and hose with tweezers inside the case.	31.58	1	1	31.58
35	Take plate holder and assemble with 5 rivets on hood.	86.22	1	1	86.22
37	Take and assemble light plate.	17.89	1	1	17.89
38	Take three filters and assemble in hood.	36.97	1	1	36.97
39	Place net cable correctly and close window.	11.86	1	1	11.86
40	Take and place hood to line.	6.30	1	1	6.30
	Change from workstation 3 to 2.	10.89	1	1	10.89
54	Replenish instructions manual in workstation.	99.30	1	22	4.51
55	Empty 75 rivets from riveter interior.	22.69	5	75	1.51
56	Provide workstation with several light plates.	107.08	1	60	1.78
57	Provide plate holders from tray to table.	76.62	1	25	3.06
58	Replenish filters on top of workstation.	47.36	3	15	9.47
97	Replenish filter box.	13.03	3	55	0.71
98	Provide sleeves.	60.58	1	150	0.40
99	Provide feedthrough bracket.	60.97	1	100	0.61
105	Fill in job sheet.	214.53	1	217	0.99
101	Introduce biometric work code.	25.56	1	217	0.12
102	Perform reading of fingerprint in biometric.	7.06	1	217	0.03
				Person Time:	491.72

Figure 9.8. *Study of methods of workstation 2 (unified)*

Line Report				
N°	Workstation	Person Time (min/unit)	Cycle Time (min/unit)	Saturation
Total	Total Line	16.46	8.27	99.55%
1	Workstation 1	8.27	8.27	100.00%
2	Workstation 2	8.20	8.27	99.11%
Standard Time (min/unit)			16.54	
Efficiency of the line			99.55%	
Imbalance coefficient			0.45%	

Figure 9.9. *Line report*

9. Balancing Improvements in Tasks with Several Participants

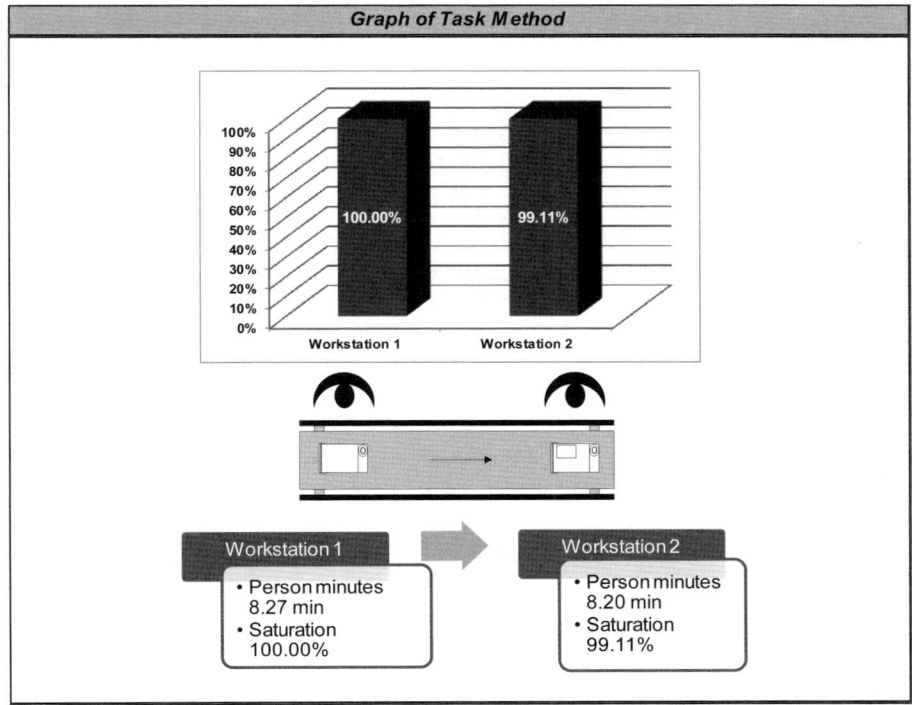

Figure 9.10. *Graph of the method of the task*

If the calculations are justified for the team of two operators:

- *Standard time = Maximum standard times of the workstations (8.27) x (1+1) = 16.54 minutes/units*
- *Coefficient of imbalance = 100 x [(2 x 8.27) − (8.27 + 8.20)] / (2 x 8.27) = 0.45%*
- *Efficiency of the line = [100 x (3.31 + 3.29)] / (2 x 3.31) = 99.55%*

In view of the data, the efficiency of the assembly line has been improved from 95% to almost 100% without monetary outlay, by eliminating a workstation. To reach these conditions, the workstation and the disaggregation of operations must be known in detail.

Example

The following example shows the implemented improvement in a bicycle assembly line. Revising the following images we can see how the saturation of the workstations is different, varying from 56 percent to 100 percent, and what generates a time waste in the stations of less saturation.

Worksta. 1	Description of Operations	Tool	Time (sec)
WS 1	Take 2 carts and place 2 carts.	pneumatic screwdriver / hammer	2.67
	Place chassis on cart (timing).		2.87
	Place sticker on bar.		9.58
	Place crown and interior protector.		25.46
	Push cart.		1.45
	Subtotal		**42.03**

Worksta. 2	Description of Operations	Tool	Time (sec)
WS 2	Take cart.	pneumatic ratchet / pneumatic riveter / pneumatic screwdriver	1.98
	Place sleeve in direction axis.		5.28
	Place back mudguard.		10.86
	Cut chain.		5.24
	Close chain.		8.67
	Take wheel and place wheel.		4.30
	Place chain in pinion and crown.		8.87
	Push cart.		1.45
	Subtotal		**46.65**

Worksta. 3	Description of Operations	Tool	Time (sec)
WS 3	Take cart.	pneumatic screwdriver	1.98
	Put 2 nuts in back wheel.		7.61
	Tighten 2 nuts.		10.47
	Check and adjust back wheel.		21.96
	Place external right nut.		5.80
	Put chainguard.		4.70
	Place 2 stickers on chainguard.		10.79
	Place 3 stickers on saddle bar and 4 on direction bar.		10.07
	Push cart.		1.45
	Subtotal		**74.83**

Figure 9.11. Study of times and methods of workstations 1, 2. and 3

Worksta. 4	Description of Operations	Tool	Time (sec)	Saturation
WS 4	Take cart.	pneumatic ratchet / pneumatic screwdriver / wrench	1.98	96.62%
	Take fork, assemble mudguard, and assemble brake and put nut.		27.00	
	Tighten brake nut.		2.46	
	Place cover.		2.85	
	Insert fork in chassis.		3.02	
	Put front wheel.		3.13	
	Put 2 nuts in front wheel		12.60	
	Tighten nuts, test wheel, and adjust wheel.		17.81	
	Push cart.		1.45	
	Subtotal		**72.30**	

9. Balancing Improvements in Tasks with Several Participants

Worksta. 5	Description of Operations	Tool	Time (sec)	Saturation
WS 5	Take cart.		1.98	78.35%
	Put screw in chainguard, check, adjust, and spin bicycle.	screwdriver	12.58	
	Place small sticker.		1.84	
	Place EEC sticker.	wrench	5.66	
	Bring brake shoe closer.	wire cutter	8.29	
	Loosen prisoner and put tool.	pneumatic ratchet	4.70	
	Take handlebars and insert cable in lever.		6.23	
	Insert cable in prisoner, tighten, put cap, remove tool, and check.	brake shoe approx. tool	15.90	
	Push cart.		1.45	
	Subtotal		58.63	

Worksta. 6	Description of Operations	Tool	Time (sec)	Saturation
WS 6 (BALER)	Take cart.		1.98	75.95%
	Take box and assemble box.		4.56	
	Staple box.		3.04	
	Turn box around.		2.10	
	Place sticker on box.		7.38	
	Insert stick (MOD-119).		4.92	
	Remove handlebars, remove fork, and place rod.	staple gun	11.11	
	Put bicycle in bag.		6.70	
	Put bag in box.		1.40	
	Put saddle in box.		2.03	
	Close box.		1.99	
	Staple box.		3.04	
	Move box to pallet and return for cart.		4.43	
	Send carts to place.		2.15	
	Subtotal		56.83	

Figure 9.12. Study of times and methods of workstations 4, 5, and 6

Worksta.	Nº Operators	Person Time (sec/unit)	Cycle Time (sec/unit)	Standard Time (sec/unit)	Saturation
Total Line	6	351.27	74.83	448.98	78.24%
Worksta. 1	1	42.03	74.83		56.16%
Worksta. 2	1	46.65	74.83		62.34%
Worksta. 3	1	74.83	74.83		100.00%
Worksta. 4	1	72.30	74.83		96.62%
Worksta. 5	1	58.63	74.83		78.35%
Worksta. 6	1	56.83	74.83		75.95%
			Line efficiency:	78.24%	
			Imbalance coefficient:	21.76%	

Figure 9.13. Report of the assembly line before the improvement

Industrial Productivity

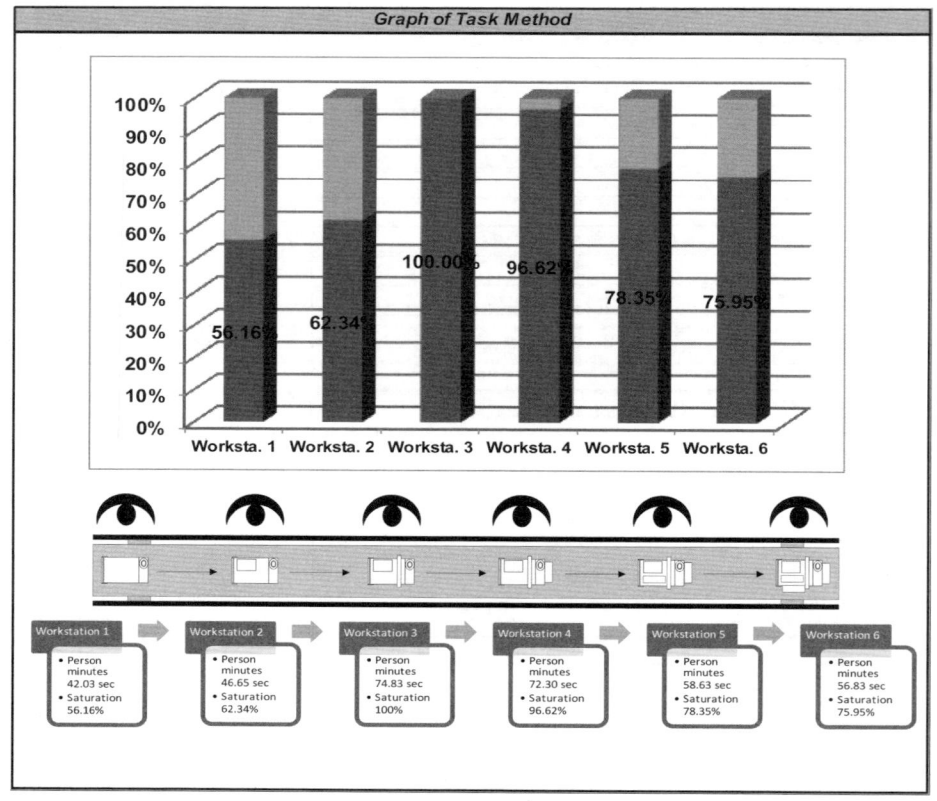

Figure 9.14. Graph of the task's method

Justifying the results:

- Coefficient of imbalance = 100 x [(6 x 74.83) − (42.03 + 46.65 + 74.83 + 72.30 + 58.63 + 56.83)] / (6 x 74.83) = 21.76%

- Efficiency of the line = [100 x (42.03 + 46.65 + 74.83 + 72.30 + 58.63 + 56.83)] / (6 x 74.83) = 78.23%

Adopted solution: In this case, a redistribution of operations between the different stations was chosen, from the most to the least saturated. Because differences in saturation were high, this solution will be more easily carried out.

9. Balancing Improvements in Tasks with Several Participants

Document 2 - Method study of the task: Bicycle assembly

Worksta. 1	Description of Operations	Tool	Time (sec)
WS 1	Take 2 carts and place 2 carts.		2.67
	Place chassis on cart (timing).		2.87
	Place sticker on bar.		9.58
	Place crown and interior protector.	pneumatic screwdriver	25.46
	Place small sticker.		1.84
	Place EEC sticker.	hammer	5.66
	Place 3 stickers on saddlebar and 4 on direction bar.		10.07
	Push cart.		1.45
	Subtotal		**59.60**

Worksta. 2	Description of Operations	Tool	Time (sec)
WS 2	Take cart.		1.98
	Place sleeve in direction axis.		5.28
	Place back mudguard.		10.86
	Cut chain.		0.00
	Close chain.	pneumatic ratchet	8.67
	Take wheel and place wheel.	pneumatic riveter	4.30
	Place chain in pinion and crown.	pneumatic screwdriver	8.87
	Put 2 nuts on rear wheel.		7.61
	Tighten 2 nuts.		10.47
	Check and adjust rear wheel.		0.00
	Push cart.		1.45
	Subtotal		**59.49**

Worksta. 3	Description of Operations	Tool	Time (sec)
WS 3	Take cart.		1.98
	Put 2 nuts in back wheel.		0.00
	Tighten 2 nuts.		0.00
	Check and adjust back wheel.		21.96
	Place external right nut.	pneumatic screwdriver	5.80
	Put chainguard.		4.70
	Place 2 stickers on chainguard.		0.00
	Tight nuts, test wheel, adjust wheel.		17.80
	Push cart.		1.45
	Subtotal		**53.69**

Figure 9.15. Study of redistributed times and methods of workstations 1, 2, and 3

Industrial Productivity

Worksta. 4	Description of Operations	Tool	Time (sec)
WS 4	Take cart.		1.98
	Take fork, assemble mudguard, assemble brake and put nut.		27.00
	Tighten brake nut.	pneumatic ratchet	2.46
	Place cover.		2.85
	Insert fork in chassis.	pneumatic screwdriver	3.02
	Put front wheel.		3.13
	Put 2 nuts in front wheel.		12.60
	Tighten nuts, test wheel, and adjust wheel.	wrench	0.00
	Push cart.		1.45
	SUBTOTAL		**54.49**

Worksta. 5	Description of Operations	Tool	Time (sec)
WS 5	Take cart.	screwdriver	1.98
	Put screw in chainguard, check, adjust, and spin bicycle.		12.58
	Place small sticker.	wrench	0.00
	Place EEC sticker.		0.00
	Bring brake shoe closer.	wire cutter	10.79
	Loosen prisoner and put tool.		8.29
	Take handlebars and insert cable in lever.	pneumatic ratchet	4.70
	Insert cable in prisoner, tighten, put cap, remove tool, and check.		6.23
	Push cart.	brake shoe approx. tool	15.90
	Subtotal		**60.47**

Worksta. 6	Description of Operations	Tool	Time (sec)
WS 6 (BALER)	Take cart.		1.98
	Take box and assemble box.		4.56
	Staple box.		3.04
	Turn box around.		2.10
	Place sticker on box.		7.38
	Insert sticker (MOD-119).		4.92
	Remove handlebars, remove fork, and place rod.	staple gun	11.11
	Put bicycle in bag.		6.70
	Put bag in box.		1.40
	Put saddle in box.		2.03
	Close box.		1.99
	Staple box.		3.04
	Move box to pallet and return for cart.		4.43
	Send carts to place.		2.15
	Subtotal		**56.83**

Figure 9.16. *Study of redistributed times and methods of workstations 4, 5, and 6*

Line Report				
Worksta.	N° Operators	Person Time (sec/unit)	Cycle Time (sec/unit)	Standard Time (sec/unit)	Saturation
Total Line	6	344.57	60.47	362.82	94.97%
Worksta. 1	1	59.60	60.47		98.55%
Worksta. 2	1	59.49	60.47		98.38%
Worksta. 3	1	53.69	60.47		88.79%
Worksta. 4	1	54.49	60.47		90.11%
Worksta. 5	1	60.47	60.47		100.00%
Worksta. 6	1	56.83	60.47		93.98%
			Line efficiency:	94.97%	
			Imbalance coefficient:	5.03%	

Figure 9.17. *Report of the assembly line after the improvement*

9. Balancing Improvements in Tasks with Several Participants

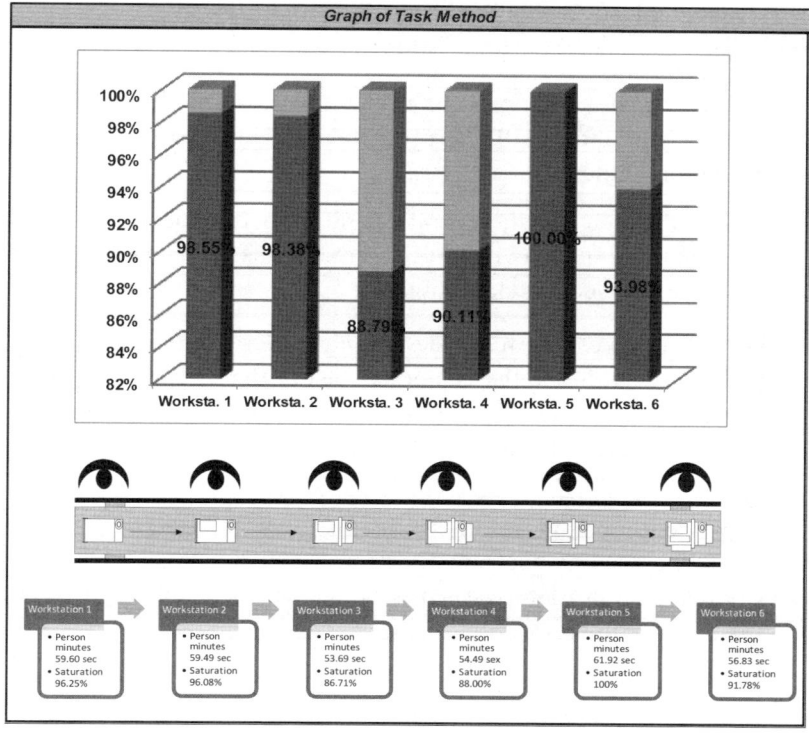

Figure 9.18. *Graph of the method after the implementation*

Due to this redistribution of operations, the saturation of the workstations only oscillated between 86% and 100%, therefore the efficiency of the chain and the balancing coefficient improved considerably:

- *Coefficient of imbalance = 100 x [(6 x 61.92) − (59.60 + 59.49 + 53.69 + 54.49 + 61.92 + 56.83)] / (6 x 61.92) = 6.87%*

- *Efficiency of the line = [100 x (59.6 + 59.49 + 53.69 + 54.49 + 61.92 + 56.83)] / (6 x 61.92) = 93.13%*

9.3. Improvement of Simultaneous Person-Person Tasks

The purpose of the improvement in simultaneous person-person tasks is to reduce the cycle time for an equal quantity of participants from the reduction of delays. The possible solutions for this include:

1. Divide the task.
2. Redistribute operations.
3. Alter workstation grouping.

Industrial Productivity

4. Redesign the workstation.

5. Overlap operations when possible.

As can be observed, the solutions are nearly the same as those applied to the assembly line works. Conceptually the problem of imbalance is the same, therefore the solutions are the same.

When analyzing tasks in which several operators participate simultaneously, it makes sense to differentiate two types of operations. They are the dependent operations and the independent operations.

- Dependent operations are those that must be executed by both operators simultaneously due to the characteristics of the operation or product. An example can be to turn around a part of large dimensions or to position it over the processed item. In these operations, operators must help each other out.

- Independent operations are those that can be executed individually, without the need of a second operator. An example can be the sanding of a wooden board of large dimensions that can be sanded by two operators or just by one operator.

Example

The following example of improvement in simultaneous person-person tasks is about a company that manufactures rubber parts, the operators must pour the component into molds. Once the component is ready, the operators proceed to extract the forged part from the mold. Due to the conditions of the place and to additives in the mixture, when the parts need to be extracted they are wet, which hinders the labor of the machine in charge of stacking them on wooden pallets. To eliminate the excess water, one of the two operators uses a propane bottle, applying heat to the surface of the parts. When revising the subtask "Dry parts," it can be observed how the second operator remains waiting.

9. Balancing Improvements in Tasks with Several Participants

Graph of the task method: Part demolding

Operator 1				Operator 2		
Subtasks of Operator 1	Sec / Unit	State	State	Sec/ Unit	Subtasks of Operator 2
Rubber part demolding.	28.45			28.45	Rubber part demolding.
Rubber part demolding.	11.26			-	Waiting time.
Dry parts.	11.50			-	Dry parts.
Load new tool.	25.67			25.67	Blow and apply mold releaser.
Waiting time.	-			7.65	Blow and apply mold releaser.

Simultaneous task report

Workstation	Nº Participants	Person Time (sec/unit)	Cycle Time (sec/unit)	Standard time (sec/unit)	Saturation
Total task	2	138.65	84.53	169.06	82.01%
Operator 1	1	76.88	84.53		90.95%
Operator 2	1	61.77	84.53		73.07%

Figure 9.19. Graph of the method and report of the task

The graph of the task returns these results; the standard time of the operation is 169.06 seconds/unit.

The objective of the analyst is then to eliminate waiting time for the second operator while the first operator was drying the parts. It was decided to give the second workstation an air gun. As they are independent operations, both operators could blow off excess water. The result of the improvement implementation was the following:

Graph of the task method: Part demolding

Operator 1				Operator 2		
Subtasks of Operator 1	Sec/Unit	State	State	Sec/Unit	Subtasks of Operator 2
Rubber part demolding.	28.45			28.45	Rubber part demolding.
Rubber part demolding.	11.26			-	Waiting time.
Dry parts.	5.75			5.75	Dry parts.
Load new tool.	25.67			25.67	Blow and apply mold releaser.
Waiting time.	-			7.65	Blow and apply mold releaser.

Simultaneous task report

Workstation	Nº Participants	Person Time (sec/unit)	Cycle Time (sec/unit)	Standard time (sec/unit)	Saturation
Total task	2	138.65	78.78	157.56	88.00%
Operator 1	1	71.13	78.78		90.28%
Operator 2	1	67.52	78.78		85.71%

Figure 9.20. Graph of the improved method and report of the simultaneous task

The standard time of the task was reduced, and the second operator, who until then remained idle, was saturated. An 8 percent improvement was obtained with the improvement implementation. In this example, the most obvious detail triggered a great improvement and, what is more important, with the help of a minimum investment cost.

9.4. Improvement of Simultaneous Person-Machine Tasks

In the production processes where operator and machine work together, frequently the operator cannot exercise 100 percent of his or her technical or physical skills.

Another aspect that has to be studied in depth by the analyst is the time in which both (machine and operator) are working. When performing the study of methods, the analyst will observe how operator and machine are operating together, asking questions that might include:

- Does the machine operate at 100 percent?
- Does the operator work at 100 percent?
- Can the saturation of either be increased?

On numerous occasions, during the time the machine is functioning, the operator remains idle during part of the process; or the contrary case could be given where the operator must reduce the speed of the machine (or even stop it) to be able to fulfill the amount of work necessary lengthening the cycle of work.

These two situations are undesirable; if the operator remains idle during the time the machine is running its saturation will be low, and when the operator slows the speed of the machine, it starts lowering its capacity. In the first scenario, the solution is to designate for the operator some preparatory operation during idle time; in the second scenario, the solution would be to increase the workforce to eliminate pauses for the machine. We will now show some practical examples of solutions to these situations.

Generally, we must always try to overlap the activities of operators with the cycle of the machine operating in such a way that the total cycle time is reduced. In addition, other recommendations function in these scenarios.

If the machine has more workload than the operator does and the operator stops:

1. **Bring other machines, either of the same type or another type, closer so that the operator can attend to it during the delays.**

9. Balancing Improvements in Tasks with Several Participants

2. **Try to increase the speed of the machine.**

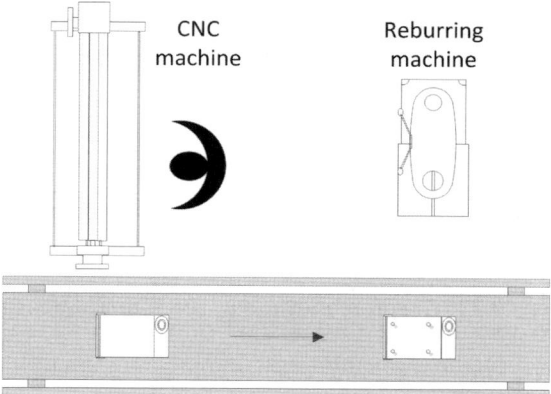

Figure 9.21. Operator attending two machines

If the operator has more workload than the machine and it stops:

1. **Study the possibility of placing more operators:** In the case of machines with an elevated cost of amortization, it could be preferable that more operators work even if they are not saturated. It will depend on the cost of each participant.

2. **Eliminate some operations from the operator who interacts with the machine:** To reduce this operator's workload, operations could be shifted so that the operator from the previous or next workstation carries them out.

3. **Invest in the improvement of the work method for its time reduction.**

Example

A company that manufactures trousers wanted to increase productivity in the fabric cutting area. The cutting area consists of a cutting machine and an operator. After performing the study of methods and times and making the graph of the task, the results were the following:

Industrial Productivity

Graph of the task method: Pattern cutting						
Operator				Cutting machine		
Subtasks of Operator	Sec/Unit	State	State	Sec/Unit	Subtasks of Machine	
Setup tasks.	307.50			-	Paused time.	
Provide fabric patterns.	679.04			325.05	Cutting and labeling time.	
				-	Paused time.	
Classification of fabric kits.	590.63			-	Paused time.	
Tasks of workstation order.	807.25			-	Paused time.	

Figure 9.22. Graph of method of the simultaneous task

The line report indicated a cycle time of the task just over 39 minutes per unit and a saturation of the machine of 13.6 percent.

Simultaneous Task Report					
Workstat.	Nº Participants	Person Time (sec/unit)	Cycle Time (sec/unit)	Standard time (sec/unit)	Saturation
Total task	2	45.16	39.74	39.74	56.82%
Operator	1	39.74	39.74		100.00%
Machine	1	5.42	39.74		13.63%

Figure 9.23. Report of simultaneous task

In this case, duplicating the number of operators in the workstation to reduce the cycle time was the solution chosen. The graph of the task would be:

Graph of the task method: Pattern cutting						
Operator				Cutting Machine		
Subtasks of Operator	Sec/Unit	State	State	Sec/Unit	Subtasks of Machine	
Setup tasks.	153.75			-	Paused time.	
Provide fabric patterns.	339.52			325.05	Cutting and labeling time.	
				-	Paused time.	
Classification of fabric kits.	295.32			-	Paused time.	
Tasks of workstation order.	403.63			-	Paused time.	

Figure 9.24. Graph of the method of the improved simultaneous task

9. Balancing Improvements in Tasks with Several Participants

Workstat.	Nº Participants	Person Time (sec/unit)	Cycle Time (sec/unit)	Standard time (sec/unit)	Saturation
Simultaneous Task Report					
Total task	3	25.29	19.87	39.74	63.63%
Operator	2	19.87	19.87		100.00%
Machine	1	5.42	19.87		27.26%

Figure 9.25. *Report of the simultaneous task after the improvement*

As can be appreciated, the situation has turned 180 degrees, now the cycle time has been reduced to half, from practically 40 minutes to 20 minutes. This way the saturation of the machine has been increased by 11.53 percent.

Example

This second example explains the improvement achieved in a workstation where one operator and one machine participate. The company manufactures chrome handles for wooden doors. The handles were placed in a tool that, once complete and after pressing a button, rotated and was introduced inside the machine. Previously, the processed handles had to be removed, in order to load the next handles to be processed. Next, the machine started its polishing cycle, leaving the operator waiting. The graph of the task would correspond to the following illustration:

Graph of the task method: Door handle polishing

Operator				Machine		
Subtasks of Operator	Sec/Unit	State	State	Sec/Unit	Subtasks of Machine	
Press button to change cart.	3.320			-	Waiting time.	
Place handles on support tool.	120.360			-	Change cart. Polishing cycle.	
Remove processed handles. Tumble second cycle and place first cycle.	-			285.230	Polishing cycle.	
Waiting time.	142.320			-	Polishing cycle.	

Figure 9.26. *Graph of the method of the simultaneous task*

As can be observed, in this task one of the participants always has to wait, never are both working simultaneously. This situation explains why the report of the task produces such improvable results.

Simultaneous Task Report				
Workstation	Nº Participants	Person Time (sec/unit)	Cycle Time (sec/unit)	Standard time (sec/unit)	Saturation
Total task	2	9.19	9.19	9.19	50.00%
Operator	1	4.43	9.19		48.26%
Machine	1	4.75	9.19		51.74%

Figure 9.27. Report of the simultaneous task

Facing this situation, the analyst together with the person in charge of the tool worked together to improve the weak 46 percent saturation of the operator. The task and the machine were studied, a variety of questions were put to the machine's operator, and a tool was designed that allowed the operator to refill and supply the handles while the machine was operating. As explained at the beginning of this example, the machine rotated and the tool was introduced in the machine, so the chroming tools were duplicated, placing them facing each other in such a way that the worker could operate on the one that was not inside the machine. With this low investment, the graph of the task changed the following way:

Graph of the task method: Door handle polishing

Operator		
Subtasks of Operator	Sec/Unit	State
Press button to change cart.	3.320	
Place handles on support tool.	120.360	
Remove processed handles. Tumble second cycle and place first	142.320	
Waiting time.	-	

Machine		
State	Sec/Unit	Subtasks of Machine
	-	Waiting time.
	120.360	Change cart. Polishing cycle.
	142.320	Polishing cycle.
	22.550	Polishing cycle.

Figure 9.28. Graph of the method of the improved simultaneous task

Simultaneous Task Report				
Workstation	Nº Participants	Person Time (sec/unit)	Cycle Time (sec/unit)	Standard time (sec/unit)	Saturation
Total task	2	9.19	4.81	4.81	95.52%
Operator	1	4.43	4.81		92.19%
Machine	1	4.75	4.81		98.85%

Figure 9.29. Report of the improved simultaneous task

The operator's saturation improved by 42 percent and the machine's by 45 percent, both surpassing 87 percent, doubling the productive capacity. In practice, it will not always be so easy to achieve such an improvement, which is why all the tools described throughout the book must be used.

9.4.1. Interference with Machines

As we previously described, an operator and a machine participate in some tasks simultaneously. Such tasks will be composed by operations that the operator produces while the machine is working or while it is paused. Other operations will be performed by the machine itself, without direct intervention of the operator. However, what occurs when just one operator has to attend several machines at the same time? It may happen that while attending one, a failure or stop occurs in any of the others. In this case, the paused machines would stop producing until the operator stops attending the stopped machine. These interruptions, when several machines are stopped at the same time waiting for the attention of the operator, are called "machine interferences."

> *Machine interference* refers to several machines waiting to be attended by the operator who is in charge of them.

When the study of times and methods is performed in teams with several machines, the analyst must analyze the method, in order to design the sequence that generates the best balance and, therefore, the minimum quantity of interferences.

In these tasks, the analyst applies a supplement for interference to the standard time of the task. This supplement for interference is the time corresponding to the inevitably lost production for the simultaneous stop of two or more machines attended by one operator.

The calculation of this supplement is quite complex because of the amount of variables that can be present in each moment, including the number of machines, the variety of machines, variations in product, operator dedication, and the reason or cause for the machine stoppage.

Using the methods and tools described, the order of operations can be established and the interference calculated for a wide range of operations with multiple machines. Improved methods from the work study that are applied in complex situations with many machines in order to evaluate the interference and calculate the corresponding supplement are based mostly in statistical procedures and calculation of odds. This approach is the most objective in making predictions without redoing the study of work. For this, formulas have been established; curves and tables that help determine the interference and therefore the probable production from different operator-machine combinations. Such systems, if used carefully, save time when studying certain particular and complex situations that involve multiple machines. Yet, the predictions made from such formulas and tables must be corroborated by studying first-hand the current factory's working conditions, in order not to miss anything.

As a general rule, the methods of work study provided in this book should be enough to calculate reliable standard times in most of the situations the analyst will face.

Questions

1. What is the balancing of productive lines?
2. Describe the available options for balancing assembly lines.
3. Frequently, what occurs in tasks where operator and machine interact?
4. If the operator has more workload than the machine during the cycle, what can be done so the machine does not stop?
5. Define dependent operations.
6. Define independent operations.
7. Define machine interferences.

Problem I

The following real example is from a white pig quartering room. In the room, a production line is divided into six workstations. The work team is composed of eight operators, with the time for each task shown in the following table.

9. Balancing Improvements in Tasks with Several Participants

Times per Process

Task	Task Time (sec)	Limiting Workstation
Take down and quarter.	150	
Go over ham.	70	
Go over bacon.	70	
Chine.	180	Chine.
Hang ham and bacon.	30	
Hang shoulder and chops.	30	

Task time limit	180
Nº of workers available	8

Workstation Design

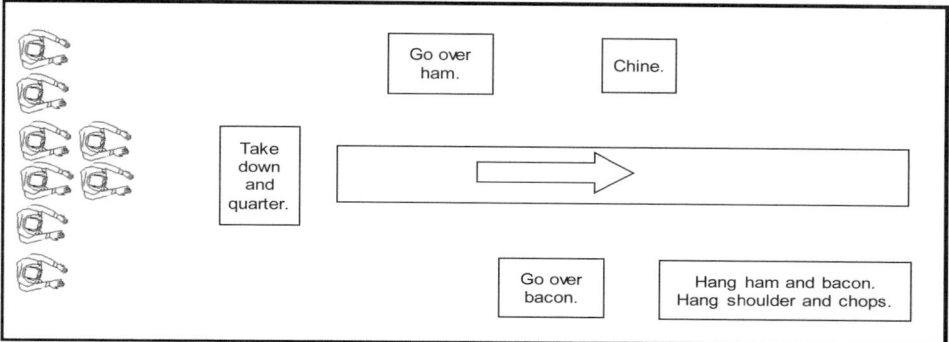

Figure 9.30. *Initial layout of the quartering room*

Once the initial situation is analyzed and available resources assessed, the following assignments are made:

Industrial Productivity

	First rebalancing of workstations						
	Workstation	Task Time (sec)	N° Initial Worker	Workstation Time	Limiting Workstation	Saturation	Waiting Time
1	Take down and quarter.	150					
2	Go over ham.	70					
3	Go over bacon.	70					
4	Chine.	180					
5	Hang ham and bacon.	30					
6	Hang shoulder and chops.	30					

Total:	6	8
Line efficiency:		Productivity
Hour production		Production
Point value		Cost
Time saving per pig		

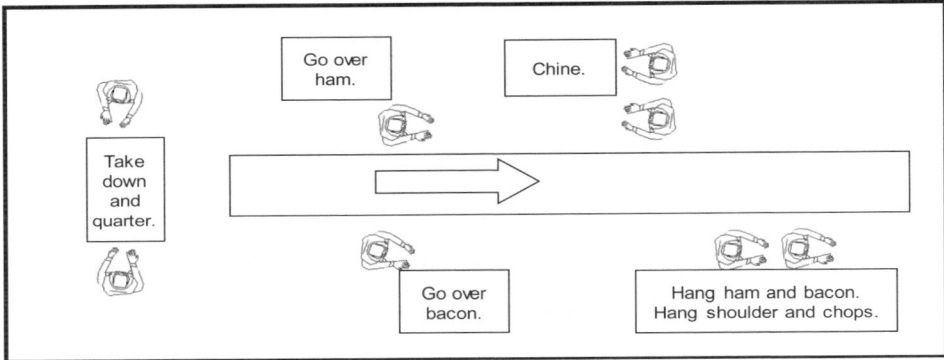

Figure 9.31. Initial assignment of resources

A first rebalancing of workstations is performed maintaining the production at 40 units/hour but reducing the number of workers and, therefore, improving the efficiency of the line and the standard time. The way to proceed is to unify the workstations 5 and 6, because they are the least saturated. This way, an operator is free.

1. Complete the data from the "First rebalancing of workstations" table after the unification of workstations 5 and 6.

9. Balancing Improvements in Tasks with Several Participants

	Workstation	Task time (sec)	N° Initial Worker	Workstation Time	Limiting Workstation	Saturation	Waiting Time
First rebalancing of workstations							
1	Take down and quarter.	150					
2	Go over ham.	70					
3	Go over bacon.	70					
4	Chine.	180					
5/6	Hang ham and bacon. Hang shoulder and chops.	60					

Totals:	5	7	
Line efficiency:		Productivity	
Hour production		Production	
Point value		Cost	
Time saving per pig			

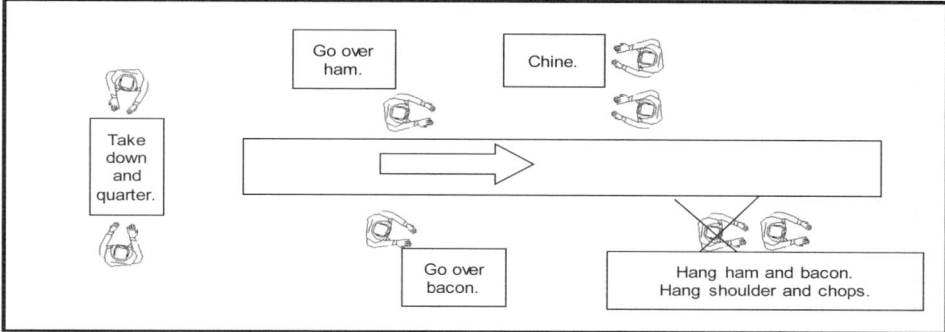

Figure 9.32. First rebalancing. Unification of workstations 5 and 6

2. Complete the data from the "Second rebalancing of workstations" table considering that the production is not limiting, anything manufactured can be sold, and keeping in mind the number of operators of each workstation.

Industrial Productivity

	Second rebalancing of workstations					
	Workstation	Task Time (sec)	Nº Initial Worker	Workstation Time	Limiting Workstation	Saturation	Waiting Time
1	Take down and quarter	150					
2	Go over ham.	70					
3	Go over bacon.	70					
4	Chine.	180					
5/6	Hang ham and bacon. Hang shoulder and chops.	60					

Totals:	5	8
Line efficiency:		Productivity
Hour production		Production
Point value		Cost
Time saving per pig		

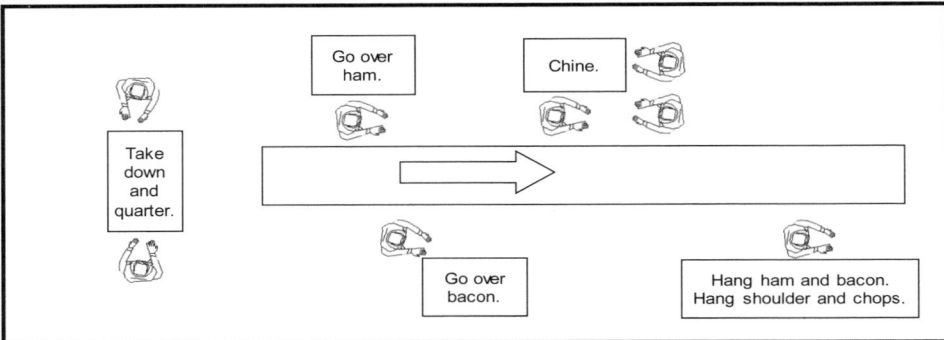

Figure 9.33. Second balancing of workstations.

	Initial Situation	Balance 1	Balance 2
Line efficiency	68%		
Production hour	40.0		
Point value (cost)	12.0		

Figure 9.34. Summary table of data

Problem 2

The following illustration shows a graph of a task's method of simultaneous operator and machine operation. Formulate proposals for improvement to reduce the cycle time of the task, and support your answer.

Graph of the task method: Mold change in injector							
Operator				Injector			
Subtasks of Operator	Sec/Unit	State		State	Sec/Unit	Subtasks of Machine	
Waiting time.	-				326.21	Injecting time.	
Provide allen wrench.	125.32				-	Waiting time.	
Provide type 1 molds.	253.02				-	Waiting time.	
Install molds in injector.	95.32				-	Waiting time.	
Waiting time.	-				312.23	Check first injection in next batch.	
Store allen wrench.	126.35				-	Waiting time.	
Store type 2 molds.	242.01				-	Waiting time.	

Simultaneous task report					
Workstat.	N° Participants	Person Time (sec/unit)	Cycle Time (sec/unit)	Standard Time (sec/unit)	Saturation
Total task	2	24.67	24.67	24.67	50.00%
Operator	1	14.03	24.67		56.88%
Machine	1	10.64	24.67		43.12%

Figure 9.35. *Graph of the method and report of the task*

Bibliography

Aguirre de Mena, Juan M., María Mercedes Rodríguez Fernández, and Dolores Tous Zamora, *Organización y métodos de trabajo* (Ediciones Pirámide, 2002).

Martín López, Milagro, María Elena Robles Rábago, Francisco José González Domínguez, and Juan Manuel Crespo Pérez, *Métodos de trabajo: Casos Prácticos* (Ediciones Pirámide, 2001).

Chapter 10

Process Improvement Criteria

Chapter 5 discussed how to build and record a process. This will deal with how to improve such processes.

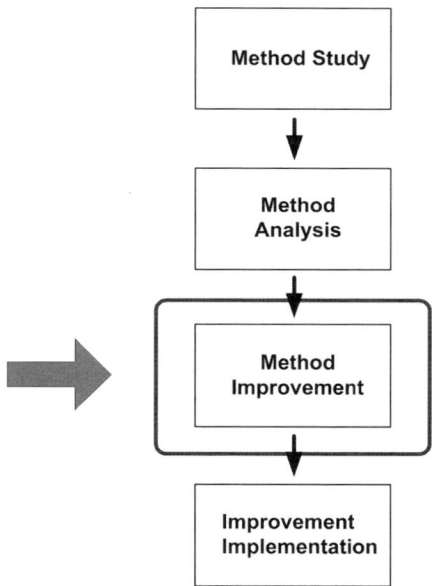

Figure 10.1. *Outline for the second part. Improvement of the method of the task*

These improvements can be made to the existing design or process. It is always preferable to improve the process on paper before setting it in motion.

10.1. Introduction: The Concept of Process Improvement

In this chapter, the main methodologies for process improvement will be shown, with the goal of eliminating non-value-adding tasks. Nevertheless, before starting to identify non-value-adding tasks we will need to remember what types of tasks we can encounter within a process. Figure 10.1 provides a list of the different tasks and their symbols.

Icon	Type of Task
○	Value-adding task
⇨	Transfer
▽	Storage
D	Delay or wait
□	Inspection
◯	Inspection-Operation
⊗	Removable task

Figure 10.2. Process symbols

From all the possible tasks that can be carried out on a material, just one of them adds value within the process. No others are needed; they do not add value and the product would have no deficiencies if they were not undertaken. However, the processes and factories are full of these types of tasks. The objective of process improvement is very clear:

> **Eliminate all tasks that do not add value to the product.**

This short and simple directive can involve great complexity when put into practice. This chapter shows the steps for minimizing the non-value-adding tasks in the process.

To eliminate all non-value-adding tasks is impossible, because some type of waste is inevitable, but the objective must be to get as close as possible. The improvement of a process is an ongoing cycle, some part can always be improved. Waste in any of its forms will always be there to eliminate, and the improvement will not end until the process only has value-adding tasks, which is when it resembles the structure of the product.

10. Process Improvement Criteria

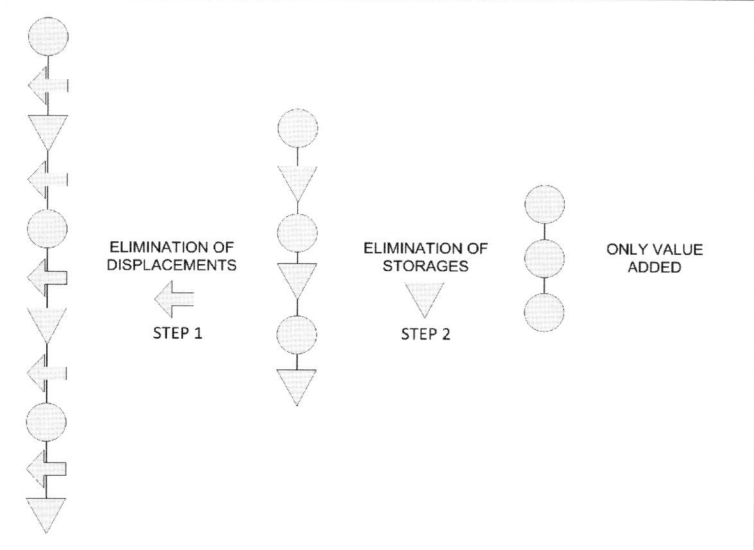

Figure 10.3. Graph of waste elimination

This graph represents the elimination of waste through the elimination of transfers and storage, which is the same as saying that the stock is reduced; the balancing is improved between the workstations or sections that compose the process and the combination of tasks. In the following images we will see how the layout will change after eliminating non-value-added tasks.

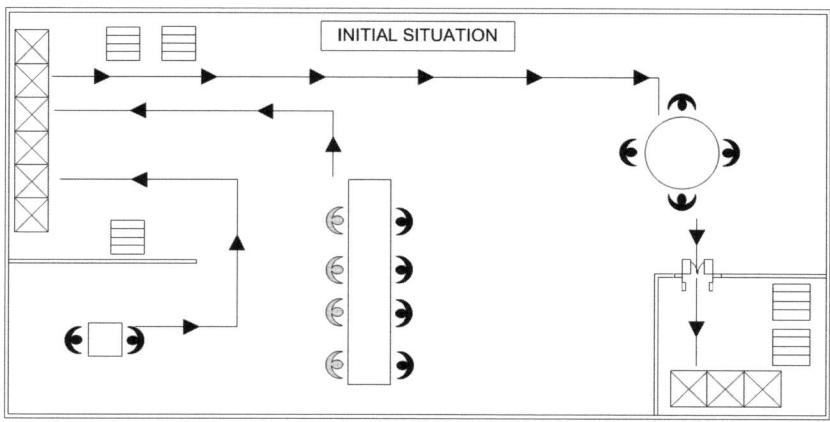

Figure 10.4. Initial situation

We start from a process full of stores and transfers. In the first phase, we will try to eliminate the transfers, improving mainly the location of storage.

Industrial Productivity

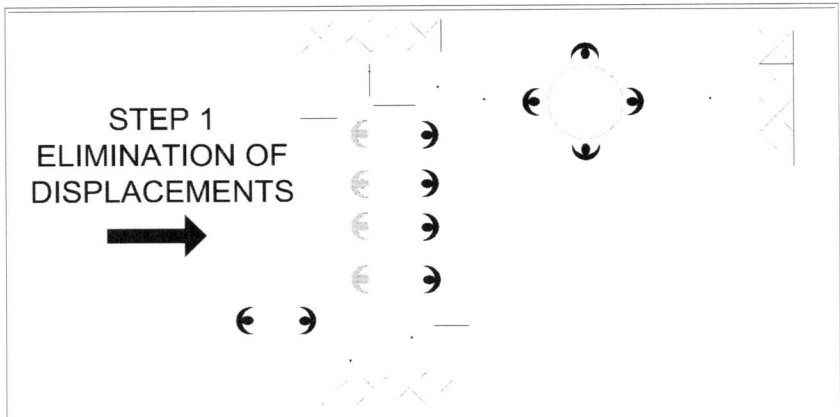

Figure 10.5. Step 1

To take the final step, once the transfers are eliminated or drastically reduced, intermediate storages must be eliminated so we end up with a distribution similar to the following:

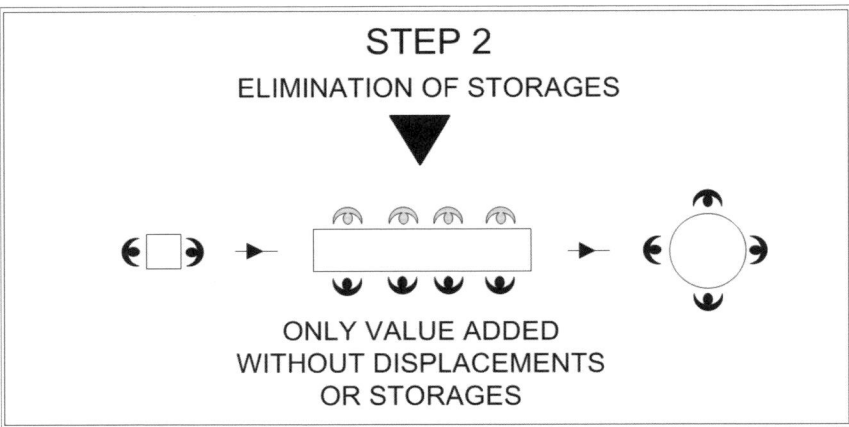

Figure 10.6. Step 2

Figure 10.7 provides a more completed improvement, which could also be valid, because the order of steps does not always have to be the same. It will depend on the situation of each process and the conditions of the factory.

10. Process Improvement Criteria

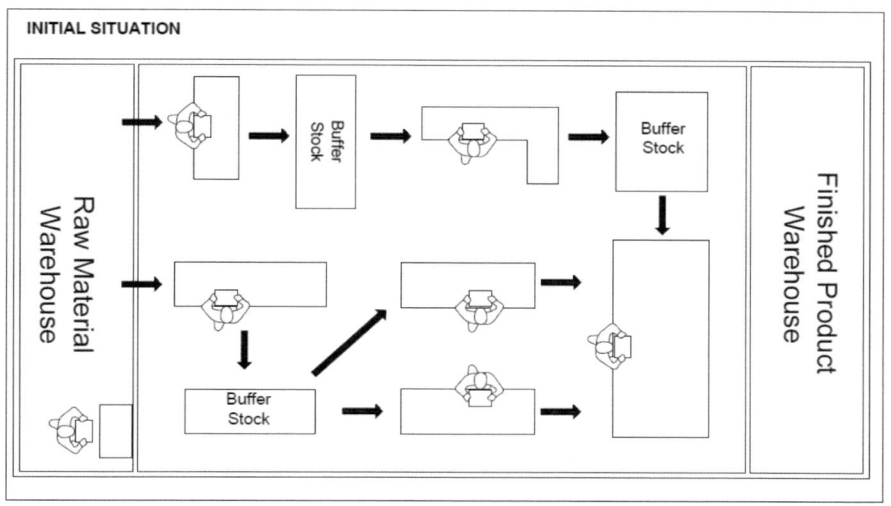

Figure 10.7. Initial situation

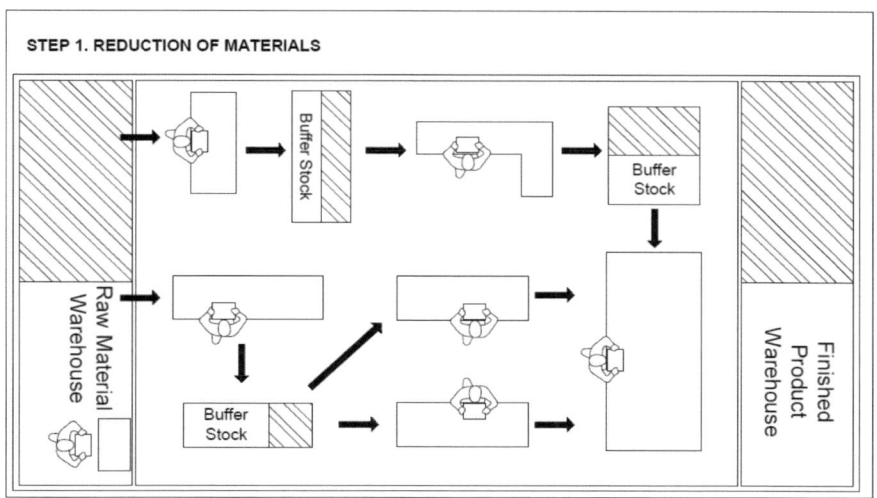

Figure 10.8. Step 1. Reduction of materials

377

Industrial Productivity

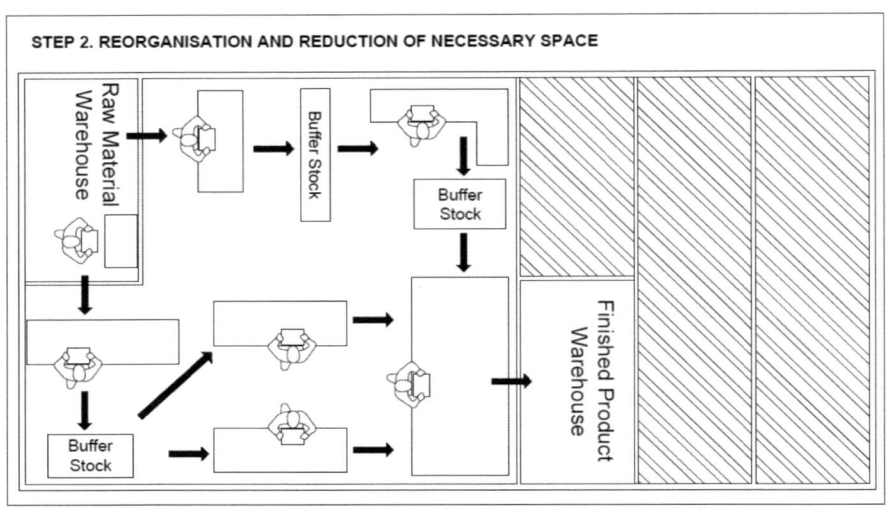

Figure 10.9. Step 2. Reorganization and reduction of necessary space

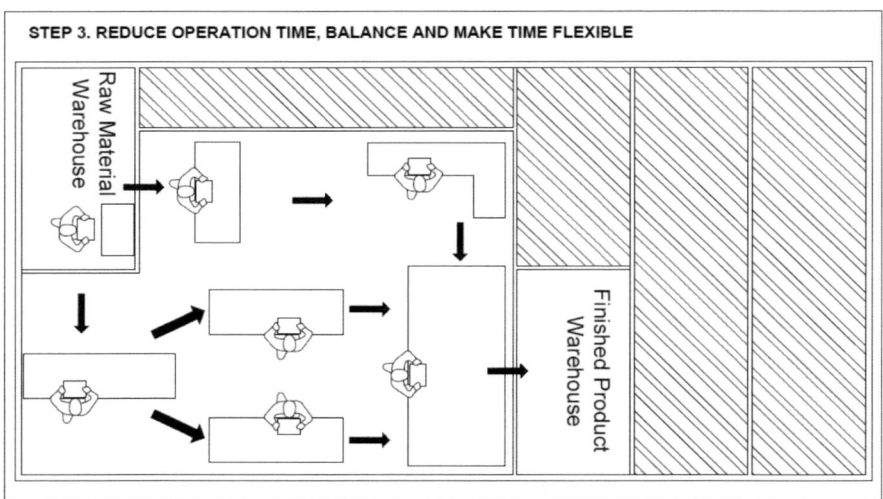

Figure 10.10. Step 3. Reduce operatory time, balance, and make time flexible

10. Process Improvement Criteria

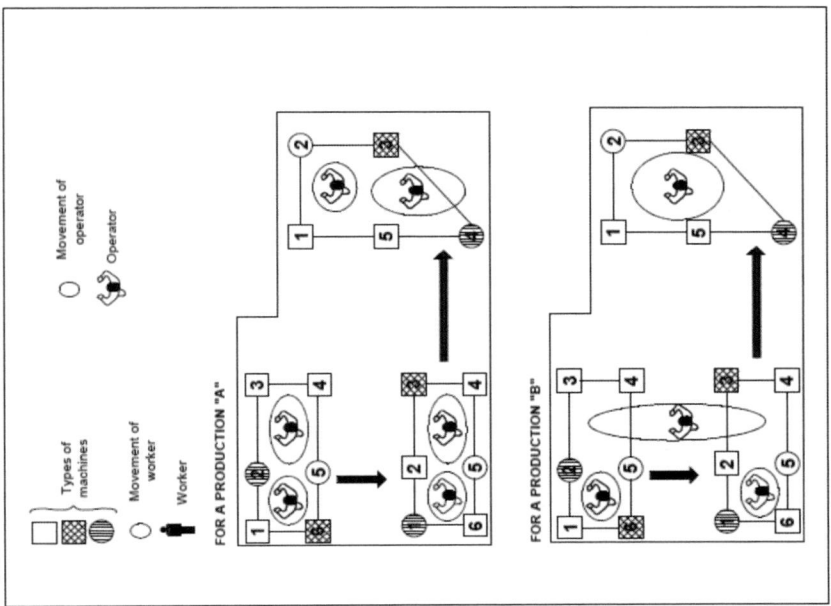

Figure 10.11. Distribution of the workstations by production

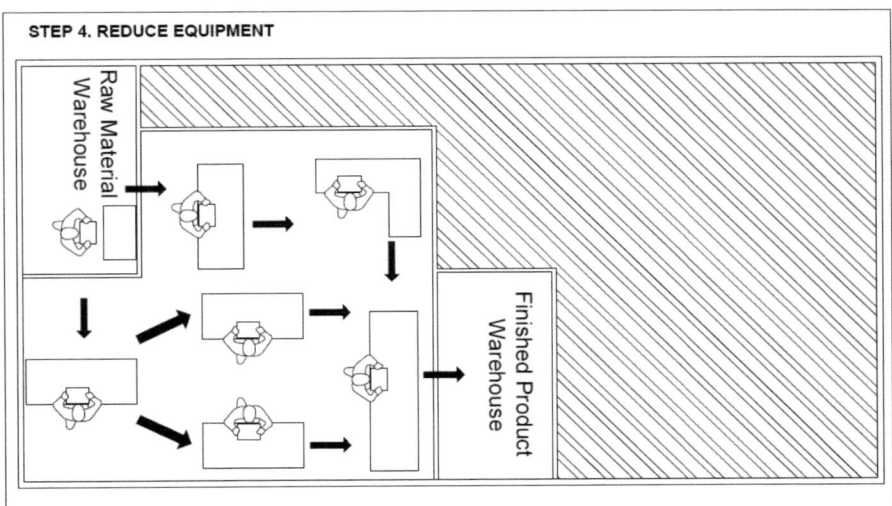

Figure 10.12. Step 4. Reduce teams

However, regardless of the order for the implementation of the process improvement, specific improvement tools considered necessary to achieve it. They include the following:

379

1. Balancing of process tasks
2. Reduction of the stocks in process
3. Reduction of space and transfers
4. Implementation of automatic means of transport

10.2. Balancing of Tasks from the Process

Before explaining how to eliminate the imbalances, we must clearly know what they are and why they occur.

An imbalance in a process is caused by the existing difference between the manufacturing capacities of the different parts that compose the process, from suppliers to customers. Given this difference of capacity in the process, the system as a whole will manufacture, if there are no problems, the same number of units that the element of minor capacity of that system is able to process. The rest of the components of the system that occur quicker than the limiting task, can either manufacture at a slower pace, making stops to equal their production to the limiting task, namely delays, or they can manufacture and store, which means storage, searches, and transfers.

In summary then, an imbalance in a process translates into waste, storage, and/or waits. Now, let us see how the imbalances can be solved. Suppose we start from the following situation:

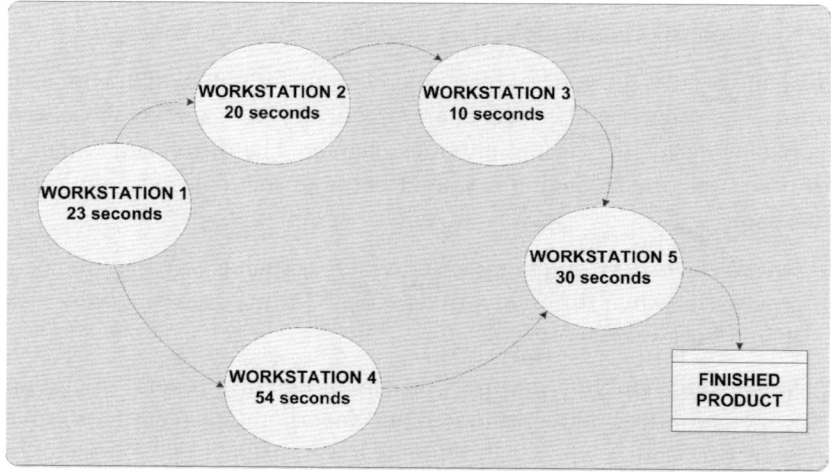

Figure 10.13. Initial situation

Although in the majority of cases it is not especially visible, in cases like the previous one the situation turns into the following:

10. Process Improvement Criteria

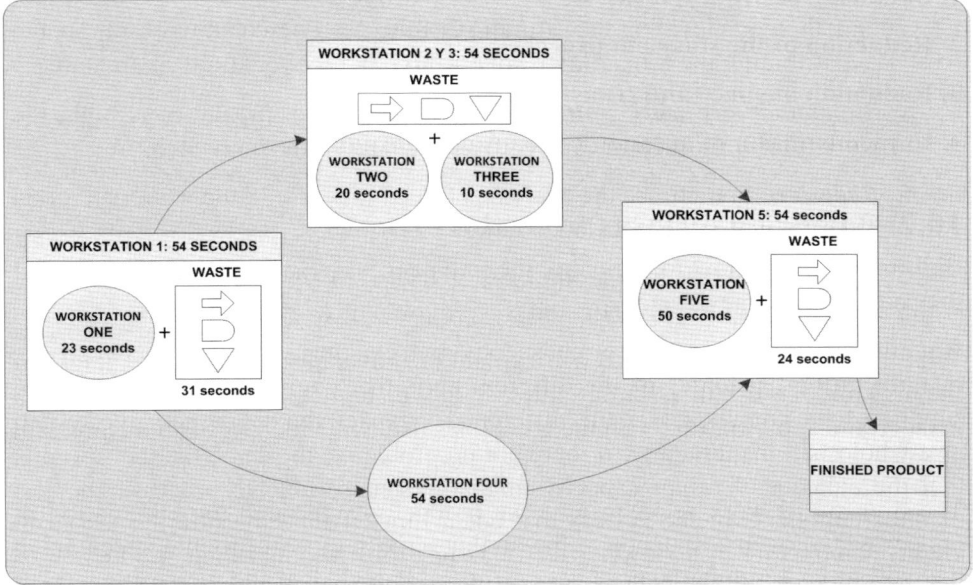

Figure 10.14. Representation with symbols

All the workstations end up producing at the pace of the slowest, occupying their time with storages, searches, waits, or transports. The situation represented in the previous graph, however, is the most optimistic possible, because it is normal that the capacity of the line is reduced by the limiting task because all the searches, storages, and transportation also affect the limiting workstation.

Roughly, and briefly, the general recommendations for reducing the imbalance are explained. The criteria and concepts are practically the same as those explained for the balancing of lines in the previous chapter. The difference is that, for the case of processes, the balancing is sought between sections and not workstations from the same line.

1. **Divide the task:** Could a task be divided in such a way that units could be processed in two different workstations? In this case, the work would be shared by several workstations.

2. **Redistribute the operations:** Consists in deleting several operations of a workstation that is oversaturated and incorporating them to a previous or later workstation whose saturation is lower, balancing the production line.

3. **Use parallel workstations:** It can be necessary when a given station has a high level of saturation to assign the work to two or more workstations so they operate in parallel. This technique consists in duplicating workstations, what would be the equivalent to assigning more operators.

381

4. ***Unify tasks:*** On other occasions, two or more tasks may be unified into one, thereby elevating the saturation of the newly created workstation and redistributing the remaining resources to other workstations on the line.

5. ***Supplementary work hours:*** In situations where imbalance is high, the work hours of a section can be raised or even shifts duplicated.

6. ***Redesign:*** Sometimes the analyst is forced to redesign the work method in order to reduce the imbalance time.

The following explains the importance of trying to find balance between the recommendations of the division and the grouping of work.

With this recommendation, we will explain the advantages and disadvantages of the division of work in assembly lines. In any discipline it is important to find a balance and apply sparingly all the guidelines that a methodology can recommend and use.

The division of work seeks to increase productivity through the elimination of unnecessary movements or non-value-adding activities for the product, specializing the workforce, limiting the necessary technical knowledge, and increasing worker dexterity, achieving a reduction in execution times without affecting productivity.

However the division of work also brings disadvantages, as there is no perfect solution. The main disadvantage is imbalance, because it is practically impossible to achieve perfect balancing in a process composed of more than one element. (The work developed by a single operator or machine is the only one that, by definition, is considered to be perfectly balanced.) Along with the imbalance, the considerable increase in handling and transport of material must be taken into account when increasing the number of components because of the accompanying increase of waste.

For large cycles, it is often recommended that the task be split to reduce the work cycle; however, when facing large imbalances, grouping the tasks together is an important. We see this approach in the following example, where productivity is improved by grouping tasks:

10. Process Improvement Criteria

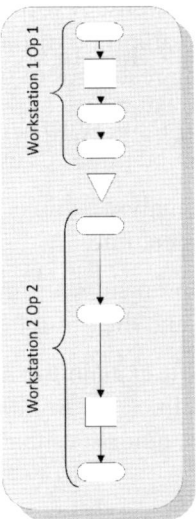

Figure 10.15. Process outline

In this situation, we have:

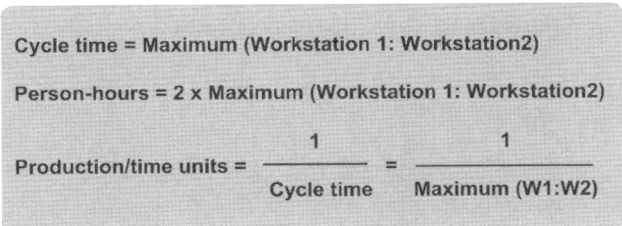

Formula 10.1

This process, in order to follow the previous example of the assembly of a bicycle, can belong to the assembly of a wheel. The first operator inspects and assembles the parts, and the second inflates and checks pressure. With this composition, the first workstation is significantly slower than the second and to breakdown the task further is not possible. So the data we have are the following:

Workstation 1: 8 seconds

Workstation 2: 4.20 seconds

The overall cycle time, then, would be equivalent to the most time-consuming process task, and the person-hours or workforce used in the process would be the cycle time multiplied by the number of people involved:

Industrial Productivity

Cycle time: 8 seconds

Person-time: 16 seconds

By applying the task grouping, the balancing of this process involves making each operator perform the complete task of assembling and inflating the wheel:

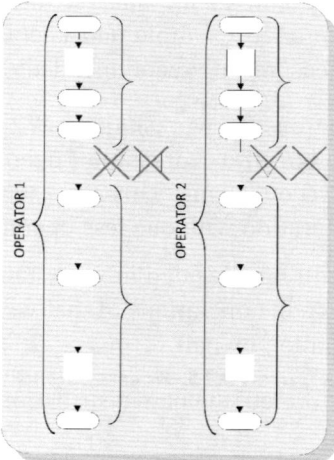

Figure 10.16. Outline of process for two operators

With this new disposition, we have an equal cycle time for each workstation that will follow the next formula:

$$\text{Cycle time} = \frac{W1 + W2}{2}$$

Formula 10.2

Every 12.2 seconds (W1 + W2) two units will be manufactured, so the cycle time for each part is 6.1 seconds, which will also coincide with the person-time. This situation perfect balancing, because a single operator participates in the process and therefore there is no possibility of losing productivity in waits, transfers, or storages.

This easy and extreme example does not mean that in every case a complete task should be grouped. In addition, we must consider the impediment of duplicating all tools to create two equal workstations. The idea is to always try to find a solution without fear of the basic principles of industrial organization that emphasize the division of work.

These recommendations try is to take advantage of the available resources without pushing for constant activity. Pushing to avoid stoppage at any cost tends to increase the stock (storage) in process.

A possible solution for the first example in which all the balancing work must be oriented to reducing the cycle of the limiting section until achieving a high utilization of the chain. The aim of the analyst must be to achieve a perfect balancing. Studying the proposed example and keeping in mind the explained guidelines, the following measures are recommended:

- To unify the operations of workstations W2 and W3 given their low saturation, the creation of a workstation denominated W23 will have a work cycle of 30 seconds/unit. This workstation with its higher cycle implies a higher saturation with one less operation.
- The free operator will be relocated in workstation W4, which is the most saturated, duplicating the operations of that workstation and reducing the cycle of this workstation by half.

Once these changes are performed, the new distribution is:

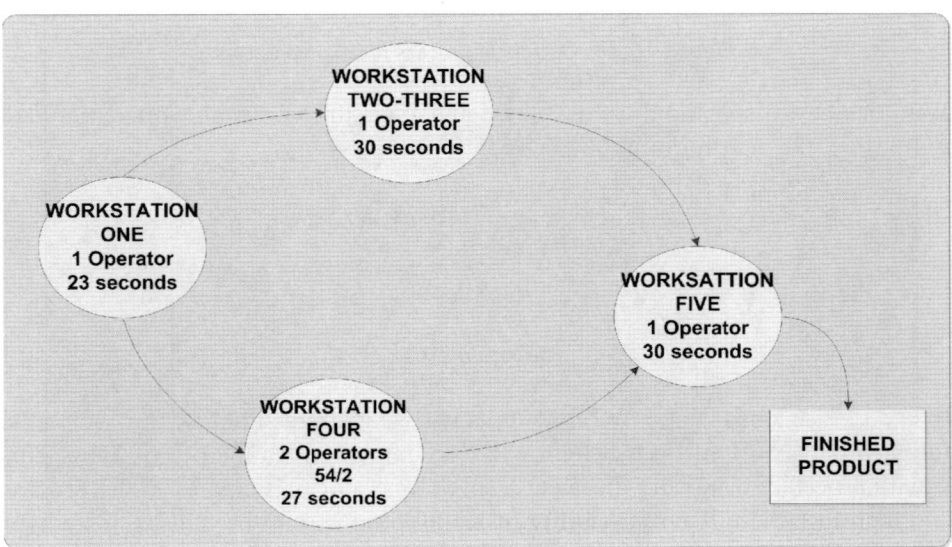

Figure 10.17. Improvement situation

With the current situation and without going into particular calculations of line balancing, we can plainly see how the level of use of the chain influences the saturation of its components, which have risen considerably. If the capacity is calculated for both cases, the quantitative improvement can be observed.

- Initial situation: Capacity = 3,600 / 54 = 66.6 units/hour
- Improvement situation: Capacity = 3,600 / 30 = 120 units/hour

In view of the results, the level of utilization of the chain is almost doubled, which matches the production obtained when the number of operators doubles.

10.3. Reduction of Stocks in Process

The stock in process includes all the materials, raw or semi-finished, existing within a plant. Excess of stock is the principal cause of waste in any company, because it requires an investment in assets and space, as well as management efforts, handling, transport, and storage that add no value to any product.

If all manuals insist that excessive stock is unnecessary and harmful, why do the vast majority of industries have it as one of their main problems? The simplest answer is that it helps cover up errors. Lack of materials and imbalances do not come to light when stock of intermediate and final goods is available. Concealed problems not only do not get solved, but they tend to get worse.

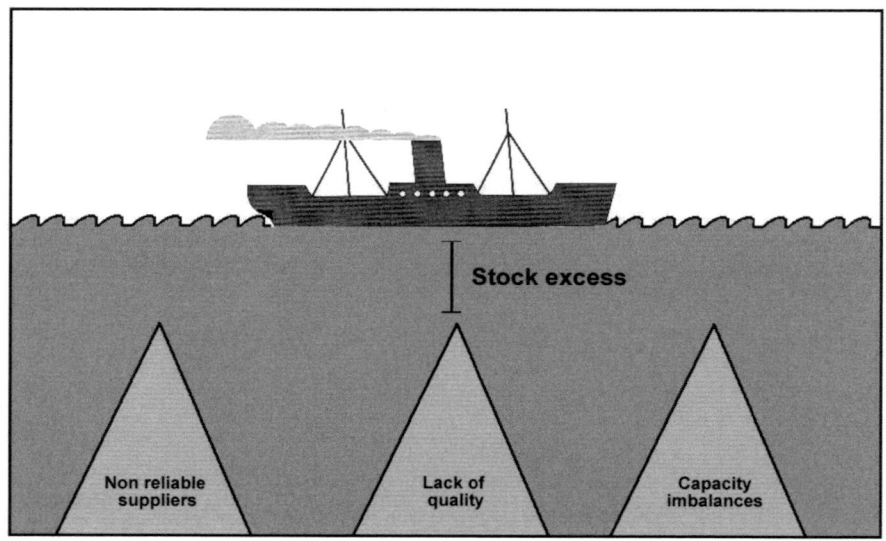

Figure 10.18. Graph of stock excess

Figure 10.18 represent the role of stock excess within a process. It simply hides serious problems. No problems are visible while any part of the process remains stopped; material batches everywhere keep work the work going. It is why alarms do not go off if a supplier fails or reprocesses occur, and so imbalances are not detected visually.

10. Process Improvement Criteria

When reducing the stock in process, the system transforms. It does not become more or less vulnerable because an error affects the situation the same way in both cases, but if it is known it becomes more obvious. A supplier error or a lack of quality is quickly detected and may possibly stop the productive process. Bottlenecks become obvious because they will be the only workstations where stock is stored in front of them. The following graph shows the change of situation when reducing the stock in process.

Figure 10.19. Graph of stock reduction

The two principal initiatives to be carried out to reduce the stock in process in a factory are adjusting the manufacturing batches to the orders and reducing the transference batch between phases. The first point is clear. To reduce the stock in process, only what is needed is manufactured. The second point is somehow less clear. The effect produced by the reduction of the transference batch in process improvement must be analyzed.

Reducing the transference batch size reduces the total time of the process and therefore the delivery time. However, it also reduces the space needed for storage, which means reducing other non-value-added tasks (search, distance of transportation, communication, amount of storage operations), which means reduction of waste.

For all these reasons, the reduction of stock in process is recommended. How the transference batch size affects the size of stock in process can be simulated, assuming that the tasks involved in the example are balanced.

Industrial Productivity

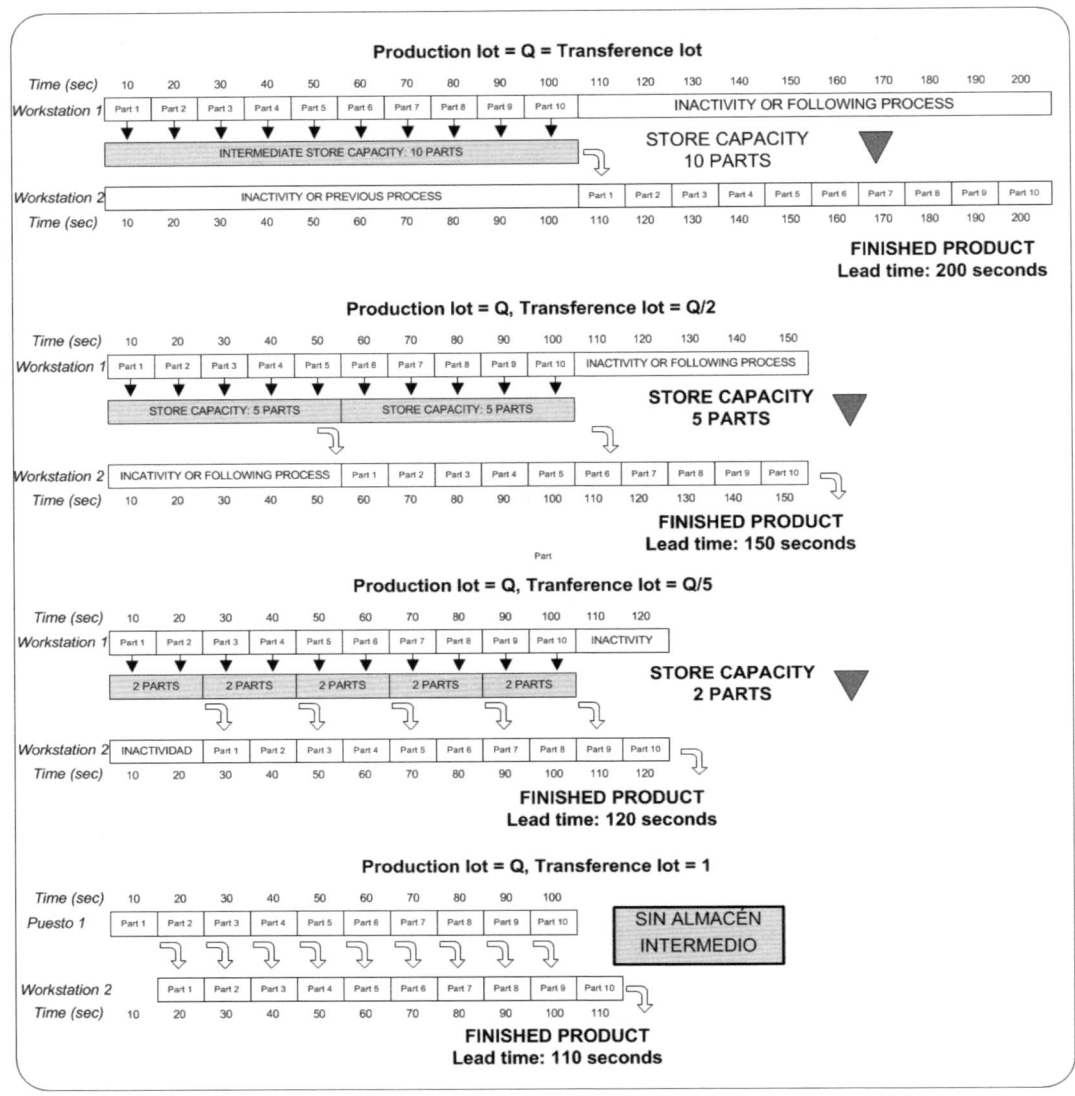

Figure 10.20. Evolution of stock by transference batch

Conclusion: The decrease in size of the transference batch reduces dramatically the need for intermediate stores and, as a consequence, non-value-added operations, such as storages, transfers, and searches.

10.4. Reduction of Available Space and Transfers

Most of the space within a factory is not occupied by workplaces or machines, but by stores. If the two previous points are applied correctly much space will be free because much stock in process is removed. **It is essential to not leave that space empty but to start reorganizing the area surrounding the machines. This way, an important part of the non-value-adding "transport or transfer" task will be avoided.** Remember from Figure 10.9 how space reorganization was achieved after the reduction of stock.

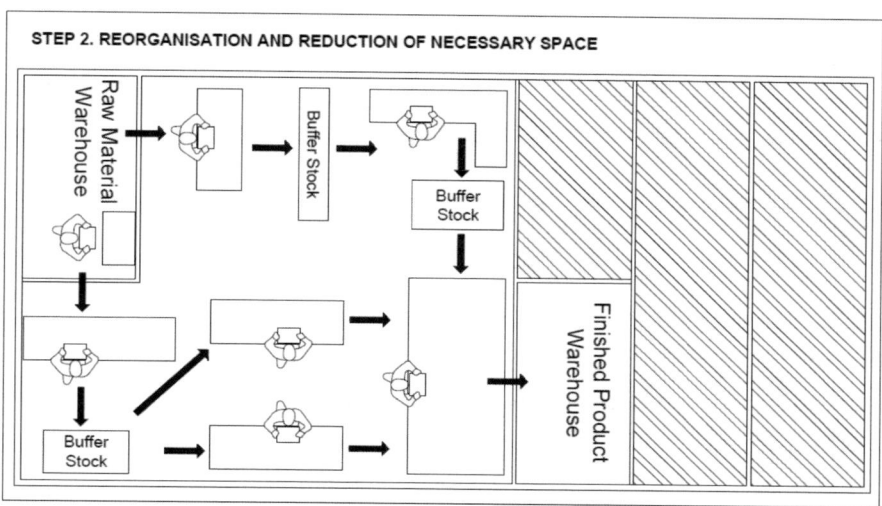

Figure 10.21. Reorganization of necessary space

On other occasions what occurs is simply that the factory or section is larger than necessary. It is commonly thought that working comfortably and without tightness is more productive. It is not the case. Instead, it generates multiple useless transfers. In these cases, it is not even necessary to reduce the stock in order to reduce space. **We must proceed to reduce it drastically, reorganizing the space and sealing the remaining areas so that no one accesses them.**

For organizing the existing space correctly, a group of tools will greatly aid in determining a layout that reduces transfers. These tools include the following:

- Definition of workstation necessities
- Matrix relation between positions
- Graph of routes
- Thread diagram
- ABC location of materials
- Analysis of operator transfers

Industrial Productivity

> A direct consequence of reduction of space is a reduction in transfers, which can be reduced by other means as well.

Before getting started in the methodologies and criteria for layout designing, a concrete explanation of this concept is helpful. The *layout* of the factory is the plant view and distribution of machines and workstations in a factory. Layout is a determinant in a process design; it is not just a plan in which the components of the system are placed whimsically, or at least it should not be. The goal in layout is that the manufacturing consumes the minimum space and reduces the movement of materials.

Given that the variety of manufacturing types is practically infinite and each type of manufacturing needs a different process and means for its execution, unique and precise rules cannot be determined. Still, with an analysis methodology of functions that compose the process and the help of concrete models, an optimum solution to the problem can be discerned.

The existing relationship among product, process, and manufacturing type is the primary factor in the layout design. The following graph presents the recommended steps to perform when designing the layout of a process:

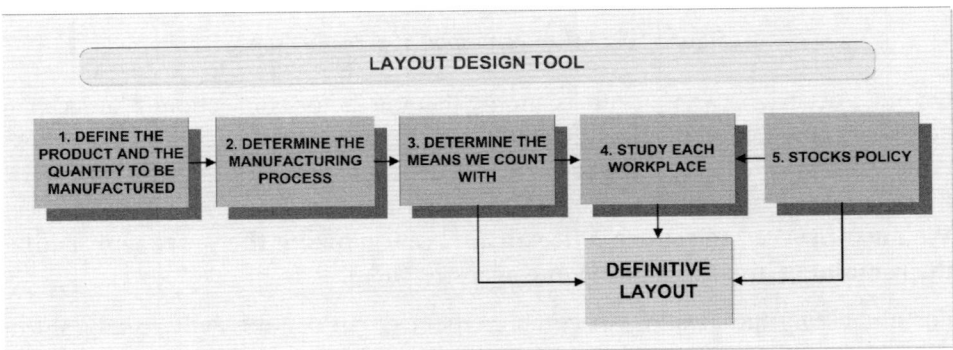

Figure 10.22. Layout design tools

In each of these phases of layout design, the objectives pursued by the process optimization need to include the following:

- Minimize equipment investments
- Use of available space effectively
- Maximize available means for comfort and security
- Minimize the manipulation of materials

10. Process Improvement Criteria

- Maximize the flexibility of the process
- Facilitate the organization of the system

Some tools that can complement the previous steps are shown next. We will start with a table that defines the necessities per workstation (Figure 10.23).

Tabla de definición de necesidades por puesto de trabajo

		Workstation 1	Workstation 2	Workstation 3	Workstation 4	Workstation 5	Workstation 6	Workstation 7	Workstation 8
Space	m2 / height / a x b								
Feeding	Raw material supply								
	Raw material departure								
	Residue departure								
	Observations of interest								
Facilities	Noise prevention								
	Electric energy								
	Natural illumination								
	Gas								
	Vapor								
	Compressed air								
	Normal water								
	ACS								
	Aspiration								
	Observations of interest								

Factory: Date:
Section: Technician:

Figure 10.23. Table of necessities definition per workstation

Table of Needs Definition per Workstation

With a simple template, the most important data that can define the location of a workstation due to space, maintenance, or type of installations needed are easily referenced.

Matrix of Relation Between Workstations

Figures 10.24 and 10.25 illustrate the matrix of the existing relationships among all workstations that compose the process. This table is extraordinarily useful to check out what activities are linked by a significant flow.

Industrial Productivity

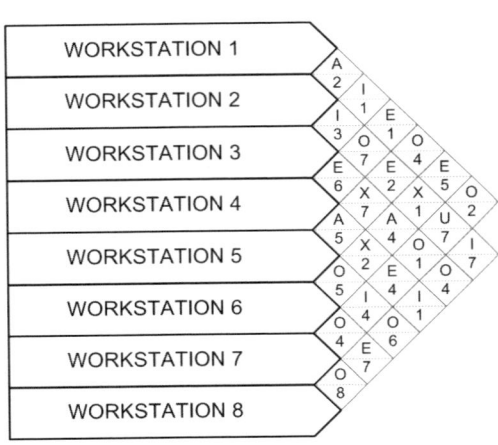

VALUE	PROXIMITY
A	Essential
E	Especially important
I	Important
O	Normal
U	Without importance
X	Not recommendable

CODE	REASON
1	Real-time information
2	Annoying noises
3	Share tools
4	Share work equipment
5	Material movement
6	Shares personnel
7	Inspection or control
8	PRL

Figure 10.24. Matrix of relation between workstations

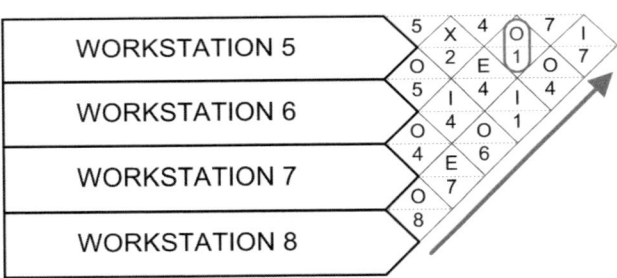

Figure 10.25. Detail of the matrix of relation between workstations

This matrix summarizes the importance of the closeness between workstations and the reason for it. In Figure 10.25, the dependence of the workstation 8 on the rest of workstations is marked with an arrow. On the other hand, the dependence between workstation 7 and 3 is circled. Consulting the tables, dependency checks out as normal due to the transference of information.

10. Process Improvement Criteria

Graph of Routes

Figure 10.26 provides a denominated graph of routes and is a useful tool for solving problems related to the transportation of materials and the layout. This graph shows the volume (e.g., tons per shift) transported between the different workstation that compose the process.

Path graph

	Workstation 1	Workstation 2	Workstation 3	Workstation 4	Workstation 5	Workstation 6	Workstation 7	Workstation 8
Workstation 1		30	45	80	32	4	3	6
Workstation 2			6	8	4	22	3	2
Workstation 3				22	14	18	3	4
Workstation 4	120				10	4	0	5
Workstation 5						6	0	2
Workstation 6			60	12	2		0	1
Workstation 7								15
Workstation 8			15	8				

Tons per shift

Figure 10.26. *Graph of routes*

This table groups the necessary information to solve the problem of equipment and workstation location in a plant. However, additional means are available for analyzing and improving the layout of a plant.

Thread diagram

Another tool for transfer analysis that should be highlighted due to its simplicity of application and its effectiveness is the thread diagram.

> The thread diagram is a scale plan or model that follows and measures with a thread the path of workers, materials, or equipment during a particular sequence of events.

Thread diagrams can be used to follow the movements of materials and products in order to know the path taken during the productive process. Nevertheless, the common use of the thread diagram is to represent the movements of workers for subsequent analysis. A thread diagram provides a quick vision of the transfers and contributes to decision making for the improvement of the process through the distribution of the workstations.

The example in Figure 10.27 shows a thread diagram corresponding to a manufacturing process in which a worker makes several transfers of necessary components for the assembly.

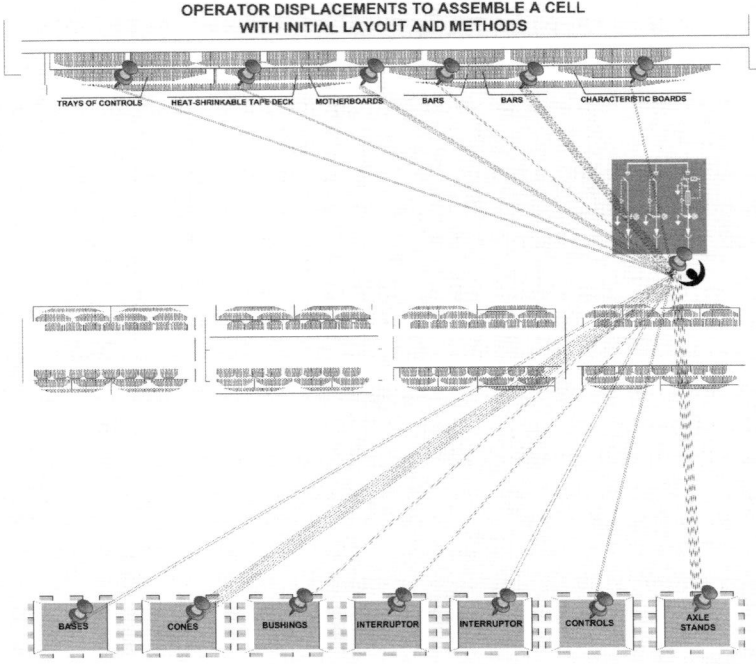

Figure 10.27. Example diagrama de hilos.

The steps to follow for the construction of a thread diagram are the following:

1. Record all the pertinent facts from a direct observation of the workstation, in particular all the spots to which the operator moves. As a supporting tool, when necessary, the filming of the process can be used.

2. Define all the spots in which the operator works. Each spot will be assigned a codification with name, letter, and number. For this step, we can use record sheets. These sheets will have a variable format that can be adapted based on the data to record and the nature of the work.

3. Once the necessary data are recorded, we will use a scaled plan where the affected work area is represented. In this plan will be placed all the machines, stores, and spots to which the operator moves. The plan will be located on a board and a pin will be placed in each place of work (previously defined) and on spots where a change of direction happens.

4. A thread of known longitude is tied to the original pin, corresponding to the starting point of the transfers.

5. The thread passes through the pins that mark the other points along the way, following the order of the record sheet, until all the movements are represented. Based on this chart of operator movements, we can observe the most frequent paths by the quantity of threads in the route; less-used routes will have less density of threads.

The completed diagram can be used to examine movements as a whole, to see where the major concentration of movements is located and what parts of the work cause more transfers. Additionally, because the original thread was measured and the plan used is in scale, subtracting the surplus thread from the total will reveal the distance travelled by the operator.

The stretches with higher density of threads show a higher relation between these two points, suggesting that changes be made in the layout, or even in the process, to reduce and optimize the transfers. The thread diagram also serves as a communication tool for explaining to directors, managers, middle managers, and workers the proposed changes. Based on this objective, a good practice would be to represent the thread diagrams for the initial and proposed process for a visual comparison with potential improvements, making it easier to convince others of the need for the change.

Following the idea that the problems of plant distribution typically have more than one solution, an example of "what must not be done" is given. At the end of this section, having explained the theoretical part, a possible solution will be explained, but it is not absolute.

Narrative

Consequences of a Poor Design of Layout.
Background

An assembly section becomes outdated in capacity and means; therefore, the decision to remodel it completely is made.

Previously, it manufactured batches of 5 to 10 units maximum, and the duration of the assembly could vary from 3 to 5 hours in function of the model. Twelve different models were manufactured and were somewhat higher in costs and deadlines compared to the competition. Technical improvements became necessary in order to maintain market share. In this scenario, two people were working with few means, and their manufacturing capacity was very low. Therefore, taking advantage of the necessity for change, management decided to perform a strategic turn and change drastically the entire section.

Objective of the Narrative

The main objective of this narrative is to explain the consequences of not paying attention to the distribution of the plant. Let us look at the chaos caused by a poor design in the distribution of a section.

Actions to Be Taken

The decision to change the section was necessary and was quickly made. The first step was to perform several changes in the rest of the factory in order to gain an important amount of space and occupy it completely.

After some thought (but not too much), they embarked on an ambitious project and, thinking big, built a line of eight independent stations. It would be possible to manufacture eight different models at the same time, giving the company greater flexibility. Because eight people would be manufacturing the same models, an important investment in training for staff was made with no doubt of its success. With this new section, the long delays and workload imbalances would surely be over. This section was the best installation in its industry, so large orders should soon be knocking on their doors.

With this layout, the material was distributed around the workstations arbitrarily to enable each station to have the same supplies for the set of 12 models, so no workstation would be penalized. The distribution is shown in the following graph:

10. Process Improvement Criteria

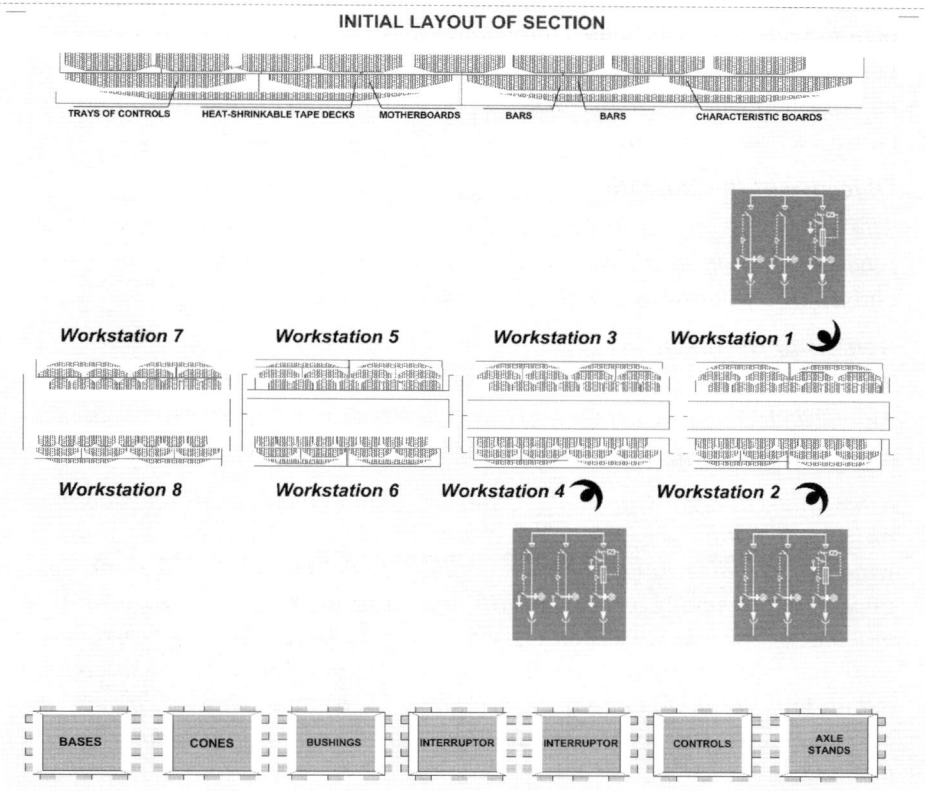

Figure 10.28. New distribution of workstation

Shortly after, the market demonstrated that their sales forecasting was too optimistic; the amortizations of this section greatly increased the price of the product and large orders were not arriving. Only enough work for three operators prompted the decision that each of these operators would work independently because the process was designed that way. Although the volume was not as expected, costs should be lower for the infrastructure of the section.

As can be observed in the previous figure, half the workstations are not needed, which means that a space that should be empty or even not exist was full of expensive tools and materials.

This oversizing of the necessary means, on top of posing important disbursement issues, normally only poses more problems. Let us see what happens to the transfers of each operator when manufacturing.

397

Industrial Productivity

After performing the corresponding data collection, the resulting thread diagram for this process is as follows:

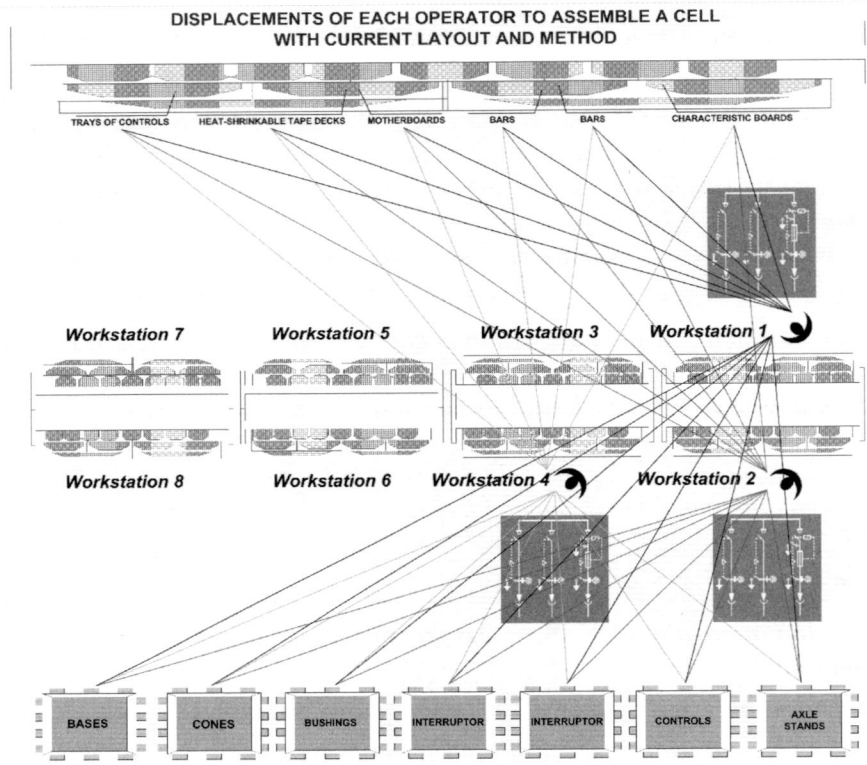

Figure 10.29. *Thread diagram of new layout*

Does the idea that some processes are designed for unproductiveness seem now so farfetched? This layout is wasteful in the extreme. The operators, following the method correctly, dedicated 37 percent of their time for transfers, supplies, preparations, and searches. In other words, for every hour of work, they dedicated more than 20 minutes to nonproductive tasks because the process required it. Add to this fact the accompanying waits, imbalances, reprocesses, and some management errors and what is obtained is a nonviable project.

Conclusion

The design was poorly planned from the beginning. It started from an erroneous base and functioned ineffectively. The layout failed to comply with everything explained so far. With the elements being far away from the workstations, there was no existing flow of any sort, and everything was transfers and searches. These transfers were only the tip of the iceberg; in this line almost nothing worked correctly, and resources were squandered.

This approach is a clear sample of how a poorly designed process generates waste precisely because it is executed according to the design.

To identify problems is just the starting point for being able to solve them. In this case, the problem is in the poor design of the section in form and substance. The next step is to propose solutions and implement the one that seems best. The complicated part of matter is the existence of several potentially superior solutions. A possible solution will be explained, but when the chapter is over, the reader will certainly be able to propose others.

Returning to the layout design, and as has been advanced; there is no single solution to define a design. Further, for each problem, the wide range of solutions is possible, each with its advantages and disadvantages. With the recommendations and methodology explained we only intended to draw a general idea of a feasible solution, somehow abstract, which should be defined differently for each individual case.

Narrative

Resolution of Poor Process Design Through Analysis with Thread Diagram

Background

A possible solution to the problem of a poor distribution of an assembly line is sought. Several solutions exist with the few data facilitated, but the proposed is designed based on forecasts that make increasing sales unlikely and an acceptable offer for disposing of the unnecessary machinery.

Actions to Be Taken

The chosen proposal is based on practically dividing the assembly into three workstations, based on the main objective of reducing the assembly time in order to decrease its cost. By reducing the work cycle and the variability of operations to be performed by each operator, their specialization will be improved.

An effort was made to improve and balance these three workstations and the final situation is shown in the following figure:

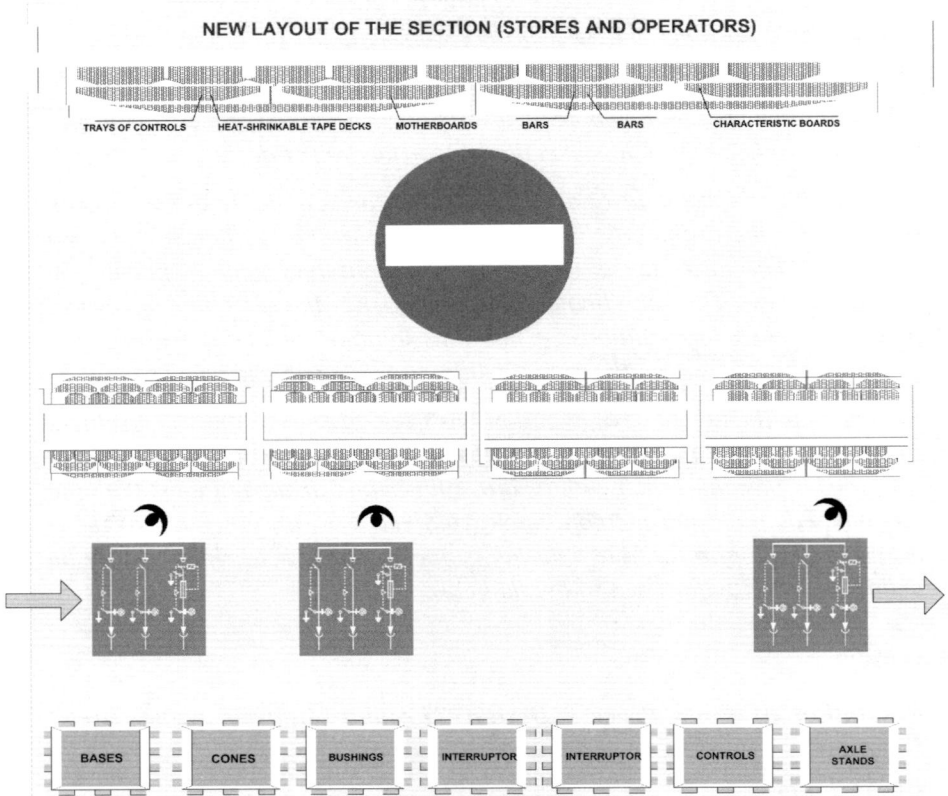

Figure 10.30. Final situation

As a preventive measure against the natural tendency of storing, use of the space "available" was prohibited. All the tools and materials were placed closer to the workstation and workers who used them. A comparison of the transfers from the previous case reveals a sensible improvement, but there is even more.

The thread diagram corresponding to the process after the improvement appears in Figure 10.31.

10. Process Improvement Criteria

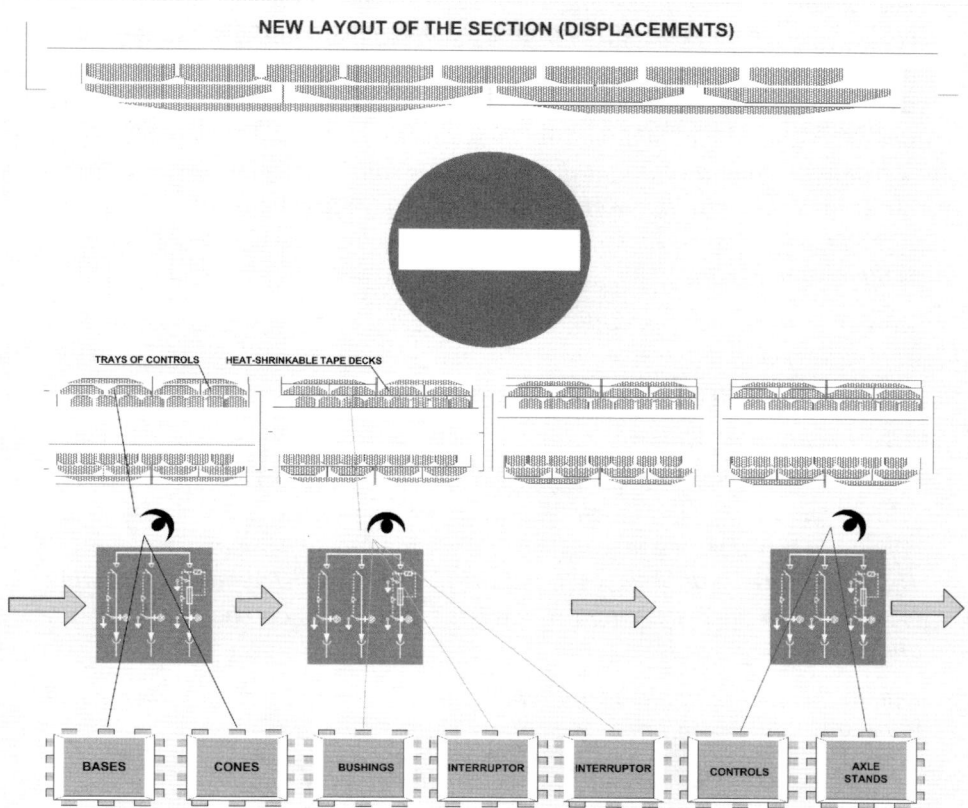

Figure 10.31. Thread diagram of final situation

With this layout, much more versatile and adequate for the amount of work performed on the line, transfers are reduced by 80 percent and searches by 60 percent. It is also true that working in assembly lines produces certain imbalances, but the unproductive time is reduced from 37 percent to 12 percent, so the line productivity is sensibly improved.

Only enough space for being able to store one unit was left between workstations; that is, a small buffer existed, so the imbalances and quality problems had to be solved in a third of the total cycle time of the part so as to avoid a stop of the whole line. The operators, in case of any problem, turned on an orange light that indicated the delay to their colleagues. If an operator finished a unit and the buffer was full, that operator must go to the workstation with the orange light and help in finding a solution for the problem. This way, no unnecessary stock developed and the resolution of problems tend to speed up, because it became everyone's problem.

Moreover, to avoid depending on the dexterity of some operators, once a week they rotated. This approach increased operators' knowledge of all three workstations, increasing their flexibility.

ABC Location of Materials

The Pareto principle can also apply to materials. In most cases, 80 percent of transfers are caused by 20 percent of the references, and conversely 20 percent of transfers are produced by the remaining 80 percent of references. This ABC classification is used, but the percentage distribution is variable based on how the distribution is done, for example, it can be 60-10, 30-40, and 10-50.

Due to this fact, a fundamental tool is the ABC analysis of movements and materials, and the solutions provided are the following:

- *Bring A articles as close as possible to the workstations.*
- *Place C articles in the highest and furthest locations.*
- *Place B articles in an intermediate location.*

Analysis of Operator Transfers

Another way to reduce the transfers is to make studies of methods of several tasks and see how many meters are traveled in each of them, as seen in Chapters 5 and 6. From there on, we must:

- *Record the method.*
- *Perform the analysis of methods focused on the operation "transfer."*
- *Propose improvements (with the tools already seen).*
- *Reduce transfers.*

10.5. Implementation of Means to Automate or Facilitate Transport

Sometimes the size of the factory may not be reduced or, due to conditioning factors, sequential work phases may not be brought closer. In these cases, in order to limit investment of operator time the transport of materials, it is necessary to think about automated transport means. Although not everything can be automated, facilitating transfers is always important.

The means for transport automation are:

1. Conveyor belts
2. Aerial trolleys
3. Auger conveyor
4. Through pipes, through pneumatic suction
5. Motorized roller conveyors
6. Bucket elevators
7. Gravity warehouses
8. Smart warehouses

Other means to facilitate transport can be:

1. Crane bridges
2. Hoists
3. Transpallet
4. Forklifts
5. Roller conveyors
6. Trolleys
7. Trucks
8. Mobile cranes

Figure 10.32 illustrates some examples of the means used for facilitating transport. However, the market offers a wide range of possibilities and even customized solutions.

Industrial Productivity

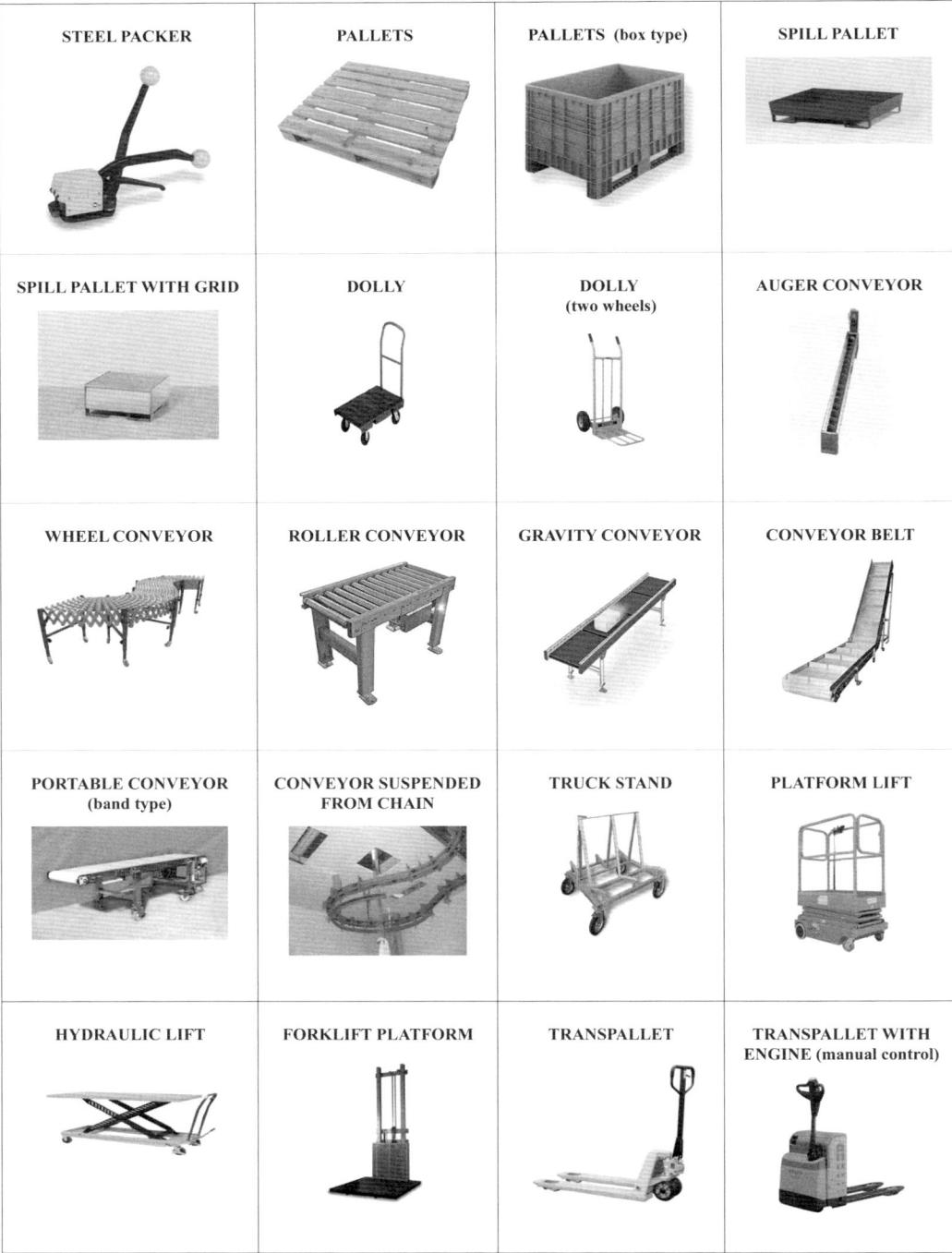

10. Process Improvement Criteria

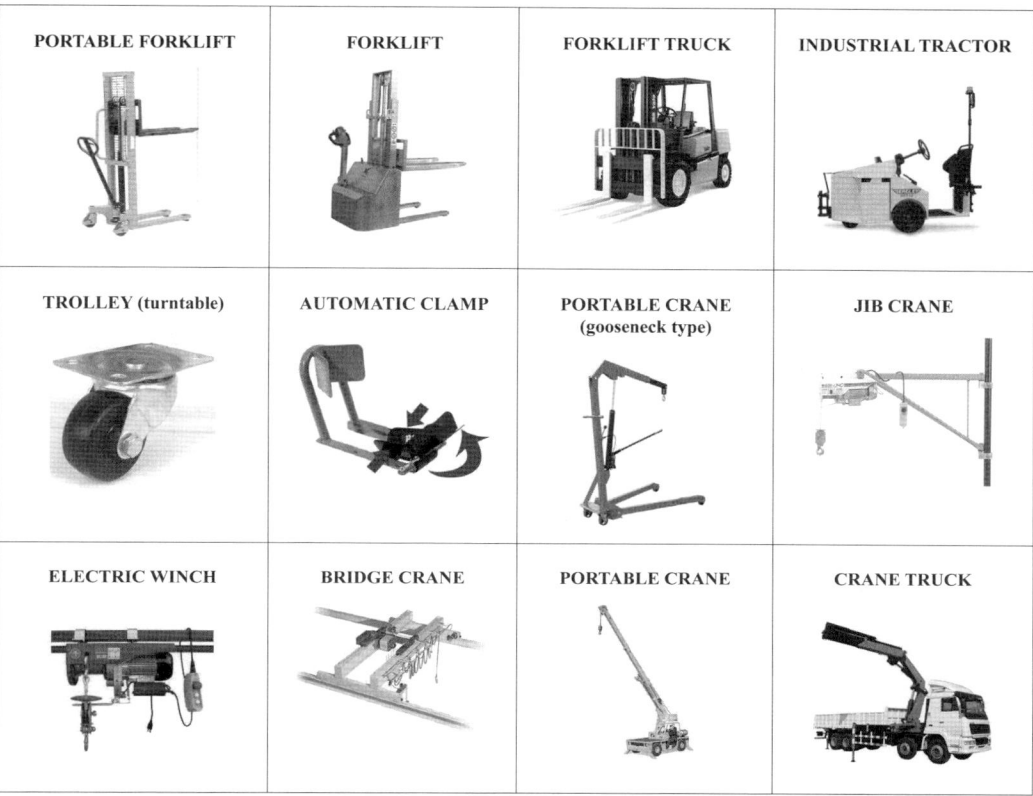

Figure 10.32. Means for facilitating or automating transportation

Narrative

Elimination of Tasks That Should Not Exist
Background

The desire for mass production can lead to mistakes in the design of processes, as we have seen. The natural tendency is for accumulation, to force large batches of semifinished products, which causes a multitude of tasks that should not exist.

A room of pig quartering had a quartering and selection process. The Serrano hams, whose weight was below a certain range, were removed from the working line and stored in a room to be deboned and used as ham later. This design entailed the following:

    a) Two workers at the end of the line classifying the Serrano hams for ham

b) *Two workers transporting the ham trolleys from the deboning room and placing them in the room for their subsequent deboning (Keep in mind the room is 800 m² and needs dedication for sorting.)*

c) *In the deboning room for ham, two workers transporting from the room to the deboning stations*

In the deboning room, four workers engaged in deboning while one worker transported hams from the room to the cold room.

The initial situation is shown in Figure 10.33.

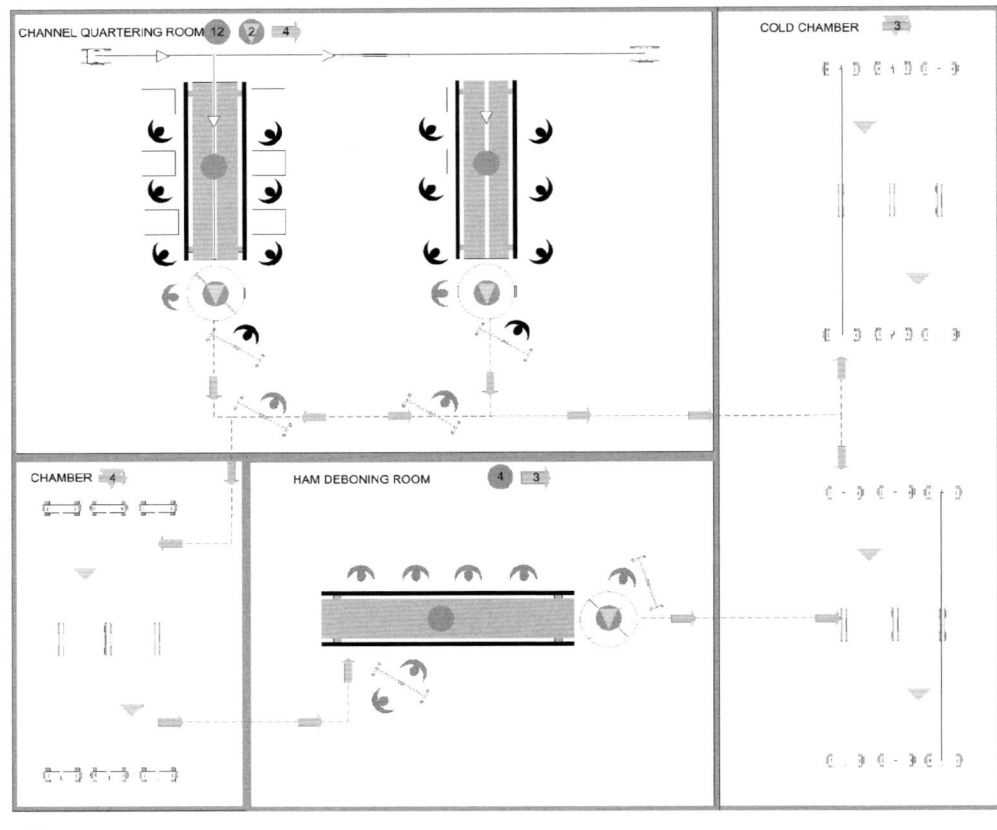

Figure 10.33. Deboning room. Initial situation

10. Process Improvement Criteria

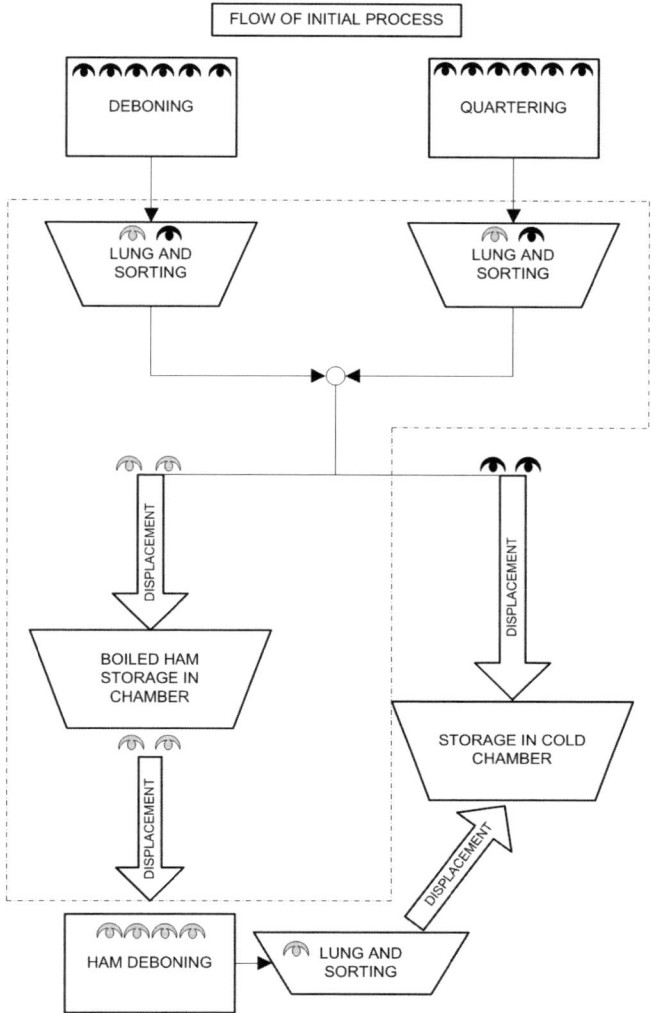

Figure 10.34. *Deboning room. Work flow in initial situation*

When it was asked why the ham was not deboned in line with the rest of the tasks, the response was that the declassifications by weight were irregular and therefore the work in line could not be balanced as work peaks may appear. The preference was, then, to develop the process as has been described. **The result, to avoid having two people from the assembly line idle in case a working peak appears, was to have four workers circling around, two classifying Serrano ham into ham. In addition, this process required an 800 square-meter room as a buffer plus the energy to keep the hams cool.**

Industrial Productivity

To the previous highlighted issues, we add that all the time that hams are in the rooms they are not finished processing and therefore cannot be billed, losing two days of income in the process.

Therefore, to perform the "Deboning of ham," a cold room and a deboning room were constructed. In addition, the commodities were moved by four workers during the workday.

Of the 11 operators working in the deboning of ham, only 5 carried out value-adding tasks; the rest did tasks whose existence was questionable. Therefore, the CwP was 11 / 5 = 2.2, which means that we invest 2.2 hours/person for each hour/person of value added.

Proposal

The graph in Figure 10.35 shows the proposed situation. In it we can clearly appreciate how the workload and layout have been improved.

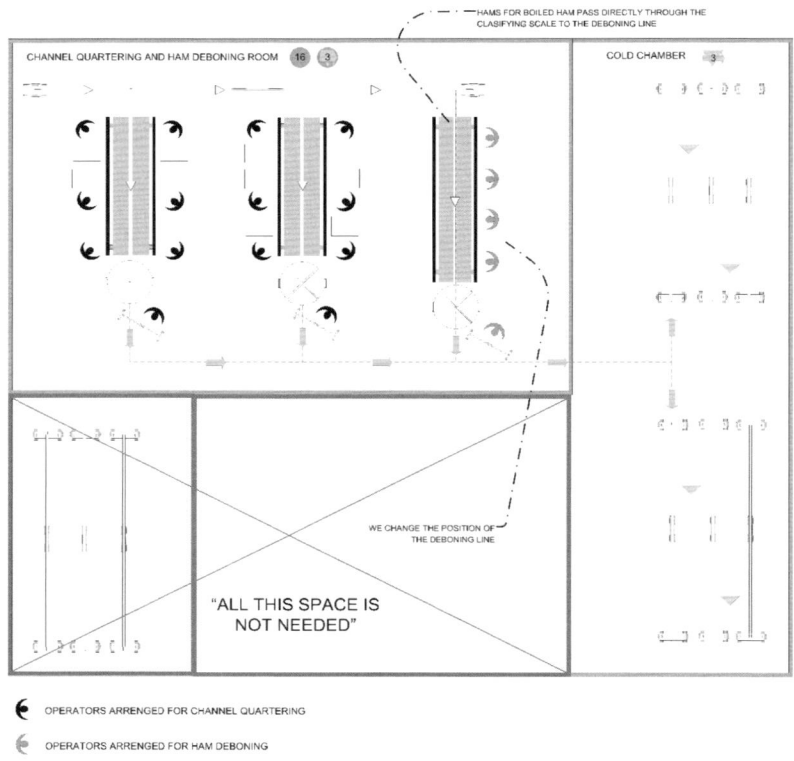

Figure 10.35. Deboning room. Proposed situation

Therefore, not only has the deboning line of ham been located in the quartering room, but following changes have occurred:

10. Process Improvement Criteria

- *Workload is reduced in the classifying stations. The quartering operators do not grab the parts that will become ham because all the parts that, by weighing, are not within the range, directly pass to the deboning line.*

- *Two unproductive jobs of exclusively transferring parts from the ham quartering room to the ham room are eliminated.*

- *Two unproductive jobs that only moved parts from the ham room to the deboning room are eliminated.*

- *A cold room is released.*

- *A workroom is released.*

Besides, as consequence of the improvement, the process duration decreases, reducing the financial cost incurred and improving the quality of the product.

A significantly simplified process flow is evident in Figure 10.36.

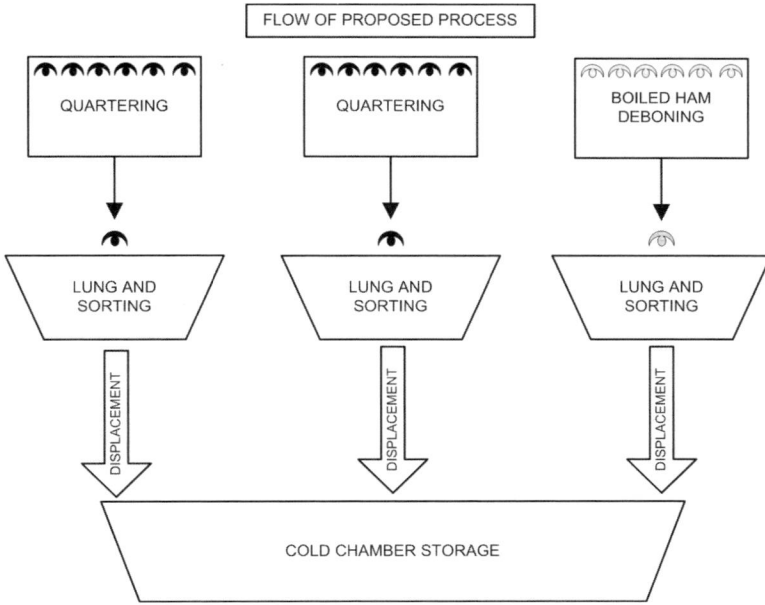

Figure 10.36. *Deboning room. Workflow improvement proposal*

In conclusion, the application of lean manufacturing principles promotes the reduction of the seven types of wastes: defects, overproduction, transportation, waiting, inventory, motion, and overprocessing. Of these wastes, overproduction should never occur, even if we are very productive doing it. Processes must be always be closely scrutinized.

Industrial Productivity

Questions

1. What is the main principle in process improvement?
2. What is the definition of a process?
3. What four main tools are used for process improvement?
4. What non-value-adding tasks cause the imbalance among tasks of the same process?
5. How can imbalance situations be solved? Cite three solutions.
6. Is specialization and division of work the best solution?
7. What non-value-added tasks cause large intermediate warehouses?
8. How is the amount of intermediate stock reduced?
9. Does the size of intermediate warehouses influence delivery deadlines?
10. How do spacious factories contribute to the productivity of work?
11. If spaces and distances between tasks cannot be reduced, what solutions can be implemented?
12. Given the typology and symbols of tasks that have been defined, what symbol will predominate in a nearly perfect process?
13. After a process improvement project, the factory will be smaller. What has to be done with the spare space?
14. What problems arise from processes of mass production in large batches?

Problem

1. The following image shows an outline from a manufacturing process.

10. Process Improvement Criteria

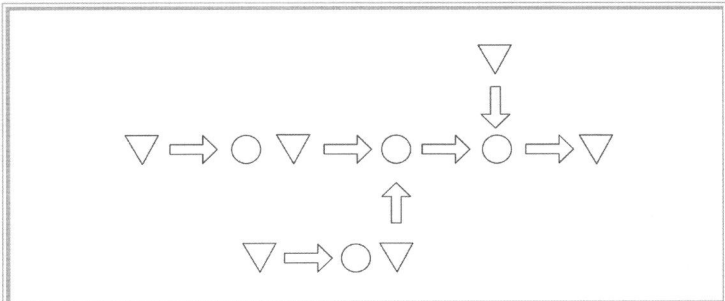

Observing the previous image and given the concepts of process improvement, the perfect process will be the following:

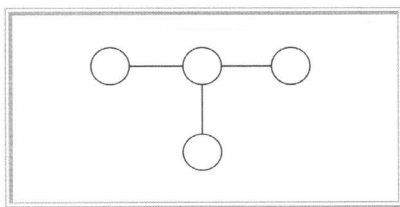

Having in mind the process improvement performed, answer the following questions:

- Is the necessary space reduced?

    ☐ Yes, therefore we could use a smaller factory.

    ☐ No, it remains the same.

- To build the perfect process we must eliminate intermediate stores, because the waiting time of a material in the stores is usually far superior to the operation time. What will happen to the lead time?

    ☐ Nothing, it will be the same.

    ☐ It can be reduced by 10 to 20 percent.

    ☐ The reduction is drastic; the manufacturing lead time will be reduced by more than 60 percent.

- To work with unit or smaller transference batches, what should be the duration times of the different tasks that intervene in a process?

    ☐ It is not relevant.

    ☐ Exactly the same.

Industrial Productivity

☐ Very similar, balancing all we can so no accumulations are produced in front of the tasks with longer duration per unit.

2. In many industries, for space and process reasons, two consecutive steps take place in different plants, so from one phase to the other the material has to be transported by truck according to the following outline.

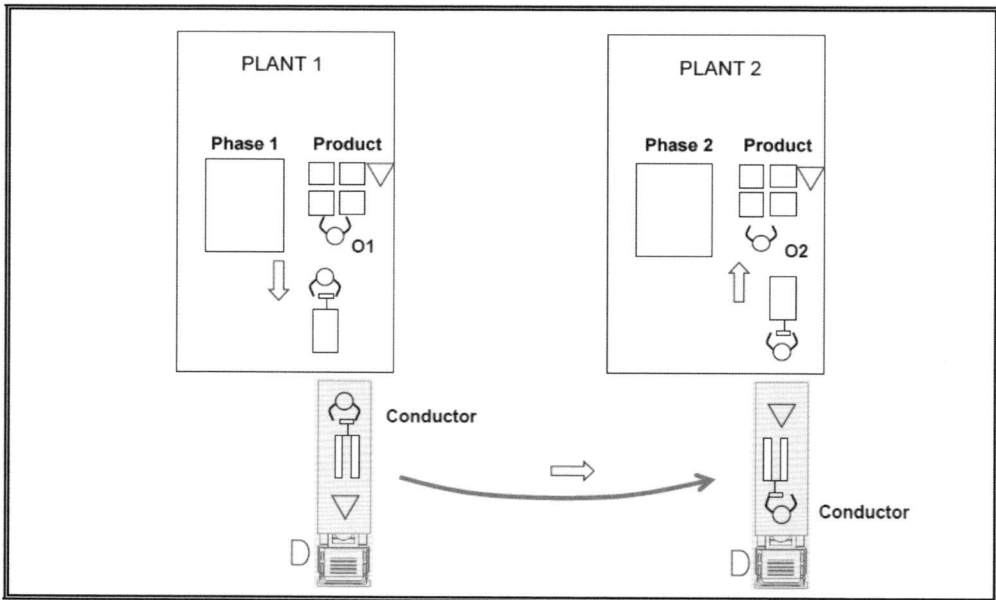

Assuming that for the load in plant 1 an operator (operator 1) loads the truck and a driver transports it to plant 2 where another operator (operator 2) unloads it in plant 2.

Operator 1 does the following tasks:

- Takes pallets from the buffer that is generated after phase 1.
- Transports it to the truck.
- Places it in the truck.

The driver

- Waits until the truck is loaded.
- Transports the material to plant 2.

10. Process Improvement Criteria

- Waits for the unloading.
- Returns with the empty truck to plant 1.

Operator 2
- Unloads the truck.
- Transports the pallets from the truck to the lung there is before phase 2.
- Places and organizes such buffer.

Given the process, locate the symbols in the previous plan in order to represent the product flow.

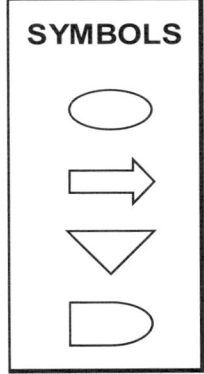

- The truck has capacity for 20 pallets and until it is not full it does not drive toward plant 2. What is the transference batch between these two phases?
- Can this process be quick in its deliveries?
- Why?
- Practical exercise: Visit a factory and collect the statistics about the amount of people who are doing non-value-adding tasks. For this exercise, collect four samples; go inside four times and without questioning anything or trying to excuse it, take a photograph in which you write down how many people you have seen:
    - Walking
    - Transporting
    - Talking
    - Searching

➤ Waiting

➤ Working on the product

When you have done so, fill in the following statistical table.

N° of sampling	N° people in plant	N° of people working on the product	N° of people doing non-value-added tasks	% of people working on the product
M	A	B	A – B	(B/A)*100
1				
2				
3				
4				

This brief study can provide a picture of the improvement possibilities for the processes.

Bibliography

Goldratt, Eliyahu M., *The Goal* (North River Press, 1984).

Harris, Rick, Chris Harris, and Earl Wailson, *Making Materials Flow* (Lean Enterprise Institute, 2003).

Jones, Dan, and Jim Womack. *Seeing the Whole* (Lean Enterprise Institute, 2003).

Kobayashi, Iwao, *20 Keys to Workplace Improvement* (TGP Hoshin, 2002).

Liker, Jeffrey K., *The Toyota Way* (McGraw-Hill, 2006).

Rother, Mike, and Rick Harris, *Creating Continuous Flow* (Lean Enterprise Institute, 2001).

Smalley, Art, *Creating Level Pull* (Lean Enterprise Institute, 2004).

Womak, James P. and Daniel T. Jones, *Lean Thinking* (Simon & Schuster, 1996).

Chapter 11

The Most Important Improvement: Ergonomics

After the study and subsequent analysis of the working method are done, the next step is its improvement. To improve the conditions in which the task is done is another of the objectives for the analyst. Ergonomics will help us in this task.

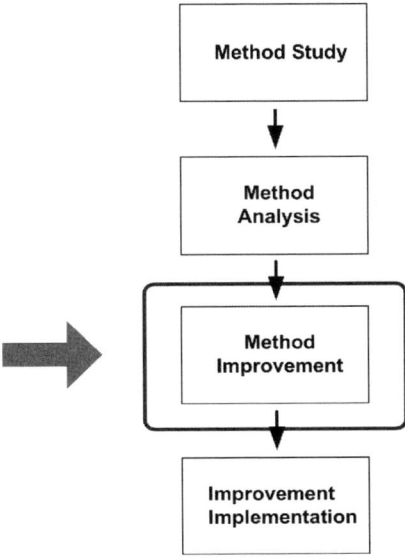

Figure 11.1. Outline of second part. Method improvement

11.1. Introduction

The word *ergonomics* comes from the Greek *ergon,* meaning "work," and *nomos,* meaning "natural laws." Frederick Taylor takes the first steps in the study of the labor activity with his work *Scientific Organization*, in which he applies the design of elemental instruments of work, such as shovels of different shapes and sizes.

Ergonomics is a scientific-technical discipline. In design, it is the study of the system formed by the human in its activity framework, related to the handling of equipment and machinery, within a specific working environment.

According to the Spanish Association of Ergonomics, ergonomics is the multidisciplinary knowledge that is applied for the adequacy of products, systems, and artificial environments to the necessities, limitations, and characteristics of users, optimizing the effectiveness, security, and well-being.

We consider ergonomics to be the most important of the improvements that can be done through the scientific study of work, because it promotes physical work that is somehow more comfortable and secure for the operator. As consequence, it is possible to obtain an increase in productivity. No one can work fast in a job if he or she feels insecure, fears an accident, or experiences fatigue in muscles and joints.

> Ergonomics is a moral obligation for the analyst.

This point is essential to this book, although we have to take into account that thorough discussion of the topic of ergonomics is beyond its scope. We must resort to other books whose references will be given. This chapter, then, is for highlighting the importance of ergonomics and giving some advice about it. In general terms, the analyst must investigate in order to solve problems such as the following:

- Fume removal
- Noise attenuation
- Temperature and relative humidity
- Weight elevation
- Uncomfortable postures
- Hard surfaces of work
- Unsecure means and conditions
- Work angle of arms

- Uncomfortable grip of tools
- Rotation in repetitive works
- Fatigue
- Working environment

11.2. Objectives of Ergonomics

The purpose of ergonomics is to design the working systems according to the capabilities and limitations of the worker, as well as the technology, equipment, and processes, so that workers can perform work more easily and comfortably, in order to achieve better productivity rates.

The way is to optimize the three previously described systems (person-machine-work environment) based on elaborated study methods of the individual, of the technique, and of the work organization.

The principal objectives of ergonomics are:

- To adapt the workplace and work conditions to the characteristics of the operator.
- To identify, analyze, and decrease work risks (ergonomic and psychosocial).
- To contribute to the evolution of work situations, not only under the approach of material conditions, but also in its socio-organizational aspects, with the purpose of performing work while safeguarding health and safety and with maximum comfort, satisfaction, and efficiency.
- To control the introduction of new technologies in organizations and their adaptation to the capabilities and aptitudes of the existing work population.
- To establish ergonomic prescriptions for the acquisition of tools and diverse materials.
- To increase the motivation and satisfaction at work.
- To reduce work accidents.
- To reduce injuries.

> In summary, ergonomics tries to adapt work to the worker instead of forcing the worker to adapt to the work, avoiding and preventing injuries and damages while achieving a noticeable improvement in productivity.

11.3. Benefits of Ergonomics

The application of ergonomics in the workplace will bring evident benefits. Roughly, it will provide the worker with healthier and safer work conditions. For the company, the benefit is the increase in productivity.

Ergonomics study different work conditions that can influence the comfort and health of the worker, factors that involve illumination, noise, temperature, vibrations, the design of tools and machinery, of footwear, and of the workplace. Likewise, ergonomics study the position, direction of materials, repetitive movements, mental workload, security and muscle-skeletal health, decision making, interaction between operator and machine, and so on.

- Benefits of ergonomics in operations include the following:
    - Reduction of work accidents
    - Reduction of injuries
    - Optimization of working methods
    - Optimization of manufacturing times
    - Increase of productivity
    - Quality improvement of the product
    - Improvement in performance of tasks with repetitive movements
    - Reduced cost of operation

- Psychological benefits of ergonomics include the following:
    - Workers with higher motivation
    - Workers with higher concentration and better perception
    - More committed workers
    - Reduction of stress
    - Improvement in quality of life
    - Improvements in the quality of work

Ergonomic investigation can be subdivided into preventive ergonomics (also known as ergonomic design) and corrective ergonomics.

11.4. Person-Machine-Work Environment Systems

When we speak about people (human factor), machines (technical factor), and environment (sociotechnical factor), we cannot treat them individually and give them independent solutions. We must try to find the concrete conditions of their interaction through the integrated *person-machine-environment* system, where the result is a set of common characteristics that should prevail over the individual characteristics of the three factors.

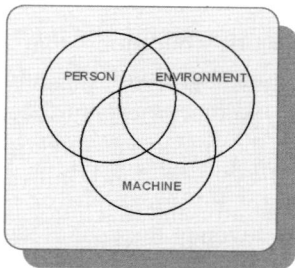

Figure 11.2. Person-machine-environment system

Ergonomics cares not so much about the primary characteristics of the three elements, but for the role of people in the person-machine-environment system. The prior analysis of tasks of the person-machine-environment system, determining the functions that individuals have to fulfill in such system, and the type and character of the activity to develop, constitutes the starting point for the design of such a system.

People and machines have different functions.

- Functions of people:
    - Correct decision making
    - Great experience that allows them to improvise better
    - Better perception and interpretation of complex situations
- Functions of machines:
    - Highly efficient for calculating, integrating, and differentiating plans.
    - Deal with predictable events more profitably
    - Useful in dangerous environments

The mission of the ergonomist will be to take into account such functions and know how to handle, intercalate, and combine them, but considering the limitations that each of them presents.

- *Preferences of the operator*: An operator who does not like the job will be more likely to create effectiveness problems, absenteeism, etc.
- *Capacity of the machine*: A machine that is not suitable for the requirements of a task will affect the efficiency of the worker in negative ways, due to low performance and potential operative imbalances the machine suffers.

Industrial Productivity

The ergonomist will face three problems when analyzing the person-machine-environment system:

1. The person-machine general comparisons may lead to an error in specific situations (e.g., the decision making of an individual with poor training can be null or wrong in certain cases given the behavior of a machine.

2. The analyst should consider how person-machine component could decrease the risk of the job and reduce time with minor costs.

3. A series of variables should be considered, such as cost, weight, size, availability, a single operator for a machine or for more than one, or several machines without operator, even at the cost of sacrificing flexibility, etc.

11.5. Analysis and Improvement of the Ergonomic System

The ergonomist must perform an initial and partial analysis of the person-machine-environment and then a total analysis of the system, and in parallel an integrated ergonomic analysis of the functions of the person-machine elements. Chapter 6 provided a checklist for method analysis; it is one of many lists designed for the analysis of ergonomics, which is to say of the environment, tools, and their effect on the operator. The analysis method is based on the following:

- Observation
- Interview
- Simulation
- Questionnaire from checklists

Based on the outcome of the analysis, different solutions can be applied to each nonconformity or improvable situation. The following lists summarize these solutions and can help the analyst to apply improvements. The instructions for the checkpoints and suggestions include:

- The analyst must get to know the principal products and production methods, the number of workers (masculine and feminine), the work schedule (including pauses and overtime), and any important working issue.

- The work area to be inspected will be defined. If it is a small business, the whole production area can be inspected. If it is a large company, the concrete areas of work must be defined for their separate verification.

- Every point will be meticulously checked. The analyst will find a way to apply each checkpoint. If the requirement is already being used or is not necessary, "NO" will be marked for "Do you propose action?" If the analyst thinks that the requisite should be met, "YES" will be marked. The section "Observations" will be used to write down any suggestions or its location.

- When the analyst has concluded, the analyst will revise the checkpoints marked with NO." The analyst will select those whose improvements seem more important and will circle "Priority" in these points.

Format

Checkpoint	Materials storage and handling	Do you propose action?		
001	1. Clear and mark transport routes.	NO	YES	Priority
	Remarks:			
002	2. Keep aisles and corridors wide enough to allow two-way transport.	NO	YES	Priority
	Remarks:			
003	3. Make the surface of transport routes even, not slippery, and without obstacles.	NO	YES	Priority
	Remarks:			
004	4. Provide ramps with a small inclination instead of small stairways or sudden height differences within the workplace.	NO	YES	Priority
	Remarks:			
005	5. Improve the layout of the work area so that the need to move materials is minimized.	NO	YES	Priority
	Remarks:			
006	6. Use carts, hand-trucks, and other wheeled devices or rollers when moving materials.	NO	YES	Priority
	Remarks:			
007	7. Use mobile storage racks to avoid unnecessary loading and unloading.	NO	YES	Priority
	Remarks:			
008	8. Use multi-level shelves or racks near the work area in order to minimize manual transport of materials.	NO	YES	Priority
	Remarks:			
009	9. Use mechanical devices for lifting, lowering, and moving heavy materials.	NO	YES	Priority
	Remarks:			
010	10. Reduce manual handling of materials by using conveyers, hoists, and other mechanical means of transport.	NO	YES	Priority
	Remarks:			

011	11. Instead of carrying heavy weights, divide them into smaller lightweight packages, containers, or trays.	NO	YES	Priority
	Remarks:			
012	12. Provide handholds, grips, or good holding points for all packages and containers.	NO	YES	Priority
	Remarks:			
013	13. Move materials horizontally at the same working height.	NO	YES	Priority
	Remarks:			
014	14. Eliminate tasks that require bending or twisting while handling materials.	NO	YES	Priority
	Remarks:			
015	15. Keep objects close to the body when manually handling materials.	NO	YES	Priority
	Remarks:			
016	16. Combine heavy lifting with physically lighter tasks to avoid injury and fatigue and to increase efficiency.	NO	YES	Priority
	Remarks:			
017	17. Provide conveniently placed waste containers.	NO	YES	Priority
	Remarks:			

Ergonomic checkpoints: Practical and easy-to-implement solutions for improving safety, health, and working conditions. Second Edition. Prepared by the International Labor Office in collaboration with the International Ergonomics Association.
Copyright © 2010, International Labor Organization

Figure 11.3. Checklist related to material storage and handling

Format

Checkpoint	Hand tools	Do you propose action?		
018	18. Select tools designed for the specific task requirements.	NO	YES	Priority
	Remarks:			
019	19. Provide safe power tools and make sure that safety guards are used.	NO	YES	Priority
	Remarks:			
020	20. Use hanging tools for operations repeated in the same place.	NO	YES	Priority
	Remarks:			
021	21. Use vises and clamps to hold materials or work items.	NO	YES	Priority
	Remarks:			

022	22. Provide hand support when using precision tools.	NO	YES	Priority
	Remarks:			
023	23. Minimize the weight of tools (except for striking tools).	NO	YES	Priority
	Remarks:			
024	24. For hand tools, provide the tool with a grip of the proper thickness, length, shape, and size for easy handling.	NO	YES	Priority
	Remarks:			
025	25. Provide hand tools with grips that have adequate friction or with guards or stoppers to avoid slips and pinches.	NO	YES	Priority
	Remarks:			
026	26. Provide tools with proper insulation to avoid burns and electric shocks.	NO	YES	Priority
	Remarks:			
027	27. Minimize vibration and noise of hand tools.	NO	YES	Priority
	Remarks:			
028	28. Provide a "home" for each tool.	NO	YES	Priority
	Remarks:			
029	29. Inspect and maintain hand tools regularly.	NO	YES	Priority
	Remarks:			
030	30. Train workers before allowing them to use power tools.	NO	YES	Priority
	Remarks:			
031	31. Provide enough space for stable postures and stable footing during power tool operation.	NO	YES	Priority
	Remarks:			

Ergonomic checkpoints: Practical and easy-to-implement solutions for improving safety, health, and working conditions. Second Edition. Prepared by the International Labor Office in collaboration with the International Ergonomics Association.

Copyright © 2010, International Labor Organization

Figure 11.4. Checklist related to hand tools

Format

Checkpoint	Machine safety	Do you propose action?		
032	32. Design controls to prevent unintentional operation.	NO	YES	Priority
	Remarks:			
033	33. Make emergency controls clearly visible and easily accessible from the natural position of the operator.	NO	YES	Priority
	Remarks:			
034	34. Make different controls easy to distinguish from each other.	NO	YES	Priority
	Remarks:			
035	35. Make sure that the worker can see and reach all controls comfortably.	NO	YES	Priority
	Remarks:			
036	36. Locate controls in sequence of operation.	NO	YES	Priority
	Remarks:			
037	37. Use natural expectations for control movements.	NO	YES	Priority
	Remarks:			
038	38. Limit the number of foot pedals and, if used, make them easy to operate.	NO	YES	Priority
	Remarks:			
039	39. Make displays and signals easy to distinguish from each other and easy to read.	NO	YES	Priority
	Remarks:			
040	40. Use markings or colors on displays to help workers understand what to do.	NO	YES	Priority
	Remarks:			
041	41. Use symbols only if they are easily understood by local people.	NO	YES	Priority
	Remarks:			
042	42. Make labels and signs easy to see, easy to read, and easy to understand.	NO	YES	Priority
	Remarks:			
043	43. Use warning signs that workers understand easily and correctly.	NO	YES	Priority
	Remarks:			
044	44. Use jigs and fixtures to make machine operation stable, safe, and efficient.	NO	YES	Priority
	Remarks:			
045	45. Purchase machines that meet safety criteria.	NO	YES	Priority
	Remarks:			

Checkpoint		Do you propose action?		
046	46. Use feeding and ejection devices to keep the hands away from dangerous parts of machinery.	NO	YES	Priority
	Remarks:			
047	47. Use properly fixed guards or barriers to prevent contact with moving parts of machines.	NO	YES	Priority
	Remarks:			
048	48. Use interlock barriers to make it impossible for workers to reach dangerous points when the machine is in operation.	NO	YES	Priority
	Remarks:			
049	49. Establish safe procedures for forklift driving by modifying the workplace and providing adequate training.	NO	YES	Priority
	Remarks:			
050	50. Inspect, clean, and maintain machines regularly, including electric wiring.	NO	YES	Priority
	Remarks:			

Ergonomic checkpoints: Practical and easy-to-implement solutions for improving safety, health and working conditions. Second Edition. Prepared by the International Labor Office in collaboration with the International Ergonomics Association.

Copyright © 2010, International Labor Organization

Figure 11.5. *Checklist related to machine safety*

Format

Checkpoint	Workstation design	Do you propose action?		
051	51. Adjust the working height for each worker at elbow level or slightly below it.	NO	YES	Priority
	Remarks:			
052	52. Make sure that the workplace accommodates the needs of smaller workers.	NO	YES	Priority
	Remarks:			
053	53. Make sure that the workplace accommodates the needs of taller workers.	NO	YES	Priority
	Remarks:			
054	54. Place frequently used materials, tools, and controls within easy reach.	NO	YES	Priority
	Remarks:			
055	55. Provide a stable multipurpose work surface at each workstation.	NO	YES	Priority
	Remarks:			
056	56. Make sure that workers can stand naturally, with weight on both feet, and perform work close to and in front of the body.	NO	YES	Priority
	Remarks:			
057	57. Allow workers to alternate standing and sitting at work as much as possible.	NO	YES	Priority
	Remarks:			

Industrial Productivity

058	58. Provide standing workers with chairs or stools for occasional sitting.	NO	YES	Priority
	Remarks:			
059	59. Provide sitting workers with good adjustable chairs with a backrest.	NO	YES	Priority
	Remarks:			
060	60. Use height-adjusted computer workstations and arrange related computer peripherals within easy reach.	NO	YES	Priority
	Remarks:			
061	61. Provide eye examinations and proper glasses for workers using a visual display unit (VDU) regularly.	NO	YES	Priority
	Remarks:			
062	62. Provide a sound and stable footing and sufficient guarding arrangements for work in high places.	NO	YES	Priority
	Remarks:			
063	63. Increase safety and comfort of driving cabins and seats of vehicles used at the workplace.	NO	YES	Priority
	Remarks:			

Ergonomic checkpoints: Practical and easy-to-implement solutions for improving safety, health and working conditions. Second Edition. Prepared by the International Labor Office in collaboration with the International Ergonomics Association.
Copyright © 2010, International Labor Organization

***Figure 11.6.** Checklist related to workstation design*

Format

Checkpoint	Lighting	Do you propose action?		
064	64. Increase the use of daylight and provide an outside view.	NO	YES	Priority
	Remarks:			
065	65. Use light colors for walls and ceilings when more light is needed.	NO	YES	Priority
	Remarks:			
066	66. Light up corridors, staircases, ramps, and other areas where people may walk or work.	NO	YES	Priority
	Remarks:			
067	67. Light up the work area evenly to minimize changes in brightness.	NO	YES	Priority
	Remarks:			
068	68. Provide sufficient lighting for workers so that they can work efficiently and comfortably at all times.	NO	YES	Priority
	Remarks:			
069	69. Provide local lights for precision or inspection work.	NO	YES	Priority
	Remarks:			

Format

Checkpoint	Premises	Do you propose action?		
070	70. Relocate light sources or provide shields to eliminate direct and indirect glare.	NO	YES	Priority
	Remarks:			
071	71. Choose an appropriate visual task background for tasks requiring close, continuous attention.	NO	YES	Priority
	Remarks:			
072	72. Clean windows and maintain light sources.	NO	YES	Priority
	Remarks:			

Ergonomic checkpoints: Practical and easy-to-implement solutions for improving safety, health and working conditions. Second Edition. Prepared by the International Labor Office in collaboration with the International Ergonomics Association.
Copyright © 2010, International Labor Organization

***Figure 11.7.** Checklist related to lighting*

Checkpoint	Premises	Do you propose action?		
073	73. Protect workers from excessive heat.	NO	YES	Priority
	Remarks:			
074	74. Protect workers from cold work environments.	NO	YES	Priority
	Remarks:			
075	75. Isolate or insulate sources of heat or cold.	NO	YES	Priority
	Remarks:			
076	76. Install effective local exhaust systems that allow efficient and safe work.	NO	YES	Priority
	Remarks:			
077	77. Increase the use of natural ventilation when needed to improve the indoor climate.	NO	YES	Priority
	Remarks:			
078	78. Use air-conditioning systems to provide an indoor climate conducive to the health and comfort of people.	NO	YES	Priority
	Remarks:			
079	79. Improve and maintain ventilation systems to ensure good workplace air quality.	NO	YES	Priority
	Remarks:			
080	80. Keep the office work area in good order to increase the efficiency and comfort of people using the area.	NO	YES	Priority
	Remarks:			
081	81. Provide enough fire extinguishers within easy reach and be sure that workers know how to use them.	NO	YES	Priority
	Remarks:			

Industrial Productivity

082	82. Recycle wastes to make better use of resources and protect the environment.	NO	YES	Priority
	Remarks:			
083	83. Mark escape routes and keep them clear of obstacles.	NO	YES	Priority
	Remarks:			
084	84. Establish evacuation plans to ensure safe and rapid egress from the worksite.	NO	YES	Priority
	Remarks:			

Ergonomic checkpoints: Practical and easy-to-implement solutions for improving safety, health and working conditions. Second Edition. Prepared by the International Labor Office in collaboration with the International Ergonomics Association.

Copyright © 2010, International Labor Organization

Figure 11.8. Checklist related to premises

Format

Checkpoint	Hazardous substances and agents	Do you propose action?		
085	85. Isolate or cover noisy machines or parts of machines.	NO	YES	Priority
	Remarks:			
086	86. Maintain tools and machines regularly in order to reduce noise.	NO	YES	Priority
	Remarks:			
087	87. Make sure that noise does not interfere with verbal communication and auditory signals.	NO	YES	Priority
	Remarks:			
088	88. Reduce vibration affecting workers in order to improve safety, health, and work efficiency.	NO	YES	Priority
	Remarks:			
089	89. Choose electric hand-held equipment that is well insulated against electric shock and heat.	NO	YES	Priority
	Remarks:			
090	90. Ensure safe wiring connections for equipment and lights.	NO	YES	Priority
	Remarks:			
091	91. Label and store properly containers of hazardous chemicals to communicate warnings and to ensure safe handling.	NO	YES	Priority
	Remarks:			
092	92. Protect workers from chemical risks so that they can perform their work safely and efficiently.	NO	YES	Priority
	Remarks:			

093	93. Identify confined spaces requiring entry permits and take adequate control measures to render the space safe for entry and work.	NO	YES	Priority
	Remarks:			
094	94. Protect workers from biological risks by minimizing exposure to biological agents and isolating potentially contaminated areas.	NO	YES	Priority
	Remarks:			

Ergonomic checkpoints: Practical and easy-to-implement solutions for improving safety, health and working conditions. Second Edition. Prepared by the International Labor Office in collaboration with the International Ergonomics Association.
Copyright © 2010, International Labor Organization

Figure 11.9. Checklist related to hazardous substances and agents

Checkpoint	Welfare facilities	Do you propose action?		
095	95. Provide and maintain good changing, washing, and sanitary facilities to ensure good hygiene and tidiness.	NO	YES	Priority
	Remarks:			
096	96. Provide drinking facilities and hygienic eating areas to ensure good performance and well-being.	NO	YES	Priority
	Remarks:			
097	97. Provide rest facilities for recovery from fatigue.	NO	YES	Priority
	Remarks:			
098	98. Provide easy access to first-aid equipment and primary health-care facilities at the workplace.	NO	YES	Priority
	Remarks:			
099	99. Provide a place for workers' meetings and training.	NO	YES	Priority
	Remarks:			
100	100. Clearly mark areas requiring the use of personal protective equipment.	NO	YES	Priority
	Remarks:			
101	101. Provide personal protective equipment that gives adequate protection.	NO	YES	Priority
	Remarks:			
102	102. Ensure regular use of personal protective equipment by proper instructions, adaptation trials, and training.	NO	YES	Priority
	Remarks:			
103	103. Make sure that everyone uses personal protective equipment where it is needed.	NO	YES	Priority
	Remarks:			

Industrial Productivity

104	104. Make sure that personal protective equipment is acceptable to the workers and that it is cleaned and maintained.	NO	YES	Priority
	Remarks:			
105	105. Provide proper storage for personal protective equipment.	NO	YES	Priority
	Remarks:			

Ergonomic checkpoints: Practical and easy-to-implement solutions for improving safety, health and working conditions. Second Edition. Prepared by the International Labor Office in collaboration with the International Ergonomics Association.

Copyright © 2010, International Labor Organization

Figure 11.10. Checklist related to welfare facilities

Format

Checkpoint	Work organization	Do you propose action?		
106	106. Solve day-to-day work problems by involving groups of workers.	NO	YES	Priority
	Remarks:			
107	107. Consult workers on improving working-time arrangements.	NO	YES	Priority
	Remarks:			
108	108. Involve workers in the improved design of their own workstations.	NO	YES	Priority
	Remarks:			
109	109. Consult workers when there are changes in production and when improvements are needed for safer, easier, and more efficient work.	NO	YES	Priority
	Remarks:			
110	110. Inform and reward workers about the results of their work.	NO	YES	Priority
	Remarks:			
111	111. Train workers to take responsibility and give them the means to make improvements in their jobs.	NO	YES	Priority
	Remarks:			
112	112. Train workers for safe and efficient operation.	NO	YES	Priority
	Remarks:			
113	113. Provide up-to-date training for workers using computer systems.	NO	YES	Priority
	Remarks:			
114	114. Provide opportunities for easy communication and mutual support at the workplace.	NO	YES	Priority
	Remarks:			

11. The Most Important Improvement: Ergonomics

115	115. Consider workers' skills and preferences in assigning people to jobs and providing them with opportunities to learn new skills.	NO	YES	Priority
	Remarks:			
116	116. Set up work groups, each of which collectively carries out work and is responsible for its results.	NO	YES	Priority
	Remarks:			
117	117. Improve jobs that are difficult and disliked in order to increase productivity in the long run.	NO	YES	Priority
	Remarks:			
118	118. Combine tasks to make the work more interesting and varied.	NO	YES	Priority
	Remarks:			
119	119. Set up a small stock of unfinished products (buffer stock) between different workstations.	NO	YES	Priority
	Remarks:			
120	120. Assign responsibility for day-to-day cleaning and housekeeping.	NO	YES	Priority
	Remarks:			
121	121. Provide short, frequent pauses during continuous precision or computer work to increase productivity and reduce fatigue.	NO	YES	Priority
	Remarks:			
122	122. Provide opportunities for physical exercise for workers.	NO	YES	Priority
	Remarks:			
123	123. Encourage full participation by women and men workers in finding and implementing work improvements.	NO	YES	Priority
	Remarks:			
124	124. Assist migrant workers to perform their jobs safely and efficiently.	NO	YES	Priority
	Remarks:			
125	125. Assign appropriate workload, facilitate teamwork, and provide adequate training for young workers.	NO	YES	Priority
	Remarks:			
126	126. Adapt facilities and equipment to workers with disabilities so they can do their jobs safely and efficiently.	NO	YES	Priority
	Remarks:			
127	127. Give due attention to the safety and health of pregnant and nursing women.	NO	YES	Priority
	Remarks:			
128	128. Take measures so that older workers can perform work safely and efficiently.	NO	YES	Priority
	Remarks:			

Industrial Productivity

129	129. Adjust the workplace to the culture and related preferences of workers by taking a user-centred approach.	NO	YES	Priority
	Remarks:			
130	130. Involve both managers and workers in conducting ergonomics-related risk assessment as part of occupational safety and health management systems.	NO	YES	Priority
	Remarks:			
131	131. Establish emergency plans to ensure correct emergency operation, easy access to facilities, and rapid evacuation.	NO	YES	Priority
	Remarks:			
132	132. Learn about and share ways to improve your workplace from good examples in your own enterprise or in other enterprises.	NO	YES	Priority
	Remarks:			

Ergonomic checkpoints: ractical and easy-to-implement solutions for improving safety, health and working conditions. Second Edition. Prepared by the International Labor Office in collaboration with the International Ergonomics Association.

Copyright © 2010, International Labor Organization

Figure 11.11. Checklist related to work organization

Note:

- For the application of these checklists, it is recommended to use the quoted book: *Ergonomic checkpoints: Practical and easy-to-implement solutions for improving safety, health and working conditions.*

- This book explains the points from the checklist with accompanying images.

- This simple manual can provide great help to anyone dedicated to the analysis and improvement of methods. It is an invaluable sourcebook, even for those who are not ergonomists.

11.6. Ergonomics and Safety

The person-machine-environment system configures an operative system that contains a series of inputs, the functional structure resulting in the accident, and a series of outputs that result.

11. The Most Important Improvement: Ergonomics

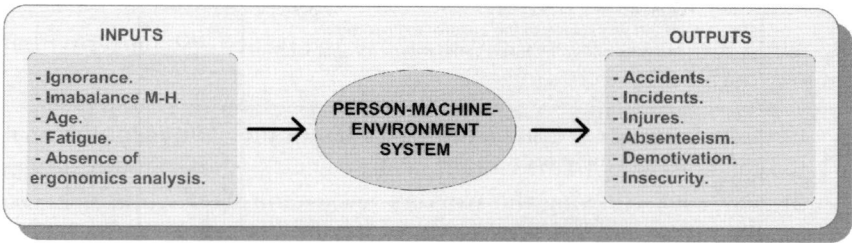

Figure 11.12. Inputs and outputs

Every activity entails risk, some of it hidden, and a certain degree of uncertainty. Ergonomics tries to reduce hidden risk and level of uncertainty. Every accident is the result of the combination of physical risks and human errors. However, from the point of view of the activity of the person-machine-environment system, it is understandable that many times the accident is consequence of a human misconduct.

The importance of security lies mainly in preventing the accident, in increasing the level of preventability and in reducing the negative socioeconomic effects. The ergonomic study of accidents is based on the analysis of certain casual models.

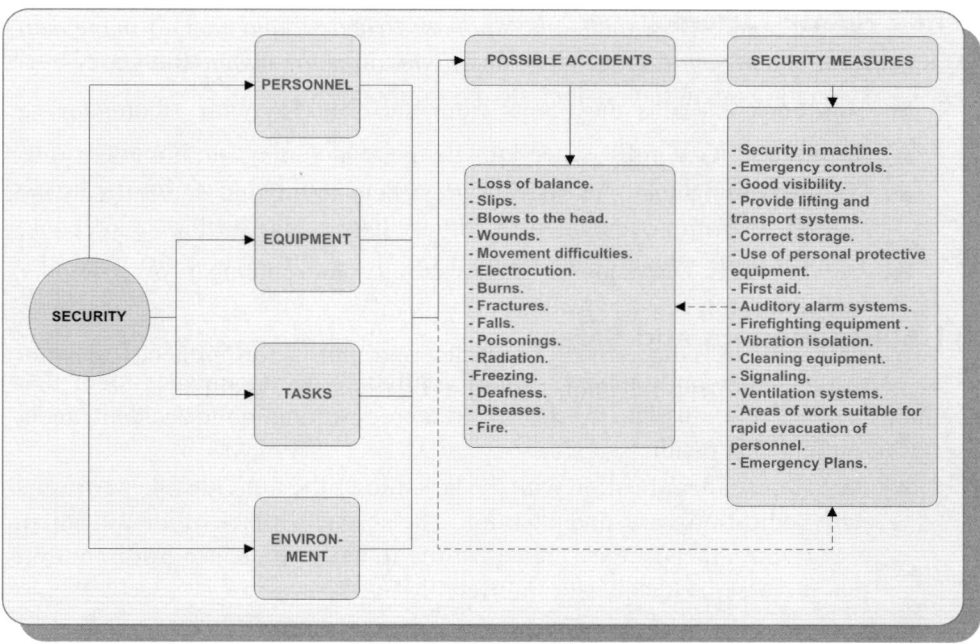

Figure 11.13. Ergonomic study of the accidents

433

11.6.1. Ergonomic Factors

These factors that intervene in the behavior of the person-machine-environment system may include the following:

- *Equipment design:* A standardized design of the equipment that matches the characteristics of the worker, with specific studies of the critical points of accidents, allowing the workers to develop their work in lower risk conditions.

- *Workstation design:* The design of the workstation accommodates the worker and promotes better working conditions and fewer high-level risks in the tasks.

- *Equipment and tools:* They must be designed to take into account their use and to reduce the risk of accidents.

- *Communication:* The absence of signs or indicating symbols or their misinterpretations are caused by human error.

- *Environment:* The low level of healthiness within the working environment, the physical agents (noise, illumination, etc.), and the work environment (temperature, ventilation) itself affect the activity of the worker.

11.6.2 Human Factors

Human error is inherent in most tasks; those who do not make anything are never wrong. The main human factors include the following:

- *Knowledge:* Generally, when knowledge, which plays an important role, is combined with experience, the effectiveness of behavior for the task is increased.

- *Mental skill:* Distractions or low ability to remember or recognize something can cause accidents.

- *Personality:* Temperament, character, and motivation influence operator behaviour, or misbehavior, and can therefore cause accidents.

- *Experience.*

- *Motivation:* Identification with the task allows the individual to perform it with dedication, care, and attention. The absence or lack of identification, along with other factors, creates in the individual a sense of discomfort that increases reluctance or indifference about the job.

11.7. Ergonomics and Fatigue

The third part, dedicated to time studies, discusses how execution times are incremented through the application of several supplements, including rest. These coefficients indicate the fatigue that comes from a certain type of task and the rest that an operator needs for recovery after each unit produced. Chapters in that part of the book include the tables that determine which supplements have to be applied to each type of task or operation. The tables of rest coefficients are in the appendixes. The rest supplement is determined by the ergonomic factors, that is, environment and tools or machines. These tables show quantitatively that the worse the conditions (temperature, noise, weight, vibrations, monotony, etc.), the greater the rest supplement needed and the more time invested in performing the operation.

> Rest supplement tables quantify the effect that ergonomics has in productivity, because the execution time of a task will be reduced proportionally to its rest supplement.

Although we advance a bit to the third part of the book, the following tables of rest supplements for the use of tools based on their weight and the existing noise in the work area indicate their role in the work process. Applying these rest supplements to the time studies will be discussed in later chapters.

TABLES OF REST SUPPLEMENTS	
(Used by Personnel Administration Ltd., London)	
1. Fixed-value supplements	**Supplement**
Supplement for personal needs	5
Base supplement for fatigue	4

2. Variable supplements	**Supplement**
Supplement for working on feet	2
Supplement for awkward position	
Slightly uncomfortable	0
Uncomfortable (inclined)	2
Very uncomfortable (stretched)	7

3. Supplement for use of strength or muscular energy to lift, throw, or push (weight lifted in kilograms)	
Kilograms	Supplement
2.5	0
5	1
7.5	2
10	3
12.5	4
15	5
17.5	7
20	9
22.5	11
25	13
30	17
35.5	22

4. Supplement for poor illumination	**Supplement**
Slightly under the recommended illumination	0
Well below	2
Absolutely insufficient	5

Figure 11.14. Extract from the tables of rest supplements

11.8. Images and References

Figure 11.15. Object transport

Industrial Productivity

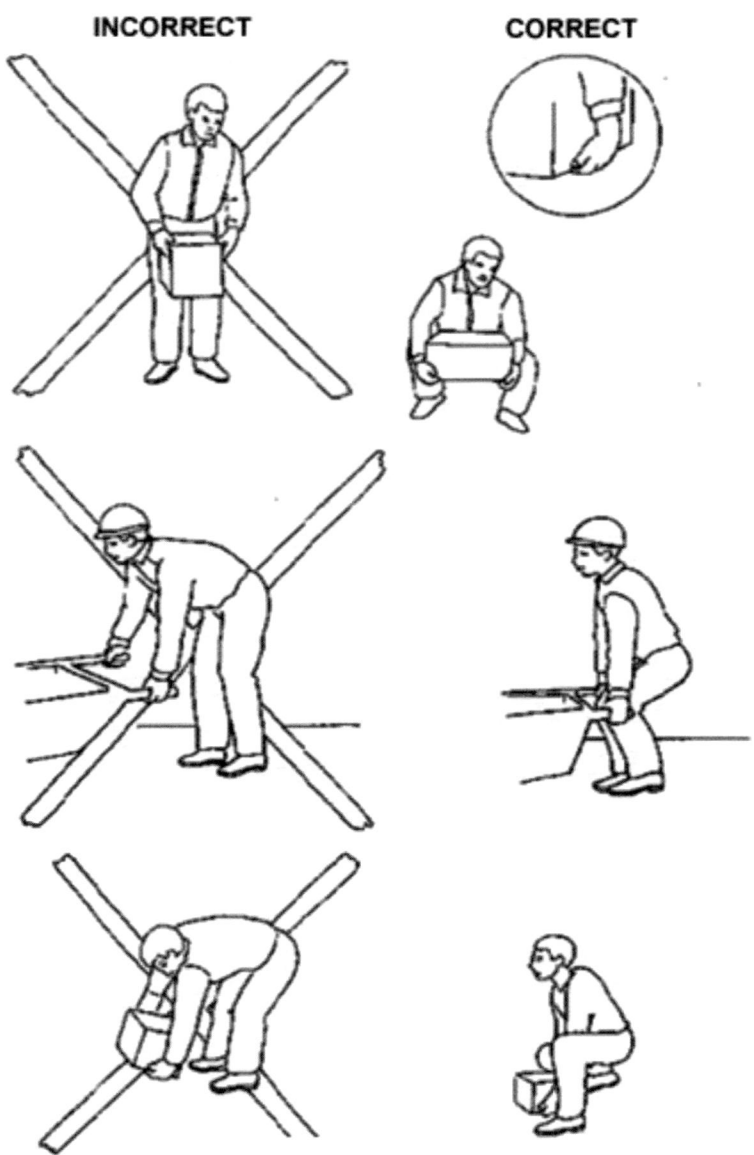

Figure 11.16. Object lifting

11. The Most Important Improvement: Ergonomics

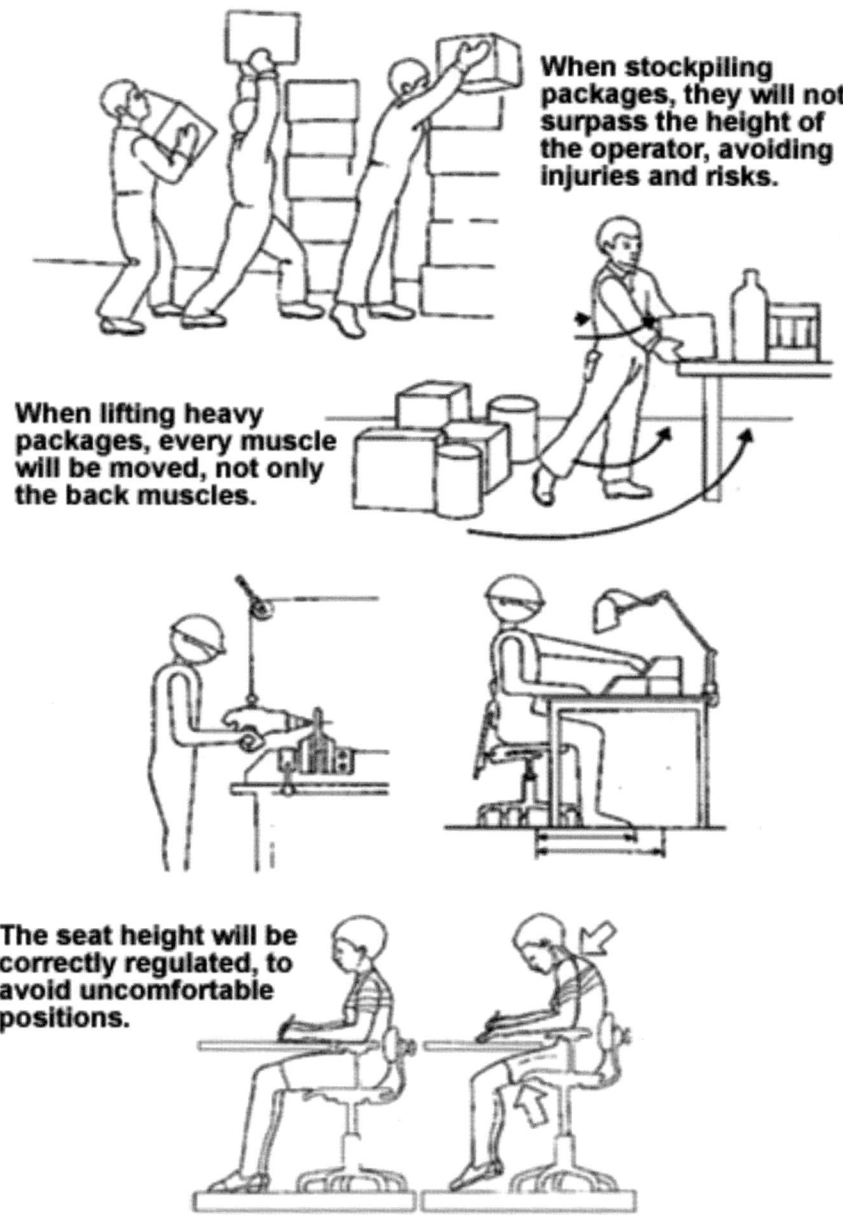

Figure 11.17. Uncomfortable postures

Industrial Productivity

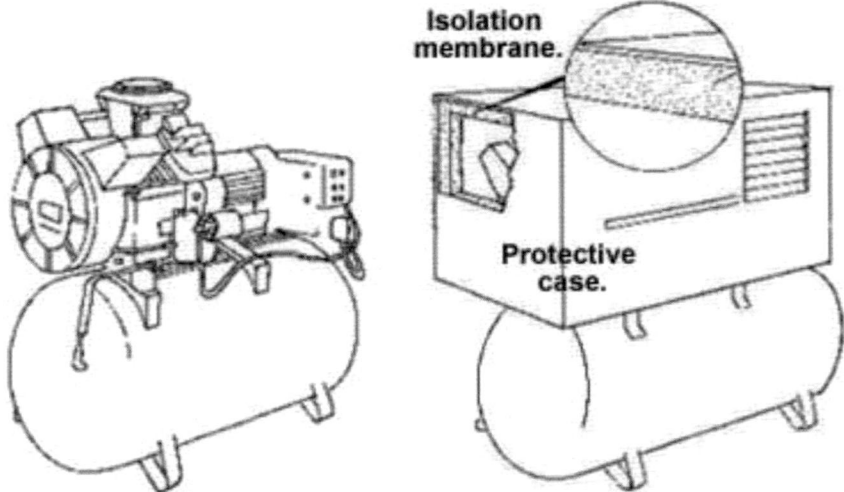

Vacuum cleaners will be used to clean the floor, with the purpose of avoiding the creation of dust clouds.

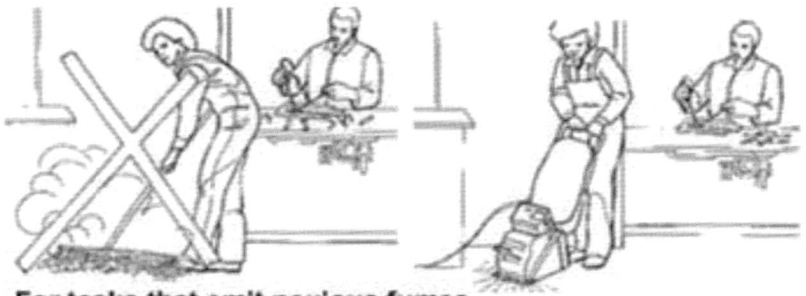

For tasks that emit noxious fumes, extractors will be installed.

Your health and safety at work: A collection of modules
Copyright (C) International Labour Organisation

Figure 11.18. Elimination of dust, fumes, and noise attenuation

11. The Most Important Improvement: Ergonomics

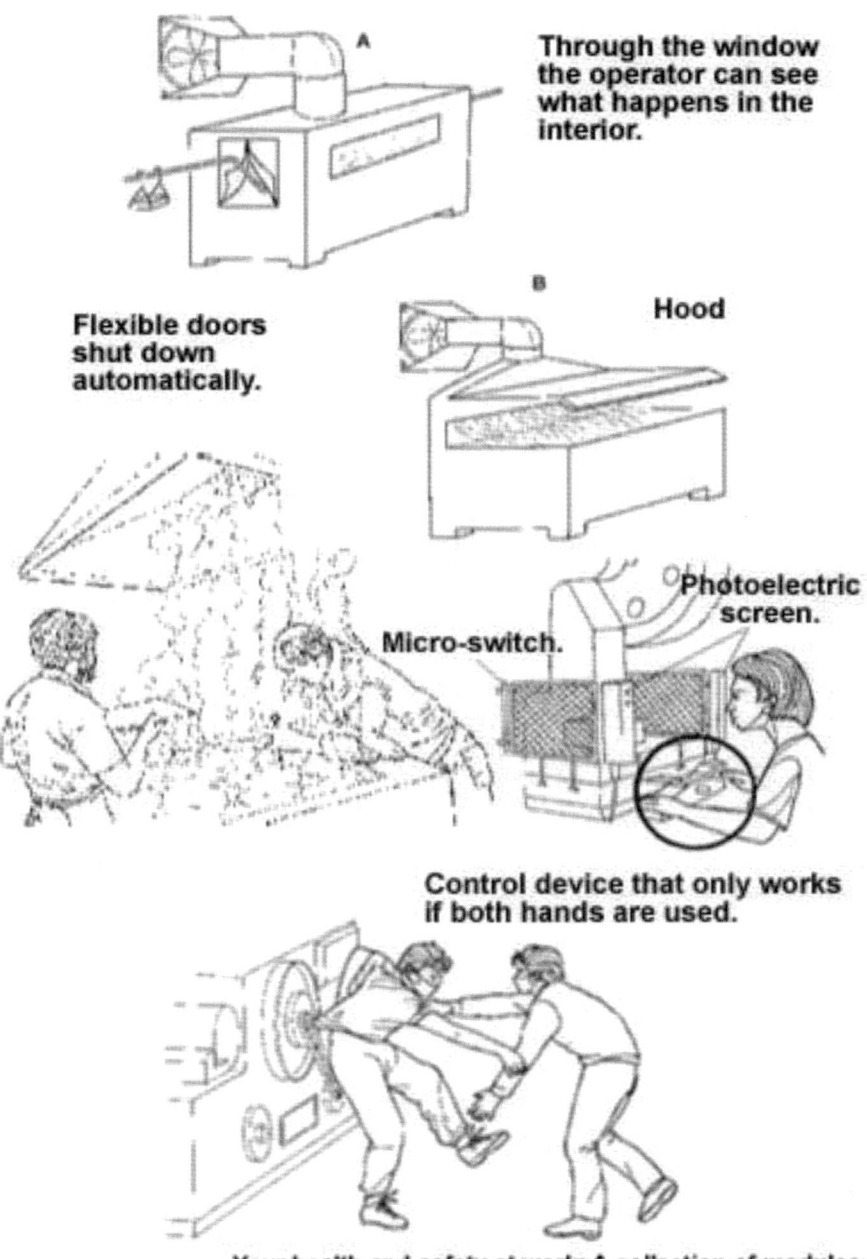

Figure 11.19. Control devices

Questions

1. Describe five generic problems regarding ergonomics in a factory.
2. What supplements quantify the productivity loss caused by poor ergonomic conditions?
3. Which are the principal benefits of ergonomics?
4. Indicate five types of lists for ergonomic solutions based on the area they study.
5. What three factors does ergonomics study as a whole?
6. Indicate the analysis methods used for ergonomics.
7. How is the application of rest supplements related to the use of muscular force?

Bibliography

Barrau Bombardo, Pedro, Enrique Gregori Torada, and Pedro R. Mondelo, *Ergonomía 1. Fundamentos* (Ediciones UPC, 2001).

Cavassa, Ramirez, "Ergonomía y productividad" (*Limusa*, 2000).

de Pablo Hernández, Carmela, "Manual de ergonomía. Incrementar la calidad de vida en el trabajo" (Alcalá grupo editorial, 2004).

Falzon, Pierre, *Ergonomics* (Presses Universitaires, 2004).

Fernandez, Jeffrey E., Robert J. Marley, Salvador Noriega, and Gabriel Ibarra, "Ergonomía ocupacional. Diseño y administración del trabajo" (*International Journal of Industrial Engineering*).

Guérin, Daniellou, Duraffourg, Kerguelen, and Laville, *Understanding and Transforming Work: The Practice of Ergonomics* (Anact Editions, 2006).

Kanawaty, George, *Introduction to Work Study* (Geneva: International Labor Organization, 1992).

Menéndez Montañes, Concha, "Ergonomía para docentes: análisis del ambiente de trabajo y prevención de riesgos" (*Grao*, 2006).

Reason, James, *Human error* (Cambridge University Press, 1990).

Sánchez, Yolanda, "Salud laboral. Seguridad, higiene, ergonomía y psicología" (*Ideas propias*, 2006).

Chapter 12

Innovation and Implementation

After the existing elements for the improvement of working methods have been described and the possible improvements in the working method detected, those improvements will have to be implemented. A priori an improvement can provide great economic savings and improve the quality of the workplace, but if it is not implemented, its benefit is zero.

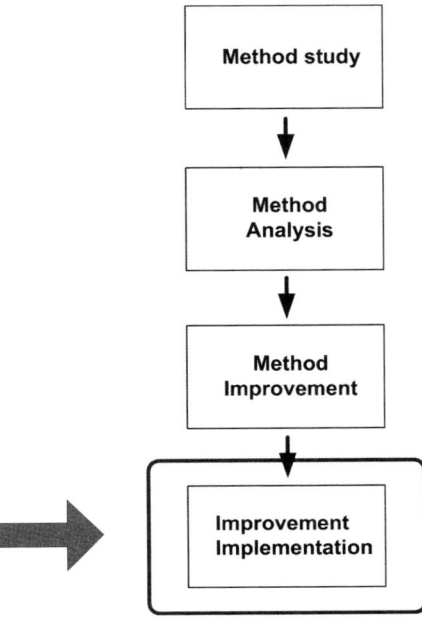

Figure 12.1. Outline of second part. Improvement implementation

443

12.1. Introduction and Definition

Once the process is finished and the idea or ideas accepted, the following step is to set the improvement in motion, to implement it and make the idea start to generate benefits. Innovation can be defined as follows:

$$\text{An idea} \rightarrow \text{Implementation} \rightarrow \text{Benefit generation}$$

The last is important. If an innovation does not generate benefits, we must return to the initial process as the preferred situation. Innovation requires two stages once the idea is approved:

1. Plan of action and implementation
2. Achievement of results and verification of the viability of the innovation

Innovation is not creativity or imagination; innovation is action and implementation.

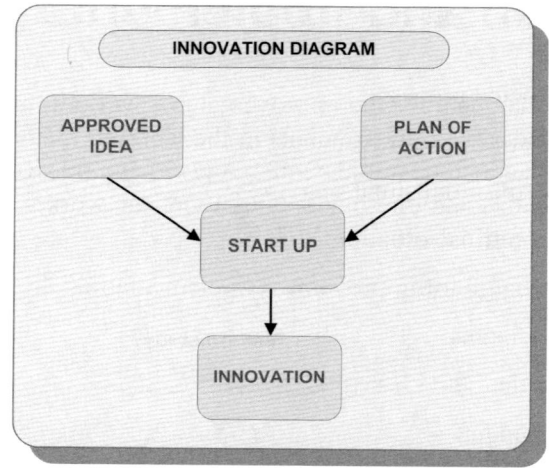

Figure 12.2. Innovation diagram

This chapter looks at the aspects to keep in mind for the implementation of the accepted improvements.

12.1.1. Implementation of Innovation

The implementation of any improvement or project requires the following aspects:

- Designation of people in charge
- Assignment of available time to perform the works
- Time scheduling
- A budget

It is necessary to know who will perform the innovation, how much time that person can dedicate to the planned innovation, a schedule with dates and milestones, and the available budget. If these assignments are not made, it will not be possible to implement the improvement. In many industries, a typical phrase is "We have many good ideas, but we never carry them out." For an idea to be put in motion, it must be supported by planning, person-time, and money.

It is also necessary to correctly define the state of the operation, task, or process to be improved and desired state after the improvement to know whether it has been achieved (standard time, line saturation, process time, etc.). Because the impetus behind adopting the improvement is expected profitability, present and desired states are calculated in numerical terms. This way provides a clear milestone indicating when the improvement is implemented.

When putting into practice an improvement, we propose an agreement be recorded that shows the following fields:

- Date
- Task or affected process
- Description of the improvement
- Parameters of initial situation
- Parameters of final situation
- Person in charge for improvement implementation
- Other participants
- Assigned time
- Assigned budget
- Deadlines, with an attached Gantt when necessary
- Other attached documentation:
    - Record of improvement proposal (see Chapter 7), which contains:
        · Summary of the improvement
        · Amortization
        · Advantages
        · Description of the improvement and sketch
        · Current and proposed method
    - File for improvement acceptance (see Chapter 7)

Example

Improvement Implementation Record				
Date 1:	2/15/2012	Implemented: ☐ YES ☒ NO	Implementation level (%):	51.23%
Date 2:	2/20/2012	Implemented: ☒ YES ☐ NO	Implementation level (%):	89.34%
Date 3:		Implemented: ☐ YES ☐ NO	Implementation level (%):	
Note: Implementation level is the percentage between obtained and expected improvement.				89.34 %
Budget spent:		1,040 $		
Hours spent:		16 Person-hours		
Final improv. obtained:		4.96 $/unit		
Annual saving obtained:		19,641.60 $/year		
Brief description of obtained results: A drilling template has been designed and manufactured to avoid having to make measurements. In addition, maintenance operators moved and installed the column drill next to the workstation. Several non-value-adding operations have been eliminated. Operators claim they are pleased with the ergonomics improvement and suffer less from back pains.					

Figure 12.3. Example of improvement implementation record

The problem with improvements normally is the time management of the people who will implement them. The best advice in this regard is setting an order and not opening too many fronts. It is preferable to finish a single improvement and then advance to the next than it is to implement ten improvements in parallel. It is best to focus on one project at a time, concentrating efforts and objectives.

> Many times, when improvements are not put into practice, it is because we fail to assign exclusive time for their implementation.

12.1.2. Verification of Results

An innovation is something that finally has to be economically viable. Even a brilliant idea is useless if it is not profitable. Paradoxically, though, the simpler the idea is, the better the results it gives.

The method improvement should also reduce the person-time execution of the task. When selecting the idea, a simulation and/or extrapolation of results should have been carried out in such a way that, in principle, the idea will be classified as viable. Once the idea is launched and implemented, we have to check to ensure that results, even if not quite as expected, lead to a reduction in time compared to the previous scenario.

This result validation of the new method may require, in some cases, additional time to accommodate a learning and resistance curve. In many others, however, the result will be almost immediate. The efficiency, speed, and reliability in the implementation of the perfected method will be proportional to its simplicity.

Once the method is implemented and work is done according to it with a real time savings, it can be said that an innovation has been performed.

The procedure or complete cycle of implementation is reflected in Figure 12.4 and developed in the next section. According to the figure, monitoring must be frequent and tangible. The implementation cannot be improvised, nor can effective monitoring.

Format

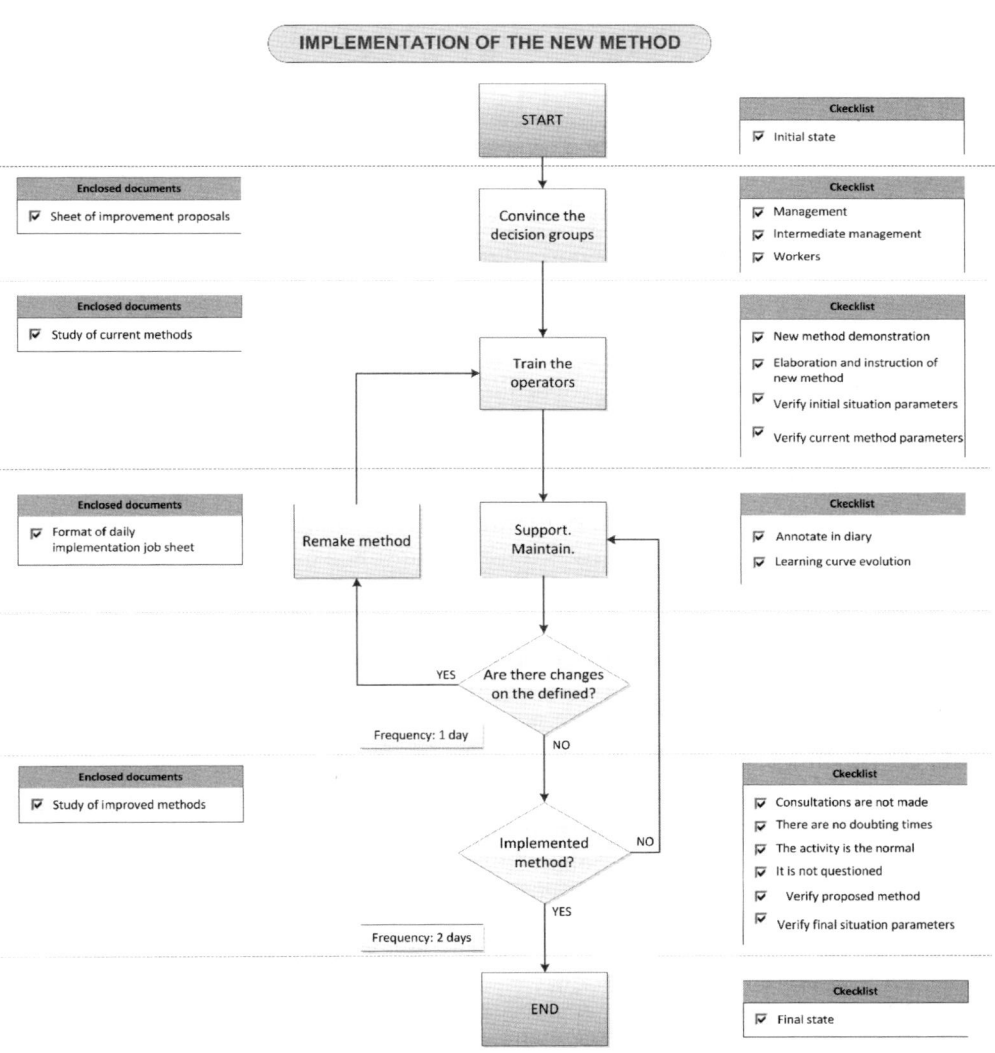

Figure 12.4. Implementation procedure for the new method

447

12.2. Implementation and Resistance to Change

12.2.1. Implement the Perfected Method

An analyst must convince three large decision-making groups in order to be able to perform an improvement: the managers, the workers, and the middle managers. Supposing the work is technically well done, the implementation work requires more human and diplomatic qualities than technical. In this case, inspiring credibility is the analyst's greatest asset.

> The work of analysis can be perfect. If any of the decision-making groups does not trust the analyst, the improvement will not be implemented.

The implementation of the new method can be subdivided into these principal stages:

1. Obtain the support of the decision-making groups:

    a) The management

    b) The department or workshop manager

    c) The affected operators and their representatives

2. Teach the new method to workers.

3. Monitor closely the progress of work to ensure it is executed as planned.

If changes are proposed that influence the workers in the operation, as usually happens, the workers' representatives must be consulted as soon as possible. The plans to change the distribution of the workforce must be studied carefully to minimize disorders or discomfort. We must not forget that even workers who perform operation on their own are not isolated entities in the workshop or company where they work. If not part of a team, perhaps the worker belongs to a section or department and is accustomed to the same colleagues and spends lunchtime with them. Even if they work at a distance that prevents them from talking, they can see each other occasionally and engage in conversation. They have adapted to one another, and if one is transferred abruptly, even if it is no farther than the other end of the workshop, that worker is removed from the current social circle and will feel its absence.

When it is a work team, the bonds are even tighter and breaking them up can have serious consequences for productivity, even with method improvement. The analyst must take into account all these aspects of social character to avoid a strong resistance. It is always preferable for those involved to perform the change. Hence we reiterate what was said at the beginning of the previous paragraph: **Before implementing, consult.**

Once the three decision-making groups have been convinced of the idea, the next step is training the people affected by the change and having them, as much as possible, contribute to the change process. The more people understand the change, the easier it is to gain their acceptance. If the change is implemented without participation—in addition to losing workers' suggestions and contributions of interest—an analyst is likely to encounter rejection and a sense of imposition from those affected by the change. If the changes concern a team, it normally is preferable to maintain discussions with the group as a whole, rather than individually with each of the members. That way, the group can collectively express its point of view as well as individual objections.

12.2.2. Strategies to Convince Each Decision Group

Convince Middle Managers

The middle managers are affected by the improvement; they will understand it as an indirect reproach to how they previously worked. Analysts have to be especially delicate in this case to avoid confrontations and always have to be respectful of the work of others. The middle manager is dedicated to the management of his or her section, not to method analysis, which is why he or she would perhaps not realize improvements that may seem obvious and for which the analyst was called in to accomplish. **In this case, the key is sensitivity and respect.**

Management

Management is easily convinced when an economic saving is demonstrated and more if the improvement needs no investment. If an investment is needed, managers will require a short amortization deadline.

Workforce

The workforce will be convinced if we demonstrate effort savings and an improvement in ergonomic conditions. For this reason the analyst must try, in each method improvement he or she intends to implement, to affect improvements in working conditions. This way, two results are achieved:

1. Facilitate the implementation.
2. Improve the working conditions for workers.

On the other hand, the reduction or displacement of workplaces directly affects the workers.

12.2.3. Training and Professional Adaptation of Workers

The level of professional adaptation that workers need will depend entirely of the nature of the job. It will be greater for jobs that entail a high component of manual skill in which traditional methods have been applied for a long time. In these cases, one possible approach is to film/video the old methods and the new ones, contrasting them as a way to demonstrate the performance of the new movements. Each job will be treated in accordance to its own circumstances.

In the training or professional adaptation of operators, the most important habit to create is the one of performing the task correctly. Habit constitutes a priceless element for increasing the productivity while reducing the necessity of a conscious reflection.

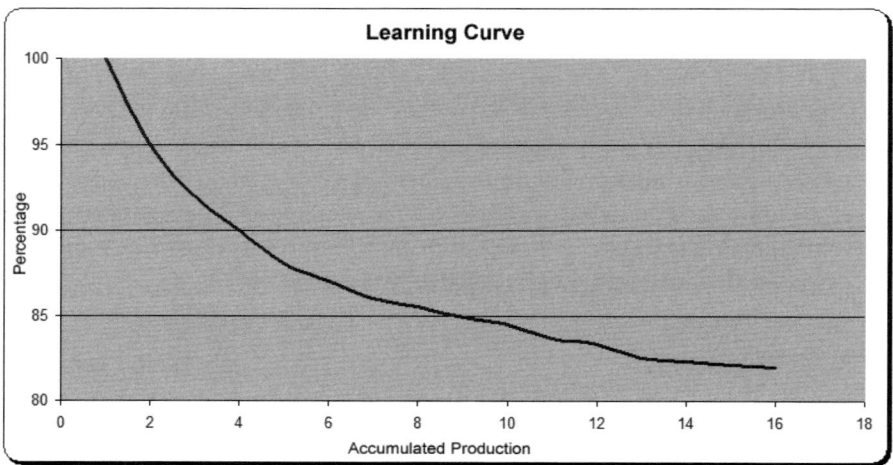

Figure 12.5. Learning curve ($k = 95\%$)

The more standardized the new method and the more thorough training, the faster learning will be. If, in addition, the analyst supervises the implementation, clarifying issues and correcting errors, the path will be much easier. The documentation or training aids can include the following:

- List of operations near the machine or workstation
- Images, either plans or photographs
- Recorded videos of operators who have master the new method
- Any information that will help increase understanding as to why a new method is not implemented arbitrarily and how it will bring an improvement

The following figures provide several generic files of the new process. The set of these documents is named "Operations Manual" or "Manufacturing Book."

BASIC TRUCKS	2 AXIS MECHANIC TIPPER	WORKSTATION A : AXIS PREASSEMBLY
		ASSEMBLY PROCESS

INDEX

1. SHEET OF PARTS AND MATERIALS..................HPM 002 13
2. SHEET OF OPERATION INSTRUCTIONS.............HIO 002 13
3. SHEET OF LIST OF CHANGES..........................HLC 002 13

ENGINEERING		QUALITY			
PERFORMED BY:	APPROVED:	APPROVED:			
Demetrio Lozano			CODE: 002 13	PAGE: 1 of 5	REV.:
	Benjamín Pérez Pérez	Antonio Hormero.		DATE: 10 / 11	

Figure 12.6. Operations manual

BASIC TRUCKS	2 AXIS TIPPER TRUCK	WORKSTATION A : AXIS PREASSEMBLY	NUMBER: 13
			SHEET: 2 of 5 REV.:
		MATERIAL SHEET	

CODE	DESCRIPTION	N°
M001650	FLAT WASHER 45D*24,5D UJA0037	16
9031136	NUT M22X1,50*29 MM. U-JA0036-1	16
9031137	ROD BUSHING *** U-JA0033-1	16
9031139	STAB. BUSHING U-JA0030-1	4
9031198	BOLT ROD M24*2 * U-JA0034-1	8
9031200	STAB. ROD. UJA0325 M24*2	2
9031108	BOLT IN U L=380 MM U-JA0020-5	8
9031225	BOLT SEAT IN U. U-JA0044-1	4
9031250	WAS. D25*D100*6 MM * U-JA0032-1	2
9031251	WAS. D27*D063*6 MM * U-JA0035-1	8
9031252	WAS. D33,3*D63,5*1,5 U-JA0097-1	8
9031253	WAS. D52,4*D101*1,5. U-JA0097-2	2
9031331	SPRING 13H E/E1310 (31256)	4
9031302	FIX ROD L=425 U-JA-023/6	2
9031258-01	CLAMP ADJUST. ROD DC(RH)	2
9031258-02	CLAMP ADJUST. ROD IZ(LH)	2
9031258-03	STUD ROD GRADUAB.L=291	2
9000023	SCR M16x1'5x65 DIN-960-8.8 CIN	4
9000526	SCR.AUT.M16x1,50 DIN-985.8 CIN	4
9031309	STABILIZER U-JB0154-001 S/T	2
9031314	SOP. AXIS RED.127 (FA) UJA-0027	4
9000047	SCR M12x1,75x35 DIN933-8.8 CIN	1
9001042	WASHER D.12 DIN-125 CINCA	1
9000538	NUT AUT.M12x1,75 DIN-985.8 BIC	1
9000008	SCREW M-14X1,5X40	18
9000509	NUT AUTOBLOC.M-14X1,5	18
9001080	WASHER D.14 DIN-125 CINC.	18

Figure 12.7. Material sheet

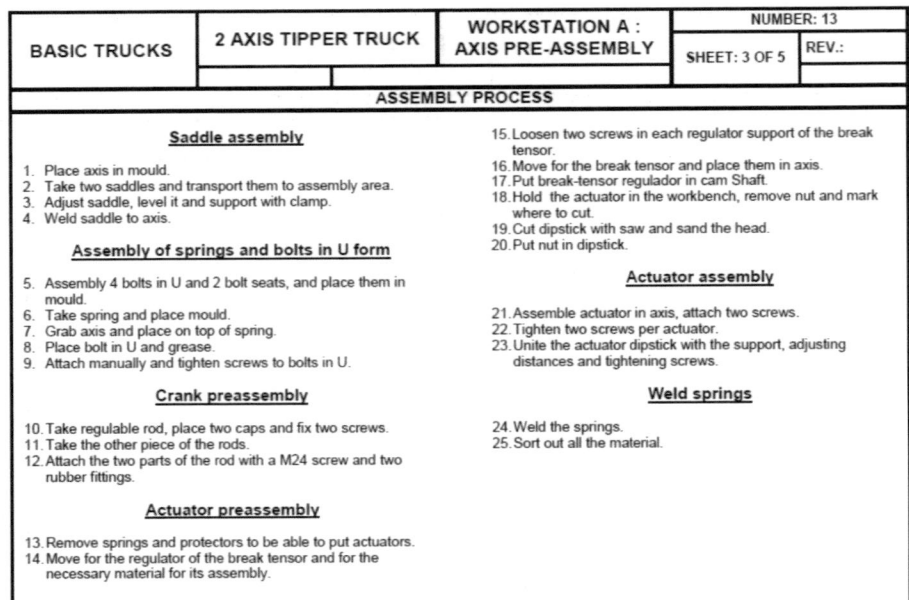

Figure 12.8. Assembly process

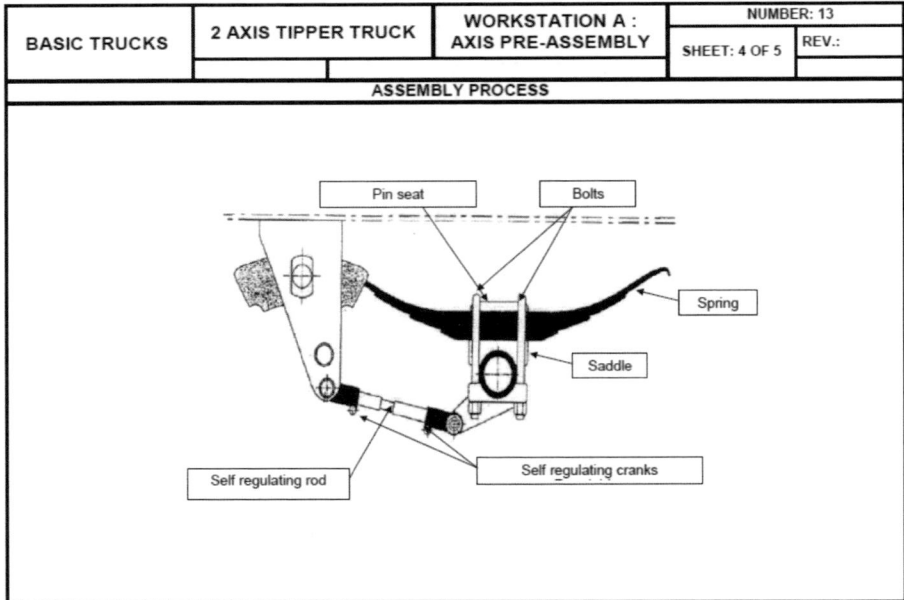

Figure 12.9. Sketch or assembly plans

BASIC TRUCKS	2 AXIS TIPPER TRUCK	WORKSTATION A : AXIS PRE-ASSEMBLY	NUMBER: 13	
			SHEET: 5 of 5	REV.:
HOJA DE LISTA DE CAMBIOS					
REV.	DATE	CHANGE DESCRIPTION	OBSERVATIONS	

Figure 12.10. Suggestion sheet for improvements

When learning a new set of movements, the operator quickly acquires mastery and reduces the necessary time to perform movements quickly at the beginning. The rate of improvement soon becomes slower, however; it commonly takes a great deal of practice to achieve a really high and constant speed, even if the adoption of modern methods for accelerated training will considerably reduce the necessary time.

Experiments show that in the first learning stages, in order to obtain optimum results, the rest periods between practice periods must be longer than the proper practice periods. This situation changes, however, when the operator begins to master the new method and acquires speed; then the rest periods can be much shorter.

12.2.4. Mentor the Change

The simple fact of changing the way things are done presents a challenge in the performance of a task. Therefore, change must be well prepared and planned, free of incidents and incidentals; otherwise barriers to its implementation will arise. When introducing the new method, the following aspects must be addressed:

- Are necessary materials available?
- Are tools for the new method available and correctly ordered?

- Is the workplace clean and tidy?
- Is the method documentation prepared?
- Are those who will be affected informed?
- Is the situation free from any incidences, that is, urgency, lack of supplies, or serious damages?

When the previous points are under control, the green light will be given to implement the change. At the beginning, the results, although from the better method, may return lower production. This situation is normal; it is a function of the learning curve. The analyst should monitor the day-by-day evolution of the productivity to see if objectives are being fulfilled.

12.2.5. Maintenance of the New Method

Without a short-term follow-up, due to human nature, operators will return to doing things as they did before. It is necessary to persevere and monitor the compliance with the new method, not stopping until the new method is totally assimilated and becomes habit.

As we know, for implementing the new method it is necessary to define it and specify it. But on occasion, devising a new method implies imagining a future situation that, once put into practice, can and must be modified and corrected. If so, the new method would have to be redefined and specified again, fixing a new time.

> The work of the analyst is not finish when he or she defines the new method, but when that method is implemented.

Depending on the relevance of the implementation, it may be convenient to complete a daily report of the progress that includes the evolution, results, and incidences of the implementation. The following figure shows the implementation diary of the improvement accepted at the beginning of the chapter.

12. Innovación e implantación

\multicolumn{6}{c	}{**Improvement implementation job sheet: Decorative assembly**}
\multicolumn{6}{l	}{Responsible for implementation: Joe Padilla}
\multicolumn{6}{l	}{Implementation deadline: 5 days}
\multicolumn{6}{l	}{Person-hours assigned: 18 person-hours}
\multicolumn{6}{l	}{Budget assigned: $1,200}
Date	Area-Section	Computed hours	\multicolumn{2}{c	}{Budget invested}	Comments- Incidences
2/13/2012	Assembly and mechanization area	1.5 hours	$	80	Moved the drill column from the assembly area to the work area. Maintenance personnel previously installed an energy input and a compressed air input for the machine. Mechanization operators are pleased with the change.
2/14/2012	Engineering	0.5 hours	$	17	The engineering staff took action and revised the piece plans for the drilling template. A sketch of the template was drawn.
2/15/2012	Engineering-Maintenance	9 hours	$	821	Maintenance personnel along with engineering supervision manufactured the drilling template of the piece.
2/16/2012	Engineering-Production-Maintenance	3.5 hours	$	105	The validity of the drilling template is checked, processing several pieces with it. Quality and validity of the processed parts confirmed. Slight modifications were necessary.
2/17/2012	Engineering-Production	0.5 hours	$	17	Several pieces are processed with the changes made the day before. The improvement is terminated. Operators of the mechanization area are pleased with the improvements implemented, which will considerably reduce the task and the risk of failure.
2/20/2012	Production-Quality	2 hours	$	-	Various surveys are conducted to check the quality of a batch of parts processed with the new drilling template. None detected for any nonquality parts checked.
2/21/2012	Production-Quality	0,5 hours	$	-	Various surveys are conducted to check the quality of a batch of parts processed with the new drilling template. None detected for any nonquality parts checked.
\multicolumn{2}{	c	}{Total}	0.00 hours	\multicolumn{2}{c	}{1,040.00 €}	

Figure 12.11. Example of record for improvement implementation

This daily report includes all the steps followed until implementation is complete. Only then can we know the level of implementation of the improvement. At this moment two distinctions should be made: level of quantitative improvement and level of qualitative improvement. The first of which is shown in Figure 12.3 and is obtained from dividing the annual saving obtained by the annual saving expected.

$$\text{Quantitative implementation level} = \frac{\text{Annual saving obtained}}{\text{Annual saving expected}}$$

The second level, measured later, will indicate lower absenteeism by notably improving the ergonomic conditions of the workplace and reducing work risks. This level compares the amount of sick leaves in the affected workplace before and after the improvement.

12.2.6. Summary

The stage of analysis still leaves the other parts: start-up and implementing the idea. On occasion, this point is forgotten, which means great ideas without any result. In fact, it is sometimes preferable to stop the work of study and analysis of more methods until those already proposed are implemented. **The work of study, analysis, and improvement is only amortized when implemented.** To hand over recommendations to managers is not finishing the work.

Questions

1. What is innovation?
2. Compare and contrast innovation and creativity.
3. What are the minimum requirements for implementation of an idea?
4. When has an innovation actually occurred?
5. What three large steps are necessary for the implementation of the new method?
6. If a change affects the habits, number of workers, equipment, and, in general, the environment of workers, what must be done?
7. Before a new method can be implemented, what motivates management?
8. In what ways can a new method affect a middle manager?
9. What is the best way to convince workers of the importance of a change?
10. How can the learning time for a new method be reduced?
11. When does the work on a method end?

Bibliography

Carballo, Roberto, *En la espiral de la innovación* (Ed. Díaz de Santos, 2004).

Gallego, Fabio, *Aprender a generar ideas: Innovar mediante la creatividad* (Ediciones Paidós Ibérica S.A., 2001).

Hidalgo Nuchera, Antonio, Gonzalo León Serrano, and Julián Pavón Morote, *La gestión de la innovación y la tecnología en las organizaciones* (Ed. Ediciones Pirámide, 2002).

Chapter 13

Study and Analysis of Administrative Processes

13.1. Introduction

Of all the existing working methods, this group deserves a separate chapter: It is the study of methods and processes of administrative tasks. Besides, in developed countries, these tasks already have more weight than industrial tasks.

In this chapter we learn to develop administrative processes and to apply criteria for their improvement. The definition of processes for administrative works includes the following:

- Save time in communications.
- Eliminate differences in performance between workers due to standardization.
- Make tasks and processes easier to delegate.
- Reduce the risk of errors.

The potential for improvement in the execution times of administrative tasks is significant. Administrative tasks usually encompass billing, order processing, correspondence, accounting, financial records, and so on. Nevertheless, believing that administrative tasks are reduced to the personnel performing these jobs is a mistake.

Industrial Productivity

> All knowledge workers perform administrative tasks: accountants, doctors, lawyers, engineers, architects, managers, and executives. In fact, we can say that in most cases, the administrative load exceeds 75 percent of working hours, with the rest of the time dedicated to the specific knowledge of each profession or specialization.

For this reason, improving the productivity of the administrative component is important to the output of the knowledge workers. If improvements can reduce the time dedicated to routine tasks, they can then increase the time dedicated to knowledge, enabling to improve contributions to companies and to society.

It seems sensible to make a scientific study of industrial works, but the same is not done with administrative, office, or knowledge tasks. In this kind of works, **being productive results first from having a method and performing it without unnecessary repetition or rework. The second way to achieve productivity is to be focused on what is being done.**

Even though process construction has already been developed in Chapter 5, we treat it here again because administrative tasks pose a special case. First we will learn to construct a process from disordered tasks. The processes need to be graphically represented and therefore diagrams will be used. We explain what a diagram is and how this easy and powerful tool is developed.

- The diagram of a working process is a graphic representation that shows schematically all the steps to follow in order to perform a job or activity according to a process or procedure.
- In a process diagram, each of the steps to follow is represented with a symbol that will correspond to the type of represented operation. Besides, it will include information deemed necessary for its analysis.
- The goal of a process diagram is to present a clear image of the task sequence or events that compose it and their possible variations or routes to follow.

> A process diagram is the graphic representation that illustrates the sequence or succession of tasks.

The diagram will represent the process as it currently is with all its defects and inefficiencies. It will be a working document, a means to achieve better activities.

13.2. Elaboration and Representation of an Administrative Process

To start the construction of a process, we must have a clear idea of the contributions we will obtain with its elaboration.

> The aim of diagramming a process is to determine the sequence of operations that compose it, so it can be standardized, used, and improved.

With the elaboration of a process diagram, we have to establish *what it must be* and *how it must be* in order to create the guidelines to follow for the correct and complete fulfilment of the work cycle. Every process has the following elements:

1. Title of the process
2. Objective of the process
3. Client
4. Suppliers
5. Participants
6. Beginning: Initial milestone
7. End: Final milestone
8. Tasks or events of the process
    8.1 Sequence of tasks
    8.2 Rationale of the tasks
9. Inputs and outputs

What we will learn in this chapter is to define and represent an administrative process and improve it. Even the formats are flexible; the final form of a process will be the following (Figure 13.1):

Industrial Productivity

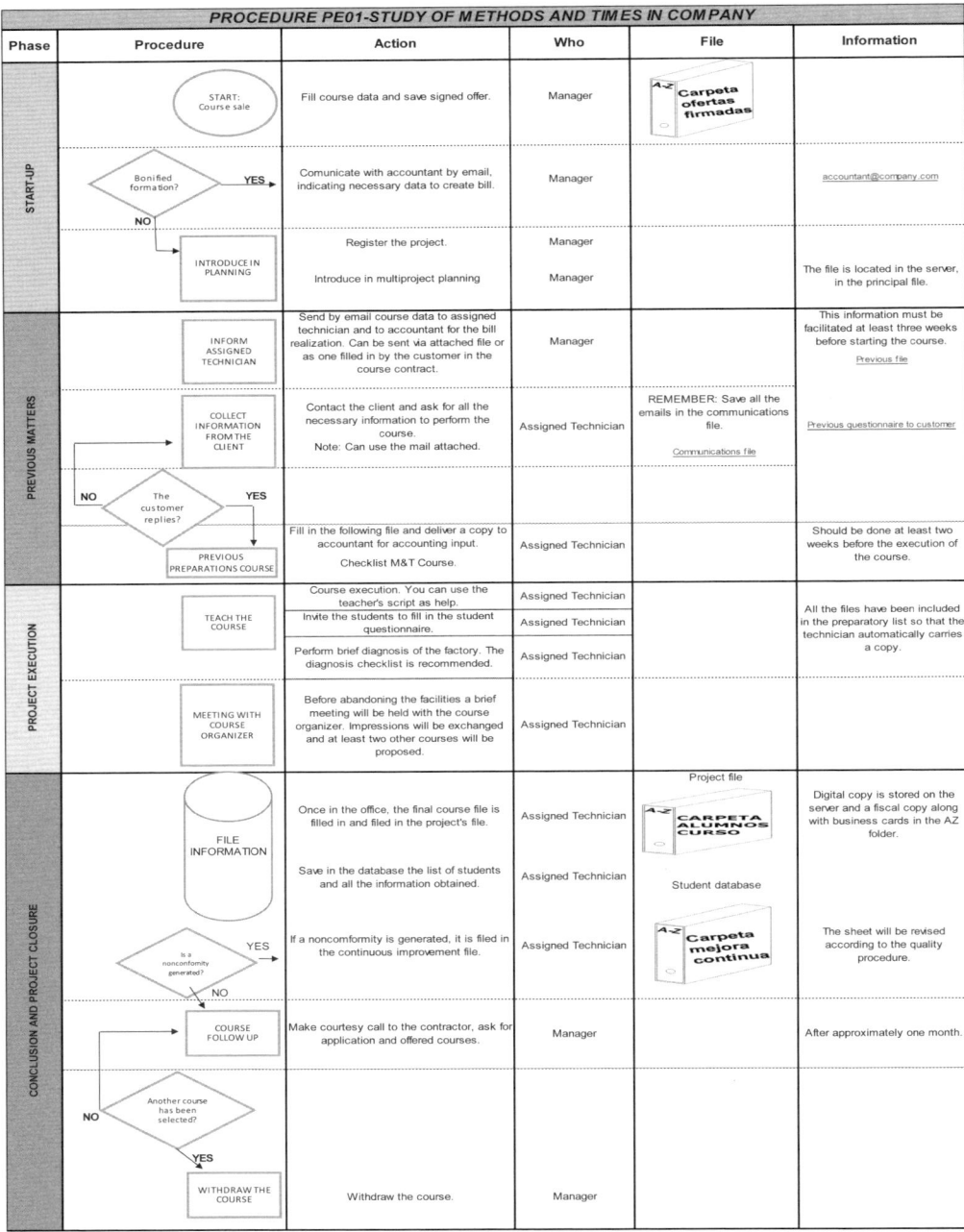

Figure 13.1. Example of process diagram

To build a process is creative work that requires certain level of abstraction as well as great knowledge of the process. A relatively simple methodology is needed for building a process; however, it must be followed with discipline and avoiding the temptation to take shortcuts.

Example

All the elements that occur in the "Quotation" process will be described, followed by the steps for developing the corresponding process diagram.

Title of the process
Quotation.

Objective of the process
The budgeting process identifies and defines the steps to follow for the request for quotation, the quotations, and contract signing.

Client
Quotation solicitor.

Suppliers
Possible subcontractors.

Messenger.

Participants
Designed technician.

Possible subcontractors.

Client.

Beginning: Initial milestone
The commercial department provides a description of the work for which a bid is being prepared.

End: Final milestone
Quotation delivered to client.

Tasks or events of the process
First, all the tasks and events that take place in the process development will be noted. When writing them down, do not worry about the order.

Tasks and events of the process
Develop budget.
Request for quotation.
Send quotation to client.
Convert to pdf.
Sign contract.
Receive quotation signed by client
Receive RFQ from suppliers.
Verify data and content of quotation.
Have the quotation accepted by the client.

Tasks are classified in two groups. The first group includes the tasks that are always performed to obtain the output of the process. The second group includes the tasks that are only performed sometimes.

Tasks that are always performed	Tasks that are only performed sometimes
Develop quotation.	Receive quotations from suppliers.
Request for quotation to suppliers.	Request for quotations to suppliers again.
Convert to pdf.	Sign contract.
Verify data and content of quotation.	Have the quotation accepted by the client.

Inputs and outputs of the process

Inputs	Outputs
Quotations from suppliers.	Quotation.
	Signed contract.

Once all the elements of the process are defined, we will go on to perform the diagram. The following steps are necessary for its fulfilment:

1. *The first step consists of taking a blank sheet. As we have said, developing a process is a work of creativity. If we are going to create our process, it means we start from scratch; that is, we are faced with a blank sheet.*

13. Study and Analysis of Administrative Processes

Industrial Productivity

2. *Tasks that always occur are ordered sequentially.*

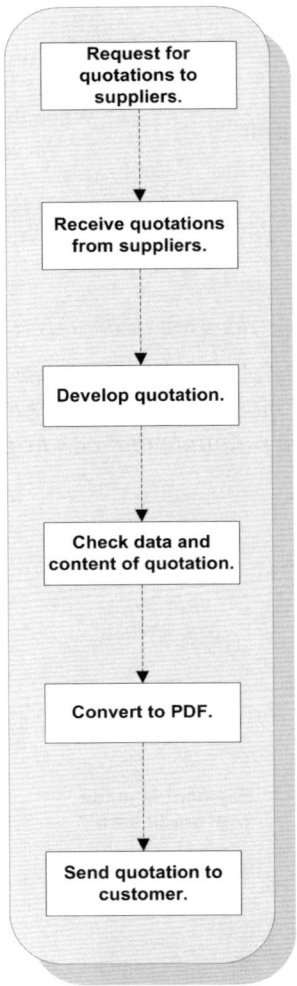

Figure 13.2. *Essential steps for quotations*

3. *Tasks and events that sometimes occur are written down either sequentially or in parallel, and also when and why they occur.*

Tasks and events that sometimes occur	When and why they occur
RFQ to suppliers again	When not enough quotations have been received. When quotations received do not meet our objectives.

464

13. Study and Analysis of Administrative Processes

Revision of quotation	When the former has not been accepted by the client. When any error has been detected.
Submit the quotation again	When the previous has not been accepted by the client.
Signed contract	When the client accepts the quotation sent.

All these tasks are subject to decision diamonds (conditionals).

During the development of a process, situations arise in which we have to decide between two or more alternatives. **The diagram must describe and contemplate the entire rationale that can be provided by the different events.**

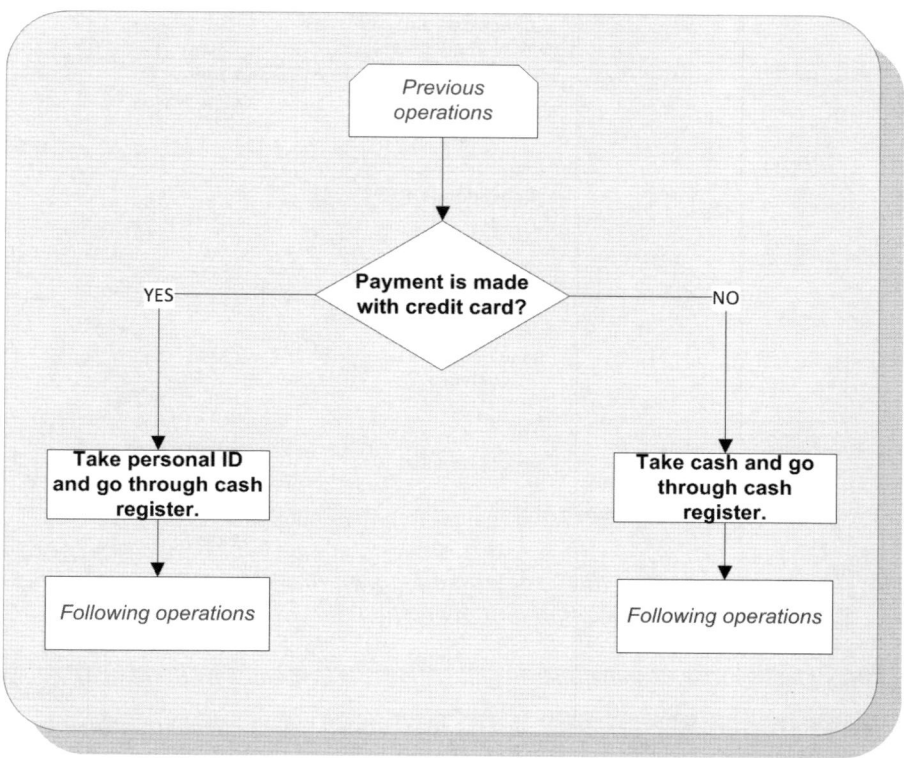

Figure 13.3. *Alternative trajectories*

Industrial Productivity

4. *With fields filled and tasks occasionally given cleared, and when or why they are given is known, the decision diamonds and the representation of tasks in parallel can be represented in our process diagram. The following format is proposed for the creation of the process diagram.*

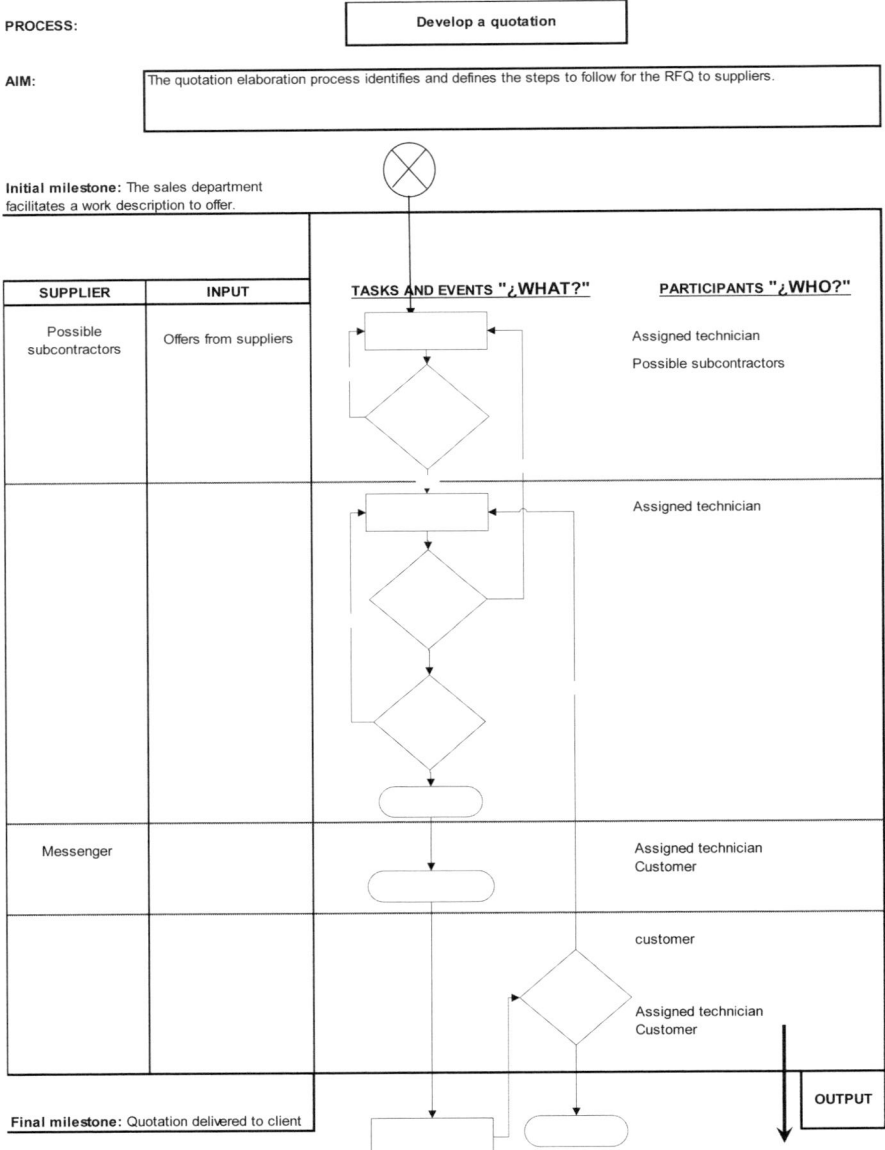

Figure 13.4. *Process diagram of "Quotation"*

13. Study and Analysis of Administrative Processes

With the diagram represented, we will know the rationale for the process.

Besides, the diagram's format can include all the necessary information and respond to the questions that are formulated to the process: **what, how, when, where it is performed, with what is it performed**, *and so on, according to the following generic format:*

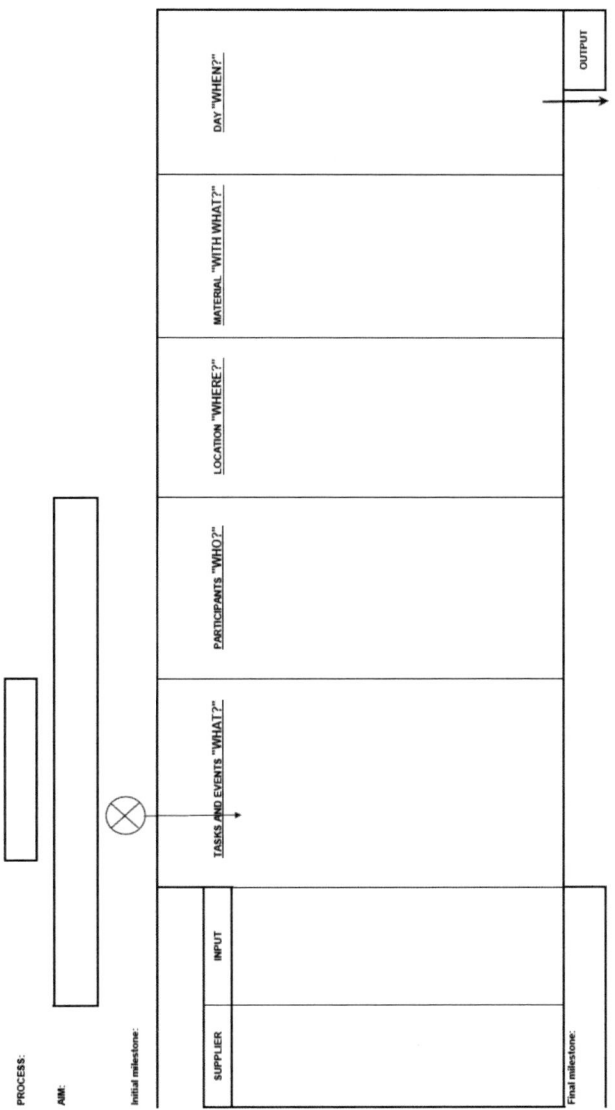

Figure 13.5. *Generic format of process diagram*

467

Process diagrams must be drawn. Normally, companies have procedures written in prose, which often go unread because they can be complicated. When developing a process, use a symbol that will help everyone understand visually the task it represents.

13.3. Improvement of Administrative Processes

Once the process is built and represented by a diagram, the next step is to analyze and study the possible improvements.

> The objective of improving the process is (1) reducing its time in order to reduce delivery deadlines, obtain more capacity to serve the clients, and reduce internal costs; and (2) securing the process and the result.

Process improvement consists in optimizing effectiveness and efficiency, improving also the controls, reinforcing the internal mechanisms for responding to contingencies and demands of new and future clients. The improvement of processes must constitute a cycle that achieves a continuous improvement of the process.

> When creating and improving a process, it is necessary to keep in mind that developing processes does not provide improvements. For this reason, the development of a process has to be finished, with benefits realized from the performed improvement, before starting the next.

Many of the improvements are just common sense, but the diagramming helps to see non-value-adding tasks and invites a redefining of the processes. When a process "has always been done that way" and is totally assimilated, it is hard to think that it can be done in a better way. The diagram and its symbols help to overcome this prejudice and expose many unnecessary time losses.

The main techniques for process improvement are listed:

1. Locate and eliminate non-value-adding tasks.
2. Place checkpoints.

    - Make checklists.

    - Place checkpoints near the possible places where errors are made.

    - Remove looping tasks causing inspection.

    - Try to eliminate checkpoints securing quality and results.

3. Office layout.
4. Make procedures and tasks easier to delegate; create technical instructions.
5. Application of tidiness and cleanliness in offices: 5S.
6. Combine tasks with previous and/or posterior process.
7. Process grouping. Technique for perfect balancing.

In general, the analysis techniques seen in Chapter 6 can be applied; they consist of interrogatory techniques using preliminary and background questions. It may seem that background questions are only applicable to industrial tasks, but with some level of abstraction, they may be applied also to office tasks. The same is applicable to the improvement techniques seen in Chapter 7.

Two steps of improvement can be made to the designed process of quotation elaboration shown in Figure 13.6:

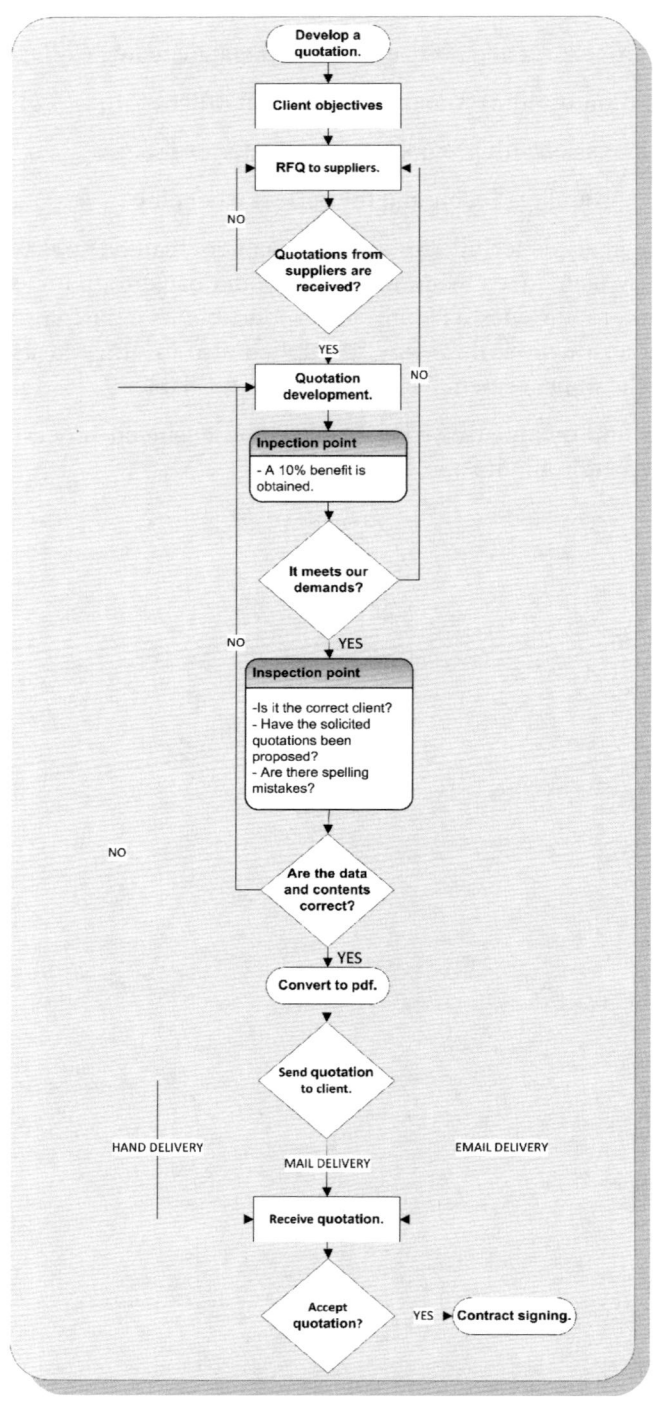

Figure 13.6. Process of budgeting with checkpoints

13. Study and Analysis of Administrative Processes

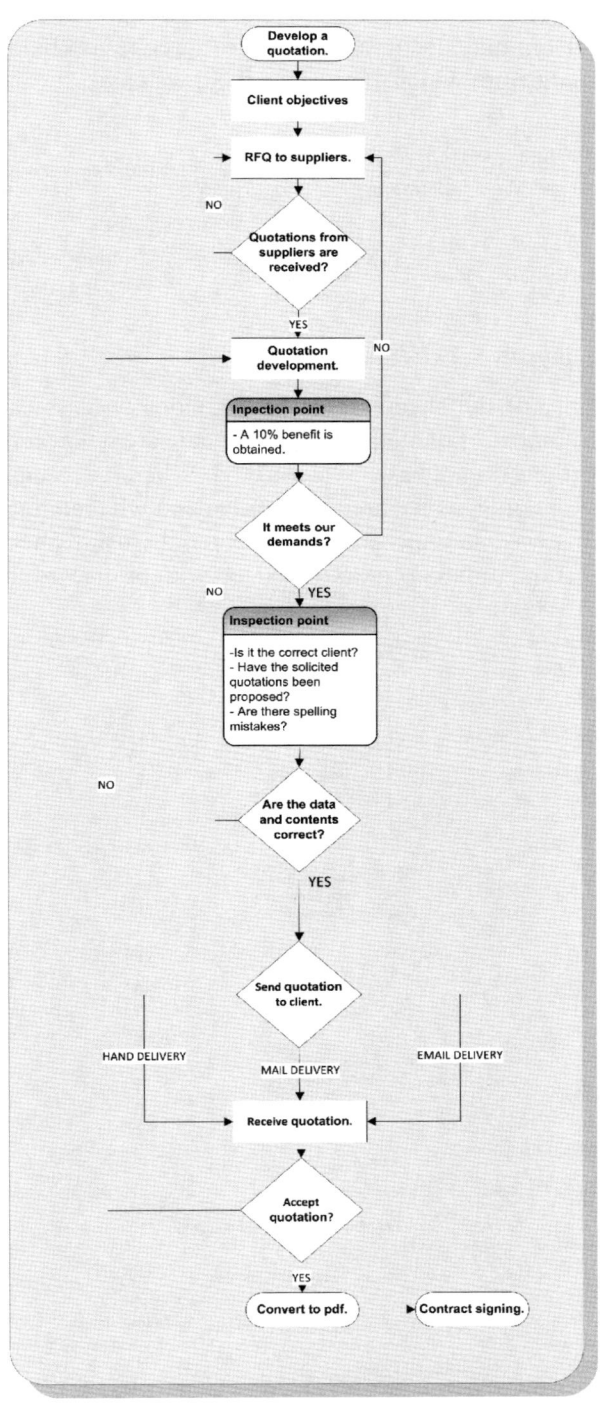

Figure 13.7. Process of budgeting with checkpoints

If this improvement is assessed, and considering that converting a quotation into pdf can take 10 minutes, with an average of three revisions per offer and 20 quotations per month from which 10 are accepted, we have:

$$Initial\ Cycle = \frac{10\ min}{conversion} \times \frac{2\ conversion}{quotation} \times \frac{20\ quotations}{month} = 600\ min/month = 10h/month$$

$$Current\ Cycle = \frac{10\ min}{conversion} \times \frac{1\ conversion}{quotation} \times \frac{10\ accepted.quotations}{month} = 100\ min/month = 1.67h/month$$

The result is a savings of 8.33 hours/month.

With the correct use of the checkpoints, the previous process can be improved and optimized. A number of quotations that are made are not accepted. Therefore, many of the quotations do not have to be offered. When redacting quotations, we know in what sectors or areas we are competitive and what conditions have to be given to be so. This way, an important improvement by using checkpoints will be the disposition of some initial criteria to proceed with or discard the quotation, as shown in Figure 13.8:

13. Study and Analysis of Administrative Processes

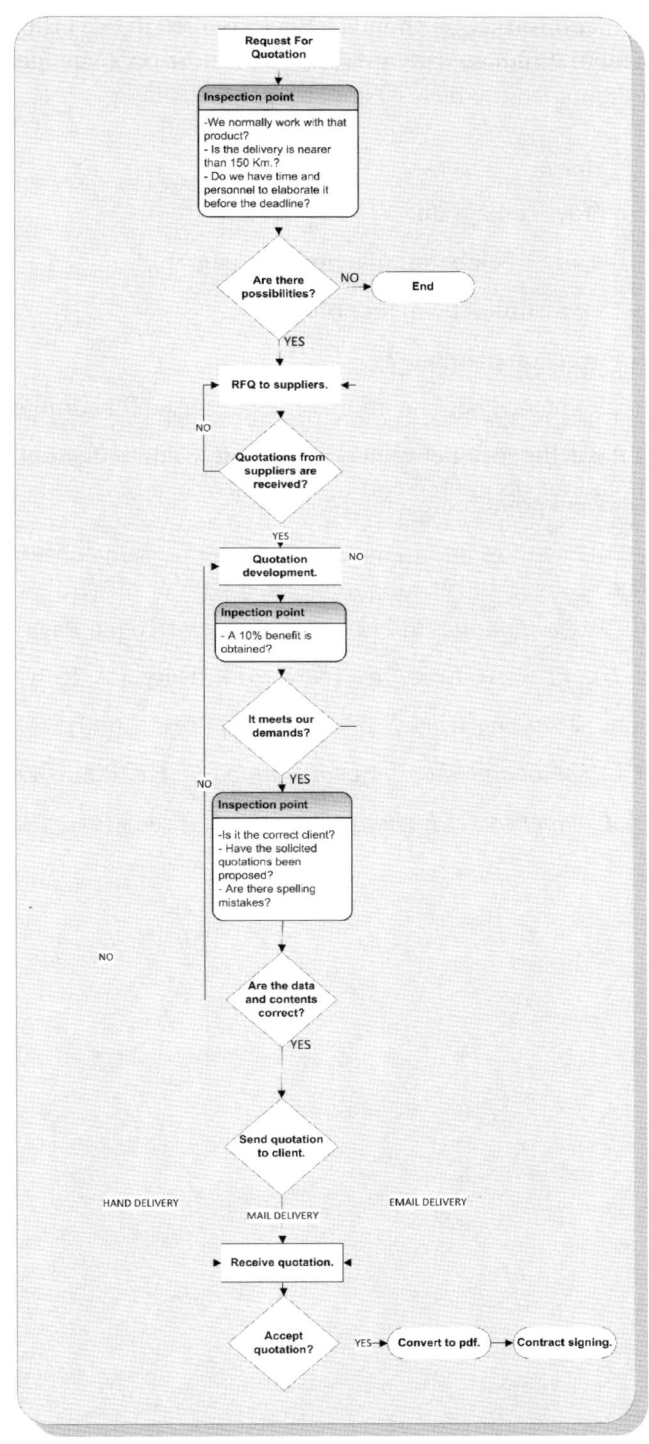

Figure 13.8. Process of budgeting with new checkpoint.

You can find further information about the topic covered in this chapter in the book by this same author *Productivity in Administrative Tasks* (Marcombo Technical Editions).

Questions

1. What is a process diagram?
2. What is the aim of elaborating a process diagram?
3. What tasks constitute the main process?
4. What is a decision diamond?
5. Can the rules of analysis and improvement be used for administrative tasks?
6. What is the difference between administrative and industrial tasks?
7. How is a checkpoint represented?

Bibliography

Chang, Richard Y., *Continuous Process Improvement* (Kogan Page, 1999).

Drucker, Peter, *The Effective Executive* (New York: Harper & Row, 1967).

Galloway, Dianne, *Mapping Work Processes* (Asq Press, 2000).

Kremer, Roger J., *The Lean Office: Pocket Handbook* (RK Publishing Co., 2005).

Porter, Michael, *Competitive Advantage* (New York: Free Press, 1985).

PARTE III
MEDICIÓN DE TIEMPOS

1. MANT
2. WASTE IN WORK DESIGN
3. WASTE BY LOW PERFORMANCE
4. WASTE BY MANAGEMENT FAILURES

Part	Aim	Initial Situation	Final situation
Part 1: Diagnosis	We start from a manufacturing execution times and we want to know what caused them.		
Part 2: Methods	We study and improve the work method of a task to reduce its necessary execution time. The same with processes.		
Part 3: Time measurement	With a defined and improved method we time the task through various techniques to be able to establish a standard, this implies time improvements.		
Part 4: Operations planning	With standard times we can manage production, dimensionate, make decisions, etc. Waste by management failures is reduced.		
Part 4: Productivity control	With standard times productivity can be controled reducing the waste by low performance.		

Chapter 14

Foundations of Work Measurement

14.1. Definition and Evolution of Time Measurement

In the third part of the book will be discussed the techniques regarding work measurement. Once the method is defined, the following step is to measure the work. The definition of work measurement is:

> The application of techniques to determine the time a skilled worker invests in performing a defined task, making it according to a standard (method) of execution established.

This introductory chapter covers the following topics:

1. The different existing techniques for work measurement and their development
2. The concept of standard time, which is derived from work measurement
3. The importance of standard time

The evolution of work measurement has a long history.

1. Leonardo da Vinci (1452–1519) systematically studied earth excavations with shovels.
2. Engineer Jean Perronet (France, 1760) performed the first recorded attempt to measure the time of manufacturing operations. He described the complete productive process of a pin factory.

3. Charles W. Babbage (1820), British mathematician, conducted a series of time studies in the production of common pins.

4. Frederick W. Taylor (1881) began his work studying methods and times.

5. Frederick W. Taylor (1911) published *The Principles of Scientific Management*. He used manual timekeeping to determine the manufacturing time:

    - Divide the task into elements or operations.

    - Observe more than one work cycle.

    - Establish a department of methods and times.

6. Charles Bedaux (1916) established a management consulting company in Cleveland and his great success allowed him to create a multinational company. The Bedaux Method consists of time measurement linked to the activity or performance of the operator. The scale of Bedaux Activity is the 60-80, where 60 is normal activity and 80 refers to optimum activity. The same method can be used to measure the productivity of workers by comparing the work done with the normal time.

7. MTM has its origin in the United States in the 1940s. It was developed by Maynard, Schwab, and Stegemerten from the Methods Engineering Council while consulting with Westinghouse Brake and Signal Corporation. In 1948, the book *Methods–Time Measurement* was published; in it the MTM was clearly defined along with its rules of application as used in the United States and other industrialized countries. The USA/Canada MTM Association for Standards and Research was formed in 19501 by users of MTM. Afterwards derived systems were developed, including the MTM-2, MTM-3, MTM-V, MTM-C, MTM-M, and others.

14.2. Concept of Standard Time

The definition of standard time (ST) is:

> The time required for a generic operator, fully qualified and trained, working at a normal rhythm, to perform a task according to the established method. It is determined by adding the assigned time for each of the elements or operations that compose the task affected by the corresponding fixed or variable rest supplement, and the proportion of frequential tasks. It is measured in "person time" (person-hours or person-minutes) and in "machine time."

Properly understanding this definition will require several chapters in order to explain the supplements, the normal pace, frequential, as well as other important concepts.

> Conceptually, the standard time is the cost of performing a work measured in "person time." Therefore, these data must take into account everything that this work entails, besides its proper execution. For this reason, the standard time is increased with rest supplements and other types of supplements, expanding with frequential operations that arise because of the task at hand, even if they are not part of its cycle.

We will also refer to the standard time as *point value*.

The calculation of the standard time of a task will depend on the nature of the task, whether it is open work or limited, whether operators work in an assembly line where the pace is defined by the chain, and so on. Those conditions and differences in work are summarized in Figure 14.1.

Industrial Productivity

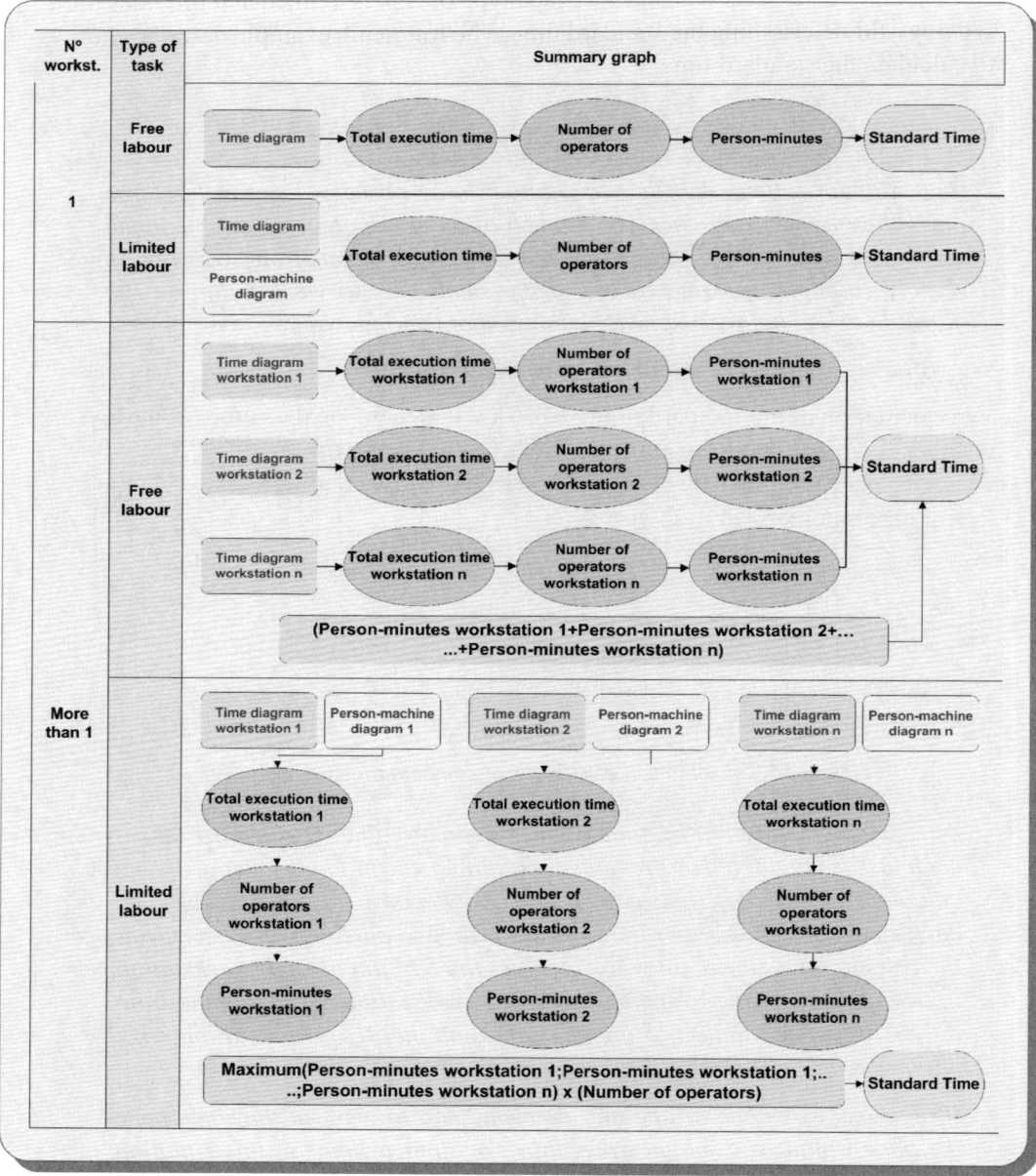

Figure 14.1. Outline for the calculation of standard time (ST)

14. Foundations of Work Measurement

As originally discussed in Chapter 5, each type of task is defined and provides the typology for determining the standard time. The following example describes how to calculate the standard time.

Example

The standard time will be calculated in a process formed by three workstations, with an operator in each of them. The type of work is open work, but workstation 2 needs the semifinished products from workstation 1, and supplies work-in-process at the same time to workstation 3. The formula to use in this case will be the sum of the three values.

Workday: 1 Hours

Workstation 1		
N° of operators	1	
Cycle time 1 operator	3	Min
Cycle time 1 operator	3	Min
Units/Hour	20	

Stock in 1 hour: 8

Workstation 2		
N° of operators	1	
Cycle time 1 operator	5	Min
Cycle time 1 operator	5	Min
Units/Hour	12	

Stock in 1 hour: -18

Workstation 3		
N° of operators	1	
Cycle time 1 operator	2	Min
Cycle time 1 operator	2	Min
Units/Hour	30	

Workstation	Cycle
Workstation 1	3
Workstation 2	5
Workstation 3	2

Limiting cycle	5
N° of operators	3

Line capacity (Units/Hour)	12
Line efficiency	67%
Standard time	10

Figure 14.2. *Example of calculation of standard time for open work*

After each workstation is studied and the point value or standard time of each task is calculated as previously explained, the following step will be to calculate the standard time of the whole line. Because it is open work, where each operator can exercise the work according to personal characteristics, the calculation of the point value includes **the ST sum of each workstation.** *As we observe in the example, the ST of workstation 1 is 3 minutes/unit, the ST of workstation 2 is 5 minutes/unit, and the ST of workstation 3 is 2 minutes/unit, for a total of 10 person-minutes/unit.*

If the work was done in line and everyone had to work at the same pace, the pace would be 5 minutes per unit. For limited labor in this situation, the standard time of such work would be **the result of multiplying the maximum ST by the number of operators**, *3 x 5 = 15 person-minutes/unit.*

Industrial Productivity

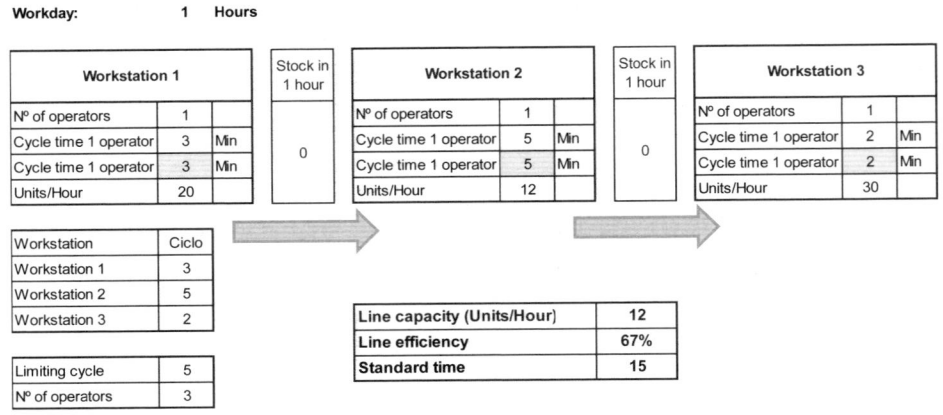

Figure 14.3. Example of calculation of standard time for limited labor (ST)

14.3. Importance of the Standard Time (ST)

Standard time is the raw material for production management.

To understand the importance of standard time, we will look at what would happen if a factory did not measured the work of its tasks and products:

1. Would we be able to know the manufacturing cost?
2. Would we know if the performance of the work teams is acceptable?
3. Would we know if deviations from the standard occur? Would we know the causes of the deviations?
4. Would we be able to calculate how many hours are needed for a certain production?
5. Could we know how many operators are necessary?
6. Would we know if a determined machine is going to be enough for a certain quantity of production?
7. Could we evaluate with precision whether one method is better than another?
8. Can we evaluate the profitability of the possible acquisition of a machine?
9. Can the lead times be calculated?

NO

The industries that do not determine standard times for their normal production are in the hands of circumstances and their works may go out of control. The fourth part of this book is dedicated to the application of standard times, where its usefulness is more easily seen. Without standard times, effectively managing production is not possible.

14.4. General Methods to Measure the Standard Time (ST)

A variety of techniques can be applied to work measurement:

1. Estimation
2. Historical data
3. Tables with normalized data
4. Systems of predetermined times (MTM)
5. Sampling
6. Timekeeping

The following sections explain briefly the characteristics of each of these techniques.

14.4.1. Estimation

This technique is carried out by direct observation and must be performed by a highly experienced analyst. It must only be used for the following circumstances:

1. Less-repetitive measurements. For example, the bearings of a machine that are exchanged once a year.
2. For working processes where it is not profitable to apply a more exhaustive, and therefore more expensive, method (e.g., the time determination of riveting trims on finished shoes because of the large variety of trims and changes in models every 6 months).

Figure 14.4 provides a summary table of advantages and disadvantages of the use of this technique of work measurement:

	Advantages
1	Cost savings derived despite failure to conduct new time studies for each new process or any modification of the existing ones.
2	Elimination of interruptions caused by the time study.
3	Standard times for new tasks can be calculated before they are performed.
4	Previous time studies can be applied with greater assurance that the values are correct and acceptable, both for workers and for the management of the company.

Industrial Productivity

	Disadvantages
1	Calculated times may not have the desired accuracy especially if many elements are not found in the table; if few standard elements have associated times, this technique is not feasible.
2	Because a company's conditions vary from others' situations, it is unwise to use data from other companies.

Figure 14.4. Advantages and disadvantages of the estimation

14.4.2. Historical Data

This technique is based on the determination of the standard times from the data obtained in similar works or as consequence of the comparison with other known times. With the knowledge of other data, standard times can be deduced.

The use of historical data is maybe one of the most overlooked approaches for work measurement. This situation is such because methods are not controlled by historical data and therefore it would be impossible to establish a standard. In order to measure work based on historical data, each employee or supervisor records the time required to perform each operation. For example, if the operation is to drill a certain type of hole in 100 parts, the time per unit will be recorded. Afterwards, when the work is performed again, the time per unit will also be recorded and compared with the previous data. This way, it is possible to maintain continuous control of the time spent per unit and also control the deviations from the historical average.

For some workers the approach of using historical data can be preferable, because the work in itself is used to develop a standard. Stopwatches are not mandatory and flexibility in method is allowed, thereby driving innovation without the need to establish a new standard. This approach can be especially effective when coupled with a wage incentive plan, where the goal is to make continuous improvements to historical levels. From the times recorded in previous measurements of that same operation performed, the time can be calculated by applying the following formula:

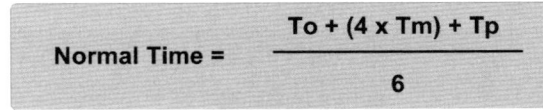

$$\text{Normal Time} = \frac{T_o + (4 \times T_m) + T_p}{6}$$

Figure 14.5. Normal time for historical data

Where:

- T_o = Optimistic time

- T_m = Modal time
- T_p = Pessimistic time

This second method of work measurement can be used in the following cases:

- Methods are clear.
- Method improvement is not possible.
- The manufactured product does not vary.
- No technological changes or obsolescence has occurred.
- A great amount of data for the processes are available.

This system does not presuppose an improvement and does not allow modification of any element, because data would no longer be valid.

Example

A worker in a furniture factory has written down the time invested in assembling model A. Worker annotations are the following:

Model performed	A	A	A	A	A	A	A
Time (minutes)	3	5	4	7	4	2	4

The optimistic time is 2 minutes, the pessimistic time is 7 minutes, and the modal is the most often repeated, in this case 4 minutes. Applying the formula we have:

$$\text{Expected time} = [2 + (4 \times 4) + 7] / 6 = 4.16 \text{ minutes}$$

14.4.3. Table of Normalized Data

This technique is used to measure working times at a company, based on tables of data from typical situations collected over time by the company. Operations that are common to many tasks performed in the organization are specifically described. With these tables the standard times of new works can be calculated or existing times modified in order to reflect the changes produced in the working processes.

	Advantages
1	Eliminate the rating of activity.
2	Establish consistent times.
3	Allow establishment of standard time before actual production.
4	Permit adjustments of standards due to slight changes in the method.

	Disadvantages
1	May require more training from analysts.
2	It is more difficult to explain to workers.
3	May have problems when including small variations in the method.
4	May be inexact if extended beyond the reach of the data used in its development.

Figure 14.6. Advantages and disadvantages of normalized data

14.4.4. Systems of Predetermined Times (MTM)

The use of systems of predetermined times for the observation of operation execution times limits the observation to what is already recorded for the necessary gestures; consequently they are performed without the use of any timekeeping. Standard times for each complex operation can be obtained from the tables where the execution times of each gesture are quantified by type and several characteristics.

The MTM system offers time data for fundamental movements such as reach, turn, locate, drop, and let, with the purpose of establishing the required time of a task performed according to a method of execution. The basis of any system of predetermined times is the fact that variations in the required time to perform the same movement are clearly small for different operators who have received adequate training. Most systems have been made through thousands of time studies in controlled situations; the times for each basic movement have been established by averaging, which makes these data highly reliable. The MTM systems are based on cataloged times for each type of movement, rather than on direct observation of activity-time values. The MTM breaks down the task into greater detail than we get with the normalized data technique and is usable by the different companies of a sector. The main difference with time study is that it does not alter the productive activities.

The calculation of the total time of task execution will imply following the next procedure:

1. Separate the task into micro-motions or basic human movements (reach, take, move, etc.), as if it was a film, frame by frame.

2. Check the time values that the MTM tables assign to each of the movements in order to determine the normal times for each micro-motion.

3. Finally, all the normal times obtained will be added to determine the duration of the task. The value of each normal time does not include personal supplements. Logically the pertinent supplements must be added, an aspect that will be developed in detail later.

Figure 14.6 shows an example of MTM table.

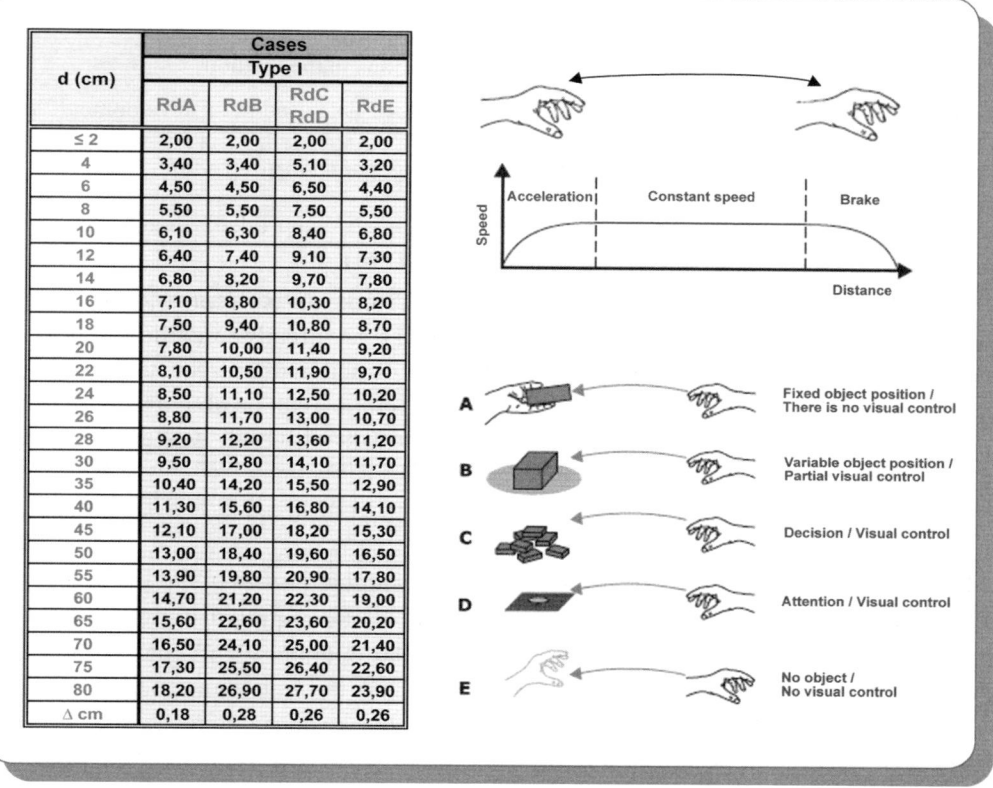

Figure 14.7. Example of MTM table

	Advantages
1	Requires a detailed record of the method, movements, tools, and any other item used.
2	Stimulates work simplification.
3	Eliminates the rating of activity.
4	Allows standards to be set before starting the actual production.
5	Allows adjustment of standards to accommodate slight changes in the method.
6	Provides standards that are more consistent.

	Disadvantages
1	Depends on the complete description of method, tools, etc., for obtaining more accurate standard times.
2	Requires more training of analysts.
3	Can be more difficult to explain to workers.
4	Needs more time to establish standards.
5	Requires other data sources for elements of the process controlled by machines.

Figure 14.8. Advantages and disadvantages of systems of predetermined data

14.4.5. Time Measurement Through Sampling

This system involves performing for a certain period of time a large number of instantaneous observations of certain work elements, either in groups or individually (machines, processes, or workers), for determining whether they meet certain conditions.

Each observation leads to a record of what occurs at that instant in the workplace; afterward, the Methods and Times Office uses statistical formulas to indicate the percentage or frequency of a certain circumstance (normally timeouts or causes of the stops) in the work elements observed.

The following summary table (Figure 14.8) shows the advantages and disadvantages in the application of this system to the measurement of work:

	Advantages
1	Analysts do not need to be highly trained, unless wanting to determine basic times.
2	Does not interfere with the activity of operators.
3	The study can be delayed temporarily without having a major impact on the results.
4	When instantaneous observations are made over a long period, the worker has almost no chance to change the study results.
5	The study duration is long, minimizing the effects of short-term variations.

	Disadvantages
1	In many cases no record of the method used by the operator is available.
2	Not advisable for short-cycle and repetitive tasks; in this case, time study is more advisable.
3	Workers can intentionally change their activity when they notice they are being watched.
4	If the analyst does not follow the paths and random times established, sampling will be biased.

Figure 14.9. Advantages and disadvantages of measurement through sampling.

14.4.6. Timekeeping

Timekeeping uses a stopwatch in order to record the time of the activity; that is, the performance with which the operator has carried out the operation. In order to analyze the time spent performing work, several measurements must be taken of several people at different times of the day. This approach will cover all the possibilities the operations may offer. Before using the stopwatch, the analyst must preview the task under consideration in order to define clearly the initial milestone and final milestone of each operation that compose the task.

Each operation is assigned a time. All times will jointly generate the normal time of execution of the operation. With such a large sample, the result is reliable. The next step is to add the relevant rest supplement to each operation, which will entail obtaining the corrected time of the operation. These calculations will be explained later.

	Advantages
1	Only method that directly measures the time it takes the operator.
2	It allows detailed observation of the complete cycle and method.
3	Can cover elements that occur less frequently.
4	Provides fast accurate values for elements controlled by the machine.
5	It is simple to explain and learn.

	Disadvantages
1	Requires marking employees' activities.
2	Does not require keeping detailed records of method, movements, and tools.
3	Noncyclic elements are not easily evaluated.
4	Standard based on the bias of an analyst who studies a worker using a single method.

Figure 14.9. Advantages and disadvantages of timekeeping

14.5. Systematic Procedure for Timekeeping

The stages of timekeeping are:

1. ***Work selection***: The task subject of study will be determined.

2. ***Record the information:*** As in the study of methods, what is done in a certain task is studied and broken down.

3. ***Examine the task:*** Recorded data will be analyzed and an initial and final milestone established for each element and operation to measure.

4. ***Timekeeping and measurement:*** Each operation of the task under study is measured with the chosen measurement method.

5. ***Compile and define:*** All the operations are grouped in the study of methods and times, and supplements, frequential, and other relevant factors are applied in order to obtain the standard time of the task.

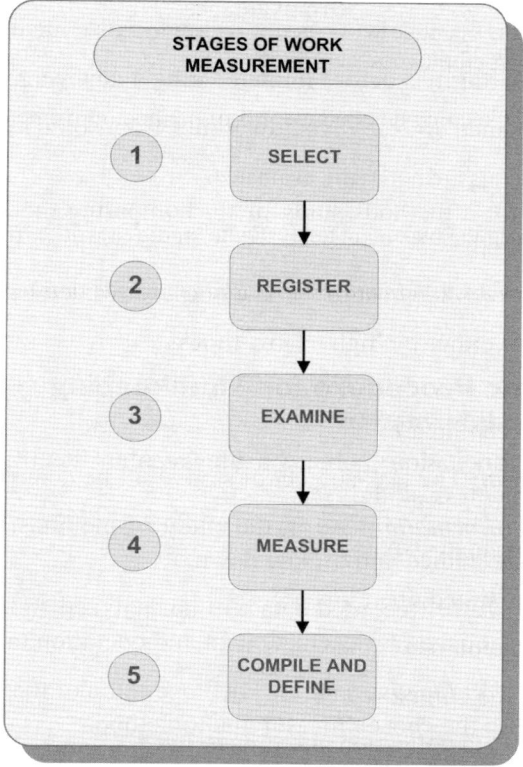

Figure 14.10. Stages of work measurement

From this procedure, the standard time (ST) of the task will be calculated.

14.5.1. Work Selection

As in the study of methods, the first thing we have to do in the time study is to select the work that is going to be studied. Previously in Chapter 5, we described the factors to take into account when choosing a task to study: ergonomics, CwM, and the weight of the task in the productive process. We also have to take into account other aspects:

1. Novelty of the task, not executed previously (when product, component, operation, or the series of activities are new)

2. Change of material or method, which requires a new standard time

3. Complaints from operators or their union representatives about the standard time of a task

4. Delays caused by a slow operation that holds up the next and possibly the previous tasks, because work is not following its course and accumulates
 5. Setting standard times before implementing a new wage incentive system
 6. Low performance or excessive downtimes from some machine or group of machines
 7. Preparation for a methods study or for comparing the advantages of two possible methods
 8. Apparently excessive cost of some work, as revealed by an analysis
 9. Possible error either by high or low times

14.5.2. Record the Information

The study of the workstation includes a timekeeping identification, as well as identifying data of the task study:

- Name of the analyst
- Name of the timed operator
- Name of the company
- Address of the company
- Date of the data collection and processing
- Name and code of the task on which the study is conducted
- Sketch of the workstation with the path that is going to be timed, as well as machines or tools that are used in that workstation

14.5.3. Examine the Task

Break Down the Task into Operations or Elements

The breakdown into operations follows the same criteria as explained in Chapter 5 for describing the method and includes the following:

1. Before proceeding to the division of a task into small operations, the analyst must observe the operator for several work cycles. If possible, it is better that the analyst determine the operations the task is composed of before initiating the study.
2. Manual operations must be differentiated from the ones performed with a machine. In manual activities it is the operator who can reduce the time of execution according to interest, dexterity, or skill. However, the machine-times can be external to the operator; they depend on the technical characteristics of the machine and therefore, the operator cannot exert any

influence on them, with the exception of paying attention to machine, which makes them work better.

3. The manual operations with the machine stopped and the machine running must be differentiated from one another. Manual operations performed while the machine is waiting can affect the duration of the work cycle due to the activity of the operator. Manual operations executed while the machine is running do not modify the duration of the cycle but influence the saturation of the operator.

4. The operations that need different efforts will be separated from one another, with the purpose of facilitating the work of the analyst in the fulfillment of the future time study that will determine the standard time of execution of the task and to which will be applied different fatigue coefficients. This point will be widely discussed in this part of the book, which is dedicated to time studies.

5. The operations that compose a work process must be easily recognizable, thanks to the delimitation of operations through an initial and final milestone.

6. Operations must be within a duration interval of 8 to 100 seconds. This delimitation is because time intakes less than 8 seconds are hard to measure, and the milestones of the operation will be diffuse and complicated to establish and prone to errors. For operations whose execution time is higher than 100 seconds, the performance of the operator can vary during that time interval.

The breakdown of the task into operations is necessary to:

- Describe the operation sequence.
- Know exactly how work is performed.
- Classify the operation according to its typology in order to give it its corresponding treatment.
- Be able to perform the time measurement.

Classification of Operations

The operations or elements of work can be classified based on the following main criteria:

- According to the work cycle:
    - Regulars: Those elements that always appear in each work cycle and therefore their frequency of apparition is constant and regular.

- Irregulars: Necessary operations that do not happen in all the cycles, neither do they appear regularly or periodically.

- Frequential: Operations that do not happen in every work cycle but their apparition is regular, periodical, and predictable. Its repercussion can de calculated precisely.

- Strange: Elements that are not necessary to complete the work cycle but do happen, therefore, insofar as possible must be eliminated.

- According to the performer:
    - Manual elements are performed by the operator and can be without machine, or *free*, whose duration depends on the activity of the operator; and with *machine*, where the work of the person involves feeding or helping the machine. These last are classified in turn into elements with the machine stopped or running. These elements or operations should be clear before performing the time study, with the purpose of not committing any error.
    - The machine elements are work elements performed by the machine. They can be with *automatic machine*, which do not require the operator, but only their vigilance; or with *machine of manual advance*, where the machine works with the help of the operator at certain moments.

- According to the typology of the operation the operator performs.

Delimitate the Operations: Definition of Initial Milestone and Final Milestone of the Operation

It is important to define clearly the initial milestone and final milestone in the operations for the purpose of avoiding mistakes in timekeeping. Frequently, an analyst does not identify clearly the beginning and end of an operation, and this circumstance triggers errors in the time study. This error can be of low importance in the time study of tasks of long duration (several hours); however, this error will acquire more importance in time studies of tasks of short duration (2–3 minutes).

Determine the Size of the Sample

Much of what will be described in Chapter 17 about sampling, the statistical level of confidence, and the tables of random numbers, is equally applied here. In this case, it is not about establishing a proportion but about calculating the average value representative of each operation. This way the problem consists in determining the size of the sample or the number of operations that must be performed for each operation, given a level of confidence and a predetermined margin.

14.5.4. Timekeeping and Measurement

Once initial milestone and the final milestone are identified and the description of operations articulated, the timing can start. Two main procedures involve a stopwatch:

- Accumulative timekeeping
- Timekeeping with return to zero

In accumulative timekeeping, the stopwatch works uninterrupted for the entire study. It is started at the beginning of the first operation of the first cycle and does not stop until the study is over. At the end of each operation, the time on the stopwatch is written down, and the duration of each operation is obtained by making the respective subtractions after ending the study. With this procedure, we record all the time the work is under observation.

In the timekeeping with return to zero, times are taken directly. After the end of each operation, the stopwatch is returned to zero and is started again for the next operation timing, without the mechanism stopping for a moment.

In all time studies, it is common to verify the total time by a wristwatch or a wall clock. That way the time when the study is made is also written down, which can be important because it is likely that the operator fulfills the cycle in less time at the beginning of the day than at the end, due to the effect of fatigue.

14.5.5. Compile and Define: Study of Methods and Times

After calculating the time for each operation and identifying the rest supplements to apply, we will proceed to group all the information in order to build the study of methods and times. Chapter 16 provides examples of completed studies of methods and times.

Questions

1. Define work measurement.
2. Define standard time (ST).
3. Indicate three methodologies of time measurement.
4. What are the stages of work measurement?
5. From which elements is time calculated with MTM?
6. Indicate three aspects that need to be considered for the study of work.
7. Indicate several identifying data of the task when performing the study of times.
8. Why is the breakdown of tasks into operations necessary?

Bibliography

Kanawaty, George, *Introduction to Work Study* (Geneva: International Labor Organization, 1992).

Chapter 15

Prerequisites for Determining the Standard Time

The work of time measurement and calculation of standard time requires a series of minimum conditions to ensure result validity. These conditions include:

- Training of the analyst
- Training of the operator
- Evaluation of the work pace
- Compliance level of the working method
- Physical environment and general work conditions
- Necessary material

This chapter addresses each of these points.

15.1. Trained Analyst, Required Competencies

The times and methods analyst must have solid knowledge of the different techniques for determining standard and manufacturing times, but also must have other types of skills and competencies.

In the technical part, the analyst relates to the task under study. The final objective of the technician is to determine the necessary amount of time to perform the task under study, taking into account different factors, but principally considering the method used. It is essential to know exactly what is and is not necessary in order to perform a task. If the materials and tools used are unknown, the calculated time will not be precise; its only reference is the method used by the observed operator or operators. Therefore, it is highly recommended that an analyst be accustomed to performing manual labor, even that the analyst tries to perform various work cycles to check the level of difficulty and precision required.

It should also be considered that operators in the section or workstation that is the subject of study may be reluctant to perform a work study, because they normally equate a standard time with an increase their workload. The idea of the work study may also stir apprehension about the possible consequences if the standard time calculated is greater than the particular way an operator has for performing the work.

This difficulty emphasizes the need for certain social skills in the analyst, such as kindness, comprehension, patience, and total availability for communication with the operators in order to resolve doubts they may have concerning the study. The analyst must try to look for the highest level of cooperation from the operator, because the attitude of the operator can noticeably affect the necessary time for performing the study satisfactorily.

The operator knows the workstation the best and is the person who can help in correctly carrying out the study. Therefore an operator's help is invaluable. Facing a condescending, distant, or unclear attitude from the analyst, the operator is less likely to collaborate and more likely to vary the work pace or perform the operations more slowly. Complaints are more likely as are nonconformity to any type of incidence and unwillingness to respond correctly to any type of question raised.

In summary, the analyst needs both technical and social skills.

Technical skills:

- Knowledge of the time measurement techniques
- Knowledge of the product
- Knowledge of the materials used
- Knowledge of the tools and machines
- Previous experience or at least familiarity with the work

Social skills:

- Empathy (understanding how the operator feels, as no one likes to be timed)
- Communication skills, especially listening
- Consideration
- Availability/approachability

15.2. Qualified Operator, Learning Curve

Before beginning the study of a task, an important factor is the selection of the operators for the study of standard time. Theoretically, the type of operator that is studied is not relevant, but reality indicates that the observation of operators can affect the result of the study considerably.

Therefore, one of the prerequisites is to find a qualified operator on which to perform the study, one who has passed the learning cycle and has adequate skills for performing the work. Each work requires different skills, some of them inherent to the person, such as strength or physical endurance, level of concentration, capacity to absorb information, good insight, and mental agility, are skills or knowledge that can be acquired through time. Operators acquire skills and knowledge through a combination of training and imitation of colleagues. Although with correct training, the attitude of operators can be improved, experience is the most influential. The experience of operators contributes to their movement precision, the ability to increase the work pace, and a capacity to react quickly to signs and to anticipate and overcome difficulties. All these skills are certainly obvious when comparing an experienced operator with an inexperienced one.

The duration of the training stage will depend on the difficulty and precision that the work requires, but usually fluctuates from a minimum of two weeks to a maximum of six months. The evolution of apprenticeship refers to the increase in productivity that is produced through accumulated experience. It is a graphic representation of workforce hours per unit and number of produced units. It normally has the shape of a negative exponential distribution, and is no more than a line that shows the existing relationship between production time and accumulated experience.

Another consideration is the amount of mistakes or errors, or the number of accidents in relation to the number of produced units. The learning curve is, literally, a graphical record of cost improvement as operators gain experience and increase the number of total manufactured units.

Figure 15.1 is an example of the learning curve.

Industrial Productivity

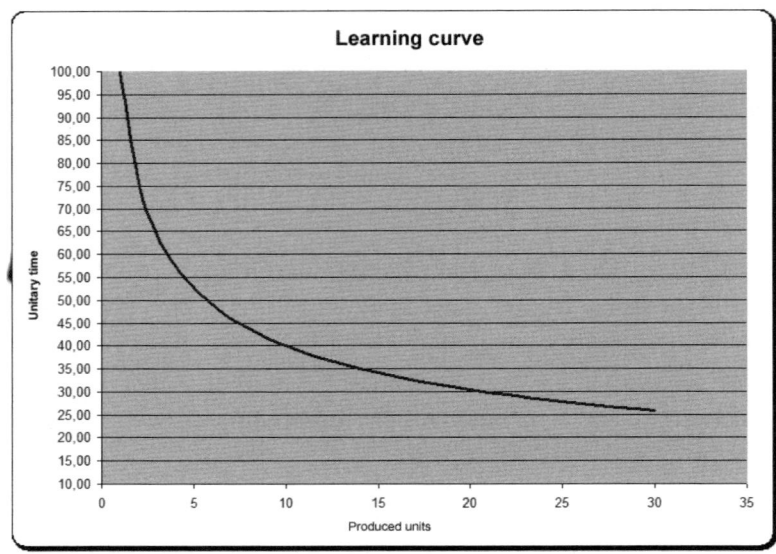

Figure 15.1. Example of learning curve

The slope of a learning curve varies as a function of the training necessary to develop the work. Expressed in a simple way, it could be said that the slope of the curve will depend on what an operator learns in each cycle performed. If it is a long and complex process, little will be learned, relatively speaking, in each cycle, so many cycles will be needed to become proficient with the numerous aspects of such process. If, on the contrary, it is a short and simple work cycle, most details of the process will be known after manufacturing only a few units.

The majority of industries, through careful recruiting, adequate training, and a knowledge-recycling program, ensure that the majority of their employees reach those minimum requirements to perform the work. It is not an easy task, but the analyst must search among the available workforce operators with an acceptable level of aptitude and attitude. The desired profile is an operator who is trained and used to that workstation, and who is capable and motivated to perform this work.

15.3. Normal Work Pace, Scales, and Valuation Methods

After observing several operators performing the same work, it is apparent how they do not work at the same rate. Even the same operator, day to day, even hour to hour, does not perform the exact same amount of work, even if the conditions are reproduced accurately because of variations in the work pace. The concept of work pace is equivalent to activity. This topic will be discussed in greater detail in this subsection.

Example

The task of putting on protective gloves is timed on two occasions for the same operator.

In the first timing, the operator is focused on the task and with quick movements, takes the gloves from the table, puts one on and then the other one; consuming a time of 5 seconds.

Later, returning from a break, the operator performs the same operation, but remains talking to a colleague, without paying much attention to the action itself, and takes 7.5 seconds to perform the same operation.

If it is the same work, why does such a difference between the necessary times to perform it occur? **Due to the variation of work pace.**

In the previous example, the operator, by changing the work pace, can increase or reduce the execution time of a task noticeably. **Therefore, awareness of this factor is essential for the time calculation of an operation.**

The activity or work pace with which a task is developed depends on several factors in addition to movement speed. In Chapter 16, referring to timed studies of methods and times, the discussion will focus on how to correct for work pace variations through activity judgment, but at this point we will concentrate on the aspects of which it is composed, measurement scales and valuation methods.

Work pace must be understood as the quantity of work developed per time unit. The normal pace or normal activity is the rate at which an operator must carry out work, on average, through the workday.

The following classification of work paces will help to better understand the concept:

- *Deficient work pace, clearly below normal pace*: An operator who clearly loses time, shows a lack of interest in work, takes too long in obtaining supplies, manipulates materials excessively, making it seem that the work is more difficult than it really is, keeps the workstation in disorder, and conveys an attitude that is not collaborative.

- *Normal or average work pace*: Works with consistency, seems honest when performing work, plans with priority before executing, performs work without hurrying but without purposely losing time.

- *Excellent work pace, clearly above normal pace*: An average-skilled operator who works quickly, minimizing the time losses and inquiring about the work being performed, working at a pace that can be kept up with effort throughout the day.

Industrial Productivity

The technique of work measurement understands that these differences are principally the result of variations in activity or pace. Therefore, the execution time will be determined by this concept: better activity corresponds with less execution time and, conversely, worse activity corresponds with a greater execution time.

Activity or pace is the level of fulfillment of three factors (Caso Neira, 2003):

- Commitment to the work method
- Precision of movements
- Speed of movements

A fourth factor, consistency, needs to be considered when performing measurements of long duration. (Figure 15.2)

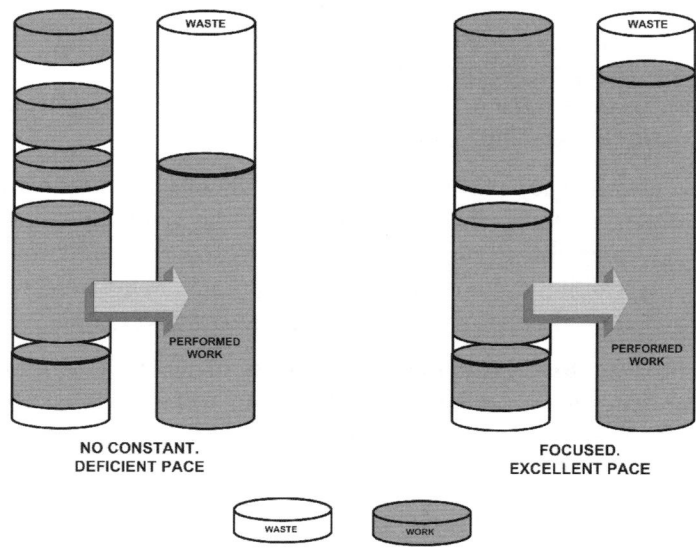

Figure 15.2. Comparison of the effect of consistency in the work pace (activity)

When these four factors are achieved at a controlled level, a specific activity will be obtained; a greater compliance with them will translate to a greater activity. If this level is reduced, activity will decrease. If movements are quick and precise, but not committed to the work methods, the result can be a low activity.

The activity, as a function of the nature of the work, evolves throughout the day, due to accumulated muscular fatigue. Such evolution is represented in Figures 15.3 and 15.4.

15. Prerequisites for Determining the Standard Time

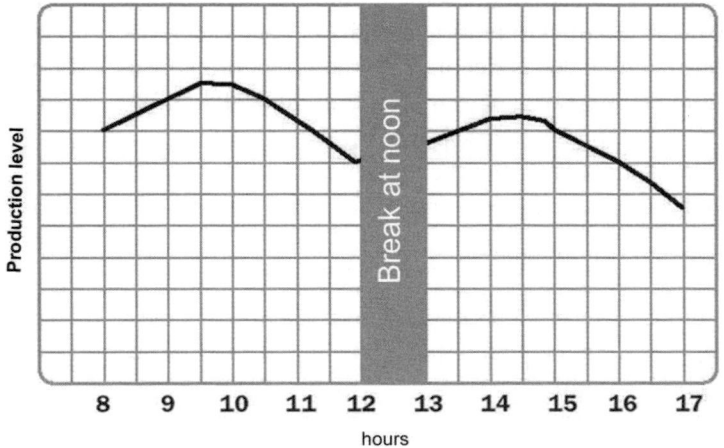

Figure 15.3. Performance in highly muscular work

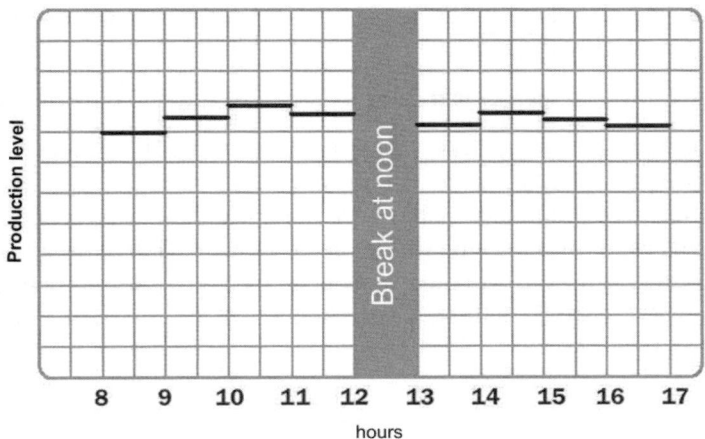

Figure 15.4. Performance in light muscular work

In order to measure activity it is necessary to have a determined scale (Bedaux, centesimal, etc.) where several basic points are defined:

- Null activity or absolute repose
- Normal activity
- Optimum activity

505

Each scale defines the maximum score or minimum score with which equal activity performed in a measured operation is rated. Theoretically, normal activity is that which can be fulfilled by an operator in these conditions (Caso Neira, 2003):

- Normally
- Trained and adapted to the workplace
- Throughout the day
- Taking a break that compensates the effort
- Without suffering a permanent decrease in physical or mental faculties

According to practical experience in numerous studies, it has been proven that workers motivated by performance (primed by achieved productivity) can accomplish one-third more work than those who are not. The scales for activity measurement are:

- Bedaux 60-80, where 60 is the normal activity and 80 the optimum activity
- Centesimal 100-133, where 100 is the normal activity and 133 the optimum activity
- BSI 75-100, where 75 is the normal activity and 100 the optimum activity

As observed, the optimum activity is 33 percent higher than normal activity. In practice, optimum activity can be achieved by 50 percent of the operators who work with incentives. Statistically has been observed that 96 percent of a group of operators reaches normal activity. Based on these levels, that optimum and normal activities are reached by the quoted percentages of the working population, and for the purpose of analysts having a reference point, a set of activity patterns has been established.

15. Prerequisites for Determining the Standard Time

ACTIVITY				Performance description	Comparable walking speed (km/h)
60-80	75-100	100-133	90-120		
Bedaux	BSI	Centesimal	WTM		
0	0	0	0	No activity.	0
40	50	67	60	Very slow, akward, and insecure movements; the operator seems half asleep and uninterest in the work.	3.2
60	75	100	90	Constant, determined, leisurely, as a worker well managed and watched over; seems slow but does not lose time intentionally while observed.	4.5
80	100	133	120	Active, capable, as average skilled operator; meets with ease the level of quality and precision required.	6.4
100	125	167	150	Very fast; the operator acts with great security, skill, and coordination of movements, above-average skilled worker.	8
120	150	200	180	Exceptionally fast, concentrated, and intense effort without probability of lasting through long periods; achieved only by a few exceptional workers.	9.6

Source: Adapted from Engineering & Allied Employers (West England) Association, Department of Work Study.

Figure 15.5. Activity scale table

An analyst who knows these patterns will compare them to the activity with which an operator develops the operation being observed and will mark it. This subjective valuation is known as "activity judgment." Activity always needs to be evaluated and marked before writing down the time so as not to be conditioned by our judgment. That way, in the timing sheet, the activity column must always precede the time column.

The training method for a correct evaluation of the activity for an operation consists of performing four levels of activity evaluation. In each of these levels or phases, five practices will be done; the difference between the levels is the precision required of the technician. All the practices will be performed in groups of at least three people, with at least one of the three being a senior technician who will determine the activities and indicate to the junior technicians the corrective factor.

Industrial Productivity

The practices performed in the different levels are the same:

- Level 1: Evaluation of walking activities
- Level 2: Evaluation of card distribution activities
- Level 3: Evaluation of video activities with comparison of employees
- Level 4: Evaluation of activities without comparison of employees
- Level 5: Evaluation of activities in the factory

Note: These exercises use the centesimal scale (100-133).

Level 1:

The technician has to accomplish activities, differentiating only between three intervals from the activity table: low activity, normal activity, and high activity. A data collection will be done that will later be processed to determine whether the technician is prepared to move on to the next level. The activities that correspond to each interval can be seen in the following table:

Intervals	Activity
Interval of Low Activity	60
	65
	70
	75
	80
	85
Interval of Normal Activity	90
	95
	100
	105
	110
	115
Interval of High Activity	120
	125
	130
	135
	140

Level 2:

This level consists of the same practices as in level 1 but with a 10 x 10 precision. A data collection will be made that later on will be processed to determine whether the technician is prepared to move on to the next level. The table shows what activities are used.

The analysis with a score table by activity elements is introduced, including base activity, methodology, precision, speed, and difficulty coefficient.

Activity
60
70
80
90
100
110
120
130
140

Level 3:

At this level, the same as in level 2 is carried out but with a 5 x 5 precision. A data collection will be made that later on will be processed to determine whether the technician is prepared to move on to the next level.

Level 4:

Accomplishment of activity without help of tables and with an individual corrective factor.

Example

TABLE OF ACTIVITY ACCOMPLISHMENT				
Activity		Km/Hour	Sec/m	10.00 m
Bedaux	Centesimal			
43	67	3.00	1.20	12.0
44	70	3.13	1.15	11.5
46	75	3.36	1.07	10.7
49	80	3.58	1.01	10.1
51	85	3.81	0.95	9.5
54	90	4.03	0.89	8.9
57	95	4.25	0.85	8.5
60	100	4.50	0.80	8.0
63	105	4.70	0.77	7.7
66	110	4.93	0.73	7.3
69	115	5.15	0.70	7.0
72	120	5.37	0.67	6.7
75	125	5.60	0.64	6.4
78	130	5.82	0.62	6.2
80	133	5.96	0.60	6.0
81	135	6.04	0.60	6.0
84	140	6.27	0.57	5.7
87	145	6.49	0.55	5.5
90	150	6.72	0.54	5.4
93	155	6.94	0.52	5.2
96	160	7.16	0.50	5.0
100	167	8.00	0.45	4.5
120	200	9.60	0.38	3.8

Figure 15.6. Table evaluating walking activities

15. Prerequisites for Determining the Standard Time

The following table shows a comparison of the operation of card distribution to be able to define the level of performance or activity.

Example

DISTRIBUTE 40 CARDS			
Activity		**Time**	
Bedaux	Centesimal	Minutes	Seconds
42	65	0.60	36.0
44	70	0.56	33.4
46	75	0.52	31.2
49	80	0.49	29.3
51	85	0.46	27.5
54	90	0.43	26.0
57	95	0.41	24.6
60	100	0.39	23.4
63	105	0.37	22.3
66	110	0.35	21.3
69	115	0.34	20.3
72	120	0.33	19.5
75	125	0.31	18.7
78	130	0.30	18.0
81	135	0.29	17.3
84	140	0.28	16.7
87	145	0.27	16.1
90	150	0.26	15.6

Figure 15.7. Table evaluating card distribution

Methods and work requirements must be carefully defined. For comparing the performance of an operator, the distributor must have a specific description of the following example, indicating the distance of the four distributed hands and the techniques used to take, move, and leave the cards.

The normal activity pattern corresponds to a 1.68m person who walks with 75 centimeter steps without load, through horizontal ground with no obstacles

in normal environment conditions (temperature 25°C and 40% relative humidity) at a speed of 1.25 m/s, equivalent to 4.5 Km/h and who performs work with consistency and systematically.

Which operator is being analyzed in an operation being studied makes little difference. For the same work, a person who invests less time and is more precise will have a better qualification than another person who invest more time or is less precise. The relationship between time and activity is given through the following equation:

Time x Activity = Constant

In order to comply:

Time 1 x Activity 1 = Time 2 x Activity 2

Normal Time x Normal Activity = Observed Time x Observed Activity

Example 1

This example looks at the operation "Leave mask and gun."

First operator observed: (centesimal scale 100-133)

- *Invests 10 seconds in "Leave mask and gun" = clock time.*
- *Operator is not very quick or precise; the granted mark is Activity 90.*
- *The normal necessary time for "Leave mask and gun" is 10 x 90/100 = 9 seconds.*

We multiply the 10 seconds by 90, because it is the activity of that person, and divide it by 100 to obtain the time it would take at normal activity.

Second operator observed:

- Invests 7.5 seconds in "Leave mask and gun" = clock time.
- Operator is quick and precise; the granted mark is Activity 120.
- The normal necessary time for "Leave mask and gun" is 7.5 x 120/100 = 9 seconds.

Therefore, independently of whom we have observed, the necessary time to "Leave mask and gun" is 9 seconds.

Example 2

To travel a distance of 10 meters at normal activity takes 8 seconds. Calculate the execution time for an optimum activity in the Bedaux scale and for optimum activity in the centesimal scale.

Observation of 8 seconds at activity 60, normal activity in Bedaux activity (optimum activity in this scale is 80):

- *Time at optimum pace = (Tn x An) / Ao = (8 x 60) / 80 = 6 seconds*

In both cases the result is the same, because independently on the scale used the normal and optimum times of a task are the same.

Example 3

After performing an exhaustive time study, it is determined that to perform a task takes 12 seconds. Days later, timing an operator we observe that the same task is performed in 9 seconds, what is the activity of the task: 80, 90, 95, or 133? Use the centesimal scale.

To solve this exercise, calculations are not needed, because the only possible solution is 133. If at normal activity the operator takes 12 seconds and later performs that task in less time, the only possibility is that the operator has done the task more quickly and precisely. Therefore, the operator must be qualified with a higher activity. From the four possible solutions, only 133 fulfills that requirement.

Example 4

The execution time of a task at normal activity is 15.50 seconds. We observe how an operator, when performing that task, spends 19.37 in one occasion, 12.92 in another, and 15.50 seconds in the third. Calculate the activity in centesimal scale, in each of the cases:

- *First case, real execution time of 19.37 seconds:*

    Real activity = (Tn x An) / Tr = (15.5 x 100) / 19.37 = 80

- *Second case, real execution time of 12.92 seconds:*

    Real activity = (Tn x An) / Tr = (15.5 x 100) / 12.92 = 120

- *Third case, real execution time of 15.50 seconds. In this case performing the calculation is unnecessary, because when the execution and the normal time coincide, the activity level of the operator is the normal activity, which in this case is 100.*

Example 5

For a task can be executed in 10 seconds when performing the work at a 75-activity pace, calculate the amount of cycles per hour that can be done at normal and optimum activity (Bedaux scale).

We begin by calculating the execution time of the task at normal activity, Activity 60:

- *Normal time = (T x A) / An = (10 x 75) / 60 = 12.5 seconds*
- *Production per hour = 3600 / Tn = 3600 / 12.5 = 288 cycles / hour*

In order to calculate the production at optimum activity, it will consist in increasing the normal production by 33 percent:

- *Optimum production per hour = Pn + 33% = 288 x 1.33 = 383 cycles / hour*

15.4. Execution Standard, Work Specification, and Standard Operation Procedure

The working method must be recorded and stabilized. The variability in the execution of the task must be the lowest possible. If not, it will be difficult to establish precisely a standard time.

Example 1

Differences between operators when performing the same operation.

At an assembly line from an automotive company, the following worksheet is posted:

"Assemble wheel completely, measuring pneumatic pressure, fixing with four screws, and tightening with pneumatic tool."

In the assembly line four operators will perform the same assembly, which consists in placing four wheels on a vehicle that comes through the line, with each operator assembling one wheel. With such unspecific instructions, operators perform the task in completely different ways. Some carry out the pressure check with some of the wheels already assembled and others not. Each operator has a different method for handling the wheel, screws, and the pneumatic tool as well. It is difficult to specify the correct way or what operator we should take as reference when each of them has a method with advantages and disadvantages.

Example 2

Differences between operators when performing the same operation.

In the same automotive assembly line, the following worksheet is used:

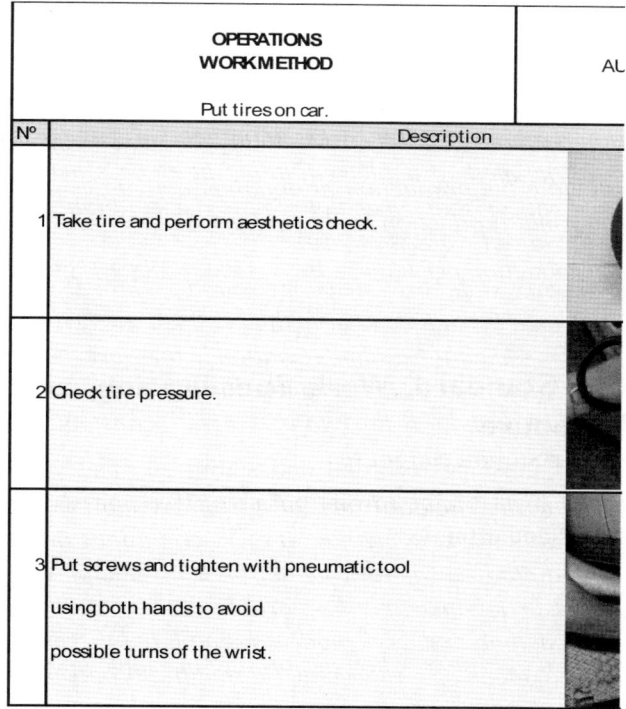

Figure 15.8. *Example of worksheet*

Although the working method is specified in an instructions sheet, when observing the work of the four operators, three of them take the wheel, inspect it, check the pressure, place it, underpin a screw, press that screw with a pneumatic gun, and repeat that operation for each screw.

A fourth operator performs the task nearly the same way but first places the four screws and then uses the pneumatic gun to tighten them one after another, until setting the wheel perfectly, performing the task in less time than the other operators. The four operators follow the essence of the rules, but do not perform the task the same way.

From this example, independent of the level of description, we can see a certain looseness in the operatory mode in which the interpretation is left to the person performing the task. This is what is known as method level.

Method level *means that the process design (i.e., the designed work method) differs from the way in which those instructions are carried out, which is known as* work mode.

When a task is initially designed, clear work standards are set but with a certain approximating character. The reason is that from a technical office it is impossible to pick up all the characteristics of a workstation that does not exist yet. Therefore, at the beginning of the method implementation, differences between the method and the work mode will arise as operators improvise solutions to the difficulties not addressed by the initial work standard.

The efficiency of a work standard will be measured by how it matches the work mode, which will mean it has left a clear method defined. In the previous examples despite the efforts in specifications, some variation in the work mode was apparent, but the method level achieved in the second example cannot even be compared with the first. The work standards have to be "alive," constantly adapting to the variations that a workstation can present.

In trying to determine the standard time of a task, we must begin with a clear, implemented, and stable working method. If these conditions are not present, we will be conducting a study of a work mode, or a particular way of work, but not of the task. A time study must not be started until a method is stable and the differences between method and work mode are small. In other words, the work to perform is completely clear and determined through a procedure that adjusts to the characteristics of the performed work.

15.5. Physical Work Environment, Applicable Requirements and Standards, and Organizational Aspects

The physical conditions under which work is done can influence the way a task is executed. In some cases, reducing the fatigue or increasing the comfort or health of environment in general are needed. Numerous factors can alter work conditions, but in general, the most representative ones include the following:

- Illumination
- Noise
- Temperature
- Vibrations
- Radiation
- Exposure to toxins

For example, excess temperature results in slower movements and the reason the operator is more tired and fatigued. Therefore, it is important that the conditions in which timing is done are the usual inside the factory. Otherwise, the observed times will not be reliable. In addition, if timing is done in extraordinarily favorable conditions, they will also be erroneous.

In summary, the conditions and background for the timing must be as close as possible to the normal conditions in the factory.

Furthermore, the task to be measured must be free from incidences in order to observe the method and time without interruptions or variations. The incidences, as seen in the first part of this book, can be caused by lack of materials, imbalances in workload, breakdowns, defects, and errors in information. The repeated existence of incidences breaks the pace and introduces multiple operations external to the method that sometimes are difficult to separate.

15.6. Materials for the Time Study

Materials necessary for performing a time study can vary in function according to the type of measurement system performed.

Every study has two parts: the first part is data collection and the second is data processing. Data collection requires the following materials:

- **Writing materials:** Paper and writing tool. A folder or clipboard is recommended to facilitate note taking even while in a standing position.

- **Stopwatch:** Available in a wide range of styles and capabilities, stopwatches can perform in almost any unit—seconds, minutes, thousandths of an hour—and can be found in both analogical and digital formats or with memory. Some are even capable of sending the information to a computer in real time, thus avoiding having to take note of the time reading. Without further specifications or specific agreements regarding the accuracy of the measuring means, the time measurement obtained is considered valid.

Industrial Productivity

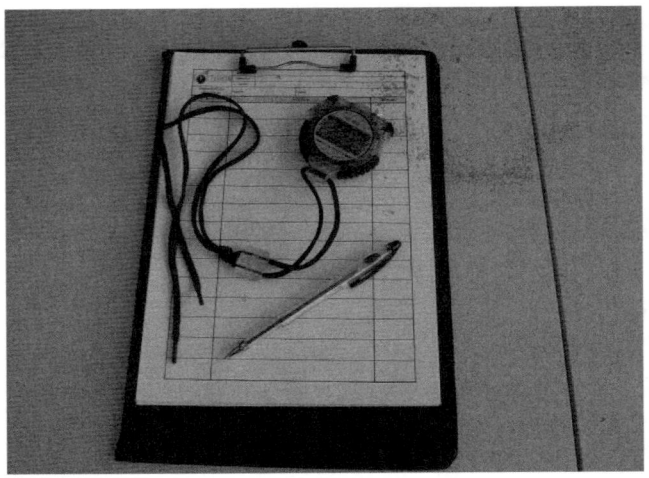

15.9. Writing materials and stopwatch

- **MTM tables:** If the study is made using a system of predetermined times, such as MTM, those tables are needed.

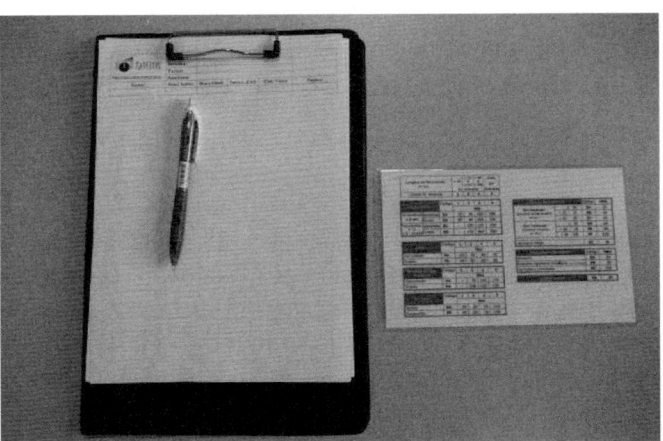

15.10. Writing materials and MTM table

- **Elements for distance measurement:** A tape measure of 1 to 5 meters to check distances to objects or even longer for measuring transfers is necessary for timekeeping. A laser range finder allows for measuring much faster or in inaccessible areas.

15. Prerequisites for Determining the Standard Time

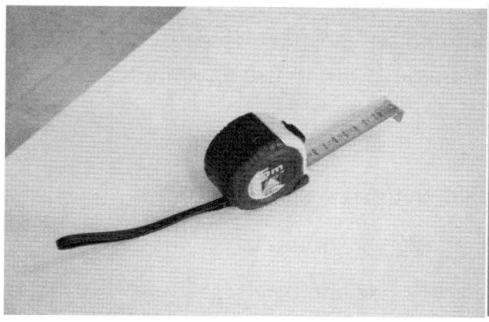

15.11. Distance measurement elements

- **Dynamometer:** For the establishment of times through MTM, it is necessary to know the weight of the parts that are handled. If this information is not provided, the part has to be weighed.

- **Camera:** For an accurate record of the working method, photographs can be used with the layout or for determining the precise method of operation, and it can be much easier to transmit certain information.

- **Videotaping equipment:** For long tasks, it is difficult to make the data collection in the workstation. In this case, a video camera is convenient. For MTM calculation it is absolutely indispensable.

15.12. Videotaping equipment

519

For data processing, as a rule, it is essential to prepare a written report, typically in the form of a word-processed document and spreadsheet. Because this format greatly facilitates this task, it is almost unthinkable not to use a computer.

Questions

1. List at least three technical skills that an analyst should have.
2. List at least three social skills that an analyst should have.
3. What is represented in a learning curve? Explain briefly.
4. List the main factors that influence the work pace.
5. List two rating scales of activity.
6. What is the walking speed that is considered to correspond to normal activity?
7. If an operator takes 10 seconds to perform a task and the activity mark was 80 in centesimal scale, what would be the runtime if the activity had been 100?
8. Based on the data from question #7, if we calculate the time of an activity to be 133 in centesimal scale, what would be the result?
9. Briefly describe the differences between work mode and work method.
10. Indicate at least four basic tools that an analyst must have.

Bibliography

Caso Neira, Alfredo, *Production Incentive Systems* (Ed. Fundación Confemetal, 2003).

MTM Manual (MTM Spanish Association).

Chapter 16

Time Study with Timekeeping

16.1. Introduction: Timekeeping Techniques

Generally, no facet of company management can do without a correct determination of the runtimes for the different operations that are developed in them. In other words, an adequate policy of work measurement is essential.

The time study is a work measurement technique used for recording work and activity times for the operations of a defined task, performed under certain conditions. The purpose of time study is an analysis of the data and calculation of the required time to perform the task according to an established method of execution. Ultimately, time study contributes standards of performance for the execution of a task.

In order to perform this task, the first thing the analyst must do is to pick the tool or technique for performing the timekeeping. Several of them are described here.

1. Use of the stopwatch: It is the method used most extensively. Chapter 14 described the two main procedures for timing with a stopwatch:

- Accumulative timekeeping: In accumulative timekeeping, the stopwatch runs uninterrupted throughout the study. It is started at the beginning of the first operation of the first cycle and does not stop until the study is over.

- Timekeeping with return to zero: In this procedure, the stopwatch is returned to zero at the end of each operation and started again for the next operation without the mechanism stopping for a moment.

Industrial Productivity

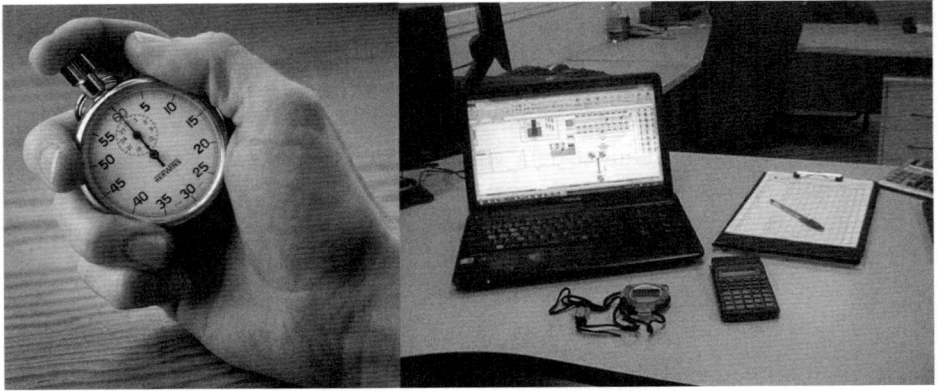

Figure 16.1. Use of the stopwatch

2. Videotaping: Video cameras are the ideal devices for recording the operator's methods and the elapsed time to perform the task without losing any detail. When recording and then viewing a task, the analyst can record all details of the method used. The biggest advantage of using the camcorder is being able to pause and review how the task is performed as many times as necessary. In addition, suggestions for improvement to the method used can be provided more easily than with the stopwatch procedure. For the study, the timer may be used while viewing the task, using the method best suited to the requirements of the study. Another advantage of the video camera recording is that with specific software, the methods and times studies are almost automatic. With digital video cameras and editing software on PC, the time and methods studies can be performed almost in parallel. This software allows analysts to identify the initial and final milestones of each recording operation while analyzing the task. Subsequently and semiautomatically, they generate time studies calculating the frequency of occurrence for each event. Video recordings are also useful for training analysts in timing methods; they allow for practicing with already solved examples. Today, in racing competitions, the Formula 1 teams use the camcorder in order to correct mistakes and optimize tire exchanges in the race.

Figure 16.2. Use of video camera and office processing

3. Use of PDA: The majority of electronic systems offer additional functions to be able to perform time studies. With the installation of specific software, the task of data transcription from data sheets to the computer is eliminated, improving the precision of the calculations. These systems transfer the data to the personal computer for the subsequent data analysis. A team of analysts can perform a great number of studies in a short period, and using this approach allows for studies to be analyzed by numerous analysts simultaneously. However, it is important that the person who performs the study examines these analyses before publishing and validating the results.

Figure 16.3. Use of PDA

In any of the three cases, the result is a summary sheet of the study that will contain the same information, standard time, unit cost, and other relevant statistics.

This chapter explains the methodology of work measurement through timekeeping: timing, recognition of activities, and the compilation of data for obtaining the standard time. It is one of the most important chapters of the book because work measurement through timekeeping is the most widespread.

16.2. Stages of the Timekeeping Study

The stages of the time study through timing are defined in Figure 16.4.

Industrial Productivity

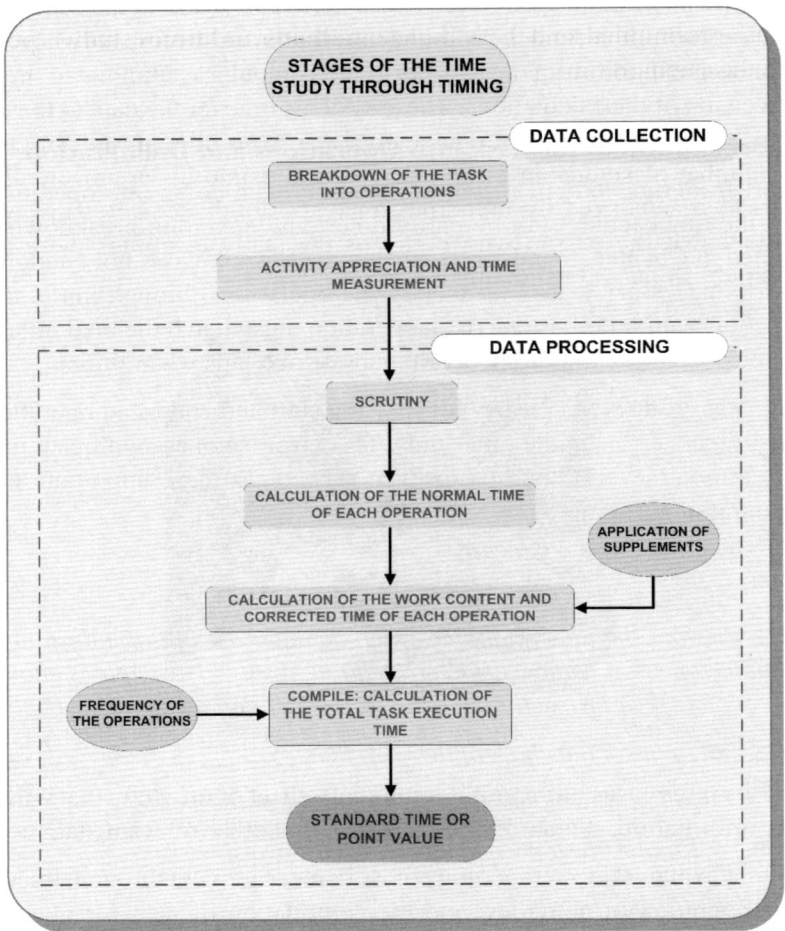

Figure 16.4. Stages of time study through timing

A task is composed of a set of operations that can be of different types. Its duration will be measured using any of the techniques described previously. Before the time record, the analyst must value and assign an activity. For each operation, a determined number of measurements must be taken based on its complexity, dimension, repetition, and importance.

After taking the necessary number of measurements, each operation the task is composed of will be scrutinized to obtain its *normal time*. The analyst should be as detailed as possible to be fair and avoid deviations. The objective is to derive calculated times that are correct and, therefore, fair for the company and workers.

To each normal time will be added supplements, obtaining the *corrected time* of each operation. The following step will be to calculate the frequency of each operation, the number of times it repeats. Finally, all the data from the different operations are compiled, and the complete **methods and times** study is performed to obtain the standard time.

16.2.1. Breakdown of the Task into Operations and Delimitation

If we start from the study of methods already broken down into operations, this phase of the timekeeping will be partly done. The operation breakdown criteria is explained in Chapters 5 and 14. However, the breakdown is not enough for the timing; it is necessary to delimit clearly the operations through initial and final milestones. The initial milestone of an operation must match the final milestone of the previous operation in order to avoid gaps or overlaps when timing.

Often the analyst does not clearly identify the start and end of an operation. This situation triggers errors in the time study. This error is not as significant in studies of long duration (several hours); however, it becomes more important in studies of short duration (2–3 minutes).

Example

For facilitating the understanding when defining the initial milestone and final milestone that compose each operation, a solved example is shown of the task "Retrieve instruction booklet from shelf and take to workbench."

- *Stand up from the chair of the workbench:*
    - *Initial Milestone: Beginning of body movement.*
    - *Final Milestone: Start movement toward shelf.*
- *Move toward the shelf:*
    - *Initial Milestone: Start movement toward shelf.*
    - *Final Milestone: Stop in front of shelf.*
- *Reach for book from shelf:*
    - *Initial Milestone: Stop in front of shelf.*
    - *Final Milestone: Touch book with hand.*
- *Take book from shelf:*
    - *Initial Milestone: Touch book with hand.*
    - *Final Milestone: Start movement to turn around.*
- *Turn around to return to the table:*
    - *Initial Milestone: Start movement to turn around.*
    - *Final Milestone: Begin movement toward table.*

- *Scroll to the table:*

    -Initial Milestone: Begin movement toward table.

    - Final Milestone: Stop in front of table.

- *Put book on the table:*

    - Initial Milestone: Stop in front of table.

    - Final Milestone: Touch book to the table.

As can be appreciated in the example, the final milestone of each operation coincides with the initial milestone of the next operation.

	Breakdown sheet and delimitation of operations				
Task:	Provision instructions book	Company:	Patterson Assemblies		**Patterson Assemblies**
Date:	2011/07/13	Process:	90/39A00		
Analyst:	Jason Hayes	Area:	Decorative assembly		
Operator:	Jeremy Alexander				
#	Description of the operation	Type	Initial milestone		Final milestone
1	Stand up from the chair of the worktable.	○	Beginning of body movement.		Start movement toward shelf.
2	Move toward the shelf.	⇨	Start movement toward shelf.		Stop in front of shelf.
3	Reach for book from shelf.	○	Stop in front of shelf.		Touch book with hand.
4	Take book from shelf.	○	Touch book with hand.		Start movement to turn around.
5	Turn around to return to the table.	○	Start movement to turn around.		Begin movement toward table.
6	Move to the table.	⇨	Begin movement toward table.		Stop in front of table.
7	Put book on the table.	○	Stop in front of table.		Touch book to the table.
8					
9					
10					

Figure 16.5. *Definition of initial milestone and final milestone*

The level of detail varies with the level of precision needed. To achieve a precise study of methods and times, the breakdown needs to be sufficiently broad. However, for a time study with stopwatch, having to measure so many short-timed operations is laborious and does not provide greater accuracy. Therefore, we must achieve a balance between the two terms in function of desired accuracy and work objectives.

16.2.2. Determination of the Number of Measurements for an Operation

After delimiting correctly each operation and establishing its initial milestone and its final milestone, the analyst will calculate the number of observations or measurements needed to obtain the normal time of each operation with a certain level of precision. This task can be done using two methods.

1. **Mundel Table:** This table indicates the number of observations necessary to obtain a ±5% deviation with a 95% probability.

MUNDEL TABLE							
(A - B) / (A + B)	Initial Series		(A - B) / (A + B)	Initial Series	
	5 measures	10 measures		5 measures	10 measures
0.05	3	1	0.28	93	53
0.06	4	2	0.29	100	57
0.07	6	3	0.3	107	61
0.08	8	4	0.31	114	65
0.09	10	5	0.32	121	69
0.1	12	7	0.33	129	74
0.11	14	8	0.34	137	78
0.12	17	10	0.35	145	83
0.13	20	11	0.36	154	88
0.14	23	13	0.37	162	93
0.15	27	15	0.38	171	98
0.16	30	17	0.39	180	103
0.17	34	20	0.4	190	108
0.18	38	22	0.41	200	114
0.19	43	24	0.42	210	120
0.2	47	27	0.43	220	126
0.21	52	30	0.44	230	132
0.22	57	33	0.45	240	138
0.23	63	36	0.46	250	144
0.24	68	39	0.47	262	150
0.25	74	42	0.48	273	156
0.26	80	46	0.49	285	163
0.27	86	49	0.5	296	170

Figure 16.6. Mundel Table for calculating the number of measurements

The procedure to calculate the number of measurements is the following:

1. An initial series of five (or ten) time measurements is taken for the operation that is the object of study.
2. The highest measurement (A) and the lowest measurement (B) are taken.
3. The remainder is divided by the sum of the maximum and minimum.

Industrial Productivity

$$\frac{A - B}{A + B}$$

Formula 16.1

4. The result of this division is checked in the previous table, which will indicate the number of observations that must be measured.

To illustrate this calculation method, a solved exercise is offered.

Example

Calculation example of the number of measurements using the Mundel table.

- *The times taken are: 4, 4.03, 4.12, 6, and 5.19*
- *A = 6 and B = 4*
- *Result of the formula = 2/10 = 0.2*
- *According to the Mundel table, 47 is the number of necessary measurements.*

2. Statistical method: The goal is to obtain the representative average value for each operation. With the statistical method a number of initial measurements are performed and then the following formula is applied for a confidence level of 95.45% and a margin of error of ±5%:

$$n = \left\{ \frac{40\sqrt{(c \sum x^2) - (\sum x^2)}}{\sum x} \right\}^2$$

Formula 16.2

Siendo:

- n = number of measurements to be done
- c = number of initial measurements
- $\sum$ = sum of values
- x = value of the measurements

Here we solve the problem from the previous example using the statistical method.

Example

Calculation example for the number of measurements with the statistical method.

- *The same data from the previous example will be used: 4, 4.03, 4.12, 6, and 5.19. If we calculate the squares and the sum of them, we will have the following summary table:*

x	x^2
4	16
4.03	16.24
4.12	16.97
6	36
5.19	26.94
$\sum x = 23.34$	$\sum x^2 = 112.155$

- $c = 5$, *number of initial observations*

- *Substituting in the previous formula* $\rightarrow n = 47.12 \approx 47$ *measurements, the same result as given by the Mundel table*

In practice, the necessary measurements are defined based on the experience of the analyst. For this, the following factors have to be taken into account:

- **Weight of the operation:** *Importance of the operation in the task. We must not forget that with the study of times and methods the goal is to improve. Excessive detail in determining operations that in the end are not important in the task makes the study unprofitable.*

- **Level of observed dispersion:** *Either of the two methods explained will help the analyst to be more effective when timing, adjusting the number of observations as a function of their dispersion.*

- *Level of measurement difficulty.*

It is normal to have an accuracy of 95%. However, for operations with little repetition and less weight within the task, a lower level of confidence is appropriate. Always keep in mind the cost-benefit relationship involved.

16.2.3. Timekeeping: Record of Activity and Time

The time recorded with a stopwatch and the recognized activity for the measurements of each operation are central to time study. Once the specification requirements of the working method are completed and the task is divided into its different operations, we can address the proper timing. It consists in writing down activity marks and the clock time for each of the operations that compose a complete work cycle.

Each measurement will have a qualified activity and a timed time, in that order. Each operation is measured a determined number of times as a function of the result obtained with either of the two methods explained, making as far as possible the timings in different moments of the day and week. With such a wide sampling accompanied by careful scrutiny, the obtained result is reliable. The most common errors committed in time measurement are reading errors and pulsation errors, with the admissible error $\pm 1\%$. Chapter 15 explained how to value the work pace and how to value activity; according to these criteria the activity in each measurement of the operations will be marked.

> The activity of an operation always has to be evaluated and valued before writing down its time. Therefore, on a timing sheet, the activity column must precede the time column.

Figure 16.7 contains a basic format sheet for activity and times collection of the operations from the studied task.

Format

Format of timing sheet												
Task:			Company:						Logo of the company		
Date:			Process:						^		
Analyst:			Area:						^		
Operator:									^		
	Description of the operation || Measure.	1	2	3	4	5	6	7	8	9	10
1	|| A										
^	|| T										
2	|| A										
^	|| T										
3	|| A										
^	|| T										
4	|| A										
^	|| T										
5	|| A										
^	|| T										
6	|| A										
^	|| T										
7	|| A										
^	|| T										
8	|| A										
^	|| T										
9	|| A										
^	|| T										
10	|| A										
^	|| T										
11	|| A										
^	|| T										
12	|| A										
^	|| T										
13	|| A										
^	|| T										
14	|| A										
^	|| T										
15	|| A										
^	|| T										

Figure 16.7. *Format of timekeeping sheet*

Industrial Productivity

As shown in the timekeeping sheet, the activity box (A) is found before the time box (T). As previously mentioned, the activity of the operation must always be marked before the time to help the analyst avoid being influenced by the duration when rating the activity of an operation.

It is also important to complete all the required data from the activities and times sheet. Forgetting details may delay the fulfillment of the methods and times study.

We will show several examples of timekeeping sheets properly completed. In the first example, the activity has been recognized in the 100-133 scale and in the second example, the scale is 60-80.

Example

		Format of timing sheet													
	Task:	Frame check		Company:	Ectrodus Welding				*Ectrodus*						
	Date:	2008/12/04		Process:	Frame assembly				*Welding*						
	Analyst:	Teresa White		Area:	Finishes										
	Operator:	Jacob Brown													
	Description of the operation		Measure.	1	2	3	4	5	6	7	8	9	10		
1	Take location go/no go gauge.		A	100	100	80	90								
			T	2.36	2.4	3.12	2.75								
2	Perform check in frame welder.		A	100	105	90	100	80							
			T	12.32	11.95	13.95	12.49	14.23							
3	Deposit device in location.		A	100	100	110	90								
			T	2.3	2.4	1.9	3.02								
4	Take clean cloth and apply degreaser.		A	100	100	90	110	115							
			T	6.3	6.45	7.56	5.92	4.96							
5	Apply layer of degreaser in frame.		A	95	100	100	90	90							
			T	10.23	9.96	9.89	10.53	10.63							
6	Clean frame with help of clean cloth.		A	100	100	90	110	115	110	90					
			T	35.26	34.29	40.23	31.25	30.98	31.27	40.1					
7	Take barcode reader.		A	100	100	110	90	85							
			T	2.2	2.35	1.85	2.78	2.98							
8	Read barcodes from tracing label.		A	100	100	100									
			T	3.6	3.5	3.6									
9	Remove label and adhere to checked frame.		A	90	100	100	95	95							
			T	6.63	7.01	7.12	6.89	6.96							
10	Take frame and deposit in adjacent workstation.		A	100	100	100	95	105							
			T	18.95	19.01	19.1	20.98	17.95							
11			A												
			T												
12			A												
			T												
13			A												
			T												
14			A												
			T												
15			A												
			T												

Figure 16.8. Format of timing sheet completed (scale 100-133)

Example

	Format of timing sheet													
Task:	Box assembly		Company:	Alcan Cardboards			*Alcan Cardboards*							
Date:	2009/05/07		Process:	Quality check										
Analyst:	David Harris		Area:	Dispatch										
Operator:	Georgia Martin													
	Description of the operation	Measure.	1	2	3	4	5	6	7	8	9	10
1	Take a cardboard box.	A	60	65	55							
		T	3.34	2.98	3.79							
2	Assemble cardboard box.	A	60	60	65	55	60	50				
		T	13.45	13.89	12.89	14.23	13.87	15.63				
3	Take precinct roll holder.	A	60	60	65	65	55					
		T	13.25	13.23	12.95	12.98	14.54					
4	Precint cardboard box by its base.	A	60	60	80	60	60	70	70	60		
		T	24.53	24.01	19.21	25.42	25.31	22.53	22.31	24.68		
5	Deposit precinct roll holder on auxiliary table. Turn around cardboard box.	A	60	65	60							
		T	7.51	6.87	7.32							
6	Provision seal and buffer. Place seal to identify order.	A	60	60	55							
		T	3.3	3.32	3.65							
7	Deposit seal and buffer. Deposit assembled box.	A	60	60	60	55	65					
		T	4.53	4.65	4.76	5.32	4.21					
8		A										
		T										
9		A										
		T										
10		A										
		T										
11		A										
		T										
12		A										
		T										
13		A										
		T										
14		A										
		T										
15		A										
		T										

Figure 16.9. Format of timing sheet completed (scale 60-80)

16.2.4. Calculation of the Normal Time of an Operation: Scrutiny

Previously, we described how to perform the data collection during timekeeping when measuring a task whose standard time is going to be calculated. The next step after the data collection is the determination of the normal time for each operation:

Industrial Productivity

> The normal time is the necessary time for the execution of an operation working at a normal activity.

In practice, to calculate the normal time of each measurement, the following mathematical expression is used:

$$\text{Normal Time} \times \text{Normal Activity} = \text{Observed Time} \times \text{Observed Activity}$$

Formula 16.3

Or also this similar expression:

$$\text{Normal Time} = \frac{\text{Observed Time} \times \text{Observed Activity}}{\text{Normal Activity}}$$

Formula 16.4

How do we calculate the normal operation time with a given amount of measurements? When making repeated time and activity measurements of an operation, we have a series of values from the operations, from which the analyst must determine the representative time and activity of the observed operation. This determination is performed by an operation called scrutiny, which uses the series of observed values to deduce a time and activity value for each operation that will allow us to calculate the normal time.

> A scrutiny is a set of mathematical operations that return as a result the most repeated time and the activity observed for such time within a range. The most repeated time is called modal value.

A scrutiny must be made for each of the operations performed in the task, this way the normal times of all the operations that compose a task will be defined. At this point several examples explain how to calculate the normal time of an operation through scrutiny.

Example

After taking a sufficient number of measurements in the factory, the analyst is ready to start processing data. The first operation measured is "Place pallet to unload" and the list of data collected is as follows:

16. Time Study with Timekeeping

Activity	Time	Activity	Time
75	13,94	65	15,52
55	25,56	65	15,71
65	15,87	65	15,34
75	13,56	65	15,66
60	16,98	70	14,35
65	15,65	60	15,71
60	16,56	70	14,29
60	16,54	65	15,21
75	13,92	65	15,43
55	25,65	65	15,54
65	15,89	65	15,31
75	13,59	65	15,66
60	16,99	70	14,31
65	15,62	60	15,78
60	16,59	70	14,18
60	16,51	65	15,19
65	15,59	65	15,69
65	15,69	65	15,62
65	15,34	65	15,33
65	15,67	65	15,69
70	14,31	60	16,42
60	15,71	60	15,65
70	14,21	70	14,23
65	15,32	65	15,21

The first step is to normalize the times taken in order to ascertain the dispersion level of the measurements. For this, the times collected are multiplied by the activity marked in the data collection and divided by the normal activity, which in the Bedaux scale is 60. As an example, we calculate the first time of the list:

$$\text{Normal } T_1 = \frac{T_1 \times A_1}{A_n} = \frac{13.94 \times 75}{60} = 17.43$$

Formula 16.5

When performing the same operation on the other times, you get the following list:

Industrial Productivity

Activity	Time	Normal Time	Activity	Time	Normal Time
75	13,94	17,43	65	15,52	16,81
55	25,56	23,43	65	15,71	17,02
65	15,87	17,19	65	15,34	16,62
75	13,56	16,95	65	15,66	16,97
60	16,98	16,98	70	14,35	16,74
65	15,65	16,95	60	15,71	15,71
60	16,56	16,56	70	14,29	16,67
60	16,54	16,54	65	15,21	16,48
75	13,92	17,40	65	15,43	16,72
55	25,65	23,51	65	15,54	16,84
65	15,89	17,21	65	15,31	16,59
75	13,59	16,99	65	15,66	16,97
60	16,99	16,99	70	14,31	16,70
65	15,62	16,92	60	15,78	15,78
60	16,59	16,59	70	14,18	16,54
60	16,51	16,51	65	15,19	16,46
65	15,59	16,89	65	15,69	17,00
65	15,69	17,00	65	15,62	16,92
65	15,34	16,62	65	15,33	16,61
65	15,67	16,98	65	15,69	17,00
70	14,31	16,70	60	16,42	16,42
60	15,71	15,71	60	15,65	15,65
70	14,21	16,58	70	14,23	16,60
65	15,32	16,60	65	15,21	16,48

Now, to get a much more reliable time, all times that have a deviation higher than 33%, both upper and lower, compared to the average of the normalized times should be removed. The next step is to calculate the average of the standard times, calculate the ±33% of the average value, and eliminate all the times that are out of this range. (Note: The percentage deviation can be changed depending on the dispersion in time we want to allow.)

Superior deviation (+33%)	22,60
Average value	16,99
Inferior deviation (−33%)	11,38

16. Time Study with Timekeeping

As you can observe from the timetable, two normalized times fall outside that range. These two data are removed from the list of normalized times. After this filter, the initial table appears like this:

Activity	Time	Normal Time	Activity	Time	Normal Time
75	13,94	17,43	65	15,71	17,02
65	15,87	17,19	65	15,34	16,62
75	13,56	16,95	65	15,66	16,97
60	16,98	16,98	70	14,35	16,74
65	15,65	16,95	60	15,71	15,71
60	16,56	16,56	70	14,29	16,67
60	16,54	16,54	65	15,21	16,48
75	13,92	17,40	65	15,43	16,72
65	15,89	17,21	65	15,54	16,84
75	13,59	16,99	65	15,31	16,59
60	16,99	16,99	65	15,66	16,97
65	15,62	16,92	70	14,31	16,70
60	16,59	16,59	60	15,78	15,78
60	16,51	16,51	70	14,18	16,54
65	15,59	16,89	65	15,19	16,46
65	15,69	17,00	65	15,69	17,00
65	15,34	16,62	65	15,62	16,92
65	15,67	16,98	65	15,33	16,61
70	14,31	16,70	65	15,69	17,00
60	15,71	15,71	60	16,42	16,42
70	14,21	16,58	60	15,65	15,65
65	15,32	16,60	70	14,23	16,60
65	15,52	16,81	65	15,21	16,48

As mentioned at the beginning of this chapter, the modal value is the most frequent value within a range, so the next step for the analyst is to divide this list into intervals. For calculating the number of intervals, the square root of the sampling size is calculated and rounded to the nearest whole number. For example:

537

Industrial Productivity

$$N° \text{ intervals} = \sqrt{\text{Sample size}} = \sqrt{48} = 6.93 \rightarrow 7$$

Formula 16.6

In this case, we will proceed to divide the list into seven intervals and seek the highest and lowest time on the list. As you can see, the times are 13.56 and 16.99. To calculate the increase in intervals the following formula applies:

$$\text{Increment} = \frac{\text{Higher T} - \text{Lower T}}{\text{Intervals}} = \frac{16.99 - 13.56}{7} = 0.49$$

Formula 16.7

With the intervals known, the analyst will be able to complete the scrutiny, as shown in the following table:

Operation		Activity						
Time	Activity / N° of Repetitions							
13,56								
14,05								
14,05								
14,54								
14,54								
15,03								
15,03								
15,52								
15,52								
16,01								
16,01								
16,50								
16,50								
16,99								

Once the time column is completed, the row is completed with the value of the activity. In the case studied, the boxes are filled with activities ranging from 50 to 75 with an increment of 5. The result will be the following table

16. Time Study with Timekeeping

Operation		Activity					
Time	Activity / N° of Repetitions	50	55	60	65	70	75
13,56							
14,05							
14,05							
14,54							
14,54							
15,03							
15,03							
15,52							
15,52							
16,01							
16,01							
16,50							
16,50							
16,99							

The last step is to fill the grid with the times listed. The second column will serve to make the sum of all times that fall within the range.

Operation		Activity					
Time	Activity / N° of Repetitions	50	55	60	65	70	75
13,56 / 14,05	IIII						IIII
14,05 / 14,54	IIIII III					IIIII III	
14,54 / 15,03							
15,03 / 15,52	IIIII IIII				IIIII IIII		
15,52 / 16,01	IIIII IIIII IIIII IIIII			IIII	IIIII IIIII IIIII		
16,01 / 16,50	I						
16,50 / 16,99	IIIII I			IIIII			

The data show that more times are found in the 15.52–16.01 interval. We will now calculate the average modal interval:

- *16.01 + 15.52 = 31.53 / 2 = 15.76 for a 65 activity value, because it is the column where most observations are found.*

Finally, a last calculation expresses this time at normal activity or, put another way, normalizes it:

$$\text{Normal Time} \times \text{Normal Activity} = \text{Observed Time} \times \text{Observed Activity}$$

Substituting values:

$$\text{Normal Time} = \frac{\text{Observed Time} \times \text{Observed Activity}}{\text{Normal Activity}} = \frac{15.76 \times 65}{60} = 17.07$$

Formula 16.8

The analyst can ensure that the normal time consumed performing the operation "Place pallet to unload" has a value of 17.07 seconds.

The following summary shows the detailed calculations made in the example:

16. Time Study with Timekeeping

Scrutiny			
Date:	Unload of defective material	Date:	2010/09/09
Operation:	Place a pallet to unload	Company:	White Arma
Analyst:	Jayla Marin	Process:	90/39A00
Operator:	Stuart Parker	Area:	Logistic platform

White Arma

Summary of measurements

Activity	Time	Activity	Time
75	13.94	65	15.54
55	25.56	65	15.69
65	15.87	65	15.34
75	13.56	65	15.66
60	16.98	70	14.35
65	15.65	60	15.71
60	16.56	70	14.29
60	16.54	65	15.21

33 Sup. Dev. (%)

22.86 Maximum v.
17.19 Average v.
11.52 Minimum v.

33 Inf. Dev. (%)

Time	OPERATION Activity/Repetitions	ACTIVITY				
		50	55	60	65	70	75
13.56–14.05	//						//
14.05–14.54	//					//	
14.54–15.03							
15.03–15.52	//				//		
15.52–16.01	••••••			/	•••••		
16.01–16.50							
16.50–16.99	///			///			

Modal interval	15.76
Most repeated activity	65

Normal Activity	60
Normal Time	17.07

541

Example

A new example of the operation "Take and assemble pin" will be solved.

Activity	Time	Activity	Time
110	6,43	95	8,21
100	7,89	110	6,54
85	11,98	105	7,24
100	7,76	100	7,65
125	4,21	95	8,24
95	8,32	125	4,56
100	7,67	105	7,01
95	8,45	80	16,56
100	7,58	85	14,32

Now, we will normalize the data:

Activity	Time	Normalized Time	Activity	Time	Normalized Time
110	6,43	7,07	95	8,21	7,80
100	7,89	7,89	110	6,54	7,19
85	11,98	10,18	105	7,24	7,60
100	7,76	7,76	100	7,65	7,65
125	4,21	5,26	95	8,24	7,83
95	8,32	7,90	125	4,56	5,70
100	7,67	7,67	105	7,01	7,36
95	8,45	8,03	80	16,56	13,25
100	7,58	7,58	85	14,32	12,17

In order to achieve a more reliable time, we eliminate all the times with a deviation greater than ±33%.

16. Time Study with Timekeeping

Superior deviation (+33%)	10,78
Average value	8,11
Inferior deviation (−33%)	5,43

After this filter the initial table will be:

Activity	Time	Normalized Time	Activity	Time	Normalized Time
110	6,43	7,07	95	8,21	7,80
100	7,89	7,89	110	6,54	7,19
85	11,98	10,18	105	7,24	7,60
100	7,76	7,76	100	7,65	7,65
95	8,32	7,90	95	8,24	7,83
100	7,67	7,67	125	4,56	5,70
95	8,45	8,03	105	7,01	7,36
100	7,58	7,58	-	-	-

We will proceed to divide the list into seven time intervals and search for the highest and lowest on the list. As can be observed, those times are 11.98 and 4.56. For calculating the increase in the intervals, the following formula is applied:

$$\text{Increment} = \frac{\text{Higher T} - \text{Lower T}}{\text{Intervals}} = \frac{11.98 - 4.56}{7} = 0.49$$

Formula 16.9

After calculating the intervals, the analyst will be able to complete the scrutiny, as shown in the following table:

Industrial Productivity

Time	Operation Activity/ N° of Repetitions	\multicolumn{9}{c}{Activity}
		85	90	95	100	105	110	115	120	125
4,56 – 5,62	I									I
5,62 – 6,68	II						/ II			
6,68 – 7,74	IIII				III /	II				
7,74 – 8,80	IIIII			IIII /	/ II					
8,80 – 9,86				/						
9,86 – 10,92			/							
10,92 – 11,98										
10,92 – 11,98	I	I								

In view of the data, more times are contained in the range 7.74–8.80. Afterwards we calculate the interval ends of the modal average and the, result is 8.27 with a marked activity of 95, because it is the column with the most measurements. Finally, a last calculation consists of expressing this time at normal activity, which is the same as saying to normalize it:

$$\text{Normal Time} = \frac{\text{Observed Time} \times \text{Observed Activity}}{\text{Normal Activity}} = \frac{8.27 \times 95}{100} = 7.86$$

Formula 16.10

Figure 16.11 shows how the methods and times study is being built once we have the normal time of operations. This will require scrutinizing individual operations.

Document 2 - Study of methods and times of the task: Insert placement

Description of operation	Type of operation	Distance (meters)	Normal time (sec)
Provide panel. Remove protector paper.	○		9.33
Provide set of bits for drill.	○		5.90
Move toward following workstation.	⇨	20.00	16.00
Deposit panel on worktable.	○		1.90
Search and provide plans.	▭		57.91
Perform drill markings with pencil and ruler.	⟲		206.20
Store plans in closet.	▽		54.42
Take panel.	○		2.00
Move toward manual mechanizing area.	⇨	100.00	80.00
Deposit bits and panel on auxiliary table. Clear working area.	▽		5.78

Figure 16.11. Methods and times study: Normal time of each operation

16.2.5. Supplement Application

The normal time is the time it takes to execute an operation at normal activity. However, during the workday, the operator has to perform other types of tasks than those made at his or her workstation: use the restroom, rest from fatigue, troubleshoot, clean office, don safety gear, and so on.

The study of methods and times attempts, for simplicity and consistency, to load the times dedicated to these tasks to the main operation. The mathematical tool for doing so is the supplements, which would imply that it is shared among all tasks carried out throughout the day and the operations within these tasks. It would be distributed in proportion to the duration of the same. Possible supplements are:

- Rest supplements
- Incidence supplements
- Start and end of workday supplements
- Cleaning supplements
- Adjustment supplements

Once the different supplements have been calculated, the normal time of each operation will be incremented the following way:

Rest supplements

The rest supplement takes into account personal necessities and fatigue. The resulting time after applying all the rest supplements is named, according to the ILO, **Work content**.

The book *Introduction to Work Study* from the International Labor Organization indicates the following:

> *It should be noted that when it comes to time study, which is necessarily based on the measurement of work with numeric values, the term "work" not only applies to the physical or mental work done, but it includes a fair amount of rest necessary for inaction or recovery from fatigue caused by such work.*

> Work content of a task or operation is the normal time plus the applicable rest supplements.

Based on the conditions and type of operation, the percentage of time the task has to be incremented to include the values of rest supplements. In this book we recommend finding these values in the table provided by *Personnel Administration Ltd (London)* due to its scientific stringency and its simple application in the studies of methods and times. This table is provided in Appendix I. The supplements are expressed in percentages and only have to be applied to the operations corresponding to person-time, either person-time with machine stopped or person-time with machine running, never to a machine-time or to a cycle with the exception of the supplements by personal necessities, as we will see later on. The principal objective of any rest supplement is to increase the normal time of an operation, without diminishing its physical conditions. In 1999 the differences between the supplements applied to men and women were eliminated.

The two types of rest supplements are:

1. Fixed to the task: supplements that correspond to general conditions from the workplace.

2. Variables of the operation: An additional supplement that has to be added to the fixed supplement for each operation and varies in accordance with what has to be performed and how it fatigues the operator.

Calculation of supplement fixed to the task

According to the tables provided in Appendix I, and for normal working conditions in which work must be done while standing, for example, the fixed supplement of the task will be:

- Basic supplement for personal necessities: 5%
- Basic supplement for fatigue: 4%
- Basic supplement for working in standing position: 2% (whenever the operation is done standing)
- Total: 11%

Imagine the workshop where the work is done has some uncomfortable conditions, which are:

- Intermittent and strong noise: 2%
- Poor illumination, far below the recommended: 2%

To the 11% previously calculated we add the implications of these noise and illumination conditions; therefore, the fixed supplement of the task is 15%.

If the manager of the workshop would invest in soundproofing, in good illumination, and in means to be able to perform the work while seated, the fixed supplement would be 9%; that is, the time of the operation would be 6% lower due to a lower fatigue of the operator. **The 9% (5% fatigue and 4% personal necessities) is called constant supplement: it is always applied.**

For fixed supplements, tables include value factors such as:

- Temperature and relative humidity
- Illumination
- Noise
- Constant fatigue (9%)

Calculation of the additional supplement of the operation

What has been previously discussed affects the totality of the task development; however, within the task is a whole breakdown of operations that are not subject to the same fatigue. For example, if an operator works with a machine that includes operations pushing buttons and operations loading and unloading parts, then loading parts logically causes more fatigue than pushing buttons. According to these tables, if the parts weight more than 5 kilograms, 1% should be added to the fixed supplement. If they weighted 20 kilograms, then it would be 9%.

For the additional supplement of the operation, the value factors include:

- Weight of the load
- Working postures
- Level of concentration

Industrial Productivity

- Types of displacements
- Tedium and monotony
- Mental tension
- Action over objects
- Use of tools
- Intellectual works

Whatever tables are used, it is important that they are well assimilated.

$$\text{Rest Supplement} = \text{Fixed rest supplement} + \text{Additional supplement}$$

Formula 16.11

Consequently, the work content of the operation will be obtained:

$$\text{Work Content} = \text{Normal Time} \times (1 + \text{Rest Supplement})$$

Formula 16.12

Example

For work content calculation of the operation "Place a pallet to unload" studied previously in the scrutiny, whose normalized time is 17.07 seconds, the corresponding basic or fixed supplements will be applied:

- *Supplement for personal necessities: 5%*
- *Supplement for fatigue: 4%*
- *Supplement for working in standing position: 2%*

Whether it is pertinent to include any other type of supplement must be considered. A wooden pallet weights approximately 17.5 kilograms, so it is necessary to revise the value from the table of rest supplements. The operator, in order to place the wooden pallet has to use muscular strength, so the analyst must consult the supplement value for the studied operation.

17.5 kilograms → 7%, so to the total of fixed supplements, must be added the corresponding to the use of strength. Thus, we have:

Rest supplements = Fixed supplements + Additional supplements = 11 + 7 = 18%

The following step is to calculate the work content of the operation:

Work content = 17.07 x (1 + 0.18) = 20.14 seconds for the operation "Place a pallet to unload"

The previous example takes from the table the value corresponding to the operation described. In other cases, the tables give a range of values, between which we have to search for the adequate value.

Example

How will the supplement of the operation "Push trolley on rails" be determined? (Note: The trolley weights 200 kilograms.)

- *Basic supplement for personal necessities: 5%*
- *Basic supplement for fatigue: 4%*
- *Basic supplement for working in a standing position: 2%*

If we consult the tables to apply a supplement for pushing the trolley, these values are showed:

$$\text{For } 100 \text{ Kg} \rightarrow 15\%$$

$$\text{For } 400 \text{ Kg} \rightarrow 30\%$$

For intermediate loads, as it is our case, we must calculate the value through interpolation:

- *The load variation is: 400 – 100 = 300 Kg*
- *The variation in the supplement value is: 30 – 15 = 15%*
- *The variation in the supplement value per kilogram: 15 / 300 = 0.05*

For the 200 kilograms from our case:

- *For 100 Kg → 15%*
- *The load variation is: 200 – 100 = 100 Kg x 0.05 = 5%, which added to the initial 15% results in a total 20%*

In summary, the total value of the supplement to apply is: 5 + 4 + 2 + 20 = 31%

In other cases, the corresponding values of a certain operation are obtained through the addition of several elements.

Example

For a displacement with a dense load of 30 Kg carried in arms, through soil in good condition.

The supplement would be:

- *Displacement coefficient → 8%*
- *Load supplement → 12%*

Summarizing, the total value of the supplement to apply is: 5 + 4 + 2 + 20 = 31%

Example

What would be the supplement of the operation "Add sand in concrete mixer to make cement mortar"?

As the mixture is prepared at ground level, the operator must shovel from the pile of sand to the concrete mixer orifice, which is higher than the pile. Therefore, the shovelling is done from a low to a high position, so the adding supplement is:

- *Supplement for indirect projection → 25%*

Example

What is the additional supplement for the operation "Weld cap in steel tank"? To perform this operation, the operator had to weld the cap in an uncomfortable posture. While performing the cap welding, the operator had to use the hammer to level the cap, constantly hitting the object. On the other hand, analyzing the work environment, it is a job with inadequate illumination, accentuated in night shifts when solar light through windows or skylights is absent. Because it was a boiler shop, noise was continuous and loud from the use of hammers, drills, and other tools.

The total supplements to add to the operation are:

- *Supplement for uncomfortable postures → 7%*
- *Supplement for the use of drill → 30%*
- *Supplement for loud noises → 5%*
- *Supplement for insufficient illumination → 5%*

The total value of the supplement to apply is: 7 + 30 + 5 + 5 = 47%

Example

What would be the supplement of the operation "Brush wooden door"? The carpenter who performs this operation must assemble the door in its corresponding ironwork. Once this operation is made, the operator checks that the door opens and closes correctly, so that the interior part of the door does not touch the floor. Using both hands passes the brush back and forth, repeatedly, until removing the imperfection.

The supplement is:

- *Supplement for sway, wood brushing → 15%*

Supplement for beginning and end of workday

Normally, it is not possible to be at workstation from the start of the workday to the end. It depletes the productive capacity and has to be considered in the standard times. The best way is through supplements. This supplement for start and end of the day depends a lot on the labor agreement and the sector. For some sectors, the workday is considered in the workplace, and in this case, this supplement would not be considered. For other sectors, the workday is considered from the entry to the industrial compound until the exit of the same.

For example, in food industries, the operators have to be equipped with clothes and footwear that they cannot wear from their homes and even sanitize their hands and boots after entering. At the end of the workday, it will be the same but the other way around. In this case, workday times include time the worker is not operating. To calculate the supplement for start and end of the workday the following data needs to be handled:

- Workday length
- Allowed time for the start and end of the workday

If the length of the workday is 8 hours (480 minutes) and the time allowed is 15 minutes, the supplement will be:

$$\frac{15}{(480-15)} = 0.032 \rightarrow 3.2\%$$

In general, for the times granted per workday (for a determined cause), the formula to use in order to calculate the corresponding supplement is:

$$\text{Supplement} = 100 \times \frac{\text{Granted Time (cause)}}{\text{Workday length - Granted Time (cause)}}$$

Formula 16.13

Industrial Productivity

This type of supplement can also include the starting of a machine; the offset time from the starting of production until workers can begin to work, due to delays in other tasks; the shift takeover that involves a time for the transference of information, and so on.

Supplement for incidentals

Incidentals are incidents that should not occur. These incidents can be of two types:

- Long term
- Short term

Long-term incidents will never be taken into account in the standard time and will be marked as incidentals in the work order. Short-term incidents, because it would take longer to write them down in the work report than to solve them, have to be assumed in the standard time by a supplement for incidentals.

To calculate this supplement, a sampling needs to be done (that will be seen in the following chapter) to determine what amount of time of the workday incidentals occupy, which will be assumed in the standard time. Generally they will include micro-stops and weird elements. A times study needs to record the number of times these elements appear and their duration to be able to determine a correct statistic.

The ideal is to refine the method, supplies and tools until it would not be necessary to include this supplement. If, for example, a sampling showed an incidental time of 10 minutes and the workday had 8 hours, the supplement would be:

$$\frac{10}{(480-10)} = 0.021 \rightarrow 2.1\%$$

The formula to apply to calculate the corresponding supplement for unexpected events would be:

$$\text{Unexpected event supplement} = 100 \times \frac{\text{Unexpected event Time}}{\text{Workday length - Unexpected event Time}}$$

Formula 16.14

It is important to be clear and to record what causes are included within the supplement for incidentals and what causes are not. The reason is that when annotating incidents and stop-times that do not require production, time that was already included in the rest supplement may be included, effectively counting it twice. These concepts are developed with greater detail in Chapter 20, which is dedicated to productivity control and incentive systems.

Other supplements

Analogously to the previous supplements, others can be added such as:

- Cleaning supplement: applied when cleaning the machine or the workplace is included in the workday (This supplement is calculated from the cleaning time and the duration of the workday.)
- Supplement for adjustments of machines and tools
- Supplement for company politics

The calculation formula will be the one that has been seen generically, which depends on the time allowed for each cause in the workday and on the duration of the workday. Generally, the time consumption contributed by a concrete activity within the workday, and that is not specifically measured with its standard time, must be taken into account as supplement or unproductive time. The objective must always be to eliminate any cause that generates a supplement or unexpected events. If elimination is not an option, it is preferable to have it as a supplement always, because this unproductive time is never precisely ranged; therefore, the supplement is distributed in each quantified operation and repetition performed.

Supplement application

A clarification should be made at this point. As indicated throughout this chapter, the sum of normal time plus the quantity of rest supplements that are applicable to one operation is denominated **work content**. On the other hand, the sum of normal time plus the quantity of all the supplements (rest, incidentals, special, etc.) that are applicable to one operation, is denominated **corrected time**.

> The corrected time of an operation is the normal time plus all the supplements that are applicable to it (rest, incidentals, specials, etc.).

The following illustration shows graphically the explained concepts:

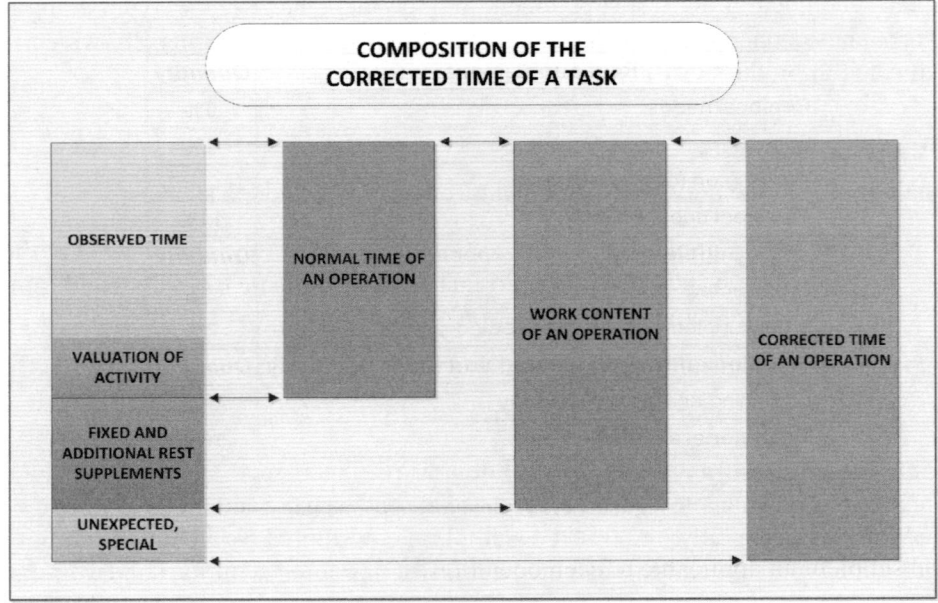

Figure 16.12. Composition of the corrected time of an operation

For the application of all the supplements, two distinctions are made:

- Supplements applicable to the task
- Supplements applicable to operations

Supplements applicable to the task include:

- Fixed rest supplement
- Supplement for beginning and end of workday
- Supplement for incidentals
- Other supplements

The supplement applicable to the task will be the sum of all the supplements and we will call them **general supplements**. They will be calculated for the task in question:

16. Time Study with Timekeeping

General Supplements	
Rest supplements	*Quantity*
Personal needs	5%
Fatigue	4%
Working on foot	2%
Total rest supplements	**11%**
Supplements for unexpected events	*Quantity*
Unexpected	2%
Total supplements for unexpected events	**2%**
Supplements for beginning and end of workday	*Quantity*
Beginning and end of workday	3%
Total general supplements	**16%**

Figure 16.13. General supplements

The supplement applicable to each operation is:

- Additional rest supplement of the operation

This will be specified for each operation and added to the general supplement of the task in order to obtain the total supplement of the operation.

Total operation supplements = Total general supplements + Additional rest supplements to the operation

Formula 16.15

Therefore, the corrected time of the operation will be calculated using the following expression:

Corrected Operation Time = Normal Time x (1 + total Operation Supplements)

The following diagram summarizes the steps to follow to calculate the corrected time of an operation.

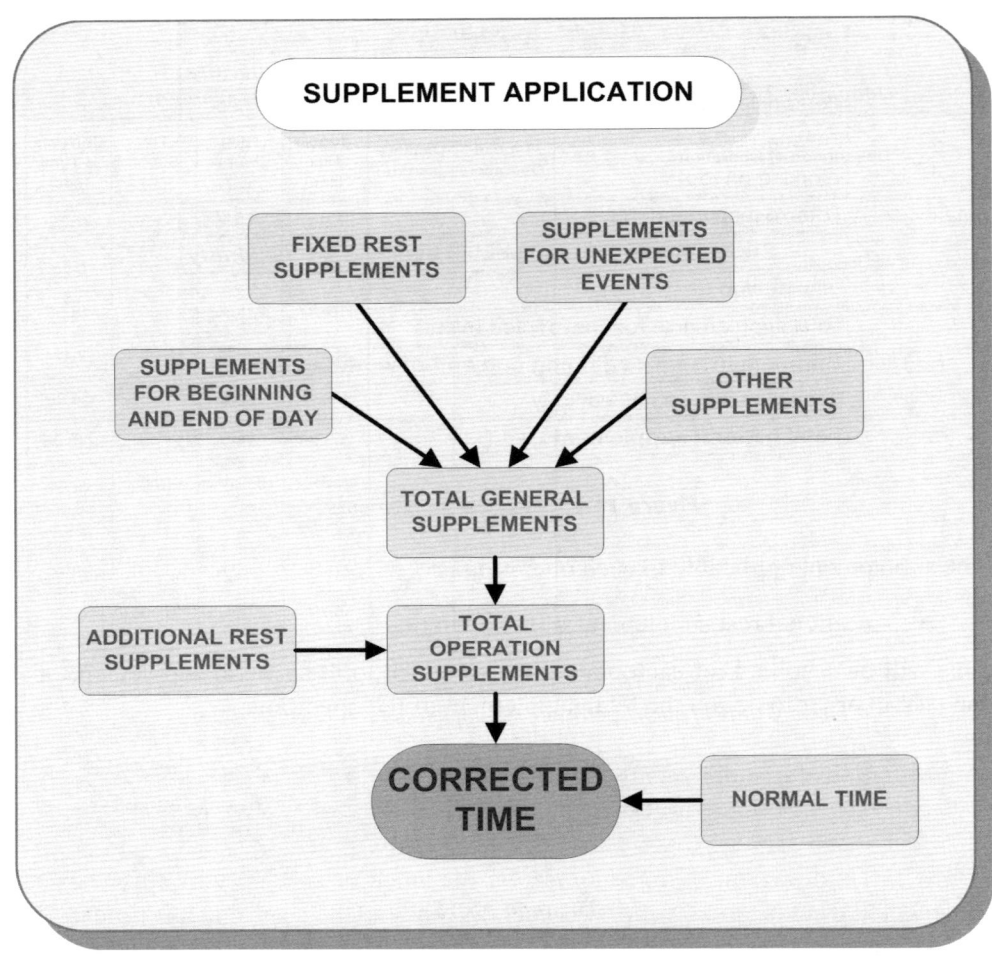

Figure 16.14. Application of supplements

Example

Document 2 - Study of methods and times of the task: Insert placement							
Description of Operation	Type of Operation	Distance (meters)	Normal Time (sec)	Addit. Suppl. (%)	Tot. Suppl. (%)	Corrected Time (sec)
Provide panel. Remove protector paper.	◯		9.33	2.00%	13.00%	10.54
Provide set of bits for drill.	◯		5.90	0.00%	11.00%	6.55
Move toward following workstation.	⇨	20.00	16.00	2.00%	13.00%	18.08
Deposit panel on worktable.	◯		1.90	2.00%	13.00%	2.15
Search and provide plans.	▭		57.91	0.00%	11.00%	64.28
Perform drill markings with pencil and ruler.	◌		206.20	0.00%	11.00%	228.88
Store plans in closet.	▽		54.42	0.00%	11.00%	60.40
Take panel.	◯		2.00	2.00%	13.00%	2.26
Move toward manual mechanizing area.	⇨	100.00	80.00	2.00%	13.00%	90.40
Deposit bits and panel in auxiliary table. Clear working area.	▽		5.78	2.00%	13.00%	6.53

Figure 16.15. Methods and times study:
Normal time of each operation + Supplements = Corrected time

Considerations for supplements:

> The rest times spent by operators (time for lunch or snacks) will never be deducted from the total workday (generally 8 hours), because that rest time is considered when calculating the corrected time or work content of each task with the application of the basic supplement for fatigue. The production must be calculated for the total of the workday, without discounting rests or others that have already been taken into account in the supplements.

These considerations will be demonstrated with a practical example.

Example

A bolt manufacturing company recently performed a methods and times study for the mechanizing of certain type of bolt. The result has been a standard time of 2.4 minutes/unit. This standard time includes all the applicable supplements that have been explained in this chapter. In order to

Industrial Productivity

calculate the production required of operators, the duration of the workday must be taken into account. Daily, the operators stop their work for a period of 20 minutes to take a coffee or snack. This stop in the middle of the workday is not stipulated in the labor agreement. What is the required production?

Option 1: *Data: 480 minutes – 20 minutes of rest = 460 minutes → 460 minutes / 2.4 minutes/unit = 192 units produced*

If these calculations were performed, we would be making a mistake. We must recall how it has been mentioned that these stops are not stipulated in the labor agreement; they do NOT have to be discounted from the total of the workday, so the correct calculation would be:

Option 2: *480 minutes / 2.4 minutes/unit = 200 units produced, the number of units enforceable*

Option 2 is the correct answer. *In the chapter dedicated to productivity control, these aspects will be explained in greater detail, as the duration of the workday can be affected by other factors such as incidentals. The enforceable or expected production of a certain quantity of unit responds to the following formula:*

$$\text{Required Production (units)} = \frac{\text{Workday lenght}}{\text{Standard Time}}$$

Formula 16.16

16.2.6. The Study of Methods and Times: Data Grouping

The next step in the study of times and methods is to calculate the total running time of a task. As has been described, the studied task has been broken down into small operations based on different criteria. Such operations have been timed by performing a corresponding scrutiny that generated the normal time of each of the operations. Subsequently, the necessary supplements are added to the normal time to determine the corrected time for each operation.

The next thing the analyst must carry out is to define the frequency with which each operation is repeated within the studied task. Normally, each of the operations that compose a task are repeated a number of times, but it does not have to be the same number for each operation. Multiplying the corrected time of each operation for the number of times that it is repeated within the task will generate the total corrected time of each operation. The sum of all the total corrected times will be the total execution time of a task.

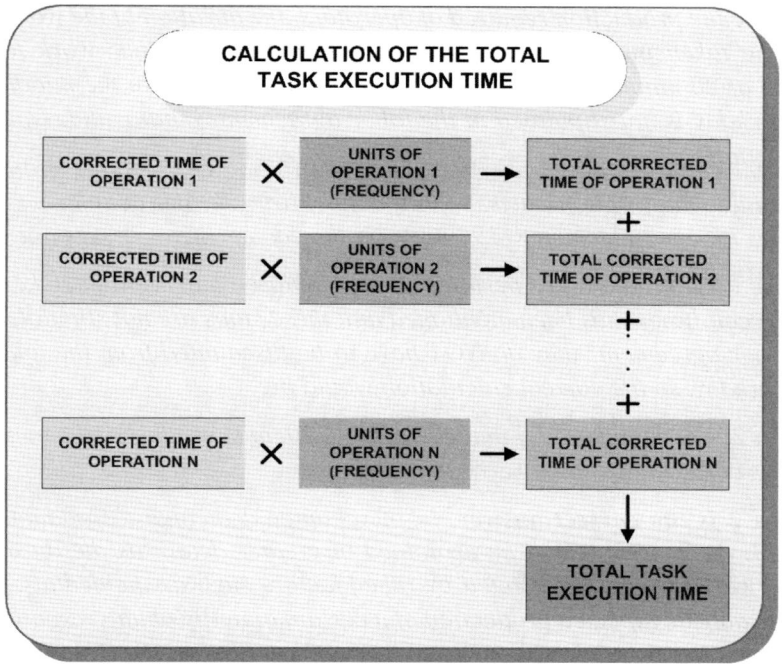

Figure 16.16. Calculation of the total execution time of a task

Example

In the operation "Manufacture of wooden blocks," and starting from the following elemental values:

- *Move table and trace: 15.00 sec.*
- *Drill a hole: 11.10 sec.*
- *Saw: 12.90 sec.*

What is the total execution time of the task if four holes must be made in the part?

The total execution time of the task would be:

- *Move table and trace: 15.00 sec. x 1 = 15.00 sec.*
- *Drill a hole: 11.10 sec. x 4 = 44.40 sec.*
- *Saw: 12.90 sec. x 1 = 12.90 sec.*

Therefore, the total execution time of the task "Manufacture of wooden blocks" is: 15.00 + 44.40 + 12.90 = 72.30 sec.

Therefore, 4 is the frequency of the operation "Drill a hole." It is the number of times that the operation is repeated in the total operation.

Example

The total time is required for the task "Drill 10 holes in a wooden strip." The analyst, once the task is observed and having performed the appropriate studies, reaches the next step (the corrected time of each operation is shown):

- *Supply pneumatic drill, drill bit setup: 16.77 sec.*
- *Connect compressed air intake: 9.54 sec.*
- *Drill a hole in wood strip: 13.34 sec.*
- *Put drill in desk and disconnect air intake: 8.45 sec.*

Then, the analyst must apply the frequency to each operation.

- *Supply pneumatic drill, drill bit setup: 16.77 sec. x 1 = 16.77 sec.*
- *Connect compressed air intake: 9.54 sec. x 1 = 9.54 sec.*
- *Drill a hole in wooden strip: 13.34 sec. x 10 holes =133.4 sec.*
- *Put drill in desk and disconnect air intake: 8.45 sec. x 1 = 8.45 sec.*

Therefore, the total execution time of the task "Drill 10 holes in a wooden strip" is: 16.77 + 9.54 + 133.4 + 8.45 = 168.16 sec.

In practice, the analyst must face studies of diverse characteristics, where the value of frequencies will depend on several factors.

To facilitate this task and provide a tool where the frequency of an operation (or any other parameter the studied operations depend on) can be easily modified, the **methods and times study** is developed.

> The methods and times studies are reality simulators and try to reflect the rationale that occurs in a task in order to quantify the necessary work time.

In the following figure, the study of methods and times is still under construction. Here we add the column "Units," in which the frequency of the operation is written down and the column "Total Corrected Time."

16. Time Study with Timekeeping

Description of Operation	Type of Operation	Distance (meters)	Normal Time (sec)	Addit. Suppl. (%)	Tot. Suppl. (%)	Corrected Time (sec)	Units	Total Corrected Time (sec)
Provide panel. Remove protector paper.	○		9.33	2.00%	17.00%	10.92	2.00	21.83
Provide set of bits for drill.	○		5.90	0.00%	15.00%	6.79	1.00	6.79
Move toward following workstation.	⇨	20.00	16.00	2.00%	17.00%	18.72	1.00	18.72
Deposit panel on worktable.	○		1.90	2.00%	17.00%	2.22	1.00	2.22
Search and provide plans.	▭		57.91	0.00%	15.00%	66.60	1.00	66.60
Perform drill markings with pencil and ruler.	◌		206.20	0.00%	15.00%	237.13	2.00	474.26
Store plans in closet.	▽		54.42	0.00%	15.00%	62.58	1.00	62.58
Take panel.	○		2.00	2.00%	17.00%	2.34	2.00	4.68
Move toward manual mechanizing area.	⇨	100.00	80.00	2.00%	17.00%	93.60	1.00	93.60
Deposit bits and panel on auxiliary table. Clear working area.	▽		5.78	2.00%	17.00%	6.76	1.00	6.76

Figure 16.17. *Studies of methods and times: Frequency and total corrected time*

The study of methods and times can be constructed for a manufacturing unit or a batch of work (multiple units). If done for a unit, the frequency ("Units") will refer to the repetitions that a work cycle has and the standard time will be the sum of the total corrected time of the operations. If done for a batch, the frequency is the repetitions per unit and per batch size and the standard time is the sum of the corrected times divided by the batch size. The result should be the same, the second way of calculating it takes into account more explicitly the batch size in the standard time of the part. The batch size affects the standard time due to the preparation tasks and noncyclical tasks. An example of this process will be explained, using the previous example "Drill 10 holes in wooden strip."

Example

Suppose we must perform this same task in eight wooden strips.

If we make the calculation for the batch of eight strips:
- *Supply pneumatic drill, drill bit setup: 16.77 sec. x 1 = 16.77 sec.*
- *Connect compressed air intake: 9.54 sec. x 1 = 9.54 sec.*
- *Drill a hole in wooden strip: 13.34 sec. x 10 holes x 8 s =1067.2 sec.*
- *Leave drill in desk and disconnect air intake: 8.45 sec. x 1 = 8.45 sec.*

Therefore, the total execution time of the task "Drill 10 holes in a wooden strip" is:

- *16.77 + 9.54 + 1067.2 + 8.45 = 1,101.96 sec. becomes the standard time as a result of dividing 1,101.96 by 8 strips → 137.75 sec/strip*

If we perform the calculation for a strip:

- *Supply pneumatic drill, drill bit setup: 16.77 sec. x 1 = 16.77 sec. → 16.77 sec. / 8 strips = 2.096 sec./strip*

- *Connect compressed air intake: 9.54 sec. x 1 = 9.54 sec. → 9.54 sec. / 8 strips = 1.19 sec./strip.*

- *Drill a hole in wooden strip: 13.34 sec. x 10 holes x 8 strips = 1067.2 sec. → 1067.2 sec. / 8 strips = 133.4 sec./strip.*

- *Put drill in desk and disconnect air intake: 8.45 sec. x 1 = 8.45 sec. → 8.45 sec. / 8 strips = 1.056 sec./strip.*

Therefore, the standard time of "Drill 10 holes in a wooden strip" is:

- *2.096 + 1.19 + 133.4 + 1.056 = 137.75 sec./strip is the standard time, the same result as performing the operation in the previous way.*

Both ways are valid; it depends on how we want to represent the information.

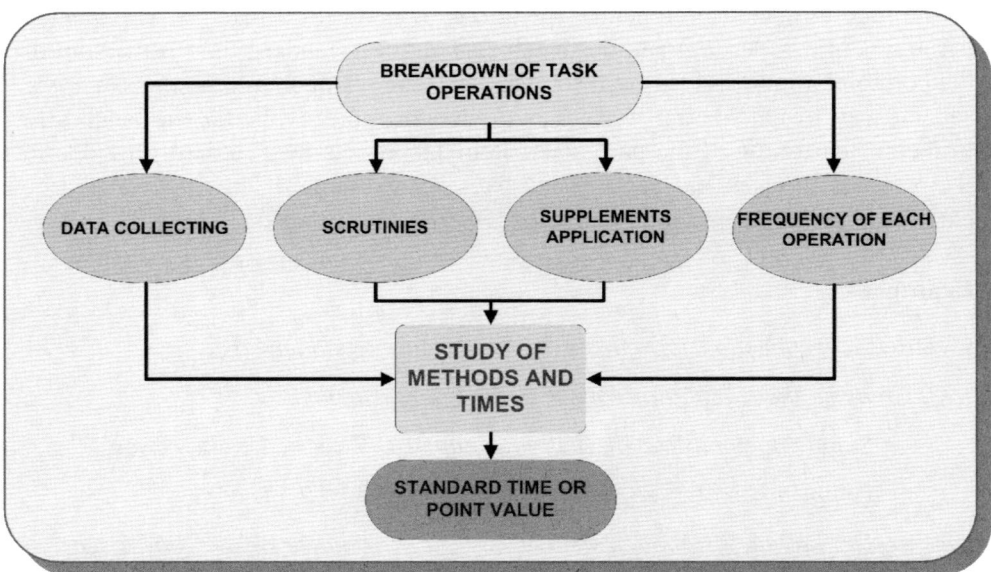

Figure 16.18. Data grouping for the study of methods and times

16. Time Study with Timekeeping

A similar example to the previous will be used to explain in a clearer way each of the elements that participate in the fulfillment of the methods and times study of the task. It has been divided into two parts or documents:

- *Document 1*: Task data and summary of the study of times and methods
- *Document 2*: Study of times and methods of the task

Document 1 details each and every parameter that affects the calculation of the total execution time of the task along with data relative to the study. Document 2 shows the breakdown of the studied task into operations, its frequency, applicable supplements, and so on. We have identified each of the tables of the study and provided a brief explanation of each field.

Document 1: Task data and summary of the study of methods and times.

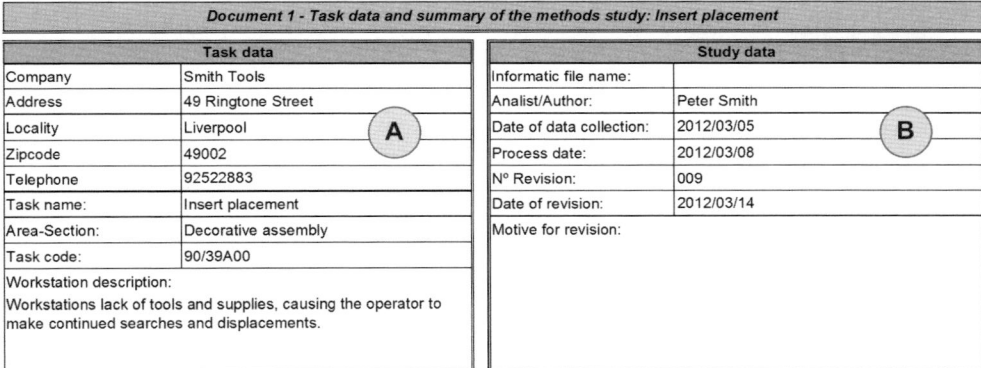

Figure 16.19a. Document 1: Task and study data

Industrial Productivity

Parameters of order / product		
Description of ordered parameter	Quantity	Units
Quantity of pannels to process.	2,00	pannel
Quantity of inserts per pannel.	4,00	inserts

Technical parameters		
Description of technical parameter	Quantity	Units
Speed on foot.	0,80	sec/metres
Distance from Assemble Area 1 to 2.	120,0	metres
Distance from Injected Area to supervisor.	10,0	metres
Distance from drilling workstation to packaging	20,00	metres

Suplements		
Rest supplements		Quantity
Personal needs.		5%
Fatigue.		4%
Being on foot.		2%
Total rest supplements.		11%
Supplements for unexpected events		Quantity
Unexpected.		2%
Total supplements for unexpected events		2%
Supplements for beginning and end of workday		Quantity
Beginning and end of workday		2%
Total general supplements		15%

Statistical parameters		
Description of statistical parameter	Quantity	Units
Quantity of inserts injected per kit.	264,00	units/kit
Average quantity of inserts per pannel.	24,00	units

Figure 16.19b. Document 2: Parameters and general supplements

Cuadro resumen de métodos y tiempos	
Description	Min/Unit
Standard time.	16,91
Workforce cost (€/hour)	35,00
Worforce cost per unit (€/unit)	9,87
Total displacements (metres)	152,00
Clasification of operations	Min/Unit
Total value adding operations.	7,37
Total non value adding operations.	9,54
Total displacements.	2,03
Total storages.	0,79
Total waits.	0,00
Total inspections.	0,00
Total inspection-operation.	1,26
Total searches.	0,55
Total eliminable operations.	4,92
Total communications.	0,00
Waste by method coefficient (CwM)	1,56

Figure 16.19c. Document 1: Summary table of methods and times

A) *Task data:* Shows the location of the company to which the task object of study belongs as well as identifies the task and briefly describes the workplace where such task is executed.

16. Time Study with Timekeeping

B *Study data:* Shows the name of the analyst and of the operator who executed the studied task, the date of the data collection, the date of study processing, and the number of revisions. These data are important for future work-method modifications.

C *Parameters of the Order/Product:* These types of parameters are relative to the dimension of the order and the physical characteristics of the product and their possible variants.

D *Technical parameters*: Parameters whose value is measureable (e.g., the cutting speed of a table saw, the distance between two locations, etc.).

E *Statistical parameters:* Parameters that can influence the frequency and/or time of the operations, whose value is not fixed from one cycle to another and, therefore, are not precise. We have to perform statistical analysis for their calculation.

F *Supplements:* Percentage supplements that are applied to the normal time, either rest supplements, incidentals, or beginning and end of the workday, etc.

G *Summary table of times:* Shows the resulting data from the study.

- **Standard time (or point value):**

    - For a study made for of a unit product:

$$\text{Standard Time} = \sum \text{Corrected time of each operation}$$

Formula 16.17

    - For the study made of a work batch:

$$\text{Standard Time} = \frac{\text{Total task execution time}}{\text{Batch/order size}}$$

Formula 16.18

Industrial Productivity

- **Workforce cost:** indicates the cost of workforce per hour.
- **Workforce cost per unit:** indicates the workforce cost that each unit produced will have in that task.
- **Total displacements**: indicates the quantity of distances traveled in producing a unit.
- **Classification of operations:** quantity of each operation based on its type, either transfer, storage, added value, etc. When analyzing each task in order to improve it, we will focus our attention on those operations that are non-value-adding.

The standard time in the example task "Placing inserts in panels" from the study of methods and times is as follows:

- The total execution time of the task: 2,029.42 seconds → 33.82 minutes
- The batch size: 2 panels
- Standard time: 33.82 minutes / 2 units = 16.91 minutes/unit

Document 2: Methods and times study of the task: Calculation of standard time.

Description of operation	Type of operation	Distance (Metres)	Normal time (sec)	Addit. Suppl. (%)	Tot. Suppl. (%)	Corrected Time (Sec)	Units	Total Corrected Time (secs)
Provision pannel. Remove protector paper.	○		9,33	2,00%	17,00%	10,92	2,00	21,83
Provision set of bits for drill.	○		5,90	0,00%	15,00%	6,79	1,00	6,79
Displacement towards following workstation.	⇨	20,00	16,00	2,00%	17,00%	18,72	1,00	18,72
Deposit pannel on worktable.	○		1,90	2,00%	17,00%	2,22	1,00	2,22
Search and provision of plans.	▯		57,91	0,00%	15,00%	66,60	1,00	66,60
Perform drill markings with pencil and ruler.	⟲		206,20	0,00%	15,00%	237,13	2,00	474,26
Store plans in closet.	▽		54,42	0,00%	15,00%	62,58	1,00	62,58
Take pannel.	○		2,00	2,00%	17,00%	2,34	2,00	4,68
Displacement towards manual mechanizing area.	⇨	100,00	80,00	2,00%	17,00%	93,60	1,00	93,60
Deposit bits and pannel in auxiliary table. Clear working area.	▽		5,78	2,00%	17,00%	6,76	1,00	6,76
						Total task execution time:		758,04
						Tiempo Estándar:		379,02

Figure 16.20. Document 2: Methods and times study of the task

16. Time Study with Timekeeping

(1) *Description of the Operation:* This field must describe the operation using technical and concise language, without leaving out any important characteristic of the operation.

(2) *Type of Operation:* The graphic representation of the type of operation indicates everything that is non-value-adding or inspection-operations, and therefore should be eliminated.

(3) *Distance (meters):* The distance traveled is used to calculate the time of transfer operations. The distance in traveled meters is multiplied by the constant 0.80 seconds/meter. (This value comes from the normal pattern of activity for walking, converting the units of 4.5 km/hour to 0.80 sec/m.) This box will be filled in when the operation requires transfer.

(4) *Normal Time (sec):* The normal time of the operation in seconds can be obtained with any of the time measurement systems described. In the case of timekeeping, they are obtained through scrutiny.

(5) *Addit. Suppl. (%) [Additional Supplements]:* Exclusive supplements from each of the operations that compose the process diagram, which are due to the conditions of the workplace or the nature of the performed operation.

(6) *Tot. Suppl. (%) [Total Supplements]:* It is the sum of the fixed supplements for all the operations of the F table, along with the additional supplements of each operation.

(7) *Corrected Time (sec):* It is the normal time once all pertinent supplements are applied.

(8) *Units:* Corresponds to the frequency of the operation during the fulfillment of a task. Each operation will have its unit.

(9) *Total Corrected Time:* Obtained from multiplying the corrected time by its frequency ("Units"), it is the total corrected time of each operation expressed in seconds.

(10) *Total execution time of the task:* It is the sum of the total corrected times of the operations.

(11) *Standard Time:* If the study of methods and times has been made for one unit, it will be the same as the total execution time of a task. If it has been calculated per batch, it will be divided between the batch units.

16.3. Time Studies with Machines

16.3.1. Concepts and Definitions

Work cycle with machine

The work cycle with machine consists of different components:

From/for the machine:

- *Machine stopped*
- *Machine running*

From/for the operator:

- *Operations of stopped machine:* correspond to operations performed by the operator outside the machine time, when the machine is stopped
- *Operations of running machine:* operations performed by the operator within the machine time, when the machine is running

As described in Chapter 5, within the work cycle with machine, it may or may not be in operation, which needs to be taken into account when performing the study of times and methods.

Figure 16.21 illustrates the described concepts:

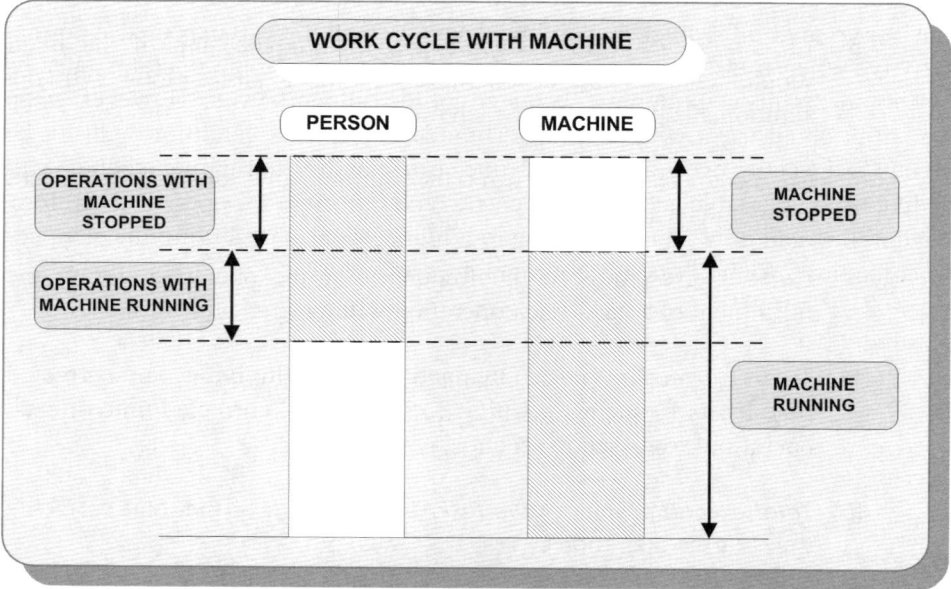

Figure 16.21. Work cycle with machine

Limited work

Until now we have treated studies of methods and times where the amount of work the operator can perform is not subject to limit. Because it is open work, the activity of the operator depends exclusively on the individual person. Open works are, in general, purely manual. What happens when the operator cannot deploy all his or her skills or abilities? How are operations affected? What considerations must be made? To this circumstance, we apply the label **limited work**.

> Limited work is that in which the operator who executes it cannot deploy all the capacity of which he or she is able, for some reason beyond the control of the individual operator, such as the machine, the characteristics of the proper work, or the intervention of other operators.

When performing a study of methods and times, several operations performed by an operator could be executed freely, more slowly or quickly, and others will be limited by the machine with which they interact.

The machine plays an important role when performing the methods and times study. Its influence not only applies to the speed at which it manufactures a part, but also to the quality of the materials, the conditions of the workplace, the characteristics of the part to process, the preparation and supply time of the part, among others.

According to the activity scales (Bedaux 60-80 and centesimal 100-133), a task can be executed 33% quicker at optimum activity than if it was executed at normal activity. When a task is free, when no conditions outside the operator alter its development, this condition will be given for the full work cycle. However, when we speak about tasks with machines (limited labor), this condition will not be given for the entire cycle because the time corresponding to running machine will be fixed and invariable and will not depend on the work of the operator, therefore, the duration can only be reduced due to a higher work pace during the stopped-machine time. We will see this point graphically.

Industrial Productivity

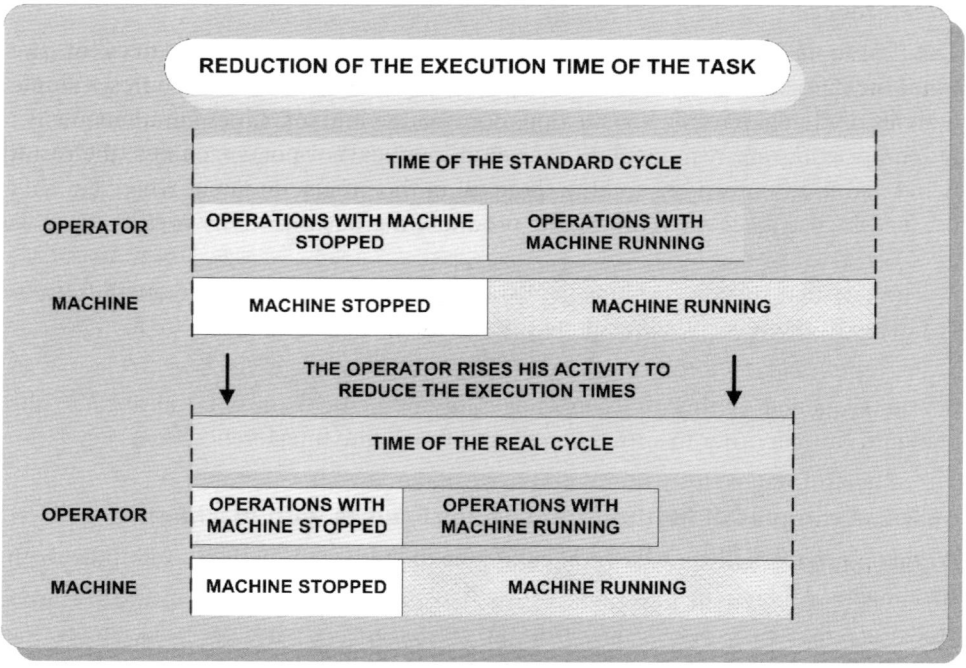

Figure 16.22. Reduction of the execution time of the task

As observed in Figure 16.22, the period of time that can be reduced due to the operator's skills is that in which the machine is stopped. So if we wish to calculate the optimum time to execute a task, whenever it is performed with a machine, we must use the following formula:

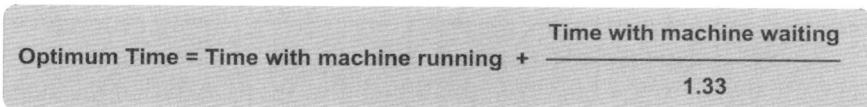

Formula 16.19

Never will a machine time be divided by 1.33 to calculate the optimum time of an operation or a task. The motive is that the machine time is limiting and is supposed to be fixed. Time can only be reduced during the stopped machine part of the cycle.

Interferences

The last concept that still requires explanation is the **interferences of the machines**. So far we have seen tasks in which a single operator handles a single machine. What happens when the operator uses several machines simultaneously? Often operators are responsible for several identical (or not) machines; the result is the inability to always attend to them all in the precise moment when it would be necessary, triggering delays in the production process.

> The fact that several machines are waiting to be attended by the operator in charge of them is called machine interference.

As consequence of these circumstances, a supplement must be applied to the standard time in order to soften the effect of machine interference.

16.3.2. Examples of Methods and Times Studies with Machines

At this point we will show several examples of studies of methods and times with machines.

Example

A factory makes handles for doors and drawers. Figure 16.23a shows the graph of the task.

Graph of the task method: Doorknob polishing

Operator			Plishing machine		
Subtasks of the Operator	Sec/Unit	State	State	Sec/Unit	Subtasks of the Machine
Push button to change cart.	3.320			-	Waiting time.
Place doorknobs on polishing tool.	120.360			-	Waiting time.
Waiting time.	-			285.230	Polishing cycle.
Remove processed doorknobs.	142.320			-	Waiting time.

Figure 16.23a. *Graph of the task method*

All the tasks (or operations in this case) performed by the operator and by the machine are simultaneously grouped in the column labeled "Subtasks," indicating in each moment the state of the participant, for both the operator and the machine. Each task will have attached its pertinent study of times and methods (similar to the study of a free task) that will justify the value obtained in each block. The following figure displays the study of times and methods of the task "Remove processed handles."

Industrial Productivity

Document 2 - Study of methods and times of the task: Remove processed doorknobs								
Description of Operation	Type of Operation	Distance (Metres)	Normal Time (sec)	Addit. Suppl. (%)	Tot. Suppl. (%)	Corrected Time (sec)	Units	Total Corrected Time (sec)
Remove flanges from doorknob. Take down security flanges.	◯		16.35	0.00%	6.00%	17.33	1.00	17.33
Remove doorknob batch and deposit in transport cart.	◯		112.03	0.00%	6.00%	118.75	1.00	118.75
Seal job order.	◯		5.88	0.00%	6.00%	6.23	1.00	6.23

Workstation	N° Operators	Standard Time	Saturation
Remove processed doorknobs	1	2.37%	48.26%

Figure 16.23b. *Study of methods and times of the task*

Then, the "Report of the simultaneous task" contains the same information as the previous preliminary studies, such as saturation of the participants, standard time, cycle time, work time, or number of participants.

Report of the simultaneous task				
Workstation	N° interveners	Work time (minutes/unit)	Cycle time (minutes/unit)	Standard time (minutes/unit)	Saturation
Total task	2	9.19	9.19	9.19	50.00%
Operators	1	4.43	9.19		48.26%
Machines	1	4.75	9.19		51.74%

Figure 16.23c. *Report of the simultaneous task*

The work time of each participant corresponds to operating time, without including the waiting time to which the operator is subjected by other participants (for an operator it would be the same as saying person-time).

- Cycle time = 9.19 minutes/unit
- Standard time = 9.19 minutes/unit, when multiplying 9.19 minutes by one operator

Example

For an example of the task of packing a table, the graph of the task method will be as follows:

16. Time Study with Timekeeping

Graph of the task method: Table packaging		

Operator				Baler		
Subtasks of the Operator	Sec / Unit	State	State	Sec / Unit	Subtasks of the Machine
Take table from packaging area and move to the entrance of baler.	33.30			-	Pause time.
Place quality labels on table.	66.60			-	Pause time.
Put table in baler and activate.	22.20			-	Pause time.
Waiting time.	-			100.00	Packaging time per unit.
Remove table from baler.	33.30			-	Pause time.

Report of the simultaneous task						
Workst.	N° interveners	Work time (minutes/unit)	Cycle time (minutes/unit)	Standard time (minutes/unit)	Saturation	
Total task	2	255.40	255.40	255.40	50.00%	
Operators	1	155.40	255.40		60.85%	
Machines	1	100.00	255.40		39.15%	

Figure 16.24. Graph of the method and report of the simultaneous task

As observed in the example, during operator performance of the task, the machine waits; and when the machine performs its task, it is the operator who is idle. In these conditions, in order to calculate the standard time, it is necessary to add the times of the operator, both of operation and of waiting.

- Cycle time = 255.40 seconds
- Standard time = 255.40/60 = 4.25 minutes/unit, this value is multiplied by the number of operators, that in this case is one operator

Example

A trousers plant has a cutting area in which a machine performs the pattern cutting. The functioning of this machine is simple; the operator supplies a roll of cloth, loads the program of pattern cutting and then collects the cutting patterns, while the machine continues to work. The work outline could be: preparation time, processed time, and workplace ordering time.

Because the machine is managed by a personal computer, it must process the information to cut the cloth patterns. Pattern shapes and sizes are variable, and as a result, the operator remains idle, while waiting for the machine to finish cutting a cloth. The opposite may also occur: due to the size and shape of the patterns, they are easily cut by the machine that supplies the operator with large amounts of patterns, keeping the operator totally busy. In this particular scenario and for the trousers that were going to be cut, the machine invests less time in cutting the cloth patterns, and the operator *experiences maximum saturation. In order to avoid this situation and reduce the cycle time of the task, the two operators are provided whenever this situation occurs.*

Graph of the task method: Pattern cutting

Operator				Machine		
Subtasks of the Operator	**Sec / Unit**	**State**	**State**	**Sec / Unit**	**Subtasks of the Machine**	
Preparatory tasks.	153.75			-	Pause time.	
Provision of fabric patterns.	339.52			325.05	Cutting and labeling time.	
				-	Pause time.	
Classification of fabric kits.	295.32			-	Pause time.	
Workstation ordering.	403.63			-	Pause time.	

Figure 16.25a. *Graph of the task method*

Applicable supplements	
Personal needs	5.0%

Report on the simultaneous task					
Workst.	**N° interveners**	**Work time (minutes/unit)**	**Cycle time (minutes/unit)**	**Standard time (minutes/unit)**	**Saturation**
Total task	3	25.29	20.86	41.73	60.60%
Operators	2	19.87	20.86		95.24%
Machines	1	5.42	20.86		25.97%

Figure 16.25b. *Report of the simultaneous task*

- *Cycle time = 20.86 minutes/unit*
- *Standard time = 41.73 minutes/unit, multiplying 20.86 minutes by two operators*

In this example, the box "Applicable supplements" appears after the graph of the task method instead of being included in the study of methods and times of each task, as previously explained. In the following section, we will justify the application of the supplements for personal needs in works with machines.

16.3.3. Supplement Considerations for Tasks with Machines

Considerations when applying rest supplements

When a task is cataloged as limited work, the analyst, when applying the rest supplements, must differentiate the fatigue supplement from the supplement for personal needs. The reason is that the supplement for personal needs must be applied to the whole work cycle, which logically includes the machine-running time and the operations performed by the operator while the machine is paused. The rest supplement for personal needs must correspond to the totality of time that the operator remains in the factory, while the fatigue supplement is necessary for the task in itself (without including the waiting time), applying to the exact amount of work performed. How to deal with this situation will be shown in this subsection.

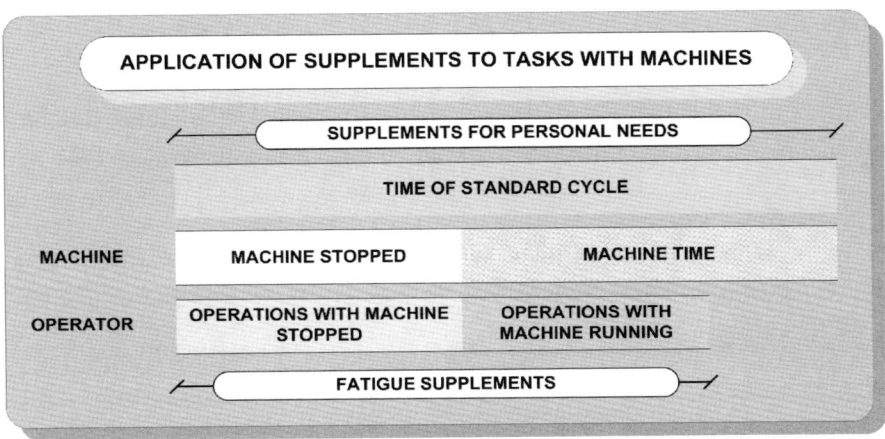

Figure 16.26. Considerations for the application of supplements in tasks with machines

Once the applicable supplement is calculated by the analyst, the analyst needs to confirm whether the operator can use this supplement as a whole or only in part within the cycle time or if this supplement must be added to the cycle time with the purpose of obtaining the real cycle time. What does this mean? If the cycle time is large and includes time periods in which the operator remains idle, it is possible that the operator can make use of these supplements in those idle periods. For supplements due to personal needs this possibility is considered only in idle periods of more than 10 minutes, provided that they are uninterrupted and the operator can leave the machine operating automatically without supervision.

However, it is much more common that the supplement for personal needs is applied to the total time of the cycle, because it is a waiting time of short duration. Suppose a task has a machine cycle of 2 minutes and a waiting time of 52 seconds. Obviously, the operator has no chance to use such supplement for personal needs during the machine-running cycle. The same occurs with the fatigue supplements, the operator can use brief spaces of waiting time to relax. Any period of less than 30 seconds cannot be considered as useful time to recover. For periods between 30 and 90 seconds, the useful time for resting must be calculated by subtracting 30 seconds from the real duration period and multiplying the result by 1.5. The following table provides an example for these different situations:

Uninterrupted waiting time	Calculation time	Time usable for rest
30 seconds	-	-
60 seconds	30 seconds	45 seconds
75 seconds	45 seconds	67.5 seconds
90 seconds	60 seconds	90 seconds

Source:
Introduction to Work Study © 1996, **International Labor Organization.**

The following illustration shows how to proceed for calculating the fatigue supplements of work with machines, based on the waiting time.

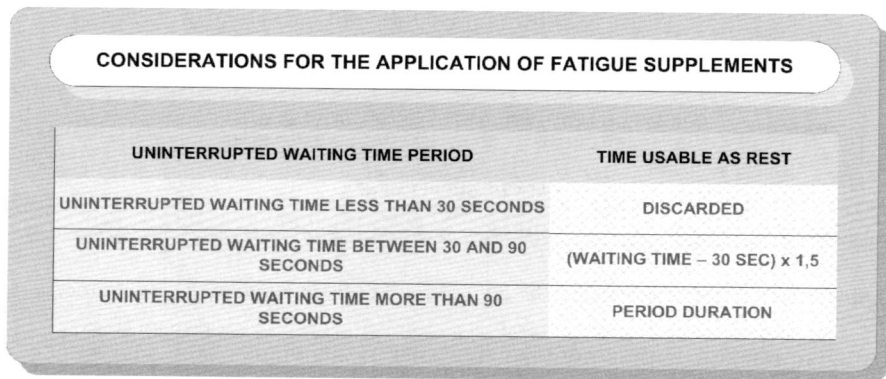

Figure 16.27. Considerations when applying supplements for fatigue

Therefore, the way the rest supplement should be treated depends at the same time on the duration of the cycle and the characteristics of the operations performed with the machine running, being able to distinguish four scenarios:

- The supplements for personal needs and fatigue must be applied entirely outside the cycle time.

16. Time Study with Timekeeping

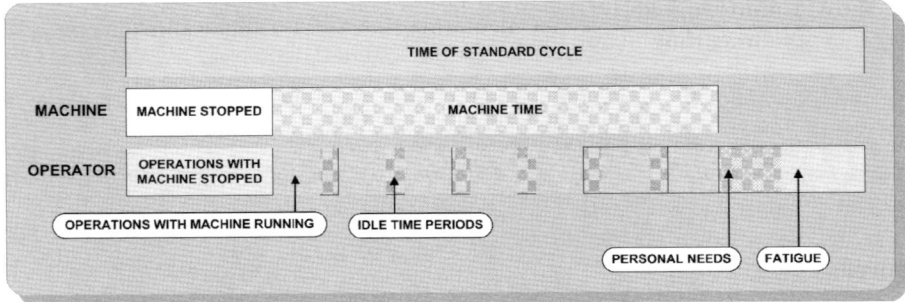

Figure 16.28. Scenario 1: Both supplements are applied outside the cycle time

- The supplements for personal needs must be applied outside the cycle time, but the fatigue supplement can be applied entirely inside it.

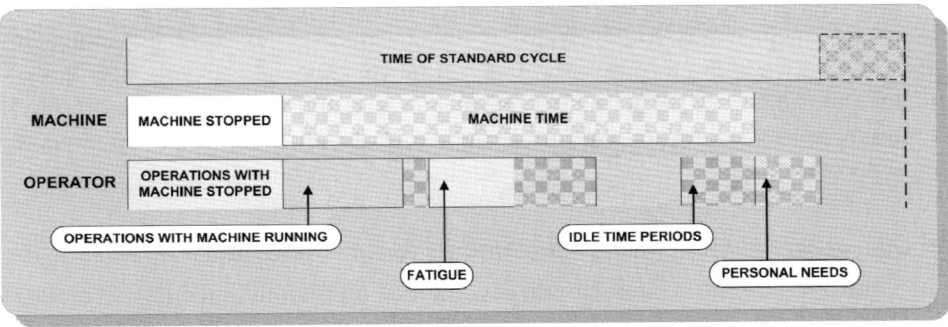

Figure 16.29. Scenario 2: Supplement for personal needs applied outside the cycle time

- The supplements for personal needs and a part of the fatigue supplements can be applied outside the cycle time, but the rest of the supplement for fatigue can be applied within the cycle.

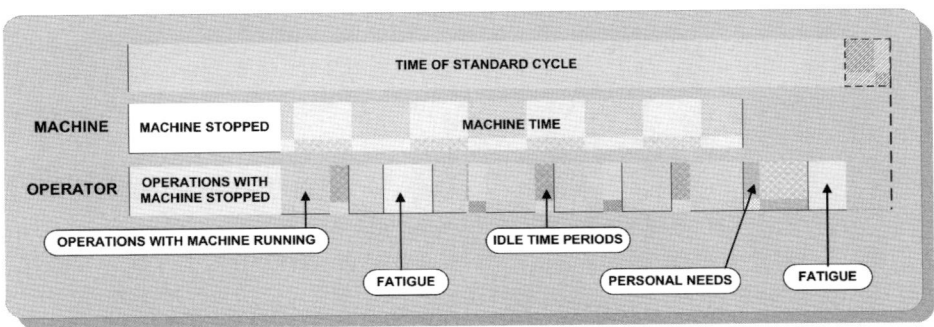

Figure 16.30. Scenario 3: Fatigue supplement applied inside and outside the cycle time

Industrial Productivity

- The supplements for personal needs and the fatigue supplement can be applied entirely inside the cycle time.

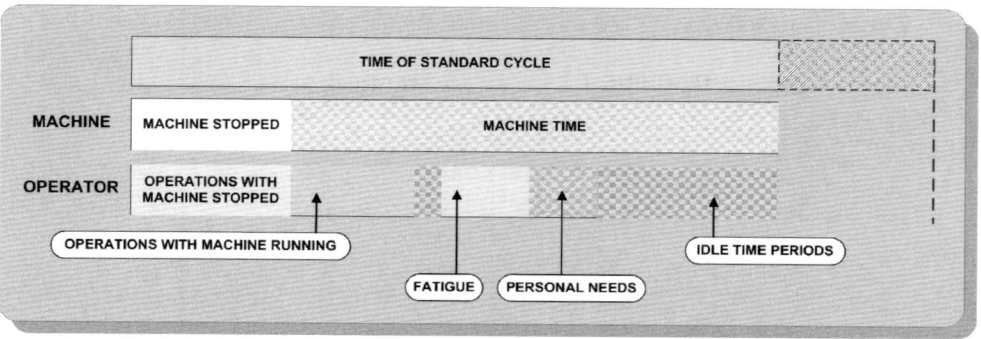

Figure 16.31. Scenario 4: Both supplements are applied entirely inside the cycle time

Observing the previous four scenarios, we see that the existing difference in cycle time between the four possibilities can be checked, so logically it will also influence in the daily production. Consequently, the analyst should bear in mind all these aspects in order to avoid prejudicial mistakes for both the company and the group of workers.

Considerations when applying supplements for machine interferences

When one operator must interact with several machines simultaneously, at certain times, any of them can stop, and will remain in that position until the operator ends the supervision of the machine being handled at that moment. For this reason, an interference supplement must be applied to consider these times the machine stops. Figure 16.32 portrays the effect of the interference on an operator interacting with two machines.

16. Time Study with Timekeeping

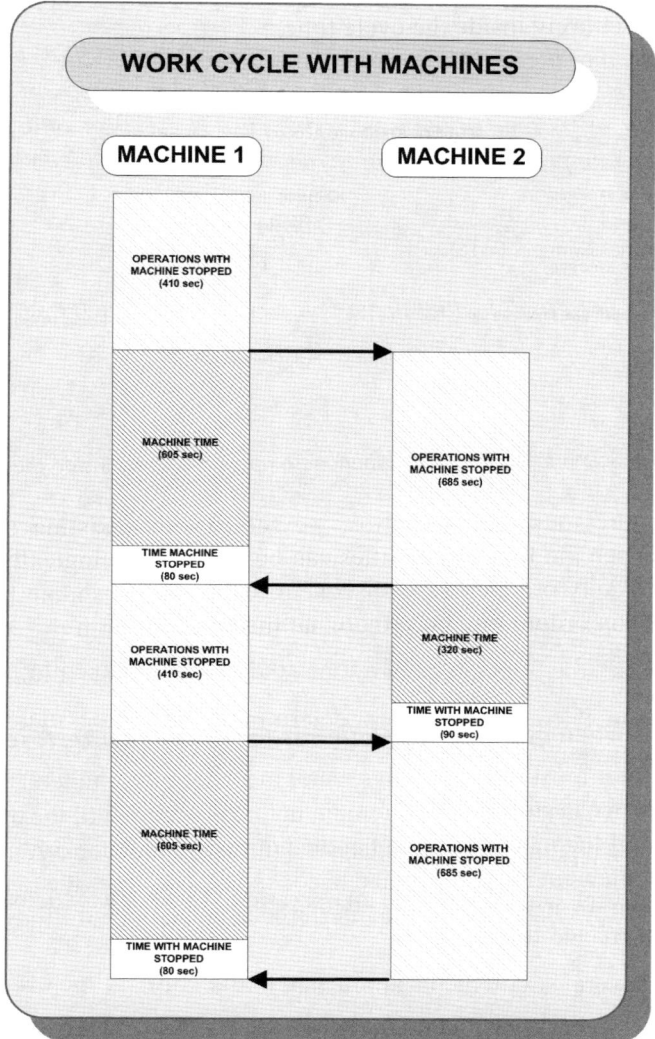

Figure 16.32. Machine interferences

As shown, while the operator is handling machine 2, machine 1 waits to be handled. In the same way, when the operator handles machine 1, machine 2 remains waiting. Calculating interference supplements requires a study of times and methods, which determines the total time that any machine remains stopped. These precise measurements need to be done for several days and after a sufficient amount of data is obtained, the analyst performs the scrutiny as if it was another operation. We will solve the example of Figure 16.32:

Example

After performing the study of methods and times, we see that during each work-cycle, machine 1 waits for 80 seconds, while machine 2 waits for 90 seconds. The cycle time of the task in this case is 2,190 seconds. Knowing the data, we can proceed to calculate the interference supplement:

$$\frac{170}{(2190-170)} = 0.0841 \rightarrow 8.41\%$$

The formula used to calculate the supplement for unexpected events would be:

$$\text{Interference supplement} = 100 \times \frac{\sum \text{Interference Times}}{\text{Cycle Time} - \sum \text{Interference Times}}$$

Questions

1. List the existing timekeeping techniques.
2. What are the four stages of a time study with timekeeping?
3. What are the methods used for determining the number of data collections of an operation?
4. What is a scrutiny?
5. What two parameters are measured through timekeeping?
6. What is the work content of an operation? In what way does it differ from the corrected time?
7. List several supplements applicable to the normal time of an operation.
8. What are the studies of methods and times?
9. What does *limited work* mean?
10. What is meant by machine interference?

Problem I

1. Given the following group of samples of activity and time, perform the scrutiny that will generate the normal time of the operation.

Activity	Time	Activity	Time
3,99	80	6,56	70
6,78	75	5,32	80
9,05	60	13,26	50
8,48	60	8,58	60
10,23	50	8,59	60
12,36	55	8,62	60
8,87	60	7,1	75
8,56	60	4,01	80
7,98	65	9,62	55

Problem 2

2. Operations of the task "Process square steel plate" include the following:

- Take square plate from steel plate: 5.76 sec.
- Polish one face of the plate: 14.1 sec.
- Round a corner: 9.9 sec.
- Take drill: 13.98 sec.
- Make a hole with the drill: 13.44 sec.
- Leave drill on workbench: 18.78 sec.
- Leave processed plate: 6.72 sec.

Considering the normal times shown for each operation and keeping in mind that the operator must polish both faces of the plate, round all the corners, and make five holes, calculate the standard time of the task. The weight of the plate is 10 kilograms.

Bibliography

Kanawaty, George, *Introduction to Work Study* (Geneva: International Labor Organization, 1992).

Chapter 17

Work Sampling and Structured Estimating

Much of the material in this chapter is based on the book *Introduction to Work Study*, and used with permission of the International Labor Organization (1996).

> Work sampling is a method of finding the percentage occurrence of a certain activity through statistical sampling and random observations

17.1. The Need for Work Sampling

Work sampling (also known as "activity sampling," "ratio-delay study," "random observation method," "snap-reading method," and "observation ratio study") is, as the name implies, a sampling technique. Let us first see why such a technique is needed.

In order to obtain a complete and accurate picture of the productive time and idle time of the machines in a specific production area, it would be necessary to observe continuously all the machines in that area and to record when and why any of the machines were stopped. It would of course be quite impossible to do this unless a large number of workers spent the whole of their time on this task alone—an unrealistic proposition.

If it were possible to note at a glance the state of every machine in a factory at a given moment, however, it might be found that, say, 80 percent of the machines were working and 20 percent were stopped. If this action was repeated 20 or more times at different times of the day and if each time the proportion of machines working was always 80 percent, it would be possible to say with some confidence that at any one time 80 percent of the machines will be working.

Because it is not generally possible to do this either, the next best method involves making tours of the factory at random intervals, noting which machines are working and which are stopped, and noting the cause of each stoppage. This approach is the basis of the **work sampling** technique. When the sample size is large enough and the observations made are indeed at random, the probability is high that these observations will reflect the real situation, plus or minus a certain margin of error.

17.2. A Few Words About Sampling

Unlike the costly and impractical method of continuous observation, sampling is mainly based on **probability**. Probability has been defined as "the extent to which an event is likely to occur." A simple and often-mentioned example that illustrates the point is that of tossing a coin. When we toss a coin two outcomes are possible: that it will come down "heads" or that it will come down "tails." The law of probability says that we are likely to have 50 heads and 50 tails in every 100 tosses of the coin. Note that we use the phrase "likely to have." In fact, we might have a score of 55–45, say, or 48–52, or some other ratio. But it has been shown that the law becomes increasingly accurate as the number of tosses increases. In other words, the greater the number of tosses, the more chance we have of arriving at a ratio of 50 heads to 50 tails. This suggests that the larger the size of the sample, the more accurate or representative it becomes with respect to the original "population," or group of items under consideration.

We can therefore visualize a scale where, at one end, we can have complete accuracy achieved by continuous observation and, at the other end, doubtful results derived from a few observations only. The size of the sample is therefore important, and we can express our confidence in whether the sample is representative by using a certain **confidence level**.

17.3. Establishing Confidence Levels

Let us go back to our previous example and toss five coins at a time, and then record the number of times we have heads and the number of times we have tails for each toss of these five coins. Let us then repeat this operation 100 times. The results would resemble those in Figure 17.1 or graphically as in Figure 17.2.

17. Work Sampling and Structured Estimating

If we considerably increase the number of tosses and in each case toss a large number of coins at a time, we can obtain a smoother curve, such as that shown in Figure 17.3.

Combination		Number of Combinations
Heads (p)	Tails (q)	
5	0	3
4	1	17
3	2	30
2	3	30
1	4	17
0	5	3
		100

Figure 17.1. Proportional distribution of "heads" and "tails"
(100 tosses of five coins at a time)

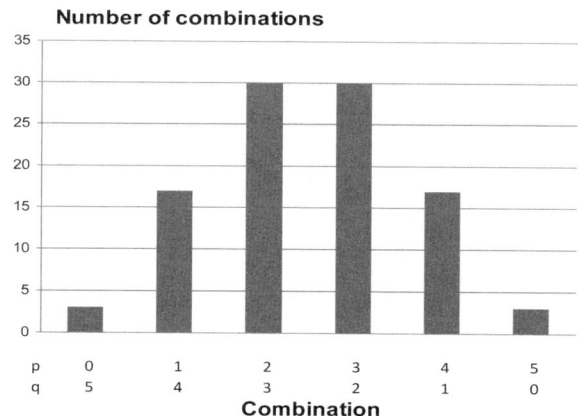

Figure 17.2. Proportional distribution of "heads" and "tails"
(100 tosses of five coins at a time).

585

Industrial Productivity

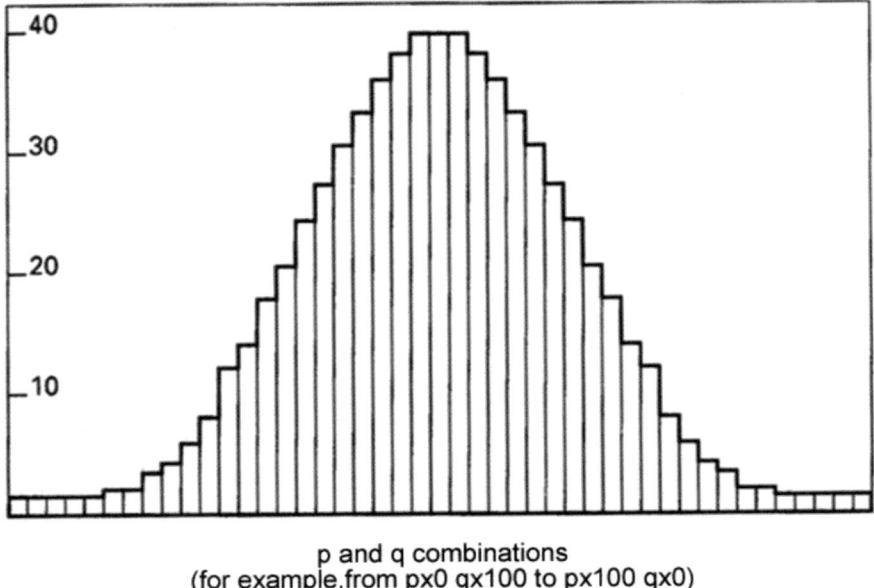

p and q combinations
(for example, from px0 qx100 to px100 qx0)

Figure 17.3. *Distribution curve showing probabilities of combinations when large samples are used*

This curve, called the **curve of normal distribution**, may also be depicted as shown in Figure 17.4. Basically, this curve tells us that, in the majority of cases, the tendency is for the number of heads to equal the number of tails in any one series of tosses (when p = q, the number of tosses is a maximum). In few cases, however, p is markedly different from q due to mere chance.

Curves of normal distribution may take many shapes. They may be flatter or more rounded. To describe these curves we use two attributes: $\bar{x}$, which is the average or measure of central dispersion; and a, which is the deviation from the average, referred to as standard deviation. Because we are dealing with a proportion in this case, we use op to denote the standard error of the proportion.

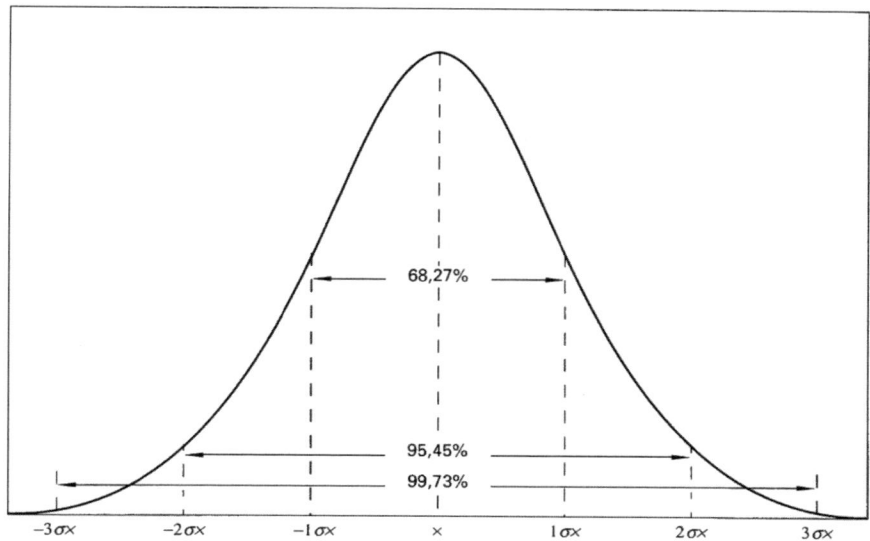

Figure 17.4. *Curve of normal distribution*

The area under the curve of normal distribution can be calculated. In Figure 17.4, one op on both sides of $\bar{x}$ gives an area of 68.27% of the total area; two op on both sides of $\bar{x}$ gives an area of 95.45%; and three op on both sides of $\bar{x}$ gives an area of 99.73%. We can put this in another way and say that, when free of bias in our random sampling, 95.45% of all our observations will fall within $\bar{x} \pm 2\ op$ and 99.73 percent of all our observations will fall within $\bar{x} \pm 3\ op$.

It is in fact the degree of confidence we have in our observations. To make things easier, however, we try to avoid using decimal percentages; it is more convenient to speak of a 95% confidence level than of a 95.45% confidence level. For simplicity, we can change our calculations and obtain:

- 95% confidence level or 95% of the area under the curve = 1.96 *op*
- 99% confidence level or 99% of the area under the curve = 2.58 *op*
- 99.9% confidence level or 99.9% of the area under the curve = 3.3 *op*

In this case, if we take a large sample at random we can be confident that in 95% of the cases our observations will fall within ±1.96 *op*.

In work sampling the most commonly used level is the 95% confidence level.

17.4. Determination of Sample Size

As well as defining the confidence level for our observations we have to decide on the margin of error that we can allow for these observations. We must be able

Industrial Productivity

to say that: "We are confident that 95% of the time, this particular observation is correct within ±5%, or 10%," or whatever other range of accuracy we may decide on.

Let us now return to our example about the productive time and the idle time of the machines in a factory. Two methods of determining the sample size would be appropriate for this example: the statistical method and the nomogram method.

17.4.1 Statistical Method

The formula used in this method is:

$$\sigma p = \sqrt{pq/n}$$

Where:

- op = standard error of proportion
- p = percentage of idle time
- q = percentage of working time
- n = number of observations or sample size we wish to determine

Before we can use this formula, however, we need to have at least an idea of the values of p and q. The first step is therefore to carry out a number of random observations in the working area. Let us assume that some 100 observations were carried out as a preliminary study and at random, and that these showed the machine to be idle in 25% of the cases (p = 25) and to be working 75% of the time (q = 75). We thus have approximate values for p and q; in order now to determine the value of n, we must find out the value of op.

Let us choose a confidence level of 95% with a 10% margin of error (that is, we are confident that in 95% of the cases our estimates will be ± 10% of the real value).

At the 95% confidence level:

1.96 op = 10

σp = 5 (approx.)

We can now go back to our original equation to derive n:

$$\sigma p = \sqrt{pq/n}$$

$$5{,}1 = \sqrt{25 \times 75 / n} \rightarrow n = 75 \text{ observations.}$$

If we reduce the margin of error to ± 5%, we have

1.96 op = 5

σp = 2.5 (approx.)

$$2{,}55 = \sqrt{25 \times 75 / n} \rightarrow n = 300 \text{ observations}$$

In other words, to reduce the margin of error by half, the sample size will have to be quadrupled.

17.4.2 Nomogram Method

An easier way to determine sample size is to read off the number of observations needed directly from a nomogram such as the one reproduced in Figure 17.5. Taking our previous example, we draw a line from the "percentage occurrence" ordinate p (in this case 25-75) to intercept the "error (accuracy required)" ordinate (say, 5%) and extend it until it meets the "number of observations" ordinate n, which it intercepts at 300 for the 95% confidence level. It is a quick way of determining sample size.

17.5. Making Random Observations

Our previous conclusions are valid provided that we can make the number of observations needed to attain the confidence level and accuracy required, and also provided that these observations are made **at random**.

To ensure that our observations are in fact made at random, we can use a random number table such as the one in Figure 17.6. Various types of random number tables exist, which can be used in different ways. In our case let us assume that we shall carry out our observations during a day shift of eight hours, from 7 a.m. to 3 p.m. An eight-hour day has 480 minutes, which may be divided into 48 ten-minute periods.

We can start by choosing any number at random from our table, for example by closing our eyes and placing a pencil point somewhere on the table. Let us assume that in this case we pick, by mere chance, the number 11 which is in the second block, fourth column, fourth row. We now choose any number between 1 and 10. Assume that we choose the number 2; we now go down the column picking out every second reading and noting it down, as shown below (if we had chosen the number 3, we would pick out every third figure, and so on).

11 38 45 87 68 20 11 26 49 05

Industrial Productivity

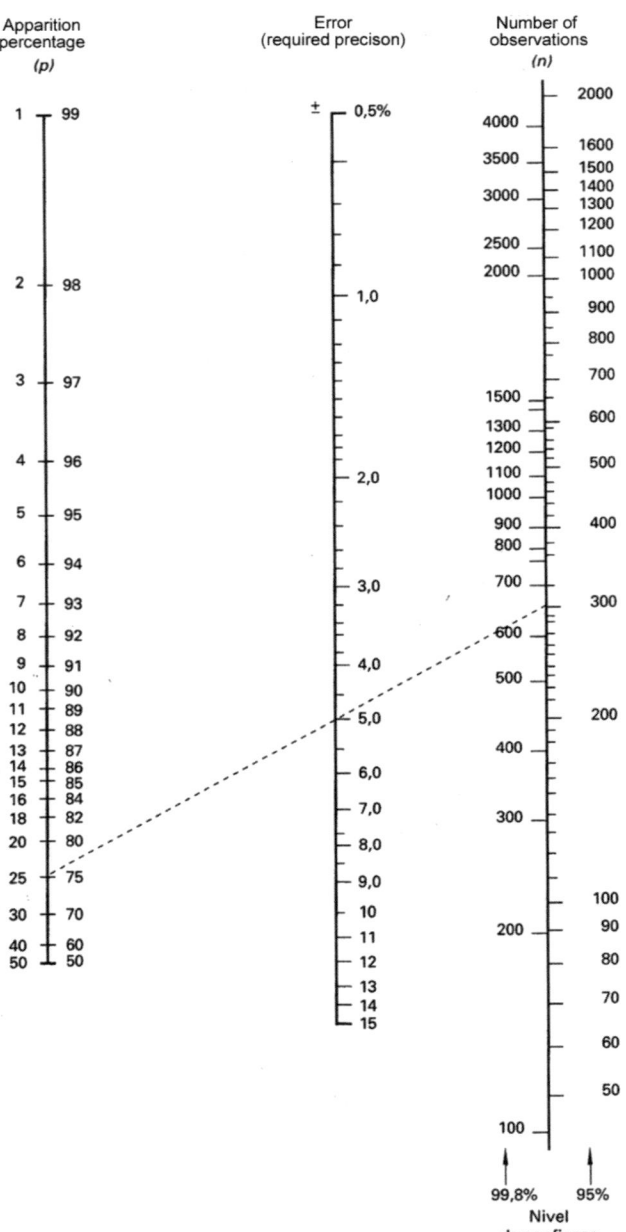

Figure 17.5. Nomogram for determining number of observations

17. Work Sampling and Structured Estimating

49 54 43 54 82	17 37 93 23 78	87 35 20 96 43	84 26 34 91 64
57 24 55 06 88	77 04 74 47 67	21 76 33 50 25	83 92 12 06 76
16 95 55 67 19	98 10 50 71 75	12 86 73 58 07	44 39 52 38 79
78 64 56 07 82	52 42 07 44 38	15 51 00 13 42	99 66 02 79 54
09 47 27 96 54	49 17 46 09 62	90 52 84 77 27	08 02 73 43 28
44 17 16 58 09	79 83 86 19 62	06 76 50 03 10	55 23 64 05 05
84 16 07 44 99	83 11 46 32 24	20 14 85 88 45	10 93 72 88 71
82 97 77 77 81	07 45 32 14 08	32 98 94 07 72	93 85 79 10 75
50 92 26 ⑪ 97	00 56 76 31 38	80 22 02 53 53	86 60 42 04 53
83 39 50 08 30	42 34 07 96 88	54 42 06 87 98	35 85 29 48 39
40 33 20 38 26	13 89 51 03 74	17 76 37 13 04	07 74 21 19 30
96 83 50 87 75	97 12 25 93 47	70 33 24 03 54	97 77 46 44 80
88 42 95 45 72	16 64 36 16 00	04 43 18 66 79	94 77 24 21 90
33 27 14 34 09	45 59 34 68 49	12 72 07 34 45	99 27 72 95 14
50 27 89 87 19	20 15 37 00 49	52 85 66 60 44	38 68 88 11 80
55 74 30 77 40	44 22 78 84 26	04 33 46 09 52	68 07 97 06 57
59 29 97 68 60	71 91 38 67 54	13 58 18 24 76	15 54 55 95 52
48 55 90 65 72	96 57 69 36 10	96 46 92 42 45	97 60 49 04 91
66 37 32 20 30	77 84 57 03 29	10 45 65 04 26	11 04 96 67 24
68 49 69 10 82	53 75 91 93 30	34 25 20 57 27	40 48 73 51 92
83 62 64 11 12	67 19 00 71 74	60 47 21 29 68	02 02 37 03 31
06 09 19 74 66	02 94 37 34 02	76 70 90 30 86	38 45 94 30 38
33 32 51 26 38	79 78 45 04 91	16 92 53 56 16	02 75 50 95 98
42 38 97 01 50	87 75 66 81 41	40 01 74 91 62	48 51 84 08 32
96 44 33 49 13	34 86 82 53 91	00 52 43 48 85	27 55 26 89 62
64 05 71 95 86	11 05 65 09 68	76 83 20 37 90	57 16 00 11 66
75 73 88 05 90	52 27 42 14 86	22 98 12 22 08	07 52 74 95 80
33 96 02 75 19	07 60 62 93 55	59 33 82 43 90	49 37 38 44 59
97 51 40 14 02	04 02 33 31 08	39 54 16 49 36	47 95 93 13 30
15 06 15 93 20	01 90 10 75 06	40 78 78 89 62	02 67 74 17 33
22 35 85 15 33	92 03 51 59 77	59 56 78 06 83	52 91 05 70 74
09 98 42 99 64	61 71 62 99 15	06 51 29 16 93	58 05 77 09 51
54 87 66 47 54	73 32 08 11 12	44 95 92 63 16	29 56 24 29 48
58 37 78 80 70	42 10 50 67 42	32 17 55 85 74	94 44 67 16 94
87 59 36 22 41	26 78 63 06 55	13 08 27 01 50	15 29 39 39 43
71 41 61 50 72	12 41 94 96 26	44 95 27 36 99	02 96 74 30 83
23 52 23 33 12	96 93 02 18 39	07 02 18 36 07	25 99 32 70 23
31 04 49 69 96	10 47 48 45 88	13 41 43 89 20	97 17 14 49 17
31 99 73 68 68	35 81 33 03 76	24 30 12 48 60	18 99 10 72 34
94 58 28 41 36	45 37 59 03 09	90 35 57 29 12	82 62 54 65 60

Figure 17.6. Table of random numbers

Industrial Productivity

Usable figures selected from the random numbers list	Classified by numeric order	Hour of the observation*
11	05	7:50
38	11	8:50
45	14	9:20
20	15	9:30
26	20	10:20
05	22	10:40
14	26	11:20
15	38	13:20
47	45	14:30
22	47	14:50

[1] Multiply each figure by 10 minutes and start at 7:00 a.m.

Figure 17.7. Determining the sequence of time for random observations

Looking at these numbers, we find that we have to discard 87, 68, and 49 because they are too high. (Because we have only 48 ten-minute periods, any number above 48 has to be discarded.) Similarly, the second 11 will also have to be discarded because it is a number that has already been used. We continue with our readings to replace the four numbers we have discarded. Using the same method, that is choosing every second number after the last one (05), we now have:

14 15 47 22

These four numbers are within the desired range and have not appeared before. Our final selection may now be arranged numerically and the times of observation throughout the eight-hour day worked out. Thus our smallest number (05) represents the fifth ten-minute period after the work began at 7 a.m. Thus our first observation will be at 7.50 a.m., and so on.

17.6. Conducting the Study

17.6.1 Determining the Scope of the Study

Before making our actual observations, it is important that we decide on the objective of our work sampling. The simplest objective is that of determining whether a given machine is idle or working. In such a case, our observations aim at detecting one of two possibilities only:

17. Work Sampling and Structured Estimating

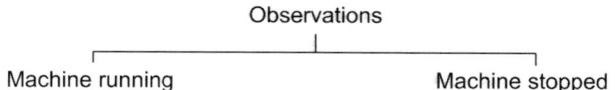

Figure 17.8

We can, however, extend this simple model to try to find out the cause of the stoppage of the machine:

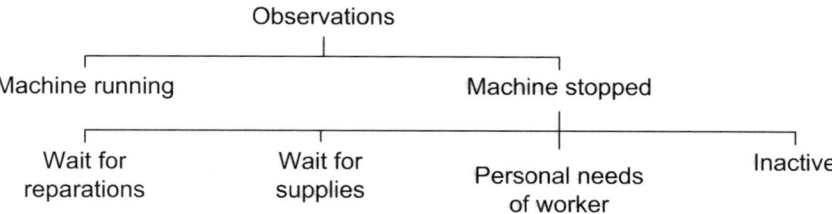

Figure 17.9

Again, we may be interested in determining the percentage of time spent on each activity while the machine is working:

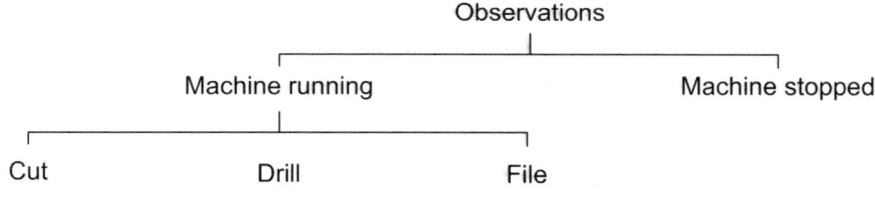

Figure 17.10.

Or perhaps we may wish to get an idea of the percentage distribution of time when the machine is working and when it is idle, in which case we combine the last two models.

We may also be interested in the percentage time spent by a worker or groups of workers on a given element of work. If a certain job consists of ten different elements, by observing a worker at the defined points in time we can record the element at which he or she is working and therefore arrive at a percentage distribution of the time he or she has been spending on each element.

The objectives of the study will determine the design of the recording sheet used in work sampling, as can be seen in Figures 17.11, 17.12, and 17.13.

17.6.2 Making the Observations

So far we have taken the first five logical steps in conducting a work sampling study. To recapitulate, these consist of the following:

- Selecting the job to be studied and determining the objectives of the study
- Making a preliminary observation to determine the approximate values of p and q
- In terms of a chosen confidence level and accuracy range, determining n (the number of observations needed)
- Determining the frequency of observations, using random number tables
- Designing record sheets to meet the objectives of the study

An additional step to take is that of making and recording the observations and analyzing the results. In making the observations, it is essential from the outset that the work study person is clear about what is to be achieved and why. Ambiguity should be avoided when classifying activities. For example, if the engine of a forklift truck is running while the truck is waiting to be loaded or unloaded, it should be decided beforehand whether this means that the truck is working or idle. It is also essential for the work study person to contact the people he or she wishes to observe, explaining to them the purpose of the study, indicating to them that they should work at their normal pace and endeavoring to gain their confidence and cooperation.

The observation itself should be made at the same point relative to each machine. The work study person should not note what is happening at the machines ahead, because it tends to skew the study. For example, in a weaving department, the observer may notice a loom that is stopped, just ahead of the one he or she is observing. The weaver may have it running again by the time the observer reaches it. The observer would, by noting it as idle, be giving an untrue picture of the situation.

The recording itself consists simply of making a stroke in front of the appropriate activity on the record sheet at the proper and predetermined time. No stopwatches are used.

The analysis of results can be calculated readily on the record sheet. It is possible to find out the percentage of effective time compared with that of delays, to analyze the reasons for ineffective time and to ascertain the percentage time spent by a worker, groups of workers, or a machine on a given work element. These, in themselves, provide useful information in a simple and reasonably quick way.

17. Work Sampling and Structured Estimating

Date:	Observer:		Study n°:	
Number of observations: 75			Total	Percentage
Machine running	||||‑||||‑||||‑||||‑||||‑||||‑||||‑||||‑||||‑||||‑||||‑||		62	82,7
Machine stopped	||||‑||||‑||||		13	17,3

Figure 17.11. *Example of a simple work sampling record sheet*

Date:		Observer:		Study n°:	
Number of observations: 75				Total	Percentage
Machine running		||||‑||||‑||||‑||||‑||||‑||||‑||||‑||||‑||||‑||||‑||||‑||		62	82,7
Machine stopped	Repair	||		2	2,7
	Supplies	||||‑|		6	8,0
	Needs				1	1,3
	Inactive	||||		4	5,3

Figure 17.12. *Work sampling record sheet showing machine utilization and distribution of idle time*

	Work elements									
Date: Observer: Study n°: Number of observations: 75	1	2	3	4	5	6	7	8	9	10
Worker number 1										
Worker number 2										
Worker number 3										
Worker number 4										

Figure 17.13. *Work sampling record sheet showing distribution of time on ten elements of work performed by a group of four workers*

17.7. Rated Work Sampling

In Chapter 18 we shall discuss the problem of rating a worker's performance relative to a conceived standard pace. Thus qualified workers who work according to a specified method and who are motivated to apply themselves to work briskly but naturally without overexertion are said to be working at 100% standard rating on the performance scale. As will become apparent in that chapter, rating is an important factor in deriving a time for an operation because not all workers work at the same pace. As a result, a work study person must take into consideration the pace of work when timing a study.

This rating of pace can be combined with work sampling to give what is known as **rated work sampling** or **rated activity sampling**.

In this method, observations are made at fixed intervals rather than at random times. When using fixed interval sampling, care must be taken to ensure that the fixed interval selected does not coincide with a natural cycle in the work. Such a coincidence would distort the results. Generally, if the interval is short enough when compared to the overall job cycle time, normal variations in the work will keep this problem from occurring.

During the sampling study, in addition to the activity being undertaken at the instant of the observation, a recording is also made of the pace of the worker using a performance rating scale. This rating can be used to modify the results of the study through the process of extension (converting observed times to basic times), which is discussed in Chapter 18.

17.8. Group Sampling Techniques

As the name suggests, these techniques are designed for the measurement of work carried out by groups of workers. They are sometimes referred to by the term *high-frequency sampling* because, when used for the measurement of short-cycle work, they use fixed short-time intervals with the observer in constant attendance. They are similar to time study but have the advantage of allowing the observer to cover the work of the entire group. Group sampling techniques may make use of rating systems.

Consider a simple example of three workers each producing the same parts by a process that involves only hand tools. The sampling is carried out at 0.5 minute intervals and involves the categories of "working" and "not working" only. The sampling observations have been rated, making it an example of both rated activity sampling and group sampling.

The sampling sheet would look as shown in Figure 17.14.

Time	Operator 1		Operator 2		Operator 3	
	Working	Without working	Working	Without working	Working	Without working
9.00	85		90		80	
9.005	90				85	
9.01	90		90			
9.015						
9.02	95					
9.025						

Total observation time = 250 min.
Number observations of each operator = 500 min.
Total number of observations - working = 1370 min.
                                       - without working = 130 min.
Average valuation of the three workers = 87% (based on 100% uniform performance)
= 62

From where, total working time = 1370 × 0,5 = 685 min.

Conversion to basic time = $\dfrac{685 \times 87}{100}$ = 596 min.

Basic min. per part = $\dfrac{596}{62}$ = 9.6 min.

If the valuation is not taken into consideration, the sampling results per group would be = $\dfrac{685}{62}$ = 11.04 min.

Figure 17.14. Sampling register sheet of valued work

17.9. Using Work Sampling

Work sampling—either individually or by group, with or without rating—is widely used. It is a relatively simple technique that can be used advantageously in a wide variety of situations, such as manufacturing, service, and office operations. Apart from providing a quick result, it is a fairly low-cost method and one that is less controversial than time study. The information derived from work sampling can be used to provide for a more equitable distribution of work in a group and, in general, to provide the management with an appreciation of the percentage of and reasons behind ineffective time. As a result it may indicate where method study needs to be applied, materials handling improved, or better production planning methods introduced, as may be the case if work sampling shows that a considerable percentage of machine time is spent idle, waiting for supplies to arrive.

17.10. Structured Estimating

Estimating is probably the earliest "measurement" technique. People have always used the basis of past experience to predict future events. Normally, however, simple estimates are too unreliable to be used as the basis of effective planning and control. The accuracy of estimating depends on the experience of the estimator in the field in which he or she is estimating. Structured estimating techniques are an attempt to make use of this fact and at the same time to impose a structure and a discipline on the estimating process so that results derived from it can be treated with confidence.

The advantages of estimating are that:

- It is cheap to apply, and therefore may be the only technique appropriate to one-off jobs.
- It can be used to predict times for work that has not been observed and thus can be used as a basis for price estimating for large, one-off jobs.

Estimating is normally used where the required time values do not demand great detail. Thus, such techniques are useful in long-cycle work and in situations where aggregated measurement data are used for planning, control, or payment over reasonably lengthy time periods.

17.10.1. Analytical Estimating

Analytical estimating is a combination of estimating and synthesis from standard data. The technique is based on the fact that if jobs are broken down into constituent elements and individual elements are measured or estimated, errors in those individual times will be random and will compensate for one another to leave an overall time that will be within acceptable limits. Similarly, when a number of jobs are combined into a larger time accumulation (such as the workload for a given week), individual errors in job times will be random and compensated by one another, leaving an overall time that is acceptable.

The estimating is normally carried out by a worker who is skilled in the area of work being measured and who has been trained in work study techniques. The estimator then:

- Breaks a job into elements.
- Applies any standard or synthetic data that are available.

- Carries out measurement on elements that are considered to warrant such effort and expenditure.
- Estimates any remaining elements using his or her experience and knowledge of the working conditions, safety factors, etc.

Element times that are estimated may then be incorporated into the standard data for future use, although such data should be revalidated at intervals.

17.10.2. Comparative Estimating

Comparative estimating relies on the identification and measurement of "benchmark" jobs of known work content against which all other jobs to be measured are compared. The benchmark jobs are selected to encompass the whole range of work involved and to represent intermediate points on the overall scale of job. These benchmark jobs are measured with some precision using an established work measurement technique.

The next stage is to identify time bands or slots, which are determined by statistical analysis and may not be of equal width. Commonly, a logarithmic progression is selected with each slot being allocated a basic or standard time equivalent to its midpoint.

Thus:

Interval	1	2	3	4
Extension (min)	0-30	31-60	61-120	121-240
Basic time	15	45	90	180
Each reference work is assigned to the right interval.					

Figure 17.15.

Each of the benchmark jobs is assigned to the appropriate slot.

When estimating work subsequently, the estimator refers to the benchmark jobs and compares the job being measured. On the basis of experience, he or she makes a comparison of the work content of the job to be estimated with a number of the benchmark jobs. When he or she is satisfied that the correct slot for the job has been identified, he or she assigns the slot basic time to that job. Because this time is to be combined with others to give a total workload over a long period, the fact that this one time is "inaccurate" does not matter. It is dangerous, however, to use such individual times outside the planned period designed to offer the statistically correct error compensation period.

Because of the high setup cost of this system (in terms of measuring all the benchmark jobs, training estimators, etc.), comparative estimating is most suitable for situations involving a lot of long-cycle, nonrepetitive work. A common area of application is in maintenance work, where the work is similar but no two jobs may be identical. To reduce the setup time, it is possible to "import" data on benchmark jobs from another organization (such as a consulting firm). If imported data are used, it is important to validate the data (as with any imported standard data) in their field of operation through carrying out some comparative studies.

Questions

1. What is the work sampling?
2. Define probability.
3. What parameters are used to describe normal distribution curves?
4. What confidence level is most commonly used for a random sample of large size?
5. List the two existing methods for sample size determination.
6. List five logical steps for making observations when performing a study.
7. Indicate the advantages of estimating over other techniques of study.

Bibliography

Kanawaty, George, *Introduction to Work Study* (Geneva: International Labor Organization, 1992).

Chapter 18

Predetermined Time Standards

Much of the material in this chapter is based on the book *Introduction to Work Study*, and used with permission of the International Labor Organization (1996).

18.1. Definition

Predetermined time standards (PTS), also referred to as predetermined motion time systems (PMTS) or synthetic time standards, are advanced techniques that aim to define the time needed for the performance of various operations by derivation from preset standards of time for various motions and not by direct observation and measurement. These techniques are not normally considered suitable for trainees to use until they have gained a real understanding of, and considerable experience in, work study practice. They will also require specialized PTS training. The essential nature of these standards will be explained in this chapter.

> A predetermined time standard is a work measurement technique whereby times established for basic human motions (classified according to the nature of the motion and the conditions under which it is made) are used to build up the time for a job at a defined level of performance.

As the definition indicates, PTS systems are techniques for synthesizing operation times from standard time data for basic motions. Synthesis and standard data are discussed more fully later in this book.

The nature of PTS systems can be easily illustrated by reference to a simple work cycle, such as putting a washer on a bolt. The operator will reach for the washer, grasp the washer, move the washer to the bolt, position it on the bolt, and release it.

Many operations consist, broadly speaking, of some or all of these five basic motions. To these are added other body motions and a few other elements. Figure 18.1 illustrates the components of a basic PTS.

By examining a given operation and identifying the basic motions of which it is composed, and by referring to PTS tables that indicate standard times for each type of motion performed under given circumstances, it is possible to derive a standard time for the operation as a whole.

Motion	Description
Stretch arm	Move hand to destination.
Grab	Obtain control of the object with fingers.
Move	Change position of object.
Position	Align object and position one on others.
Release load	Let go of the object.
Body movements	Movements of feet and body.

Figure 18.1. Components of a basic PTS

18.2. Origins

The pioneer of motion classification was Frank B. Gilbreth, whose "therblig" subdivisions of hand or hand and eye motions were the key concept in the development of motion study. Two main ideas underlying Gilbreth's approach were that the act of making a detailed critical analysis of work methods stimulates ideas for method improvement; and that the evaluation of alternative work methods can be achieved by a simple comparison of the number of motions, the better method being the one requiring fewer motions.

The credit for adding the time dimension to motion study is attributed to A. B. Segur, who in 1927 stated that "within practical limits the time required for all experts to perform true fundamental motions is a constant." Segur developed the first predetermined time standards, calling his system Motion Time Analysis. Little is known publicly about the system because he exploited it as a management consultant and bound his clients to secrecy.

The next important development was the work of J. H. Quick and his associates, who originated the Work Factor system in 1934. Like Segur's system, it was employed on a management consultancy basis and little information was published about it. However, it was eventually adopted by a large number of companies and is now in active use.

A considerable number and variety of PTS systems were produced during and following World War II. Among these was a system that has become widely used throughout the world, Methods-Time Measurement (MTM). Because of its importance, MTM will be used here to illustrate establishing predetermined time standards.

MTM was first developed by three men working on the system at the Westinghouse Electric Corporation in the United States: H. B. Maynard, G. J. Stegemerten, and J. L. Schwab. Their findings were published, and thus, for the first time, full details of a PTS system were made freely available to everyone. MTM has also set up, in various countries, independent nonprofit MTM associations to control the standards of training and practice and to continue research into and the development of MTM. These associations have established an international coordinating body, the International MTM Directorate. In 1965 a simplified form of MTM known as MTM-2 was developed, which led to a rapid increase in the use of the system. In addition, a number of other systems were also derived for particular categories of work such as maintenance work or office work intended to permit a faster and easier derivation of standard times.

18.3. Advantages of PTS Systems

PTS systems offer a number of advantages over stopwatch time study. With PTS systems, one time is indicated for a given motion, irrespective of where such a motion is performed. In stopwatch time study it is not so much a motion as a sequence of motions making up an operation that is timed. Timing by direct observation and rating can sometimes lead to inconsistency. A PTS system, which avoids both rating and direct observation, can lead to more consistency in setting standard times.

Because the times for the various operations can be derived from standard time tables, it is possible to define the standard time for a given operation even before production begins, and often while the process is still at the design stage. This advantage of PTS systems allows the work study person to change the layout and design of the workplace and of the necessary jigs and fixtures in such a way that the optimum production time is achieved. They also make it possible, even before starting the operation, to draw up an estimate of the cost of production, which obviously could be valuable for estimating and tendering purposes or for budgeting. PTS systems are not too difficult to apply and can be less time-consuming than other methods when time standards for certain operations are being determined. They are particularly useful for short repetitive time cycles such as assembly work in the electronics industry.

18.4. Criticisms of PTS Systems

In view of the value of PTS systems, it is surprising that it took so long for them to become part of general work study practice. The main reason for this delay is probably the considerable number and variety of systems that have been produced, together with the fact that many of them could be obtained only by employing consultants. At present, more than 200 such systems exist. This proliferation has led to complaints from management, trade unions, and work study specialists.

Furthermore, any PTS system is rather complicated. It is not easy to learn, and a work study person needs a good deal of practice before being able to apply it correctly. The task of learning enough about the various systems to be able to judge their claims and their relative merits is an almost impossible one. For example, some systems do not go into sufficient detail in defining a certain motion. They might, for instance, give the same time for the movement both of an empty cup and of one full of water, or for the movement of a dry brush and of one laden with paint, which must be moved with care. PTS systems cannot also cope readily with movements made under abnormal conditions, for example, movements made when the worker is wearing protective clothing or when the movements are made in an abnormal position, such as a worker reaching into a confined space behind a pipe. The situation was made more complicated by the lack of freely available information on many systems, whose tables were considered to be the property of their developers and were thus not available for publication.

Some work study researchers also questioned the basic assumptions of PTS systems. In part, these criticisms were justified, although some appear to have arisen through misinformation or misunderstanding. PTS systems do not, as was claimed, eliminate the need for the stopwatch, any more than they eliminate method study or work sampling. Machine time, process time, and waiting time are not measurable with PTS systems, and occasional or incidental elements are often more economically measured by using other techniques. In fact, it is difficult to obtain 100 percent coverage in a plant using only a PTS system, and for certain operations such as batch production or nonrepetitive jobs the use of such a system can be an expensive proposition.

One type of criticism stems from a too literal interpretation of the basic assumption of Segur, quoted earlier. In fact, absolute constant times are not implied. The times indicated in PTS tables are averages, and the limits associated with the averages are small enough to be neglected in all practical circumstances.

Another common criticism is that it is invalid to add up times for individual small motions in the way required by PTS systems because the time taken to perform a particular motion is influenced by the motions preceding and following it. It is unfair to criticize the more important PTS systems on these grounds, because not only were these relationships clearly recognized by their originators but also special provision was made to ensure that the essential correlations were maintained. In the case of MTM, for example, it was achieved by establishing subdivisions of the main classes of motions and by creating special definitions and rules of application to ensure their essential linking. The relationships are also preserved in simplified systems such as MTM-2.

It has also been declared that the direction of the motion influences the time—for example, that it takes longer to cover the same distance when moving upward than when moving downward— and that no PTS system isolates this variable. MTM researchers would agree that the direction of the motion is an important variable. However, they argue that in a single work cycle the operator will not be reaching only upward, nor always away from the body, nor making only counterclockwise turns: he or she will reach downward or toward the body or make clockwise turns also, and so justify the use of average values.

Levels of data in NTPD systems

1st level MTM-1	2nd level MTM-2	3rd level MTM-3	Higher level i.e.:MTM-V
RELEASE, STRETCH ARM, GRAB	TAKE	MANIPULATE	The combinations form simple and complex elements
MOVE, PLACE	PUT		
RELEASE			

Figure 18.2. PTS data levels: Basic motions

18.5. Different Forms of PTS Systems

A work study person is likely to encounter a number of different forms of PTS systems and will therefore find it useful to understand the main ways in which the systems vary, as well as differences in levels and scope of application of data, motion classification, and time units.

18.5.1. Data Levels

Figure 18.2 illustrates data levels by means of the official international MTM systems: MTM-1, MTM-2, and MTM-3.

The first level comprises the motions RELEASE, REACH, GRASP, MOVE, POSITION, RELEASE. At the second level these motions are combined: in MTM-2, for instance, the motions are GET and PUT. At the third level, the motions have been further combined as HANDLE, to give a description of the complete work cycle. Beyond the third level no completely clear-cut rules have yet been articulated, and methods of classification vary according to the work area for which the data are intended.

18.5.2. Scope of Application of Data

PTS systems vary as regards the universality of their application. It is difficult to explain this concept exactly, but Figure 18.3 attempts some clarification.

Scope	NTPD System	Field of Application
Universal	MTM-1, -2, -3 Work Factor	Transferable throughout the world and applicable to all sectors of manual activity
General	Master Clerical Data (office) MTM-V (workshop)	Transferable only within an activity sector
Specific	Basic data for certain departments of a factory	Not transferable without validation studies

Figure 18.3. Scope of application of data

Figure 18.3. First of all, systems of universal application cover all work anywhere, including motion data at the MTM-1, -2, or -3 levels and for the Work Factor systems. Second, some data relate to a main occupation (e.g., office work, maintenance work, or some kinds of production work). Examples of these systems are Master Clerical Data for the office and MTM-V, the Swedish MTM Association data for machine shops. Finally, the least general category deal with the specific data systems that are developed for use in particular factories or departments. These data are not transferable without validation studies.

18.5.3. Motion Classification

PTS systems provide information about manual work cycles in terms of basic human motions. Differences between the criteria adopted for the classification of these motions include, broadly speaking, two main sets:

- Object-related classification
- Behavior-related classification

The object-related classification is employed in the majority of PTS systems (including Work Factor, Dimensional Motion Times, and MTM-1) and virtually all the data systems relating to main occupational groups or specifically designed for use within a plant. In an object-related system, reference may be made to characteristics of parts (such as grasping a 6 x 6 x 6 mm object), or to the nature of the surrounding conditions (such as reaching out to an object that is jumbled with other objects, or reaching out to an object that is lying flat against a surface). The classification is, however, not entirely object-related because motions such as RELEASE LOAD or DISENGAGE have behavioral definitions.

Unlike most systems, MTM-2 employs exclusively behavioral concepts, which is also true of MTM-3, Master Standard Data, and a few less well-known systems. The behavior-related systems classify motions according to what they look like to an observer: for example, a movement of the empty hand for a distance of between 5 and 15 centimeters followed by a grasping action made by a simple closing of the fingers defines the GET motion in the MTM-2 system (see, for example, Figure 18.5).

18.5.4. Time Units

No two PTS systems have the same set of time values, partly due to the fact that different systems have different motion classes and the time data therefore refer to different things. Again, the choice of the basic unit (fractions of a second, minutes, hour) may vary, and some systems follow the practice of adding contingency allowances to motion times, whereas others do not. A final major cause of variations arises from the differences in the performance level implied in the time data. The methods adopted for standardizing, normalizing, or averaging the motion times are not uniform. Consequently, PTS time data are divided into one of two sets: Work Factor systems, which express their data in minutes; and MTM systems, expressed in time measurement units (tmu) of one hundred-thousandth of an hour or about one twenty-eighth of a second. The MTM time values, which were derived mainly from film analysis of a variety of industrial operations (the method was to count the number of "frames" occupied by each motion), were standardized using the well-known "Westinghouse" or "Levelling" system. The times stated are those achieved by an experienced operator of average skill, working with average effort and consistency under average conditions. **The performance level, MTM 100, is therefore somewhat less than BSI 100. A public statement by the United Kingdom Institute of Management Services and the MTM Association suggests that MTM 100 equals BSI 83.**

18.5.5. Other Considerations

Some important properties of PTS systems are less easy to establish and to compare than the aspects discussed in the previous subsections. Examples include the precision and accuracy of the time data, speed of application, methods description capability, and learning time. The lack of reliable, detailed information and, to some extent, the lack of agreed design criteria hamper comparison of these properties.

18.6. Use of PTS Systems

The system most likely to be used by the work study person is MTM-2. The following categories constitute the MTM-2 system. Each will be explained in detail in the following subsection.

Category	Code
Get	GA, GB, GC
Put	PA, PB, PC
Regrasp	R
Apply pressure	A
Eye action	E
Foot motion	F
Step	S
Bend and arise	B
Weight factors	GW, PW
Crank	C

Figure 18.4. MTM-2 symbols

	Code	GA	GB	GC	PA	PB	PC
Distance	0 - ≤ 5 cm	3	7	14	3	10	21
	>5 - ≤ 15 cm	6	10	19	6	15	26
	>15 - ≤ 30 cm	9	14	23	11	19	30
	>30 - ≤ 45 cm	13	18	27	15	24	36
	>45 cm	17	23	32	20	30	41

Time in TMU

Figure 18.5. MTM-2 data card for GET and PUT

Code	A	R	C	R	F	S	B
TMU	14	6	15	7	9	18	61

Figure 18.6. MTM-2 data card

GW	1 TMU per kg, starting from ≥ 2 kg weight/effort per hand
PW	1 TMU per each 5 kg, starting from ≥ 2 kg weight/effort per hand

Figure 18.7. MTM-2 data card

The MTM-2 system provides time standards ranging from 3 to 61 tmu as shown on the data card reproduced in Figure 18.5. As stated, 1 tmu equals one hundred-thousandth of an hour.

TMU	Seconds	Minutes	Hours
1	0,036	0,0006	0,00001
27,8	1		
1.666,7		1	
100.000			1

Figure 18.8. Time units

18.6.1. MTM-2 Categories

1. GET (G): GET is an action with the predominant purpose of reaching out with the hand or fingers to an object, grasping the object and subsequently releasing it.

The scope of GET:

- Starts: with reaching out to the object
- Includes: reaching out to, gaining control, and subsequently releasing control of the object
- Ends: when the object is released

Selection of a GET is done by considering three variables:

1. Case of GET—distinguished by the grasping action employed
2. Distance reached
3. Weight of the object or its resistance to motion

Cases of GET are judged by the following decision model:

Industrial productivity

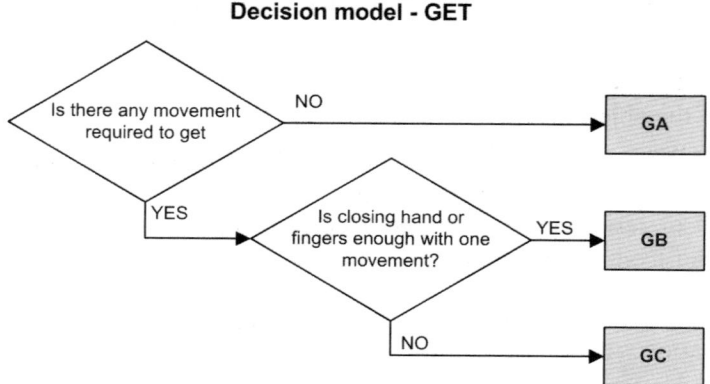

Figure 18.9. *Modelo de decisión – TOMAR.*

- An example of GA is putting the palm of the hand on the side of a box in order to push it across a table.
- An example of GB is getting an easy-to-handle object, such as a one-inch cube, which is laying by itself.
- An example of GC is getting the corner of a page of this book in order to turn it over.

Distance is a principal variable in GET, and five distance classes are provided. Distances are judged by the upper limits of the classes, which are 5, 15, 30, 45, and over 45 cm. The code 80 is assigned to the highest class. Distances are estimated from the path of travel of the hand, less any body assistance.

Centimeters		Distance
Over	Not over	range
0,0	5,0	5
5,0	15,0	15
15,0	30,0	30
30,0	45,0	45
45,0	-	80

Figure 18.10.

2. GET WEIGHT (GW): GET WEIGHT is the action required for the muscles of the hand and arm to take up the weight of the object.

The scope of GET WEIGHT:

- Starts: with the grasp on the object completed

- Includes: muscular force necessary to gain full control of the weight of the object
- Ends: when the object is sufficiently under control to permit movement of the object

GET WEIGHT occurs after the fingers have closed on the object in the preceding GET. It must be accomplished before any actual movement can take place. When the weight or resistance is less than 2 kg per hand, no GW is assigned. When resistance exceeds 2 kg, 1 tmu is assigned for every kg including the first two.

3. PUT (P): PUT is an action with the predominant purpose of moving an object to a destination with the hand or fingers.

The scope of PUT:

- Starts: with an object grasped and under control at the initial place
- Includes: all transporting and correcting motions necessary to place an object
- Ends: with object still under control at the intended place

Selection of a PUT is done by considering three variables:

1. Case of PUT—distinguished by the correcting motions employed
2. Distance moved
3. Weight of the object or its resistance to motion

Cases of PUT are judged by the following decision model:

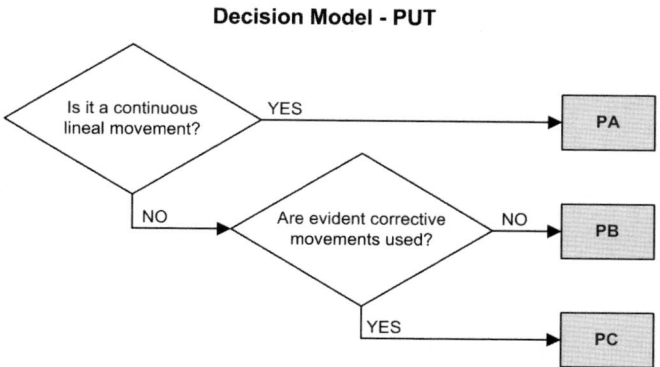

Figure 18.11. Decision model: PUT

- An example of PA is tossing aside an object.
- An example of PB is the action of putting a 12 mm ball in a 15 mm diameter hole.

- An example of PC is inserting a Yale or similar key in a lock.

A correction is not likely to be confused with a short PA. A correction is a short unintentional motion at the terminal point; a PA is purposeful, usually of easily discernible length.

The motion distance is handled in a similar manner to GET.

When an engagement of parts follows a correction, an additional PUT will be allowed when the distance exceeds 2.5 cm.

4. PUT WEIGHT (PW): PUT WEIGHT is an addition to a PUT motion, depending on the weight of the object moved.

The scope of PUT WEIGHT:

- Starts: when the move begins
- Includes: the additional time, over and above the move time in PUT, to compensate for the differences in time required in moving heavy and light objects over the same distance
- Ends: when the move ends

PW is assigned when resistance to movement exceeds 2 kg per hand. Weights are calculated as in GET WEIGHT. Between 2 kg and 5 kg, 1 tmu is allowed and coded PW 5; between 5 kg and 10 kg 2 tmu are allowed and coded PW 10; and so on.

5. REGRASP (R): REGRASP is a hand action with the purpose of changing the grasp on an object.

The scope of REGRASP:

- Starts: with the object in the hand
- Includes: digital and hand muscular readjustment on an object
- Ends: with the object in a new location in the hand

A single REGRASP consists of not more than three fractional movements.

Digital and muscular readjustments, while performing an APPLY PRESSURE, are included in APPLY PRESSURE. A REGRASP should not be assigned in combination with APPLY PRESSURE.

If the hand relinquishes control and then secures another grasp on the object, the action will be a GET, not a REGRASP.

- An example of R is changing the grasp on a pencil in order to get into the position for writing.

6. APPLY PRESSURE (A): APPLY PRESSURE is an action with the purpose of exerting muscular force on an object.

The scope of APPLY PRESSURE:

- Starts: with the body member in contact with the object
- Includes: the application of controlled increasing muscular force, a minimum reaction time to permit the reversal of force and the subsequent releasing of muscular force
- Ends: with the body member in contact with the object, but with muscular force released

The minimum dwell time covers mental reaction time only. Longer dwells, in holding actions, must be separately evaluated.

APPLY PRESSURE applies to the action of exerting muscular force on an object to achieve control, to restrain or to overcome resistance to motion. The object is not displaced more than 6 mm during the action of APPLY PRESSURE.

APPLY PRESSURE, which can be performed by anybody, is recognized by a noticeable hesitation while force is applied.

- An example of A is the final tightening action made with a screwdriver or spanner.

7. EYE ACTION (E): EYE ACTION is an action with the purpose of either recognizing a readily distinguishable characteristic of an object or shifting the aim of the axis of vision to a new viewing area.

The scope of EYE ACTION:

- Starts: when other actions must cease because a characteristic of an object must be recognized
- Includes: either muscular readjustment of the lens of the eyes and the mental processes required to recognize a distinguishable characteristic of an object; or the eye motion performed to shift the aim of the axis of vision to a new viewing area
- Ends: when other actions can start again

A single eye focus covers an area 10 cm in diameter at 40 cm from the eyes. Recognition time included is sufficient only for simple binary decisions.

- An example of E is the action of determining whether a coin is showing head or tail.

8. FOOT MOTION (F): FOOT MOTION is a short foot or leg motion when the purpose is not to move the body.

Industrial productivity

The scope of FOOT MOTION:

- Starts: with the foot or leg at rest
- Includes: a motion not exceeding 30 cm that is pivoted at the hip, knee, or instep
- Ends: with the foot in a new location

FOOT MOTION is judged by the decision model for FOOT MOTION and STEP.

9. STEP (S): STEP is either a leg motion with the purpose of moving the body or a leg motion longer than 30 cm.

The scope of STEP:

- Starts: with the leg at rest
- Includes: either a motion of the leg where the purpose is to achieve displacement of the trunk; or a leg motion longer than 30 cm
- Ends: with the leg at a new location

STEP or FOOT MOTION is judged by the following decision model

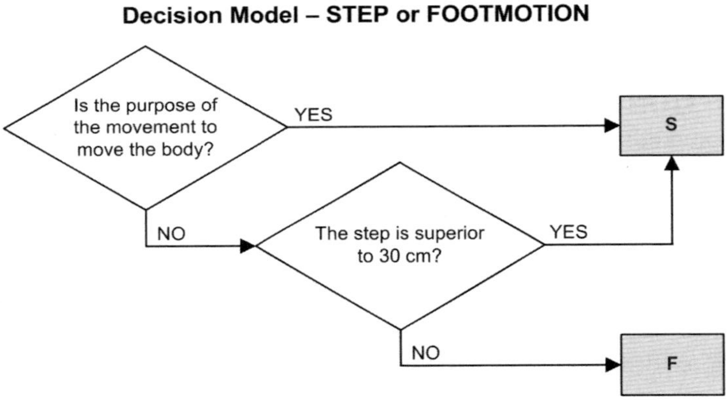

Decision Model – STEP or FOOTMOTION

Figure 18.12. Decision model: STEP or FOOT MOTION

To evaluate walking, count the number of times the foot hits the floor.

- An example of F is depressing a foot pedal in a car.
- n example of S is making a single step to the side to enable the arm to reach further.

10. BEND AND ARISE (B): BEND AND ARISE is a lowering of the trunk followed by a rise.

The scope of BEND AND ARISE:

- Starts: with motion of the trunk forward from an upright posture
- Includes: movement of the trunk and other body members to achieve a vertical change of body position to permit the hands to reach down to or below the knees and subsequently arise from this position.
- Ends: with the body in an upright posture

The criterion for BEND AND ARISE is whether the operator is able to reach to below the knees, not whether he or she actually does so. Kneeling on both knees should be analyzed as 2B.

11. CRANK (C): CRANK is a motion with the purpose of moving an object in a circular path of more than half a revolution with the hand or finger.

The scope of CRANK:

- Starts: with the hand on the object
- Includes: all transporting motions necessary to move an object in a circular path
- Ends: with the hand on the object when one revolution is completed

The two variables to consider in applying the CRANK motion are:

1. The number of revolutions
2. Weight or resistance

The time value of 15 tmu per revolution may be used for any crank diameter and applies to both continuous and intermittent cranking. CRANK applies to motions in a circular path regardless of whether the axis of cranking is perpendicular to the plane of rotation.

The number of revolutions should be rounded to the nearest whole number. The weight or resistance influences the time for moving an object. The rules of adding GW and PW to PUT motions also apply to CRANK. PW applies to each revolution, whether continuous or intermittent. GW is applied once only to a continuous series of revolutions, but to each revolution where these are intermittent.

No correcting motions as applied to PUT are included in CRANK. If correcting motions occur in putting the object at the intended place an extra PUT must be allowed.

- An example of C is turning a hand wheel through one revolution.

18.6.2. Training Requirements

In the preceding subsection the essentials of the MTM-2 system were outlined. To obtain an adequate understanding of the system, however, a trainee will require at least two weeks of formal training in MTM-2 theory and practice, followed by guided application on the shop floor with an MTM instructor. A trainee who is already competent in work study practice should reach a reasonable standard on the use of MTM-2 after about a month of guided application. MTM-1 will require a longer training period. It is helpful if part of this training can be carried out in a plant where MTM standards are already in use. When trainees find that their own analyses compare closely with established standards, their confidence builds rapidly. Without guidance it is difficult for a trainee to learn how to use MTM adequately.

Most PTS training courses end up with an examination in which the trainee carried out a measurement study of a real or simulated job, sometimes on film. Only if a specified pass mark is obtained in this examination is the trainee certified to apply the PTS in question at the place of work as a consultant in that particular PTS system.

18.7. Application of PTS Systems

PTS systems can be applied in three main ways:

1. Direct observation of the motions used by the operator
2. Mental visualization of the motions needed to accomplish a new or alternative work method
3. From analysis of a film/video taken of the operator at the place of work

The overall approach adopted when one of the PTS systems, such as MTM-2, is used for direct observation is not too different from that adopted for making a time study (see Chapter 16). Indeed, a person experienced in the procedures described in that chapter—selecting the job, approaching the worker, recording job information, breaking it down into elements, making allowances, and compiling total job times—is well equipped to become a good PTS practitioner. The main difference in the approach is that at the point in the total time study procedure where the observer is ready to time and rate the work cycle, he or she will instead make an MTM-2 analysis and then enter the motion times on the analysis sheet from the MTM-2 data card. The calculation of allowances, completion of the documentation, and issuing of the job times are then done in much the same way as in a time study. If the same type of summary sheets can be used, so much the better. The study summary sheet and the short-cycle study form can be adapted to summarize the information from the MTM-2 analysis sheets.

18.7.1. Choosing the Operator

In the choice of operator to be observed, it is just as desirable to have a cooperative, good-average worker for PTS analysis as it is for time study. Exceptionally fast or abnormally slow performances are difficult for time study specialists to rate, and they present problems for PTS analysts too. The superskilled operator combines and overlaps motions in a manner beyond the capabilities of the average worker, while an abnormally slow or reluctant operator will make separate, one-handed, hesitant motions that the average operator will perform smoothly and simultaneously. The rules and motion combination tables of the MTM system, like those of other systems such as Work Factor, provide information for adjusting the observed motion pattern to that applicable to the good-average worker; this additional work can, however, be avoided by an intelligent choice of operator in the first place. Of course, the experienced PTS analyst may also study extreme performances with advantage. The performance of an exceptionally fast operator may give clues as to how all operators might be trained to reach a higher-than-average performance level, and the study of slow operators would show where difficulties are being encountered and whether further training might eliminate them.

18.7.2. Recording Job Information

In recording job information, it is important to remember that distance is a significant variable in PTS systems. The plans for the workplace layout should therefore be accurately drawn to scale to help in judging or checking the length of motions shown in the analyses.

18.7.3. Breakdown into Elements

In PTS systems the division of the operation into work elements follows the same principles as for time study. The breakdown can be made much finer, if required, because the difficulty of timing short elements does not arise. If necessary, the break points can also be changed easily and without having to retime the cycle. This flexibility is illustrated in Figure 18.13, which shows a common work cycle—that of fitting a nut and washer on a stud. For example, if a change of method eliminates the need for a washer, the appropriate motions (GC30, PC30, PA5) and time (56 tmu) can easily be removed from the analysis. Finger turns can also be readily separated from spanner turns and, indeed, from the fitting actions and subsequent turns.

Example

Document 2 - Study of the task: Fitting a nut and washer on a stud					
Description of Operation	MTM Element	Code	TMU	Q	F	Total TMU
Fit washer.	Get washer.	GC	30	23	1	1	23
	Move washer to stud located at 30 cm.	PC	30	30	1	1	30
	Fit stud	PA	5	3	1	1	3
Fit nut and turn down by hand.	Get nut.	GB	15	10	1	1	10
	Move nut to stud located at 15 cm.	PC	15	26	1	1	26
	Place nut on stud.	PA	5	3	1	2	6
	Turn down nut by hand (take).	GB	5	7	1	6	42
	Turn down nut by hand (place).	PA	5	3	1	6	18
Tighten nut using spanner.	Get spanner.	GB	30	23	1	1	23
	Move spanner to nut.	PC	30	30	1	1	30
	Turn down nut with wrench.	PA	15	6	1	1	6
	Give final tightening.	A		14	1	1	14
			Total task execution time (TMU): ||		231

Figure 18.13. Example: Fitting a nut and washer on a stud

18.7.4. Allowances and Job Times

Problems of rating are not part of a PTS system such as MTM-2, because the times have been rated once and for all. All that needs to be done is to add up the motion times and transfer the totals to the study summary sheet. If times are to be issued at BSI 100 and not MTM 100, the tmu total from the study summary sheet should be multiplied by 0.83. (If times are issued in standard minutes, the total tmu can be divided by 2,000.) **It should be understood that the general relationship between the scales applies only to the time totals, and most definitely not to the individual motion times shown on the MTM data cards. Converting individual motion times is quite improper because they are not improved uniformly when a higher performance of a cycle time is achieved.**

The times for low control motions (such as GA and PA) are improved only a little compared with those for the highly complex motions (such as GC and PC).

18. Predetermined Time Standards

The issue is, however, more complicated than this because one would also need a different set of motion combinations when considering a different performance level. Some sophisticated MTM users prefer to issue values at MTM 100.

Rest and other allowances are added in exactly the same way as for time study, in order to give the total job time.

18.7.5. Visualization

When the work study person does not have the opportunity of observing the work cycle (e.g., when designing a new work method or constructing alternative methods during method study of an existing job), he or she must mentally visualize the motions needed. Figures 18.14 and 18.15 give an example of a PTS problem that can be solved by visualization of the various motions involved, as can be seen from Figure 18.16.

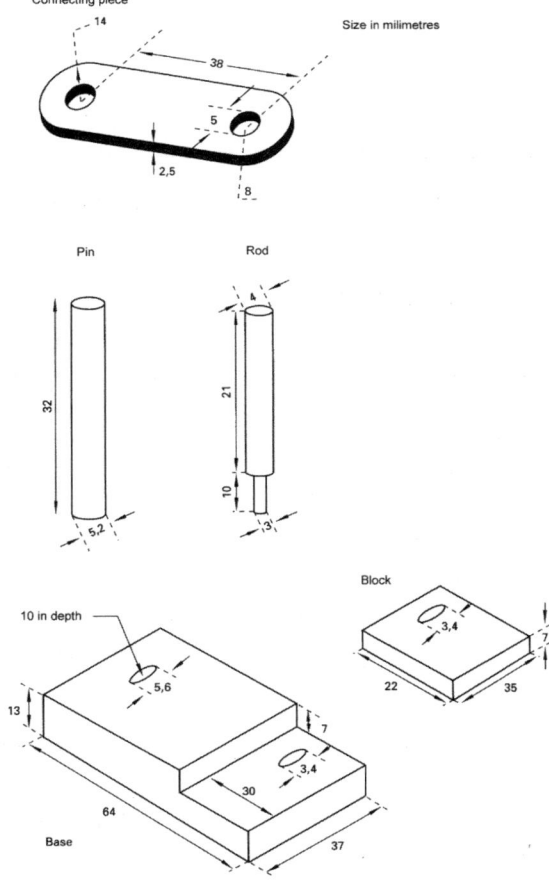

Figure 18.14. Base assembly

619

Industrial productivity

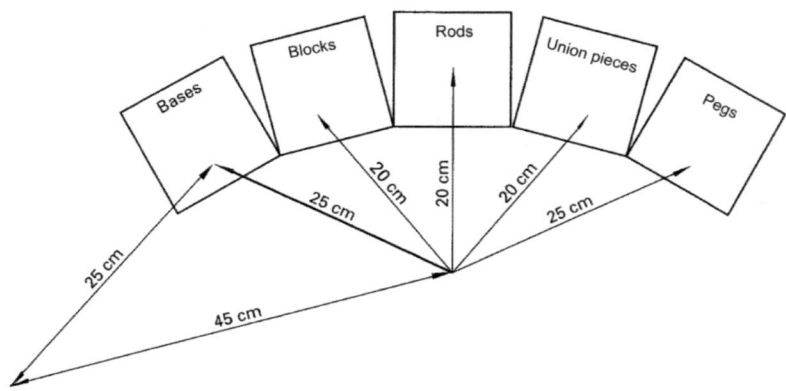

Figure 18.15. Base assembly workplace layout

The ability to visualize motion patterns depends on the study person's intelligence and on practical experience. The more familiar he or she is with work study, the more readily the person can picture the motions necessary to pick up and fit parts together, as well as visualizing which motions can be performed together easily and which motions are difficult to carry out simultaneously (Figure 18.16).

In designing work methods, it can be helpful to use a methods laboratory. However, when motion analysis is undertaken, caution is necessary, just as it is with time standards. The experiments with new methods will probably be performed by the work study person or by colleagues, and it is important that they should bear in mind that their own performances will generally fall far short of those achieved by the regular shop-floor operators. Even when shop-floor operators are assisting in the methods laboratory, their performance of a new work cycle will fall short of the standard they will achieve after sufficient practice in working the cycle under shop-floor conditions.

In both these instances the rules for work design, particularly those of the motion combination possibilities expected of the average experienced operator, must be used to arrive at a correct shop-floor method.

It is in the work design process that a work study person who chooses to use an MTM-2 system, for example, will reap the benefit of a full training in the detailed MTM-1 system on which MTM-2 was founded. However, at a minimum the classification details of MTM-1 together with the basic motions which make up the MTM-2 motions and the rules covering the combination possibilities of the basic motions must be understood, particularly in relation to practice opportunity, area of normal vision, and difficulty of handling. With this knowledge it will become evident, for example, that in designing the workplace for the parts to be kept in tote pans, a separate GC with either hand will be required. It will also be apparent that even expert operators cannot perform these motions simultaneously, because each motion involves a kind of minute searching and selecting activity, because the objects are jumbled together. Similarly, the work study specialist will know that putting loose-fitting round plugs into round holes can be done with both hands simultaneously, provided that the workplace is designed so that the targets are within the area of normal vision as defined above under EYE ACTION. The rules provide many such guidelines.

18.7.6. PTS Systems and the Broader Techniques

The nature and value of PTS systems should now be reasonably clear. If a work study person intends to become a specialist, for example in MTM, full training in MTM-1 and MTM-2 and in all the advanced techniques outlined in this book will be necessary. In the more general case, where both work study and other jobs will probably be undertaken as well (such as production planning and control—a common combination in small plants, particularly in developing countries), an MTM-2 training may be sufficient.

However, it is most important that the study person should not lose sight of the fact that the PTS technique is a fine precision tool. Before getting down to minute detail, examining what can be accomplished by using the broader, simpler approaches should come first. In companies where work study practice has not yet been introduced, intelligent broad thinking will usually reveal ways of bringing about considerable initial improvements in productivity.

\multicolumn{9}{c}{MTM-2 Analysis Sheet}
Operation:	Base assembly			Company:				
Date:	2010/02/12			Task:				
Analyst:	Tucker Campbell			Process:				
Operator:	Franklyn Evans			Area:	Assembly			
N°	ANALYSIS OF LEFT HAND ELEMENTS		Code		TMU	Code		ANALYSIS OF RIGHT HAND ELEMENTS
1	Get base from box.		GC	30	23	G....		Get pin from box.
2					14	GC	5	
3	Put base on bench.		PA	30	30	PC	30	Locate pin to base.
4	Get block from box.		GC	30	23	G....		Get stud from box.
5					14	GC	5	
6	Move block stud.		P....		30	PC	30	Locate stud through block.
7	Assist location.		P....		26	PC	15	Fit assembly to base.
8					23	GC	30	Get connector from box.
9	Assist location.		GB....		30	PC	30	Locate to stud.
10	Locate to pin.		PC	5	21			
11	Pick up assembly.		GB	15	10			
12	Place on conveyor.		PA	80	20			
	Total task execution time (TMU):				264			

Figure 18.16. MTM-2 analysis sheet, base assembly

Industrial productivity

1. REACH - R

Distance (cm)	Time (tmu) A	B	C o D	E	Hand in motion A	B	Class and description
2 or less	2,0	2,0	2,0	2,0	1,6	1,6	A. Reach to object in fixed location, or to object in other hand or on whichother hand rests.
4	3,4	3,4	5,1	3,2	3,0	2,4	
6	4,5	4,5	6,5	4,4	3,9	3,1	
8	5,5	5,5	7,5	5,5	4,6	3,7	
10	6,1	6,3	8,4	6,8	4,9	4,3	
12	6,4	7,4	9,1	7,3	5,2	4,8	B. Reach to single object in location which may vary slightly from cycle to cycle.
14	6,8	8,2	9,7	7,8	5,5	5,4	
16	7,1	8,8	10,3	8,2	5,8	5,9	
18	7,5	9,4	10,8	8,7	6,1	6,5	
20	7,8	10,0	11,4	9,2	6,5	7,1	
22	8,1	10,5	11,9	9,7	6,8	7,7	C. Reach to object jumbled with other objects in a group so that search and select occur.
24	8,5	11,1	12,5	10,2	7,1	8,2	
26	8,8	11,7	13,0	10,7	7,4	8,8	
28	9,2	12,2	13,6	11,2	7,7	9,4	
30	9,5	12,8	14,1	11,7	8,0	9,9	
35	10,4	14,2	15,5	12,9	8,8	11,4	D. Reach to a very small object or where accurate grasp is required.
40	11,3	15,6	16,8	14,1	9,6	12,8	
45	12,1	17,0	18,2	15,3	10,4	14,2	
50	13,0	18,4	19,6	16,5	11,2	15,7	
55	13,9	19,8	20,9	17,8	12,0	17,1	
60	14,7	21,2	22,3	19,0	12,8	18,5	E. Reach to indefinite location to get hand in position for body balance or next motion or out of way.
65	15,6	22,6	23,6	20,2	13,5	19,9	
70	16,5	24,1	25,0	21,4	14,3	21,4	
75	17,3	25,5	26,4	22,6	15,1	22,8	
80	18,2	26,9	27,7	23,9	15,9	24,2	

Figure 18.17. Methods-Time Measurement application data in tmu: REACH

II. MOVE - M

Distance (cm)	Time (tmu) A	B	C	Hand in motion B	Weight up to (Kg)	Static constant (tmu)	Dinamic factor	Case and description
2 or less	2,0	2,0	2,0	1,7	1	0	1,00	
4	3,1	4,0	4,5	2,8				
6	4,1	5,0	5,8	3,1				
8	5,1	5,9	6,9	3,7	2	1,6	1,04	
10	6,0	6,8	7,9	4,3				A. Move object against stop or to other hand.
					4	2,8	1,07	
12	6,9	7,7	8,8	4,9				
14	7,7	8,5	9,8	5,4				
16	8,3	9,2	10,5	6,0	6	4,3	1,12	
18	9,0	9,8	11,1	6,5				
20	9,6	10,5	11,7	7,1				
					8	5,8	1,17	
22	10,2	11,2	12,4	7,6				
24	10,8	11,8	13,0	8,2	10	7,3	1,22	
26	11,5	12,3	13,7	8,7				B. Move object to approximate or indefinite location.
28	12,1	12,8	14,4	9,3				
30	12,7	13,3	15,1	9,8	12	8,8	1,27	
					14	10,4	1,32	
35	14,3	14,5	16,8	11,2				
40	15,8	15,6	18,5	12,6				
45	17,4	16,8	20,1	14,0	16	11,9	1,36	
50	19,0	18,0	21,8	15,4				
55	20,5	19,2	23,5	16,8				
					18	13,4	1,41	
60	22,1	20,4	25,2	18,2				C. Move object to exact location.
65	23,6	21,6	26,9	19,5	20	14,9	1,46	
70	25,2	22,8	28,6	20,9				
75	26,7	24,0	30,3	22,3				
80	28,3	25,2	32,0	23,7	22	16,4	1,51	

Figure 18.18. Methods-Time Measurement application data in tmu: MOVE

18. Predetermined Time Standards

IIIA. TURN - T

Weight (kg)	Time (tmu) for degrees turned										
	30°	45°	60°	75°	90°	105°	120°	135°	150°	165°	180°
Small: (0) to (1)	2,8	3,5	4,1	4,8	5,4	6,1	6,8	7,4	8,1	8,7	9,4
Medium: (1) to (5)	4,4	5,5	6,5	7,5	8,5	9,6	10,6	11,6	12,7	13,7	14,8
Large: (5.1) to (16)	8,4	10,5	12,3	14,4	16,2	18,3	20,4	22,2	24,3	26,1	28,2

Figure 18.19. Methods-Time Measurement application data in tmu: TURN

IIIB. APPLY PRESSURE - AP

Complete cycle			Components		
Symbol	tmu	Description	Symbol	tmu	Description
APA	10,6	AF + DM + RLF	AF	3,4	Apply force
			DM	4,2	Remain minimum time
APB	16,2	APA + G2	RLF	3,0	Release force

Figure 18.20. Methods-Time Measurement application data in tmu: APPLY PRESSURE

IV. GRASP - G

Case	Time (tmu)	Description
1A	2,0	Pick up grasp - small, medium or large object by itself, easily grasped.
1B	3,5	Very small object or object lying close against a flat surface.
1C1	7,3	Interference with grasp on bottom and one side of nearly cylindrical object. Diameter larger than 12 mm.
1C2	8,7	Interference with grasp on bottom and one side of nearly cylindrical object. Diameter 6 to 12 mm.
1C3	10,8	Interference with grasp on bottom and one side of nearly cylindrical object. Diameter less than 6 mm.
2	5,6	Regrasp.
3	5,6	Transfer grasp.
4A	7,3	Object jumbled with other objects so search and select occur. Larger than 25x25x25 mm.
4B	9,1	Object jumbled with other objects so search and select occur. 6 x 6 x 3 and 25 x 25 x 25 mm.
4C	12,9	Object jumbled with other objects so search and select occur. Smaller than 6 x 6 x 3 mm.
5	0	Contact, sliding or hook grasp.

Figure 18.21. Methods-Time Measurement application data in tmu: GRASP

V. POSITION - P

Class of fit		Symmetry	Easy to handle	Difficult to handle
1. Loose	No pressure required	S	5,6	11,2
		SS	9,1	14,7
		NS	10,4	16,0
2. Close	Light pressure required	S	16,2	21,8
		SS	19,7	25,3
		NS	21,0	26,6
3. Exact	Heavy pressure required	S	43,0	48,6
		SS	46,5	52,1
		NS	47,8	53,4

* Distance moved to engage - max. 25 mm.

Figure 18.22. Methods-Time Measurement application data in tmu: POSITION

VI. RELEASE - RL

Case	Time (tmu)	Description
1	2,0	Normal release performed by opening fingers as independent motion.
2	0	Contact release.

Figure 18.23. Methods-Time Measurement application data in tmu: RELEASE

VII. DISENGAGE - D

Class of fit		Easy to handle	Difficult to handle
1.	Loose - Very slight effort, blends with subsequent move.	4,0	5,7
2.	Close - Normal effort, slight recoil.	7,5	11,8
3.	Tight - Considerable effort, hand recoils markedly.	22,9	34,7

Figure 18.24. Methods-Time Measurement application data in tmu: DISENGAGE

VIII. EYE TRAVEL AND EYE FOCUS - ET and EF

Eye travel time $= 15{,}2 \times \frac{T}{D}$ tmu, with a maximum value of 20 tmu,

where $T =$ the distance between points from and to which the eye travels,

$D =$ the perpendicular distance from the eye to the line of travel T.

Eye focus time $= 7{,}3$ tmu.

Figure 18.25. Methods-Time Measurement application data in tmu: EYE TRAVEL and EYE FOCUS

IX. BODY, LEG AND FOOT MOTIONS

Description	Symbol	Distance	Time (tmu)
Foot motion			
Hinged at ankle	FM	Up to 10 cm	8,5
With heavy pressure	FMP		19,1
Leg or foreleg motion	LM	Up to 15 cm	7,1
		Each additional cm	0,5
Sidestep			
Case 1: Complete when leading leg contacts floor	SS-C1	Less than 30 cm	Use REACH or MOVE time
		30 cm	17,0
		Each extra cm	0,2
Case 2: Lagging leg must contact floor before next motion can be made	SS-C2	Up to 30 cm	34,1
		Each extra cm	0,4
Bend, stoop or kneel on one knee	B.S.KOK		29,0
Arise	AB.AS.AKOK		31,9
Kneel on floor - both knees	KBK		69,4
Arise	AKBK		76,7
Sit	SIT		34,7
Stand from sitting position	STD		43,3
Turn body 45 to 90 degrees::			
Case 1: Complete when leading leg contacts floor	TBC1		18,2
Case 2: Lagging leg must contact floor before next motion can be made	TBC2		37,2
Walk	W-M	Per metre	17,4
Walk	W-P	Per pace	15,0
Walk - obstructed	W-PO	Per pace	17,0

Figure 18.26. Methods-Time Measurement application data in tmu: BODY, LEG, AND FOOT MOTIONS

X. SIMULTANEOUS MOTIONS

REACH			MOVE			GRASP			POSITION			DISEN-GAGE		CASE	MOTION
A,E	B	C,D Bm	A	B	C G2	G1A G1C G5	G1B	G4	P1S P2S	P1SS P2SS	P1NS D1D P2NS	D1E	D2		
*W O		*W O	*W O		*W O	*W O			**E D	**E D	**E D		**E D		
			X X				X X X							A, E	REACH
	X		X X ■			X X ■ X X X			■ ■			X		B	
X X ■	X ■ ■ ■					X ■ ■ ■ ■ ■ ■ ■ ■ ■						X	■ ■	C, D	
							X X X						A, Bm	
						X X ■ X X X			■ ■			X		B	MOVE
					X ■	X ■ ■ ■ ■ ■ ■ ■ ■ ■						X	■ ■	C	
									■ ■ ■				■ ■	G1A, G2, G5	
							■ ■ X		■ ■ ■ ■ ■ ■				■ ■	G1B, G1C	GRASP
									■ ■ ■ ■ ■ ■			■	■ ■	G4	
									X ■ ■ ■ ■ ■ ■			■	■ ■	P1S	
									■ ■ ■ ■ ■ ■			■	■ ■	P1SS, P2S	POSITION
									■ ■ ■ ■ ■ ■			■	■ ■	P1NS, P2SS, P2NS	
												X	X X	D1E, D1D	DISENGAGE
													X X	D2	

□ = EASY to perform simultaneously.
☒ = Can be performed simultaneously with PRACTICE.
■ = DIFFICULT to perform simultaneously, even afetr long practice. Allow both times.

Motions not included in above table: TURN - Normally EASY with all motions except when TURN is controlled or with DISENGAGE.
APPLY PRESSURE, CRANK - May be EASY, require PRACTICE, or DIFFICULT. Each case must be analysed.

POSITION - Class 3 - Always DIFFICULT. DISENGAGE - Class 3 - Normally DIFFICULT. RELEASE Always EASY. DISENGAGE. - Any class may be difficult if care must be exercised to avoid injury or damage to object.
W = Within the area of normal vision, i.e. r=10 cm, d=40cm.
O = Outside the area of normal vision, i.e. r=10 cm, d=40cm.
E = EASY to handle.
D = DIFFICULT to handle.

Source: Official International MTM-1 Data, © International MTM Directorate and MTM Association for Standards and Research. Tables reproduced by kind permission of the International MTM Directorate.

Figure 18.27. Methods-Time Measurement application data in tmu: SIMULTANEOUS MOTIONS

Questions

1. What is PTS?

2. List the components of a PTS system.

3. List some PTS systems and indicate their scope.

4. List the categories that compose the MTM-2 system and their corresponding codes.

Problem

Perform the analysis and break down into elements the operation "Take five steps, grab an object (1 kg), take five steps, and leave it on table."

Document 2 - Task Study						
Operation Description	MTM Element	Code	TMU	Q	F	Total TMU
Take five steps, grab an object (1 kg), take five steps, and leave it on table.						
					Total task execution time (TMU):	

Figure 18.28.

Bibliography

Kanawaty, George *Introduction to Work Study* (Geneva: International Labor Organization, 1992).

Chapter 19

Development of Standard Data and Time Formulas: Methods Study and Parameterized Times

19.1. Introduction and Concepts

So far we have worked with time studies where the parameters remained constant. One of the objectives of the study of methods and parameterized times is to be able to know the standard time of a task for producing goods, based on certain variables of such goods, without needing to study each of them. For this, it is necessary:

1. Standard data: Operation times that are common to different tasks and products.

2. Time formulas: Solutions to the variation of frequency and the normal times of the operations based on product variables and batch size.

3. Database containing both the standard data and their formulas and equations in order to use them in the construction of studies of methods and times for each task.

We feed these data from the study of methods and parameterized times into a computer program that will return a standard time from basic times, time formulas, and the parameters of each order or product.

Industrial productivity

Nowadays companies often have a wide variety of products or even brands whose life in the market is relatively short. What sectors might deal with this problem?

For example, in the shoe industry a shoe model has a lifetime of six months, along with a great variety of models from competitors. Actually, automobile companies offer made-to-order cars, where the equipment and finish can be personalized. In the fashion world, apparel companies feature catalogs of clothes and accessories that change each season.

If an analyst had to study the manufacturing process of all the models and goods and each of their variants one by one, cost and time would make the endeavour nonviable. A study of methods and times has to provide a greater benefit than the cost to conduct it.

The studies of methods and parameterized times offer a solution to this problem, from mathematical formulas and variables. They are also a potent tool for calculating costs, making quotations, and performing simulations of options and materials.

An analyst performing the studies or using the tools needs to consider all factors that may influence the execution time of the task, such as batch size to produce, the number of different screw references, the necessary quantity of rivets, quantity of transportable kilograms, elevator speed, lifetime of the blade, and distance between workstations are some of the parameters and the ways in which they may be manipulated, depending on the studied reference. The analyst must know the task well, along with the characteristics of the product or service. In this chapter, you will learn about the calculation of the standard time of a product or good with variables from time formulas and standard data.

Standard data can be obtained from any of the studied measurement techniques based on the characteristics of the task and the precision desired. The most common techniques are timekeeping and PTS (MTM) systems.

19.2. Principles for Elaborating Standard Data and Time Formulas

As has been described, the total corrected time of each operation is calculated from the following formula:

> Normal Time x Supplements x Units Repeated = Total Operation Time

Each component of the equation may vary for a particular operation based on several parameters. In this section we look at how to calculate the total corrected time of an operation using formulas. The most relevant variable in the variation of the standard time of the task normally is "Repeated units" of the operation.

19.2.1. Calculation of the Normal Time Component

Chapter 16 described how to calculate the normal time of an operation through timekeeping and scrutiny. This section examines the calculation of normal time of an operation based on specific variables.

For obtaining the normal time of an operation through variables, all aspects, conditions, or factors that can modify their value must be taken into consideration. Therefore, the following premises will be followed:

1. *Variables identification:* The analyst will not overlook anything and will question whether any aspect, as small as it may seem, might affect the normal time of the operation, from the width of the cutting disk, to the weight and volume of a material transported by a crane.

2. *Calculate the value of the normal time based on variables*: A formula or algebraic expression will be developed that will establish the normal time of the operation before the production, using values or known variables typical of the operation.

- *Manual labor:* Variables will be fixed and scrutiny made. Once the analyst has identified the variables that can influence obtaining the normal time of the operation, those variables will be fixed in the methods and times study and verifications will be performed. After checking, the analyst will implement the possible corrections in the study of methods and parameterized times. The following case provides an example.

Example

A footwear company offers in its product catalog a type of athletic shoe. According to the characteristics of this range, all the shoes have the sole stitched manually to the rest of the shoe, so great skill and dexterity are required. The analyst performed a study of methods and times for a shoe model made of pigskin and used the time for that same task with shoes made of cowhide, goat, or plastic. In this way, the analyst can use that study of times and methods for the rest of ranges and models without needing to measure them all. The time invested in sewing a shoe was the following:

- *Nautical model with rubber sole + pigskin = 309 seconds/unit*

This datum is the starting point for the analyst. All the models are sewn in the same way: the sole is the same, the material used to sew is similar in all the models, and the linear distance is similar. The only factor that changes from one model to another is the type of skin. So the following step is to determine whether this factor really influences the execution time of the task. The results are as follows:

- *Nautical model with rubber sole + cowhide = 339.9 seconds/unit*

- *Nautical model with rubber sole + goatskin = 321.5 seconds/unit*
- *Nautical model with rubber sole + plastic = 402 seconds/unit*

A scrutiny has to be made from a great number of data collections in order to obtain a series of data as reliable as possible that comply with an equation of the type:

$$\text{Time} = K + Bx$$

The data that are going to be listed are from B. K is supposedly taken into account in another standard datum, normally a constant that corresponds with the preparation. x is the length of the sewing.

Afterwards, based on the design sketches the sewn length must be confirmed to know the sewing speed. If the sewing distance is 49 cm, we will have:

- *Sewing speed in pigskin = 0.158 centimeters/second*
- *Sewing speed in cowhide = 0.144 centimeters/second*
- *Sewing speed in goatskin = 0.152 centimeters/second*
- *Sewing speed in plastic = 0.122 centimeters/second*

Once these results are obtained, the following step is to compare it with the rest of models from the other ranges. The analyst should check and keep an eye on the possible variables that influence in the time duration of the hand-sewn shoe. It is possible that the previous models are also offered with a different type of sole or different shoe design, factors that should be considered.

This list of data would be the standard data. Once obtained and calculated, we would proceed in the following way:

1. File them in a standard database.
2. Use them in the construction of methods and times, which implies that it would not be necessary to measure again the time of these operations, because what changes in calculating the standard time is the frequency, units, length, etc.
3. For the previous case, the sewing lengths would be measured for every type of shoe and multiplied by the sewing time that depends on the type of skin.

19. Development of Standard Data and Time Formulas: Methods Study and Parameterized Times

■ *Works with machines:* A set of data will be taken (the most representative and whose validity is proven) as a starting point for being able to build a mathematical expression that calculates, from the defined variables, the normal time of the operation.

What variables will influence the cutting speed of a blade? Well the type of blade, the amount of material to cut, the width of the material roll and the degree of wastage are some of the variables that influence the cutting speed. Afterwards we will solve an example to assimilate correctly what has been explained. **In machine-times is where time formulas appear, although time can also be a constant.**

Example

A shirt company has a fabric cutting section. This company produces a wide variety of shirts of different sizes, materials, and finishes. During the fabric cutting for the tailoring of these shirts, the analyst obtained a list of data groups that resulted in the following:

- *For cutting 30 fabrics with a material wastage level of 11%, the speed was 16 m/s.*

- *For cutting 52 fabrics with a material wastage level of 22%, the speed was 15 m/s.*

The analyst studied the relationship between the different parameters:

- *The a variable relates the quantity of fabrics.*

- *The b variable relates the level of material wastage.*

Therefore:

- *Equation: $30a + 11b = 16$*

- *Equation: $52a + 22b = 15$*

Solving the equations system with two unknowns, we will have:

- *$a = 2.125$*

- *$b = -4.34$*

Subsequently, the analyst extracted another group of data from the list of variables and repeated the same process until the equation system resulted in new values for a and b. Later the analyst repeated this process until obtaining a large enough sample to have reliable data. These data are presented in table and graph formats.

Industrial productivity

System	Nº of fabrics	% wastage	Speed
System 1	55	23.50	15.00
System 2	53	23.62	16.23
System 3	53	21.32	15.32
System 4	52	21.21	14.32
System 5	51	22.63	16.32
System 6	49	19.98	16.25
System 7	32	10.50	14.99
System 8	31	10.26	16.02
System 9	31	11.30	14.23
System 10	30	11.01	15.63
System 11	29	10.30	16.38
System 12	29	10.95	16.54
System 13	29	10.84	16.46
System 14	27	9.65	17.00
System 15	20	5.32	14.32
System 16	19	9.00	15.55
System 17	15	3.23	16.10

Figure 19.1.

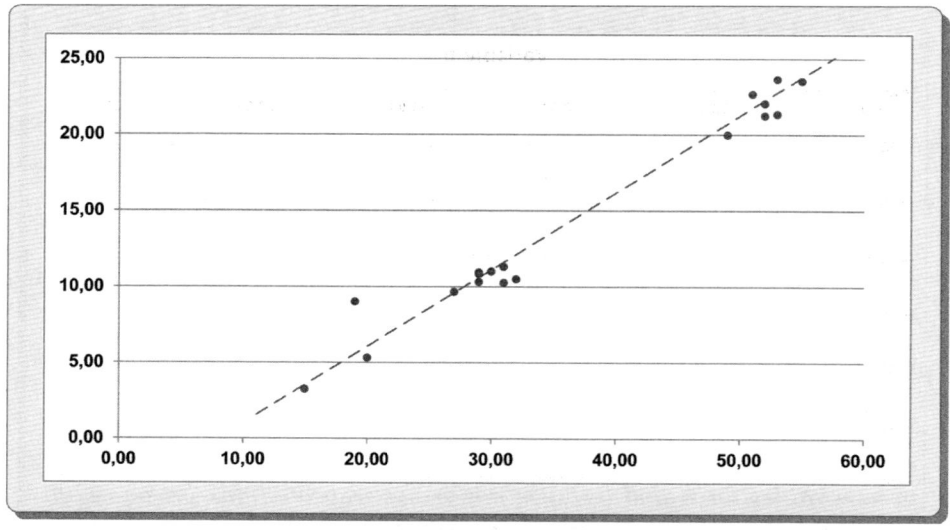

Figure 19.2. Representation of points

In the graph, the number of fabrics is plotted on the x axis and the level of material wastage on the y axis. Observing the representation of points we see how they take the shape of a straight line. On other occasions they may have a parabolic or other shape. The next step is to solve the systems of equations in order to calculate the values of the variables a and b.

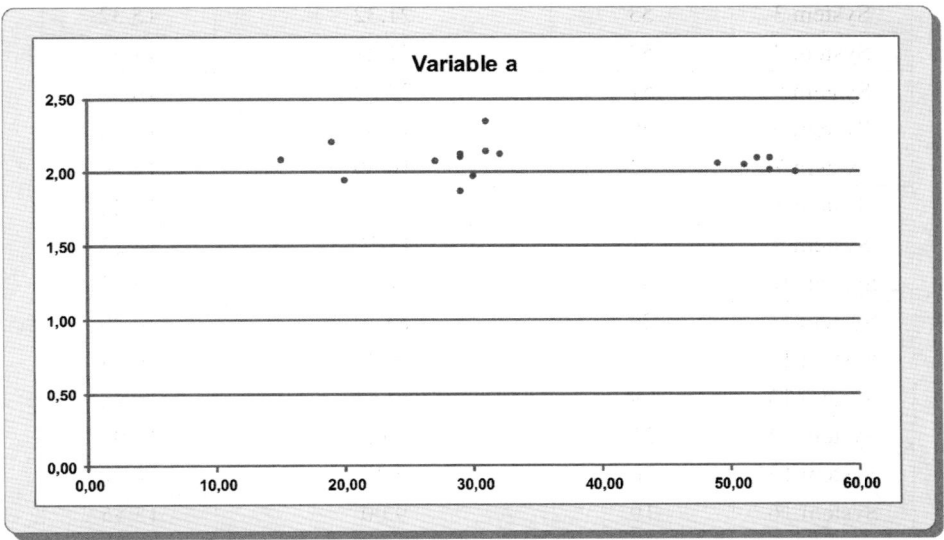

Figure 19.3. Representation of the a variable

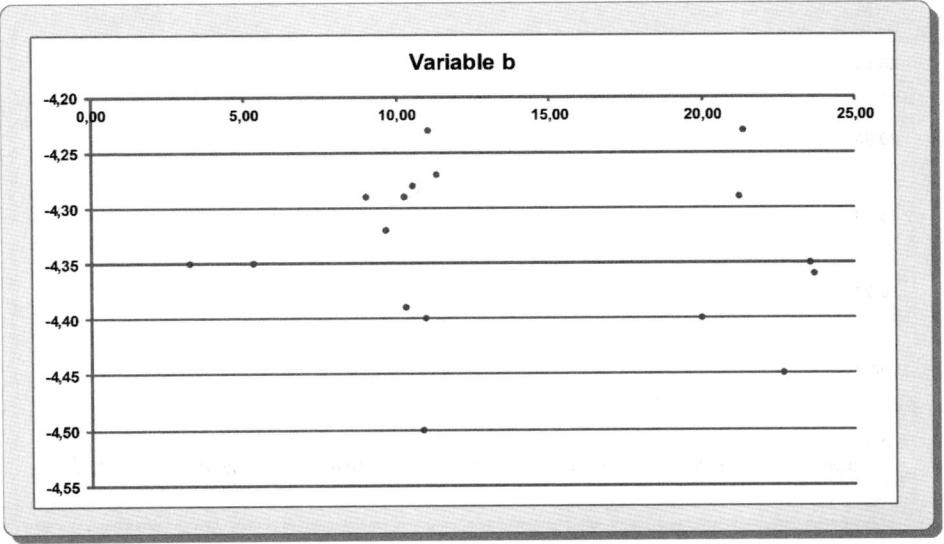

Figure 19.4. Representation of the b variable

Industrial productivity

Once the analyst has calculated the set of values for a and b, and each of the variables are plotted in a graph, a scrutiny will be made:

- $a = 2.08$
- $b = -4.34$

Therefore, the mathematical expression is:

- *Cutting speed = (2.08 x n° fabrics) – (4.34 x Wastage level)*

The appearance of the equation may be different depending on the number and the variables used to obtain them. We will now see a new model for the calculation of the normal time of an operation.

Example

In a metal processing company, a bridge crane is used to supply steel-plate coils to a hydraulic press. In order to calculate the motion speed of the crane, the analyst concluded that it depended only of the weight of the coils. From the data list, the following set of data was extracted:

- *For 2-ton coils, the time was 3 sec/meter.*
- *For 0.66-ton coils, the time was 1 sec/meter.*

Therefore:

- *Equation: $2a = 3$*
- *Equation: $0.66a = 1$*

Solving, we have several values for the a variable: 1.51 and 1.50. Logically, a larger sampling would have to be done.

Afterwards, we will repeat the same process. On this occasion we will choose two new groups of data and obtain new values for a. We will repeat the process until we have volume of data large enough so as to obtain reliable data. After performing the scrutiny of variable a, we have the following mathematical expression:

- *Time (sec/meter) = 1.507 x Coil weight*

On other occasions, the analyst will not have such an arduous task. Normally, the variables related to the machine are supplied by the manufacturer of the machine, facilitating the work of the analyst.

In the case of these two examples, what we have is a time that depends on some variables and an equation; they are examples of time formulas. What would be done is:

19. Development of Standard Data and Time Formulas: Methods Study and Parameterized Times

1. File the time formulas and their already-calculated constants in a database.

2. Perform the study of times, substituting the formula in the time box, because time is not a constant.

3. The methods and times study should include the parameters or variables that influence the time formulas.

4. Remember that if the formula calculates the speed, we will put the inverse of speed (1/speed) in the times study.

5. Equally, the frequency or units will be substituted in the table of methods and times.

3. Results checking: Because it is an extrapolation and interpolation of results from the characteristics of a good or product, it is important to subject the formula to an operational test and to considerate the possible deviation of its result. For this reason, we should include a supplement increase for unexpected events in extrapolated operations as a cushion for the possible deviations in time. This supplement will be calculated with the variance (S2 or σ2), which is obtained in the checks.

19.2.2. Calculation of the Rest Supplement Component

Another of the total operating time components is the additional rest supplement. As was described in Chapter 16, once the normal operating time of an operation has been calculated, the following step is to increase it with the application of supplements.

These supplements are applied as a function of the characteristics and conditions of the operation in question. This means that when performing the time parameterization, the analyst must pay special attention to the variables that can affect the conditions of an operation and its rest supplement. One operation can be "Load wooden board." If we are conducting a study of methods and parameterized times, the weight and size of the boards can mean a different additional rest supplement.

To carry out the calculation of the additional rest supplement, the following aspects must be taken into consideration:

- Identify what variables affect the application of rest supplements. Normally, for an operation, it will be weight.

- Formulate the equations that calculate the supplements as a function of variables.

A simple case can be a table that reeds and loads supplements as a function of the parameter "product weight." We will discuss an example to explain the calculation of this component of the equation.

Industrial productivity

Example

A wooden furniture manufacturing company for kitchens acquires the laminated wooden boards from a supplier and buys the metal sheets with a different finish from another supplier. This company is responsible for assembling the two finish sheets to the wooden laminated board. Such laminated wooden board can have several thicknesses. In order to perform this task, an operator is responsible for supplying a press by depositing piles of boards in the press covering. It will apply a layer of glue in each layer and will stick together two sheets of wooden veneer. Afterwards, a second operator will store the processed board.

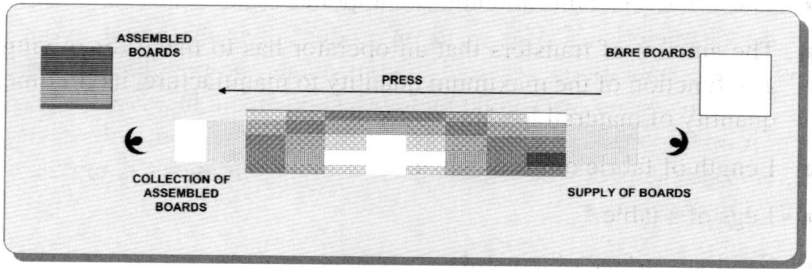

Figure 19.5.

The first operator receives piles on pallets of the same height, independently of the thickness of the boards. Therefore, the quantity of boards varies as a function of thickness. For the case studied by the analyst, the operator supplied the press with boards of 0.4 m x 0.8 m x 0.016 m for a pile height of 1.75 meters. If wood density is 900 kilograms/cubic meter, we will have:

- Board weight = (0.4 m x 0.8 m x 0.016 m) x 900 kg/m3 = 4.61 kg/unit. If we revise the rest supplement table, an additional 1% has to be applied to the operation.

Weight (kg)	2,5	5	7,5	10	12,5	15	17,5	20	22,5	25	30	35,5
Supplement (%)	0	1	2	3	4	5	7	9	11	13	17	22

What supplement must be applied to 0.72 m x 1 m x 0.016 m boards?

We will proceed analogously:

- Board weight = (0.72 m x 1 m x 0.016 m) x 900 kg/m3 = 10.37 kg/unit. If we revise the rest supplement table, an additional 4% has to be applied to the operation.

All these conditions will be indicated in the parameter table of the study of methods and parameterized times and must be considered with the use of mathematical formulas.

19.2.3. Calculation of the Units Component

Ultimately, the calculation of the last component of the equation involves the units. Such component will be defined by the number of times that an operation is repeated in order to manufacture a product unit or batch as a function of the parameters. The difficulty of calculating this parameter can vary with the task subject of study, which can be defined, for example, in the following ways:

- The amount of bolts and nuts a component has
- The amount of transfers that an operator has to make for mixing paints as a function of the maximum quantity to manufacture, its lifetime, or the quantity of material loads
- Length of fabric or shoes sewn
- Legs of a table
- Sanding surface of a board

The first case will be simple and involves consulting the list of materials (LOM) for the component in order to know those units. The second case is more complex. For it we will resort to the previous example of the wooden board press. At the end of the chapter, several examples are supplied to clarify these concepts.

Example

As explained in the previous example, two operators were in charge of supplying and stockpiling the processed boards. The pile of boards awaiting processing always has the same height, independent of the board thickness, which means that for the same amount of boards, the greater the thickness the greater the quantity of board piles that must be supplied to the operator. For the case under study, the quantity is 240 units, of 4.5 centimetres in thickness, being supplied in piles of 175 centimeters in height. In order to calculate the number of pallets needed we will proceed the following way:

- *175 centimeters/pile / 4.5 centimeters/board = 39 boards/pile*
- *240 boards / 39 boards/pile → 7 board piles must be supplied to the operators*

Industrial productivity

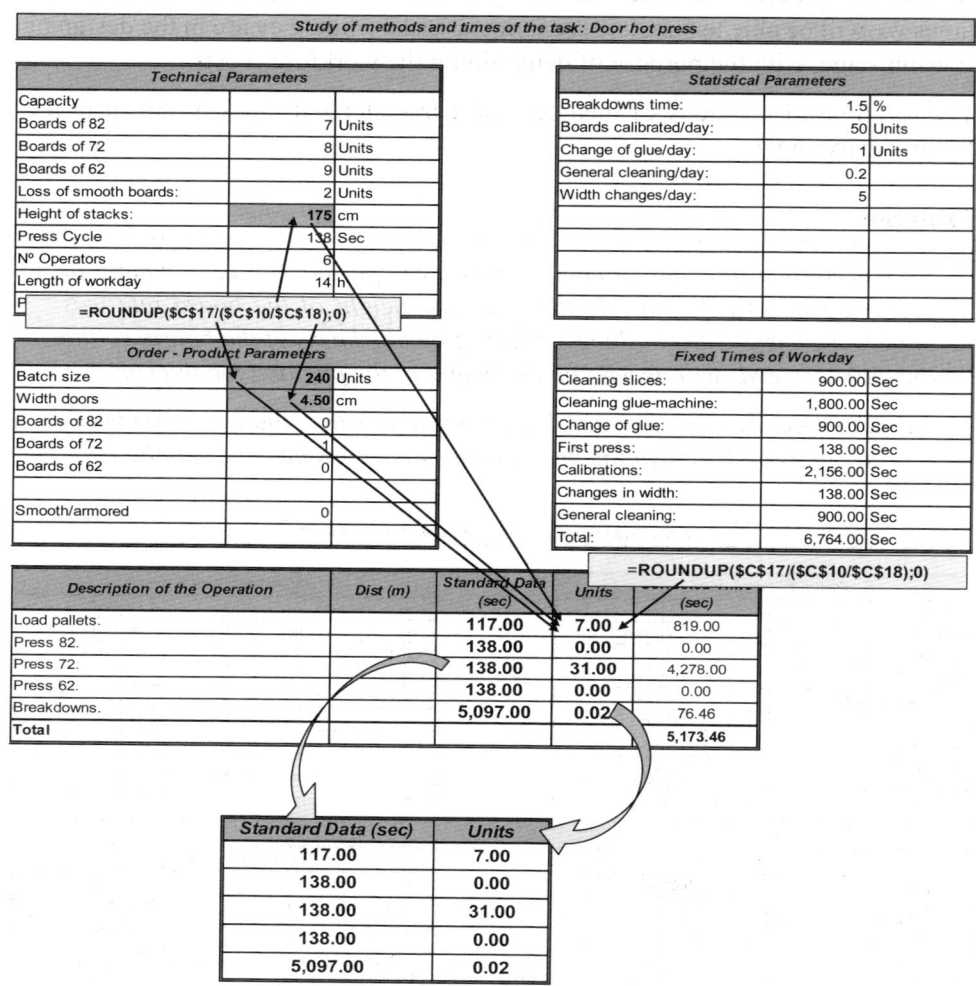

Figure 19.6.

19.3. Handling of Variable Elements: The Study of Methods and Parameterized Times

The handling of the study of methods and parameterized times will be similar to what has been seen so far. The difference will be in times not being obtained from a new timekeeping but from standard data; or time formulas and frequencies will not be constant but will depend on the parameters that vary from one task or product to another: batch size, rest supplements, lengths, types of material, drill gauge, product weight, and so on.

19. Development of Standard Data and Time Formulas: Methods Study and Parameterized Times

As previously described, when designing a study of methods and parameterized times we will be able to simulate scenarios or tasks while they are in the design or start-up stage, with the purpose of determining the workforce costs.

The handling of the study of methods and parameterized times is shown in the following example.

Example

> We will use the previous example, where two operators were in charge of supplying wooden boards. In this task, the height of the board pile was always the same, 175 cm, independent of the thickness of the board, so the number of boards will depend on the height of the pile and the thickness.
>
> We will proceed to simulate another scenario. For this, the size of the batch is 1,000 units of 3.3 cm in thickness. How many piles must be supplied?

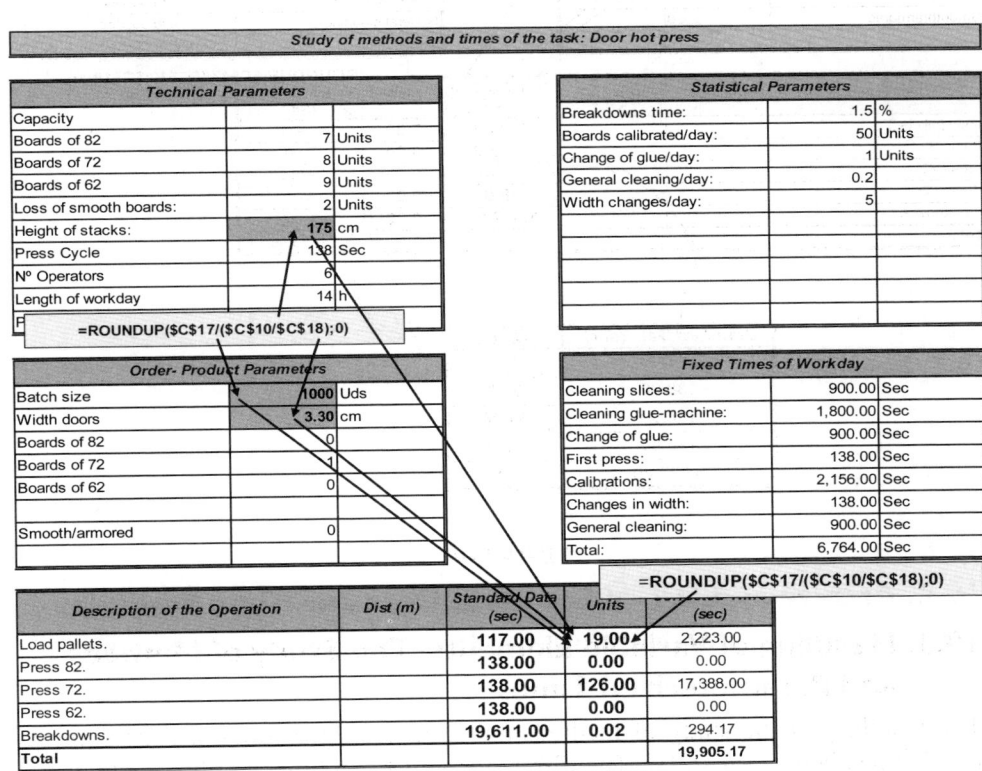

Figure 19.7.

Industrial productivity

Substituting the new values in the table of the order parameters, we will obtain the amount of board piles that have to be supplied. What will happen if the height of the piles is elevated to 185 cm?

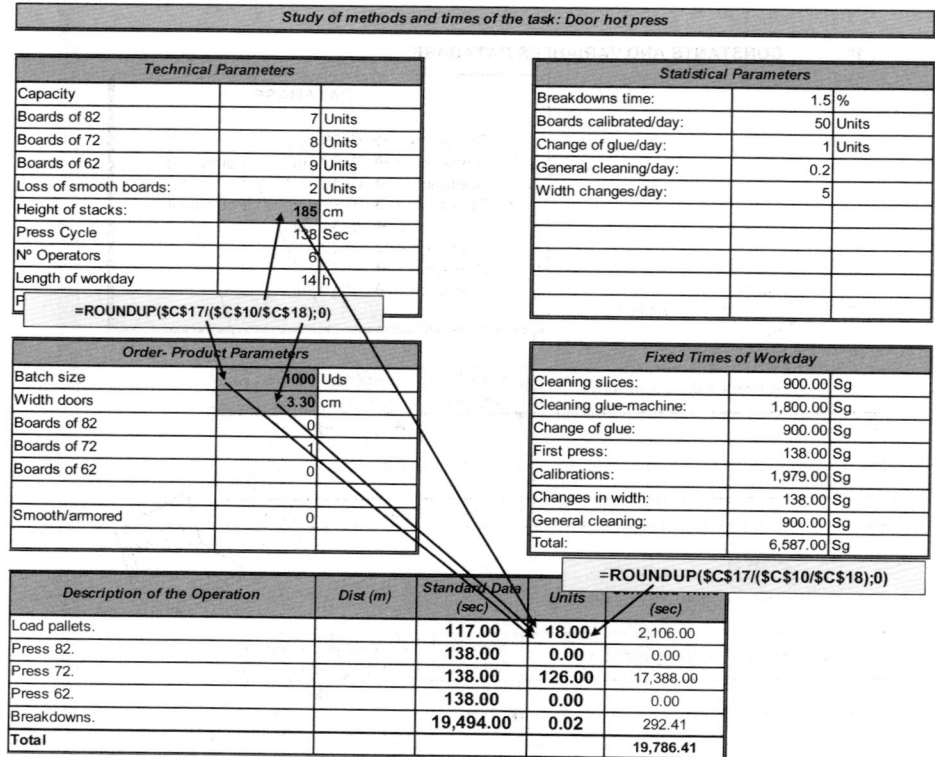

Figure 19.8.

When we modify the table of technical parameters, automatically the value of the operation "Load pallet" is updated.

19.4. Archive and Use of Standard Data and Time Formulas

Once standard data have been calculated and time formulas elaborated, we proceed to:

1. File them in databases.

2. Use them in the construction of studies of methods and times.

3. Update them as a function of technological changes in machinery, tools, or work methods.

19. Development of Standard Data and Time Formulas: Methods Study and Parameterized Times

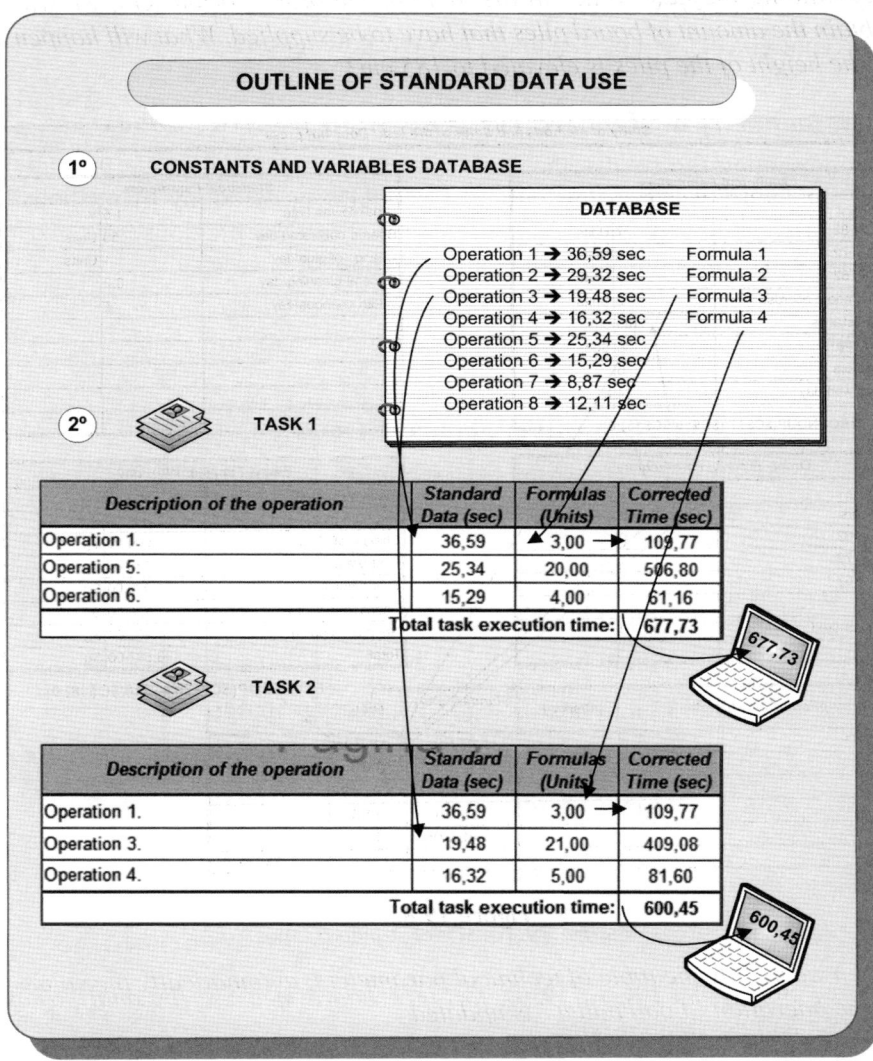

Figure 19.9. Using standard data and time formulas

19.5. Presentation of Results

The presentation of results from the time studies from standard data and time formulas will need to include, at a minimum, the following:

- Summary of the resulting standard times of the goods
- The construction of the study of methods and parameterized times that justify those standard times

Industrial productivity

- Justification of the formulas and standard data

These requirements will be explained in the following sections.

19.5.1. Summary of Standard Times Resulting from the Goods

When presenting the results, the analyst must make a list showing the standard times obtained from the substitution of variables in the study of methods and parameterized times for each good or reference. From the previous example, a list is made of standard times divided by the thickness of boards:

Example

List of Standard Times		
Item	sec/unit	min/unit
13 mm boards	23.65	0.394
16 mm boards	24.28	0.405
19 mm boards	24.28	0.405
25 mm boards	24.91	0.415
33 mm boards	25.55	0.426
38 mm boards	26.18	0.436
45 mm boards	26.82	0.447
51 mm boards	26.82	0.447

Figure 19.10. List of standard times

As we can see in Figure 19.10, for each board measure the analyst has calculated the standard time.

19.5.2. Study of Methods and Parameterized Times

Along with the elaborated list will be attached the study of methods and parameterized times, which justifies the results obtained and that, in case of doubts, can be consulted to verify the standard times. The presented study of methods and times from the example would resemble Figure 19.11.

19. Development of Standard Data and Time Formulas: Methods Study and Parameterized Times

Example

Study of methods and times of the task: Door hot press

Technical Parameters

Capacity		
Boards of 82	7	Units
Boards of 72	8	Units
Boards of 62	9	Units
Loss of smooth boards:	2	Units
Height of stacks:	175	cm
Press Cycle	138	Sec
N° Operators	6	
Length of workday	14	h
Paradas	1	

Statistical Parameters

Breakdowns time:	1.5	%
Boards calibrated/day:	50	Units
Change of glue/day:	1	Units
General cleaning/day:	0.2	
Width changes/day:	5	

Order- Product Parameters

Batch size	240	Units
Width doors	5.10	cm
Boards of 82	0	
Boards of 72	1	
Boards of 62	0	
Smooth/armored	0	

Fixed Times of Workday

Cleaning slices:	900.00	Sec
Cleaning glue-machine:	1,800.00	Sec
Change of glue:	900.00	Sec
First press:	138.00	Sec
Calibrations:	1,979.00	Sec
Changes in width:	138.00	Sec
General cleaning:	900.00	Sec
Total:	6,587.00	Sec

Description of the Operation	Dist (m)	Standard Data (sec)	Units	Corrected Time (sec)
Load pallets.		117.00	7.00	819.00
Press 82.		138.00	0.00	0.00
Press 72.		138.00	31.00	4,278.00
Press 62.		138.00	0.00	0.00
Breakdowns.		5,097.00	0.02	76.46
		Total task execution time (sec):		5,173.46
		Standard Time (sec/unit):		21.56

Figure 19.11. Example of study of methods and parameterized times

Example

Document 1 - Task data and summary of the study of methods and times

Order/Product Parameters

Field	Quantity	Units
Batch size	10.00	units

Technical Parameters

Field	Quantity	Units
Number of thermometers.	2	
Number of valves.	2	
Number of parts/tool.	2	
Tool surface.	0.65	m2
Nylon sheet surface.	0.46	m2
Sealant perimeter.	3.98	ml
Number of holes.	2	
Quantity of drills that can be performed.	20	
Number of scrapings that can be performed.	5	
Speed of person on foot.	0.80	sec/ml
Elevator speed.	1.25	sec/ml
Distance from table to parking.	14.00	m
Distance from table to shelves.	25.00	m
Distance from shelves to parking.	20.00	m
Distance toward tool- able.	5	m
Distance to cart of demolded parts.	12	m

Statistical Parameters

Field	Quantity	Units
Remove nylon and scum.	70.11	sec/m2
Remove nylon sheet.	44.37	sec/m2
Tool scraping.	18.65	sec/ml
Tool blowing.	46.37	sec/m2
Application of demolding liquid.	34.48	sec/m2

Supplements

Personal needs.	5%
Fatigue.	4%
Stand.	2%
Unexpected.	1%
Beginning and end of day.	1%
Total general supplements	13%

Figure 19.12a. Example of task data and parameters

645

Industrial productivity

As can be observed, the technical parameters and workstation layout are inserted as a function of the calculation of normal times. (See Figure 19.12b.)

Document 2 - Study of methods and times of the task							
Description of the Operation	Type of Operation	Distance (meters)	Standard Data (sec)	Additional Suppl. (%)	Total Supplements (%)	Units	Total Corrected Time (sec)
Remove thermometers.	○		4.32	0.00%	13.00%	20	97.63
Accumulate thermometers.	○		18.84	0.00%	13.00%	20	425.78
Remove valves.	○		2.99	0.00%	13.00%	20	67.57
Take valves and thermometers to worktable and get scraper.	⇨	5.00	0.80	0.00%	13.00%	1	4.52
Remove nylon layer and scum with help of scraper.	○		70.11	0.00%	13.00%	6	513.19
Throw removed material to garbage container.	○		10.25	0.00%	13.00%	10	115.83
Remove nylon layer without drilling.	○		44.37	0.00%	13.00%	5	230.03
Provision drill and template.	○		13.00	0.00%	13.00%	1	14.69
Take bit in drill to sharpen.	⇨		54.86	0.00%	13.00%	1	61.99
Sharpen bit in drill.	○		45.31	0.00%	13.00%	1	51.20
Place bit in drill.	⇨		53.09	0.00%	13.00%	1	59.99
Connect drill to compressed air outlet.	○		6.89	0.00%	13.00%	1	7.79
Place template to drill.	○		5.59	0.00%	13.00%	20	126.33
Perform hole and clean drilled area.	○		17.83	10.00%	23.00%	20	438.62
Remove template from drill.	○		4.78	0.00%	13.00%	20	108.03
Take pattern and drill to tool table.	⇨	5.00	0.80	0.00%	13.00%	1	4.52
Remove perimeter tape with help of scraper.	○		18.65	0.00%	13.00%	40	838.77
Provide wooden wedge and pot.	○		13.00	0.00%	13.00%	1	14.69
Extract part from tool with help of scraper.	○		28.67	0.00%	13.00%	10	323.97
Retake part paperworks.	○		53.47	0.00%	13.00%	1	60.42
Check paperwork with part.	○		22.84	0.00%	13.00%	10	258.09
Fill in part paperwork.	○		21.73	0.00%	13.00%	10	245.55
Take demolded part to delivery cart.	⇨	12.00	0.80	0.00%	13.00%	1	10.85
Deposit part in delivery cart.	○		5.34	0.00%	13.00%	1	6.03
Return delivery cart.	⇨	12.00	0.80	0.00%	13.00%	1	10.85
Take scraper to sharpen.	⇨	5.00	0.80	0.00%	13.00%	1	4.52
Sharpen scraper.	○		8.81	0.00%	13.00%	1	9.96
Return from sharpening scraper.	⇨	5.00	0.80	0.00%	13.00%	1	4.52
Remove residues of resin and tool tape with use of scraper.	○		18.65	0.00%	13.00%	40	838.77
Take and connect compressed airgun.	○		28.29	0.00%	13.00%	1	31.97
Remove dust and dirt with help of compressed air gun, removing with scraper possible residues of tape.	○		46.37	0.00%	13.00%	6	339.43
Carrry compressed air gun. Get demoliding liquid and cloth.	⇨		24.19	0.00%	13.00%	2	54.67
Apply demoliding liquid with cloth to the tool.	○		34.48	0.00%	13.00%	5	178.77
Carry demoliding liquid to worktable.	⇨	5.00	0.80	0.00%	13.00%	1	4.52
Take label from tool.	○		10.35	0.00%	13.00%	10	116.96
Fill in label from tool.	○		12.17	0.00%	13.00%	10	137.52
					Total task execution time (sec):		5,818.54

N° Operators	Standard Time (sec/unit)	Standard Time (min/unit)
1	581.85	9.70

Figure 19.12b. *Example of study of methods and parameterized times*

19.5.3. Formula Justification

Finally, all that remains pending is justification of the mathematical formulas used to calculate the normal time of each operation. As explained in section 19.3, when obtaining the mathematical expression that generates the normal time or standard datum of an operation, the aspect or format of the expression may vary, from a second-degree equation to a linear equation. When calculating the variables on which each of the parameters depend, the fulfillment of a scrutiny or a mathematical programs such as Mathlab, Orcad, or similar can be used. On other occasions the use of scrutiny or mathematical programs will not be necessary, because the parameter from which the normal time or standard data of an operation depends can be facilitated by the manufacturer of the machine.

In any case, the following points need to be clarified:

1. Operations with variable times
2. Performed data collection
3. Obtained formulas
4. Rationale for the operation that explains such formulas

19.6. Examples of Parameterized Studies

Example

A company of processed-metal products needs to know the standard times of all its products. This company makes auxiliary components for industrial vehicle dashboards. Such components are manufactured from a steel sheet. That press is in charge of making the preshapes that afterwards will be assembled to the rest of components and will be installed in the vehicle.

The company has a wide catalog of metal components, each of them with different size, shape, hardness, resistance, and so on, which implies a need for the company to have a raw material stock. For this stock, the company has a warehouse where it stores the different types of steel sheet coils, each of them in a predetermined location. This situation makes the time for loading and unloading coils variable, because each one is at a different distance in location. For this task, the company installed a large tonnage bridge crane.

To perform the study of methods and times of this task, the analyst followed the guidelines described in Chapter 3. The analyst studied the behavior of the bridge crane in charge of supplying the raw materials to the press, breaking it down into transversal and longitudinal transfers and lifting and lowering speed in order to determine conditions:

Industrial productivity

- *Longitudinal transfer time: 1 second/meter*
- *Transversal transfer time: 0.50 seconds/meter*
- *Lifting and lowering time: 29 seconds*

Once we know the behavior of the bridge crane, we only have to carry out the sequence of operations and calculate the normal time of each of them. We will focus on the operation "Transport coil to table," which includes the lifting, longitudinal transfer, transversal transfer, and the lowering of the clamping hook with the coil.

The machine speeds will be substituted in the technical parameters of the study of methods and times.

The same way, the roll forming machine times are calculated (speed of sheet passing) and packaging.

In this case, where sheets are manufactured for construction, each order has different measures in order to adapt to the building site. It is not possible to have a standard time for sheet unit; we have to calculate the time of each order and to do so we have to resort to a study of methods and parameterized times.

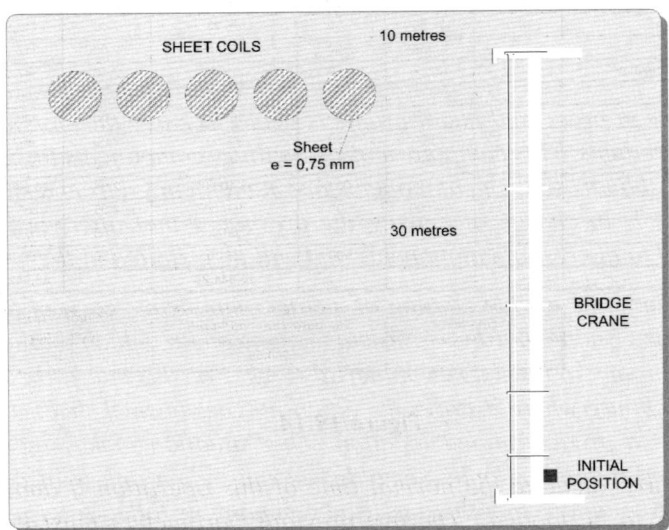

Figure 19.13.

Knowing the distances and speeds, we are able to calculate the normal time of the operation.

- *29 sec. + (30 meters x 1 sec./meter) + (10 meters x 0.5 sec./meter) + 29 sec. = 108 seconds for the operation "Transport coil to table"*

19. Development of Standard Data and Time Formulas: Methods Study and Parameterized Times

Study of methods and times of the task: Outline

Technical Parameters

Coil width:	1250	mm
Longitudinal speed crane:	1	m/sec
Transversal speed crane:	0.5	m/sec
Time up/down crane:	29	sec
Speed passing plate:	3.29	sec/ml
Steel density:	7850	Kg/m3
Coil weight:	8000	Kg
Profiling machine power:	15	Kw
Power of crane:	15	Kw
Energy cost:	0.085	Euros

Statistical Parameters

Distance to coil store	30	m
Distance of coil transport	10	m
N° coils that are moved in store:	4	coils
D. store	15	m
Coil changeovers	1.5	changes
per order	0.25	changes
Profile changes		

=$C$8+($H$5/$C$6)+($H$6/$C$7)+$C$8

Profile and order parameters:

Plate thickness:	0.75	mm
Profile type:		
N° plates/package:	40.00	sheets
Total meters of order:	4000.00	m
Plate average length:	7.00	m
Different measures:	2.00	Units
Order weight:	29,437.5	Kg
	29.4	Tn

=$C$8+($H$5/$C$6)+($H$6/$C$7)+$C$8

Description of the Operation	Dist (m)	Standard Data (sec)	Units	Corrected Time (sec)	N° Operators	Person Time (sec)	Operation Code
Inspect note		25.00	1.00	25.00	1.00	25.00	
Place crane	45	74.00	1.00	74.00	1.00	74.00	B CRANE
Change profile		3605.96	0.25	901.49	2.00	1,802.98	B CRANE
Remove current coil		258.00	1.00	258.00	2.00	516.00	B CRANE
Weight and discharge		15.00	1.00	15.00	2.00	30.00	B CRANE
Transport to store		108.00	1.00	108.00	2.00	216.00	B CRANE
Unleash		62.64	1.00	62.64	2.00	125.28	B CRANE
Take new coil		427.92	1.50	641.88	2.00	1,283.76	B CRANE
Transport to table		108.00	1.50	162.00	2.00	324.00	B CRANE
Place on table		37.50	1.50	56.25	2.00	112.50	B CRANE
Place on mandrill		105.90	1.50	158.85	2.00	317.70	
Place plate on profiling machine		182.50	1.50	273.75	2.00	547.50	
Program machine		148.00	1.00	148.00	2.00	296.00	
Collect data of new coil		112.00	1.50	168.00	2.00	336.00	
Take to sampling area		15.00	1.50	22.50	2.00	45.00	
Make free check		122.60	1.50	183.90	2.00	367.80	
Profile		3.29	4000.00	13,160.00	2.05	26,978.00	B CRANE
Measure change		100.00	1.00	100.00	2.05	205.00	
Wait to pack		0.00	1.00	0.00	2.05	0.00	B CRANE
End of note		25.00	1.00	25.00	2.00	50.00	
TOTAL				16,544.26		33,652.52	

N° Operators	Standard Time (min/unit)	Standard Time (hour/unit)
2	560.88	9.35

Figure 19.14.

How will we calculate the normal time of this operation if another type of coil has to be loaded? The five previous parameters must be defined in the technical parameter table and the distances must be defined in the statistical parameter table. The previously stated parameters must be linked to the said operation, so that when operating in any of them the normal time is modified according to the change performed. For the rest of similar operations the procedure would be identical. Another example follows.

Example

In this example, we will be able to check the advantage of making a study of methods and parameterized times. It is a footwear assembly workshop in which operators sew each of the leather pieces to shape the shoe before attaching the sole and heel. Initially, the analyst performed a study of methods and parameterized times for this workshop.

Study of methods and times of task: Footwear sewing

Statistical Parameters		
Length bobbin stitching 1.	1,500.00	cm
Length bobbin stitching 2.	1,500.00	cm
Length bobbin stitching 3.	1,500.00	cm
Quantity checked per note	25.00	pares
Quantity shoes per pair	2.00	zapatos

Model Parameters		
Sewing parts	4	units
Total stitches	5	units
Length stitching 1	8.40	cm
Length stitching 2	5.00	cm
Length stitching 3	0.00	cm
Total length of stitches	13.40	cm
Hammer	1.00	cm
N° transfers	4	units

Description of the Operation	Distance (m)	Standard Data (sec)	Units	Total Corrected Time (sec)
Inspect note.		25.00	1	25.00
Provide pack of parts. Remove elastic rubber.		6.14	8	49.12
Prepare sewing machine.		15.00	1	15.00
Put elastic rubber. Deposit in transport box.		7.51	8	60.08
End of note.		10.00	1	10.00
Provide two tanning parts. Unfold one over the other.		5.70	150	855.00
Place on sewing head.		1.60	250	400.00
Sew stitch 1.	=$D$7*$D$8	4.20	50	210.00
Sew stitch 2.		3.75	50	187.50
Sew stitch 3.		0.00	50	0.00
Conclude.		1.45	500	725.00
Stockpile sewing cut.		2.00	250	500.00
Cut threads with help of scissors.		0.00	250	0.00
Take hammer. Mash stitch.		0.00	50	0.00
Change bobbin. Mount finished bobbin in sewing machine side.		41.50	0	18.54
			Total task execution time (sec):	3,055.24

N° Operators	Standard Time (sec/pair)	Standard Time (min/pair)
1	122.21	2.04

Figure 19.15.

This study considers only the number of times that each operation is repeated, without any in-depth study of the operation. The case studied deals with the shoe assembly of size 35 (EU), describing three types of stitching, each of them with a duration and frequency. The stitching longitude is obtained from the shoe design. In several of the following examples, the longitude of Stitch 2 is changed.

19. Development of Standard Data and Time Formulas: Methods Study and Parameterized Times

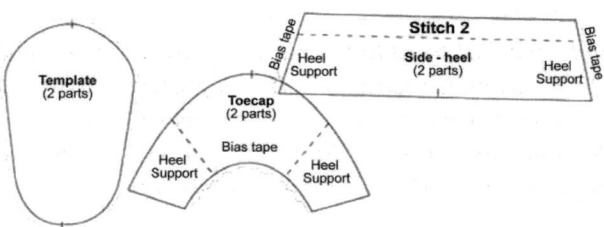

Figure 19.16.

As seen in Figure 19.16, stitch 2 is made in the heel of the shoe. We will now study in depth the operation:

- Longitude of stitch 2 → 5 centimeters
- Time spent performing the stitch → 3.75 seconds
- Speed of stitch 2 → 3.75 sec / 5 centimeters = 0.75 seconds/centimeter (the standard datum to make a centimeter with stitch 2)

Study of methods and times of task: Footwear sewing

Statistical Parameters			Model Parameters		
Length bobbin stitching 1.	1,500.00	cm	Sewing parts	4	units
Length bobbin stitching 2.	1,500.00	cm	Total stitches	5	units
Length bobbin stitching 3.	1,500.00	cm	Length stitching 1	8.40	cm
Quantity checked per note	25.00	pares	Length stitching 2	5.00	cm
Quantity shoes per pair	2.00	zapatos	Length stitching 3	0.00	cm
Speed of stitch 1	0.50	sec/cm	Total length of stitches	13.40	cm
Speed of stitch 2	0.75	sec/cm	Hammer	1.00	cm
Speed of stitch 3	1.00	sec/cm	N° transfers	4	units

Description of the Operation	Distance (m)	Standard Data (sec)	Units	Total Corrected Time (sec)
Inspect note.		25.00	1	25.00
Provide pack of parts. Remove elastic rubber.		6.14	8	49.12
Prepare sewing machine.		15.00	1	15.00
Put elastic rubber. Deposit in transport box.		7.51	8	60.08
End of note.		10.00	1	10.00
Provide two tanning parts. Unfold one over the other.		5.70	150	855.00
Place on sewing head.		1.60	250	400.00
Sew stitch 1.		0.50	420	210.00
Sew stitch 2.	=$D$10	0.75	250	187.50
Sew stitch 3.		1.00	0	0.00
Conclude.	=$D$7*$D$8*$I$7	1.45	500	725.00
Stockpile sewing cut.		2.00	250	500.00
Cut threads with help of scissors.		0.00	250	0.00
Take hammer. Mash stitch.		0.00	50	0.00
Change bobbin. Mount finished bobbin in sewing machine side.		41.50	0	18.54
		Total task execution time (sec):		3,055.24

N° Operators	Standard Time (sec/pair)	Standard Time (min/pair)
1	122.21	2.04

Figure 19.17.

651

Industrial productivity

Subsequently, we will modify the cell units, multiplying the standard datum by the total quantity of centimeters in the 25 pairs (50 units) in order to know the total time for this operation. The procedure for the rest of operations susceptible of being parameterized will be similar, collecting a set of data large enough to obtain reliable data once the scrutiny is made, as has been described in this chapter.

After performing the study of methods and parameterized times, we will be able to simulate and know the manufacturing times for the rest of the sizes of the shoe model studied, without needing to study them one by one. What will be the standard time of the size 48 model? We will only have to revise the patterns of that shoe design; we will measure the longitude of stitch number 2 for the size 48 shoe, which for this example is 12.56 cm and we will substitute it in the study.

Study of methods and times of task: Footwear sewing

Statistical Parameters		
Length bobbin stitching 1.	1,500.00	cm
Length bobbin stitching 2.	1,500.00	cm
Length bobbin stitching 3.	1,500.00	cm
Quantity checked per note	25.00	pairs
Quantity shoes per pair	2.00	shoes
Speed of stitch 1.	0.50	sec/cm
Speed of stitch 2.	0.75	sec/cm
Speed of stitch 3.	1.00	sec/cm

Model Parameters		
Sewing parts	4	units
Total stitches	5	units
Length stitching 1	18.56	cm
Length stitching 2	12.56	cm
Length stitching 3	0.00	cm
Total length of stitches	31.12	cm
Hammer	1.00	cm
Nº transfers	4	units

Description of the Operation	Distance (m)	Standard Data (sec)	Units	Total Corrected Time (sec)
Inspect note.		25.00	1	25.00
Provide pack of parts. Remove elastic rubber.		6.14	8	49.12
Prepare sewing machine.		15.00	1	15.00
Put elastic rubber. Deposit in transport box.		7.51	8	60.08
End of note.		10.00	1	10.00
Provide two tanning parts. Unfold one over the other.		5.70	150	855.00
Place on sewing head.		1.60	250	400.00
Sew stitch 1.		0.50	928	464.00
Sew stitch 2.	=$D$10	0.75	628	471.00
Sew stitch 3.		1.00	0	0.00
Conclude.	=$D$7*$D$8*$I$7	1.45	500	725.00
Stockpile sewing cut.		2.00	250	500.00
Cut threads with help of scissors.		0.00	250	0.00
Take hammer. Mash stitch.		0.00	50	0.00
Change bobbin. Mount finished bobbin in sewing machine side.		41.50	1	43.05
		Total task execution time (sec):		3,617.25

Nº Operators	Standard Time (sec/pair)	Standard Time (min/pair)
1	144.69	2.41

Figure 19.18.

The standard time of different shoes has been calculated without needing to measure each of them, all from standard data and the parameterization of model variables.

19. Development of Standard Data and Time Formulas: Methods Study and Parameterized Times

Questions

1. Indicate the usefulness of the parameterized time studies.
2. List the variables or components that have to be taken into consideration when performing a study of parameterized times.
3. For the calculation of the normal time component, how will the procedure be conducted once the data are obtained and calculated?
4. Once the time formulas are obtained, what is the procedure?
5. Indicate the basis for obtaining the standard data.
6. Indicate the basis for obtaining the rest supplements.
7. How will the results be presented?

PART IV
APLICATION OF STANDARDS

1. MANT
2. WASTE IN WORK DESIGN
3. WASTE BY LOW PERFORMANCE
4. WASTE BY MANAGEMENT FAILURES

Part	Aim	Initial Situation	Final situation
Part 1: Diagnosis	We start from a manufacturing execution times and we want to know what caused them.		
Part 2: Methods	We study and improve the work method of a task to reduce its necessary execution time. The same with processes.		
Part 3: Time measurement	With a defined and improved method we time the task through various techniques to be able to establish a standard, this implies time improvements.		
Part 4: Operations planning	With standard times we can manage production, dimensionate, make decisions, etc. Waste by management failures is reduced.		
Part 4: Productivity control	With standard times productivity can be controled reducing the waste by low performance.		

Chapter 20

Operations: Production Management

20.1. Introduction and Concepts

According to the development of *the theory of waste measurement*, discussed in the first part, one of the principal waste factors in industries is caused by management failures. Within the components of this waste factor, the one that produces more losses is the waste from imbalances. In this case, the imbalance discussed is not the one treated in the second part, which comes from different standard times of the tasks or assembly lines. The imbalance that is produced by a poor operation planning is due to the difference between workload and work capacity.

The imbalances in a factory limit productive capacity, producing oversaturation in certain resources and leaving others idle. This imbalance leads to increased manufacturing costs, noncompliance with deadlines, and the discomfort among workers who see that even if they work hard, the production is not enough.

> We understand production management as the discipline whose objective is to coordinate the company's agents and available resources within a given environment in order to be able to serve clients, as a function of the agreements adopted with them, at the lowest possible cost.

Production management constitutes a fundamental arena for the elimination of waste, in particular, waste from management failures. In production management, we take into account the temporary scenario (long, medium, short or very short term) on which we are working. For this reason, the structuring of this part is done from a long-term planning (periods of 1 or several years) perspective, up to very short-term planning (periods of 1 day or even hours). The planning and control cycle of production can be described, roughly, in the following figure, and each point will be explained in its corresponding section in the chapter.

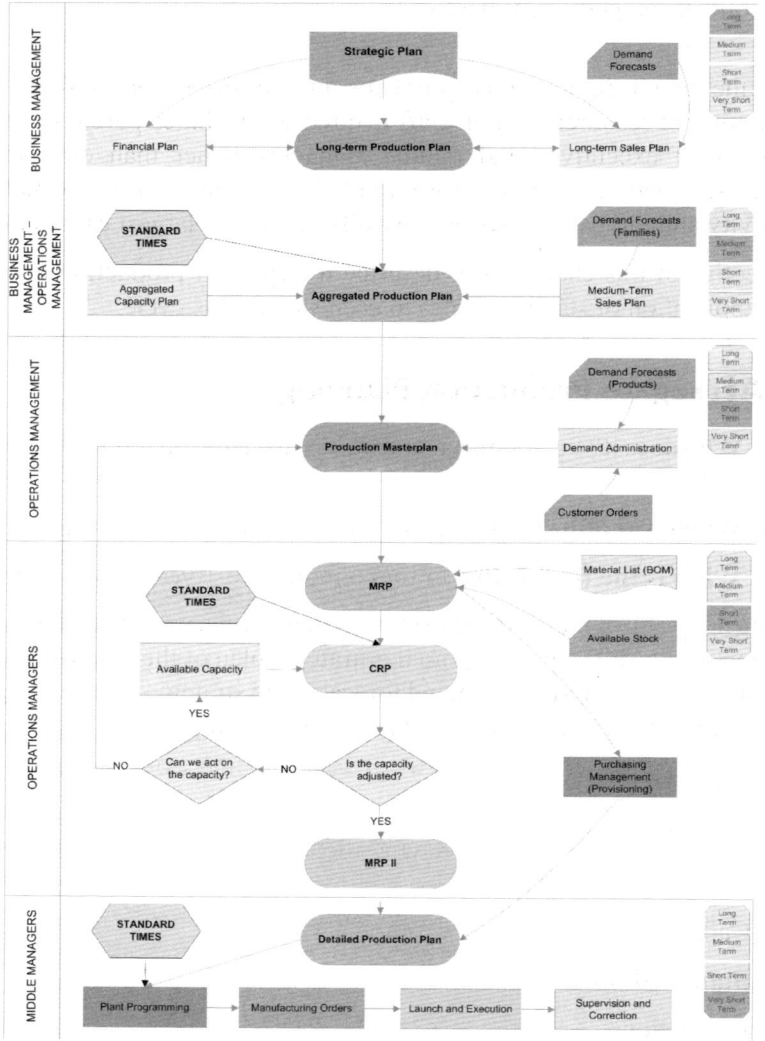

Figure 20.1. Planning and control cycle of production

So far, the cycle of production management is described. The first step for reducing costs or "manufacturing at the lowest possible cost" is to develop this cycle, which requires knowing the standard times of the tasks for different products. Standard times are the power supply for the scientific performance of the different production plans, either in the long term or short term. For this reason, we must ensure their correct calculation and application.

> Without the development of a times study within the organization, standard times cannot be known, and consequently, the diverse production plans cannot be developed scientifically.

One of the major productivity problems in industries comes from a wrong dimensioning of resources. Often staff is hired or machines purchased according to opinions of executives and middle managers rather than on scientifically based decision making. The result is an imbalance of the capacity, which reduces productivity and increases costs. It is usually one of the largest causes of waste.

The objective of this chapter is to describe the cycle of production management and the application of standard times to each step of this cycle.

20.2. Aggregate Production Planning

> **Who does it?** Senior management, based on information from production and sales

> **When is it done?** After the long-term production planning

> **What is the time frame?** From 6 months to 1 year, monthly accrued

Recalling the graph of the production management cycle, we note that the aggregate production plan (APP) emerges from the strategic plan of the organization, which, taking into account long-term demand forecasts and strategic objectives, generates a sales plan for that time frame. The inputs to the aggregated plan are:

- Forecasts
- Company plans
- Available resources
- Capacity
- **Standard times**
- Restrictions
- Unit costs

After doing simulations, the aggregate plan will return the following:

- Medium-term production plan
- Stock levels

- Resource availability: workforce and machines
- Subcontracting
- Objective cost of the plan

Domínguez Machuca, in his book *Operations Management,* defines it the following way:

> A production plan in the medium term, feasible from the point of view of capacity, allows achievement of the strategic plan as effectively as possible in relation to the tactical objectives of the operations subsystem.

The outline of the process for developing an aggregate production plan is shown in the following figure:

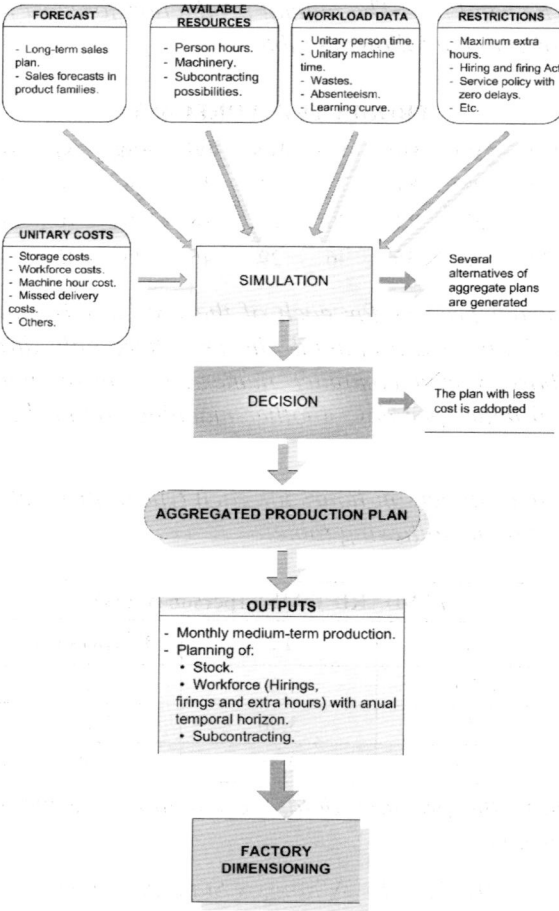

Figure 20.2. *Process outline of APP elaboration*

20. Operations: Production Management

> The aggregate plan reports the approximate dimension that the factory must have and its resources in order to meet its delivery schedules, given some restrictions and policies, at the lowest cost.

The following example shows the dimensioning of a factory, starting from a production forecast, the workload generated, the number of operators required, and the saturation of machines. **This example demonstrates the importance of knowledge of the standard times.**

Example

Generic scenario of plant dimensioning from production forecasts

In this example, the dimensioning of a factory is done for three different products (P1, P2, and P3). The annual production forecast for these three products is shown in the following table:

	\multicolumn{12}{c	}{PRODUCTION FORECAST}
	Jan	Feb	Mar	Apr	May	Jun	Jul	Aug	Sep	Oct	Nov	Dec
P1	70	40	95	87	75	53	47	34	70	80	100	70
P2	10	5	22	13	20	20	18	10	10	15	17	10
P3	40	32	43	35	46	29	46	25	45	42	32	30

The manufacturing process for each of the products is consists of three phases. Phase 1 and 2 are manual phases, where only direct workforce intervenes. Phase 3 is a computer numerical control that can work a maximum of 16 hours per day. Another machine cannot be acquired due to its cost.

The standard times in person-hours for each type of product in each phase are summarized in the following table:

	\multicolumn{4}{c	}{STANDARD TIMES (person-hours)}
	F1	F2	F3 (person)	F3 (machine)
P1	8,20	4,20	2,40	2,70
P2	7,40	3,90	2,10	3,40
P3	5,90	2,45	1,38	1,50

Keeping in mind the previous data, we calculate the monthly workload through the formula:

$$Workload = N° \text{ units} \times Standard\ Time$$

Industrial productivity

Month	Units	Product	F1	F2	F3 (h)	F3 (m)
January	70,00	P1	574,00	294,00	168,00	189,00
	10,00	P2	74,00	39,00	21,00	34,00
	40,00	P3	236,00	98,00	55,20	60,00
	TOTAL PER PHASE		884,00	431,00	244,20	283,00
February	40,00	P1	328,00	168,00	96,00	108,00
	5,00	P2	74,00	19,50	10,50	17,00
	32,00	P3	188,80	78,40	44,16	48,00
	TOTAL PER PHASE		553,80	265,90	150,66	173,00
March	95,00	P1	779,00	399,00	228,00	256,50
	22,00	P2	162,80	85,80	46,20	74,80
	43,00	P3	253,70	105,35	59,34	64,50
	TOTAL PER PHASE		1195,50	590,15	333,54	395,80
April	87,00	P1	713,40	365,40	208,80	234,90
	13,00	P2	96,20	50,70	27,30	44,20
	35,00	P3	206,50	85,75	48,30	52,50
	TOTAL PER PHASE		1016,10	501,85	284,40	331,60
May	75,00	P1	615,00	315,00	180,00	202,50
	20,00	P2	148,00	78,00	42,00	68,00
	46,00	P3	51,90	48,45	47,38	47,50
	TOTAL PER PHASE		814,90	441,45	269,38	318,00
June	53,00	P1	434,60	222,60	127,20	143,10
	20,00	P2	148,00	78,00	42,00	68,00
	29,00	P3	171,10	71,05	40,02	43,50
	TOTAL PER PHASE		753,70	371,65	209,22	254,60
July	47,00	P1	385,40	197,40	112,80	126,90
	18,00	P2	133,20	70,20	37,80	61,20
	46,00	P3	271,40	112,70	63,48	69,00
	TOTAL PER PHASE		790,00	380,30	214,08	257,10
August	34,00	P1	278,80	142,80	81,60	91,80
	10,00	P2	74,00	39,00	21,00	34,00
	25,00	P3	147,50	61,25	34,50	37,50
	TOTAL PER PHASE		500,30	243,05	137,10	163,30
September	70,00	P1	574,00	294,00	168,00	189,00
	10,00	P2	74,00	39,00	21,00	34,00
	45,00	P3	265,50	110,25	62,10	67,50
	TOTAL PER PHASE		913,50	443,25	251,10	290,50

October	80,00	P1	656,00	336,00	192,00	216,00
	15,00	P2	111,00	58,50	31,50	51,00
	42,00	P3	247,80	102,90	57,96	63,00
	TOTAL PER PHASE		1014,80	497,40	281,46	330,00
November	100,00	P1	820,00	420,00	240,00	270,00
	17,00	P2	125,80	66,30	35,70	57,80
	32,00	P3	188,80	78,40	44,16	48,00
	TOTAL PER PHASE		1134,60	564,70	319,86	375,80
December	70,00	P1	574,00	294,00	168,00	189,00
	10,00	P2	74,00	39,00	21,00	34,00
	30,00	P3	177,00	73,50	41,40	45,00
	TOTAL PER PHASE		825,00	406,50	230,40	268,00

The previous workload calculation does not consider any type of waste. But as we have seen during the development of the book, waste is present in production, so it is necessary to consider it when analyzing whether an aggregate production plan can be fulfilled.

In the case of the factory from this example, the ratio of waste (CwF) is 1.16. Considering the following formula, the new monthly workload is calculated.

$$\text{Workload} = \text{N° units} \times \text{Standard Time} \times \text{CwF}$$

Formula 20.1

The results obtained are shown in the following table:

Month	Units	Product	F1	F2	F3 (h)	F3 (m)
January	70,00	P1	665,84	341,04	194,88	219,24
	10,00	P2	85,84	45,24	24,36	39,44
	40,00	P3	273,76	113,68	64,03	69,60
	TOTAL PER PHASE		1025,44	499,96	283,27	328,28
February	40,00	P1	380,48	194,88	111,36	125,28
	5,00	P2	42,92	22,62	12,18	19,72
	32,00	P3	219,01	90,94	51,23	55,68
	TOTAL PER PHASE		642,41	308,44	174,77	200,68

Industrial productivity

Month						
March	95,00	P1	903,64	462,84	264,48	297,54
	22,00	P2	188,85	99,53	53,59	86,77
	43,00	P3	294,29	122,21	68,83	74,82
	TOTAL PER PHASE		1386,78	684,57	386,91	459,13
April	87,00	P1	827,54	423,86	242,21	272,48
	13,00	P2	111,59	58,81	31,67	51,27
	35,00	P3	239,54	99,47	56,03	60,90
	TOTAL PER PHASE		1178,68	582,15	329,90	384,66
May	75,00	P1	713,40	365,40	208,80	234,90
	20,00	P2	171,68	90,48	48,72	78,88
	46,00	P3	60,20	56,20	54,96	55,10
	TOTAL PER PHASE		945,28	512,08	312,48	368,88
June	53,00	P1	504,14	258,22	147,55	166,00
	20,00	P2	171,68	90,48	48,72	78,88
	29,00	P3	198,48	82,42	46,42	50,46
	TOTAL PER PHASE		874,29	431,11	242,70	295,34
July	47,00	P1	447,06	228,98	130,85	147,20
	18,00	P2	154,51	81,43	43,85	70,99
	46,00	P3	314,82	130,73	73,64	80,04
	TOTAL PER PHASE		916,40	441,15	248,33	298,24
August	34,00	P1	323,41	165,65	94,66	106,49
	10,00	P2	85,84	45,24	24,36	39,44
	25,00	P3	171,10	71,05	40,02	43,50
	TOTAL PER PHASE		580,35	281,94	159,04	189,43
September	70,00	P1	665,84	341,04	194,88	219,24
	10,00	P2	85,84	45,24	24,36	39,44
	45,00	P3	307,98	127,89	72,04	78,30
	TOTAL PER PHASE		1059,66	514,17	291,28	336,98
October	80,00	P1	760,96	389,76	222,72	250,56
	15,00	P2	128,76	67,86	36,54	59,16
	42,00	P3	287,45	119,36	67,23	73,08
	TOTAL PER PHASE		1177,17	576,98	326,49	382,80
November	100,00	P1	951,20	487,20	278,40	313,20
	17,00	P2	145,93	76,91	41,41	67,05
	32,00	P3	219,01	90,94	51,23	55,68
	TOTAL PER PHASE		1316,14	655,05	371,04	435,93

December	70,00	P1	665,84	341,04	194,88	219,24
	10,00	P2	85,84	45,24	24,36	39,44
	30,00	P3	205,32	85,26	48,02	52,20
	TOTAL PER PHASE		**957,00**	**471,54**	**267,26**	**310,88**

The following graphs show the monthly workload generated for the fixed production in each of the phases.

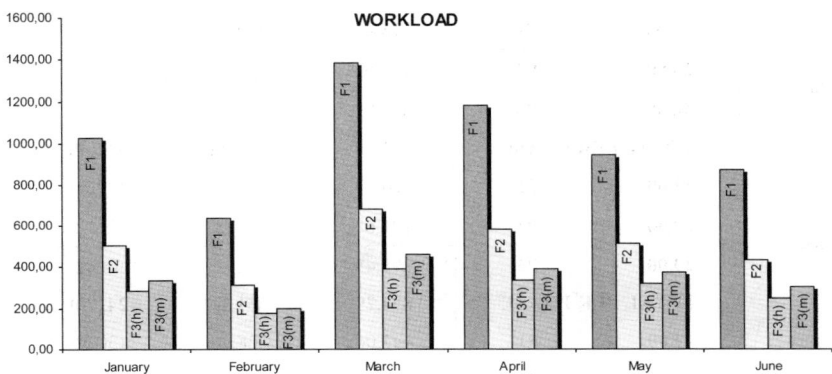

Figure 20.3

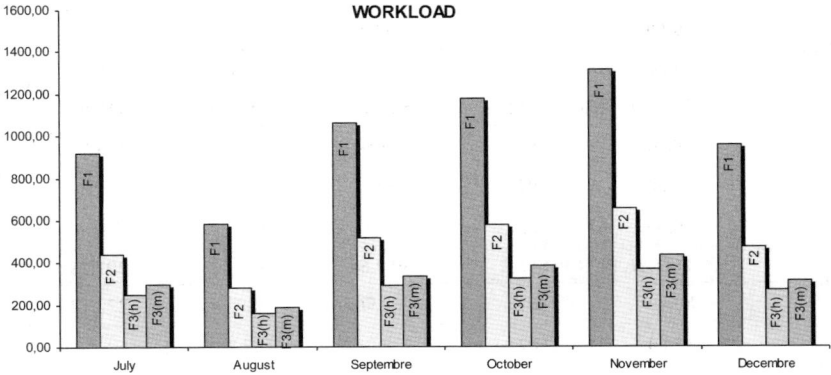

Figure 20.4

Industrial productivity

The following tables show a summary of the total workload generated for the production indicated.

	January	February	March	April	May	June
Total (p·h)	1808.67	1125.62	2458.26	2090.73	1769.85	1548.10
Total (m·h)	328.28	200.68	459.13	384.66	368.88	295.34

	July	August	September	October	November	December
Total (p·h)	1021.32	1865.11	2080.65	2342.23	1695.80	0.00
Total (m·h)	189.43	336.98	382.80	435.93	310.88	0.00

Based on the workdays in each month, and with the objective of meeting the sales plan, the following data can be deducted:

1. Staff required
2. Hours the machine will have to work

The following table summarizes the number of workdays in each month:

WORKDAYS												
Month	Jan	Feb	Mar	Apr	May	Jun	Jul	Aug	Sep	Oct	Nov	Dec
Days	20	19	23	21	22	22	21	23	22	21	22	22

Considering an 8-hour workday and an absenteeism of 4 percent, we can calculate the available capacity according to the following formula:

$$\text{Available Capacity} = \text{Month workdays} \times \text{Workday hours} \times (100 - \text{Absenteeism}(\%))$$

Formula 20.2

The available capacity per month and per person is summarized as follows:

AVAILABLE CAPACITY (person-hours/person month)												
Month	Jan	Feb	Mar	Apr	May	Jun	Jul	Aug	Sep	Oct	Nov	Dec
AC	154	146	177	161	169	169	161	177	169	161	169	169

The next step is to deduce the number of operators required by dividing the workload by the hours per month of each operator.

$$\text{N° of Necessary Operators} = \frac{\text{Workload}}{\text{Available Capacity}}$$

Formula 20.3

20. Operations: Production Management

The number of operators required, calculated according to the previous formula, is summarized in the following tables:

NECESSARY RESOURCES (N° of operators)						
Month	January	February	March	April	May	June
Workload (p·h)	1808.67	1125.62	2458.26	2090.73	1769.85	1548.10
Capacity (p·h/h)	153.60	145.92	176.64	161.28	168.96	168.96
Necessary operators	12	8	14	13	10	9

NECESSARY RESOURCES (N° of operators)						
Month	July	August	September	October	November	December
Workload (p·h)	1605.88	1021.32	1865.11	2080.65	2342.23	1695.80
Capacity (p·h/h)	161.28	176.64	168.96	161.28	168.96	168.96
Necessary operators	10	6	11	13	14	10

In the table, we have dimensioned the factory according to the production forecasts; we know how many people are necessary, but we do not know where to place them. The next step is to calculate the number of operators required for each of the phases. For this purpose, we use the same formula as in the previous case.

The following tables show theses calculations:

PHASE	Month	January	February	March	April	May	June
	Days	20.00	19.00	23.00	21.00	22.00	22.00
PHASE 1	Workload (p·h)	1025.44	642.41	1386.78	1178.68	945.28	874.29
PHASE 1	Capacity (p·h/h)	160.00	152.00	184.00	168.00	176.00	176.00
PHASE 1	Necessary operators	6	4	8	7	5	5
PHASE 2	Workload (p·h)	499.96	308.44	684.57	582.15	512.08	431.11
PHASE 2	Capacity (p·h/h)	160.00	152.00	184.00	168.00	176.00	176.00
PHASE 2	Necessary operators	3	2	4	3	3	2
PHASE 3 (h)	Workload (p·h)	283.27	174.77	386.91	329.90	312.48	242.70
PHASE 3 (h)	Capacity (p·h/h)	160.00	152.00	184.00	168.00	176.00	176.00
PHASE 3 (h)	Necessary operators	2	1	2	2	2	1

669

Industrial productivity

PHASE	Month	July	August	September	October	November	December
	Days	21.00	23.00	22.00	21.00	22.00	22.00
PHASE 1	Workload (p·h)	916.40	580.35	1059.66	1177.17	1316.14	957.00
	Capacity (p·h/h)	168.00	184.00	176.00	168.00	176.00	176.00
	Necessary operators	5	3	6	7	7	5
PHASE 2	Workload (p·h)	441.15	281.94	514.17	576.98	655.05	471.54
	Capacity (p·h/h)	168.00	184.00	176.00	168.00	176.00	176.00
	Necessary operators	3	2	3	3	4	3
PHASE 3 (h)	Workload (p·h)	248.33	159.04	291.28	326.49	371.04	267.26
	Capacity (p·h/h)	168.00	184.00	176.00	168.00	176.00	176.00
	Necessary operators	1	1	2	2	2	2

NECESSARY RESOURCES (N° of operators)

NOTE: *Once the calculation for the number of operators required per phase is done, it may happen that the sum of these operators has a slight variation with the initial estimation for the entire factory due to rounding. If for instance in the month of January in phase 1, 6.4 operators are needed according to the calculation, it will be in our hands to have, at this stage, 6 operators, supplying that saturation with punctual aids or, instead, locating 7 operators, assuming the cost for idle time or increasing saturation.*

In any case, this decision will be scientific and will allow us to raise awareness of the production situation, anticipating it and eliminating surprises and unexpected events.

The evolution graph in Figure 20.5 shows the number of operators required each month.

20. Operations: Production Management

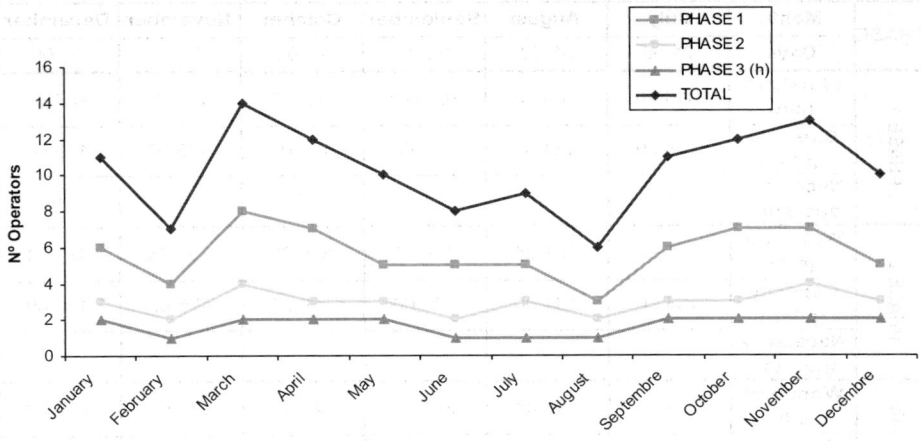

Figure 20.5

After calculating the number of operators required, we calculate the hours that the machines are required to work daily in each of the months. To do this, the monthly workload in person-hours (p-h) is divided by the days of the month.

$$\text{Machine hours necessary per day} = \frac{\text{Monthly machine workload}}{\text{Days of month}}$$

If we consider that the machine can only work 16 hours a day, we get its saturation.

$$\text{Saturation (\%)} = \frac{\text{Machine workload}}{\text{Machine available capacity}} \times 100$$

Applying the previous equations, we calculate the machine-hours per day and also machine saturation. The results are shown in the following table:

Industrial productivity

MACHINE SATURATION						
Month	January	February	March	April	May	June
Workdays	20	19	23	21	22	22
Workload (m·h)	328.28	200.68	459.13	384.66	368.88	295.34
Capacity (m·h/m)	320.00	304.00	368.00	336.00	352.00	352.00
m·h necessary per day	16.41	10.56	19.96	18.32	16.77	13.42
Machine saturation (%)	102.59%	66.01%	124.76%	114.48%	104.80%	83.90%

MACHINE SATURATION						
Month	July	August	September	October	November	December
Workdays	21	23	22	21	22	22
Workload (m·h)	336.98	382.80	435.93	310.88	0.00	0.00
Capacity (m·h/m)	336.00	368.00	352.00	336.00	352.00	352.00
m·h necessary per day	16.05	16.64	19.81	14.80	0.00	0.00
Machine saturation (%)	100.29%	104.02%	123.84%	92.52%	0.00%	0.00%

The following graph shows the comparison between workload and available capacity of the machine; through it, checking the machine saturation graphically for each of the months is possible.

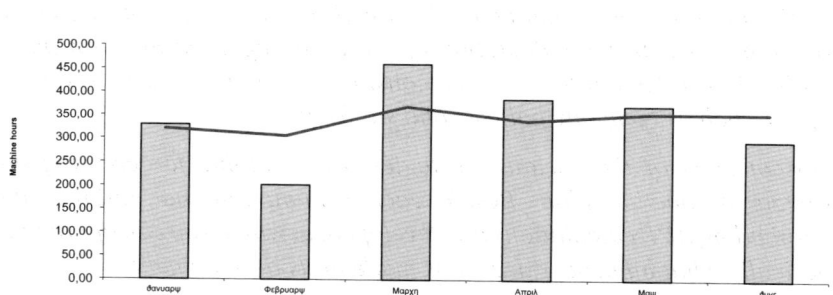

Figure 20.6

The bars represent the workload and the line represents the available capacity for that month, which varies depending on the days available for each of them. (Remember that the machine can work 16 hours a day, so this parameter is constant.)

In the months in which the machine has low saturation, the bars will be below the line. By contrast, in the months in which there is oversaturation, the bars will exceed the line, indicating that the machine cannot produce the demanded units.

Conclusions to dimensioning

With the development of the previous calculation, we already have data on the number of workers that the factory must have and we know the possibilities of other limitations.

From these results, several questions can be raised:

- *The number of operators required varies with each month. Is it better to hire and fire or pay for overtime?*

- *Another option is to stockpile during the months of less workload in order to reduce the workload in peak months. Is this option better than the previous?*

- *The machines have limitations and during some months the amount of work to do exceeds those limitations. Is the cheapest solution to work on Saturdays or, on the contrary, to accumulate stock in the months of less workload so as to compensate when demand is greater?*

Answers to these questions are the decision-making work the chief operating officer and chief executive officer. Because the work done is scientifically based, decisions must be supported by calculations or numerical estimates.

From the calculation of standard times and workload, the remaining variables may be deducted: stocks, recruitments, dismissals, and so on. To simulate and find the best operation and be able to make decisions, different strategies of action are simulated, which will result in different aggregate production plans. In the calculation of these aggregate production plans not only will production forecasts be considered, but more variables come into play, such as company policies and stocking.

Details of each of the various strategies are available for creating the aggregate production plan. Beside each explanation that follows, the corresponding APP calculations are developed, in which you can appreciate numerically what influences decisions made in its development.

Creation of the Aggregate Plan and Action Strategies

Two possibilities in developing an aggregate plan are derived primarily from the predicted demand. On one hand, we can act on the demand and on the other, on capacity.

Acting on **demand**, we raise it when it is inferior to the productive capacity and we decrease it when it is superior, always trying to balance demand with capacity. Balance is achieved by actions such as promotions (advertising), reduction of prices, and delayed services, among other options. We act on **capacity**, increasing or decreasing it, adjusting it to the demand. It is achieved by varying overtime, subcontracting, and so on.

Based on the situation, two aggregate planning strategies emerge, named *hunting strategy* and *levelling strategy*. A third is called *mixed strategy*, which is the optimal combination of the other two.

- **Hunting strategy:** Manufacture what is demanded and adjust the resources to demand
- **Levelling strategy:** Maintain resources at a constant level of occupancy and store for valleys and peaks in demand
- **Mixed strategy:** Combine hunting and levelling strategies

The strategy will be characterized by the best combination between costs and restrictions. The more restrictions a business has (e.g., you cannot store or deliveries have to be immediate or workers cannot be fired, etc.), the easier it is to decide.

20.3. Master Production Schedule (MPS)

> **Who does it?** Operations director and commercial director

> **When is it done?** After the aggregate production plan

> **What is the time frame?** From 1 year to 1 week

Once the aggregate production plan is developed, we will have an analysis plan by product brands. At this point, we have to take a step forward in the level of detail. Products by brand should be broken down and their deliveries specified, which results in the master production schedule (MPS).

We can define the master production schedule as:

> A detailed production plan that establishes, based on customer orders and demand forecasts, how many final products must be produced and in what time frames.

20.3.1. Creation of the Master Production Schedule

To develop a master production schedule it will be necessary to carry out a decomposition process. This process may have two origins: the aggregate production plan, or the sales plan in the medium term (composed of medium-term sales forecasts and already closed orders) if we do not have an aggregate production plan. The beginning of the process of creating the MPS is shown in Figure 20.7.

20. Operations: Production Management

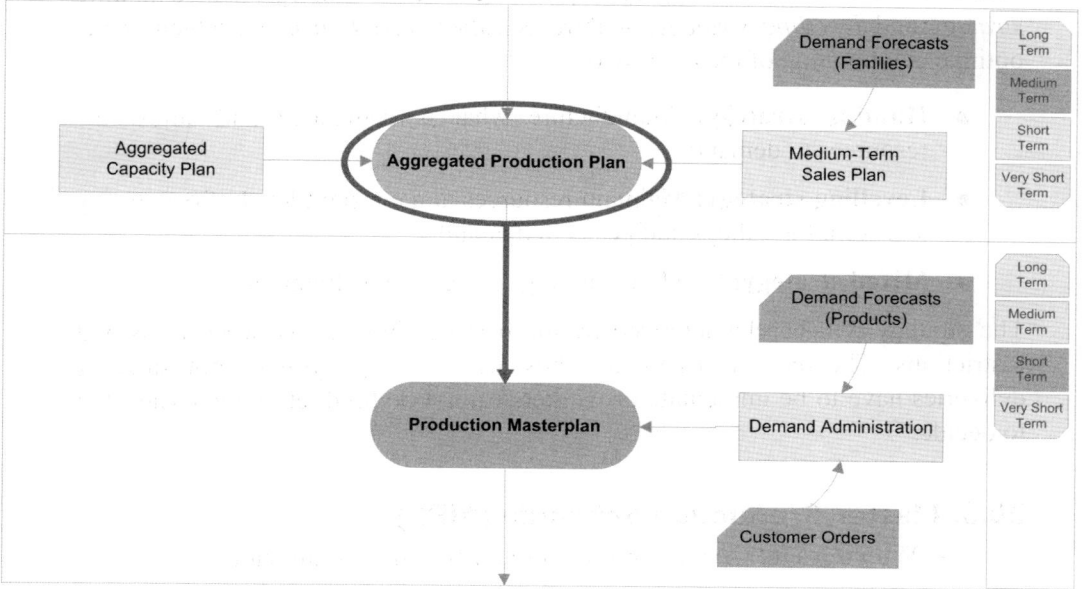

Figure 20.7. MPS feeding diagram

The first step for developing the MPS is to break down the aggregate production quantities (product brands) into product units. In order to perform this step, the cycle time to consider in the MPS will be detailed in shorter periods, going from months in the medium term to weeks or days. Thus, the quantities of products may be split up over time, specifying more closely the moment in which they are needed and reflecting more accurately the activities to develop.

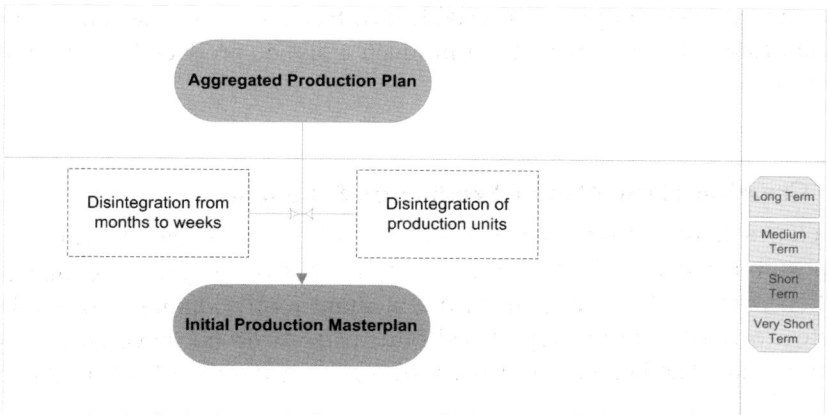

Figure 20.8. MPS creation diagram

675

With the breakdown of production in product units into weekly periods of time, we will have an initial MPS, which may be compared with the forecast of short-term sales, closed orders with customers, deliveries of open orders, orders in process, and the available stock in the short term, resulting in the MPS.

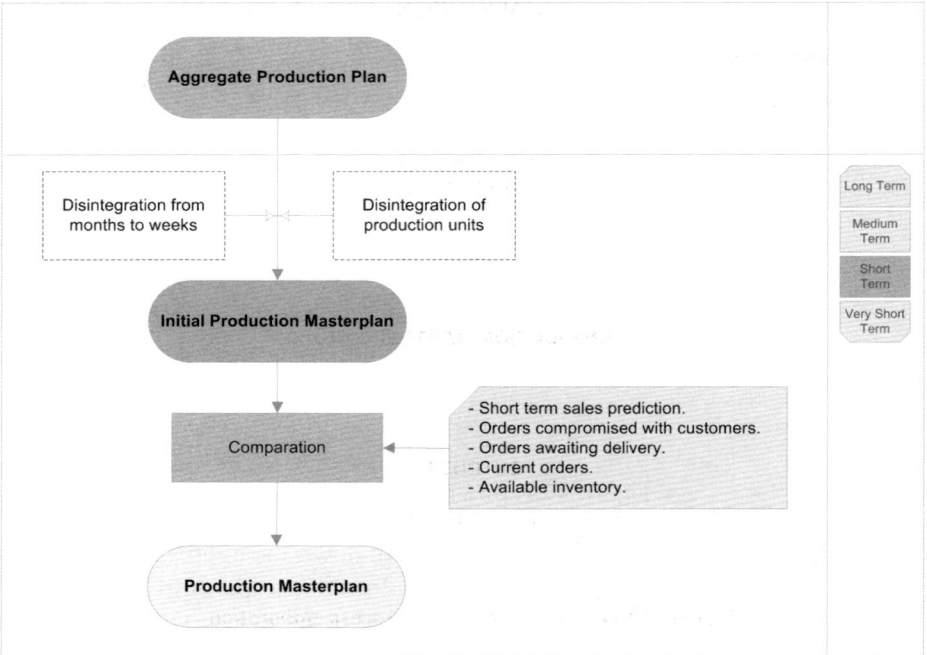

Figure 20.9. MPS creation diagram

The outline of the process for developing a master production schedule is shown in Figure 20.10.

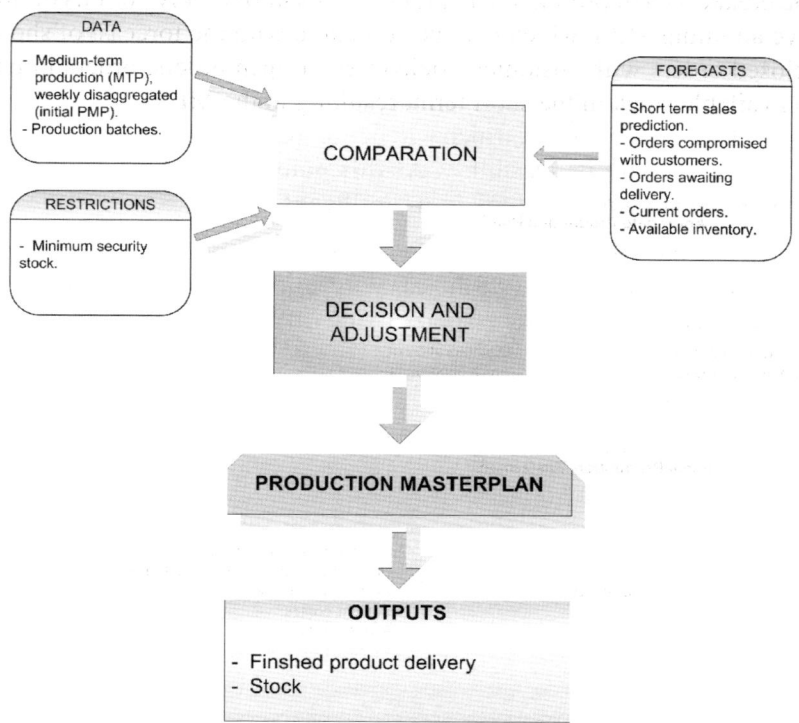

Figure 20.10. MPS diagram for process elaboration

Although the MPS development phase is beyond the scope of this book, we look at the "decision and adjustment" phase here because it depends on the standard times. As will be seen in the MRP II section, the MPS viability will depend on its capacity to carry it out, and the capacity is compared with the workload, which is calculated from the standard times. An MPS example that starts from an APP and considers two possible finished products, P1 and P2, follows:

MPS OUTPUT									
Month	1				2			
Medium-term forecast (brand units)	8,250				10,500			
Weeks	1	2	3	4	1	2	3	4
MPS initial P1	0	3000	0	3000	0	3000	0	3000
Final stock (available + SS)	375	1875	750	2625	1125	2625	750	1875
MPS initial P1	0	0	2625	0	2625	0	0	2625
Final stock (available + SS)	750	0	1688	750	2250	1125	75	1500

Industrial productivity

It is called "proposed" because, according to the Mundel table in Figure 16.6, it cannot be final until it has been contrasted with the capacity, which is in turn compared with the standard times. Subsequently, after calculating the proposed MPS, the material requirements planning (MRP) and the capacity requirements planning (CRP) are developed, which will be compared with the available capacity in the factory to verify its feasibility. **At this point the standard time and the waste coefficients come into play in a significant way.**

In the event that the MRP is not feasible with the capacity, we will proceed to adjust it by adapting it to the demand. If the capacity adjustment made is not enough to meet the demand, we will make changes to the MPS. The cycle followed appears in Figure 20.11:

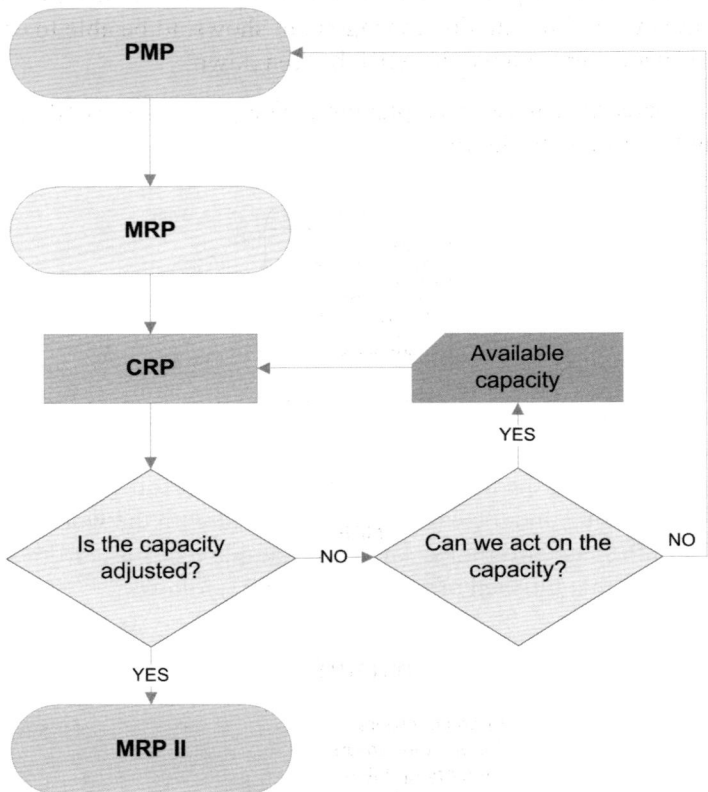

Figure 20.11. Cycle for MRP approval

20.4. MRP *(Material Requeriments Planning)*

- ➢ **Who does it?** Planning manager
- ➢ **When is it done?** After the MPS
- ➢ **What is the time frame?** Generally from 1 to 2 weeks accrued per day, although this period can be modified based on the type of company

The MPS developed and adapted to the characteristics of the demand constitutes the input for the development of the MRP, which must be submitted for approval after the capacity calculation, because both the lack and excess of capacity will adversely affect the company profits. The MRP does not take into account the standard times (it is planned for infinite capacity); however, it will be treated as a part of the cycle of production management and decision making. As the chart from the cycle of production management shows, to be able to calculate the capacity, it is necessary to have the MRP broken down.

MRP means material requirements planning. The process of MRP elaboration is presented in the following figure:

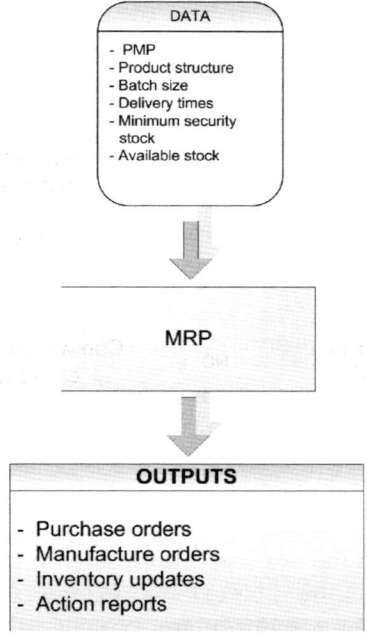

Figure 20.12. MRP elaboration process

For the development of an MRP system, it is necessary to take into account some requirements of finished products and their composition, which is contained in the "product structure."

20.4.1. The Product Structure

The product structure is a file that shows the sequence in which raw materials are manufactured and assembled, the parts that are bought and the subassemblies needed to form the final product. Each element in the product structure has an associated number, which corresponds to the number of units required for a final product.

> To be able to calculate the MRP production plan, the product structure is necessary.

Figure 20.13 provides a possible product structure.

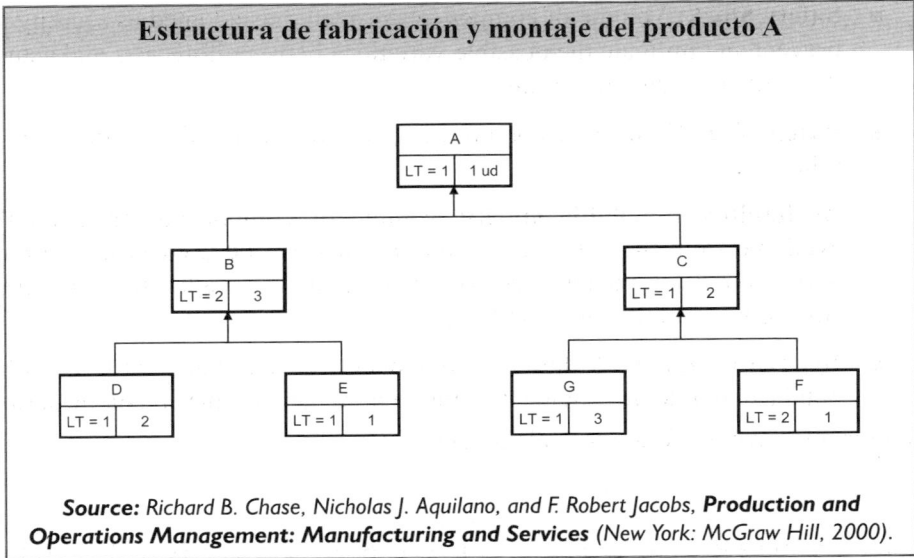

Source: Richard B. Chase, Nicholas J. Aquilano, and F. Robert Jacobs, **Production and Operations Management: Manufacturing and Services** (New York: McGraw Hill, 2000).

Figure 20.13. Manufacture and assembly structure of product A

As can be observed in the figure, item A is the final product of our manufacturing, which is composed of three units of product B and two of product C. In turn, the items B and C are subassemblies in the manufacturing process, composed by the components located in the last level (D, E, G, and F). These components can be raw materials, or inputs, from an external manufacturing process. In the box marked LT, the lead time for the corresponding item is written down. For clarity, it will be the time it takes to supply item G or the time it takes to make the assembly of C.

20.4.2. MRP Development

Once we have developed the product structure, we must consider:

- The measurement unit for the lead time (seconds, hours, days, etc.)
- Base period for production planning, which should coincide with the lead time units
- Number of periods to plan

The calculated levels in the MRP development are:

- **Gross requirements:** Volume of components or materials that we need to have available at the end of a period for the next process
- **Safety Stock:** Volume of components or materials adopted as security to prevent and mitigate the possible variations between forecasts and actual demand or production failures
- **Batch Size:** Number of components that are requested or ordered as a minimum
- **Availability (available stock):** Volume of components or materials available from the previous period and that can be used in the current period to meet immediate needs (When calculating availability, the safety stock does not fall below the fixed value.)
- **Net requirements:** Volume of components or materials that have to be obtained in order to provide the gross requirements at the end of the period

These levels have the following relationship:

> Net R. = Gross R. − Availability − Programmed Receptions + Security Stock

Formula 20.6

What We Need − What We Have = What We Have to Manufacture

After this calculation, work orders are launched based on their delivery deadlines in order to meet the schedule. The MRP system operates according to Figure 20.14.

Industrial productivity

Period	1	2	3	4	5
Gross requirements M					600
Availability M			LT = 2		10
Net requirements M					550
Launch of planned order M			550		
Gross requirements CM		LT = 1	550	2 units needed for the next	
Availability CM			10		
Net requirements CM			540		
Launch of planned order CM		540			
Gross requirements EM			1100		
Availability EM			0		
Net requirements EM			1100		
Launch of planned order EM		1100			
Gross requirements A			1100		
Availability A			0		
Net requirements A			1100		
Launch of planned order A		1100			
Gross requirements R			1100		
Availability R			90		
Net requirements R			1010		
Launch of planned order R		1010			
Gross requirements CR		1010			
Availability CR		5		1 unit needed for the next	
Necesidades netas CR		1005			
Launch of planned order CR	1005				
Gross requirements LLR		1010			
Availability LLR		0			
Net requirements LLR		1010			
Launch of planned order LLR	1010				

Figure 20.14. MRP calculation

Figure 20.14 shows orders and launches, that is, how much to order and when to do so in order to comply with planning. Regardless of the standard manufacturing times of each phase, this could be a manufacturing planning. However, when applying the calculations of capacity and workload, this planning must be validated; it must be determined to be feasible. The system used to perform this validation and/or correction is the MRPII, which is discussed in the following section. **Without standard times being calculated and implemented correctly, this check cannot be done.** Many companies stay at planning on the MRP level, without comparing the results with actual workloads and often fail in their planning and calculations of resource requirements.

20.5. Manufacturing Resource Planning (MRPII)

As stated in the introductory chapter, MRP II means manufacturing resource planning, which involves the planning of all elements needed to carry out the master production schedule—not only materials to manufacture and sell, but factory capacities in workforce and machines—responding to the questions concerning how much and when it will be produced, and what resources are available for it. This planning system was born from MRP in the mid-1970s. It emerged from the deficiencies of the MRP, which calculates material quantities but not necessary resources for their manufacturing. MRP II needs standard times for its elaboration.

While the APP serves for dimensioning, the MRP II calculates capacity more precisely. The MRP II is the audit tool for MPS. At this point, standard times play an important role. Without them, this tool cannot be fed and therefore cannot be used. As mentioned throughout this book, imbalance equals unproductiveness. Failure to use standard times in factory dimensioning results in imbalances and therefore manufacturing wastes. We are so repetitive in this aspect because few companies are actually successful in applying standard times.

The MRP II system is a tool for planning, simulation, execution, and control that promotes achievement of production targets efficiently by adjusting capacity (workforce, machines, subcontracting, etc.), stocks, costs, and production times. Such adjustments can only be made by knowing the required capacity to carry out the production plan (from the units to manufacture and their standard time) and the available capacity of the factory. When such information is available, MRP II may be applied.

20.5.1. Capacity

This section studies the concept of productive capacity, a parameter used in confirming the feasibility of the developed MRP.

> Manufacturing capacity or productive capacity is the amount of product or service that can be achieved with a given productive structure for a certain time.

The study of capacity is essential for business management because it allows analysis of the usage level of each resource in the organization, along with the opportunity to optimize them.

Industrial productivity

> The capacity requirements planning (CRP) determines the necessary capacity level to complete the production plan and determine whether the plan is feasible or whether requirements have to be balanced according to the available capacity. Consider that each stage of the production process requires time from machines and workforce. Information from the MRP can be used to consider factors such as lot sizes, lead times, inventory levels, and safety stock.

The capacity has to adapt to the workload as a function of demand involves an initial dimensioning and subsequent decision. The flowchart in Figure 20.15 illustrates the process.

20. Operations: Production Management

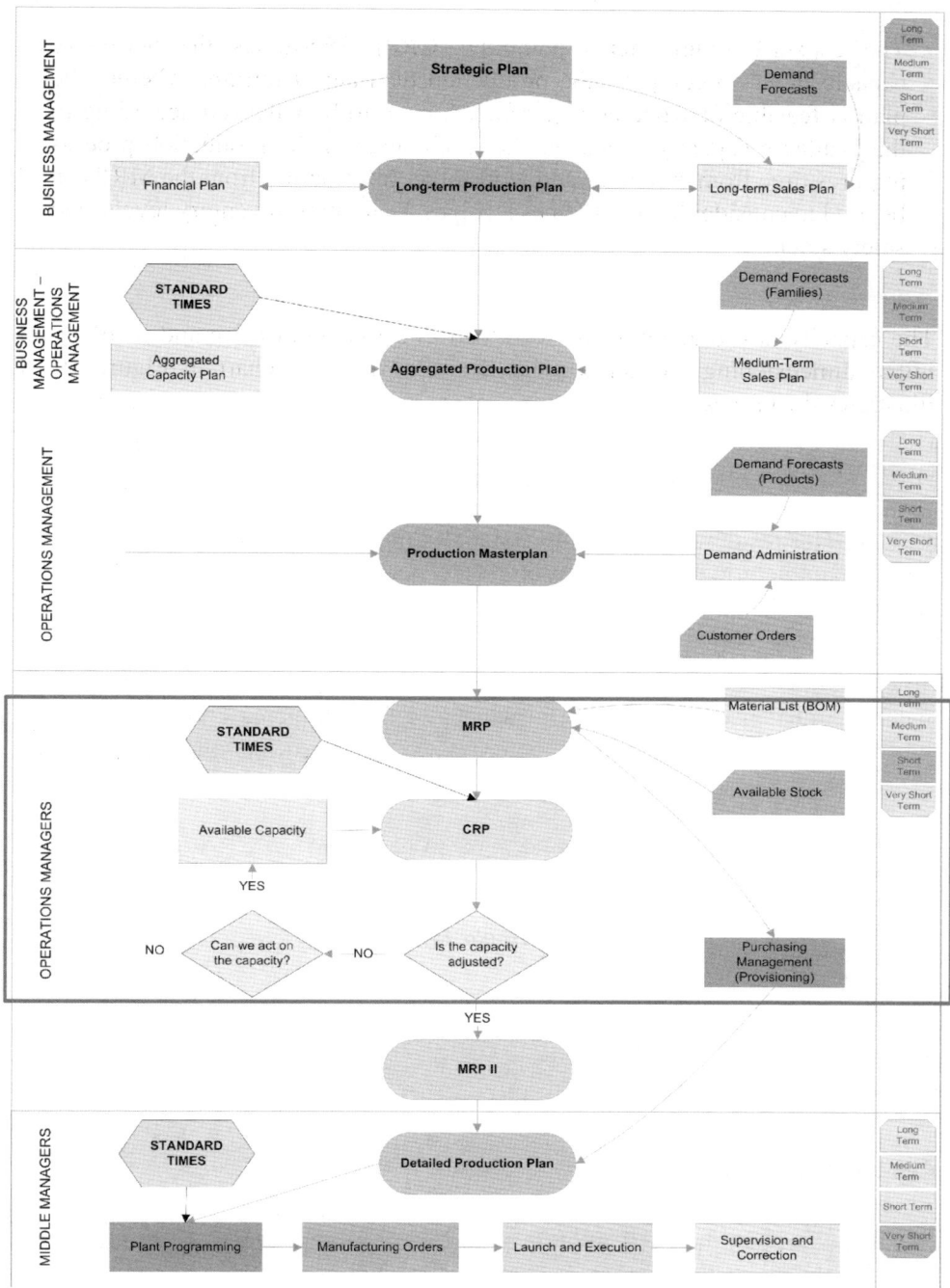

Figure 20.15. Cycle of productivity planning and control: CRP

As seen in the graph, the compatibility between the CRP and the capacity available will result in an approved MRP. Conversely, if capacity is not adjusted to demand, we must take measures for its adaptation. These measures may focus on the capacity adjustment (increase or reduction of workforce, overtime, outsourcing, layoffs). If these adjustments are not enough, we will resort to the modification of the MPS. We should study, for each case, the viability and sustainability of the measures that can be adapted and, in the case that several of them are viable, which one is more beneficial to the interests of the company. For this assessment, it is necessary to study and understand both required capacity and available capacity (workload vs. available capacity), which is discussed next.

CRP: Workload

The CRP will determine the capacity needed to meet the demand planned in the MRP. Therefore, the input for the creation of the CRP is based on output from the MRP, the planned production. For the creation of the CRP, we calculate workforce hours (person-hours) and machinery (machine-hours) required to meet the demand. This result will be given by the multiplication of the units to manufacture by the manufacturing time for that product. Therefore, the CRP will be the result of adding a new line to the MRP where the number of hours required for each phase of the product structure is indicated.

However, waste will exist in the factory due to several reasons such as lack of material, imbalances, and low performance, which will increase the time to carry out each task. The workload for each item is determined by the following formula:

$$CRP = Q \times Standard\ Time \times CwF$$

Formula 20.7

Where:

CwF = the manufacturing waste

Q = the quantity of units to manufacture

Available Capacity

After the development of the MRP and once the capacity requirements are calculated through the CRP, in order to test its feasibility, it will be necessary to establish the available capacity for the planning horizon considered. At first it is obvious that if the decisions made in the long term were adequate, the size of the fixed structure should have been established for meeting the demand needs in the most favorable conditions. The available capacity can be calculated for the desired period (a day, a week, a month, etc.). The formula is:

> Available Capacity (AC) = Nº Operators x Workday Hours x Nº Workdays

Formula 20.8

In this case, capacity would be calculated in person-hours; it could also be done in machine-hours. The number of days determines the period for which we want to calculate the capacity.

20.5.2. MRP II Calculation Process

As previously explained, the MRP system can be carried out more fully by taking into account the resources required (people and equipment) and the available capacity, which is precisely what the MRP II system proposes. *In fact, MRP operates as if capacity was infinite.* The MRP is calculated or developed regardless of standard times. It is in a subsequent step that the capacity is evaluated and adjusted to the workload, and in that step standard times do enter the equation. The necessary and available capacity adjustment will be done through an iterative process. Before obtaining the approved MRP II, we simulate the adjustment between required workload (CRP) and available capacity (AC), making appropriate corrections.

20.5.2.1. Comparison Between CRP and AC (Workload vs. Available Capacity)

Supposing we already have both data, the CRP and the AC. By contrasting them, we obtain important information, the saturation that would occur if daily production orders were launched as proposed in the MRP. A saturation above 100 percent means that, at a normal pace, the workforce will be unable to achieve the production suggested. By contrast, a saturation lower than 100 percent means that on that day, idle time occurred. This step is important for that reason: its setting is crucial for achieving an acceptable productivity and the compliance required in both production and delivery deadlines. The simulation could be as follows:

CRP vs. AC

DAY	-4	-3	-2	-1	0	1	2	3	4	5	6	7	8	9	10
CRP (s.h.)	0,00	314,34	716,92	984,79	890,28	1145,66	1123,66	1123,39	998,23	1023,16	1004,71	1047,68	278,14	20,69	0,00
Nº workers	95	95	95	95	95	95	95	95	95	95	95	95	95	95	95
AC (s.h.)	760,00	760,00	760,00	760,00	760,00	760,00	760,00	760,00	760,00	760,00	760,00	760,00	760,00	760,00	760,00
Saturation	0,00%	41,36%	94,33%	129,58%	117,14%	150,74%	147,85%	147,81%	131,35%	134,63%	132,20%	137,85%	36,60%	2,72%	0,00%
Deviation	760,0	445,7	43,1	-224,8	-130,3	-385,7	-363,7	-363,4	-238,2	-263,2	-244,7	-287,7	481,9	739,3	760,0
Accumulated deviation	760,0	1205,7	1248,7	1024,0	893,7	508,0	144,4	-219,0	-457,3	-720,4	-965,1	-1252,8	-771,0	-31,7	728,4

As evident in the saturation, intermediate days exceed 100 percent. As a workaround, we could spread the workload between adjacent days that are less saturated, or take temporary measures for increasing capacity. In any case, we can see in the table that the accumulated deviation at the end of the period is positive, which means that it can cope with the expected demand with the considered capacity (95 workers). Graphically it looks like this:

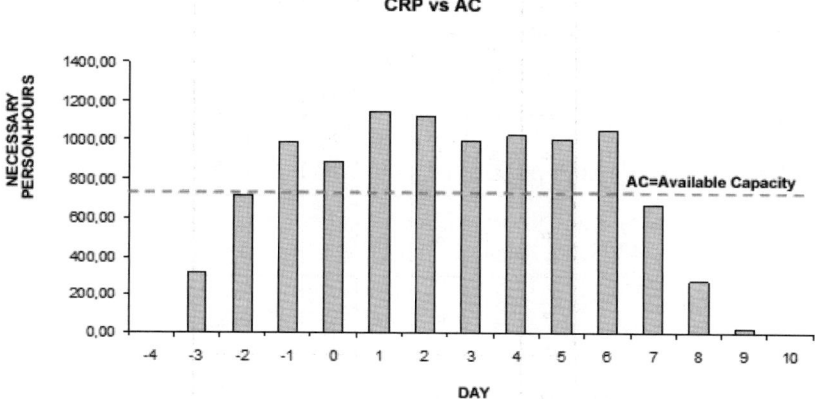

Figure 20.16. CRP vs. AC graph.

To be able to solve intermediate saturations we will act on the launch of production orders, bringing them forward or delaying them in order to distribute the workload.

The output produced by this tool shows us whether the capacity is in line with the expected demand and what the level of saturation is. The following possibilities can be obtained from this interpretation:

- *If capacity is in line with demand*, the level of saturation is close to 100 percent.
- *If capacity exceeds demand*, saturation will be low and we will try to advance orders, work against store or give holidays, if there is time for reaction.
- *If capacity is less than demand*, we have to increase the first. This increase can be accomplished by hiring, overtime, subcontracting, and so on. In any case, choosing the mechanism of increase will be based on the company's policy, costs, and restrictions.

If with the increase the demand is not satisfied, the MPS should be modified to match it. Although that situation will be difficult to achieve, we will try to come close to it. The target is 100 percent saturation.

20.5.2.2. How to Balance the Capacity and the Workload

Sometimes, due to a different rationale based on production, we face work demands that, with the current resources available, are not enough to meet this demand. Other times, however, the opposite occurs and we find idle resources that raise production costs.

In these situations, measures must be taken in order to adapt the capacity to the workload and that way not to change production plans. Here are some measures aimed at adjusting capacity to the workload.

1. Increase or decrease the size of the workforce
2. Work overtime in saturated sections
3. Schedule holidays in periods of low workload
4. Exchange personnel between sections: personnel moves from sections with low workload to saturated sections or bottlenecks
5. Outsourcing
6. Create or delete shifts
7. Use flexible workdays

These measures do not affect the MPS; they are only intended to modify capacity to suit the requirements. Always try not to change the MPS. In the event that avoiding changes is not possible, that the capacity cannot be readjusted, resort to varying the MPS, advancing or delaying orders and/or quantities.

20.5.2.3. MRP II Output

Once the simulation is finished, the launched production orders reorganized, and the available capacity requirements balanced (trying not to alter the MPS), the MRP II output is obtained. Here the production planning loop is closed and the results are:

- The MPS approved and executed.
- The MRP derived from that MPS.
- Manufacturing resources that comply with the MRP, that is, a CRP (workload) adjusted to the AC (available capacity).
- A launch plan, which will be the guide for middle management for executing the production. It will be this plan that says what and how much to produce, when to do so, and in what workstations. Such plans must be adequate to the actual conditions that arise in the manufacturing plant.

Narrative

Capacity dimensioning in sausage factory

The objective of this narrative is to develop an MRP II from simulations. What we have seen in the theoretical part cannot be clear enough or make us think that the format is unique, so we provide examples. It is important to see that the format is flexible, that the priority is to adjust capacity to demand, and that it can be done with simple tools. In this case, a spreadsheet was enough to build a MRP II. Of course, the simpler and shorter the manufacturing process is, the easier it is to perform and manage the MRP II.

Background

In this case, we present a company that makes fresh sausages. It is a highly perishable product, with no more than 4 or 5 days until spoilage. For distribution and trade issues it should be sold virtually the same day it is made. Because we are unable to work against store, workloads are highly variable, because they depend directly of the market.

Actions to Be Taken

Planning in this factory, as such, was virtually nonexistent. Orders were collected without any control, without capping, and the problems for having peaks in production occurred daily so workers had to work overtime in the afternoon.

Operators lengthened the manufacturing processes when they sensed overtime was needed so as to ensure a minimum of three extra hours. This annoyed both parties because management felt that they were being scammed, and many workers still had doubts about the profitability of working overtime due to the effort it posed.

An indispensable tool for production planning is a MRP II, that is, a necessary-workforce planner. In this case, we are face the problem of company management having little technical training and real problems when working with computer programs.

Therefore, it was decided to develop a computerized tool that was simple to handle, a "daily planner."

Industrial productivity

WORK ASSIGNED TO FILLER A				
PRODUCT	Kg to produce	Kg / person hour (normal)	Kg / person hour (optimum)
Sausage	400.00	45.33	60.57
Spanish sausage	400.00	70.67	88.67
Small sausage	150.00	54.00	62.29
Small Spanish sausage	150.00	42.67	56.73
Long chistorra	110.00	46.33	61.73
Small chistorra	110.00	36.67	47.83

Nº of operators assigned to the section	3
Time spent normal activity (maximum deadline)	8 hours and 44 minutes
Time spent optimum activity (minimum deadline)	6 hours and 45 minutes

OUTSIDE DEADLINE

NOTE: The boxes Kg/person-hour do not indicate standard time, but work pace, which is the inverse of the standard time.

We distribute the workload among the different fillers, regulating the amount of kilograms for the different products to manufacture, until all operators have enough work to be able to meet their 8 hours of work.

The factory implemented an incentive system, so the time spent performing the work is expressed in a range. The maximum deadline the operators have for completing the workload is the time consumed at a normal average activity, which is required. This concept will be further explained in the next chapter. Operators are required to comply with this performance, but are not required to surpass it, which is where performance bonuses come in to encourage operators to work above this rate.

On the other hand, the minimum deadline corresponds to the optimum activity, the maximum average pace at which operators should work.

Knowing these intervals and the availability of workers to stay in the afternoon for working overtime, planning was closed. In the afternoon, after the deadline for placing orders, the production manager could distribute the load of orders to the different work teams knowing in advance whether they can serve all orders the next day without having to work overtime.

A simulation of workload distribution follows:

20. Operations: Production Management

Product	Total Kg to Manufacture	Remaining Kg
Sausage	3500,00	3500,00
Spanish sausage	300,00	300,00
Small sausage	100,00	100,00
Small Spanish sausage	200,00	200,00
Long chistorra	100,00	100,00
Short chistorra	100,00	100,00

Initially the data to load into the planner are the total kilograms to produce, according to the orders that had been received throughout the day. Next to it is listed the kilograms missing. Not having done any more steps, logically the scheduler indicates that everything has yet to be done.

The next step to take is to start distributing the workload into the different fillers. We begin with filler A. We will saturate it until it has work to complete 8 hours at normal activity.

The following example shows the workload at a filling machine:

WORK ASSIGNED TO FILLER A

PRODUCT	Kg to produce	Kg / person hour (normal)	Kg / person hour (optimum)
Sausage	1100.00	45.33	60.57
Spanish sausage	0.00	70.67	88.67
Small sausage	0.00	54.00	62.29
Small Spanish sausage	0.00	42.67	56.73
Long chistorra	0.00	46.33	61.73
Small chistorra	0.00	36.67	47.83

Nº of operators assigned to the section	3
Time spent normal activity (maximum deadline)	8 hours and 06 minutes
Time spent optimum activity (minimum deadline)	6 hours and 04 minutes
OUTSIDE DEADLINE	

It is decided that filling machine A will be dedicated solely to making sausage, so it will make 1,100 kg. It also tells us that this work will take eight hours and six minutes, so it does not make the day. The data presented in the summary table are the following:

Industrial productivity

Product	Total Kg to manufacture	Remaining Kg
Sausage	3,500	2,400
Spanish sausage	300	300
Small sausage	100	100
Small Spanish sausage	200	200
Long chistorra	100	100
Short chistorra	100	100

Now the data have changed. The plan now indicates that only 2,400 kg of sausages are left to make after subtracting what filling machine A is going to make.

Product	Total Kg to manufacture	Remaining Kg
Sausage	3,500	0
Spanish sausage	300	0
Small sausage	100	0
Small Spanish sausage	200	0
Long chistorra	100	0
Short chistorra	100	0

A simulation distributes workloads so that no workstation exceeds 8 hours, based on four filling machines:

WORK ASSIGNED TO FILLER A

PRODUCT	Kg to produce	Kg / person hour (normal)	Kg / person hour (optimum)
Sausage	1050.00	45.33	60.57
Spanish sausage	0.00	70.67	88.67
Small sausage	0.00	54.00	62.29
Small Spanish sausage	0.00	42.67	56.73
Long chistorra	0.00	46.33	61.73
Small chistorra	0.00	36.67	47.83

N° of operators assigned to the section	3
Time spent normal activity (maximum deadline)	7 hours and 44 minutes
Time spent optimum activity (minimum deadline)	5 hours and 47 minutes

WITHIN THE DEADLINE

20. Operations: Production Management

WORK ASSIGNED TO FILLER B

PRODUCT	Kg to produce	Kg / person hour (normal)	Kg / person hour (optimum)
Sausage	1050.00	45.33	60.57
Spanish sausage	0.00	70.67	88.67
Small sausage	0.00	54.00	62.29
Small Spanish sausage	0.00	42.67	56.73
Long chistorra	0.00	46.33	61.73
Small chistorra	0.00	36.67	47.83

Nº of operators assigned to the section	3
Time spent normal activity (maximum deadline)	7 hours and 44 minutes
Time spent optimum activity (minimum deadline)	5 hours and 47 minutes

WITHIN THE DEADLINE

WORK ASSIGNED TO FILLER C

PRODUCT	Kg to produce	Kg / person hour (normal)	Kg / person hour (optimum)
Sausage	1100.00	45.33	60.57
Spanish sausage	0.00	70.67	88.67
Small sausage	0.00	54.00	62.29
Small Spanish sausage	0.00	42.67	56.73
Long chistorra	0.00	46.33	61.73
Small chistorra	0.00	36.67	47.83

Nº of operators assigned to the section	3
Time spent normal activity (maximum deadline)	7 hours and 45 minutes
Time spent optimum activity (minimum deadline)	5 hours and 50 minutes

WITHIN THE DEADLINE

WORK ASSIGNED TO FILLER D

PRODUCT	Kg to produce	Kg / person hour (normal)	Kg / person hour (optimum)
Sausage	300.00	45.33	60.57
Spanish sausage	300.00	70.67	88.67
Small sausage	100.00	54.00	62.29
Small Spanish sausage	200.00	42.67	56.73
Long chistorra	100.00	46.33	61.73
Small chistorra	100.00	36.67	47.83

Nº of operators assigned to the section	3
Time spent normal activity (maximum deadline)	7 hours and 21 minutes
Time spent optimum activity (minimum deadline)	5 hours and 40 minutes

WITHIN THE DEADLINE

As can be observed, the work has been distributed so that none of the workstations should have trouble completing their work within normal working hours. Now the production summary indicates that no work is left to be done.

This way we achieve effective planning in an extremely simple way, work is distributed equally to all workstations and the existence of overtime is controlled, without being left to the criteria of operators.

Conclusion

In this narrative, you can see what the concept of MRP II (manufacturing resource planning) is:

1. We start from a master production schedule; in this case the master plan consists of the orders of the day, nothing more and nothing less.

2. The master plan is inflexible and cannot be modified downward or upward (because we cannot store).

3. Therefore, we can only work on capacity.

4. Each filler has its simulator and the workload is simulated against the capacity until they are at an acceptable level of balance.

5. When it reaches this level, the work is assigned to each filling machine for the workday.

6. Planning has established what each manufacturing resource has to do.

20.6. Bottleneck management

20.6.1. Introduction

The management of bottlenecks is a special study case of workload (required capacity) against available capacity. The importance of the correct understanding of the issues that bottlenecks can cause in a factory is explained and, therefore, the vital need to consider them during production planning. Identifying these issues is imperative in order to optimize the productivity of the entire manufacturing plant. The physical progress of production orders is subject to a multitude of possible incidents that lead to delays and failure to meet the plan. From all of these, the most harmful are those that cause manufacturing bottlenecks.

A limiting resource is the one that has the lowest production speed in an assembly line production process. It can be a machine, a manual process, or a slow material-handling equipment that transports commodity products or raw material from a machine in one area to another machine in another area. If in addition, the capacity of this resource is not enough to supply the needs of the market, we have a bottleneck.

20. Operations: Production Management

For this reason, if capacity is adjusted to that bottleneck, any incident that may occur in it and cause a loss of time and/or production will be difficult to recover. We dedicate time to this phenomenon in order to give some advice about its treatment.

Consider that no matter the capacity sections have on their own, what generates finished product is the process; and it is not possible to manufacture more units than allowed by the limiting resource, although less is possible. To better understand what a bottleneck entails, the following narrative describes a bottleneck and the possible solutions to the situation.

Narrative

Non-elimination of bottleneck in metallic processed industry

In this narrative, we can see how a blatantly obvious situation caused a great loss of productivity. This industry has 240 operators of which 70 percent perform manual labor and 30 percent interact with a machine.

The company management was obsessed with two things:

1. To increase production

2. The low productivity of the factory

Before thinking that operators do not work, it is always good to assess whether they can work, that is, whether the factory is properly balanced. Assembly line tasks form a chain and all workstations are part of the process for any of the units produced. The factory will make a maximum number of units that corresponds to the capacity of the smallest or slowest machine or workstation.

The factory production at the time was 2,800 units/day with the workforce it had. To achieve the correct productivity, it should produce 3,200 units/day. That rate was achievable because the sector considered normal a ratio of 13.3 units/operator per day. This company was at 11.6. However, it was necessary to take a second step, once productivity was achieved; it had to reach 4,000 units/day to cover the high general expenses the company.

Having analyzed the factory and its capacities, the analyst observed that a heavy machine had a capacity that did not exceed 2,800 units per day. Therefore, the first objective of reaching a productivity of 3,200 units with 240 operators was unachievable, because the machine could produce no more units in 18 hours of work each day, and the other hours were necessary for maintenance and tool exchanges. Furthermore, it must be highlighted that expanding the production capacity of this machine would cost approximately $1.5 million, which the company could not afford.

Considering the situation as stated, we propose thinking backwards in order to achieve the productivity. We set the production to 2,800 units a day and recalculate the remaining tasks that have overcapacity due to the bottleneck caused by this machine.

Based on a rough estimate, then, the number of staff needed to meet this production with normal productivity ratios would be 2,800/13.33 = 210 operators. Logically, we would study in detail machine by machine and workstation by workstation in order to achieve this result, but for defining the overall strategy to adopt, the aggregated plan would work this way.

It may sound wrong but the factory had only one way to increase productivity, which was to dispense with 30 operators. A social solution consisted of having these personnel perform some tasks that were outsourced. But management did not want to hear about lowering the production. The situation was not about lowering production, but being realistic about what could be manufactured and adjusting the means to the maximum output achievable, which meant lowering expectations.

But the workforce was not adjusted to the ratio of normal production for 2,800 units/day, so solutions were sought to increase the production of that machine. While they were searching for them, they were losing money every day for lack of productivity, which could have provided an immediate solution.

Various solutions were proposed:

- *Make the machine work on Saturdays and Sundays for making a store and recovering through the week. It did not work, operators did not go on Saturdays and Sundays, so for lack of control, what was necessary was not produced. In addition, the factory had to be opened for that machine, which entailed further expenses.*
- *An attempt was made to outsource the semifinished product manufactured by that machine, but no other manufacturers could be found.*

These options did not work, but without a new analysis, management insisted that 4,000 units a day had to be done and asked factory managers to dimension the workforce for this new challenge. Thus, 4,000 units / 13.3 = 300 workers, so they decided to hire 60 people more without having solved the bottleneck that could manufacture no more than 2,800 units/day!

They tried to solve the problem with a third shift at night, but it did not work. This night shift yielded no better results than the weekends. Furthermore, breakdowns and maintenance were much more expensive because they were made in parallel to the operators who were working in the machine and who had to stop because the machine had no free time now.

The environment in the factory was untenable, and the production was still under 2,800 units, but this time with 300 workers. Productivity was down to 9.3 units per worker and per day.

What can we learn from this point?

- *If the CRP says that a certain production can be achieved, it may not be achieved. However, if it says that the production is not going to be achieved, surely it will not be. This means that when it says yes, it is maybe; and when it says no, it is certainly not.*

- *Things are as they are, not as we think they are, or how we want them to be, or as we need them to be.*

- *All measures taken to increase production in the bottleneck were logical, but before dimensioning the factory, thinking about the day when the bottleneck is solved, we need to solve the bottleneck. Consider that the production will not increase even though we increase the resources, if the bottleneck is still the same, so an urgency to increase production must first focus on solving the bottleneck.*

- *When overheads force you to sell more, think first about how to reduce them. Selling more requires more overhead spending and forces you to adjust margins. Selling 2,000 units of whatever product per day is done much more comfortable than selling 4,000 units.*

- *Production has to be taken very seriously.*

Note: *For these cases, the book* The Goal *by Eliyahu M. Goldratt is highly recommended.*

20.6.2. Solutions to Bottlenecks

After reading the example about the bottleneck, a list of solutions is provided that will help to identify and solve bottlenecks.

1. Diagnose and identify.

Before looking at how to solve or address a bottleneck, we must identify it. In the CRP it will appear as the resource with more saturation. We can observe it graphically:

Industrial productivity

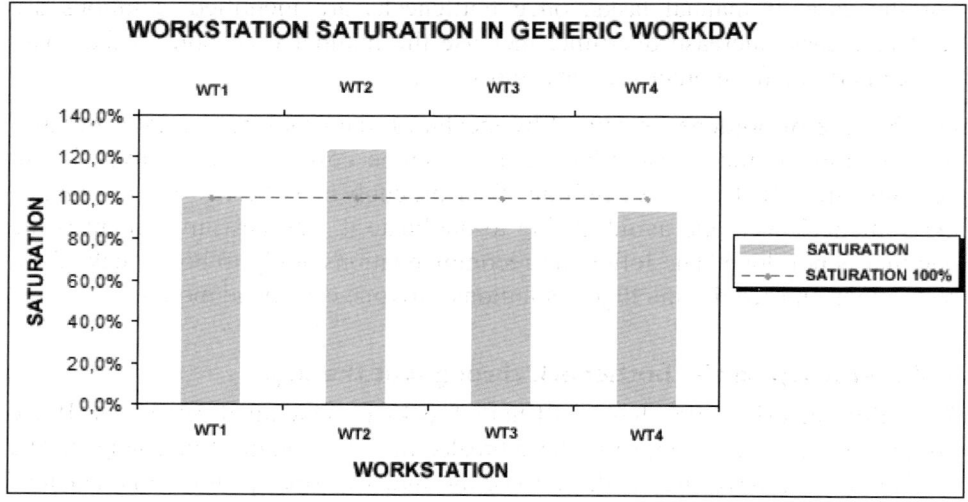

Figure 20.17. Graph of workstation saturation

That is, in a typical day, we see that WS1 (workstation 1) is 100 percent saturated, WS3 and WS4 are working below their capacity, and WS2 cannot meet the average production at normal pace. It is quickly evident that the bottleneck is in WS2.

Physically, what comes before the bottleneck generates a stock of semifinished product whereas the sections that come after this task are short of work. Graphically:

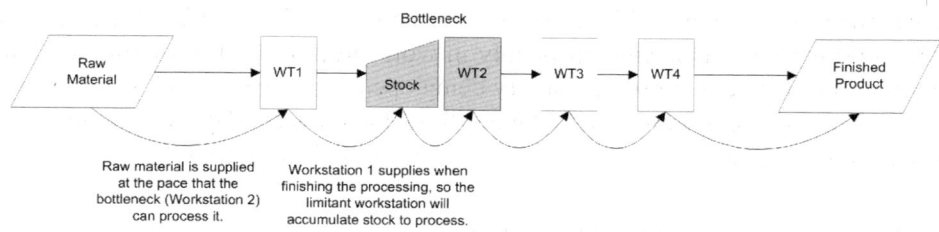

Figure 20.18. Stock in bottleneck

Bottlenecks might be variable; they can change, depending on the workstation saturation of the production mix. In addition, depending on how long the process is, partial restrictions may exist.

The most important step in order to solve a bottleneck is to identify it.

We could classify bottleneck into two different groups:

- Manual tasks

- Machine-dependent tasks, which are so for restrictions or production capacities

For the case of manual tasks, once bottlenecks are identified, solutions are relatively easy: increase overtime, increase the number of people in that task, move operators from other sections, and so on.

For the case of bottlenecks caused by machines, the problem is greater because the limitation is more restrictive. If the machine costs $30,000, maybe it can be duplicated. If it costs $2 million, then probably it is best to try to manage the bottleneck well and avoid having to duplicate it. The best investment is the one that is not done. The following recommendations apply to bottlenecks from restrictions and require intelligent solutions. Anyone can spend money.

2. Avoid stopping the bottleneck throughout the day.

Typically, factories often have half-hour breaks or scheduled rest stops. If the bottleneck machine is subject to these breaks, the situation must be changed. The workers should have the break, but not the machine (except for a maintenance operation). We must organize shifts and substitutions so that the machine does not stop.

Consider an example of why this concept is so important: In the previous narrative, when the bottleneck machine operators took their break, so did the machine. Let us calculate the cost of this break for this machine.

Given that we can only produce as many units as the bottleneck can, a 40-minute stop of the machine was a 40-minute stop of the whole factory. Those 40 minutes have to be multiplied by 240 operators to calculate losses for the capacity imbalance. or 160 hours. If the cost of one hour is $15, it is $2,400 per day or $576,000 per year. This amount is only in workforce costs; it does not take into account the cost per hour of the factory being opened or the margin lost for unsold units, that is, the opportunity cost of not selling 266 units per day. With these costs, it seems reasonable to give a solution to the bottleneck stop, right?

3. Place an older machine in parallel.

Many times, assuming an older machine is obsolete, we invest in a new machine because it helps to have a higher yield per operator. It is a good approach if the gain in productivity exceeds the cost of the new machine (it is not always clear). If we are talking about a bottleneck machine, the recommendation is to leave the old machine in parallel. Do not look at the maximum productivity of the workstation but seek the maximum productivity of the process. Although this old machine causes a low yield to operators that operate it, productivity gains will accrue to the rest of the factory.

Normally, factories keep the old machines, which can help overcome the bottleneck.

4. The bottleneck manufactures only the necessary.

Oftentimes, mass production and large batches require the manufacturing of products that nobody has asked for, which forces a delay in the manufacturing of items that have been ordered and results in pressure from customers because of these delays.

The aim is to show that the bottleneck is already limited so that manufacturing products not demanded and that are not going be billed either is a problem.

5. Put a quality control before the bottleneck.

6. Monitor the bottleneck more frequently.

7. Organize the bottleneck supply.

8. Minimize the time for machine changing.

You can expand your knowledge about the topic covered in this chapter in the book by the same author *Stocks, Processes and Operations management* (Marcombo, Technical Editions).

Questions

1. What is production management?
2. What application has standard time in operations management?
3. What is the main cause of waste in production management?
4. When performing the simulation of the aggregate production plan, what strategy will we try to choose?
5. In the previous question, we defined the information obtained from the MRP. What information is added by the MRP II?
6. What do you get from the comparison between workload (CRP) and available capacity?
7. In the case of having a capacity below demand, what steps can we take?
8. What is a limiting resource?
9. List four possible solutions to bottlenecks.
10. After completion of the MRP II, what is the next step to take in process planning?

Problems

1. A factory produces three different products: P1, P2, and P3. For the process to produce each unit, five steps are necessary: S1, S2, S3, S4, and S5.

   The waste coefficient is homogeneous in all phases and is Cd = 1.15.

   The standard times in hours of each product type for each phase are:

	S1	S2	S3	S4	S5
P1	0.37	0.81	0.21	1.56	1.22
P2	0.56	1.04	0.43	1.85	1.67
P3	0.19	0.30	0.15	0.85	0.44

   This factory makes weekly master plans; the weekly orders are grouped and released every Monday.

   By default, the operators defined for each phase are:

   S1: 1 operator

   S2: 2 operators

   S3: 1 operator

   S4: 3 operators

   S5: 3 operators

   In week 5, the master plan is as follows:

   P1: 38

   P2: 28

   P3: 17

   What will the workload (CRP) in person-hours be that week in each phase?

   NOTE: Do not forget the waste coefficient.

Units	Product	F1	F2	F3	F4	F5
38	P1	16.19	35.61	9.18	68.17	53.41
28	P2	17.89	33.39	13.85	59.57	53.67
17	P3	3.62	5.79	2.93	16.62	8.69
TOTAL PER PHASE		37.69	74.79	25.96	144.36	115.77

   * Calculation of values considering the coefficient of waste.

Given the operators who, by default, work at each stage, what is the capacity available in each phase for that period?

- One-week period: 5 days
- Workday hours: 8 hours/day

Phase	F1	F2	F3	F4	F5
N° Operators	1	2	1	3	3
Available capacity (p-h)	40	80	40	120	120

Compare the workload with the available capacity and calculate the level of saturation. Remember that:

Phase	F1	F2	F3	F4	F5
Workload (p-h)	37.69	74.79	25.96	144.36	115.77
Available capacity (p-h)	40	80	40	120	120
Saturation (%)	94.24%	93.49%	64.89%	120.30%	96.47%

- Do you think the workload is well balanced between phases? No.
- Which is the limiting stage? Phase 4.
- Do you think the master plan will be met? No.
- Why? Because one of the phases has insufficient capacity to meet the workload.

Bibliography

Chase, Richard B., Nicholas J. Aquilano, and F. Robert Jacobs. *Operations and Supply Management* (New York: McGraw-Hill, 2000).

Domínguez Machuca, José Antonio, *Dirección de operaciones* (New York: McGraw-Hill, 1995).

Goldratt, Eliyahu M., *The Goal* (Barrington, MA: North River Press, 1984).

Heredia Álvaro, José Antonio, *La gestión de la fábrica: Modelos para mejorar la competitividad* (Díaz de Santos, 2004).

Vollmann, Thomas E., William L. Berry, D. Clay Whybark, and F. Robert Jacobs, *Manufacturing Planning and Control for Supply Chain Management* (New York: McGraw-Hill, 2005).

Womak, James P., and Daniel T. Jones, *Lean Thinking* (New York: Simon & Schuster, 1996).

1. MANT
2. WASTE IN WORK DESIGN
3. WASTE BY LOW PERFORMANCE
4. WASTE BY MANAGEMENT FAILURES

Part	Aim	Initial Situation	Final situation
Part 1: Diagnosis	We start from a manufacturing execution times and we want to know what caused them.		
Part 2: Methods	We study and improve the work method of a task to reduce its necessary execution time. The same with processes.		
Part 3: Time measurement	With a defined and improved method we time the task through various techniques to be able to establish a standard, this implies time improvements.		
Part 4: Operations planning	With standard times we can manage production, dimensionate, make decisions, etc. Waste by management failures is reduced.		
Part 4: Productivity control	With standard times productivity can be controled reducing the waste by low performance.		

Chapter 21

Productivity Control and Incentive Systems

21.1. Introduction and Concepts

Measuring times and having a standard are essential for production management, but they are by no means enough. All the standard times we have in a list, book, or manufacturing sheet are useless if productivity is not controlled and its compliance not monitored.

If we cannot ensure the compliance with the standard times:

Can we plan?

Can we know costs a priori?

Can we evaluate the performance of the production factors?

Can we range the permanent deviations in costs that we have once the manufacturing is done?

Will we know the causes of the deviations?

NO

Therefore, enforcing the standard times is absolutely essential, and the tool to do so is the control of productivity.

Productivity control is totally assumed in the collective agreements. Moreover, the agreements consider productivity incentives and even suggest them as a means so that operators who have a performance above normal may perceive a greater remuneration. By controlling productivity, we will have a tool for continuous improvement. Deviations in cost and in execution times will be given by two major groups of causes (as seen in the waste measurement theory).

1. The incidents caused by management problems: lack of materials, breakdowns, imbalances, etc.
2. A performance below average

By controlling the productivity we may identify and quantify the causes and therefore attack them. Without this tool, these causes that are not disaggregated, would go unnoticed. Endemic time losses, reiterated for years and for which there is no reaction, will be highlighted, generating all kinds of complaints and suggestions for improvement once productivity control is implemented. Time losses are always assigned to a cause and every cause has a culprit.

Incentive systems can make operators earn more money; and with the same manufacturing infrastructures, more is produced and fixed costs are diluted. However, incentive systems cannot be initiated without control of productivity.

The objectives of productivity control and incentive systems include the following:

- To ensure standard times are met with a small margin of error
- To range production costs
- To identify the causes of time losses and quantify them
- To pay a bonus to operators who have a performance above normal

21.1.1. Measurement Units of Productivity

In a manufacturing process, materials are involved along with a necessary execution time for the material transformation processes in which the workforce is involved. **Productivity** is a ratio that measures the level of utilization of the influencing factors when making a product, so thus it is necessary to control productivity. The higher the productivity of our company, the lower the production costs are and, therefore, our competitiveness within the market will increase.

> Productivity is a ratio that measures the relationship between the production performed and the number of factors or inputs used to achieve it.

21. Productivity Control and Incentive Systems

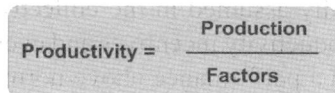

Formula 21.1. *Productivity formula*

The formulation of productivity can be contemplated in three ways:

- **Total productivity:** the ratio between total production and all the factors used
- **Multifactorial productivity:** associates final production with several factors, usually labor and capital
- **Partial productivity:** the ratio between the final production and a single factor

In these quotients, both numerator (production) and denominator (factors) will be expressed in the same units, usually in monetary units. To mention productivity is to mention the term *efficiency*, which measures how or to what extent they used each of the factors or resources in the conversion process necessary to obtain the product.

> Efficiency measures the relationship between inputs and outputs, seeks to minimize the cost of resources ("doing things right"). In numerical terms, it is the ratio between the current production obtained and the standard production expected.

Efficiency is responsible for the "means" and the effectiveness of the "ends." Efficiency and effectiveness are interrelated: an operator can be efficient but ineffective. For example, an operator who makes many units of product A in a short time is highly efficient, but if the operator really should have made product B, that operator is ineffective. Productivity is a combination of both concepts. By increasing the productivity of a company, it will be more competitive in its sector by reducing manufacturing costs.

Figure 21.1. *Relationship between productivity and competitiveness*

It is vital to carry out productivity control in an industrial enterprise. Companies need to increase their productivity, because it entails a better use of resources and therefore the ability to achieve more production with the same resource

Industrial productivity

consumption, or to produce the same with less consumption. Any option that does not involve one of these two options does not increase productivity.

Of all the resources controlled by a company in the process of making a product, the most important is people, the **workforce factor**. If to increase productivity is to optimize the use of factors, and if the most important of these is the workforce, we need to consider human activity patterns in order to define and standardize rules or procedures.

21.1.2. Bedaux System

The Bedaux system measures workforce in minutes or work points. The final outcome of the work study, once all the phases it consists of are finished, is obtaining the point-value of a task, that is to say, the standard time. The point value is the time required to perform a particular task at normal activity, including rest time. It is expressed in person-minutes. Each task will have a certain point value (number of minutes or points) multiplied by the number of units produced, its result is the value in work points. The sum of all the work points in a day will indicate the amount of work performed.

The main advantage of this system is that visually it is simple to quantify work by points (e.g., person-minutes) and in this way compare it with the time taken in checking its level of utilization. The following example performs a calculation of the points earned in one workday.

Example

A worker uses a full workday of 8 hours to make the following number of items:

Reference	Manufactured Units
A	12
B	5
C	10
D	3
E	7

A worker uses a full workday of 8 hours to make the following number of items:

21. Productivity Control and Incentive Systems

Reference	PV (p-min)
A	15.6
B	14.32
C	15.6
D	3.34
E	9.66

Comparing both tables of values, we obtain the following result for that day:

Reference	Manufactured Units	PV (p-min)	Points Earned
A	12	15,6	187,2
B	5	14,32	71,6
C	10	15,6	156
D	3	3,34	10,02
E	7	9,66	67,62

Total: 492,44 puntos

These points obtained are compared with the time that the operator has spent actually performing these tasks. This time is called *dedicated time*. The possible results of this comparison are shown in the following diagram:

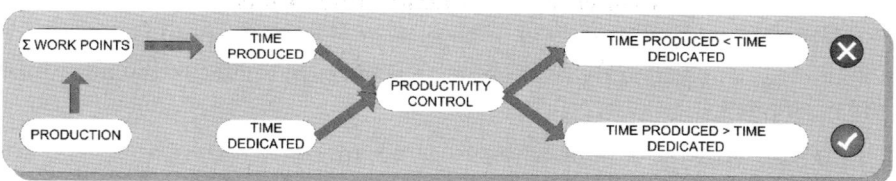

Figure 21.2. *Basic steps of productivity control*

If the comparison results in an excess of dedicated time, it will be interpreted as performance at low activity. The company will not be adjusting to costs, will loose productivity and therefore will be less competitive. If on the contrary an excess of produced time is synonymous with high performance, the company will adjust to the costs and be much more competitive and productive.

Throughout the chapter the descriptions of prescribed actions will depend on the result of the comparison between standard time and time spent. Standard time is synonymous with enforceable time, and therefore, it requires compliance of the operator or group of operators in return for a fixed salary. Similarly, when the time spent is less than the points awarded, the operator or group of operators will have achieved performance above the required level (bonus points), which may be paid by the company.

21.1.3. Activity Calculation

The third part of the book dealt with and measured work pace based on a subjective evaluation and on scales (the most common are the 100-133 and the 60-80). An essential part of this chapter looks at calculating the productivity by the calculation of activity.

> For timekeeping, activity is calculated at the time the work is performed. For the control of productivity, the activity is calculated based on a production performed in a given period.

The business management, by controlling productivity and with a good incentive system must ensure that the level of activity complied by all its staff is the highest possible within acceptable limits, because much of the productivity achieved depends directly on this parameter. Therefore, we will explain how to calculate the activity achieved by an operator from the execution time and from the production achieved.

As explained earlier, it should be understood that execution time and activity are inversely proportional (to higher activity, lower execution time) but achieved production and activity are directly proportional (to higher activity, higher production). From these premises, some equations will be discussed that relate the activity achieved, the execution time, and the actual production. For the calculation of achieved activity from an execution time, the following formula should be applied:

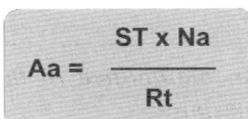

Formula 21.2. *Activity calculation*

Where:

Aa = Achieved activity

ST = Standard time, which is the execution time that corresponds to normal activity

Na = Normal activity (The numerical value corresponding to the scale used must be placed.)

Rt = Real time of execution, or running time

In order to study the relation between production and achieved activity, a new concept must be introduced, which is produced time, Tp. The concept of produced time should be understood as the time required to perform a specific number of parts with the standard time. To calculate it we will use the formula:

$$Tp = ST \times \text{Manufactured Parts}$$

Formula 21.3. Standard time calculation for batch of the same reference

When different pieces are being made, which would mean different standard times, the formula would be:

$$Tp = \sum ST \times n° \text{ of part}$$

Formula 21.4. Standard time calculation for batch of different reference

The time allowed for production is the time at normal activity of a unit multiplied by the number of units to be manufactured. Once this produced time is known, for calculating the activity obtained from a production, it should be compared with the current execution time:

$$Aa = \frac{Tp \times Na}{Rt}$$

Formula 21.5. Activity calculation from runtimes

Example

Average activity calculation maintained in the development of a work making use of the execution times

Two operators jointly manufactured 14 parts, with a standard time of 19 person-minutes/part, for which they have used 2 hours. We proceed to calculate, step by step, all the data needed for the activity, using the Bedaux scale. The only noteworthy detail is the necessity to always work with the same units.

Industrial productivity

Time produced = Manufactured parts x Standard time per piece

Tp = 14 x 19 = 266 minutes

Actual execution time (in minutes) = Time spent x Number of operators

Rt = 120 minutes x 2 operators = 240 minutes

$$Ac = \frac{266 \times 60}{240} = 66,5$$

It is clear that the activity achieved by the operator is 66.5 measured with the Bedaux scale (60-80), more than 6 points above the required, which means they have worked above the enforceable performance.

21.2. Convenience of Productivity Control

Productivity control is essential for implementing the time study, which must have been previously done in our plant. The control of productivity is the comparison between the standard time of the operation (work produced) and the actual execution time (time spent), thereby obtaining from this comparison real information about the deviations that exist in our factory. Without productivity control, time implementation is simply impossible.

> **STANDARD TIME vs. REAL EXECUTION TIME**

***Formula 21.6.** Productivity control*

In most cases, this equality is not satisfied, because:

> **REAL EXECUTION TIME = STANDARD TIME + INCIDENCE TIME + LOW PERFORMANCE**

***Formula 21.7.** Decomposition of the execution time of a task*

The real execution time of a task consists of standard time or point value and time losses, that is, workforce waste, stops or waits by the operator, imbalances in production lines, lack of material to process, and so on. Because of productivity control, all inefficiencies that should be improved will come to light and therefore, we will know what percentage of the workforce is wasted.

> **WITHOUT PRODUCTIVITY CONTROL COSTS CANNOT BE ENSURED. EVERY TASK NOT MEASURED OR CONTROLED IS A "BOTTOMLESS PIT" OF HOURS.**

Figure 21.3. Importance of productivity control

21.3. Convenience of the Incentive Systems

The main objective of an incentive system is to invite workers to be more productive, because if they reduce the standard time of manufacturing, they will receive in exchange an improvement in their salary.

> The main and most important benefit that an incentive system provides will be an increase in production without the need to increase working hours or make investments. It improves the efficiency of all the factors involved in production.

Figure 21.4. Effect of productivity increase

Furthermore, the implementation of an incentive system will bring these other benefits. One of them is the reduction of workforce cost, because operators achieve a higher performance within the workday, without increasing the number of hours of the workday.

1. Wages increase for workers, as they receive a higher salary because of their higher than required performance.

2. Improvement of work methods is realized as all non-value-adding operations would surface, such as imbalances in production lines, low saturation, etc.

3. Reductions of overhead are attributable to the product:

    - Energy
    - Management
    - Amortizations

4. Benefit is obtained from the sale of a greater production.

21.4. Productivity Control

The first part of this chapter explained what to really understand when it comes to productivity, the factors that can make it vary, and some ways to measure it, along with the convenience of controlling and encouraging its continued rise. The minimums necessary to design and implement an adequate productivity control for a factory will be explained in the following section. Figure 21.5 is an outline that summarizes the calculation of productivity:

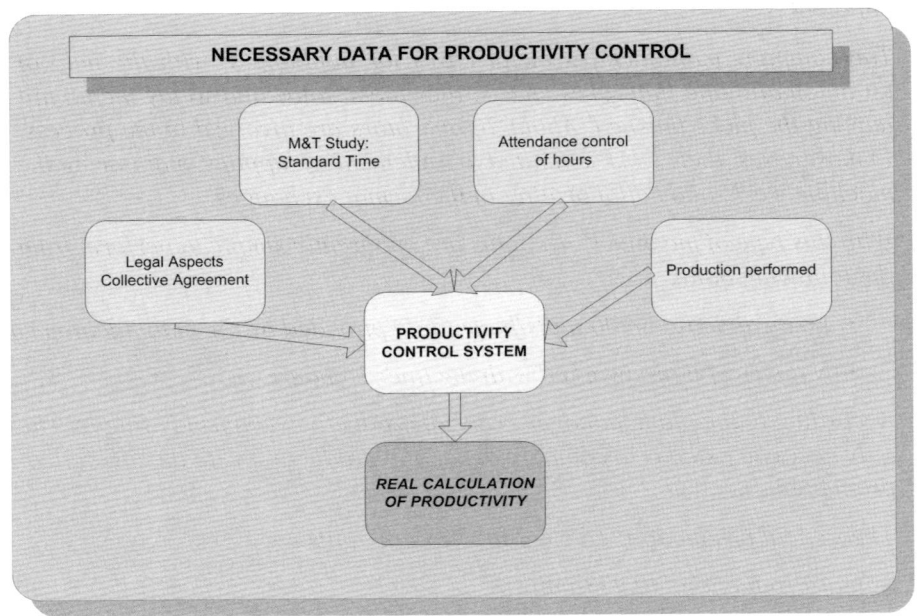

Figure 21.5. Productivity control outline

21.4.1. What Is Productivity Control?

A productivity control system is much broader than a report of the current situation compared to what it should be. Much more than a graph that shows how well or how poorly we have done, it tries to identify each of the causes of delays in the execution of work and to quantify the delays. The first step in order to solve a problem is to identify and understand the problem in depth, which is the main objective of a productivity control system. Typically, in the absence of complete and current information on the situation, the problems cannot be identified or in many cases they are confused. Given a fact as common as a delay in the manufacturing of a product, it is not known what action to take, because the only information we have is usually that something has gone wrong, because we have not met the standard.

21. Productivity Control and Incentive Systems

The following real example shows the information that business management receives about the production executed on any day.

Narrative

Lack of information on high-capacity assembly line

A company with serious management problems and with a huge lack of useful information about the state of the factory can only be regarded as impotent.

The company manufactures metal cases for appliances, with the help of an automatic line that takes sheets, dies them, folds and welds them until leaving the piece finished. About 20 operators are involved in the process. In most cases, their work is limited to replenishing supplies, monitoring the machine work, and collaborating in the format exchanges.

With this type of machines, accounts are apparently simple to perform from the following data:

- *Line capacity: 6,200 units/hour (data provided by the manufacturer)*
- *Number of hours worked with the line: 16 hours*

According to the plant manager criteria, productivity control is simple. The only necessary step is to compare the actual production with the theoretical production.

Theoretical production: 16 x 6,200 = 74,400 units

Actual Production: 40,933 units

Line performance: $= \dfrac{40.933}{74.400} \times 100 = 55\,\%$

However, what is the meaning of these datum? For every 100 units the factory has had the opportunity to manufacture, it has manufactured only 55. How is this possible? Has something happened? Of course, information collected from middle managers includes the fact that an operator was sick in one of the shifts, that to complete the task three format changes were needed, and that a mechanical problem led to downtime.

The manager went downstairs to the factory floor to try to discover the source of the problem. Upon arriving at the line, he found it stopped because the line was undergoing a format exchange and the operators were talking in a huddle. He approached them and asked what was happening; they answered that they were waiting for the warehouse to supply the new tool and raw material in order to initiate the exchange. The director criticized their attitude, but the operators answer that it was not their problem and that they were clearly doing everything possible.

The plant manager was about to continue asking for explanations and go to the warehouse section. Word preceded him and everyone seemed busy, running through the halls and preparing everything needed to start making the new reference. The director blamed the section manager for his lack of anticipation and involvement. The response made the director blush even more: "This format change was not planned; it has been communicated on the fly."

The responsibility got pushed away more and more. In his plant nobody was responsible for anything when the format exchange was caused by a rush order and when they did not have enough raw materials to work the complete shift with the reference that was planned, so making the exchange did not seem a bad choice. Something had also failed in the sales, purchasing, and planning departments.

He continued to seek explanations in several departments. When he arrived at his office, the first shift had already concluded and he decided to find out what the productivity had been on that fateful day. The surprise was enormous when he discovered that the productivity of this first turn was 58%, higher than achieved in the previous day.

"Now I really do not understand a thing!"

So, what happened yesterday that led to an even worse outcome?

The most worrisome part of the situation is that nobody has a clear and concise answer. In summary, it could be said that productivity control is a system that is responsible for collecting information from the factory, sorting it out, and classifying it. Without any doubt, this tool helps to verify where the errors are and, therefore, facilitates taking corrective measures.

21.4.2. Necessary Data for Productivity Control

When carrying out the productivity control for a factory or section, we must have the following information:

> Data needed to control productivity:
>
> - Amount of work performed (e.g., the type and quantity of produced parts)
> - Time spent doing the work, occurred incidences, and controlled hours
> - Standard time of the task, result of the time study conducted
> - Basic information about the legal framework (collective agreement, workers' rights)

It is now necessary to classify the types of hours that compose the workday. Depending on whether the task is measured, if stops occur in the manufacturing process for causes beyond the operator or by any other cause, and so on, to each space of time when different situations occur will be referred to in one way or another.

- **Noncontrolled hours:** the time, measured in person-hours, in which the operator performs a task that has not been measured and, therefore, the performance achieved by that operator is not known

- **Controlled hours:** the time, measured in person-hours, in which the operator performs a task that has been measured and, therefore, the performance achieved by that operator can be known

- **Incidence hours:** the time, measured in person-hours, in which the operator cannot do the assigned job due to causes beyond the operator's control

- **Presence hours:** the time, measured in person-hours, spent by the worker in the workplace (The addition of controlled hours, noncontrolled hours, and incidence hours should coincide with the presence hours.)

Another kind of hour classification is the following:

- **Normal hours:** hours that correspond to a normal workday

- **Extra hours/Overtime:** hours are performed outside normal hours that are more expensive than normal hours and therefore important to control (Neira, 2003)

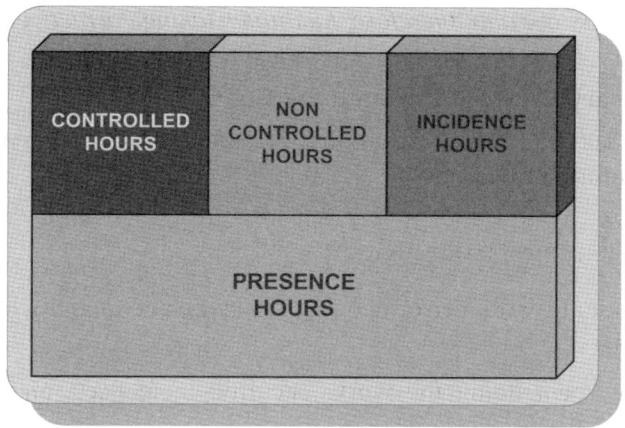

Figure 21.6. Cast of presence hours

Performance can only be studied within controlled hours. In noncontrolled hours the performance of any operator or group of operators cannot be checked, so it must be reduced from the total time of the workday for productivity calculation.

> The productivity control should minimize the amount of noncontrolled hours and incidence hours.

> NON CONTROLLED HOURS → CHAOS

Formula 21.9. Consequences of the absence of productivity control

Knowing the details needed for productivity control and knowing what kind of hours should be taken into account, the next step will be to collect the data regarding them, which will be done by a work report system.

21.4.3. Work Reports

What is a work report? A work report is a file or document (digital or printed) that contains all the necessary information for controlling productivity. The work reports feed the control of productivity. They describe, for a particular period of time, the work done, the time spent performing it by an operator or group of operators, and the incidences that occurred as well as quantify them. The work report system has different rationales; however, they shall contain at least the following terms:

Minimum information that a work report will contain

- Presence time
- Incidence time and its causes
- Noncontrolled time
- Actual production
- Identification of operator or operators affected by this report
- Identification of work report supervisor

The aim of the work report system:

- To conduct a control of the time spent on a task
- To perform a control on actual production, quantifying it
- To quantify the stops and incidences

Operators generally must complete their work reports correctly. Depending on the needs of the company, their content may vary, but at all times, the accuracy of the information it contains must be ensured. Therefore, it is important that such report is monitored by some manager or the supervisor of that section. As a general rule, monitoring provides a level of control that prevents work report information from being solely dependent on the personnel involved who may have a biased interest in the outcome. For this reason, the person who validates the work reports does not get any benefit that may test his or her impartiality.

Currently, automatic plant control systems are able to collect and display real-time production data, such as quantities, times, incidents, and breakdowns, thereby facilitating the work of operators and managers.

21.4.4. Examples of Work Reports

The examples of work reports shown here provide a number of diverse formats.

Example

In this simple example of work report, we can find all the necessary information for a work performed by a single operator.

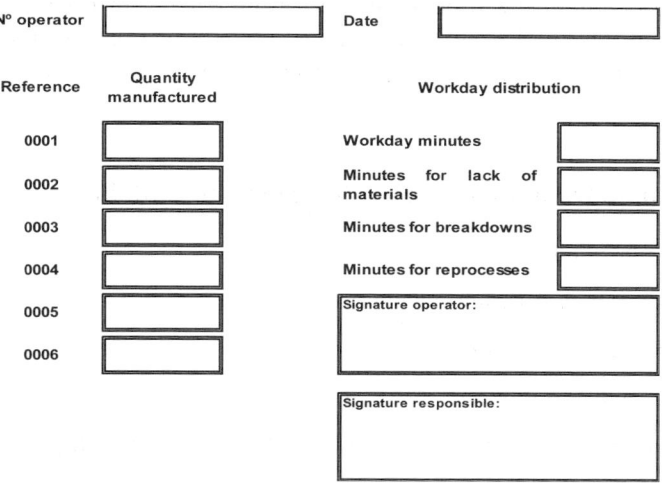

Figure 21.7. *Example of work report*

So far we have not commented on the importance of monitoring the work. In many cases operators do not understand the importance of the information contained in the work reports and fail to fill them out properly. It should be mandatory that the person directly responsible for the operator validates the document, in order to verify that everything in it is correct and truthful. Without this control, productivity control relies too much on the honesty and involvement of the operators who fills in the report.

The following examples provide some sheets already filled in, giving us the opportunity to check the information they can contain.

Example

> *Another production line has had problems when performing its work, but the report shows no noncontrolled hours and an incidence of one hour. In this case the inaccuracy of this report is demonstrated, because the stop was caused by lack of material, but this fact is not reflected anywhere, so this information does not transcend. Not being validated by any supervisor, it is not possible to corroborate, a week later, for example, whether the assembly line was really stopped for one hour due to lack of materials or for any other reason.*

21. Productivity Control and Incentive Systems

WORK REPORT FOR PEPPERS PACKAGING LINE

Code	Category	Name	Presence Hours	Hours at Control	Noncontrolled Hours	Incidence Hours
A01	1st Officer	Murray Murphy	8	8	0	0
A02	Assistant	Graham Reed	8	8	0	0
A03	Specialist Operator	Caren Cook	8	8	0	0
A04	Operator	Jamie Ward	8	8	0	0
A05	Operator	Clark Sanchez	8	8	0	0
A06	Operator	Halley Brook	8	8	0	0
A07	Operator	Kai O'Meara	8	8	0	0
A08	Operator	Chad Richardson	8	8	0	0
			64	64		

Initial Hour:	7.00
Final Hour:	15.00

Presence Hours	64.00
Noncontrolled Hours	0.00
Incidence Hours	0.00
Hours at Control	64.00
Nº of workers:	8.00
Dedicated minutes:	3,840.00

Work Order

Trays of peppers	11,000.00
Point Value:	0.392
Total Points:	4,312.00
PRODUCTIVITY	**1.12**

Figure 21.8. *Filled-in work report, containing incidentals and noncontrolled hours*

In the basic structure for a work report system, necessary information is collected to obtain data on the productivity, but not all the information required is collected. Depending on the rationale of the tasks, the systems can be different, because they are for individual tasks, teams, or reference types.

723

Examples

Another type of work report identifies each incident and describes it. Moreover, each of these incidents is verified by a supervisor.

OPERATOR		Anthony King		Date:	2011/06/28	
SECTION	TIMETABLE					
Workstation 1	Start hour	8:00				
	Finish hour	11:00				
Workstation 2	Start hour	11:00				
	Finish hour	14:00				
Workstation 3	Start hour	14:00				
	Finish hour	16:00				
Workstation 4	Start hour					
	Finish hour					
Workstation 5	Start hour					
	Finish hour					
Noncontrolled Time	Start hour					
	Finish hour					

AFFECTED SECTION	TIMETABLE		INCIDENCE DESCRIPTION		SUPERVISED BY:
1	Start hour	8:00	Stop by lack of material.		Line supervisor
	Finish hour	8:15			
1	Start hour	10:00	Jam in cutting machine. Maintenance has to fix it.		Maintenance
	Finish hour	10:25			
3	Start hour	14:30	Maintenance operations. cleaning of glue injectors.		Line supervisor
	Finish hour	15:15			
	Start hour				
	Finish hour				
	Start hour				
	Finish hour				

Figure 21.9. *Example of work report*

As you can see in Figure 21.9, each incident is described and quantified, and its veracity monitored by a supervisor.

In order to measure the waste in manufacturing, a productivity control system is necessary and examples of it are provided. To be able read correctly the waste and its causes, the work report should indicate how many hours are attributed to each of these causes: lack of materials, breakdowns, information defects, imbalance, or rework. Knowing the causes makes it easier to find solutions.

That being the case, are we productive? Are we meeting the required standard times? Answering these two questions requires being able to interpret the data obtained through the work report system.

21.4.5. Productivity Calculation

As consequence of the daily data collection through the work report system and its subsequent study, actual information from the factory will be obtained. At this point we will know the actual deviations between the standard time and the actual time, that is, the deviations of the production costs.

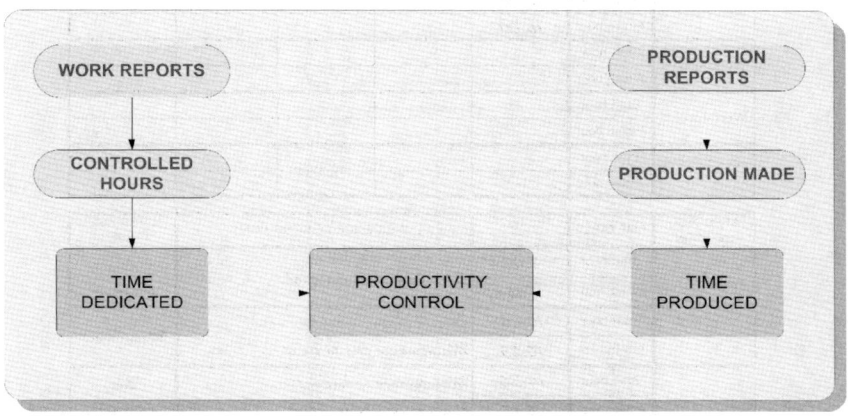

Figure 21.10. Necessary data to calculate productivity

The introduction to this book included definitions and formulas for calculating the activity achieved in a period of time. The calculation of productivity, in cases of open work consists of applying such formulas to the controlled time of the workday. In cases of limited work or work with machines use other calculation methods that will be shown later. **The calculation of productivity is equivalent to the calculation of the activity obtained in the controlled time.**

In the following examples, the calculation in different situations and with different activity scales will be shown, focusing on those that are most used, the 100-133 and 60-80.

Example

We will now retake the examples shown above, concerning two packaging lines of peppers and onions. Subsequently we will calculate the productivity ratio.

Industrial productivity

WORK REPORT, PEPPERS PACKAGING LINE

Code	Category	Name	Presence Hours	Controlled Hours	Noncontrolled Hours	Incidence Hours
A01	1st Officer	Murray Murphy	8	8	0	0
A02	Assistant	Graham Reed	8	8	0	0
A03	Specialist Operator	Caren Cook	8	8	0	0
A04	Operator	Jamie Ward	8	8	0	0
A05	Operator	Clark Sanchez	8	8	0	0
A06	Operator	Halley Brook	8	8	0	0
A07	Operator	Kai O'Meara	8	8	0	0
A08	Operator	Chad Richardson	8	8	0	0
			64	64	0	0

Initial Hour:	7.00
Final Hour:	15.00

Presence Hours	64.00
Noncontrolled Hours	0.00
Incidence Hours	0.00
Controlled Hours	64.00
N° of workers:	8.00
Dedicated minutes:	3,840.00

Work Order	
Trays of peppers	11,050.00
Point Value:	0.392
Total Points:	4,331.60
PRODUCTIVITY	**1.13**

Figure 21.11. *Work report and achieved productivity calculation*

In the first example, the production line had no incidence or had not performed unmeasured work, therefore presence hours coincided with controlled hours.

Once the monitoring of productivity is performed, the total number of controlled hours spent becomes minutes spent:

- 64 controlled hours x 60 minutes/hour = **3,840 minutes dedicated**

The production line packed 11,050 trays of peppers; the time study conducted earlier in the line indicated that the standard time is 0.392 minutes/pepper, multiplied by the number of peppers, which will give us the achieved time:

- 0.392 minutes/unit x 11,050 units = **4,331.60 points earned** (equivalent to time produced)

The next step is to compare the two, to show the productivity:

- *Points earned / minutes spent = 4,331.60 / 3,840 =* **1.13**

Going one step further, we can calculate the activity that has rendered the entire production line, during controlled time (Bedaux scale is used, 60-80):

- *Activity achieved = (4,331.60 / 3,840) x 60 =* **68**

Then we can ensure that during the controlled time, the productivity of the line is 13% greater than the required minimum.

Example

Se calcula la productividad de la línea de cebollas a continuación.

Code	Category	Name	Presence Hours	Controlled Hours	Noncontrolled Hours	Incidence Hours
A01	1st Officer	Murray Murphy	8	5.5	1.5	1
A02	Assistant	Graham Reed	8	5.5	1.5	1
A03	Assistant	Caren Cook	8	5.5	1.5	1
A04	Operator	Jamie Ward	8	5.5	1.5	1
A05	Operator	Clark Sanchez	8	5.5	1.5	1
A06	Operator	Halley Brook	8	5.5	1.5	1
A07	Operator	Kai O'Meara	8	5.5	1.5	1
A08	Operator	Chad Richardson	8	5.5	1.5	1
			64	44	12	8

Initial Hour:	8.00
Final Hour:	16.00

Presence Hours	64.00
Noncontrolled Hours	12.00
Incidence Hours	8.00
Controlled Hours	44.00
N° of workers:	8.00
Dedicated minutes:	2,640.00

Work Order	
Trays of onions	5,768.00

Figure 21.12. Work report and achieved productivity calculation

Therefore:

- *44 controlled hours x 60 minutes/hour =* **2,640 *minutes spent***
- *0.432 minutes/unit x 5,768 units =* **2,491.78 *points earned***
- *Minutes earned / Minutes spent = 2,491.78 / 2,640 =* **0.943**
- *Activity achieved = (2,491.78 / 2,640) x 60 =* **57** *(Bedaux Scale 60-80)*

So the line productivity was 5.7% below the required level. Therefore, the line has not been productive, has not met the required performance and the factors that have caused this situation should be reviewed.

Examples

This example provides another alternative format for storing the necessary data for productivity control. In it, we can see a working team from a factory of wooden tables, composed by nine operators, which is located in the different sections that make up the area. Each team is independent from each other, so that the conditions and incidences that may arise during the workday are different.

21. Productivity Control and Incentive Systems

SECTION	Surname 1	Surname 2	Name	Category	Workday	Absence	CUT N° Wst.	CUT Hours Prod	CUT 1 No Cntrl	SAND N° Wst.	SAND Hours Prod	SAND 2 No Cntrl	VARNISH N° Wst.	VARNISH Hours Prod	VARNISH 4 No Cntrl	GLUE N° Wst.	GLUE Hours Prod	GLUE 2 No Cntrl	SUMMARY HOURS Hours Prod	SUMMARY HOURS N° Wst. No Cntrl	SUMMARY HOURS 9 Absence
CUT	Alvarez	Sanchez	Antonio	Workman	7,00	1,00	6,00		1,00										6,00	1,00	1,00
SAND	Jimenez	Pascual	Pedro	2nd Officer	8,00	0,00				5,00		3,00							5,00	3,00	0,00
VARNISH	Ovejero	Perez	Juan Carlos	Workman	8,00	0,00				5,00		3,00							5,00	3,00	0,00
VARNISH	Alonso	Sanchez	Angel	Assistant	8,00	0,00							7,00		1,00				7,00	1,00	0,00
VARNISH	Muñoz	Padilla	Jonathan	Assistant	8,00	0,00							6,00		2,00				6,00	2,00	0,00
VARNISH	Parrilla	Ortiz	Juan	2nd Officer	8,00	0,00							7,00		1,00				7,00	1,00	0,00
VARNISH	Valcarce	Silva	Luis Antonio	workman	8,00	0,00							8,00						8,00	0,00	0,00
GLUE	Perez	Montalban	Jacinto	1st Officer	8,00	0,00										8,00			8,00	0,00	0,00
GLUE	Lopez	Prados	Candido	Section Manager	8,00	0,00										8,00			8,00	0,00	1,00
							6,00		1,00	10,00		6,00	28,00		4,00	16,00		0,00	60,00	11,00	

MINUTES DEDICATED	360	600	1.680	960
STANDARD TIME	15,50	14,30	12,30	17,32
UNITS PRODUCED	25	51	159	45
WORK POINTS	388	729	1.956	779

ACTIVITY	65	73	70	49

Figure 21.13. Work report and achieved productivity calculation

As the reader will notice, the rest periods taken by operators is never discounted to the total workday (8 hours, usually), because that time off is considered when calculating the corrected time of each task in the study of methods and times, along with the implementation of fatigue-based supplement. If it was not done that way, we would be assigning that time twice.

Narrative

Increase in production thanks to productivity control I.

This story continues describing the wanderings of the production manager from the metal cases factory.

Weeks passed and data fluctuated, but production did not reach 60% of its theoretical level. Business management began to get impatient. This year accounts were not good, competition had increased, customers were becoming more demanding, and the company had settled in their low productivity. The need for change was urgent: A productivity control system would be implemented based on a new time study.

The beginning was difficult. A study of methods and times infuriated operators; instead of taking it as a change for the better, they interpreted this move as distrust in them and that what the company wanted was for them to work more. The increase in productivity, meaning to manufacture more without consuming further resources is usually interpreted as having to work harder, instead of working more efficiently.

All explanations were poorly received, but work continued and some months later, finally, information was being correctly collected. At last a detailed time report was produced that was necessary for gathering information about every task performed in the section.

A few weeks later, the data was more than relevant:

- The real production of the line only reached 5,500 units/hour, far from the 6,200 promised by the supplier. An urgent meeting was planned with workers, in order to train them to make a correct tuning of the machines.

- Each time the machine was stopped for more than three minutes, it was necessary to reset part of the line and wait until it reached the proper temperature, which meant approximately 10 minutes.

- *At the beginning of the day, after each rest (two per shift), in the shift changes, and after each format exchange, those 10 minutes required for reset were lost again in the production.*

- *In some cases, by decision of the line supervisors, the speed was lowered because, in their opinion, it worked much better that way.*

- *Format exchanges in the line consumed about twice the standard time. In the absence of so much noise, because the machine remained stopped, operators took advantage of this time to talk among themselves.*

- *The stops for lack of material consumed about 10% of the day. The cause was a total lack of foresight.*

Now, enough detailed information allowed work to proceed in a clear direction. The following steps were taken:

- *A tense meeting between management and the supplier, explaining the situation and the consequences of the contract breach signed by the parties, resulted not only in a revamped setup, but the supplier also agreed not to charge for monthly revisions for the coming year. Besides the revision savings, this measure increased the speed of the machine by 10% compared to the previous speed.*

- *Unable to reduce the time to reset the machine, it was decided to extend the workday of middle managers by 20 minutes (with compensation), to start 10 minutes before and to overlap with the next turn 10 minutes, plus their rest timetable would not match the rest of the squad. This change allowed workers to start working with the machine without having to wait for the reset. It also made compensating six people financially to work 20 minutes more an excellent trade-off for a greater than 6% increase in operating time of the machine and of the entire workforce.*

- *They prevented the ability for anyone to manipulate the speed of the machine without the approval of the manager on duty.*

- *The changeover time, just by being controlled, fell nearly 15%, without any direct attempts at its improvement.*

- *The warehouse was equipped with two more operators, because it was the bottleneck. They were also provided with the necessary information to anticipate changes in order to reduce the waiting time for lack of material. These measures were expected to reduce waiting times at least 5%.*

After several long months of hard work, finally a productivity increase remained constant through all shifts, above 82%. By controlling *productivity, workers started working better, but not above what was required. The situation was very tense at the beginning, because it started from a noncontrolled situation, in which all errors were completely ignored. In the changes, everyone was made accountable for his or her actions. After several months of study, improvements, and implementations, the improvement initiative became routine. Management and workers reduced their differences in order to share the goal of having a productive plant.*

21.4.6. Productivity Calculation in Limited Works

On many occasions, particularly when working with machines or assembly lines, an operator faces numerous possibilities of constrained production capacity, which affects the attainable level of productivity. For these cases, the methodologies explained so far are not valid and would lead to erroneous results. In the following figure we can graphically visualize the problem when an operator works in a limited system, for example, in parallel with a machine.

Figure 21.14. Sequence of operations in works with machines

The operator can vary the pace of work at will in an open system. But when trying to reduce the cycle of the task in a limited system, an operator faces the existing limitation in the part that works in parallel with the machine. Machine time cannot be reduced by raising the operator's work pace; machine time will stay fixed.

This situation poses a problem because when limiting the reduction of the task cycle, we also limit the maximum achievable level of productivity for the operator. Whatever happens, the machine time will remain unchanged. To avoid this problem, a change in the formulas must be made, as shown in the following formula, where MT is the machine-time.

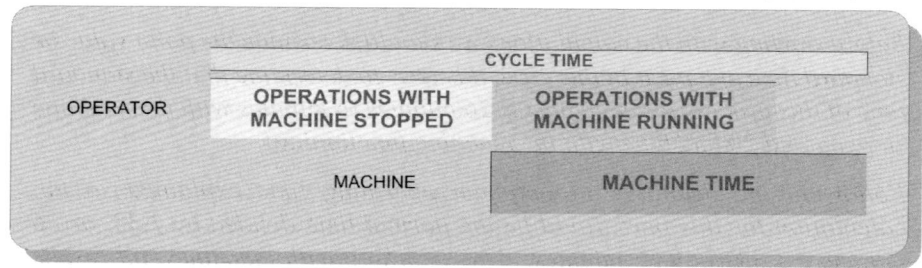

$$\text{Activity achieved} = \frac{\text{Standard Time}}{\text{Real Time}} \times An \rightarrow Aa = \frac{ST - MT}{Rt - MT} \times An$$

Formula 21.10. Activity calculation

It is about removing the control machine time, which is accomplished by subtracting from both the standard time and the real execution time. This adjustment makes it possible to compare the free time of the standard cycle with the actual cycle, and in this way to be able to determine the actual productivity level reached by the operator.

These new calculations are discussed in the following examples.

Example

Productivity calculation in limited work

A laser cutter of sheets, to which the operator supplies the veneer sheets and starts the cutting cycle. These operations require 6 minutes of the operator. The machine has a 20-minute cycle, cutting and stacking the finished parts. Once this task is done, the starting point of the cycle is reexecuted. The operator takes 24.7 minutes to perform a cycle. What activity has the operator worked at?

Before starting with the calculations we should determine the point value or standard time of a part. In this case, it is easy to determine that the standard time of this process for each part is 26 minutes (6 minutes with the machine stopped and 20 machine with the machine functioning).

Following the definition of optimum operating time explained so far, calculation for this part would be the normal time divided by 1.33, or 26 minutes / 1.33 = 19.55 minutes. When working with machines, all results should be analyzed carefully, so the previous result indicates that an operator who increased the pace of work could reduce the execution time up to 19.55 minutes. But does this mean that he would eventually make a piece in less time than it takes the machine to cut and finish the piece? We appear to have done something wrong in this calculation because it returns an absurd result. It makes no sense to apply this value when calculating productivity.

To calculate the productivity (pace or activity) achieved by the operator, the following formula is applied:

$$Ac = \frac{TE - TM}{Tr - TM} \times 100 = \frac{26 - 20}{24{,}7 - 20} \times 100 = 127.6$$

After using a correct formula we can see how the operator is working at a rate close to optimum, which does not result in a drastic reduction in the execution time. (Note that if the formula of open work had been used, the work rate obtained from this calculation would be 105, which is incorrect.)

21.4.7. OEE: Productivity Calculation in Machine Works

The OEE is a productivity calculation system specifically for working with machines and can obtain more precise data on the existing problems than using the usual method of calculation. It is an alternative to the calculation of productivity in limited work shown earlier.

What is OEE? The OEE (overall equipment effectiveness) is a percentage ratio that measures the productive efficiency of industrial machinery. This ratio is used to measure the performance and productivity of those lines where production machinery has a great influence. The OEE advantage over other systems is that it measures in a single indicator all key parameters in industrial production:

- Availability
- Efficiency
- Quality

For example, having a 37% OEE means that for every 100 good parts that the machine could have produced it only has produced 37. It is said that it includes all the basic parameters, because from the analysis of the three reasons that form the OEE, it is possible to know whether what is missing has been lost for availability (the machine was stopped some time), efficiency (the machinery operated at less than full capacity), or quality (defective units were produced). Its beginnings are uncertain but it appears to have been created in a Toyota factory. Today it has become an international standard recognized by major industries.

How is it calculated? The OEE is obtained by multiplying three percentage indicators: availability, performance, and quality.

$$OEE = AVAILABILITY \times PERFORMANCE \times QUALITY$$

Formula 21.11. OEE formula

Where:

- **Availability:** How long has the machine or equipment been running against the time that it was planned to be working?
- **Performance:** During the time it has been functioning, how much has been made (good and bad) as a function of what was possible at ideal cycle time?
- **Quality:** How many correct items have been manufactured at the first attempt, regarding the total production (Good + Bad)?

The value of OEE allows classifying one or more production lines, or an entire plant, with respect to the best of its kind and that already has reached the level of excellence:

- OEE < 65%. Unacceptable. Results in important economic losses and very low competitiveness.
- 65% < OEE < 75%. Regular. Acceptable only if we are in process of improvement. Results in economic losses and low competitiveness.
- 75% < OEE < 85%. Acceptable. Continue improvements to exceed 85%. Results in light losses and slightly low competitiveness.
- 85% < OEE < 95%. Good. Results in good competitiveness.
- OEE > 95%. Excellent. Results in excellent competitiveness.

21.4.7.1. Availability

The availability results from dividing the time the machine has been producing (operating time = OT) by the time that the machine could have been producing. The time that the machine could have been producing (planned production time = PPT) is the total time minus the periods in which it was not planned to produce for legal reasons, holidays, lunch, and scheduled maintenance, which are called *planned stops*.

$$\text{AVAILABILITY} = (OT / PPT) \times 100$$

Formula 21.12. Availability calculation

Where:

- PPT = Total working time – Planned downtime
- OT = PPT – Stops and/or breakdowns
- Availability = a value between 0 and 1, usually expressed as a percentage

21.4.7.2. Performance

Performance is calculated by dividing the number of parts actually produced by the number of parts that could be produced. The number of parts that could have been produced is obtained by multiplying the time that the machine has been running by the nominal production capacity of the machine.

Nominal capacity means the capacity of the machine/line stated in the specifications of the manufacturer, also known as maximum or optimal speed equivalent to ideal performance (maximum/optimum) of the line/machine. It is measured in number of units/hour. Instead of using the nominal capacity, ideal time cycle can be used.

Ideal cycle time is the minimum cycle time the process is expected to take under optimal circumstances.

- Ideal cycle time = 1 / Nominal capacity

The nominal capacity or ideal cycle time is the first value to be established. In general, this capability is provided by the manufacturer, but it is usually an approximation and can vary considerably, depending on the operating conditions of the machine or line. To calculate it, measurements are recommended in order to determine the true value. The nominal capacity shall be determined for each product (including format and presentation) based on two possible scenarios:

- Data exists: It will be the maximum value specified by the manufacturer for the machine or line.
- No data: The value corresponding to the best 4 hours from a total of 400 hours of operation are chosen.

The value will always refer to the final product obtained by the line. The performance takes into account any loss of speed, expressed on a per unit basis or percentage of the actual cycle or real capacity with respect to the ideal.

Performance = Ideal cycle time / (Operating time / Total n° units)

Performance = Total n° units / (Operating time x Maximum speed)

$$\text{PERFORMANCE} = \text{IDEAL CYCLE TIME} / (\text{OPERATION TIME} / \text{TOTAL N° OF UNITS})$$
$$\text{OR}$$
$$\text{PERFORMANCE} = \text{N° TOTAL DE UNIDADES} / (\text{OPERATION TIME} \times \text{MAXIMUM SPEED})$$

Formula 21.13. Performance calculation

Includes:

- Speed losses for small stops
- Speed losses for speed reduction

Efficiency is a value between 0 and 1, so it is usually expressed as a percentage.

21.4.7.3. Quality

This loss in speed comes from the time taken to manufacture defective products, which must be estimated and added to downtime, because during that time correct products were not manufactured. Therefore, the loss of quality involves two types of losses:

- Quality losses, equal to the number of units poorly manufactured
- Losses of production time, equal to the time taken to make the faulty units

And depending on whether units can to be reprocessed, losses include:

- Rework time
- Cost to discard, recycle, etc., the invalid units

It takes into account all losses in product quality, expressed on a per unit basis or percentage of nonconforming units with respect to the total number of units produced.

QUALITY = N° OF ACCEPTED UNITS / TOTAL N° OF UNITS

Formula 21.14. Quality calculation

The units produced can be approved, good, nonapproved, bad, or rejected. Sometimes nonapproved units can be reprocessed and become approved units. The OEE only considers correct units the ones approved the first time, not the reprocessed ones. Therefore, the units that will subsequently be reprocessed must be considered rejections. Consequently, quality results from dividing the correct parts produced by the total produced parts, including reprocessed or discarded parts. Quality is a value between 0 and 1, so it is usually expressed as a percentage.

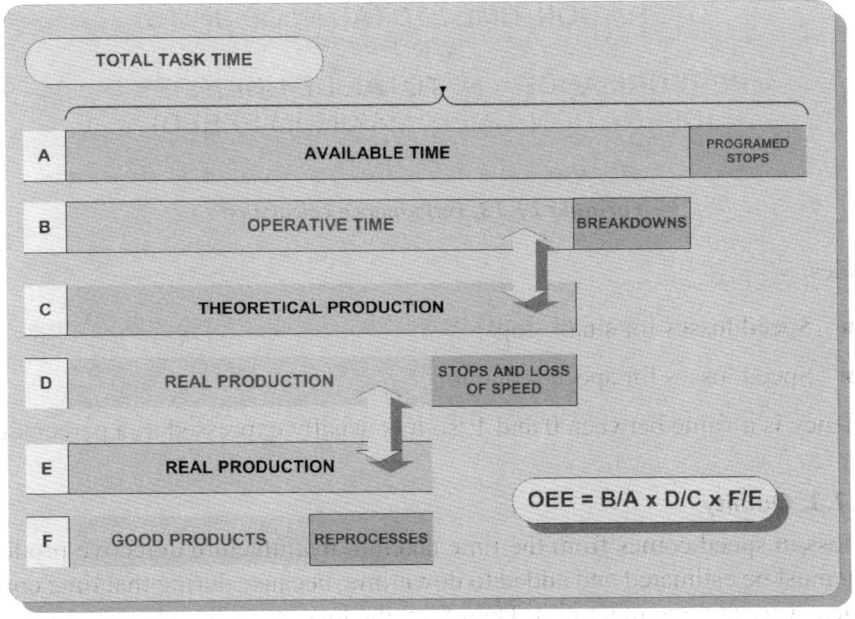

Figure 21.15. Breakdown of available time according to the OEE

Example

In the following OEE resolution example of a plate-molding machine for beverage cans, the manufacturer showed in specifications how the machine was able to process 1,500 plates per hour.

Work report:

- *Presence hours: 8 hours*
- *Stop hours: 0.75 hours*
- *Controlled hours: 7.25 hours*
- *A parts manufactured = 7,500 units*
- *Defective A parts manufactured = 45 units*

We proceed to calculate the OEE:

OT = 7.25 hours

PPT = 8.00 hours

*Availability = (7.25 hours / 8 hours) x 100 = **90.62%***

At first sight, for a 7.25-hour workday, as in our case, the expected production should be 10,875 units, a figure much higher than the achieved.

*Performance = (7,500 units / 10,875 units) = **68.9%***

Finally, we proceed to calculate the quality.

*Quality = [(7,500 − 45) / (7,500 units produced)] = **99.4%***

*OEE = 90.62 x 68.9 x 99.4 = **62.06%** → **Unacceptable***

*The low rate is mainly due to a poor performance of the machine, which varies from the 1,500 units/hour defined by the manufacturer. It actually produced **1,035 units/hour**.*

21.4.7.4. OEE Results

OEE is, therefore, an easily understandable tool for the improvement process in a company.

- It is infallible when clearly identifying where the problem is.
- It displays priorities clearly.
- It facilitates the task of correctly selecting the necessary specific improvements.
- The results of the improvement actions undertaken are quickly observed.

21. Productivity Control and Incentive Systems

- It is a simple and easy indicator to understand by all the people involved.

The main problems that affect the productivity of a machine or line are clearly identified by the OEE and grouped into the following six groups:

- Loss of maintenance time
- Loss of availability time
- Loss of idle time
- Loss of speed reduction
- Loss of quality time
- Loss of miscellaneous time

21.4.7.5. How to Use the OEE

We must keep the perspective that the OEE is a productivity control system that requires exactly the same information as a system of open work, only such information is grouped into six types of losses, as previously seen. Subsequently, we will explain how to make the information collection from the work reports.

Work Reports for OEE

Machine operators must record the data losses in paper format. Then, the six big losses are recorded. The operator or supervisor encodes the data after shift changes. So in a work report from a section that works by the OEE monitoring system, the following fields become compulsory:

Information collected by an OEE work report

- Presence time
- Production completed
- Identification of operator or operators affected by this sheet
- Identification of the work report supervisor
- Time spent on maintenance
- Time lost due to lack of availability
- Idle time
- Time working below rated speed
- Time producing nonapproved parts
- Time lost due to other causes

21.4.7.6. Analogies Between OEE and CwF

WMT is designed for tasks that mainly involve workforce, so no major differences exist between the two systems. The following step-by-step reasoning demonstrates these similarities. First we set the following hypothesis: standard time is equivalent to what the OEE defines as:

$$\text{Ideal Cycle Time} = 1/\text{Nominal Capacity}$$

The standard time is not possible to achieve, because waste will always cause the real time to be greater than standard.

$$\text{Real Time} = \text{CwF} \times \text{Standard Time}$$

As for the term OEE:

$$\text{Ideal Cycle Time} = \text{OEE} \times \text{Real Time}$$

Clearing from both formulas the real time variable and considering that Standard Time equals Ideal Cycle Time (in machine-time), we obtain:

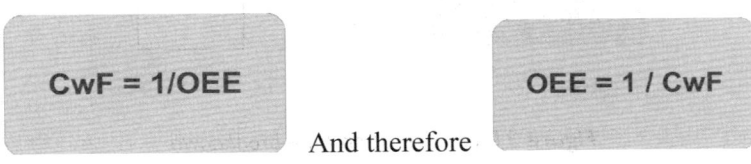

CwF = 1/OEE   And therefore   OEE = 1 / CwF

Formula 21.15.   *Formula 21.16.*

The smaller the CwF, the greater the OEE. Managing the CwF, we can get to the continuous improvement of OEE.

21.4.8. Productivity Evaluation of Middle Managers

So far the whole chapter development has focused in the productivity calculation of workers in the time corresponding to controlled hours. The controlled hours are only one component of the total duration of the task; another part, as already mentioned, is a waste for incidents, from management failures.

21. Productivity Control and Incentive Systems

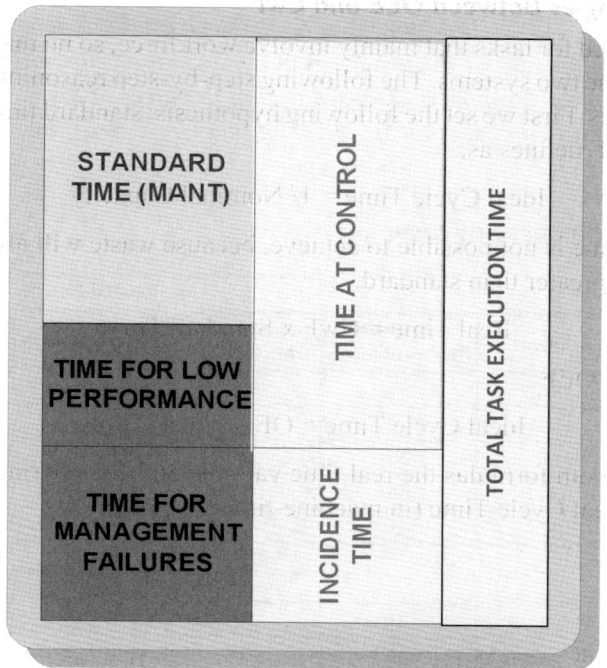

Figure 21.16. Execution time breakdown

This waste can be and indeed often is, greater than the waste from low performance. Furthermore, one waste leads to another waste; a high performance cannot be required of operators when the manufacturing process of a product is packed with incidents. The productivity control, through recording incidents and their classification, may return detailed information about the causes of waste per incidence.

Waste for incidents will always be greater than zero. The key is to set and assume a waste goal and, based on this, measure the efficiency in management. The incidences will be lower with greater management productivity.

> The productivity of middle managers should be measured from the incidents and noncontrolled hours.

Example

This example calculates the productivity of the person in charge of the line from the next work report and knowing that the level of losses assumed by the company for this section is 7%. The work report of the section is as follows:

GENERAL WORK REPORT ON PLANT

Code	Section	Available Person-Hours	Lack of Materials	Breakdowns	Reprocesses
A01	Cut	16	0.5	1	0
A02	Attach	80	0	16	0
A03	Mill	32	1	0	0
A04	Weld	64	0.25	8	0
A05	Paint	8	1	0	0
			2.75	25	0

Clm	1%
Cmt	13%
Crp	0%

Figure 21.17.

In this work report, each section has a number of hours available. How those hours are separated into controlled hours and incidence hours is indicated.

We will use the first section, the A01, for an estimate of the efficiency with which that section was managed:

- *Person-hours available: 16 hours*
- *Incidents due to lack of material: 0.5 hours (3.1% of total time)*
- *Incidents due to breakdowns: 1 hour (6.3% of total time)*
- *Incidents due to reworks: 0 hours*

$$\text{Loss of productivity for management} = \frac{0{,}5 + 1 + 0}{16} \times 100 = 9{,}4\,\%$$

The calculation results in a figure slightly above the target of 7%, which is mainly due to maintenance problems. For all the other sections we have the following results:

GENERAL WORK REPORT ON PLANT

Code	Available Person-Hours	INCIDENCES							
		Lack of Materials		Breakdowns		Reprocesses		Total
		PH	%	PH	%	PH	%	%
A01	16	0.5	3.10%	1	6.30%	0	0.00%	9.40%
A02	80	0	0.00%	16	20.00%	0	0.00%	20.00%
A03	32	1	3.10%	0	0.00%	0	0.00%	3.10%
A04	64	0.25	0.40%	8	12.50%	0	0.00%	12.90%
A05	8	1	12.50%	0	0.00%	0	0.00%	12.50%

Figure 21.18.

Except for A03, the sections have serious problems. We can confirm that management is not being effective.

At this point, we should stop and think about this exercise. The results, above our goal, are clearly negative. But what would have happened if our goal was 15%? Clearly we should congratulate ourselves on a good job. Although the data were the same, all sections would be below the target.

This demonstrates the importance of setting an ambitious goal, because our objective should be 0% of waste from management. But we must be realistic. We need to see where we really are and what means we have to reach the ultimate goal and, from there, set some short-term achievable objectives.

21.5. Productivity Control Implementation

This section shows how to implement a productivity control system, explaining the steps and deadlines that must be followed and enforced, as well as the aspects that must be taken into account when doing so. The implementation process should follow an order, so here we develop the process to follow.

The implementation process of productivity control affects working conditions and demands of workers, so the first thing we should look at is the legal aspects.

21.5.1. Legal aspects

The following excerpt from a collective agreement can be used as an example of the information that can be found regarding the implementation of productivity. It corresponds to a part from the manufacturers agreement of tiles, bricks, and clay components.

Example

State Collective Agreement of tiles, bricks and clay component manufacturers (in force between 2006 and 2008).

Article 31. Work organisation.

The technical organisation and work practice subject to the rules and guidelines of this Agreement and the various laws, is the exclusive management power of the company, subject to the terms of this agreement and the Statute of workers.

Article 32. Productivity.

The performance tables agreed in the 1983 Agreement will continue to apply in full during the term of this agreement.

The normal yield tables agreed will affect all other provinces that have no others in force, when signing this document. In those provinces or companies with current performance with normal or minimal character, shall continue to apply provided they meet the conditions of work considered normal and agreed in this State Agreement.

Will be considered as normal performances that to date have been agreed as minimal. For those workplaces where there is no established performance or comparison module, normal performance is taken as the one developed by the employee during the trial period.

The signing parties of the agreement will create a commission to determine new workplaces, their performances, and the elimination of those that are obsolete. This committee shall have such work completed before the end of term of the agreement.

Article 33. Methodology, application and productivity control.

The productivity or normal performance tables that are agreed in this agreement, and in the different provincial agreements conform to the general principles that are described below:

1. *In each table there will be a detailed description of the initial state of the work and where it is done, which should be applied to the table with the conditions that should be required.*

2. *The table of productivity or performance will describe most clearly and accurately the work or production units to perform.*

3. *The mentioned table should describe the state in which the workplace should be left after completing the tasks, object of measurement and inspection.*

4. *The table mentioned will contain a detailed explanation of the general conditions to be satisfied for the correct application of the same, which shall specify:*

   - *Quality or conditions of the materials to be used, with the maximum precision, its nature, characteristics, location, etc.*

   - *Conditions of auxiliary means to be used in the performance of work, such as machinery, tools in general, safety and hygiene elements and devices, and in general all auxiliary equipment necessary for the proper performance of the work.*

   - *Climatic and weather conditions that affect the applicability of the table and the health of workers (temperature, environment, humidity). In this sense, factors influencing them for reasons of temperature, humidity, cold, etc. will be calculated.*

5. *Tables must contain time frames that should require a normal activity per worker or team of workers, depending on whether the work is done individually or collectively. In those work units with measured performance, whose fulfilment requires a computer, its composition will be determined.*

6. *The productivity or normal performance tables contain necessary guidelines for carrying out the inspection or measurement of the works subject to the same, in case that from any dispute arises a conflict, both by workers and employers.*

Article 34. Preparation of productivity or performance tables.

The completion of this study has been done by observations or samplings, taking into account all the constraints that contribute to the fulfilment of a given work under observation.

The concretion of each of the performance units either individually or collectively approved, has been agreed between the parties.

In those industry sections whose characteristics do not meet the normal conditions that must be met according to the methodology expressed, for a correct and normal performance of work will not be applied under any circumstances the productivity or performance tables approved, until existing anomalies are not remedied.

Likewise for the application of these performance tables, is essential the existence of Staff Delegates, Company Committee or Union Delegate if by the number of employees of the company correspond its existence, and as agreed in this agreement.

When for reasons, whatever these may be, beyond the control of workers, whether for machinery breakdowns, bad weather, etc. they are unable to do the work assigned in the tables under measured performance, they will receive the daily wage that the agreement stipulates.

If by obvious flaws in its production, either party believes that one or several production units were technically poorly developed, will resort to the Productivity Joint Subcommittee, to obtain its reprocessing.

Article 36. Work reports.

The worker, in companies where so is established or will be established, shall be obliged to draw up and sign a daily or weekly work report. In case of disagreement over the work done, the legal representatives of workers must get involved (Company Officer, Company Committee or Union Delegate).

For exceptional impediments to the writing of that sheet, it will be written by or in the presence of a representative of the worker and the worker himself.

The sheet the company will facilitate, shall contain at least the following sections:

- *Company name.*
- *Section.*
- *Name of the worker.*
- *Work timetable.*
- *Observations, allegations and incidents.*
- *Production.*

Similarly will be required, where work reports are performed, that companies hand the worker given proof of having delivered the work reports.

Reading the previous extracts of different collective agreements can be seen how its structure is very similar in most cases, as all agreements are based on the premises of the Workers' Statute, which have evolved in function of gaps and needs in each sector or company.

Below is a summary, in general terms, of all legal aspects to consider before attempting to implement a productivity control system:

1. *For carrying out any practical work organisation, Business Management shall inform the Committee. The advance of this notice will vary for each case, being stipulated in most cases a period of 15 days.*

2. *The company will be responsible for implementing any productivity control system, being obliged to deliver a detailed copy to the Committee before the trial period.*

3. *The duration of the trial period can be variable, in several agreements it is set at 30 days. In others it has a period of 2-3 months. What is required is the existence of this trial period, regardless of its duration.*

4. *The last day of the trial period, the company committee will submit a report to business management. If it is positive, the system will start automatically, if it is unfavourable, the company has 10 days to decide or else it will create a conflict or lawsuit between them.*

5. *Some definitions should be taken into account, such as normal activity, optimum activity, machine-time, normal enforceable performance, optimum performance or rest supplement.*

6. *In every agreement are collected the reasons that may lead to a revision of the productivity control system. Mostly, the causes are:*

    - *Improvement or changes in the working method.*
    - *Miscalculations.*
    - *Achieving performance of 133 or 140. This aspect is variable in each agreement, as it varies the performance achieved to revision the system and varies the percentage of the workforce that achieves this performance. In several agreements if 75% of the staff reached the optimum (133), the system should be revised, in other agreements, to modify the system, 100% of staff must achieve a performance of 140. As we see, both the percentage of the workforce and the performance vary depending on the agreement reached.*

7. *As for limited jobs, several agreements stipulate concessions that the company must make to the worker, when he is not able to exercise his job with a higher than required performance, due to causes outside his control. That is why the company should give a stipulated value through agreement, during the execution of limited work. The calculation of monetary incentive in this situation is described in detail in the third section of this manual.*

An agreement can also indicate when the operator must fill out a work report, what data it should contain, and an acknowledgment of receipt of the report.

The structure of a collective agreement is often similar, varying only in aspects such as amounts, deadlines, and so on. It is therefore advisable, before the time study prior to the implementation of productivity control, to revise the collective agreement to avoid making mistakes.

Industrial productivity

> **Legal aspects to consider in an implementation**
>
> - Before starting any work, workers should be informed in advance.
> - Before the initiation of the trial period, workers or their representatives must have a copy of all documentation.
> - A trial period should be conducted before implementing definitely the control.
> - The last day of trial, workers or their representatives will submit a report to the company. If the report is favorable, work can start, if not, the company has 10 days to decide.
> - It must clearly indicate what reasons make revisions to the system necessary.

After explaining all aspects and legal conditions facing the implementation of any production control system, the next step for a company in order to increase productivity may be the introduction of an incentive system. The basic difference between a control system and a productivity incentive system is that with the former, a performance greater than required is not rewarded. By contrast, the incentive system rewards performances above the enforceable and stipulates the amount of that reward.

The implementation of an incentive system will be explained later, along with its legal considerations, its benefits, how to pay the required higher performance, and other notable aspects when starting it up.

> **BEFORE STARTING WITH THE DEVELOPMENT OF A SYSTEM FOR PRODUCTIVITY CONTROL, THE FIRST STEP IS TO READ THE COLLECTIVE AGREEMENT.**

Figure 21.19.

21.5.2. Implementation Outline for Productivity Control

After describing legal aspects to be taken into account when implementing the productivity control, a graph can show the steps to follow to achieve the implementation goal. The implementation process can be divided into three sections, each consisting of several stages. First, we must remember that to start the first phase we need an updated study of methods and times.

The work report system is an important aspect; it is the tool that will collect all the necessary information, whose most important information is the production performed, a minimal quantification and breakdown of the timetable, and some sort of verification. It is also mandatory in this first part to develop a document that explains clearly the rules of the system to be installed, so that all parties concerned see how to calculate their productivity.

Afterwards, the simulation block conducts quality tests of the time study. To this end, the work reports must be completed to later compare the time spent and the time allowed for performing the tasks. In this case, the analyst must not forget that the comparison needs to look at the actual execution time, that is, the total controlled hours. At this correction stage, errors are detected and can be corrected before the final implementation.

The last block is the final implementation of the study. The path can be more or less complicated, but the goal is always the same, the **IMPLEMENTATION**. We give the committee a copy of the time study conducted, the data collection system, and a manual of productivity control. After the committee studies the information, they may or may not agree with it, coming to a joint agreement for its implementation or deciding against implementation.

Industrial productivity

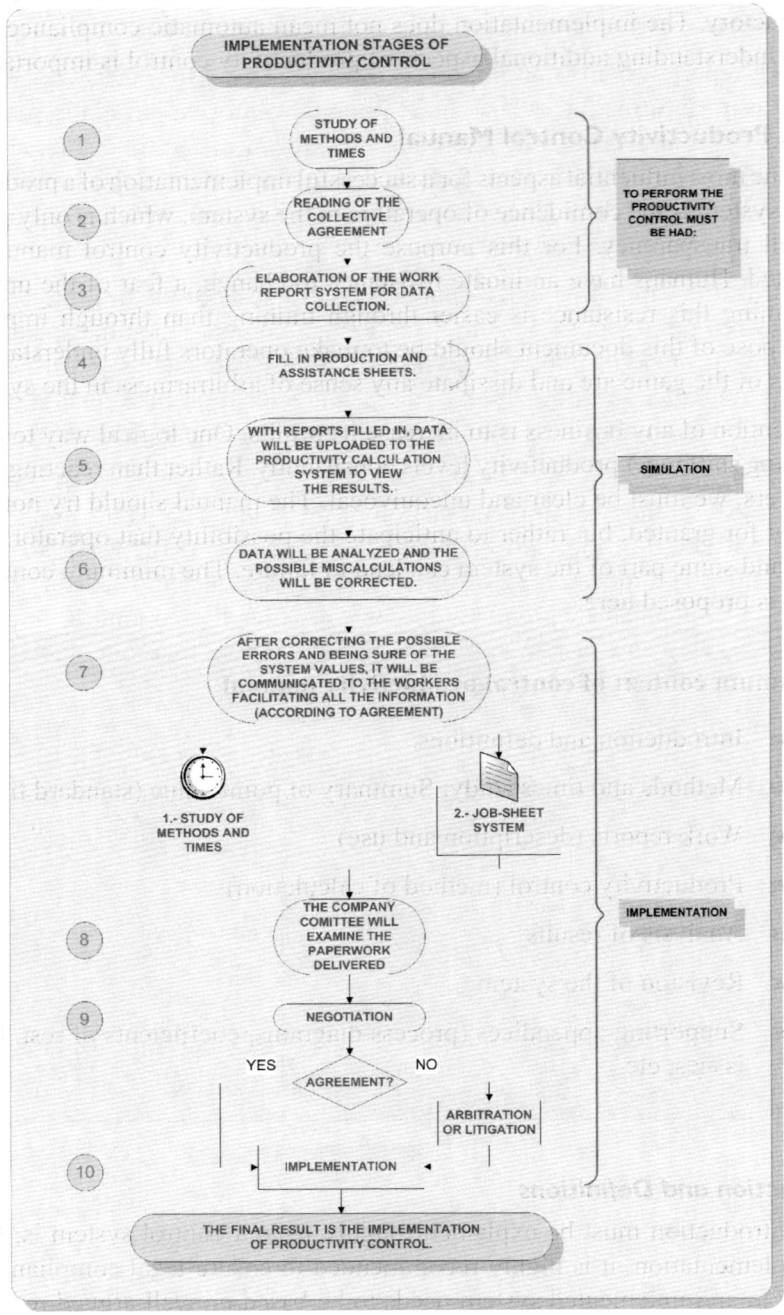

Figure 21.20. Implementation outline for productivity control

After implementation of productivity control, its effects will begin to be noticed in our factory. The implementation does not mean automatic compliance of goal times. Understanding additional aspects of productivity control is important.

21.5.3. Productivity Control Manual

One of the most influential aspects for a successful implementation of a productivity control system is the confidence of operators in the system, which is only possible with full transparency. For this purpose the productivity control manual must be created. Humans have an innate resistance to change, a fear of the unknown. Overcoming this resistance is easier through training than through imposition. The purpose of this document should be to make operators fully understand what the rules of the game are and dissipate any sense of arbitrariness in the system.

The intention of any business is to increase its profits. One logical way to do so is by helping staff meet productivity levels consistently. Rather than reacting to fears of workers, we must be clear and unequivocal. The manual should try not to take anything for granted, but rather to anticipate the possibility that operators do not understand some part of the system can lead to failure. The minimum content of a manual is proposed here:

Minimum content of control productivity manual

- Introduction and definitions.
- Methods and times study: Summary of point value (standard time)
- Work reports (description and use)
- Productivity control (method of calculation)
- Analysis of results
- Revision of the system
- Supporting appendices (process diagrams, coefficients of rest, legal issues, etc.)

Introduction and Definitions

In the introduction must be explained roughly what a control system is. For the first implementation, it is highly recommended to ensure legal compliance. Any revision to an implemented system needs to be based on well-argued reasons. In addition, this document usually launches the trial period of the implementation, so it is advisable to also report the duration of the trial period.

On the other hand, it is important to include clearly defined concepts such as:

Industrial productivity

- Normal and optimal activity
- Standard time
- Activity achieved
- Time produced
- Enforceable and optimal performance
- Rest supplements
- Work reports
- Controlled hours, noncontrolled hours, etc.

Study of Methods and Times

Secondly, we must clearly show the results of the time study, that is, the standard time per unit, in person-minutes for each of the tasks from the sections subject to control. This part is informative—it should not justify the time—and will be presented in an appendix. It is about showing these results, but workers should have access to the operation breakdown of the study. In addition to indicating the standard time of each task, it may be advisable to include some information about the type of units per hour to facilitate the understanding of the work required. Operators usually understand more easily the units required per hour or day, than the person-minutes values.

Work Reports

In the third paragraph, the new work reports must be presented and, above all, the information that must appear on them. It should describe the rules for filling in the sheets correctly, how to classify the presence hours in the factory (controlled hours, noncontrolled hours, and incidence hours), and how the work reports should be validated by a supervisor. It should convey the idea that filling the work reports is not a loss of time, but that the information contained in them adds value for the operators.

It is important that operators understand that a report containing incorrect or incomplete information causes the control, to which they are subject, to be wrong. For this reason, the company will ensure the accuracy of the information contained in the reports. Supervisors who validate the information need to have unbiased interest in the outcome of the control system in order to avoid perversions of the system.

Productivity Control: Calculation Formula

The fourth part must explain how to calculate productivity, which is the comparison of the actual execution time with the standard of concrete production. In addition, this part should dispel any ambiguity of the terms involved in the calculation, because the formulas are clear and simple. Typically, the following points need to be clarified in a generic way, because ignoring them or assuming that they are understood by all parties tends to generate problems.

Standard times should not open to many discussions. They are the result of a scientific work study, and the only part that needs to be clarified is whether the times include the cleaning and preparation of the workplace, under what batch size are calculated, or other similar detail.

When it comes to the actual production, it must clarify concepts such as whether parts with quality problems are accounted; what happens if a production or part is started by an operator or equipment and ended by another; or if the work cannot be completed in a single day, what happens to the first shift, what percentage of the task can be annotated as work.

All the details concerning the actual running time would need to be clarified. This part tends to be most subject to interpretation. Productivity controls need to clarify unambiguously at the time of control implementation, what is a lack of material, a breakdown, what is meant by rework, and how these terms affect the real execution time, whether they add or subtract productivity.

Analysis of Results

After explaining the method of calculation, the report should clarify how to interpret the results. This section should avoid at all costs instilling fear. The goal is to improve control, identify problems, and not to look for whom to blame.

The most important data to be analyzed concern the productivity of workers, by checking the level of activity achieved in a given period. On the other side, we would have to check the level of incidents in that same period.

System Revision

Finally, it should clarify what reasons are sufficient for checking the system. The most commonly used are standard time changes due to improvements in working methods, process mechanization, and new process design. But the same problem continually repeats in all industries: Small changes, barely perceptible, accumulate over time and, after a few years, the system is not valid. Therefore, it is highly recommended that system checks be performed cyclically regardless of whether great changes have taken place.

Supporting Appendices

This section displays all information used when developing the system and in support of the data shown in the previous sections. At least it needs to show a justification of time, supplements used, and legal aspects to consider from any collective agreement.

21.5.4. First Effects of Productivity Control

A productivity control system should be clear to the user and easy to understand. Within the implementation block, documentation submitted to the committee must be clear and simple, leaving nothing to chance or interpretation. The manual on how to control productivity has great importance.

The innate tendency is to reject or fear something that is not understood, which is simply mistrust of something new. Therefore, the productivity control system must avoid or fully clarify ambiguous aspects or concepts. The study of methods and times as a general rule will result in a reduction of the standard times to perform each task. In this situation, the operator may feel compelled to yield more, with more production required. It is vital to change this opinion, so it must explain all the details of the study, with particular emphasis on the classification of the hours of which the day consists.

The workday consists of three types of hours: controlled hours, noncontrolled hours, and incidence hours. The total of the three types of hours results in presence hours. It is important to explain the division of the workday to workers; They must understand that the performance of the operator is controlled only during the controlled hours of the workday. During the rest of hours, we cannot verify their performance, because they are involved in works that have not been measured or in timeouts or incidences occasioned to the operator.

Now the operator will know that stop times must be attributed to the total hours of incidence. The operator will be required to indicate the duration of this incidence time and the cause of that incidence. The obligation and duty of the company, then, is to reduce or eliminate the cause of the incident in order to gain in productivity and competitiveness.

Once the productivity control system is set in motion and all work reports are working properly, the company will manage all information, as explained in this chapter.

When comparing time spent and time granted, it is possible that in the early stages of the system implementation, the result is negative. This is, when comparing the time spent and the time granted, the first is greater than the second, generating the idea that times are impossible to achieve. In most cases this difference is due more to the lack of incidence annotation than to poor performance, hence the importance of operators correctly completing the work reports.

21. Productivity Control and Incentive Systems

It is essential that in the trial phase operators understand the difference between working in controlled hours and not doing so. At first, until the operator is coupled to the system, we should try to break down barriers by improving the acquired habits.

Briefly, one could say that the first effects that occur after the implementation of a productivity control system include the following:

- Workers believe it impossible to reach an acceptable level of productivity, because they extend the work pace to the whole day. They do not know the existence of noncontrolled hours or incidents.

- Those in charge of implementation need to explain and emphasize the concept of incidence times or noncontrol and that operators should respond only to the time in control, time without incidents.

- Operators begin to learn the system and try to write down all the inefficiencies and problems.

- The business management begin to receive information on the status of the plant of which they were completely unaware.

- When knowing the causes, not just the effects, we can begin to take corrective measures.

- The productivity of the plant begins to rise as it begins to solve all existing problems.

Narrative

Increased production by controlling productivity II

This section shows an example of how a correct productivity control results in an increase in productivity.

It was an assembly line of a metallic item that was in line with a tunnel of sandblasting and painting.

At first, the assembly section performed between 140 and 150 units per day of finished product, and the item was always the same reference. The chain consisted of 12 workers and one shift per day.

The plant manager had faith and believed that more could be done, but the assembly was in line with the blasting and painting line. According to the technicians of the factory, the paint machine could not speed up the pace it was developing, so in principle could not produce more, but maybe it could win in productivity. So how can you produce more in those conditions?

In industrial organization and productivity it is necessary to start from the easy, as with everything in life. How fast does the machine produce paint? If it produces one unit every 1.8 minutes and a shift (day) has 480 minutes, a priori, the line should be able to produce 267 units/day.

This figure, 267, was considerably different from the 150 units that were actually produced, which supported the plant manager's belief that "More can be done."

After this comparison we need more detail as to why more units were not made. First of all, the lack of production of a machine is complicated when interacting with a team, and this situation requires taking many, many aspects into consideration.

When analyzing the daily work of this section we observe that it is impossible to obtain the 267 units/day under current conditions and with the organization prevailing at the time. Did it imply no hope? Not at all, it was easy work for a good technician; it was more a matter of courage than of technique. The problem was that the line operators worked five hours a day instead of the eight that are enforceable. Just that, no other technical problem or imbalance or machinery problem or anything else . . . the operators simply did not work.

The workday time was reduced by the entrances (operators were coming in later in the morning), for the morning break (longer than it had to be), and the departure time (operators were leaving sooner than the end of their shift). According to this scenario, working 300 minutes daily to 1.8 minutes per unit results in 167 units, which gets closer to the level of production actually reached.

With the diagnosis and the causes for unproductiveness already clear, completely clear even, the plant manager was proved right! Now the next step was to solve the problem. At first it seemed rather easy, a matter of simply enforcing the schedule. But the matter is more complicated and involved a high level of conflict and a strong committee.

The collective agreement stated that the company had the power over the organization of work, therefore, these steps were followed:

1. Propose and document a productivity control system for the company to evaluate the performance of workers throughout the workday. From there on, anticipating the noncontrolled hours led to a value for the required minimum daily production.

2. This documentation was delivered to the committee and the human resources department. A one-month period was allowed for review and reflection.

3. *While that deadline elapsed, the atmosphere of the section was very tense, but the section leader remained firm and did not give in to pressure.*

4. *A meeting was held with the committee, they accepted the proposal almost without reservation, just raised a few questions.*

5. *Productivity control was implemented, and the section's production increased by 60%.*

Conclusions and lessons

- *This kind of work has a highly social nature. It is not just an engineering project (it would be if only machines worked); these jobs have a significant human component that heavily influences the motivations of those involved, the work atmosphere, and numerous other work environment factors.*

Such implementations can only be carried out with conviction, perseverance, and leadership, because the results are not often easily assimilated by the different stakeholders.

21.6. Incentive Systems

A productivity control system is a tool for increasing the performance of all the elements that work together, but it has clearly identified limits, the required performance, so we could say that it is a tool that ensures that at least the minimums are met. If you need or want to further increase productivity, something in return must be offered.

Really, what is an incentive system? It entails agreements between the company and workers, through which a value is set, payable by the company, in return for an extra effort or some portion of work, always in accordance with the legal framework established by the collective agreement. Widespread and accepted production incentive systems are in use throughout industries.

A clear example of bonus payment for extra work, or incentive system, is the commissions of salespeople. Their job is to sell and, beyond a certain minimum, receive compensation in exchange. Other incentives would be payment for accomplishing targets set by leaders responsible for sections, plants, or even companies. These objective payment systems tend to value factors other than the amount of machinery, such as customer complaints, quality issues, and damage reduction, to name a few. Also in some cases, the payable bonus is not a monetary incentive; it may be a trip, company car, or even shares of the company.

This guide will discuss incentive systems to direct workforce, but it should be clear that for a system of incentives to work, to increase productivity over the performance limit, it should be based on a correct and fair productivity control.

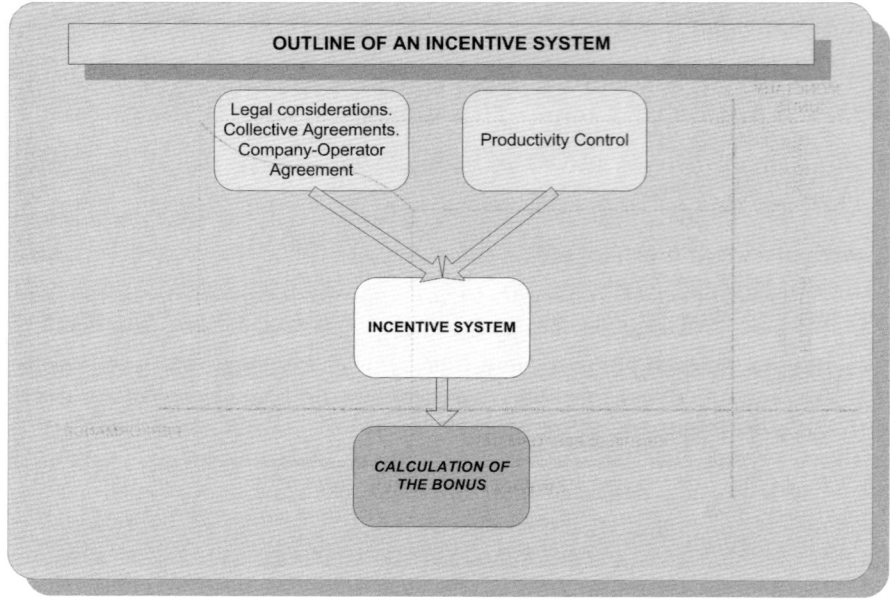

Figure 21.21. Outline of an incentive system

21.6.1. Incentive Concept in a Production Environment

The result or required performance is obtained in exchange for a fixed salary. Obtaining a result above the enforceable is voluntary, so it can be encouraged and must be agreed.

> Incentive is defined as a variable part of the salary that rewards a result above the required.

The responsibility of the company is summarized in:

- Outlining the agreement
- Providing the means for its compliance

The result is a datum that corresponds to a given level of performance, either as work performed or focusing on some aspects of it. The incentive system should be consistent with the salary system of the company.

21. Productivity Control and Incentive Systems

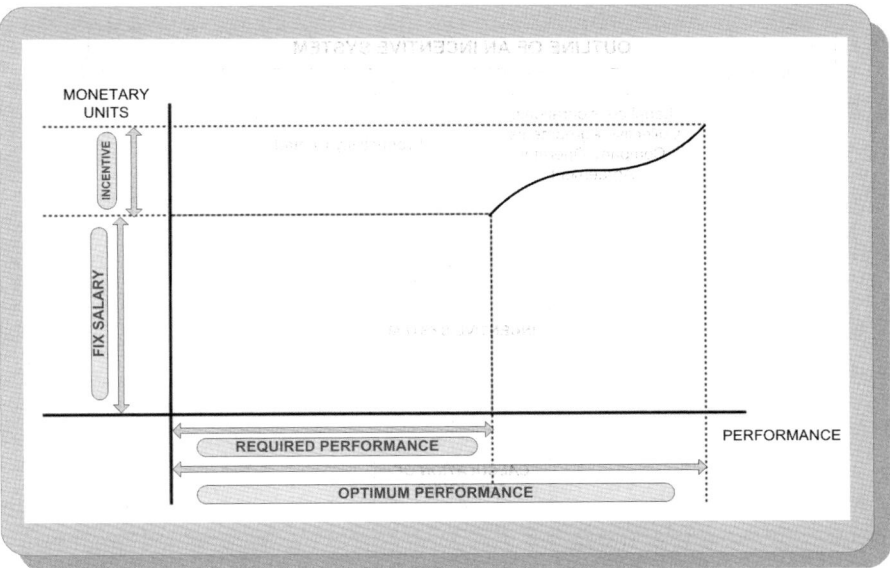

Figure 21.22. Dependence between salary and performance

Every company should be willing to give the possibility to workers to be reward for an effort above the required.

21.6.2. Incentive Calculation

To calculate the incentive we need two data:

- The amount of work performed above what is required, that is, the total of **bonus points**. Bonus points are points earned for working above the normal performance.

- **Price of bonus point** is the price that must be paid to every minute or bonus point earned.

The first of these data is obtained from the productivity control performed. The second should be reflected in the articles of the collective agreement, either its value or how to calculate it.

Industrial productivity

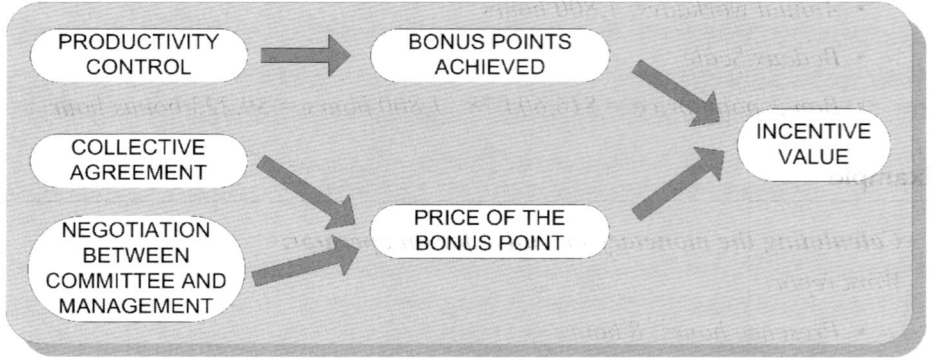

Figure 21.23. Point value calculation

Comparing the time spent performing an operation with the time obtained performing that operation, we obtain the amount of work (measured in time) that has been obtained above the required.

The bonus point price should be reflected in the collective agreement, prior to the implementation of a wage incentive system. It is the duty of management and the work committee to negotiate the price of the bonus point. Overall, even though this varies for each agreement, the price of the bonus point is calculated by dividing the annual base salary by the annual workdays.

Example

Calculate the bonus point value for an operator from the footwear sector.

- *Annual base salary: $16,604.78*
- *Annual workdays: 1,800 hours*
- *Bedaux Scale*
- *Bonus point price = $16,604.78 / (1,800 hours x 60 points) = $0.153/ bonus point.*

The agreement also stipulates that the price of the bonus hour is quantified, which is equivalent to 60 points, so the incentive to pay will be the same. In the following example we will calculate the bonus point value for the previous example.

Example

Calculate the bonus hour value for the footwear example.

- *Annual base salary: $16,604.78*

- *Annual workdays: 1,800 hours*
- *Bedaux Scale*
- *Bonus point price = $16,604.78 / 1,800 hours = $9.223/bonus hour.*

Example

Calculating the monetary incentive for an operator:
Work report:
- *Presence hours: 8 hours*
- *Noncontrolled hours: 0.5 hours*
- *Stop Hours: 0.6 hours*
- *Controlled hours: 6.9 hours*
- *Manufactured A parts = 50 units*
- *Manufactured B parts = 300 units*
- *Manufactured C parts = 32 units*

Point value of operations:
- *Point value A = 3.5 minutes / part A*
- *Point value B = 1 min / Part B*
- *Point value C = 1.25 minutes / Part C*
- *Price bonus point = **$0.09/point***

With all these data, we can carry out the calculation of monetary incentive.
- *Points dedicated = 6.9 hours x 60 points = **414 points***

Points earned:
- *Manufactured A parts = 50 units x 3.5 minutes part A = 175 points earned*
- *Manufactured B parts = 300 units x 1 minute part B = 300 points earned*
- *Manufactured C parts = 32 units x 1.25 minutes part C = 40 points earned*
- *Total minutes achieved = **515 points earned***

Now we will calculate the bonus points earned:
- *515 points earned – 414 minutes spent = **101 bonus points***

Industrial productivity

*Finally, we calculate the monetary incentive: 101 bonus points x $0.09/ bonus point = **$9.09** is the bonus achieved by the operator.*

Example

Calculating the monetary incentive with open work for an operator whose activity exceeds the optimal value.

Work report:

- *Presence hours: 8 hours*
- *Noncontrolled hours: 0.35 hours*
- *Stop hours: 0.75 hours*
- *Controlled hours: 6.9 hours*
- *Manufactured A parts = 40 units*
- *Manufactured B parts = 411 units*
- *Manufactured C parts = 96 units*

Point value of operations:

- *Point value A = 3.5 minutes / part A*
- *Point value B = 1 min / Part B*
- *Point value C = 1.25 minutes / Part C*
- *Price of bonus point = **$0.091/point***

With all these data, we can perform the calculation of monetary incentive.

- *Points dedicated = 6.9 hours x 60 points = **414 points***

Points earned:

- *Manufactured A parts = 40 units x 3.5 minutes part A = **140 points** earned*
- *Manufactured B parts = 411 units x 1 minute part B = **411 points** earned*
- *Manufactured C parts = 96 units x 1.25 minutes part C = **120 points** earned*
- *Total minutes earned = **617 points earned***

In view of the outcome, it seems to be higher than the maximum optimum achievable. We will check it out:

- (671 points earned/414 minutes spent) x 60 = **97.24**, which is higher than the optimal performance, set at 80

In this situation, we calculate the maximum bonus that the operator can reach:

- (Maximum points earned / 414 minutes spent) x 60 = 80 → **552 points** maximum achieved. So for this case, this may be the maximum amount of points earned. Performing a subtraction, we get the bonus value point earned.
- 552 points scored - 414 minutes spent = 138 bonus points

Finally, we calculate the monetary incentive: 138 bonus points x $0.091/ bonus point = **$12.56** is the bonus achieved by the operator.

21.6.3. Incentive Calculation in Limited Work

We must remember the definition of limited work. Such an event occurs when a worker performs an operation and cannot display all the activity the worker is capable of achieving due to causes outside the worker's control. These causes may be due to the machine or the characteristics of the work itself.

Generally, in works where machines are involved it is normal that they set the pace of work, limiting the possibilities for workers to achieve a given activity level.

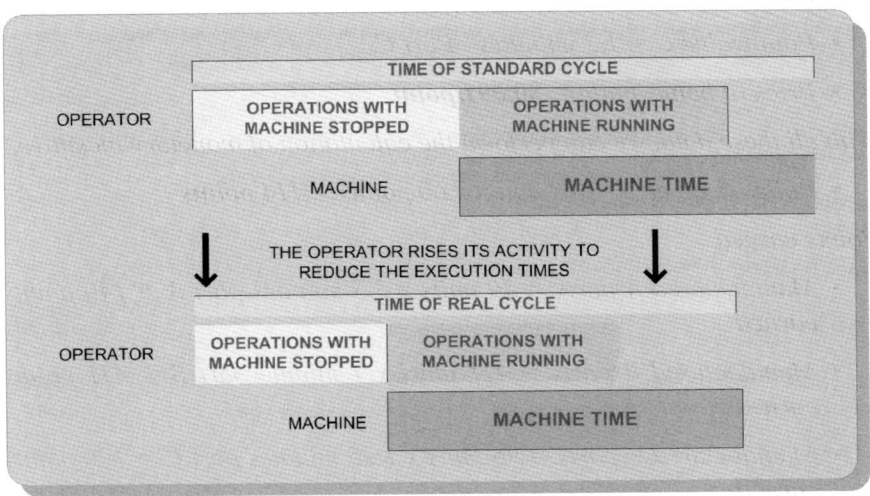

Figure 21.24. Evolution of cycle time and activity in limited works

The application of incentives for limited work can be done from the formulas for calculating productivity in limited work, subtracting the machine time from the standard time and the actual execution time.

Industrial productivity

$$Aa = \frac{ST - TM}{Tr - TM} \times An$$

Formula 21.18.

We recall that Aa is the activity achieved, ST is the standard time, and Tr is the real time. Calculations based on what was just explained for the bonus points are more complicated and therefore require more skill. In many cases, the difficulty of the calculations means that making decisions such as production or performance agreements in exchange for some compensation.

In the following example we can check out the similarities and differences of both types of calculation:

Example

Calculating the monetary incentive for limited work for an operator
The following example shows the part loading in an autoclave task.

Operation Description	Operation with Machine Stopped	Operation with Machine Running	Machine Time
1. Take parts to autoclave.		0.50	
2. Extract previous parts.	2.00		
3. Introduce parts in autoclave.	1.00		
4. Take trolley to demolding area.		0.40	
5. Curing time.			5.00
Total cycle	**3.00**	**0.90**	**5.00**

Figure 21.25.

21. Productivity Control and Incentive Systems

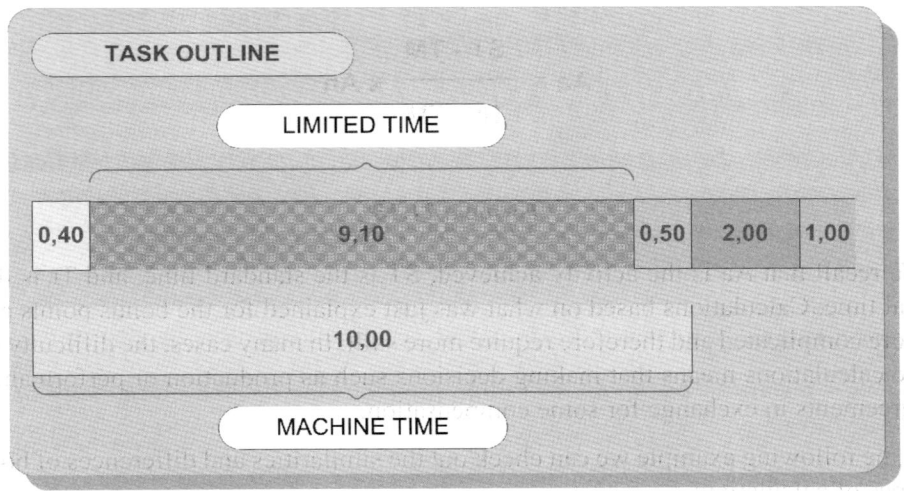

Figure 21.26.

Work report:

- *Presence hours: 8 hours*
- *Noncontrolled hours: 1 hour*
- *Stop hours: 0.75 hours*
- *Controlled hours: 6.25 hours*
- *Parts made = 50 units*

Value of operations:

- *Standard Time = 5 minutes + 3 minutes =* **8 minutes/unit**
- *Bonus point price =* **$0.078/minute**

With this information and knowing that it is a limited work, the calculation of the activity obtained is performed as described here:

- *Produced time = 8 minutes/unit x 50 units =* **400 minutes of work**
- *Real execution time = 6.25 hours x 60 minutes =* **375 minutes**
- *Minutes of machine time = 50 units x 5 minutes TM =* **250 minutes limited**

Calculate the activity achieved in centesimal scale 100-133:

$$Aa = \frac{ST - MT}{Rt - MT} \times 100 = \frac{400 - 250}{375 - 250} \times 100 = 120$$

The activity in centesimal scale obtained by the operator in this work is 120, 20% higher than required. If we want to calculate the bonus points achieved by the operator we only need to calculate the 20% of the time devoted to the task: 375 x 20$% = 75 minutes. This result means that the operator has completed work, which working at normal activity would take 75 more minutes, and so the operator must be paid for it:

- Bonus earned = Bonus points x Bonus point price = 75 x $0.078 = **$5.85**.

To perform the calculation using the same methodology as in the case of open work we should start with the calculation of point values:

- Point value A = 5 minutes + 3 minutes = **8 minutes/unit**
- Optimal time = 5 minutes + [(3 minutes / (80/60)] = **7.25 minutes/unit**

With all these data, we can do the calculation of monetary incentive.

- Minutes dedicated = 6.25 hours x 60 minutes = **375 minutes spent**
- Then calculate the amount of points earned for actual production:
- Points earned = 50 units x 8 minutes/unit = **400 points earned**

In normal conditions, the bonus the operator would get should be 25 points. Being limited work, we calculate the activity reached by the operator during the operations of open work that comprise the task. To do this:

- 375 minutes dedicated / 50 units = **7.5 minutes/unit = 7.5 points/unit**, the time the operator invested in making each unit
- 7.5 minutes/unit = 5 minutes + [3 min / (Activity achieved / 60)] → **Activity reached = 72**, which is equivalent to a **productivity ratio of 1.2 (72/60)**
- 375 minutes x 1.2 = **450 points earned**

The bonus points earned will be calculated now:

- 450 points earned – 375 minutes spent = **75 bonus points**

Finally, we just need to calculate the monetary incentive: 75 bonus points x $0.078/bonus point = **$5.85** is the bonus achieved by the operator.

As we have witnessed, both methods lead to the same result from different approaches.

Example

Calculation of the monetary incentive for limited work with several operators:

WORK REPORT ON PEPPERS PACKAGING LINE

Code	Category	Name	Presence Hours	Controlled Hours	Noncontrolled Hours
A01	1st Officer	Murray Murphy	8	8	0
A02	Assistant	Graham Reed	8	8	0
A03	Specialist Operator	Caren Cook	8	8	0
A04	Operator	Jamie Ward	8	8	0
A05	Operator	Clark Sanchez	8	8	0
A06	Operator	Halley Brook	8	8	0
A07	Operator	Kai O'Meara	8	8	0
A08	Operator	Chad Richardson	8	8	0
			64	64	0

Initial Hour:	7.00
Final hour:	15.00

Presence Hours	64.00
Noncontrolled Hours	0.00
Incidence Hours	0.00
Controlled Hours	64.00
N° of workers:	8.00
Dedicated minutes:	3,840.00

Work Order	
Trays of peppers	11,000.00
Point Value:	0.392
Total Points:	4,312.00
PRODUCTIVITY	**1.12**

Figure 21.27.

As can be seen in the pepper packaging line, the result was higher than the required; the line spent 3,840 minutes to pack 11,000 peppers. Subsequently the control of productivity was performed, comparing the time dedicated to packaging the 11,000 peppers versus time spent packaging these 11,000 peppers. As explained, after conducting a time study on the line, the point value of the operation is 0.392 minutes/pepper.

- *0.392 minutes/pepper x 11,000 peppers = 4,312 points earned*

We now calculate the bonus minutes earned:

- 4,312 earned points – 3,840 minutes spent = 472 bonus points

Afterwards we must calculate the monetary incentive, the amount of money the operator or group of operators receives for a better than required performance, which requires the bonus point value. Examining the agreement, the price is $0.105/point.

- 472 bonus minutes x $0.105/point = **$49.56,** the bonus of the line for that day

We now calculate the incentive for each operator and the presence hours:

- $49.56 / 64 controlled hours = **$0.774 /controlled hour**
- ($0.774/controlled hour) / 8 workers = **$0.0967/operator in each controlled hour**

21.7. Characteristics, Implementation, and Maintenance of an Incentive System

21.7.1. Characteristics of an Incentive System

Before implementing an incentive system, the company must study its factory to be completely sure it is ready. At first a method standardization policy should be introduced in order to achieve measurement of valid work. If different operators follow different patterns to perform a task, and if the sequence of elements is not standardized or established, the company will not be able to implement the incentive system. If the number of incidences is high, we cannot implement an incentive system, so it is vital to try to reduce to a minimum the incidences in our industry.

Without equitable standard times, an incentive system will not succeed in compensating in proportion to production. Without a tape measure, it is not possible to measure the performance. The methods and standardized times and the productivity control are the measuring tape for wage incentive applications.

Once these requirements are fulfilled, the company is ready to design the system.

An incentive system must be fair for the company and its workers. It must give operators the chance to earn 20% to 35% more than the base salary if they work at optimum activities and their efforts are ongoing. The company benefits from the additional productivity and apportioning fixed costs over a greater number of parts, thereby reducing the total unit cost.

In addition to equity, the most important attribute of a good incentive system is simplicity. The system should be fully understood by employees and by the committee. The easier it is, the easier it will be for all parties to understand it, which increases the chances of approval. The individual incentive systems are easier to understand, and these work best if they can measure the individual production.

In order to help operators associate effort with payment, payment stubs should clearly differentiate normal revenue from earnings achieved by incentives. It is good also to indicate the efficiency of the operator in the previous period.

Once installed, the company must accept responsibility for maintaining a salary incentive system. Managing an incentive system requires an objective judgment for making decisions and a detailed analysis of the complaints submitted.

The success or failure of an incentive system will depend on the level of compliance with the following:

Basic rules of an incentive system

- An incentive system should not be implemented on a faulty, unbalanced, or unfair salary structure.

- The company should be willing to give the opportunity to all workers that their efforts are primed.

- The incentive system will not function properly when:
    - Work saturation is low.
    - Materials are defective. (An inventory of suitable materials is necessary.)
    - Machines are in poor condition. (Proper maintenance is essential.)

- The incentive must be applied equitably.

- The results should be known as soon as possible, ideally on a daily basis, this way:
    - The operators will know the result of their efforts while they still remember how they worked.
    - Any claims can be addressed before the payment.

- It should clearly define the causes that force the revision and updating of the system.

- It should inform and if necessary provide training to workers in everything that the incentive system involves in a clear and sincere way. Any doubt among workers will make it difficult to correctly implement the system, possibly causing distrust.

- The incentive payment for each type of hours must be known before the implementation and should appear in the company-workers agreement.

- Always pay what was promised. Whatever the amount of bonuses and initial errors in the system approach have been committed, it is necessary to always pay the bonuses that result.

- Do not change the system, if not absolutely necessary.

To achieve high levels of productivity, the working environment conditions should encourage employees to make their best effort in order to achieve the goals of the company. Initially, most people want to work and achieve, and expect to be paid for their contribution. They wish to be involved in achieving the goals set by their company and to do a better job if they are allowed to have independence and control over their work situation. A climate of motivation must accompany any wage incentive system.

Perhaps the first requirement for establishing a proper motivational environment is to develop a management style that assumes a supporting role instead of a manager role. The goal should be to make all employees feel that it is their responsibility to comply with the objectives of the company, and it is the responsibility of the manager to help operators in the best possible way.

As a second condition, the goals of the company should be clearly stated and separated into division, department, and individual goals. It is important that the goals are realistic, highlighting both the quality and quantity, as well as the reliability and other features essential for the success of the organization. All workers must understand the company objectives and targets related to their work. These goals should be quantified so that workers can compare their achievements against the targets set.

The third requirement is constant feedback to all employees. Timely reports must contain the results for the efforts of the workers and their impact on the established goals.

Finally, each work situation must be designed so that operators are in a position of control of the assignments received. The sense of responsibility is an important source of motivation, as is the recognition of achievements.

Narrative

Incentive system based on historical data.

Here we explain the difficulties faced by a company that manufactures paper products. The company, in an effort to increase the productivity of the plant, had implemented a production incentive system, and the necessary data: the execution time of the different tasks was estimated through historical data. But the incentive system in recent months was not giving the expected results and the productivity of the company was plummeting, as were its profits.

Workloads were revised quarterly. The calculation of the workload to perform in the different workstations was calculated through the arithmetic average of the work done in the last three months and then reduced by 8%.

Initially the system worked well, especially for the company, but within a few years, everything changed. The problem is that this incentive system did not meliorate high activities but rather penalized them. For example, during three months if an operator had worked hard and on average achieved optimal performance, after the next revision that average workload achieved, reduced by 8%, would necessarily have to be done without getting any bonus. In short, high productivity, for the simple fact that it was achieved, would become normal and therefore would be rewarded, or not, as such.

Not surprisingly, the committee, in representation of workers, informed business management of the injustice of the current bonus system. The company responded that the system was what they had agreed and had no plans to undertake any changes.

Operators learn fast, and over the past year operator production underwent drastic changes. Specifically they performed only 5% more than the required workload, literally using a calculator. Thus, they received a small monthly bonus, but they lowered the compulsory production by 3% after each revision. Within one year they had driven down production by almost 12% but their bonus payment was the same.

The system did not work correctly from the beginning, because it did not reward a high productivity from workers, not at least in the long term, and eventually rewarded operators that worked less and less.

Indeed, the incentive system was designed by business management with good intentions, but had unintended consequences for the company.

Through this example we want to clarify that any system that is not fair to both parties is doomed to be useless in a short time. If the system is unfair to workers, they will not trust it and try to find an error to take advantage from it. Whether they succeed or not—and they are highly likely to succeed—the system will not be encouraging increased productivity. Instead, it will rather encourage strikes, continued fights with the committee, and disrespectful operators.

The opposite case is bonus systems that greatly benefit workers. The issue will be the money and competitiveness lost through the workforce deception. Management in some factories have not yet discovered the deception, and other factories close without ever discovering it. What is even more unfortunate is that some companies discover the deception but would rather accept the situation than face the operators.

The company of which we speak realized in time and had the courage to at least try to fix it. Luckily for them they had a manager with little willingness to give up. The solution was to perform a time study that would adjust to reality and to implement the Bedaux incentive system.

The necessary data to keep track of daily productivity can be collected from the work reports, in which each operator reflects the work done and time spent. In addition, these workloads would not change depending on what was worked in the last quarter. Workloads would remain constant as long as working conditions did not vary, avoiding deceit from either party.

After conducting the time study, it was observed that operators were working below the required performance and yet they charged bonuses. At the same time, the results expected by the company were not being realized. The company was able to demonstrate that only a fair incentive system would provide a path toward productivity and continuous improvement. The workers returned to work at a much higher activity than required, and therefore were paid a bonus in accordance with the work performed.

What should we learn this time?

- That there is only one way, with possible variants, to make the control productivity and incentive system.
- That the workers end up knowing more about an incentive system than the person who designed it. They will then either:

    Discover the ways to benefit from it.

    Report it for being an unfair system.

- On the other hand, the only way to measure work is actually measuring it. To take historical averages is a shortcut that short-circuits continuous improvement; it takes execution times achieved in the past and uses them as reference.

- We can only reward correctly when we directly relate it with a correctly measured performance.

Taking an average time as standard time has risks.

Measuring is always easier!

21.7.2. Implementation of an Incentive System

As described in previous chapters, it is necessary to consult the labor agreement of the company that wants to establish a wage incentive system, to avoid making any mistakes. That agreement describes the steps and deadlines to be met to implement such a system. Along with the guidelines described in the agreement, prior to the implementation of the incentive system, it is the responsibility of management and the work committee to reach an agreement on the bonus point price, system, and method of calculation. It should be emphasized that **the implementation of an incentive system is optional,** and both parties must agree on implementing it, so negotiations must start from both parties wanting an incentive system.

After describing legal aspects that need to be taken into account when implementing a wage incentive system, the following steps direct the achievement of the implementation goal.

The starting point must be the productivity control system fully implemented. The steps described in the previous chapters in the process of implementing the productivity control system must be followed and completed.

> WE CANNOT START TO BONUS IF THE PRODUCTIVITY CONTROL SYSTEM IS NOT IMPLEMENTED AND PROVED.

Figure 21.28.

When the productivity control system is already implemented, the obligation of the management committee is to reach an agreement on the bonus point price and the calculation system. Agreement reached, the incentive system will be implemented; if no such agreement is reached, arbitration will be needed. After solving issues with amendments or clarifications, the incentive system can be implemented in the factory.

Industrial productivity

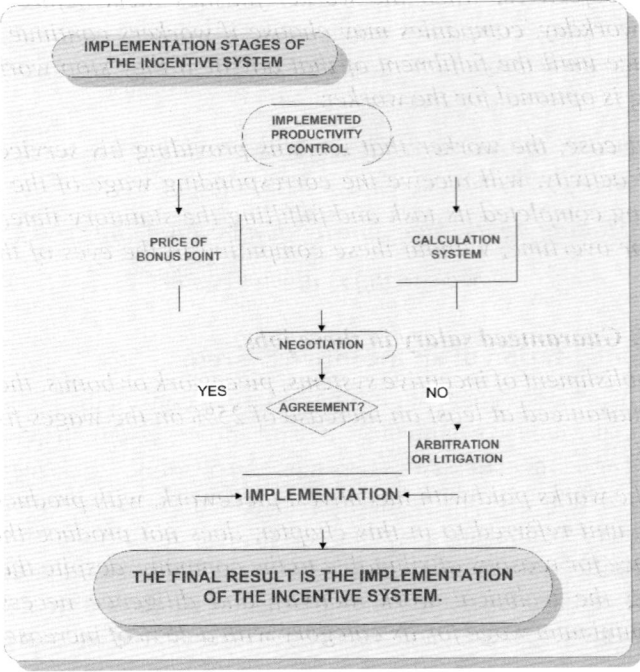

Figure 21.29. Implementation outline for incentive system

This typical pattern for the implementation of a wage incentive system occasionally encounters an exceptional situation:

- The incentive system is implemented, but operators choose not to get more points than the minimum required. They will be meeting the required points and choose not to yield more.

- During the simulation phase (for the implementation of the productivity control system), the company may choose not to implement the system after discovering that it will not be as profitable as expected.

These two situations, although they may be a bit strange, happen, and indeed are often reflected in collective agreements. For example, Article 37 of the state collective agreement of manufacturers of tiles, bricks, and clay components (in force between 2006 and 2008) states:

Example

Article 37. Working with incentives

Companies may establish for unmeasured works piecework systems or production bonuses, so that a higher than normal work performance corresponds to proportionally higher wages.

21. Productivity Control and Incentive Systems

In jobs to objectives, when the worker finishes them before the end of the legal workday, companies may choose if workers continue to provide their service until the fulfilment of that day or if they stop working. Work continuing is optional for the worker.

In the first case, the worker that remains providing his services, at least at normal activity, will receive the corresponding wage of the time spent after having completed its task and fulfilling the statutory time, with fixed charges for overtime, without these computing in the eyes of the limit set by law.

Article 38. Guaranteed salary in these jobs.

In the establishment of incentive systems, piecework or bonus, the employee shall be guaranteed at least an increase of 25% on the wages fixed by this agreement.

If any of the works paid with incentives, piecework, with production bonus or by task unit referred to in this chapter, does not produce the required performance for reasons attributable to the company, despite the employee performing the technical work, activity and diligence necessary, shall receive a minimum wage for its category with a 25% of increase.

When the reasons for the decline in performance were accidental and did not extend to the whole day, employees must be compensated for the duration of the decline with the average wages of the previous day worked.

When the reasons are not attributable to carelessness or negligence of the company and are independent from the will of workers, the affected workers will be paid with the wages from the agreement. These cases can be a lack of electricity, machinery breakdowns, forced waiting and analogous.

To accredit the right to a salary bonus in the event of the second and third paragraph, or the wage agreement mentioned in the fourth paragraph, it is essential that the worker has remained in his workplace.

Article 39. Implementation procedure, suspension and revision of the systems

1. Implementation procedure: The implementation procedure for systems of work organisation referred to in Articles 38 and 39, in companies implementing these systems or the most appropriate, shall be as follows:

- *The creation of a bonus or incentive payment system if it did not exist requires that, previously, legal representatives of workers issue the timely dictum, for which the company will provide specific data needed, such as: workers concerned, quantities, units, type of payment, etc.*

- *In order to establish rates and organisation systems sets a trial period that shall not be less than two months, or more than three.*

- *Before the end of the trial period, the legal representatives of workers may express their dissatisfaction or disagreement, reasoned and written down, to the company with the system or method tried to implement.*
- *Within ten days after receiving the letter from the legal representatives of workers, the company will decide on the issues that arise from the complaints.*
- *Against the decision of the company, legal representatives of workers may appeal to the Judicial Authority.*
- *Within a deadline under fifteen days before the implementation of the new system, the characteristics of the new organisation and the corresponding rates will be explained in the factory.*
- *Similarly will be acted in cases of the revision of the system, methods or rates that imply modifications.*

2. *Revisions: The revision of the methods and incentive rates will be done by agreement between the company and the legal representatives of workers according to Article 41.2 of the Royal Legislative Decree 1/1995, March 24. The mentioned revision should be based always in any of the following events:*

- *When activities with perceptions that exceed 100% from the ones for piecework, bonuses and analogous are repeatedly achieved, or 40% in measured activities.*
- *When the amount of work carried out does not correspond with the established.*
- *When methods and industrial processes are reformed, driven by modernisation, mechanisation or automation of the companies.*
- *When in the bonus preparations a clearly miscalculation was made.*
- *When by miscalculation or modification of methods or facilities the salary increase of 25% is not reached in unmeasured activities.*
- *When the scales or values that regulate the system of incentives suffer changes or alterations.*
- *When economic circumstances advise so.*
- *Incentives or production bonuses will be monthly paid to workers, except in cases of dismissal where they will be paid respect to the proportional performance made during that fraction of the month.*

3. *Claims of workers: In the implementation, revision and abolition of incentives, dissatisfied workers may complain to the Judicial Authority,*

without prejudice to continue observing the rules established by the company, pending the decision on how to proceed.

Article 40. Productivity incentives

1. *The remuneration of normal performance corresponds to the salary agreement.*

2. *For establishing incentives and adapting them to this agreement, the companies that already had them established should start from normal performance.*

3. *Incentives may be collective (section, work team, etc.) or individual, as determined by the company, giving priority to establishing collective incentives where its implementation is possible.*

4. *Companies may limit, proportionally reduce or even cancel incentives, individually, to all employees that by lack of aptitude or interest and attention, objectively demonstrated, jeopardise the production, without prejudice to measures that may be applicable to the case.*

5. *Incentives may be suspended generally, by sections or workers, where the ultimate goals of the system are unattainable for lack or reduction of work or in order to proceed with the reformation of facilities, in which case workers should be informed fifteen days in advance.*

6. *In companies that have established incentive compensation, production that exceeds the normal performance will be measured in bonus-hours (production hours) and each of them will be paid the amount obtained by dividing the annual salary and the annual workday in the agreement (1,800 since 1999) or the company's annual workdays, if this is less, with an increase of 2%.*

7. *When the performance of a job is difficult to measure, as it happens with certain positions (administrative, auxiliary services, storage of goods and items, etc.) and, in general, all staff that receives monthly remuneration, will necessarily establish a procedure for indirect workload assessment, if it is implemented or will be implemented in a company a system that tends to increase productivity. The remuneration for such concept that the workforce perceive will be proportional to the average perceptions of the workforce of the company, section, group, etc., to which he is part of. In addition, this criterion shall apply when establishing an incentive system in one or more sections of the company.*

8. *Matters not covered in this document are subject to the provisions in the current legislation.*

21.7.3. Distinctions of an Incentive System

When deploying and implementing a wage incentive system, it is important to have clearly identified who is going to be encouraged and what to encourage. Our factory has to be well managed and without incidents for the system to be successful. It is also necessary to consider these two distinctions:

> 1.- NEVER ENCOURAGE THROUGH A PRODUCTIVITY BONUS TO SUPERVISORS OR PERSONS IN CHARGE.
> 2.- NEVER ENCOURAGE NON CONTROLLED HOURS AND INCIDENCE HOURS.

Figure 21.30.

For the first of these distinctions, we should never motivate a person whose bonus or incentive depends exclusively on the productivity ratio of the operators for whom he or she is responsible. The reason is that when completing the incidence sheets, both operators and supervisors will want to obtain a high productivity in order to be paid more at the end of the month. Thus they may allocate the exceeding time spent in the total noncontrolled hours or incidence hours, therefore obtaining a high performance in the total controlled hours. Both operators and managers may be interested in this route to ensuring optimal wages with the complicity of those in charge.

For the second of the distinctions, the explanation is as follows and is closely linked to the first distinction. For varied reasons or negotiations between committee and management, the provisions of the collective agreement can reflect how the total noncontrolled hours and incidence hours operators should be remunerated with a performance equal to that achieved in the total controlled hours or even as optimal performance. This situation will generate more noncontrolled hours. The operator will be interested and will get higher salary at the end of the month. The company will pay more bonuses, however production will be the same.

> BEWARE WHAT YOU ENCOURAGE, IT CAN BE PROVOKED.
> NEVER MOTIVATE SOMETHING YOU ARE NOT INTERESTED IN.

Figure 21.31.

The following narrative indicates the precautions to be taken in this regard.

21. Productivity Control and Incentive Systems

Narrative

Low performance due to wrongly done and corrupted incentive system

This story deals with one of the most damaging issues that can occur in an industry: a wrong and corrupt incentive system.

The case under study involved the misfortune of permissiveness and anarchy, mistakes that all companies should strive to avoid.

The operations at this metal-processing company have a high component of machine time and machine changeover times. A long time ago, the batches were large, of many units. Today all that has changed, the batches are much smaller and the manufacturing is bound to be much more flexible. In this scenario, the machine and tool changes gain weight over the operating times.

The company had implemented a traditional incentive system based on Bedaux. Everything seemed right; however, a paradoxical problem surfaced. On one hand operators obtained maximum productivity bonuses according to the incentive system, but on the other, the company reported increasingly poor productivity data that seemed unstoppable. How could this have happened?

Quite simply, the cause was an excess of noncontrolled hours. Workers were productive during controlled time and nothing more. How could there be so many noncontrolled hours?

Simply and seriously at the same time:

1. The machine changeover times were not measured, so they were a bottomless pit in which to load noncontrolled hours in order to obtain the desired productivity in the controlled hours. Operators decided how much time to allocate to machine and tool exchanges for optimum productivity. In fact, much of the time was devoted to mathematical operations in order to balance the books.

2. The noncontrolled time is not paid as normal activity, but paid to the average productivity in the controlled hours. Thus, paradoxically, the longer they computed to noncontrolled time, the easier it was to achieve more productivity and more they got paid. The system encouraged noncontrolled hours.

3. Managers were paid by the average productivity obtained by the section.

What could the solutions to this problem be?

1. Measuring machine changeovers times and including them in the calculation of productivity as if they were a task, which in fact they are.

2. The noncontrolled hours must be paid as normal, not as incentivized, first because they are meaningless with no demonstrable productivity. Second, if we incentivize something, that something occurs and we are not interested in increasing noncontrolled hours (noncontrolled hours, which seems a technical term, means the same as chaos hours).

3. Managers cannot be paid for the individual productivity of their subordinates because the productivity bonus is due to the efforts of the person who develops a job, not who manages it. We propose that those in charge be paid for their management function. How can we evaluate it? Of course not by the productivity of individuals. Furthermore, who decides that one hour is controlled or not? Of course with the system of this company managers will be interested that workers achieve productivity, therefore, they will sign the necessary noncontrol hours. Manipulation is served. We propose that the manager's performance is encouraged by a target number for noncontrolled hours so as not to exceed a maximum of hours. If not reached, they are paid the incentive, and if it is, they are not paid the incentive.

The solutions were clear, but implementing them involved inevitable conflict. These measures would entail the following changes:

1. The noncontrolled 4 to 6 hours due to machine changeovers would be attributed to their real causes and nothing else, setting noncontrolled hours at zero.

2. Also during machine changeovers, operators would have to work at the pace marked by the time study.

3. During the working time operators should work at 140 activity to be paid for 140, and could no longer charge machine exchanges to noncontrolled hours; they would have to be productive to get paid for it.

4. Managers would not be part of the traditional bonus system, instead they must earn the bonus through good management.

Operators were perfectly willing to compromise and adapt to change as requested, but the wage bonus for the 140 activity had become an acquired right and they counted on it as a whole; for them these two concepts were their salary. Therefore, they agreed to collaborate in exchange for a wage increase, independent of the bonus.

The alternatives were few and all complicated. Leave things as they were and die, or try to enforce the changes and risk a social conflict that the company would have lost in strikes, complaints, and stops.

In our opinion, the company should have taken the second option. It is traumatic, but it is a choice between certain death and probable death.

These changes are not easy or comfortable, but that is life. It would have required an implementation process involving transfers, negotiations, layoffs, and other painful actions, but we are sure something like this has to be part of the strategy of the company, or the rest of the strategic objectives will not be needed in the medium term. In conclusion:

- *Productivity in a factory is not easy or comfortable to implement or maintain.*

- *Managers must not get paid for the productivity of their staff; they would be "judge and jury." They should get paid for their management skills; productivity must compensate those who are productive.*

- *We must leave the minimum possible tasks at no control, everything measurable must be measured. Everything not measured is a bottomless pit of hours, overtime, and noncontrolled hours. Everything not measured is chaos.*

Never encourage something that does not suit you. Paradoxically, when we incentivize something that we want, it sometimes happens and sometimes not. When we encourage something that does not interest us it always ends up happening.

21.7.4. Maintenance of an Incentive System

To be successful, an incentive system should be monitored properly. It is not maintained alone. The factory is a living entity and is subject to continuous change. For the plan maintenance to be effective, management must make all employees aware of how it works and of any changes.

A widespread and simple technique is distributing to all employees an operations instruction manual with details of the company's policies regarding the plan and the work details.

This manual must fully explain the basis of task classification, standard time, the way to rate performance, rest supplements, and the processing of complaints or suggestions. It should also describe the technique of handling unusual situations. Finally, should present the objectives of the organization and the role of each employee in their achievement.

The incentive system administrators must make frequent performance verifications, see the deviations, and determine their causes. Low performance is not only cost for administration in view of the guaranteed hourly wages, but leads to restlessness and dissatisfaction of employees. An excessively high performance is a symptom of ample standards, or the introduction of a change in method for which standards were not revised. A sufficient number of inadequate standard times can cause the whole incentive system to fail.

Industrial productivity

Often, operators who have ample standard times restrict their daily production for fear that the company may reset its standard. This restriction of production is costly for operators and for the company; the result is dissatisfaction among coworkers, who see others with "light work."

The company must conduct a periodic revision of the standards in order to ensure their validity. It is crucial that the administration of an incentive system makes constant adjustments to standard times in response to work changes. No matter how significant the change in the method of work, the standard time should be adjusted. Adding several minor improvements in methods can achieve a significant time difference and cause a loose standard time if it is not updated.

The most common causes that lead to the revision of an incentive system are discussed next.

> The nonrevision of the incentive system is always cause for long-term problems. A culture of maintenance and revision is required.

21.7.5. Causes for Change in an Incentive System

The causes that can lead to changes or updates in a wage incentive system have already been addressed in the control of productivity, and the quantity and type of these causes vary from one agreement to another. However, the following are the most common causes for change:

1. Mechanization or change of machines for others with different yield
2. Changing the quality of the material being worked with, as it can modify the standard time
3. Facility improvement to facilitate the completion of work
4. Changing the working method
5. Performances obtained by workers that do not reach a level considered normal, for reasons beyond their control
6. A numeric or mathematical miscalculation
7. When, without detriment to the quality required, a percentage of operators from the total workforce, reach during the period of one month an activity greater than the optimal

The number of workers from the total workforce to reach a performance above optimal will vary depending on the labor agreement. For example, point 6 of Article 9 from the footwear industry collective agreement, reads as follows:

Incentive fees may be revised when 140 activities are reached on an ongoing basis, or their equivalents in other scales, which will be the proof for revision. The difference between optimal and minimal activity is considered as margin of guarantee for workers.

Such an agreement provides an activity value to be able to revise the system of incentives, without quantifying the amount or percentage of the workforce that should achieve it.

In these cases, the values obtained are presented first to the affected workers, their legal representatives, and union technicians.

21.7.6. The Incentive System Manual

An incentive system needs a good and fair control of productivity in order to be implemented. Consequently, the incentive system manual must be based on the productivity control manual.

This manual should serve as a clarifying element for both parties involved, of the rules governing the system of incentives. This document should be drawn up by the company but some aspects should be negotiated with the workers, because they are not clearly defined in collective agreements.

Because an incentive system rewards operators who achieve high productivity, productivity control will determine what level of productivity has been reached and the incentive system will quantify the bonus in return. So the incentive system manual should expand productivity control.

Minimum content of the incentive system manual

- Introduction and definitions
- Methods and times study: Summary of value point
- Work reports (description and use)
- Productivity control (method of calculation)
- Analysis of results
- Compensation arrangements
- Revision of the control system and payment for productivity
- Supporting appendices (process diagrams, rest coefficient, legal aspects)

In order not to repeat the same information, only the new points added to the productivity control manual will be explained.

Introduction and Definitions

This point should be extended for an incentive system to include price of the item and, if necessary, the extended bonus.

Remuneration Arrangements

It should state unequivocally how efforts greater than required will be motivated, and how downtimes (stops or breakdowns) or work done outside the control of productivity will affect that bonus.

On the other hand, it is common to make special arrangements for some positions because of low saturation, difficulty in measuring the performance, or some other oddity. These agreements should be known by everyone involved, so they should be included in the manual in order to maintain a standard of transparency.

Revision of the Control System and Bonus Payments for Productivity

This last point should contain, in addition to the reasons that can vary the productivity control system, which usually involves reasons intrinsic to the company, the reasons that can change the bonus payment system. These reasons may well stem from sources such as new approaches in the negotiation by the company or employees, or outside the company, like changes in the national or state agreement, or agreements made in another factory of the same group.

More content about the topic covered in this chapter can be read in the book by the same author *Productivity and Incentives* (Marcombo, Technical Editions).

Questions

1. Describe at least three pieces of information to be included in a work report.
2. What documents should be consulted before starting up a productivity control implementation?
3. Briefly define what is meant by productivity.
4. Can we measure the performance of middle managers?
5. If working with a machine, and obviously the machine limits work, can we use standard methodology for calculating the performance of an operator?

6. An OEE control system would be used for what type of work?
7. What is the purpose of a productivity control manual?
8. Is it legal to apply a bonus payment system by productivity?
9. Can a drastic change in the working methodology invalidate an incentive system?
10. Once an incentive system is implemented, can we revise the times? Under what circumstances?

Problems

1. Calculate the following values related to productivity control:

    a) Data:

       Units per hour to produce at normal activity: 250 units

       Units produced: 260 units

       What activity, in the 100-133 scale, has the operator achieved?

    b) Data:

       Units per hour to produce at normal activity: 31.5 units

       Length of workday: 8 hours

       Stopped hours: 1 hour

       Units produced: 270 units

       What activity, in the 100-133 scale, has the operator achieved?

    c) Data:

       Units per hour to produce at normal activity: 25 units

       Length of workday: 8 hours

       Stopped hours: 2 hours

       Units produced: 120 units

       What activity, in the 100-133 scale, has the operator achieved?

2. The following work report from a steel mechanization line details the quantity of the different kinds of hours in the day. Complete the shaded boxes performing the operations considered appropriate:

Category	Name	Presence Hours	Controlled Hours	Noncontrolled Hours	Incidence Hours
Operator	Murray Murphy	8	6	1	1
Operator	Graham Reed	8	6	1	1
Operator	Caren Cook	8	6	1	1
Operator	Jamie Ward	8	6	1	1
Operator	Clark Sanchez	8	6	1	1
Operator	Halley Brook	8	6	1	1
Operator	Kai O'Meara	8	6	1	1
Operator	Chad Richardson	8	6	1	1
		64	48	8	8

Workday	
Initial Hour:	8.00
Final Hour:	16.00

Presence Hours	64.00
Noncontrolled Hours	
Incidence Hours	
Controlled Hours	
N° of workers:	8.00
Dedicated minutes:	

Work Order	
Steel parts per line	203.00
Point Value:	15.320
Satndard Time (min)	
Total Points:	
PRODUCTIVITY	

Figure 21.32.

Bibliography

Aguirre, J. M., Mercedes Rodríguez, and Dolores Tous, *Organización de métodos de trabajo* (Editorial Pirámide, 2002).

Caso Neira, Alfredo, *Sistemas de incentivos a la producción* (FC Editorial, 2003).

Estatuto de los Trabajadores (Editorial Tirant lo Blanch, 2003).

Synthesis

Now that the book is finished and multiple tools and methodologies have been discussed, you may perhaps have noticed the line and structuring we attempted to follow in it. On one hand, each part, each chapter was located in the precise order; on the other hand, in each chapter it is clear what waste is reduced and eliminated.

We insist that the goal of this book is pedagogy and for that reason, it is repetitive in some concepts, and in this synthesis it will continue to be in order to summarize in a few pages what it has tried to teach.

Part 1

Part 1 introduced the theory of waste measurement. According to this theory, we know that all manufacturing time contains a component that does not contribute to anything. That component is waste, and it can be divided into its different causes.

The rest of the book is dedicated to methodologies designed to reduce each of the wastes.

Parts 2 and 3

These two parts are the most extensive of the book; they focus on how to make a study of methods and processes, how to improve them, and how to measure times. Thanks to the lessons from these chapters, waste in work design (CwD)—composed in turn by waste in task method (CwM) and waste in the process (CwP)—is reduced.

What is obtained from the study of methods and times?
1. From having a nonmeasured task, we get to know how it is done and what amount of time it takes:

Industrial productivity

Summary table of methods and times		
Description	Sec/Unit	Min/Unit
Standard Time	0.91	0.02
Workforce cost	14.00	€/hour
Workforce cost per unit	0.004	€/unit
Total transfers (meters)	9,214	metres
Classification of the operations	Seg/Ud	Min/Unit
Total value-added operations ⭕	0.32	0.01
Total non-value-added operations ☁	0.58	0.01
Total moves ⇨	0.58	0.01
Total storages ▽	0.00	0.00
Total waits ◻	0.00	0.00
Total inspections ▫	0.00	0.00
Total inspection-operation	0.00	0.00
Total searches	0.00	0.00
Total removable operations	0.00	0.00
Total communications	0.00	0.00
CwM		2.81

Statistical parameters	
Description	Quantity
% of boxes of number 34 pairs	0.9%
% of boxes of number 35 pairs	2.7%
% of boxes of number 36 pairs	3.1%
% of boxes of number 37 pairs	4.5%
% of boxes of number 38 pairs	4.9%
% of boxes of number 39 pairs	9.6%
% of boxes of number 40 pairs	14.7%
% of boxes of number 41 pairs	16.1%
% of boxes of number 42 pairs	16.6%
% of boxes of number 43 pairs	13.6%
% of boxes of number 44 pairs	6.8%
% of boxes of number 45 pairs	3.3%
% of boxes of number 46 pairs	1.9%
% of boxes of number 47 pairs	1.3%

Estudio de métodos y tiempos de la tarea: Almacenaje de zapato por tallas

Code	Description of the Operation	Type	Distance (meters)	Normal Time (sec)	Addit. Suppl. (%)	Tot. Suppl. (%)	Corrected Time (Sec)	Units	Total Corrected Time (sec)
0010	Take pallet (perform maneuver to face pallet and elevate with forklift).	⭕		6.41	0.00%	14.00%	7.31	167.00	1,220.3
0020	Leave stored pallet (lower stored pallet, lower forklift, and perform maneuver for release).	⭕		10.35	2.00%	16.00%	12.01	167.00	2,005.0
0030	Move pallet taking number 34 shoes to storage location.	⇨	18.00	10.00	0.00%	14.00%	11.40	2.00	22.8
0040	Move pallet taking number 35 shoes to storage location.	⇨	26.00	14.44	0.00%	14.00%	16.46	5.00	82.3
0050	Move pallet taking number 36 shoes to storage location.	⇨	34.00	18.88	0.00%	14.00%	21.53	6.00	129.2
0060	Move pallet taking number 37 shoes to storage location.	⇨	42.00	23.33	0.00%	14.00%	26.59	8.00	212.7
0070	Move pallet taking number 38 shoes to storage location.	⇨	50.00	27.77	0.00%	14.00%	31.66	9.00	284.9
0080	Move pallet taking number 39 shoes to storage location.	⇨	58.00	32.21	0.00%	14.00%	36.72	17.00	624.3
0090	Move pallet taking number 40 shoes to storage location.	⇨	66.00	36.66	0.00%	14.00%	41.79	25.00	1,044.7
0100	Move pallet taking number 41 shoes to storage location.	⇨	66.00	36.66	0.00%	14.00%	41.79	27.00	1,128.3
0110	Move pallet taking number 42 shoes to storage location.	⇨	58.00	32.21	0.00%	14.00%	36.72	28.00	1,028.2
0120	Move pallet taking number 43 shoes to storage location.	⇨	50.00	27.77	0.00%	14.00%	31.66	23.00	728.1
0130	Move pallet taking number 44 shoes to storage location.	⇨	42.00	23.33	0.00%	14.00%	26.59	12.00	319.1
0140	Move pallet taking number 45 shoes to storage location.	⇨	34.00	18.88	0.00%	14.00%	21.53	6.00	129.2
0150	Move pallet taking number 46 shoes to storage location.	⇨	26.00	14.44	0.00%	14.00%	16.46	4.00	65.8
0160	Move pallet taking number 47 shoes to storage location.	⇨	18.00	10.00	0.00%	14.00%	11.40	3.00	34.2
							Total task execution time:		9,059.3

Figure S.1

2. Once the method is known, it can be improved.

Summary table of method		Current	Improv.	Saving	
Description		sec/unit	sec/unit	sec/unit	%
Standard Time (person time)		0.91	0.66	0.25	27%
Workforce cost ($/hour)		14.00			
Workforce cost per unit ($/hour)		0.004	0.003	0.001	27%
Total transfers (meters)		0.73	0.43	0.30	41%
Classification of Operations		sec/unit	sec/unit	sec/unit	%
Total value-added operations	○	0.32	0.32	0.00	0%
Total non-value-added operations	☁	0.58	0.34	0.24	41%
Total transfers	⇨	0.58	0.34	0.24	41%
Total storages	▽	0.00	0.00	0.00	0%
Total waits	D	0.00	0.00	0.00	0%
Total inspections	□	0.00	0.00	0.00	0%
Total inspection-operation	◯	0.00	0.00	0.00	0%
Coefficient of waste in Method (CwM)		2.81	2.06	0.75	

Figure S.2

Part 4

Part 4 discusses the application of standard times to the management of production and control. The chapter addressing operations management explains specifically how to use the standard time in the sizing of resources. Not doing so is the first cause of lower productivity in industries, and without standard time, logically, it cannot be done. Here we will learn to reduce the waste for management failures, Cm.

What is obtained with the sizing of resources and the use of simulators?

1. We start from the following situation:

   a) We do not have the standard time of tasks and products.

   b) Because we do not know the amount of time that these need, we do not know the real workload.

   c) For that reason, and facing uncertainty, we increase the capacity more than is needed.

   d) The saturation is low.

Industrial productivity

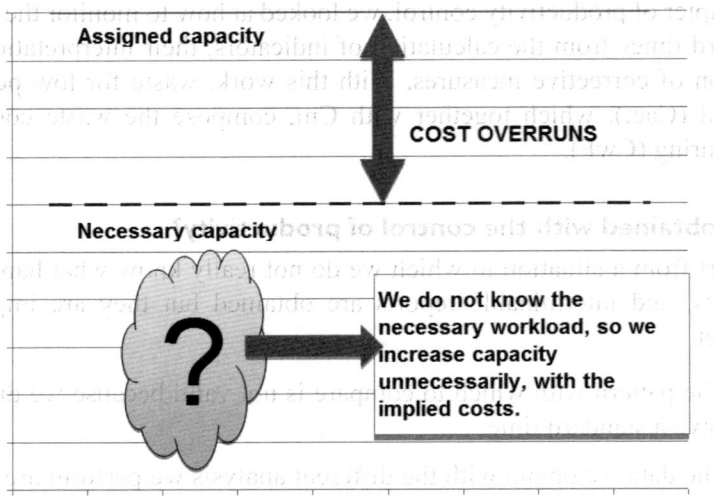

Figure S.3

e) It may also happen that we assign deficit capacities, resulting in a lack of resources to comply with the plan and the compromises.

f) Or worst of all and most frequent, we assign an excess of resources to certain tasks and do not comply with the compromises.

2. When we do have standard times and we simulate the amount of work in calculating the workload, we can adjust the capacity to it: the result usually is a considerable improvement in costs.

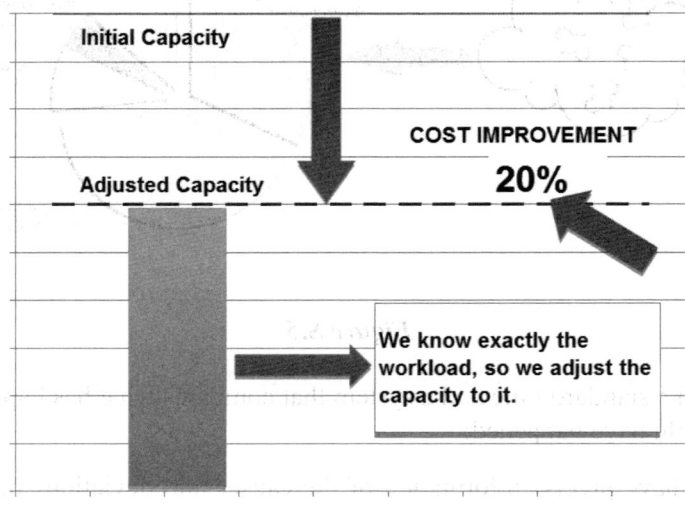

Figure S.4

790

Synthesis

In the chapter of productivity control, we looked at how to monitor the fulfillment of standard times from the calculation of indicators, their interpretation, and the application of corrective measures. With this work, waste for low performance is reduced (Cact), which together with Cm, compose the waste coefficient in manufacturing (CwF).

What is obtained with the control of productivity?

1. We start from a situation in which we do not really know what happens; data, averages, and interminable reports are obtained but they are impossible to interpret.

   - The pattern with which to compare is not valid because we did not even have a standard time.
   - The data we obtain with the different analysis we perform are confusing, contradictory, and potentially illegible.
   - We want to have so much information that what we get is misinformation.
   - Between our interpretation and reality we encounter deviations greater than 50 percent.
   - The evolution of indicators is erratic, even incoherent.
   - Finally, we have nothing: it is best to let ourselves get carried away.

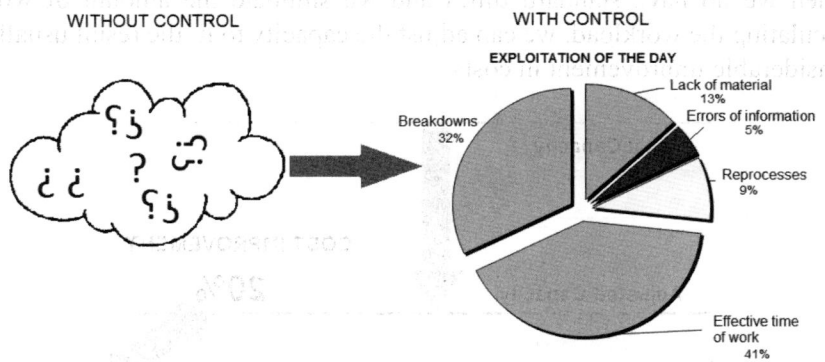

Figure S.5

2. We obtain a standard time and a system that compares what has happened with what should have happened:

   - We have precise information of the causes and deviations between one thing and the other.

Industrial productivity

- Therefore, we make correct decisions and improve, with each control, the situation.

LOGO	COMPANY NAME		Process				PROCESS TOTAL			
	Responsable:							Month		Month i
TABLE OF INDICATORS OF WASTE MANAGEMENT										
Day	∑TExUds	Activity	Cact	Management Coefficients						Cd
				Cmt	Cfm	Cdq	Cdi	Crp	Cm	
1	876,40	113,52%	-0,12	0,01	0,01	0,01	0,00	0,00	0,03	0,91
2	752,08	99,75%	0,00	0,00	0,00	0,00	0,00	0,00	0,00	1,00
3	720,87	91,02%	0,10	0,00	0,00	0,00	0,01	0,00	0,01	1,11
4	692,42	96,57%	0,04	0,06	0,00	0,01	0,00	0,00	0,07	1,10
5	709,20	95,71%	0,04	0,00	0,00	0,00	0,00	0,00	0,00	1,04
6	699,97	104,32%	-0,04	0,00	0,07	0,00	0,00	0,00	0,08	1,04
7	702,52	87,81%	0,14	0,00	0,00	0,00	0,00	0,00	0,00	1,14
8	764,63	103,33%	-0,03	0,00	0,00	0,01	0,04	0,00	0,05	1,02
9	753,53	96,61%	0,04	0,00	0,00	0,00	0,00	0,00	0,00	1,04
10	691,92	91,77%	0,09	0,00	0,00	0,00	0,00	0,06	0,07	1,16
11	764,52	95,56%	0,05	0,00	0,00	0,00	0,00	0,00	0,00	1,05
12	687,50	103,23%	-0,03	0,01	0,00	0,07	0,00	0,00	0,08	1,05
13	692,62	97,69%	0,02	0,05	0,00	0,00	0,00	0,00	0,05	1,07
14	763,02	96,22%	0,04	0,00	0,00	0,01	0,00	0,00	0,01	1,05
15	766,68	109,53%	-0,09	0,00	0,00	0,05	0,00	0,00	0,06	0,97
16	775,42	105,93%	-0,06	0,00	0,00	0,00	0,00	0,00	0,00	0,94
17	757,57	94,70%	0,06	0,00	0,00	0,00	0,00	0,00	0,00	1,06
18	709,08	96,34%	0,04	0,00	0,09	0,00	0,00	0,00	0,09	1,13
19	756,83	98,67%	0,01	0,00	0,00	0,00	0,04	0,00	0,04	1,06
20	742,57	103,86%	-0,04	0,00	0,00	0,00	0,00	0,04	0,04	1,01
TOTAL MONTH I	14.779	98,93%	0,01	0,01	0,01	0,01	0,00	0,01	0,03	1,04
OBJECTIVE			0,05	0,02	0,02	0,00	0,00	0,01	0,05	1,1
IMPROVEMENT ON OBJECTIVE			0,04	0,01	0,01	-0,01	0,00	0,00	0,02	0,06
PREVIOUS PERIOD (Month i-1)			0,02	0,01	0,01	0,05	0,02	0,00	0,09	1,11
IMPROVEMENT ON PREVIOUS PERIOD			0,01	0,00	0,00	0,04	0,02	-0,01	0,06	0,07
ACCUM. PREVIOUS PERIODS			0,02	0,01	0,01	0,03	0,01	0,00	0,06	1,08
ACCUM. IMPROVEMENT PERIODS-OBJEC.			0,03	0,01	0,01	-0,03	-0,01	0,01	-0,01	0,02

Figure S.6

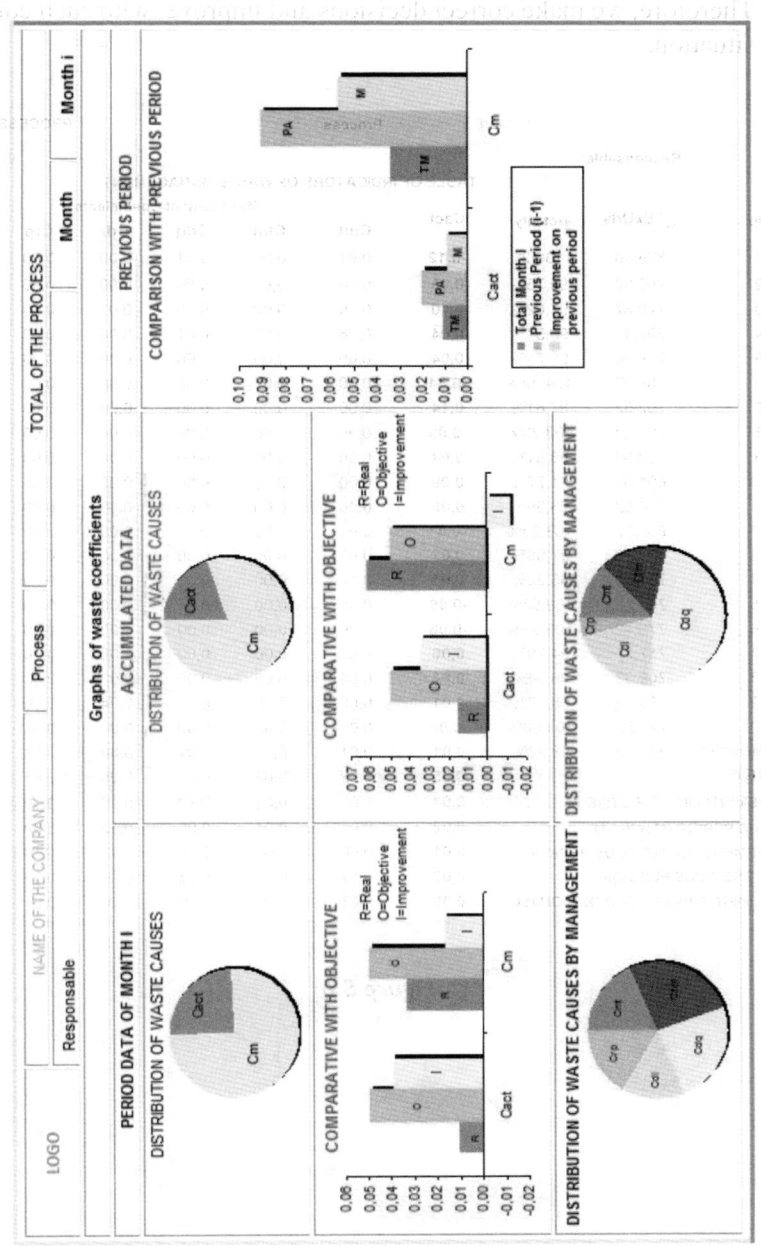

Figure S.7

Industrial productivity

The application of all the previous methods improves the total duration of the tasks:

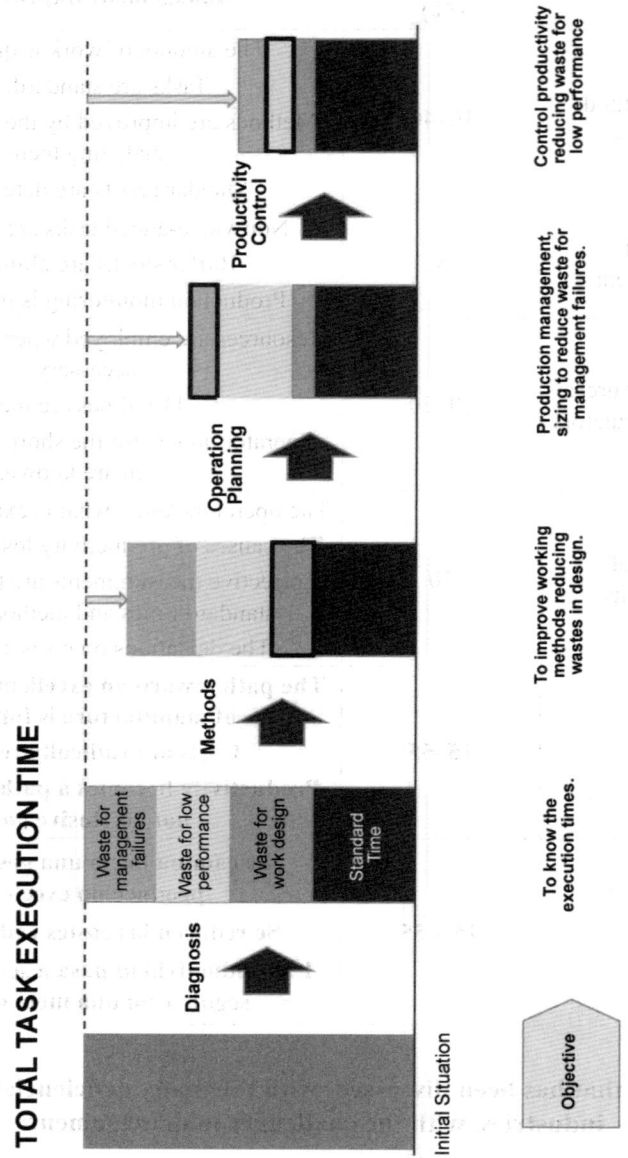

Figure S.8. A reduction of the total task execution time

Synthesis

The quantification of the improvement is estimated here; the data provided are totally real and based on experiences and improvements undertaken:

Tool	Improvement (%)	Management Improvement
Study of methods and times	10–40	The amount of work is quantified. Tasks are standardized. Methods are improved by the simple fact of analyzing them. Standard costs are determined.
Method improvement	5	Non-value-added tasks are eliminated. Buffer stocks are eliminated. Production monitoring is made easier.
Sizing of resources and use of simulators	10–20	Resources are employed where they are most necessary. Deadlines are met. Operator quotas for the short, mid, and long term are known.
Control of productivity	10	The operators know what is expected of them. The causes of productivity losses are known. Corrective measurements are taken based on standard times and methods studies. The deviations on costs are known.
Total	**15–55**	**The path toward an excellent management of manufacture is followed. Costs are radically reduced. Productivity becomes a path to follow and not an elusive goal.**
Total	15 – 55	Se camina hacia una gestión de la producción excelente. Se reducen los costes radicalmente. La productividad pasa a ser un camino a seguir y no una meta efímera.

With all that has been discussed, with the many deficiencies of most industries, with the challenges to management:

is it possible to improve productivity substantially?

Is it possible, as a nation, to be competitive?

Yes.

SOLUTIONS

SOLUTIONS

Solutions

Chapter 2 – Solutions to questions

1. Yes.
2. The waste in work design and waste in manufacturing.
3. The first, waste from method and process; the second, waste from management failures and waste from low performance.
4. Lack of materials, imbalance, and breakdowns.
5. Displacements, searches, and waits.
6. The loss of time that causes a work pace that is slower than normal.
7. Minimum amount of necessary time.
8. Yes perhaps; the reason is that the value-adding task can contain non-value-adding operations.
9. The incidences.
10. Always from the operator, watching how the operator executes the task.

Chapter 3 - Solutions to questions

1. Waste coefficients.
2. This text follows a script that reports the unproductiveness detected in different tasks and/or processes. This unproductiveness measures the waste from work design and waste in manufacturing. It is reflected in the waste maps, and improvements are proposed for the wastes.
3. They are graphs showing visually the waste in the tasks and processes.
4. Waste maps for work design, manufacturing waste maps, and maps of total waste.
5. $C_{act} = (100/Activity) - 1$
6. A waste coefficient above the target coefficient, the expiration of a period, or incidents in costs.
7. In principle it must be so; any investment should reduce the execution time of tasks. This may be due to a reduction of waste, but also due to a reduction in the standard time for the acquisition of new technology.
8. Waste from work design is the responsibility of the processes and methods department and manufacturing waste is the responsibility of the operations manager.
9. Each day.
10. No, it is erroneous information; it must be calculated by period and apportioned to the batches that have been made in that period.

Chapter 4 - Solutions to questions

1. The kaizen.

2. In the diagnosis phase, process and manufacturing engineering, application of standard times, and cycle repetition.

3. The tasks of the process; for each task, its standard time; differentiating value-added and non-value-added times, if the task is value-adding to the process; and the CwM. It also assesses from the total of the process, the CwP and CwD.

4. It records the foregoing considering the date of registration, which shows the evolution of the standard times that result from continuous improvement.

5. All coefficients related to what happens in manufacturing: Cact and Cm and their breakdown into causes.

6. Waste coefficients CwF and CwD based on a comparison with objectives. Review and revision should be done every month or when incidents require their revision.

7. In a reduction of some waste coefficients or standard time.

8. The systematization of analysis and reduction of waste in the business process.

Chapter 5 - Solutions to questions

1. Task selection, breakdown into operations, classification of operations, and representation of the working method.

2. Data entry sheet and method summary, method study sheet, additional information sheet, general considerations, sketches of the piece and workplace, task rationale, and sheet for general improvement proposals.

3. An explanatory figure that is added to the method summary when more than one participant is involved in a task.

4. Nine.

5. No, although it has some common points information may be given differently as a function of the type of task.

6. Open work, person-person simultaneous tasks, person-machine simultaneous tasks, and assembly line tasks.

7. The process captures the tasks within a factory or section with a low level of detail. The method represents operations within a task and has a greater level of detail.

8. The structure of materials that make up the finished product.

9. Processes for workshops (job shop), line processes (flow shop), hybrid, and fixed workplace.

10. To find out how it is evolving, what influence a particular investment has had, or to know how a method was done in the past; if it was appropriate, to return to the previous way of doing it, etc.

Chapter 6 - Solutions to questions

1. It is a diagnostic system that detects what is improvable. It identifies the points where potential for improvement exists.

2. Using the interrogation technique, we find preliminary questions and background questions.

3. All non-value-added or inspection-operation.

4. (1) What is done actually? (2) What is obtained in reality? (3) Why is it done? (4) Where is it done? (5) Why is it done there?

5. (1) Working conditions. (2) Materials handling. (3) Enrichment of the task. (4) Work organization.

6. Yes, micro-motions.

7. Seventeen micro-motions.

8. Eight: reach, move, grasp, release load, preposition, use, assemble, and disassemble.

9. True.

10. (1) Movements in which only the fingers are used. (2) Movements in which only the fingers and wrist are used. (3) Movements in which only the fingers, wrist, and forearm are used. (4) Movements in which only the fingers, wrist, forearm, and arm are used. (5) Movements that use the fingers, wrist, forearm, arm, and body.

Chapter 7 - Solutions to questions

1. Always.

2. Make the correct definition of the problem.

3. First the analysis of methods and processes and then the "why" diagram seeking the root cause of the problem, rather than the obvious cause.

4. Through brainstorming and/or the "how" diagram. In addition, working methods have solutions fully established and tested that may be applied.

5. The 5S, SMED (quick changeover of machines), balancing work with more than one participant, and applying the rules of motion economy.

6. A place for everything and everything in its place: order and cleanliness.

7. In observing and comparing different ways of doing things, and building or standardizing the best of each of them.

8. The ergonomic improvement as it affects not only the method, but the health of workers. The improvement is more easily accepted.

9. The experienced analyst must reduce the method improvement cycle as possible because it also has a cost. Therefore, once the study of methods has begun, for all operations possible, it is good to carry out a parallel analysis with improvement proposals based on the study and description of the operations.

10. In eliminating all non-value-added operations and reducing the time for value-added.

Chapter 8 - Solutions to questions

1. A method for improving duration of tool changeover tasks.

2. An internal operation is done with the machine stopped, and an external operation can be done with the machine running.

3. (1) Separate internal and external operations. (2) Convert internal operations into external operations. (3) Improve work methods for internal and external operations.

4. Because a faster changeover time implies a lower optimal batch size.

5. Yes, they are basic, especially in the third stage.

6. Triggers, cams, or wing nuts.

Chapter 9 - Solutions to questions

1. Equal production capacity of each of the tasks in the sequence of an assembly line or chain.

2. (1) Divide the task. (2) Redistribute operations. (3) Use parallel workstations. (4) Unify tasks. (5) Redesign.

3. The operator cannot perform at 100% technically and physically.

4. Placing more workers or reducing the current workload.

5. Dependent operations are those that must be executed by several operators simultaneously due to the characteristics of the operation.

6. Independent operations are those that can be performed individually, without assistance from another operator.

7. It is the event in which several machines are waiting to be attended by the operator in charge of them.

Chapter 10 - Solutions to questions

1. Eliminate all non-value-adding tasks.

2. It is a set of tasks that a material or materials undergo from the moment the production order is given until the product is served to the customer (internal or external).

3. Balancing of process tasks, reduction of stocks in process, reduction of space, and transfers and implementation of automated transport.

4. Storage, delay, and transfers.

5. Overtime, task redesign, and task sharing.

6. No.

7. Search, store, transfers, and communications.

8. Reducing the transference batch.

9. Yes, in fact, it is the most influential factor.

10. Nothing.

11. Automating the material transportations.

12. The circle of value-adding task.

13. Seal it, cancel it, and, if possible, sell it.

14. Intermediate stores and therefore, apparition of non-value-adding tasks.

Solutions to problems

1. - Yes, so we could use a smaller factory.

   - The reduction is drastic; the delivery time will lower manufacturing by more than 60%.

   - Very similar, balancing everything we can to avoid accumulations in front of tasks with the longest duration per unit.

2. - 20 pallets.

   - No.

   - Because we have lots of high-transfer batches, leading to further accumulation of stocks, waiting times, and limited flexibility.

Chapter 11 - Solutions to questions

1. Fume elimination, noise attenuation, weight lifting, awkward postures, and fatigue.
2. Rest supplements.
3. Healthier and safer working conditions for the operator, increasing productivity for the company.
4. (1) Handling of raw materials. (2) Manual tools. (3) Safety of machinery. (4) Workstation. (5) Illumination of the work area.
5. Person, machine, and environment.
6. Observation, interview, questionnaire, and simulation through checklists.
7. Yes, depending on the weight.

Chapter 12 - Solutions to questions

1. One idea, its implementation, and the generation of profits.
2. They are not the same thing, but innovation is the step that follows creativity; innovation thrives on creativity.
3. The designation of responsibility, allocation of time, dates, and budget.
4. When a working method consolidates and we operate according to it and with favourable results, approximated to the expected.
5. (1) To convince decision groups. (2) Train operators. (3) Foster the implementation.
6. Consult and discuss with the group. These situations require great tact.
7. The profitability.
8. The manager's image; these managers are in a position to suggest obvious things that may lead to improvements.
9. Improving working conditions (ergonomics) and involving them in the improvement.
10. With a method correctly documented and illustrated, with training, supervision, and tutelage.
11. When implemented and has become a habit.

Chapter 13 - Solutions to questions

1. The graphical representation of a process illustrating the sequence or succession of tasks.

2. The objective is to pick up the sequence of operations that compose it, as well as the rationale that follows, so that it can be standardized, used, and improved.

3. All the basic tasks required to complete the process.

4. The decision diamond is a figure that raises a question or an alternative path, or the result of an inspection point.

5. In general, yes.

6. They are more difficult to measure and have many alternative paths and replication loops.

7. Through a rectangle that displays checks to perform, followed by a decision diamond.

Chapter 14 - Solutions to questions

1. The application of techniques to determine the time it takes for a skilled worker to carry out a defined task, which is done through an established performance standard.

2. The time required for an average operator, fully qualified and trained, working at a normal pace, to perform a task according to the established method.

3. Estimation, WMT, and standardized data.

4. Select, record, examine, measure, compile, and define.

5. From the breakdown of body movements and their assessment through WMT tables.

6. (1) Change in materials and method. (2) Complaints from workers or their union representatives on the standard time of a task. (3) Possible error, either by high or low times.

7. (1) Date of data collection. (2) Name of the task. (3) Code of the task.

8. (1) Describe the operative sequence. (2) Know exactly how work is done. (3) Sort operations by type. (4) Perform the measurement of time.

Chapter 15 - Solutions to questions

1. In measurement techniques, knowledge of materials, and tools.

2. Empathy, capacity for dialogue, consideration.

3. It represents what a worker learns per cycle performed.

4. Fidelity to the method, accuracy, speed, and consistency of movements.

Industrial productivity

5. Bedaux and centesimal.

6. 4.5 km/h or 1.25 m/s.

7. 8 seconds.

8. 6 seconds.

9. The working method is the work instructions, the indications that are given to the operators in order to perform a particular job. The operation mode is the particular interpretation of each operator based on such instructions and, therefore, their way to carry them out.

10. Pen, paper, tape measure, stopwatch, or tables of predetermined times.

Chapter 16 - Solutions to questions

1. (1) Use of stopwatch. (2) Record with video camera. (3) Use of PDA.

2. (1) Breakdown of the task into operations. (2) Scrutiny. (3) Calculate the average time for each operation. (4) Compile: calculation of task execution time.

3. Mundel table and the statistical method.

4. It is a set of mathematical operations that returns the most repeated time and the activity observed for that time, within a range. The most repeated time is called modal value.

5. Time with stopwatch and activity (operator performance).

6. (1) It is the normal time plus the applicable rest supplements. (2) The corrected time also includes special supplements.

7. (1) Personal needs. (2) Fatigue. (3) Contingencies. (4) Start and end of the workday. (5) Interferences.

8. The studies of methods and times are simulations of reality that try to capture the rationale of a task, to be able to quantify the necessary work time.

9. It is that work in which the operator who executes it cannot display all the capacity of which he or she is able for some reason beyond the operator's control.

10. Machine interference is called to the fact that several machines are waiting to be attended by the worker in charge of them.

Chapter 17 - Solutions to questions

1. It is a technique using random sampling and analytical observations to determine the probability for certain activity.

2. Probability is the chance, expressed as a percentage, that an event will occur.

3. $\dot{x}$: is the average or the measure of dispersion. σ: is the average deviation, called standard deviation.

4. A 95% confidence level.

5. Statistical and nomographical.

6. (1) Select the work to be studied and determine the objectives of the study. (2) Make a preliminary observation to determine the approximate values of p and q. (3) Determine, based on the confidence level and the level of precision selected, the number n of observations required. (4) Determine the frequency of observations using random number tables. (5) Prepare recording sheets according to the study objectives.

7. It is inexpensive and thus may be the only technique suitable for works not performed in series. It can be used to predict times of a work that has not been observed and, consequently, as a basis for calculating the price of unique large works.

Chapter 18 - Solutions to questions

1. The system of predetermined times is a work measurement technique where determined times are used for basic human movements in order to establish the time required for a task carried out according to a given performance standard.

2. (1) Stretch your arm. (2) Grasp. (3) Move. (4) Place. (5) Release load. (6) Body movements.

3. (1) MTM-1, -2, -3 (transferable worldwide and applicable to all manual activity sectors). (2) MTM-V (transferable only within an activity sector).

4. 1) Take. 2) Place or position. 3) Regrasp - R. (4) Apply pressure - A. (5) Use the eyes - E. (6) Movement of the foot - F. (6) Step - S. (7) Bend and arise - B. (8) Weight factors – GW, PW. (9) Crank - C.

Solution to problems

| Document 2 - Task Study ||||||||
Operation Description	MTM Element	Code		TMU	Q	F	Total TMU
Take five steps, grab an object (1 kg), take five steps, and leave it on table.	Take 5 steps.	S		18	1	5	90
	Grab an object.	GB	5	7	1	1	7
	Take 5 steps.	S		18	1	5	90
	Leave object on table.	PA	5	3	1	1	3
				Total task execution time (TMU):			190

Chapter 19 - Solutions to questions

1. With these we can calculate the manufacturing time of the item in the design phase and so calculate the cost of manufacture.

2. (1) Normal time. (2) Rest supplements. (3) Units.

3. (1) Filing them in a standard database. (2) Use them in the construction of methods and times.

4. (1) File time formulas and constants in a database. (2) Build up the time study substituting the formula in the time box, because time is not a constant. (3) The study of methods and times should include parameters or variables that influence time formulas. (4) Remember that if the formula calculates the speed, the time study should have the inverse of speed: 1/speed.

5. (1) Identify variables. (2) Calculate the value of the normal time in function of the variables. (3) Check the variables.

6. (1) Identify the variables affected. (2) Formulate the equations that calculate supplements depending on the variables.

7. Develop a list where the standard time obtained from the substitution of variables is displayed in the parameterised time study for each item.

Chapter 20 - Solutions to questions

1. The discipline whose aim is to coordinate the various actors and available resources involved in the business and its environment, in order to serve customers according to the agreements reached, at the lowest possible cost.

2. The sizing of the resources needed to carry out a production within a specified period either in the long, medium, or short term.

3. Normally the imbalance between workload and work capacity.

4. We will have to study the three options (hunting, levelling, and mixed) and choose, for each case, which generates a lower cost in compliance with company policy.

5. The necessary resources (human and equipment) and available capacity to fulfill the MRP.

6. The saturation of each of the workstations for the production defined.

7. Making new hires and/or overtime, and even increase shifts. Outsource the work.

8. A machine, a manual process, or material handling equipment that has the lowest production rate in a production process.

9. (1) Identify it. (2) Put old machines in parallel. (3) Improve the machine changeover time. (4) Pass through the bottleneck only products that have been ordered.

10. To perform programming, launching, and monitoring activities.

Solution to problems

What will the workload (CRP) in person-hours be that week in each of the phases?

Note: Do not forget the waste coefficient.

Units	Product	F1	F2	F3	F4	F5
38	P1	16.19	35.61	9.18	68.17	53.41
28	P2	17.89	33.39	13.85	59.57	53.67
17	P3	3.62	5.79	2.93	16.62	8.69
TOTAL PER PHASE		37.69	74.79	25.96	144.36	115.77

* *Value calculation considering the coefficient of waste.*

Given the operators who, by default, work at each stage, what is the capacity available in each phase for that period?

- One week period: 5 days
- Workday: 8 hours/day

Phase	F1	F2	F3	F4	F5
Nº Operators	1	2	1	3	3
Available capacity (p-h)	40	80	40	120	120

Compare the workload with the available capacity and calculate the level of saturation. Remember that:

Phase	F1	F2	F3	F4	F5
Workload (p-h)	37.69	74.79	25.96	144.36	115.77
Available capacity (p-h)	40	80	40	120	120
Saturation (%)	94.24%	93.49%	64.89%	120.30%	96.47%

- Do you think workload between phases is well balanced? No.
- What is the limiting stage? Phase 4.
- Do you think they will meet the master plan? No.
- Why? Because one of the phases has insufficient capacity to meet the workload.

Chapter 21 - Solutions to questions

1. (1) Operator name. (2) Quantification of the work done. (3) Time spent to perform such work. (4) Incidents encountered. (5) Verification of such incidents.

2. The collective agreement.

3. Productivity is a statistical ratio that compares a production obtained with resources consumed for such production.

4. Yes, through workforce productivity control we can obtain information on how manufacturing resources are managed. Therefore, the productivity of middle managers can be monitored.

5. No, because it would lead to absurd results.

6. For work with machines.

7. It is the document that contains all the necessary information in order to be able to understand how the system works. It depicts all the rules governing that system.

8. Yes, in fact it is recommended in many collective agreements to apply bonus payment systems as a method to encourage productivity.

9. Yes, it is one of the causes that can cripple an incentive system, partially or even completely.

10. They can be checked; if the method is modified, the materials are modified or a miscalculation has been detected.

Solutions to problems

1. a) 104

   b) 122

   c) 60

2. Solutions:

   1. 8 hours

   2. 8 hours

   3. 48 hours

   4. 2,880 minutes

   5. 3,109.96 total points

   6. 1.08 productivity ratio

   7. 229.96 points earned

APPENDIX
Rest Supplements

Personnel Administration Ltd tables for the rest supplements recommended by the ILO

Table of supplements for rest in percentages of the normal times

(Used by *Personnel Administration Ltd., London*)

	Supplement
1. FIXED SUPPLEMENTS	
Supplement for personal needs	5
Base supplement for fatigue	4
2. VARIABLE SUPPLEMENTS	
A. Supplement for working while standing	2
B. Supplement for uncomfortable posture	
- Slightly uncomfortable	0
- Uncomfortable	2
- Very uncomfortable	7

C. Use of strength or muscular energy
   (Lift, pull, push) Weight lifted in kilograms:

Kilograms	Supplement
1.5	0
1.0	1
1.5	2
1.0	3
12.5	4
15.0	5
17.5	7
20.0	9
22.5	11
25.0	13
30.0	17
35.5	22

D. Poor illumination

	Supplement
- Slightly under recommended illumination	0
- Substantially below	2
- Absolutely insufficient	5

E. Atmospheric conditions

- (Heat and humidity) J. B. Shearer

Wet-bulb temperature (millicalories/cm²/seconds)	Supplement
16	0
12	0
10	3
8	10
6	21
5	31
4	45
3	64
2	100

F. Intense focus

	Supplement
- Slight precision needed	0
- Precision needed or slightly exhausting	2
- High precision or exhausting	5

G. Noise

- Continuous	0
- Intermittent and strong	2
- Intermittent and very strong/unpleasant	5

H. Mental stress

- Quite complex process	1
- Complex or attention divided	4
- Highly complex	8

I. Monotony
- Slightly monotonous   0
- Monotonous   1
- Very monotonous   4

J. Tedium
- Quite boring   0
- Boring   2
- Very boring   5

Table of efforts and fatigue coefficients
(Coefficients expressed as percentages of the normal times)

1. Horizontal progression (flat floor)   Supplement
a) Unloaded:
Walk on regular floor (cement, road, pavement, parquet, etc.)   8
Walk on irregular floor (earth, grass, etc.)   10

b) Supplements to add for carrying load:

	10 kg	carried in arms, dense or not dense bulk	2 to 5
	20 kg	carried in arms, dense or not dense bulk	5 to 8
	30 kg	carried in arms, dense or not dense bulk	12 to 20
	10 kg	carried on back or shoulders, not dense	2
20 kg		carried on back or shoulders, not dense	3 to 6
	30 kg	carried on back or shoulders, not dense	8 to 10
	40 kg	carried on back or shoulders, not dense	15 to 20
	50 kg	carried on back or shoulders, not dense	20
	60 kg	carried on back or shoulders, not dense	30
	80 kg	carried on back or shoulders, not dense	60
	100 kg	carried on back or shoulders, not dense	100
	120 kg	carried on back or shoulders, not dense	140

Industrial productivity

2. Progression on slopes between 5 and 40 cm per meter
a) Supplements per cm of gradient

Unloaded	ascent =	0.5	descent =	0.2
Loaded with 10 kg	ascent =	0.6	descent =	0.2
Loaded with 20 kg	ascent =	0.8	descent =	0.3
Loaded with 30 kg	ascent =	1	descent =	0.4
Loaded with 40 kg	ascent =	1.2	descent =	0.6
Loaded with 50 kg	ascent =	1.4	descent =	0.8
Loaded with 60 kg	ascent =	1.6	descent =	1
Loaded with 80 kg	ascent =	1.8	descent =	1.2
Loaded with 100 kg	ascent =	2	descent =	1.4
Loaded with 120 kg	ascent =	2.2	descent =	1.6

3. Vertical progression (stairs, ladders, etc.)
a) Ascent of stairs to 4 meters without landing

Unloaded	30 to 40

Carrying load, steps in good condition or average (too high or narrow, etc.)

Loaded with 10 kg	35 to 45
Loaded with 20 kg	40 to 50
Loaded with 30 kg	50 to 60
Loaded with 40 kg	60
Loaded with 50 kg	80

b) Descent from stairs

Unloaded	10 to 20
Loaded with 10 kg	15 to 25
Loaded with 20 kg	20 to 30
Loaded with 30 kg	30 to 40
Loaded with 40 kg	40
Loaded with 50 kg	50

c) Climb ladder

Unloaded	80
Loaded with 10 kg	100
Loaded with 20 kg	120

Loaded with 30 kg	150
Loaded with 40 kg	200
Loaded with 50 kg	280

4. Transportation of object by vehicle (depends on resistance)

a) Pull lorry in good condition on flat floor
   Completely loaded with 100 to 400 kg   15 to 30

b) Push lorry in good condition on flat floor
   With 100 to 400 kg load   20 to 35

c) Push wagon on flat floor
   With 100 to 500 kg load   15 to 30

d) Pull lorry manual vehicle on flat floor
   With 100 to 400 kg load   15 to 30

e) Traction of lorry in good condition on flat floor
   With 50 to 100 kg load   20 to 40

Has to be taken into account the resistance for starting movement, that is, the coefficients have to be increased.

From 5 to 10 for transports under 15 seconds (A=60).

For vehicles fitted with tires, have to be increased from 2 (flat floor) to 20 (irregular floor).

5. Transportation of objects with arms

a) Direct elevation from floor to 80 cm and from 80 cm to 1.5 m.

Centimeters	From floor to 80 cm		From 80 cm to 1.5 m	
	dense	large	dense	large
1	12 to 15	14 to 18	10 to 15	12 to 16
2	15 to 20	20 to 25	15 to 20	20 to 25
3	25 to 30	30 to 40	25 to 30	30 to 40
4	35 to 40	40 to 50	40 to 45	40 to 50
5	45 to 50	50 to 60	55 to 65	60 to 70
6	55 to 60	60 to 70	70 to 80	70 to 80
8	65 to 70	70 to 80	85 to 100	100 to 120
10	75 to 80	80 to 100	100 to 120	120 to 150

b) Indirect throw (levers)

The pressure effort made on a lever has a limit: Lifting heavy loads modifies instinctively the lever's fulcrum.

Effort coefficient:
Operator in normal posture   0 to 50
Operator bowed down   12 to 50

c) Direct throw (throwing bricks, packages, etc.)
From 1 to 20 kg   10 to 25

d) Indirect projection (to shovel)
At the same level (transportation of pile) from lower
to higher position (load wagon, excavation)   25 to 40
From higher to lower position (embankment)   20 to 40

e) Disposition (selection, superposition, reunion)

Position	0 to 10 kg.	10 to 20 kg.	20 to 30 kg.
Seated	8 to 10	10 to 14	14 to 20
Standing	10 to 12	10 to 14	14 to 20
Bowed	12 to 15	15 to 20	20 to 30

6. Action on objects

a) Apprehension (tighten and loosen)   8 to 12

b) Percussion
    Work with light or thick hammer   15 to 30
    Work with pick   25 to 30

c) Extraction (excavations, etc.)   10 to 20

d) Pressure (positive work)
    Direct pressure, drill, rivet, hammer, etc. 10 to 18

e) Counter pressure (negative work)

    Support, brake, counterweight   6 to 15

f) Swinging

File wood	10 to 14
Plane wood	15
Place in oven	12 to 30
Rinse	8 to 10
Pump	10 to 14
Saw wood	10 to 20
Saw metal	10 to 18
Roller-stamp	10 to 25
Paint	10 to 14
Sew	8 to 14
Polish	10 to 14

g) Torsion

Screw up	10 to 15
Drain by twisting	10 to 15

h) Circumduction

Handle	10 to 20
Swing	10 to 30
Pedal	14 to 40

7. Intellectual works

Read instructions sheet	12
Type	15
Write with pencil (copy)	10 to 12
Write making mental operations (add, etc.)	20 to 25